gift

ROBERT FROST

THE LATER YEARS

PREVIOUS VOLUMES

ROBERT FROST

THE EARLY YEARS

1874–1915

ROBERT FROST

THE YEARS OF TRIUMPH

1915–1938

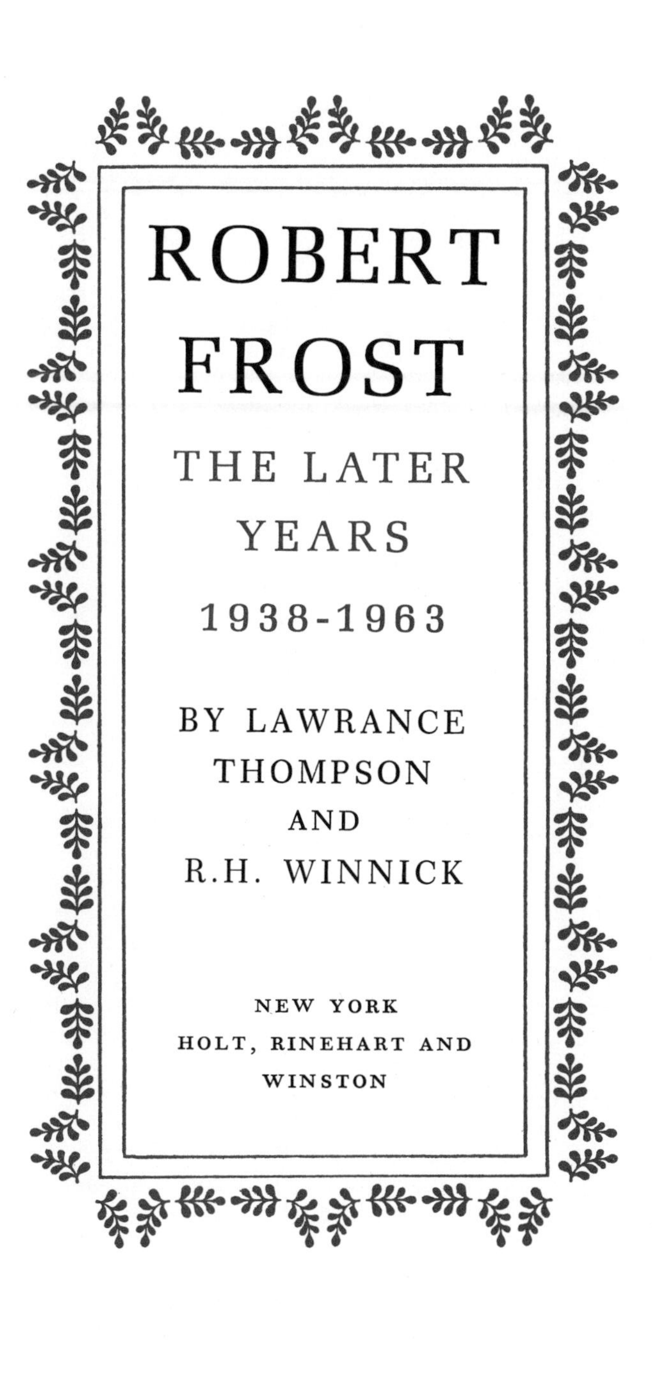

ROBERT FROST

THE LATER YEARS

1938-1963

BY LAWRANCE THOMPSON
AND
R.H. WINNICK

NEW YORK
HOLT, RINEHART AND
WINSTON

Published simultaneously in Canada by Holt, Rinehart
and Winston of Canada, Limited.

Library of Congress Cataloging in Publication Data
Thompson, Lawrance Roger, 1906–1973.
Robert Frost.
Vol. 3 by L. Thompson and R. H. Winnick.
Includes bibliographical references and index.
Contents:
[1] The Early Years, 1874–1915
[2] The Years of Triumph, 1915–1938
[3] The Later Years, 1938–1963
1. Frost, Robert, 1874–1963—Biography
I. Winnick, R. H., joint author.
PS3511.R94Z953 811'.5'2 66–20523
ISBN 0–03–017806–1 (v.3)

First Edition
Printed in the United States of America

10 9 8 7 6 5 4 3 2 1

GRATEFUL acknowledgment is made to the following for permission to reprint excerpts from their publications:

Holt, Rinehart and Winston, Publishers, for excerpts from *The Poetry of Robert Frost*, edited by Edward Connery Lathem; copyright 1916, 1928, 1934, 1947, 1949, © 1969 by Holt, Rinehart and Winston; copyright 1940, 1942, 1944, 1945, 1947, 1951, © 1955, 1956, 1958, 1960, 1961, 1962 by Robert Frost; copyright © 1968, 1970, 1973, 1975 by Lesley Frost Ballantine. For excerpts from *Selected Letters of Robert Frost*, edited by Lawrance Thompson; copyright © 1964 by Lawrance Thompson and Holt, Rinehart and Winston. For excerpts from *The Letters of Robert Frost to Louis Untermeyer*; copyright © 1963 by Louis Untermeyer and Holt, Rinehart and Winston. For excerpts from *Interviews with Robert Frost*, edited by Edward Connery Lathem; copyright © 1966 by Holt, Rinehart and Winston. For excerpts from *Robert Frost: The Years of Triumph, 1915–1938* by Lawrance Thompson; copyright © 1970 by Lawrance Thompson; copyright © 1970 by

The Estate of Robert Frost. For an excerpt from *Selected Prose of Robert Frost*, edited by Hyde Cox and Edward Connery Lathem; copyright 1939, © 1967 by Holt, Rinehart and Winston. For excerpts from *Robert Frost and John Bartlett: The Record of a Friendship* by Margaret Bartlett Anderson; copyright © 1963 by Margaret Bartlett Anderson. For excerpts from *Robert Frost: The Trial by Existence* by Elizabeth Shepley Sergeant; copyright © 1960 by Elizabeth Shepley Sergeant. For excerpts from *The Owl Among Colophons* by Charles A. Madison; copyright © 1966 by Holt, Rinehart and Winston. For excerpts from *Robert Frost: Poetry and Prose*, edited by Edward Connery Lathem and Lawrance Thompson; copyright © 1972 by Holt, Rinehart and Winston. For "The Prophets Really Prophesy as Mystics, The Commentators Merely by Statistics"; copyright © 1962 by Robert Frost.

The Atlantic Monthly Company, for excerpts from "The Agitated Heart" by Theodore Morrison; copyright © 1967 by The Atlantic Monthly Company, Boston, Massachusetts.

Doubleday & Company, Inc., and Paul Engle, for excerpts from "For an Apple Grower" from *Corn* by Paul Engle; copyright 1939 by Paul Engle.

Mrs. Valerie Eliot and Faber & Faber Ltd., for the texts of a formal toast and of a letter by T.S. Eliot; copyright © 1976 by Valerie Eliot.

The Estate of E. M. Forster, for the text of a letter by Mr. Forster to Robert Frost; copyright © 1976 by The Estate of E. M. Forster.

Maurice Greenbaum, trustee of the estate of Carl Sandburg, for "Those Who Make Poems" by Carl Sandburg; copyright 1942 by Carl Sandburg; copyright 1970 by Lilian Steichen Sandburg.

Little, Brown and Company, for excerpts from *Robert Frost in Russia* by F. D. Reeve; copyright 1963, 1964 by F. D. Reeve.

Middlebury College, for excerpts from "The Doctrine of Excursions," a Preface by Robert Frost to *The Bread Loaf Anthology*, published in 1939.

National Institute of Arts and Letters, New York, New York, for the speech delivered before the Institute in 1939 and printed in the *National Institute of Arts and Letters News Bulletin*, Vol. 5, 1939. All Rights Reserved.

The New York Times Company, for excerpts from various editorials, interview-articles, feature articles, book reviews and news stories appearing in *The New York Times* between 1939 and 1965; copyright © 1939–1965 by The New York Times Company.

The State University of New York Press, for excerpts from *Family Letters of Robert and Elinor Frost*, edited by Arnold Grade; copyright © 1972 by The State University of New York.

The University of Massachusetts Press, for excerpts from *Frost: A Time to Talk* by Robert Francis; copyright © 1972 by The University of Massachusetts Press.

The University of Oklahoma Press, for excerpts from *Robert Frost: Life and Talks-Walking* by Louis Mertins; copyright 1965 by The University of Oklahoma Press.

Wesleyan University Press for the poem entitled "Apple Peeler" in *The Orb Weaver* by Robert Francis; copyright © 1953 by Robert Francis.

A special acknowledgment is made to Mr. Alfred C. Edwards, sole trustee of the estate of Robert Frost, and former chairman and chief executive officer of Holt, Rinehart and Winston, Inc., for permission to quote from the unpublished poem, "On the Question of an Old Man's Feeling" by Robert Frost, as well as from other untitled and unfinished poems and previously unpublished letters and talks by the same author.

CONTENTS

	Preface	xi
	Introduction	xv
	Acknowledgments	xxiii
1.	A Reckless and Dangerous Mood	1
2.	Boston: A New Life	11
3.	Trials of Strength and Suppleness	25
4.	Hanging Round Education	39
5.	Friends and Neighbors	55
6.	The Death of the Dark Child	68
7.	A Witness Tree	81
8.	On the Home Front	97
9.	Dabbling in Drama	114
10.	One Step Backward Taken	129
11.	My Family Luck	142
12.	Speaking of Loyalty	165
13.	Friends Lost and Found	187
14.	The Demand for Me	211
15.	An English Diary	222
16.	Washington: The Pound Affair	247
17.	Poetry and Power	262
18.	In the Clearing	284
19.	Russia: A Final Mission	305
20.	Deeper Into Life	327
	Epilogue	346
	Appendix	351
	Notes	365
	Index	445

ILLUSTRATIONS

FOLLOWING PAGE 230

The poet at Bread Loaf, August 1938
Mrs. Bernard DeVoto

The Bread Loaf Writers' Conference staff, 1939
Middlebury College News Bureau

Frost's cabin at the Homer Noble farm, Ripton, Vermont
Bernard M. Cannon

Dartmouth's George Ticknor Fellow in Literature, with Gillie, 1944
Dartmouth College Library

Sitting for Walker Hancock, 1950
Hyde Cox

A birthday gathering at Crow Island, March 1950
Hyde Cox

The eightieth birthday dinner, Amherst, Massachusetts, March 1954
Amherst College News Service

On the way to accept an honorary degree from Cambridge University, May 1957
Howard Sochurek, Time-Life, Inc.

At the inauguration of President John F. Kennedy, January 1961
George Silk, Time-Life, Inc.

With Soviet Premier Nikita Khrushchev, Gagra, 1962
Stewart Udall

A stop on "the last go-round," November 1962
Joe Clark

Frost's last Thanksgiving at the Homer Noble farm, 1962
Anne Morrison Smyth

PREFACE

GIVEN the unusual manner in which this book came into being, the reader is entitled to some account of the collaborative effort that produced *Robert Frost: The Later Years, 1938–1963*. In August 1971, some three months after receiving a Pulitzer Prize for the second in his projected three-volume biography of Robert Frost, Professor Lawrance Thompson suffered a cerebral hemorrhage that interrupted, at an early stage, his work on Volume III. Although he had all but completed the task of assembling the biographical data needed to write this last volume, and had recorded at length in private notebooks what he had heard, seen, and provisionally concluded during and after twenty-five years as the poet's biographer and one of his intimate friends, his illness made it difficult, if not impossible, for him to continue alone.

This unhappy situation became even more so in June 1972, when, after months of apparent recovery, Thompson experienced a setback and was found to be suffering from a malignant tumor of the brain. Though surgery was soon performed by the able doctors of New York's Columbia Presbyterian Medical Center, they dared not risk complete removal of the tumor for fear of causing grievous damage to their patient's brain. Thus Thompson emerged from his surgery in markedly improved mental condition, but terminally ill.

As one of Thompson's graduate students in the English Department of Princeton University, and as one of the many devoted admirers of the man and his scholarship, I had been aware for some time of the uneven course of his recovery. Also for some time, I had hoped that Thompson's health would permit him to serve as the director of my as-yet-unwritten doctoral dissertation. But by June 1972, when the time came for me to begin that task, it had become clear that Thompson was in greater need of assistance than I. In a conversation with him shortly before his operation, we discussed an arrangement whereby that assistance might be provided. I would delay my dissertation for perhaps a year; I would, for convenience, take up residence in the Thompson home; I would serve him full-time as research assistant; and, together, we would work on the Frost biography. A few days after his operation, and after learning that he had only months to live, Thompson and I ratified that arrangement. Then, with remarkable determination and bravery, Thompson entered a race against death to complete the biography Robert Frost had authorized him to write thirty-three years before.*

In a sense he lost his race. In April 1973, after months of extensive discussion and the production, between us, of a crude first draft, Larry Thompson died. Yet with the draft, with countless notes, letters, and unpublished material at my disposal, and with the knowledge Thompson had shared with me of Frost's character and motivation, it seemed to me and to others close to the situation that Volume III might still become a reality. I am happy to say, and the present volume bears witness to the fact, that a reality, indeed, it has become.

I would like to express my gratitude to several people with whom I had the pleasure of working on the biography in the three years after Thompson's death. Particular thanks are due to Edward Connery Lathem, who made available to me the vast resources of the Dartmouth College Library and who meticulously criticized the manuscript in an early draft; to Professor Carlos Baker of Princeton University, who offered useful suggestions at every stage of my work; to Hyde Cox, who provided important insights into Frost's character based on years of close friendship with the poet; and above all to Professor and Mrs. Theodore Morrison, whose unstinting dedication to historical accuracy resulted in substantial improvements in the final manuscript. Additional thanks are offered in the Acknowledgments.

One further word on the preparation of the book: I have made every effort to carry out, herein, Lawrance Thompson's expressed intentions for the presentation and interpretation of Frost's life and poetry. In most cases, particularly those in which I could adopt or adapt from Thompson's own published or unpublished prose, this has been a relatively simple matter. But at times, when neither Thompson's instructions to me nor his writings provided guidance for the handling of a given incident or poem, I have relied on my own judgment, after

* The story of the Frost-Thompson friendship, up to the time in 1939 when Frost asked Thompson to become his "official biographer," is related in Thompson's words in the Appendix to the present volume.

appropriate research and consultation with those who knew Frost well, in formulating the biographical discussion. It is to be hoped that the narrative does not suffer unduly as a result, and that the book as a whole will nevertheless be received as the successful conclusion to Lawrance Thompson's monumental biography of Robert Frost.

R. H. Winnick

Princeton, New Jersey

INTRODUCTION

THE DAYS Robert Frost passed in solitude on the Gully farm in South Shaftsbury, Vermont, following the death of his wife on March 20, 1938, were as grim as any of his entire life. Like Frost himself, Elinor White Frost had been a difficult person to live with, and her manner of using silence to reproach and wound her husband had often caused him intense emotional pain. For Frost, the bitterest and most unforgettable silence had been Elinor's last when, dying of a succession of heart attacks in Gainesville, Florida, she had, so Frost thought, deliberately failed to summon him to her bedside to forgive him for all the pain and suffering he had caused her to endure in the course of their forty-three year marriage. That forgiveness could never now be his, and the silences of Elinor's life only added to the agony of the silence that followed her death.

Frost felt at times that he had reasons for resenting Elinor, but he could not overlook the fact that, for years, she had been the primary inspiration for his poetry. All of his books had been dedicated to her and, as he wrote to a friend after her death, "Pretty near every one of my poems will be found to be about her if rightly read."[1] Now that she was gone, Frost did not see how he could possibly continue to write poetry or, for that matter, to maintain the balanced and detached exterior he had always been able to summon for his public appearances. Unable to go on with his life, or to govern his loneliness as Elinor had always helped him do, he responded with what for him was a characteristic procedure: withdrawal.

He would perhaps have ceased to mourn in time, and resumed both his literary and his public activities, even without outside help and encouragement. But such help did come, and one source of it proved to be extraordinarily significant. Mrs. Kathleen Morrison, wife of the Harvard poet and teacher, Theodore Morrison, encouraged the distraught poet to accept an invitation to visit the Vermont home she was herself then visiting, and to benefit that summer from the friendship and support both she and her husband offered. Mrs. Morrison's kindness helped the poet immeasurably, but it also had an unforeseen result: before they had spent much time together, Frost developed a romantic interest in her, and soon came forth with a proposal of marriage—which was immediately and firmly refused.

Recognizing completely how close Frost was to what would best be described, perhaps, as a "nervous breakdown," and recognizing as well Frost's need for help in managing his normally busy public schedule, Mrs. Morrison agreed, despite Frost's expressed wish for even greater involvement, to become his part-time secretary and manager. Frost soon began to emerge from the shadow of Elinor's death and, at sixty-five, to resume his busy life of writing, teaching, and "barding around" the country. Frost had always craved public recognition, but now that he was deprived of Elinor's customary approbation, he pursued with ever greater energy the approbation of the world at large. When he was a boy, his mother had told him stories of heroes and heroines who overcame all painful hardships through actions that reflected courage, skill, cunning, wit, nobility, compassion, and persistent striving for glory. She had made him want to achieve honor and glory himself through acts of heroic accomplishment. For years, he had been forced to endure repeated frustrations and disappointments before he could realize his childhood dream of achieving honor and glory as a poet. Now that he had gained honor and glory—and a comfortable income—as America's best-known and best-loved poet, he made a conscious or unconscious decision to achieve heights of distinction that had never been achieved in America, as if he could thereby make up for the nearly forty years during which he had been regarded as no more than a high-school teacher or chicken-raiser or farmer or, what was worst of all, "riffraff."

As he entered his seventies and then eighties, becoming increasingly popular and sought-after, he took more pleasure than ever in the power he had to consist of the inconsistent, to be a bursting unity of opposites, and to make poetry out of those opposites.[2] Always a rebel, and named after one, he exercised his power by attacking, in his poetry and elsewhere, some of the prevailing tendencies of contemporary society. He conducted what amounted to a crusade in his classes at a succession of colleges and universities against the tendency to elevate science above the humanities. He attacked the tendency away from a society of self-made men—as he proudly considered himself—toward the welfare state that he thought was the legacy of the New Deal. While he liked to call himself a "liberal," the views he espoused in his last twenty-five years would more accurately be termed "conservative." He wanted to see preserved the kind of society that had been able to produce men like himself.

Frost's extraordinary rise in popularity following his return from England in 1916 had been partly due to aggressive campaigning, but it had been due even more to the quality of his verse and the attractiveness of his personality. Traveling alone to Boston shortly after landing with his family in New York, he had almost immediately been acclaimed in print as "a most agreeable personality," and as "one of the most loveable men in the world."[3] The deceptive simplicity of his poetic idiom, heightened by his personal charm, had soon resulted in invitations to read his poems in public. Always painfully shy, he had overcome his inhibitions by creating for himself the image of just a "plain New Hampshire farmer," whose New England accent gave no hint that he had spent the first decade of his life in California, or three years in England. His armor of scorn and arrogance, no longer needed, was concealed, and his audiences had no inkling of all the hurts and humiliations caused by the previous years of neglect. The poems he read to his listeners further enhanced the image of a "plain New Hampshire farmer" by expressing genuine sympathetic admiration for the virtues of back-country people who triumphed over hardship and gloried in the often-overlooked attractiveness of ordinary rural experience.

As his popularity continued to grow, he began to receive a steady flow of honors. Within a few months of his return from England, *North of Boston* became a best seller. Shortly before the publication of his next book, he was elected to membership in the National Institute of Arts and Letters. He received, and accepted, an invitation to join the faculty of Amherst College as "poet in residence," and later held similar positions at the University of Michigan, Amherst College, Dartmouth College, and Harvard University. His fourth book, *New Hampshire*, was awarded a Pulitzer Prize, the first of an eventual, unprecedented four. Soon after the publication of his *Collected Poems* (1930), which won him his second Pulitzer Prize, he was elected to membership in the American Academy of Arts and Letters. Within the space of a few short years, he had achieved a lasting place in the history of American letters.

His poetry-writing mother would have appreciated the way in which her son had achieved glory by triumphing heroically over "insuperable odds." She might have understood, even better than the poet himself, the complicated relationships between his earliest humiliations and his consequent craving for glory. In his autobiographical accounts, Frost often called attention to his evident kinship with heroes. His retelling always pointed up his struggles and triumphs, in the face of almost "insuperable odds," hurts, and humiliations. He had begun to discover his poetic gifts while still a schoolboy, he said, and yet he had been forced to suffer through a long sequence of hindrances and discouragements before winning public recognition. Toward the end of the story that he was acting out while also telling it, he never missed a chance to point out mythic roundings-off and fulfillments. Just after he was invited to England, in 1957, to receive honorary degrees from Oxford and Cambridge universities, he wrote, "It will sort of round off things I initiated with Mrs David Nutt in a small office in Bloomsbury among total strangers forty five years ago [when I was] already almost too old to bet on. There is that in it anyway. It will also sort of round off my rather great academic career in general."[4] If he was inclined to boast, when discussing fulfillments, his accomplishments exceeded his boasts.

Frustrations and tragedies repeatedly darkened his private life even as he enjoyed great public success. In his boyhood, he had been hurt and humiliated by his mother's difficulties in securing an income as a schoolteacher after the early death of his father. After graduating from high school, where he had distinguished himself as a student of Latin and Greek literature, he had been deeply injured by his temporarily unsuccessful courtship of the girl he eventually married, Elinor White. During the worst phase of the courtship, when he was convinced that he had lost out to another suitor, he was so upset that he threatened to kill himself—and unsuccessfully attempted to get himself killed in Virginia's Dismal Swamp. Although he finally overcame Elinor White's reservations about marrying him, he never completely recovered from the inner wounds suffered during the courtship. Later, he was deeply hurt again when their first child, Elliott, died at three of *cholera infantum*, after the doctor who was called in held Frost responsible for not calling him sooner. Years later, having successfully raised a family that included a son and three daughters, he lived to see death or insanity overtake all but one of his children. Marjorie, the youngest surviving child and Frost's favorite, died of puerperal fever in 1934 after giving birth to her first child. Six years later Frost's only surviving son, Carol, died by his own hand, after years of mental difficulty. Irma, too, was the victim of a mental disorder much like that which necessitated the institutionalization of Frost's sister, Jeanie, and she finally had to be placed in a mental institution herself by her anguished father. Only Lesley, who had once blamed her father for the family's misfortunes, escaped. "Cast your eye back over my family luck," Frost wrote to a friend after Irma's commitment in 1947, "and perhaps you will wonder if I haven't had pretty near enough."[5]

Frost was himself the victim of a variety of maladies, though of a less serious nature. His susceptibility to pulmonary disorders eventually forced him to flee the harsh New England winter climate and spend his winters in the South. Not long after Elinor's death, and shortly after buying the Homer Noble farm in Ripton, Vermont, he decided to buy a piece of undeveloped property in South Miami, Florida, near the home of his friend Hervey Allen. This five-acre tract, which came to be known as "Pencil Pines," was provided with a pair of prefabricated houses to which Frost repaired each winter for the remainder of his life.

As his poetic output gradually diminished, the lyricism of his earlier books gave way to poetic statements that were increasingly prophetic, aphoristic, and self-consciously philosophical. In the mid-1940s, he completed a pair of works which represented his major effort in an area that had long interested him: verse drama. *A Masque of Reason* (1945) and *A Masque of Mercy* (1947) made use of two biblical stories, that of Job and that of Jonah, to explore religious themes that had first been introduced to him in childhood by his devout mother. Always reluctant to be drawn into orthodoxy of any kind, Frost frequently seemed, in the masques, to be writing from the standpoint of a modern freethinker or worse. But the final speech of Paul in the second masque contained a prayerful utterance that Frost often repeated and applied to his own life and work:

We have to stay afraid deep in our souls
Our sacrifice—the best we have to offer,
And not our worst nor second best, our best
. . . may not
Be found acceptable in Heaven's sight.
And that they may be is the only prayer
Worth praying. May my sacrifice
Be found acceptable in Heaven's sight.[6]

It would have pleased Isabelle Moodie Frost to know how well her son had followed her own religious spirit. She would have been less pleased to see how Frost failed to outgrow certain spoiled-child habits in dealing with his closest friends. Lawrance Thompson witnessed many instances in which Frost displayed a violence of temper when imagining himself crossed or slighted or insulted that would have astonished those who saw him only in the role of the friendly, easygoing, witty Vermont farmer-poet that he himself had created. Those friends who played tennis with Frost, for example, during the annual Bread Loaf Writers' Conference he invariably attended, knew better than to allow Frost to lose a game. Whenever necessary —and it often was—his opponents would deliberately misrepresent the score in Frost's favor to avoid incurring an unsightly display of temper.

"God," Frost often said, "seems to me to be something which wants us to win."[7] Not only did Frost like to win himself, but he also coveted victories for the nation as a whole. He often found it possible to gather glory for the nation even as he gathered glory for himself. In England, in 1957, he was officially serving the State Department as an ambassador of good will when he went there to collect several honorary degrees. After participating in the inauguration of President John Fitzgerald Kennedy, he paid similar visits to Israel and Greece. His last and, in some ways, his greatest adventure was a trip he made to the Soviet Union, in 1962, just months before his death. While there, he met with Premier Nikita Khrushchev and offered the Russian leader his own vision of a "noble rivalry" between what he called the Russian and American democracies, a rivalry not in war, but in the arts, the sciences, and athletics. It was his last venture outside the United States, and a fitting capstone to his "rather great" public career.

In this volume, the authors have sought to continue the

attempt made in the first and second volumes: to offer a balanced delineation that mingles sympathy with critical detachment, in the narration and in the interpretation. The primary method employed, as before, is to select major and minor episodes of Frost's outer and inner life that dramatize the complexities of his responses to experience. The secondary method of analytical interpretation is largely relegated to the Notes.

Lawrance Thompson
R. H. Winnick

Princeton, New Jersey

PLEASE NOTE: As in the two previous volumes, Frost's often careless punctuation and erratic spelling have been amended in the present volume only when doing so seemed necessary to avoid confusion. Readers should not be surprised, therefore, to find a number of irregularities in spelling and punctuation in letters originally handwritten (that is, not dictated) by Frost. Also, it will be noted that, until 1954, Frost's age at a given birthday is referred to with quotation marks or as being "so-called." This procedure reflects the fact that, until his eightieth birthday in 1954, Frost erroneously held that he had been born in 1875 rather than 1874—an error partly attributable to the destruction of his birth records in the great San Francisco earthquake and fire in 1906.

ACKNOWLEDGMENTS

ON BEHALF of Lawrance Thompson, I take pleasure in expressing gratitude and indebtedness to all who have helped us during the various stages of our work on the manuscript of *Robert Frost: The Later Years.* In addition to those named in the Preface, my thanks go to the following, each of whom was helpful in important ways, often by making available to Professor Thompson or to me copies of Frost letters and manuscripts: Frederick B. Adams, Jr.; Hon. Sherman Adams; Charles Andrews; Lesley Frost Ballantine; Clifton Waller Barrett; Earle J. Bernheimer; Stanley Burnshaw; Mrs. Gordon K. Chalmers; Mrs. Louis Henry Cohn; Charles W. Cole; James B. Conant; Kenneth Cramer; Joan St. C. Crane; Mrs. Bernard DeVoto; Alfred C. Edwards; Valerie Eliot; Paul Engle; Mrs. Walter Fischer; Charles H. Foster; Robert Francis; Willard E. Fraser; Lillian LaBatt Frost; Michael Gibson; Jack W. C. Hagstrom; August Heckscher; Raymond Holden; John S. Van E. Kohn; Charles H. Lyttle; Archibald MacLeish; Merrill Moore; L. Quincy Mumford; Ray Nash; Jacqueline Kennedy Onassis; Franklin D. Reeve; Victor E. Reichert; Howard G. Schmitt; Eustace Seligman; Mrs. William M. Sloane III; Anne Morrison Smyth; Wilbert Snow; Dorothy Hopkins Spahr; William Tribe; Diana Trilling; Louis Untermeyer; Thomas C. Wallace; Elizabeth Whicher; Strephon Williams; Andrew Wyeth. More specific acknowledgments are made in the Notes.

Sincere thanks are also given to Princeton University, for a grant of aid from the Annan Fund, and to Mrs. Lawrance Thompson, whose encouragement of her husband and whose cooperation with his collaborator contributed to the successful completion of this work.

R. H. W.

ROBERT FROST
THE LATER YEARS

1

A RECKLESS AND DANGEROUS MOOD

I am in a reckless mood and a dangerous one left thus lying around loose in the world. Take care of me. . . .[1]

ONE MORNING late in July 1938, Robert Frost watched from a front-room window as a strange car made its way slowly up the uneven dirt road toward his Gully farmhouse in South Shaftsbury, Vermont. When it was close enough for him to see the Massachusetts license plate, he waited only a moment before taking his customary evasive action. Hurrying outside through the kitchen door, he walked quickly back of the barn, hit for the woods, and was safely out of sight before the uninvited visitor drove into the yard. As so often happened, however, his curiosity forced him to circle back to a vantage point where, through a screen of leaves, he could study the intruder. Someone he could not immediately make out—a woman perhaps forty years old, rather slight of build, with bright auburn hair—was apparently writing a note that she planned to leave. When she finished it, wedged it between the kitchen door and the jamb, and turned to walk back to her car, he recognized her: she was Kathleen Morrison, wife of Theodore Morrison of Harvard and Bread Loaf, with both of whom the Frosts had become good friends in Cambridge when, during the spring of 1936, Frost had served as Charles Eliot Norton Professor of Poetry at Harvard.[2] He had last seen them in Amherst three months ago, at Elinor's memorial service: Elinor his wife, whose death at Gainesville, Florida, in March 1938 accounted for his present self-imposed isolation. Ted Morrison, he remembered, had been one of the honorary pallbearers, and Kay, too, had shared in his mourning.[3] Frost wanted to come out of hiding and greet Kay, but before he had time to do so, she started her car and drove off.

Her note explained the purpose of her visit. Her husband, as director of the Bread Loaf Writers' Conference, was now preparing for the August session, and he wanted Frost to know that he was welcome as ever to a job at Bread Loaf, welcome to remain on campus for the two weeks of the Conference and to give as few or as many lectures as he wished. Also, Kay's note continued, she and her children—Bobby, aged 8, and Anne, almost 2—were staying with friends whom the Frosts had met, the Nathaniel Sages, in West Dover, Vermont, and they wanted Frost to spend a few days with them at their spacious summer home. Kay would pass through South Shaftsbury again after her next visit to her husband at Bread Loaf. When she did, she would stop in again. She hoped Frost then would accept the Sages' invitation and return with her to West Dover.

Frost had known Mrs. Morrison longer, if not better, than he had her husband. As Kathleen Johnston, a student at Bryn Mawr College in the class of 1921, she had been a member of the "Reeling and Writhing Club" which in 1920 brought him to Bryn Mawr for a private, three-session course in the arts of reading and writing poetry.[4] Not a poet herself, Kathleen, whose speech reflected her British parentage, had been one of those undergraduates who attended the course without submitting manuscripts for his criticism. During the next several years, they had met little or not at all, and what slight acquaintance they may have formed Frost doubtless all but forgot. But then, in 1936, Frost had come to Harvard, and Kay had joined her husband, a Harvard English instructor and a poet as well as Bread Loaf's director, in inviting Frost back to their Cambridge home at 8 Mason Street for small receptions after each of his Norton lectures.[5] Frost's growing affection for the Morrisons had led him to invite Ted to participate in the service for Elinor, and the Morrisons' reciprocated friendship had led Kay, now, to call on the grieving poet at his home in the Gully.

If there was some concern for his well-being reflected in Kay's visit and the Sages' invitation, it was not without good reason. As the Morrisons and his other close friends knew, the answer to the question of how he had been doing since Elinor's death was, simply put, not well at all. He still could not bear to sleep in the ghost-filled Gully farmhouse, but found it necessary to return every evening from long hours of aimless wandering around his farm to the Stone Cottage, where his son Carol was living with his wife Lillian, their not-quite-fourteen-year-old son Prescott, and Frost's four-year-old granddaughter, his late daughter Marjorie's child, Robin Fraser.[6] For a month during the summer, his friend from Tufts College, the poet John Holmes, had occupied the Gully farmhouse and had tried to help him get through the worst period of his bereavement.[7] But neither Holmes's expressions of sympathetic understanding nor the hours they spent walking and talking far into every night could relieve Frost of the bitterness and remorse he had felt ever since Elinor's death. He could not get it out of his mind that, in the final hours of her life, Elinor had not once asked to see him, that she had deprived him of the chance to ask her forgiveness for all the pain and suffering he had caused her in their forty-three years together. He still could not help thinking that her final silence, like so many others before, had been her way of punishing him for the bitterness of her life. What hurt him perhaps most of all was the way in which his daughter Lesley had told him, in an emotional outburst after her mother's cremation, that he was the kind of artist who should never have married, or at least who should never have had a family.[8] Was it not, he had asked himself repeatedly, a reproach he deserved?

Elinor's death continued to haunt him, but at least it had lately ceased to paralyze him completely. Only a week before Kay's visit, he had written to Professor Robert S. Newdick of Ohio State University accepting an invitation to spend a week in Columbus in the fall. He had accepted as well Newdick's offer of assistance in planning the details of his midwestern trip: "Its a great relief to have these arrangements taken off my wretched hands," Frost had written. "I say I have nothing left but work and ambition. But I sometimes doubt I have even those. I show no disposition to work and I have only ambition when it is summoned by an audience present to get me talking."[9]

Newdick, Frost knew, was not the only person eager to help him emerge from his South Shaftsbury exile and get back to work. His Harvard friends, the poets Robert Hillyer and David McCord in particular, having successfully campaigned for his election, in June, to the Harvard Board of Overseers,[10] were working hard to raise funds for a fellowship that would place him on the Harvard faculty, one to replace the position at

Amherst that he had abruptly resigned, after years of continuous employment, shortly after Elinor's death. Frost had even hinted to Arthur Stanley Pease, former president of Amherst College and now chairman of the Harvard Latin Department, that he might welcome an appointment to teach Roman classics at Harvard. But his letter to Hillyer of July 20, a few days before Kay's appearance, betrayed his growing doubt that the proposed Harvard appointment was the one he really wanted:

"See what my impulse to flight has got me into—or almost into: the Latin Dept. of Harvard College. I feel as if I might find rest there if anywhere this side of urn burial. It is a dream: but one to the realization of which there is at least one great obstacle. I mean my having been elected to the Board of Overseers. I have it plainly in writing that no one not even a seer can be at once an Overseer and an employee of the University. I am prepared to hear you say next, as I am always hearing in this irregular life of mine, that an exception could probably be made in my case. But I am tired of living outside the law. I got too much of it at Amherst, more, it turns out, than I knew I was getting. So that unless we can think of waiting a year or so and then proposing my resignation from the Board I should say it was all off. What should you say? I ought to have a year free anyway. Before I went thoroughly romantic about the classics I ought to go and muse part of the year in Greece with Lincoln MacVeagh and a few days in Rome with Santayana.[11] Do you get my dream exactly as I dream it? I had in mind a half course in all the small Latin poems that get translated into English verse. It would be for boys who had had not less than three years of Latin and who could make their own translations preferably into verse or at worst free verse. The course would be designated: Translation of Latin Poems into English verses not to be preserved. There would have to be some mischief in it for my pleasure. A good deal of memorizing of the Latin originals would be required or expected. We could look into what Waddam Jones Robinson[12] and others around us were doing. My attitude in the readings would of choice and perforce be worldly rather than scholarly. But there's the rub and the second obstacle that must be deliberately faced. First off the Latinists might think they were willing to adopt me for the cheap public support I might bring them in their decline (you neednt say I put it thus baldly), but will they in their fastidious scholarship be able to stand me on my terms for any length of time? You understand the whole point of my plan would be to treat the Latin poems as if they were still a rather accessible off hand pleasure for a number of people. They are only a little more receeded than Chaucer. Remember now *in* the days of thy Youth while the memorizing is easy, would be my motto. All this in very vague broad strokes to give you the idea, should it be worth going on with. We can't get much further without seeing each other for a talk.—Another prompting: I would be as if I had one leg in the English Department wouldn't I? Am I too nebulous? Well well well. Never mind how it comes out. A few forward-looking thoughts are what I need to keep me alive."[13]

When Mrs. Morrison returned as promised several days later, Frost told her he was not yet ready to leave South Shaftsbury for the visit the Sages proposed. He did, however, agree to participate in the Writers' Conference as Ted Morrison had suggested, and next day he sent Morrison a short message: "I'll come on Wednesday the 17th prepared to speak Thursday the 18th. So I told Kay when she looked in yesterday to cheer me up, and now I confirm it. Thanks for the job. What I need is work, you can tell Harry Hopkins. I am beyond any other kind of relief. But I am more or less Bravely yours Robert"[14]

Convinced by her visit that Frost's solitude was doing him no good, Mrs. Morrison, at the urging of the Sages and the young people in West Dover, returned to South Shaftsbury yet again to convey the Sages' invitation. This time, impulsively, the poet chose to accept. Hastily packing a suitcase, Frost climbed in Mrs. Morrison's car and rode with her to the Sages' summer home.

On the way, he confessed to Kay that he had brought with him a sheaf of unanswered correspondence to which he would sooner or later have to attend. If he could wait until the end of the Writers' Conference, said Mrs. Morrison, she would be happy to type his answers for him. Her solicitude continued after their arrival in West Dover. At the Sages' suggestion, she joined Frost on successive days for long hikes in the neighboring woods, taking part in his favorite pastime of botanizing and listening sympathetically as he unburdened himself of his accumulated troubles.

Frost enjoyed these walks with the attractive and intelligent Mrs. Morrison, but in the emotional havoc that was the aftermath of Elinor's death, their time together produced a result which neither of them had anticipated. Lonely and desperate for the companionship Elinor had always provided, Frost—who had rarely been away from his wife more than two or three days at a time in all their years together—soon began to imagine not only that the gratitude and affection he felt for Kay was love, but that she might be prevailed upon, despite her married status, fully to reciprocate that feeling. When he returned for a second visit to West Dover several days later, he astonished Kay by professing his love for her, and by following that with a proposal, amounting almost to a demand, that she leave her husband and become his wife. In his excited state of mind, he was hardly daunted when Kay told him that, happily married as she was, a marriage to him was out of the question, and that much as she might—and would continue to—care for him as a dear friend, she would never have consented to be his wife even if they were both twenty years younger and both free. When he left West Dover to spend the few days remaining before the Writers' Conference in South Shaftsbury, Frost was painfully divided between a conviction that he could prevail upon Kay to marry him, and an awareness of the possibility that she would remain adamant in her determination never to become Mrs. Robert Frost.[15]

Thinking he knew just what he wanted regarding his future domestic life, Frost found he was suddenly more sure of himself in other matters as well. On August 12, he wrote once again to Robert Hillyer: "Listen! I have scared myself with what I have set going. It won't do for me to profess Latinity. I have been warned off already. Pease though writing warmly to welcome my idea, yet winds up with the suggestion that I might like John Finley as a watcher in my classes.[16] Don't I know those bozos from of old? They are too humanistic to be human. I am only fooling myself if I think that large treatment can make them over into anything but what they are. Dont let [us] speak scornfully of them. They have their proper pride in their peculiar knowledges that I would be the last one to want to reduce. The course I propose may not belong in the Latin Department anyway. What a pity I didn't think of it for the English Department. It could have been the very same thing, Latin verse treated worldly rather than scholarly, with no regard to the purity of the period, a lot of it memorized and some of it translated into English verse and thrown away. It would have looked quaint in the catalogue as the one course in English with a prerequisite of three or four years of Latin. But it is too late to talk of this now. The Latin Department has been aroused and now it is the Latin Department or nothing. Let it be nothing. In all firmness I say it. I must not bedevil my declining years with a wantonly falsified position anywhere. I am in a reckless mood and a dangerous one left thus lying around loose in the world. Take care of me because I am Very much yours Robert"[17]

A few days later, Carol Frost drove his father to the Bread Loaf campus and left him there to prepare for a busy week of teaching and lecturing. The staff Ted Morrison had assembled included two of Frost's closest friends, Bernard DeVoto and Louis Untermeyer,[18] who were delighted to see Frost apparently emerging from his long period of bitter mourning. His first talk and reading, the following evening, was a spectacular performance, and many said that he had never been better. One of those attending was Charles H. Foster, a young poet from the University of Iowa,[19] who later recorded what he had seen and heard:

"Last night, Frost gave the best lecture I have ever heard him give. His mind was seething and rolling with metaphors and humor and he was exhausted when he was finished. . . . He said he would follow his usual custom and make up some poems on the spot. It was the most remarkable sight I have ever seen. He talked on in the direction of an idea—all around it [—] and then he said 'Here is a poem' and very slowly—changing a few words—but for the most part going ahead as one would on paper, he made his poem and it was a good poem. He called it 'Dark, Darker, Darkest.' Life is dark because life, this bright foam that catches the light, is flowing forever and ever into insanity, into poverty. Life is darker because man doesn't know how to play the stops on mankind well enough to change the situation. We must advance in a broad front and we don't know how to turn to the poor and the insane. Life is darkest because perhaps we're not meant to do anything about it. Frost said he wanted life so much he hadn't time to play with dead things—man hasn't time. . . ."[20]

It was clear from this talk, and from others he gave in the week that followed, that Frost had made a successful escape from one set of problems connected with his wife's death. But to many of the participants at Bread Loaf it was equally plain that he was by no means a man enjoying emotional peace. "Frost told me," wrote Foster in his journal after his first private conversation with the poet, "that he was a God-damned son-of-a-bitch, a selfish person who had dragged people roughshod over life. People didn't understand [him] who wanted to make him good. His rebellion looked so good, he said, but he was always a person who had his way, a God-damned son of a bitch, Charlie, and don't let anyone tell you different."[21] A week later, on the night of August 27, Frost conducted himself in a manner seemingly calculated to convince his colleagues that what he had said of himself was true. The occasion was a lecture and poetry reading by Archibald MacLeish, who had just arrived at Bread Loaf for a brief visit, and Frost, for the first time in the Conference, found himself sharing the limelight with a poet whose reputation rivaled his own. Wallace Stegner, one of the younger members of the Bread Loaf staff, has described what happened:

"Early in the proceedings [Frost] found some mimeographed notices on a nearby chair and sat rolling and folding them in his hands. Now and again he raised the roll of paper, or an eyebrow, calling the attention of his seat mates to some phrase or image. He seemed to listen with an impartial, if skeptical, judiciousness. About halfway through the reading he leaned over and said in a carrying whisper, 'Archie's poems all have the same *tune*.' As the reading went on, to the obvious pleasure of the audience, he grew restive. The fumbling and rustling of the papers in his hands became disturbing. Finally MacLeish announced 'You, Andrew Marvell,' a tour de force that makes a complete thirty-six–line poem out of a single sentence. It was a favorite. Murmurs of approval, intent receptive faces. The poet began. Then an exclamation, a flurry in the rear of the hall. The reading paused, heads turned. Robert Frost, playing around like an idle, inattentive schoolboy in a classroom, had somehow contrived to strike a match and set fire to his handful of papers and was busy beating them out and waving away the smoke."[22]

The fire was quickly extinguished, but Frost's jealousy continued to burn. After MacLeish had finished his reading, the group adjourned to Treman Cottage for drinks and conversation, and, at the urging of several of his admirers, MacLeish began to read his new radio play, *Air Raid.* Again Frost began baiting the speaker with audibly murmured comments. MacLeish refused to take offense, and the audience sat in embarrassed silence, afraid to look predator or prey in the face. Finally Bernard DeVoto, less inclined to patient acquiescence than his fellows, said something in reproof of his misbehaving friend, something like "For God's sake, Robert, let him read!" Frost said nothing in reply, but a short time later he himself took offense at a remark clearly intended for someone else, and abruptly left the room.[23]

Next morning, Sunday, Charles Foster was talking with Herschel Brickell, a member of the Bread Loaf staff, about the events of the night before, when they saw Frost walking away at top speed in the direction of Bread Loaf Mountain. Brickell ran after him, but as soon as he caught up Frost said something which made him stop and turn back. Then, without breaking stride, Frost turned to shout back to Foster, "I don't want to see you!" Later, Brickell received the summons of the troubled poet: he wanted to be driven at once to Concord Corners, Vermont, where he had a house in which his daughter Irma and her family were staying. Although he knew that Frost was scheduled to give another talk at Bread Loaf before the Conference ended, Brickell unquestioningly complied.

If Frost was seeking refuge from emotional conflict in Concord Corners, he found none. Irma, with her peculiar suspicion of all strange men,[24] refused Brickell permission to spend the night after his hundred-mile drive from Bread Loaf. When he had gone, she insisted on putting her father up in a room whose only access to the rest of the house was through the bedroom where she and her husband slept. Hurt and angered by the double insult, Frost called Brickell first thing in the morning and said that he now wanted to come back to the Writers' Conference.

He returned to a Bread Loaf alive with rumor and speculation as to the reasons for his erratic behavior. Foster agreed with Brickell's suggestion that Frost was now "raping his personality." They both concurred that all the unaccustomed whisky-drinking, all the self-abasement, all the ugliness were unlike the man they had long known and loved. Foster could not help thinking that the explanation, whatever it might be, somehow went beyond the death, five months before, of Elinor Frost. But he had no idea what else might account for so much turmoil.[25]

Bernard DeVoto and Louis Untermeyer, both of whom were privy to Frost's thoughts in a way Brickell and Foster were not, had a better understanding of the situation. They knew that much of Frost's behavior that week was related to what he felt for Kathleen Morrison. Untermeyer's natural sympathy enabled him to maintain his loyalty to his friend even though he did not approve the course he was taking. But DeVoto was deeply disturbed by the recklessness with which Frost seemed determined to interfere with the Morrison family. As he bade farewell to Frost at the end of the Conference, he scolded him for the second time in a week by saying "You're a good poet, Robert, but you're a bad man." [26]

BOSTON: A NEW LIFE

You hear from one in me now having given up life in the country for life in one of the oldest and most citified cities of the new world. Don't judge me too hardly. I have come here not to get excitement but to get away from the excitement of being alone with nature naturating.[1]

DE VOTO WAS GONE before Frost could find an appropriate way of responding to his reprimand, and soon the Bread Loaf campus was deserted except for Frost and the Morrisons. At the Morrisons' invitation, Frost moved out of the small cottage he had shared with Louis Untermeyer during the Conference, and into the Endicott house, where Ted and Kay would continue to stay until the start of the Harvard semester in late September. There, it was planned, Kay would do the secretarial work she had promised, while Frost relaxed before going on to Concord Corners.

Even before Kay set up her typewriter, however, Frost began to realize that whatever help she gave him before he left Bread Loaf, it could only provide temporary relief for a problem that, as long as he remained active as a poet and lecturer, was bound to be a continuing nuisance. What would he do when the current batch of mail was out of the way? Which of his children was willing or able to be the factotum Elinor had always been, once Kay had gone back to Cambridge? The answer was disquieting: he had three children, Lesley, Irma, and Carol, and yet they were all so bound up in their own problems, resentful of him in so many ways, that he knew he could not ask any one of them for the kind of help he needed. He had not forgotten that after Elinor's death Lesley had flatly refused to let him live with her, saying she would not let him ruin her children as he had ruined his own. Irma's response, had he asked, would have been no kinder, and Carol, while agreeing to take him in at the Stone Cottage, could scarcely take care of himself, let alone a father with whom he often did not get along.[2] Frost knew he would finally have to go it alone as far as his children were concerned. Living alone was one thing: he could get used to that, in time. But help with lecture-scheduling, proofreading, book-balancing, with the flood of routine correspondence, he would need to have. Someone had to be found.

The solution to his dilemma dawned on him suddenly, and was so clearly the answer to all his needs that he wondered at not having thought of it sooner. Whom could he find to be his secretary, his "manager," better than the woman who was even now answering his mail, who a month earlier had declined to become his wife? Kay Morrison's willingness to help him now, as a favor, might easily be turned into a permanent and formal relationship, employer and employee, in which he would pay her a salary for so many hours a week, all the year round, for —why not?—all the remaining years of his life. Yes, he decided, he would bring up the idea with Kay, and with Ted, before he left Bread Loaf.

When he did bring it up, he was delighted to find that both Kay and her husband, while not convinced of its wisdom, thought his proposal worthy of trial, and acquiesced. Kay said she would give up her present job as a part-time reader for the Atlantic Monthly Press and Little, Brown and Company, and would get in touch with her Boston friends to see about finding Frost an apartment within commuting distance of her own home in Cambridge.[3] Then, as Frost suggested, she would begin coming to him every weekday morning around half past nine, performing whatever secretarial or managerial chores needed to be done, and returning to her home and family around four in the afternoon.

It was not the salary Frost offered that induced Mrs. Morrison to take the job, but other and more important reasons. For one thing, Kay had seen enough of Frost before, during, and after the Writers' Conference to know that he was desperately in need of looking after, and that she, among all of his friends and relations, was the one now in the best position to undertake that task. She knew, also, that unless someone came forth to take Frost in hand, providing him with the encouragement and support he needed, he might never write poetry again. There was unavoidable risk, Kay knew, in continuing their association on a daily basis, but it was a risk she was prepared to run. Frost meant too much to her, as a friend and as a poet, for her to decline to help him at this critical juncture of his life.

Since Kay would soon enough be working for him after he left Bread Loaf, Frost decided not to press the matter of his typing, but to enjoy the Morrisons' company as they spent the last weeks of their summer vacation exploring the Vermont countryside in their old family Plymouth. He felt more alive than he had in months, and part of him wanted to remain with the Morrisons forever. In a few days, however, he decided it was time to go on to Concord Corners, and he prepared to make his departure. Before leaving, he asked if Ted and Kay would not accept from him, as a gift, one of the properties near his own in that hamlet in northern Vermont, making it their home base each summer in the years to come. The Morrisons were moved by the offer, but felt obliged to refuse. They already shared a family summer house in Chester, Nova Scotia. They had, moreover, already made arrangements to rent a farm in Ripton, Vermont, just a mile or so from the Bread Loaf campus, and would be living in Ripton in the coming summer whether or not they accepted Frost's generous gift.

Among Frost's first acts on settling in at Concord Corners was to write a letter to his new secretary containing, along with his plans for the coming months, much that he had been unable to express adequately face to face:

"Dear Kay: I try you with a pencil to see if a change of tool won't give me the release that a change of paper sometimes does. I am like an ocean that in its restlessness may have brought up every imaginable shape to the surface, but won't be satisfied till it brings up the sea serpent. You two rescued me from a very dangerous self when you had the idea of keeping me for the whole session at Bread Loaf. I am still infinitely restless, but I came away from you as good as saved. I had had a long lovers' quarrel with the world.[4] I loved the world, but you might never have guessed it from the things I thought and said. Now the quarrel is made up. Not that it ought to matter to anyone but me, but I can't help hoping it matters a little to my friends. The turning point for the better was on that Sunday when I seemed to behave so much worse. Stanley King's charge against me was ingratitude.[5] It will be a sensitive subject with me the rest of my life. I must be careful to avoid even the appearance of ingratitude. I am grateful to you two for your ministrations. Never doubt me. Let us pray the sea-serpent I feel so big with and about may prove to be poetic drama.

"Others to whom I should take this opportunity to acknowledge indebtedness for my relative restoration are Hershell Brickel, Bob Bailey, Fletcher Pratt, Gassner, Strauss, Stegner and those two literary girls Hassell and Negli, in about that order.[6] Hershell and Bob lead all the rest. I save Benny for a complete list by himself. There I think my obligations are met in form and my character for the moment vindicated.

"Do you want to do a little preliminary secretarial work for me on the enclosed cases? I find I *am* in a state about my lectures. I was forgetting entirely my promise of two or three days to Kenneth Sills (Pres of Bowdoin). I wish I could put off my Wyoming-Colorado-Utah and my Iowa trip till late April and get in the Bowdoin visit in November after Ohio. Maybe I could do the Johns Hopkins and Winston Salem things in November too. Another year we wont have such disorder will we? There's North Carolina and Paul Green I mustn't forget. We'll ask Paul if he still wants me at Chapel Hill. Hang it all! I keep thinking of unrecorded promises. There's a string I might do on my way south[:] Baltimore, Chapel Hill, Winston-Salem in late December or early January.

"I plan to go first to Florida and get Carol and his settled in some cheap warm spot for good and all—near Coconut Grove or even further south in Florida City or Homestead. Then I will go see Hershell for one month. Florida should take me a month what with buying a farm and giving a lecture or two I owe at Gainesville and Tellahassee. Don't get impatient with me. I am fighting a lot of engagements off.[7]

"Tears in my heart when I left you people. I wish you were in the house I am looking at over there above the lake where it in turn looks at the White Mts across the lake. Its a place I have had in mind for you if you werent so bound to Chester. Since you wont have it as a loan I am going to sell it to Benny. My love to Bobby. Tell him to write me if sawing his bat off brings up his batting average. Ever yours R."[8]

Frost's efforts to thank Kay for her friendship had begun before he wrote this letter, even before he had had the idea of making her his secretary. Midway through the Writers'

Conference, he had written a cryptic letter to John S. Van E. Kohn, a New York dealer in rare books who specialized in first editions of Robert Frost: "You have done so much for me and my books," Frost had written, "that I hesitate to ask you to do more. The nature of my request is a peculiar one. I want my two first books, first printing in first binding, and I want to pay the market price of the moment. Can you supply me with either or both? I have a very special sentimental use for them."[9] Following Frost's instructions, Kohn had sent his answer to Concord Corners, and it arrived there just ahead of Frost himself. Kohn said he could supply *North of Boston* at once from business stock, and he added that although his bookshop currently lacked a first-edition copy of the earlier volume, he would very gladly send Frost his personal copy of *A Boy's Will.* Kohn had priced the first book at $150, and thought it only fair to give Frost a larger discount than the 10 percent he normally gave to libraries and other dealers. Deciding on 15 percent, he set the price to Frost at $127.50, adding that Frost could pay him whatever it cost to replace his personal copy of *A Boy's Will.* "This is my first experience," said Kohn, "in offering a book to its author, and I am aware of an irony unflattering to myself in the asking of such a figure for a book of yours that wasn't finding buyers in England at a few shillings the copy twenty-odd years ago. I can only console myself with the reflection that this situation must be an old story to you by now."[10] Frost caught the playful tone of the dealer's letter, and his reply from Concord Corners was both playful and as cryptic as his original request:

"I am in a mood to accept any sacrifice from any man or woman. And I think it would be unromantic of me not to accept ruthlessly your romantic offer of my two firsts though one of them has to come out of your personal collection. But you are not to be allowed the only price-fixing. I enclose my check for two hundred and fifty dollars, that is to say, one hundred for *A Boy's Will* and one hundred fifty for *North of Boston.* The destination of the books is such and my obligation for favors so great there, that the more I pay for the books the more my gratification. It is a case where there is no pleasure in discounts. And there must be this understanding that when you find another copy of *A Boy's Will* you will charge me with anything it costs you above a hundred dollars. All this appeals to my imagination and you must indulge me cheerfully and without compunction. You shall be my witness that on this day I bought for two hundred and fifty dollars books of my own that twenty years before I could have bought for exactly four shillings or one dollar. The transaction flatters me I suppose. The sooner I have the books the happier I shall be."[11]

The books that were destined to be Frost's first gift to Kay Morrison arrived just a week later, and on September 10 Frost acknowledged receipt in a letter to Kohn that included an additional request: "You offer to do more for me. Let me tell you what you can start doing for me at once—finding me another first of *A Boy's Will* and another first of *North of Boston*. They will go to some one I care for only less than the person I am giving the first pair to."[12]

That person second only to Kay in Frost's affection was very likely Bernard DeVoto. Just before the first pair of books arrived, Frost had the DeVotos up to visit him in Concord Corners for the purpose he had stated in his penciled letter to Kay. But if Frost thought he could convince Benny DeVoto to buy a property next to his in the decaying hamlet of Concord Corners, he had misjudged not only his friend's real-estate plans but also the depth of his anger at the recent Writers' Conference. The DeVotos had no great desire to live in a place as remote as Concord Corners, but even if they had, the Writers' Conference had spoiled forever Benny's notion of Frost as a kind of father who could do no wrong. Frost must have sensed DeVoto's coldness, but nothing he did or said could make DeVoto take back, implicitly or explicitly, what he had said at the end of the Writers' Conference. Even an offer to buy the DeVotos a house in Cambridge, so he could have a place to go in times of loneliness, was refused. By the end of the day, Frost had to admit that if DeVoto still thought him "a good poet," he also still thought him "a bad man."[13]

Frost's liking for Concord Corners collapsed with the failure of his plans for its settlement. "You ask me where I am," he wrote to his Harvard friend David McCord. "I am where the wind never ceases blowing. . . . That's a characteristic of our hill top: on the stillest day in the summer the wind always draws knifelike across us up here. And in the fall it is almost too disturbing a foretaste of winter. No more nakedness mowing in the sun this year for me. . . . I am not going to stay up here in a bath of memories very long—I am damned if I am not for any hay fever. . . ."[14] A few days later he left Vermont for Louis Untermeyer's farm, Stony Water, in Elizabethtown, New York, which he had visited briefly before the Writers' Conference and to which he now planned to return in the company of his daughter Lesley, who had come to Vermont for a family visit. In writing earlier to invite himself back to Stony Water, Frost had also announced the success of Mrs. Morrison's efforts to find him a place to live in Boston:

"I thought of two things today the first things I have thought of since I was under the influence of your liquor at Stony Water two weeks ago in the company of that first rate fighting intellect Lee Simonson. What a good time I had that day. I had meant to report to you on it, but I had somehow got it into my head that you knew all about it already. However that may be, I am more interested now preparing you for my attempted come-back—to Stony Water. I want to come back next Monday in the car of my daughter Lesley and be left there by her after a day or two pleasantly spent on her part playing tennis with us and then be put on some train by you later in the week after some more tennis on our part exclusively and get about the business of furnishing my tenement in Boston at 88 Mount Vernon Street overlooking Louisburg Square overseeing Harvar(d) College and overlooking any little defects there may be in human nature in the rough. Dont you think so? I mean do you agree? In cutting marble and in drawing with silver point you can't undo what you have done. So may my writing be. Stet is my slogan. And if it can't stand let it set. . . ."

The continuation of the letter contained further hints of Frost's fear that his "defects" had alienated Untermeyer as they had DeVoto: ". . . I thought of you over there not two hundred miles away with your wisdom of this world, a pundit who has punned it without money and without price to all comers. All I have to do if I want advice (and I do) is to come to you in forma pauperis and not pretend it is anything else I am after. I've been crazy for the last six months. I havent known what I was doing. I wonder if you have noticed and could tell me. Thats what I'm coming over to find out. Dont talk too fast. Let it come out as it will by rambling round the subject. Do you think I am still living in this world? Tell me the truth. Dont spare me. . . ."[15]

He remained more than a week in Elizabethtown, then left with Untermeyer for the train station in Springfield, Massachusetts, stopping in Amherst to arrange for the transfer of his possessions to his new home. Soon after his train left for Boston, however, a severe hurricane swept across the state, and resulted in an adventure Frost later described in a letter to his son Carol:

"I set out from Springfield to go to Boston at a little after noon. Already the water was too high for the direct route. So my train was sent to New Haven to aim for Boston by the Long Island shore tracks. It never got further than New Haven and it was twelve hours getting there. I waited in it for half the next day and then went up to Pierson College at Yale for the next night. I had a pleasant time with friends. But I was restless to get where I could be located by Lesley should she be in trouble. So I hired a taxi for thirty dollars and came from New Haven by the Post Road one hundred and fifty miles to the St. Botolph Club 4 Newberry St. Boston Mass which will remain my address for some time to come. I saw a lot of ruin the whole way, but we had no trouble in getting through and were in no danger. The wildest time was in the train during the hurricane. The train shook and the passengers joked. Luckily the train was a sleeper from St. Louis with not many left in the sleeping cars. That gave everybody in the chair cars a chance to hire beds for the night.

"Lesley got a telephone call through to me soon after I reached here. She had been in real danger with the children. She will probably be telling you about it in a letter.

"I hear from the Morrisons that upper Vermont was probably worse damaged than in the flood of 1926. . . ."[16]

Frost's apartment was not to be ready for occupancy until mid-October, and since there was work to be done in preparation for his forthcoming lecture tour, now just three weeks away, Kay Morrison called on him at the St. Botolph Club as soon as she had returned from her abbreviated summer in Vermont. When she tried to enter the Club, however, she was stopped and informed that women were not permitted on the premises: she could not even speak to her employer in the downstairs parlor. Infuriated, Frost abruptly moved out of his room and took another in the nearby Ritz Hotel. But after a few days, exhausted by his recent exertions and apprehensive about his first lecture tour since Elinor's death, he came down with a cold that soon worsened until it was serious enough to send him to Phillips House, part of Massachusetts General Hospital. He remained there for several days before deciding he had endured hospital routine long enough. Then, rising from bed and putting on his clothes, he walked out of the hospital undismissed.

It was the second week of October when he moved in at 88 Mt. Vernon Street and with Kay's help began to unpack the boxes of books and furnishings that by now had arrived from Amherst. It was a small flat, smaller, it seemed to him, than any place he had lived in since his childhood in San Francisco. But Kay assured him that with the proper furnishings, and with his books lining the walls, it would be comfortable enough to live in at least until a larger apartment, or perhaps a small house in Cambridge, could be found. With less than a week before his first appearance at Columbia University on October 16, Frost decided not to finish unpacking until he returned from his tour. With the time remaining, he set about writing some of the letters he had owed for months to his friends. One of these was Mary Goodwillie of Baltimore, Maryland, who had long been close to the Frost family,[17] and who had asked him to speak when he could to the Friends of the Johns Hopkins Library:

"You look for me in vain in my old haunts," he wrote on October 13, "and you look for letters from me in vain. A bad correspondent seems to have become a worse. The fixtest mentionable thing about me is this apartment number 30 at 88 Mt Vernon St where I have put some books on shelves to be waiting for me when I come back worn out from my lectures. I have given up Amherst and given up the idea of settling down with any of the children. Luckily things are fine for at least two of them and if none too happily for the third surely beyond my personal powers to make any happier.[18] I am filling my immediate future full of lectures for distraction and propose to go till I almost drop. I shall welcome the chance to speak or read to your Friends of the Library. Please do pay me my usual fee (two hundred) if only to maintain my self respect. I shall need money very possibly before I get through my turn on earth. See my poem 'Provide, Provide' in *A Further Range*.[19] Money is much, particularly if it is extorted from my well-wishers; but visits with friends are more. We will have a good sit by the fire and I will tell you a lot more by intimation than I can be expected to tell outright. . . ."[20]

Another was addressed to Frost's fellow artist, J. J. Lankes, whose woodcuts had appeared as illustrations in *New Hamp-*

shire and *A Further Range*, and whose friendship with him was based in part on their shared affection for rural life:

"You hear from one in me now having given up life in the country for life in one of the oldest and most citified cities of the new world. Don't judge me too hardly. I have come here not to get excitement but to get away from the excitement of being alone with nature naturating.[21] My only happiness seems to lie in not looking behind me when I leap. Old associations are too much for me. I have to get up an interest in what is going to happen next. So for the year I am a Bostonian. . . . I thought I would have not only a city home but I would be very business like for any benefit the change might afford me. I should like to answer all my letters for a while if only by deputy. I have taken a part time secretary Mrs Kathleen Morrison who will take care of my correspondence and see to my lecture dates. . . ."[22]

Before leaving for New York, Frost wrote one more letter to the book dealer John Kohn, who had found another first-edition copy of *A Boy's Will* but who had so far been unable to secure another copy of *North of Boston*: "Never mind," Frost told him. "It isnt as important that I get the books this time as it was the first. You are goodness itself to have worked so hard on the case. Buying my own books at such an advance on the original cost was a real adventure in romantic friendship. I mus[t]nt expect to recapture that fine careless rapture. My gratitude toward one person has been satisfied as I doubt if it will ever need to be again in this world. The requirements in the second gift will be amply met I think with *A Boy's Will* alone. I guess I had as well cancel the order for *North of Boston*. Come to think of it I wouldnt want the second gift quite to equal the first gift in value. There would be poetic injustice involved. . . ."[23]

It was not that he had given up hopes of winning back the affection of Benny DeVoto. Rather, he realized that DeVoto was not likely to be won back by mere gifts, however generous, and that if he wanted to save his friendship with Benny, it would have to be by somehow neutralizing the charge that he was "a good poet" but "a bad man." Up to now, he had not seen how to do so without denying what he had long felt to be true: that he was, indeed, more a bad man than a good. But in Columbus, during his extended visit to Ohio State University and his would-be biographer, Professor Newdick, an idea came to him: Why not simply admit that he was "a bad man," that he had always been such, and that he was likely to remain so? Why not put Benny on the defensive by defending his badness, challenging his friend to accept him as he was, as he could not help being? Frost thought such an approach had a reasonable chance of success, and as soon as he could, he wrote a letter to his disaffected friend:

"Being out here with my faithful biographer inevitably puts me on the defense of my native badness. If just because I once said:

They would not find me changed from him they knew
Only more sure of all I thought was true[24]

they needn't work up a theory that my philosophy is altogether static. Any decent philosophy and all philosophy has to [be] largely static. Else what would there be to distinguish it from science? It is the same with religion: it must be the same yesterday today and forever. The only part of Genesis that has changed in three thousand years and become ridiculous is the science in it. The religion stands. My philosophy, non-Platonic but none-the-less a tenable one, I hold more or less unbroken from youth to age. But it wouldn't be fair to my flesh and temper to say that I am always tiresomely the same frost I was when winter came on last year. You must have marked changes coming over me this summer. Who cares whether they were for the worse or not? You may as a serious student of my works. But Avis and I don't give a sigh. One of the greatest changes my nature has undergone is of record in 'To Earthward' and indeed elsewhere for the discerning. In my school days I simply could not go on and do the best I could with a copy book I had once blotted. I began life wanting perfection and determined to have it. I got so I ceased to expect it and could do without it. Now I find I actually crave the flaws of human handwork. I gloat over imperfection. Look out for me. You as critic and psychoanalyst will know how to do that.[25] Nevertheless Im telling you something in a self conscious moment that may throw light on every page of my writing for what it is worth. I mean I am a bad bad man But yours R. F."[26]

At the end of October, having lectured at Ohio State and several other area colleges, Frost left Columbus and headed home. He had agreed to appear at the University of Buffalo and elsewhere along the way, but by mid-November he was back at 88 Mt. Vernon Street, where he hoped to spend most of the next few weeks forgetting his lectures as he worked with Mrs. Morrison catching up on his correspondence, or alone on his verse. He hoped also to hear some word from DeVoto in response to his letter, but none came.

The letter had had no apparent effect on Benny DeVoto, but it did, perhaps, have an effect on Frost himself. Having confessed himself to be "a bad bad man," he soon began to usurp Mrs. Morrison's time and attention in ways that she had not anticipated when she agreed to become his secretary. His recent hospitalization had taught him that illness was a convenient excuse for demanding special care, and he was not above manufacturing a malady to elicit a desired response. "Be moderately sorry for a poor old man of iron will," he wrote to Untermeyer in late November. "Nothing I do or say is as yet due to anything but a strong determination to have my own way. I may show as sick, but it is for practical purposes. I dont know what I deserve for a nature like mine. I was boasting to David McCord this very day that I was clever enough to beat my nature. Did he suppose I wasn't?

"Well among the things I don't deserve but hope to get is what I am about to propose from and for you. If you consent to do it you will be doing more than one thing to make my immediate future a joy forever. Not to beat about the bush a page longer it is: Come to Bread Loaf [next summer] and team up with me in poetry criticism four or five days a week for the two weeks of the Conference. You could go home over the week end and I could go with you. We would make the poetry consultations and clinics a joint stunt to the nation. I got up this idea and Ted Morrison took to it like live bait. I needn't go into my mixture of motives except to say that they are all honorable by now. I am growing more and more honorable every time the moon comes safely through an eclipse. (Subject for a poem.) I am really a person of good aspirations and you know I am or you wouldn't stay my indulgent friend through all my errancies the way you do. There is nothing to report on my present state of mind but that though it is better, it can still be alleviated by any kindness you will do me. I sometimes take it pretty hard to be left in a city apartment alone with the night. Dont think I haven't myself well in hand, though, and beyond the need of psychoanalysis. As I have said, I cut up no ructions but with design to gain my ends even as aforetime when I was a child in San Francisco I played sick to get out of going to school. There's a vigorous devil in me that raises me above or drops me below the level of pity. Nevertheless I sometimes weep internally with sorrow (but not as often as externally at the eyes with cold weather). Grant me my request, oh friend of many many years!"

Finally he spoke directly of Kay Morrison, the real center of the letter as she had so quickly become of his new life:

"This year I have worked hard in the open, and I think it has done me good. My secretary has soothed my spirit like music in her attendance on me and my affairs. She has written my letters and sent me off on my travels. It is an unusual friendship. I have come to value my poetry almost less than the friendships it has brought me. I say it who wouldnt have believed I would ever live to say it. And I say it with a copy of *The Independent* containing my first published poem on the desk before me. I was thrust out into the desolateness of wondering about my past whether it had not been too cruel to those I had dragged with me and almost to cry out to heaven for a word of reassurance that was not given me in time. Then came this girl stepping innocently into my days to give me something to think of besides dark regrets. My half humorous noisy contrition of the last few months has begun to die down. You have heard a lot of it and you are hearing it still a little here. I doubt if it has been quite dignified. I am told I am spoken of as her 'charge.' It is enough to be. Lets have some peace. You can figure it out for yourself how my status with a girl like her might be the perfect thing for me at my age in my position. I wish in some indirect way she could come to know how I feel toward her."[27]

It was not long before Frost found a way of informing Kay Morrison of how he felt toward her, and appropriately it was by means of poetry: a sonnet of just one sentence whose central image was a carefully constructed metaphysical conceit. His eventual title for the poem was "The Silken Tent," but when he first presented it to Kay, Frost called it "In Praise of Your Poise." As he realized when he wrote it, and Kay when she read it, it was not only the first poem he had written in many months, but one of the best he had written in his life:

She is as in a field a silken tent
At midday when a sunny summer breeze
Has dried the dew and all its ropes relent,
So that in guys it gently sways at ease,
And its supporting central cedar pole,
That is its pinnacle to heavenward
And signifies the sureness of the soul,
Seems to owe naught to any single cord,
But strictly held by none, is loosely bound
By countless silken ties of love and thought
To everything on earth the compass round,
And only by one's going slightly taut
In the capriciousness of summer air
Is of the slightest bondage made aware.[28]

TRIALS OF STRENGTH AND SUPPLENESS

The devil of it is that except for the flu threat I seem more alive than I ever was. You should see me in trials of strength and suppleness with men much younger. I even excel in some events.[1]

ON THE LAST DAY of November 1938, Robert Frost delivered a free afternoon lecture at Harvard University, and it met with a response for which the Harvard authorities had not adequately prepared. Apparently assuming that a lecture by the former Norton Professor of Poetry would draw only a few hundred people, the planners had scheduled it to take place in Room D of Emerson Hall, whose maximum capacity was 300 people. More than a thousand came. Next day, a late-coming reporter for the Boston *Evening Transcript* described the consequences of the miscalculation:

"We had just decided to retire with dignity, when of a sudden a shout went up behind us, 'New Lecture Hall!' Pell-mell the mob was on us. We ran, slipping and sliding along the paths, plunging across streets in a stream of humanity. Everyone ran except a few black-clothed old ladies, with canes, who came an hour early for seats, who would arrive at the new hall to find standing room only. . . ."

The mob scene was particularly pleasing to Frost, for he knew it would prove to skeptics that he was still in demand at Harvard. That, in turn, would aid David McCord and the "Friends of Robert Frost" in their effort to raise $4,000 for a two-year appointment for him at Harvard. In his lecture, however, Frost did not attempt to convey the impression that he approached the subject of education with Bostonian solemnity. The reporter's account continued:

"He began to speak, informally, colloquially, easily—taking his own time to find the just word, the right anecdote. His head is wrinkled in a dozen lines, his hands massive, his brow large. Colleges, he said, produce about one scholar to 999 others who go out and make money and give it back to the college to support the scholar. The excitement about adult education distresses him a little. After the age of 22 or 23, unless a man is going to be a professional scholar, a cavalier approach to knowledge recommends itself to Mr. Frost. That is the artist's way, he said. Don't go hounding after knowledge. He moved on this line of thought awhile, with sly twitching of academic tails, provoking roars of laughter. His talk is pure homespun, but it has a firm bite, a sure sense of timing. Our perceptions may be dull, but Mr. Frost reminded us yesterday of nobody so much as the late Will Rogers. . . ."[2]

The success of Frost's platform manner was nothing new, and he had been compared before to the homespun philosopher who, before his death in 1935, had typically begun his enormously popular lectures with "All I know is what I read in the papers." But even Frost was surprised by the ease with which he now approached his public appearances, after years of being terrified by the prospect of speaking before an audience. A few hours before the Harvard lecture, he had written to Lesley of the change he had noticed in his recent lecture tour:

"My fear of these things beforehand has largely left me. I have done my ten or fifteen this fall in Ohio Pennsylvania New York and Massachusetts with almost perfect calm. Something strange has come over my life. I shall never be the scared fool again that I used to be. Nothing can more than kill me. . . ."

Lesley knew her father too well to take his remark as indicating he had also overcome his lifelong fear of death. But his letter suggested that he took comfort in believing the dread event was still many years off:

"I happened to remark at the DeVoto table[3] that I might turn to prose in ten years from now and their eight year old piped up 'You, you'll be dead in ten years.' I really enjoyed the rudeness. The devil of it is that except for the flu threat I seem more alive than I ever was. You should see me in trials of strength and suppleness with men much younger. I even excel in some events. . . ."

In reminding his daughter that his mental and physical powers had not diminished with age, Frost was obliquely defending the way he had ordered his life in the months since Elinor's death. Lesley, he knew, was not sure he had been wise in declining the offer of Carol and Lillian to build an ell for his use on the Stone Cottage, and she was even less sure that Kay Morrison was, indeed, the perfect solution for his difficulties. Knowing that Lesley's disapproval of Kay would create family tensions with which he could ill afford to cope, Frost tried hard to assure his daughter that her fears were groundless, that he was capable of looking after his best interests, and that Boston, not South Shaftsbury, was where he now belonged:

"I pass the time away with the lectures and with a good deal of the society of a very few people here. Kathleen Morrison has made my apartment pleasant and taken an interest in my mail and my lecture engagements. You must be grateful to her for having helped me through my bad time. Lillian I know would have been only too glad to take care of me and make me one of the family at the farm. But the burden of that household would have been too much for my spirit. I am best as I am, though the hours alone are sometimes pretty desolate. . . ."[4]

When he visited Lesley in Washington, D.C., a week later, Frost again found it necessary to justify himself, and defend Kay, in the face of Lesley's persistent questioning. The course of the discussion can be inferred from the letter Frost sent his daughter after his return to Boston:

"You kids count with me and having you to think of and see something of means a great deal. But there are things I have to look for outside where there are no family memories for complication. You must come to be grateful to Kathleen for her ministrations. The closest criticism will discover no flaw in her kindness to me I am sure. We must all be a lot together when we can. She will press nothing of course—as she has pressed nothing. If I find myself almost a member of the Morrison family (in my entire detachment) the pressure has been all mine from the moment when both Kathleen and Ted together merely suggested that I come and live near them in Cambridge. They had forgotten the idea when I picked it up to decide me against going to live in New York. . . ."[5]

Besides his defense of his relationship with Kay, Frost's letter contained good news concerning his recent negotiations with Henry Holt and Company, with whom, for a variety of reasons, he had lately been seriously disaffected. The high point of his relationship with the firm, which had published all his books since 1915, had begun in 1936 with the appearance of his sixth collection of new verse, *A Further Range*. Brought out in an edition of 50,000 copies, it had been a Book-of-the-Month Club selection, a best seller, and had earned Frost more than $7,000 in royalties as well as his third Pulitzer Prize. Later, prompted by Frost's literary success and his personal friendship with the poet, Holt's president, Richard H. Thornton, had volunteered to supervise the editing and publishing of *Recognition of Robert Frost*, which traced the growth of Frost's literary reputation. But before the book appeared, Frost learned that Holt was planning to bring out another volume, an anthology of literary essays, which contained no reference to the poetry of Robert Frost. Enraged by the omission, he gave Thornton an ultimatum: either withdraw the literary anthology, or he would look elsewhere for a publisher of his works.

Knowing that Holt could ill afford to lose its leading author, Thornton reluctantly acceded to the request, and for a time Frost was placated. In February 1938, his Amherst friend George Roy Elliott wrote to him, "Are you going to publish your next book through Holts? Don't. Holts? / They're dolts / In need of jolts,"[6] and Frost replied by asking Elliott what he had against the firm. Perhaps, he teasingly suggested, they had refused to publish one of his books. But he acknowledged that all was not well at Holt by adding, "I'll tell you this about them, their literary department is pretty nearly on the rocks. I have my doubts of their future. This is in confidence."[7]

Over the next few months, the economic difficulties in the Holt trade department were compounded by a power struggle between Thornton and Board Chairman Herbert G. Bristol, who was seeking Thornton's removal as president. To put pressure on his adversary, Bristol urged a reduction in the monthly payments of $250 to Frost, which for several years had been given as a guaranteed advance against his royalties. Frost learned of the threat to Thornton's position, and since the level of his royalty earnings was such that there was no danger of his experiencing any real reduction in income, he went along with the reduction as a gesture of loyalty to the man who had championed his cause at Holt for the past ten years. "Make any adjustment for your comfort," he told Thornton. "I have had the feeling that my monthly check might be an embarrassment. . . . The three thousand a year was a promise of extra effort on your part to stretch the sales. I don't want it to be too much of a strain for friendship. It is necessary for me to be friends with my publishers above all things. . . . You may name $150 a month as a compromise between your fears of Mr. Herbert Bristol and your anxiety for me. Hadn't you better go the whole length for him, whatever that is. All I ask at present is what the books can earn and your assurance you will do your best for them. You understand me. I am saying use me in any way to strengthen your position."[8]

But Thornton was unable to save himself, and by the fall of 1938 Frost was thoroughly disgusted with the firm. "What's eating me at the last moment," he confessed to Untermeyer in October, "is how to compose a tactful letter to Edward Bristol to get a friendly release from Henry Holt and Co."[9] The response of the Holt management was prompt and decisive. As intent as ever to keep Frost in the firm, T. J. Wilson, the acting president, hastened to inform him that Blue Ribbon Books wished to publish a cheap reprint edition of the forthcoming Holt book, *Collected Poems of Robert Frost*, from which Frost stood to reap a guaranteed advance of $2,000.[10] At the same time, Herbert Bristol wrote to assure him that, contrary to the fears he had lately expressed, Holt had absolutely no intention of closing down the trade department of the company. "On the contrary," said Bristol, "we are seeking a man of enterprise to develop it from a source of annual loss of over $30,000 (the other branches prospering) to at least its pre-depression place. Otherwise, we should not have been so firm in our response to your suggestion of withdrawing your books." He added: "I don't know what passed between you and Mr. Thornton when your monthly stipend was reduced from $250. Your royalty earnings by and large seemed to justify the larger sum, and we are of course ready to continue it until you would call for a change. It would, of course, make the future more certain if you cared to include your prose as well as poetry, so long as you are satisfied that we are doing our part well. Mr. Wilson is trying to see you personally shortly, and can arrange details in person."[11]

A few days later, Wilson and Frost met in New York City, as Frost returned from his visit with Lesley in Washington. Their conversation was soon followed by a concrete proposal: "If you will give us all your future books, whether in verse or in prose, for publication by us, we will pay you a royalty of twenty percent of the published price on all copies sold. We will also pay you henceforth a royalty of twenty percent of the published price on all copies sold of those books by you which we published prior to the present date, December 12, 1938. Furthermore, we will pay you, during the remainder of your lifetime, the sum of $300 monthly, until you consider such payment an unfair burden to us. These monthly payments shall not be considered returnable to us under any circumstances."[12]

Never before, as Frost well knew, had an author been offered so munificent a contract. The 15 percent royalty he had been receiving was unusually good. Twenty percent was unheard of. In detailing the terms of the proposed contract to Lesley after his return to Boston, Frost could scarcely conceal his sense of triumph over the Holt management: "Kathleen had Raymond Everett in to tell us what he thought of the Holts' proffered contract. I could see it was disappointingly good from his point of view. None but a bad publisher, he said, could give an author such good terms. . . . The falling out of faithful friends is the renewal of contract much to my advantage. I didn't go for to get the better of them. I merely set out to get away from them, or make them eat crow for treating me so badly this year. I suppose Richard Thornton's quarrel with Herbert Bristol was to blame for their mishandling of me."[13]

Oddly enough, it was the new head of Holt's trade department, William M. Sloane III, who detected a serious flaw in the agreements newly arrived at by Frost and the firm. In going over various publishing contracts, Sloane was disturbed to find that Holt had agreed to permit Blue Ribbon Books to publish an edition of Frost's new *Collected Poems*, textually identical to Holt's own volume, at a list price only about a third of that of the Holt edition. Considering this a situation likely to damage sales of Holt's own volume, Sloane asked Frost, in their first meeting, if he would be willing to write a special preface to be added to the *Collected Poems* Holt was bringing out, to distinguish it from the cheaper edition.

Because he saw the validity of Sloane's argument, but more because he liked this young man who wrote books himself and loved classical literature, Frost put aside his long-standing aversion to writing anything to order, and agreed to do the piece. Within three weeks he had completed a 1,500–word preface for the Holt *Collected Poems*, a highly compressed, richly metaphorical essay on the art of poetry which he called "The Figure a Poem Makes."

He began with a discussion that reflected his continuing interest in the relationship of the sound of a poem to the sense the sound conveys. The object in writing poetry, he asserted, "is to make all poems sound as different as possible from each other," but the "greatest help towards variety" lies less in what the poet does with his words than in what he does with his "meaning," his "subject matter." In our language, Frost said, the poet has but two meters to choose from, "strict iambic and loose iambic," but "the possibilities for tune from the dramatic tones of meaning struck across the rigidity of a limited meter are endless." Beyond the sound of a poem, there is its quality of "wildness" to consider, but the wildness must be pure, the poet must be "wild with nothing to be wild about." "Just as the first mystery was how a poem could have a tune in such a straightness as meter, so the second mystery is how a poem can have wildness and at the same time a subject that shall be fulfilled." Frost then described "the figure a poem makes":

"It begins in delight and ends in wisdom. The figure is the same as for love. No one can really hold that the ecstasy should be static and stand still in one place. It begins in delight, it inclines to the impulse, it assumes direction with the first line laid down, it runs a course of lucky events, and ends in a clarification of life—not necessarily a great clarification, such as sects and cults are founded on, but in a momentary stay against confusion. . . ."[14]

Frost was pleased with the piece, and particularly so by the success with which he had adapted ideas about wildness and love—important private concerns of the moment—to the needs of an essay on poetry.[15] As he was putting the finishing touches on it, in the first week of January 1939, he was further pleased by the arrival of a letter from the National Institute of Arts and Letters, informing him that he had just been awarded the Institute's Gold Medal for "distinguished work in poetry." The writer extended Frost an invitation to attend the Annual Dinner in New York on January 18, at which time the president of the Institute, Dr. Walter J. Damrosch, would formally present the award.[16]

Frost had planned to leave for Florida well before the dinner in question, and he had undertaken lecture obligations in the South prior to the eighteenth. But the Institute's Gold Medal, which had been awarded only three times before for poetry, was worth a special trip back to New York, and he cheerfully made plans to go there after a speaking engagement in Richmond, Virginia. On the evening of the eighteenth, after accepting the Gold Medal from Dr. Damrosch,[17] he addressed the membership of the organization that had voted to honor him, and chose to speak on a subject that was both a personal favorite and appropriate to the occasion:

" 'Have you ever thought about rewards,' I was asked lately in a tone of fear for me that I might not have thought at my age. I don't know what I was supposed to think, unless it was that the greatest reward of all was self-esteem. Saints, like John Bunyan, are all right in jail if they are sure of their truth and sincerity. But, so, also, are many criminals. The great trouble is to be sure. A stuffed shirt is the opposite of a criminal. He cares not what he thinks of himself so long as the world continues to think well of him. The sensible and healthy live somewhere between self-approval and the approval of society. They make their adjustment without too much talk of compromise.

"Still an artist, however well he may fare, within and without, must often feel he has to rely too heavily on self-appraisal for comfort. For twenty years the world neglected him; then for twenty years it entreated him kindly. He has to take the responsibility of deciding when the world was wrong. He can't help wishing there was some third more disinterested party, such as God, or Time, to give absolute judgment.

Oh Time whose verdicts mock our own
The only righteous judge art thou.

"The scientist seems to have the advantage of him in a court of larger appeal. A planet is perturbed in its orbit. The scientist stakes his reputation on the perturber's being found at a certain point in the sky at a certain time of night. All telescopes are turned that way, and sure enough, there the perturber is as bright as a button. The scientist knows he is good without being told. He has a mind and he has instruments, the extensions of mind that fit closely into the nature of the Universe. It is the same when an engineer has plotted two shafts to meet under the middle of a mountain and make a tunnel. The shafts approach each other; the workmen in one can hear the pickaxes of the workmen in the other. A sudden gleam of pickaxe breaks through. A human face shows in the face of the rock. The engineer is justified of his figures. He knows he has a mind. It has fitted into the nature of the Universe. . . ."

The artist, he said, concluding his remarks, must look elsewhere for proof of his excellence:

"I should be sorry to concede the artist has no such recourse to tests of certainty at all. His hope must be that his work will prove to have fitted into the nature of people. Beyond my belief in myself, beyond another's critical opinion of me, lies this. I should like to have it that your medal is a token of my having fitted, not into the nature of the Universe, but in some small way, at least, into the nature of Americans—into their affections, is perhaps what I mean. I trust you will be willing to indulge me here and let me have it so for the occasion. But whatever the medal may or may not symbolize, I take it as a very great honor."[18]

Frost had planned, before leaving New York, to see someone under far less pleasant circumstances than the dinner of the National Institute, and he was relieved when a last-minute development permitted him to avoid the unwanted meeting. Just after receiving word of the Gold Medal and the National Institute dinner earlier in the month, he had found in his mail a letter from Eustace Seligman, a trustee of Amherst College, concerning the possibility of his returning to Amherst on something like, but less than, the former basis. "Since we met a few weeks ago," wrote Seligman, "I have had a chance to talk to Stanley King. I find that his version of what happened and yours are not 100% in accord, but I don't see any use in going into it. The important thing, however, is that, in response to my question, he said he would be only too delighted to have you continue in some part-time capacity. . . ." The trustee invited Frost's response to three essential questions: "1. If arrangements can be made to underwrite your salary by a group of alumni, will you be willing to resume a position on the Amherst faculty? 2. If you are willing, will you let me know what kind of a position you will be willing to take? Specifically, how long during each year would you be willing to stay in Amherst, what time of the year would it be, how many lectures would you want to give, and what title would you want? 3. Finally, what would your idea be as to compensation? In writing the above I am, of course, aware—having been told by Tom Lamont—that he is arranging something similar to the above at Harvard. I don't see why the two necessarily will interfere. . . ."[19]

Obviously, Amherst College in general, and President King in particular, were willing and even eager to see Frost rejoin the faculty he had abruptly quit in 1938 after eleven years of continuous employment. Still convinced that King had treated him badly, Frost had no intention whatever of working again under his administration. But he was curious to see how far Amherst was willing to go to "compensate" him for the wrongs he felt he had suffered, and he wrote back to Seligman, through Mrs. Morrison, that he would meet the trustee after the dinner in New York.

When Seligman took sick shortly before the planned encounter, and wrote to Frost inviting him to supply his views on reemployment by mail, Frost drafted a reply that revealed, perhaps better than he could have done in person, his continuing resentments of Amherst and Stanley King: "Whatever this misunderstanding is between Amherst and me," he wrote, "it bids fair to continue awhile longer. You unfortunately have a cold that keeps you from talking with me, and I unfortunately can have no views on the subject of your last letter unless you talk some into my head. The two proposals that brought me back to Amherst the last two times were entirely of George Olds and Dwight Morrow's framing.[20] I couldn't bring myself to set a value on my name example or services to any college. I have always been in a position to leave it to others to say what good I was. I haven't claimed to be much good. I appreciate your great good will as intercessor between Stanley King and me, but aren't you really afraid I have been allowed to get too far away from Amherst for rapproachment." Beneath the text of the draft, which he gave to Mrs. Morrison for retyping, he added, scornfully, "Something like the above I am sending him. They seem to me to be manoevering."[21] For the present, at least, the matter of his return to Amherst was closed.

Immediately following the National Institute dinner, Frost boarded a southbound train for Key West, Florida, where he was joined after several days by the Morrisons. They stayed at the comfortably attractive Casa Marina Hotel, where Frost had stayed during previous trips to the island, and whose manager, Peter Schutt, was by now something of an old friend. They slept late, took long walks around the picturesque town, and played tennis with Mrs. Ernest Hemingway, whose husband was then in Havana. Then, returning to the mainland, they spent a second week visiting their mutual friend of Bread Loaf summers, Hervey Allen.[22]

A highly successful novel, *Anthony Adverse*, had enabled the friendly giant, Allen, to build a good-sized estate on a tract of undeveloped pineland in South Miami, and The Glades, as the property was called, now had located on it a number of prefabricated houses in which Allen's guests stayed during their visits. The addition of Frost and the Morrisons to the two couples already there put a considerable strain on the hospitality the Allens could provide. That, however, was nothing compared to the strain Frost felt himself by the time the Morrisons left him and returned to Cambridge. After two weeks of trying to keep on an even keel among the pressures of being a guest of the Allens in company with the Morrisons, he was tense and exhausted, but grateful that there had been no major upsets.[23] "There is nothing much new about me," he wrote Lesley on February 3, "except that I came through the two weeks with the Morrisons pretty well considering all there was on all sides to dissemble. I am alone now in a rather desolated house. The plan of my well-wishers is to ship me off for a few days' change to Cuba in the company of Mr and Mrs Paul Engel who are my neighbors in another of the Allen houses."

Compounding the tensions that grew out of his relationship with Kay were Frost's concerns for Carol and his family, who had also come down to Florida for the winter and perhaps for good. As Frost had told Kay in his letter from Concord Corners, Carol was planning to buy a house and settle permanently somewhere in southern Florida, hoping thereby to break out of the pattern of failure and dependency on his father that had long since established itself on his marginal farm in South Shaftsbury. But even now Carol seemed unable to order his life in the proper manner or to accept advice from his well-intentioned father, and Frost could only bitterly report to Lesley the latest news of his son's restless wanderings in search of a happier life:

"Carol had found nothing in Homestead and given it up. When I got here he had all but decided to take a rather expensive house at West Palm Beach. I interposed to make them look Coconut Grove over. They are settled in a large house on the other side of town from me at $75 a month for February and March. Their trip down cost $200. The trip back will be another $200. The total extra cost will be upwards of $600 that might as well have gone toward a better house in South Shaftsbury. They have begun to see it that way. . . ."

As Frost knew well, Carol's problems were more psychological than economic, but he was powerless to do much more than observe the way in which Carol seemed to flirt constantly with self-destruction:

"They talk as if this were their last winter south. I am not seeing them often. It isnt good for us to be together. I remonstrate with Carol for running past stop signs and I only start an argument. He says everyone runs through them. The next day he has a small head on collision with a man uninsured. It cost us twenty five dollars. I didnt complain a word—merely said we were lucky it was no worse. He said Lillian had called his attention away to look at something. I feel all the time I ride with him his eyes are off the road ahead too often. I'm no judge and I dont want to be one. He is not well disciplined and it is too late to do anything about it. Let's not worry. Prescott is out of school. I may offer him money to do some real work for me this spring when he gets back to Vermont. . . ."

As Frost worried over Carol, he could not help thinking once again of the way in which he had seemingly damaged his children. All of them had been exposed, from their earliest years, to the high-strung personality of their father; all had developed personalities that were also high-strung. Beyond that, they all had been obliged to live with the heavy burden of a father whose fame and success they could scarcely hope to duplicate. Marjorie, Irma, Carol, and Lesley had all tried or were trying to express themselves through art, but even Lesley, the strongest of his children, seemed unable to break free of his unintended domination. "It is as if I was always present when you wrote," he told her, alluding to the children's stories she had recently seen through publication. "You have me to get over."

He finally managed to assuage his sense of guilt by reminding himself—and Lesley—that if his children were unhappy, he was too. "Me—," he complained bitterly, "I am miserable living round with people all the time. I have always had hours and days to myself alone. I feel on draught from dawn to dark. It can't last. I have no idea how it is going to be stopped though. Not as yet. My entanglement has had critical moments when it looked like openly declared trouble. The future of Europe is easier for me to see into than my own future."[24]

Hervey Allen had quickly realized that his friend's spirits were disturbingly low, and without fully understanding the cause, he had set about finding a remedy. Being temporarily tied up in work on a new novel, he had suggested that Frost and the Engles fly down by seaplane to Cuba and spend a week sightseeing around the island. Frost had grudgingly agreed to the proposal, and the Engles—Paul Engle was one of his young poet-friends at the University of Iowa[25]—were only too glad to do so too. But the trip did little to change Frost's mood. "I have just been to Cuba with Paul and Mary Engle," he wrote soon after his return. "The land is mo[no]tonously rich and full of beggars. Any souvenirs were made in Chekoslovakia Paris or the United States. There is no native art or craft. The Engles made good company and so did our grimy little Cuban interpreter who was educated at the normal school at Mansfield Penn and for three years in the American navy. I am still at a loss what harmless to do with myself. . . ."[26]

Before the return flight to Florida, completing Frost's first adventure in airborne travel, he cabled ahead

CUBA HAS BEEN GOOD GLADES WILL BE BETTER[27]

and so it proved. Freer now to spend more time with his guests, Allen displayed just the right combination of wit, wisdom, and commiseration to give Frost some comfort amidst the problems that beset him. According to Frost's later account, Allen was "the same old philosopher as of old only more so. He has many figures, parallels, and ancient and modern instances. To show his sympathy with me he says he hates to see one of the most powerful engines in the country wracking itself to pieces from running wild after the loss of its flywheel: also I remind him of a big steam boat with all its lights ablaze and the band on it playing as it passes Goat Island toward the roar of Niagara Falls. I, who never sang played read or wrote a note of music have learned for consolation to play on a 'recorder' by ear entirely the whole of The Linden Tree and Wanita. What is to become of me? Will I end up on the concert platform? That is for my friends and well-wishers to puzzle out. I am past feeling that it is any concern of mine."[28]

Continuing the account, which was contained in a letter to

Louis Untermeyer dated February 17, Frost reported that he had just received word of the publication of his new book, *Collected Poems 1939*. "I got a telegram partly in Latin from the Holts yesterday saying it was their pride to let me know that my latest book was that day on the market. The Latin gave me a stir that I never expected to have again in this world from publication." Modesty prevented Frost from repeating the text of the telegram, but it had indeed been a moving tribute from one Latinist, William Sloane, to another, Robert Frost:

> NO SATISFACTION COULD BE KEENER THAN THAT WITH WHICH WE PUBLISH TODAY YOUR COLLECTED POEMS. EXIGISTI MONUMENTUM PERENNIUS AERE.[29]

You have erected a monument more lasting than bronze, went Sloane's adaptation of Horace. Next day, Frost thanked his publisher in terms similar to those he used in writing to Untermeyer, and added, significantly, "I am happy to be in your hands."[30]

How happy he had been in the hands of Hervey Allen, during the last weeks of his winter vacation, Frost told Lesley as he was returning by train to Boston on the twenty-fifth of February. "I had a really beneficial visit at Hervey's," he wrote. "Hervey is a great friend, almost of the devotion of Louis. He has bottomless wisdom in metaphor and story. I never realized his importance to me before. He and I have reached a point of frankness where we can tell each other exactly what we want of each other. For instance he could say right out to me that for worldly reasons if for no other, he would like me to be good, but that doesn't mean too good. He recognizes that all my thinking must start from the obligations I am under to Kathleen and she under to me for what she has done to bring me back to life. He thinks as I think all can be managed right and seemly."[31]

HANGING ROUND EDUCATION

This new Harvard entanglement is no help. None at all. I am going to say in my letter of acceptance that I wonder at myself for still hanging round education after all these years. . . .[1]

AS SOON as he was back in Boston, Robert Frost began preparing for a series of five lectures he had agreed to give in Lawrence, Massachusetts, sponsored by a man named White who was a distant relative of his wife Elinor, and given by Frost the general title, "A Prospective Anthology of British and American Verse, with liberal quotations from many poets." He was still so downcast by personal frustrations, however, and by what he had seen of Carol in Florida, that when he gathered his thoughts toward the first lecture on March 2, entitled "The Success of a Single Poem," he found himself reflecting with some bitterness that for all the success of his own poems, taken singly or as a whole, his private life had little of what might be called, by him or anyone else, "success." How successful Carol and his family were, Frost had summed up in his last letter to Lesley: "They are not lucky so far in life. They catch no fish."[2] Irma and John Cone "caught no fish" either. Despite John's growing success as an architect in the firm of a man named Larson, Irma seemed to find married life excruciatingly difficult, and in recent months she had been subject to an increasing number of emotional and physical disorders. Lesley, divorced and with two young daughters, was trying to succeed as a teacher at a private school in Washington, D.C., but she was not immune from the Frost traits of extreme nervousness and irritability. As for Frost himself, he had gradually come to think that his married life had been more seriously flawed than he had ever dared to imagine while

Elinor lived, and that she had resented his success as a poet even as she had inspired his best poetic efforts.[3] The discovery, among his papers, of a letter Elinor had sent to Lesley back in 1917, gave Frost a further opportunity to reflect on why the members of his family seemed to "catch no fish":

"Somehow mixed with my own recent mail," Frost wrote to Lesley after reading it, "I found this letter of Elinor's. I suppose you must have given it to me when I was away from my desks and files and I must have put it into one of my traveling bags with the confusion of letters and manuscript I always carry around. It belongs to your early days at Wellesley. My, my, what sorrow runs through all she wrote to you children. No wonder something of it overcasts my poetry if read aright. No matter how humorous I am I am sad. I am a jester about sorrow. She colored my thinking from the first just as at the last she troubled my politics. It was no loss but a gain of course. She was not as original as I in thought but she dominated my art with the power of her character and nature. I wish I hadnt this woeful suspicion that toward the end she came to resent some thing in the life I had given her. . . . It seems to me now that she was cumulatively laying up against me the unsuccess of the children I had given her. She was a person of the soundest realistic judgment. But here I think she was radically wrong for once. She failed to see she wasn't giving you the time she patiently gave me. You are coming out all right in your way. Irma will come out all right too. (I have just had a letter from Larson to tell me how very well John is doing in his office. That gratuitously from a hard man!) A way will be found to put Carol on his feet. You'll see."

He continued the letter by reporting some bad news concerning Irma, to whose gradually deteriorating mental condition, reflected in part in an intense jealousy of her own husband's professional success, had lately been added a new physical malady:

". . . today I had a shock that was sympathetic with the way Elinor would have taken what I heard on the telephone when I called up John at Hanover. While I was lost in my travels so I couldnt be reached anyway Irma was discovered to be suffering with a large tumor and operated on at the Hanover hospital. That was last Friday. Everything went off all right and she should be at home tomorrow (Thursday March 2) with a prospect of better health than she has had. I dont suppose you realized there had been anything very wrong with her. I knew she was rather worse than she used to be. Be sure to write her a good encouraging letter. She'd like to know I told you how Larson had been bragging about John. That is I guess she would. It cant be that what a woman lays up against a man is his success out where she can only imperfectly share it. Mind you I dont care if she does. I am prepared for any sadness in the structure of the universe."

He concluded with some fatherly advice and encouragement: "Go out and get all your own success. But do it cooly and deliberately without importunate haste. Keep well, look well. A woman has to look well. You have the basic good looks to build on. In one way and another I keep hearing of you as having made your place in Washington."[4]

The first White Fund lecture, delivered the following night, was a pleasurable relief from family worries, and the Lawrence audience did not have to be reminded it was in their town, fifty years before, that Frost had discovered his interest in reading and writing poetry as a student at Lawrence High School. Frost began the lecture series by assuring his listeners his talks would be informal, with no explicit criticism of the poets in question, but with a wide-ranging selection of the verse of such men as Collins, Emerson, Longfellow, Poe, Bryant, and Sill. These, Frost said, were poets he planned to include in an anthology he was preparing for Harvard University,[5] a project he had been working on recently and which he hoped to complete within a year or two, before he "retired from this world." The format of the series was a departure for him, he continued, because he was usually expected to read only his own verse. He would follow his usual practice of saying nothing against any poem or poet, but would let his selections indicate his preferences, for, as the title of the fourth lecture suggested, he considered the anthology "the highest form of criticism." After lecturing on many poets, English and American, past and contemporary, he would return to his own verse, in a lecture entitled "If the Anthologist Includes His own Writing; with liberal quotations from his latest book."[6]

Frost's humorous, mildly ironic platform manner delighted the Lawrence audience, and the series was a great local event. His Lawrence engagements, however, were spread out over a period of two months, and he interspersed with these other lectures in Massachusetts, New York, New Jersey, and Pennsylvania. In early April, he embarked on the major phase of his lecture season, traveling to the University of Iowa for a long visit he had postponed from the previous winter.[7] There, he planned to enjoy the company of Charles Foster, Norman Foerster, and his other Iowa friends, delivering a lecture on April 13 before going on to other colleges and friends in Wyoming and Colorado.

Arrangements for the Iowa lecture had been made by Foerster, the director of the University's School of Letters, and the memory of a similar evening at Harvard, last November, invited comparisons that did not work to Foerster's advantage. The lecture was to begin at seven-thirty, in a room which Foerster's colleagues had repeatedly warned was too small to accommodate the number of people likely to seek admission. By seven o'clock, the 300-seat Senate Chamber was nearly filled. By seven-fifteen, it was jammed. By seven-thirty, the stairs leading to the hall were so crowded that Frost himself could not get in. Finally, with considerable difficulty, he made his way to the podium, only to be delayed further while an amplifier system was set up for the hundred or more students who had been unable to gain entry. Forty-five minutes later, he began his lecture, betraying no sign that the preliminary confusion had upset him in the least. When it was over, he attended a party given in his honor at Foerster's home, and still he made no reference to the events of the evening. When, however, all the other guests had at last departed, Frost turned on Foerster and tore into him in a fury. "What the hell do you think I am," he demanded, "a rural schoolteacher that nobody wants to hear? Last week I talked to two thousand in Philadelphia, and they turned five hundred away!"[8]

A more serious though less dramatic upset was occasioned by Paul Engle, who, though unavoidably absent from Iowa City during the week of Frost's visit, had previously contributed a pair of poems, and a brief eulogy honoring his friend, to the April number of *American Prefaces*, the University's literary journal. The eulogy was beyond reproach as it spoke of the "natural delight" in knowing that "on these streets where we have our home and our work, the greatest poet of a continent will soon be walking."[9] The title-page poem, "Homage to Robert Frost," was good enough to win Frost's admiration for Engle's poetic gifts. But a few pages into the issue, Frost found a second, longer poem, innocuously entitled "For An Apple

Grower," which contained, to his shock and dismay, a lengthy, poeticized version of much he had said to Engle during their visits together in Gainesville not long before, and in South Shaftsbury not long after, Elinor Frost's death. Engle's opening reference to Frost—the unnamed speaker of most of the poem—hurt Frost's pride as much as what followed violated his reticence:

Being an old man and his mind bearded
By the white memory of many years,
I listened to his voice. He talked the way
A horse drinks, with a slow deliberation,
The gulp of words big in his throat like water:

We meet it all the time with the animals.
You know how cattle lie for hours on a hill
As if the wind had roped and thrown them down,
Head hanging quiet while the hollow eyes
Stare at nothing or eternity.
Moving only the resolute, old cud.
They die that way. When the milk fever took
That gray-faced Guernsey, ill with her first calf,
I'd go into her stall last thing at night
And she'd be looking at the very corner
I'd found her watching first thing in the morning,
Her eyes full of a wild emptiness,
Waiting for something that I could not see.
So with a woman, there's that in her eyes,
When the next breath's a chance and each tomorrow
Is not just one more day but another life,
That sees beyond your hand on her damp forehead,
Through the house wall, beyond the very air.
It can't stop looking more than the heart can beating. . . .

Following this passage, Engle provided versions of other remarks Frost had made, all having Elinor as their focus:

. . . You met her once,
But late, when pain was native to her nature—
Drank it in water, heard it in hello.
She called you by your name and shook your hand.
That was an act of courage and of will

Greater than a tough man's on a terrible mountain
Climbing the massive wall of ice and wind.
Each breath gave her double nourishment—
To the declining heart, the labored living,
To the growing death, the energy of ending. . . .
No, don't bother to be kind and say
I can go back and see her broad thumb print
Worn in the worked earth. I can't learn the crippled
Lesson of comfort. At my age
You gather patience like a mold, aware
Wisdom is knowing when you can't be wise.
I'll never walk through doors that she has opened,
Or scoop up water on the hottest day
From a clear spring where she has knelt to drink.
And yet our days are here to be lived out,
The plain bread to be eaten. . . .[10]

Engle had obviously intended to honor both the Frosts when he wrote the poem, but it was hard for Frost to see it that way. What he did see was Engle's apparent intention to represent him as a doddering old man, tied to his past and with no discernible future. Engle returned to Iowa City too late to disabuse his friend, or to apologize for any errors of taste or judgment, but even if he had, Frost would probably not have listened. He had made up his mind that Engle had turned against him, and once his mind was made up he rarely, if ever, allowed it to be changed.[11]

From Iowa City Frost went directly to Laramie, where he stayed with the chairman of the Department of English at the University of Wyoming, Professor Vincil C. Coulter. Coulter had informed Frost in 1938 that the University was planning to build a Frost Poetry Library of books and manuscripts, and Frost had reciprocated by making an initial gift of nineteen inscribed books and pamphlets to serve as the nucleus of the collection. When he arrived in Laramie, he found that the collection had so far grown to only thirty volumes, but the enthusiasm of the English Department, which had charge of the "Library," was gratifying. The Wyoming student newspaper, *The Branding Iron*, spoke glowingly of the "wide acclaim" the collection was "fast achieving . . . because it is the only one of its kind in America" and went on to say that "eventually all of the works of and about Frost will be placed in the library."[12] Such interest in his works in a place so far away from New England was welcome proof to Frost that his national reputation was still as strong as ever.

After attending a dinner in his honor on the night of April 18, and lecturing in the University Auditorium the following day, Frost left Laramie and went by train to the next stop in his round of readings, Central State Teachers College in Edmond, Oklahoma. Neither he nor Mrs. Morrison, in planning the itinerary for the trip, had realized that the excursion to Oklahoma would take him halfway home, and by the time he arrived in Denver, Colorado, on the morning of April 23, he was ill and worn out. Fortunately, his friend and former student at Pinkerton Academy, John T. Bartlett, had heard well in advance that Frost was to be in the vicinity of his Boulder home in April, and on the strength of this information, he had written to Frost in March volunteering his services and his home while Frost was in the area. Receiving no word from Frost, but determined to be of use, Bartlett then wired him in Edmond two days before the poet's scheduled arrival in Denver. Frost's telegram of reply arrived on Sunday night:

> HOPE YOU CAN MEET ME IN DENVER MONDAY 8:15 A. M.[13]

During their drive together to Boulder, Frost and the Bartletts talked of all that had happened since they had last seen each other in 1935. Almost at once the talk turned to Elinor's last years and death, and John and his wife, Margaret, unaware of the Engle incident at Iowa, were disturbed and saddened to see how painfully fresh these still were in Frost's mind. By afternoon, his emotions were sufficiently under control for him to attend the Honors Convocation at the University of Colorado, and receive an honorary degree, but his illness forced him to cut short his acceptance speech before he had really finished. Afterward, he retired to rest at the home of his host, President George Norlin, and he was well enough by evening to perform again, longer and far better, at a dinner sponsored by the Honors Committee.

By prearrangement, Frost stayed that night at President Norlin's home, but he moved in next day with the Bartletts, and permitted John Bartlett to drive him back and forth, on successive days, to his other area engagements in Denver, Fort Collins, and Colorado Springs. Of these, the most important was his talk on April 28 in Colorado Springs, at the opening session of a conference on the fine arts arranged by his English poet-friend, the director of the Rocky Mountain Writers Conference, Edward Davison. After a warm introduction by Davison, who had also presented him for his Colorado honorary degree, Frost spoke on "The Trial by Market." His remarks were a further development of the ideas he had expressed at the January meeting of the National Institute of Arts and Letters.

Does the artist, he began, have any standard like the scientist's to tell him of the success of his art? Yes, he said, the artist has the "trial by market": "The fact that things go out, that I I am not an amateur, that I'm a professional, that people will pay blood money for what I've done—blood in the form of money, a mortal trial, for people care for their money. I, for instance, would just as soon give a poem I'd written to a magazine for nothing, except that I know what editors are, and I like to make them at least unhappy enough to have to part with some money. I know very well that to the world at large money talks, money speaks. Everybody has got to have it." That, however, was not enough, for artists also wanted to be safely beyond "the carp of critics." "I wish," he continued, "we had something like the prize ring where we could fight to a finish, where work went down on the mat or had its arm lifted by the judges at the end. I hate prize fights where the victory is dependent on the referee's decision; it seems too much like the arts.

"I wonder if you have thought about the assurance which I have thought of. I know it is momentary. I know that it will not permanently satisfy me. My dissatisfaction and uncertainty will return. Over and beyond all the intellectual proofs that you have to pass, beyond the money, lies something that I have thought I tasted in the affections of the affectionate. When I have thought I tasted that affection of the affectionate—not just uncritical, but something that has come through criticism to this—it sometimes seems as if art has worked and worked and finally had lifted into something, and that is the affections of the affectionate."[14]

The Associated Press ignored his thoughts on "the affections of the affectionate," but his analogy between poetry and prize fighting was good copy, and it was widely reported next day in newspapers across the country.[15] Three days later, the New

York *Times* saw fit to rebut Frost's position in an editorial entitled "Poets and Prize Rings":

"Robert Frost, speaking at a fine arts conference at Colorado Springs, is reported as wishing that poets and artists could have 'something like the prize ring where we could fight to a finish, where work went down on the mat and had its arm lifted by the judges at the end.' Mr. Frost may have his figure of speech a bit twisted. In boxing, at least, a man who goes down too often to 'the mat' (and many tired pugilists have looked in vain for mats to fall on) is less likely to get his arm lifted by the judges than to have his face lifted by the doctors.

"But a really serious question is involved—namely, whether the arts are, or ought to be, competitive in their nature. From the days of the first Olympics there have been esthetic competitions, with prizes for the winners. Often these contests have yielded small results. Aren't the loveliest flights of the human imagination made for their own sake, out of the sheer joy of creation? Mr. Frost once wrote a poem (the lines are chosen at random) beginning:

All out-of-doors looked darkly in at him
Through the thin frost, almost in separate stars,
That gathers on the pane in empty rooms.

Was he trying to outdo some one else? One doesn't think so. One thinks that he was experiencing the sheer joy of capturing a mood, a picture, a sharp, incisive thought.

"We will trust Mr. Frost to create without a judge or an opponent, save the judge of time and the opponent of the refractory material. And whatever the 'inner assurance of excellence' for which he thinks the artist longs, in his case there is an outer assurance in the gratitude and respect accorded to him by the poetry-loving public."[16]

Frost might have been pleased or upset by being so treated editorially in the New York *Times*, but he probably did not see, or even learn of, the editorial until his return to Boston. Even so, he had his own complaint about the Colorado Springs Conference, and it was that there were too many other poets present with whom he had been forced to compete for attention. As he confessed afterward to Bartlett, it was "not my kind of affair. I like a one-man show."[17]

On the last day of April, after visiting his old friend, the Denver poet Thomas Hornsby Ferril, Frost left Colorado and headed home, making several stops for more lectures along the way. When he arrived, safe but exhausted, at 88 Mt. Vernon Street, he found a letter waiting for him that was a demonstration of the affections of his friends at Harvard University. The writer was Harvard President James B. Conant:

"A group of men and women, calling themselves the 'Friends of Robert Frost,' have donated to the University a sum of money to provide for the creation for two years of the 'Ralph Waldo Emerson Fellowship in Poetry.' It is their hope and mine that you will be willing to accept appointment to this Fellowship for two years, beginning September 1, 1939. I have ventured to have this appointment made by the Corporation and sent to the Board of Overseers for confirmation next Monday. If you accept this appointment, you would be quite free to do whatever work you desired in the University during these two years. It was the hope of those who founded this Fellowship that after consultation with the Chairman of the English Department you might make arrangements for meeting groups of young men interested in poetry and possibly give a series of lectures if you so desire. From my own point of view, you are quite free to come and go as you wish and I only hope that you will enjoy this method of coming in contact with some of the students in the College who are interested in poetry. I am sure that you will have much to give them. . . ."[18]

Frost's reaction to the Harvard invitation, which was the culmination of more than a year of work on the part of David McCord, Robert Hillyer, and others, was curiously unenthusiastic. Perhaps because he was exhausted from the rigors of his Western trip, perhaps because he and President Conant had not gotten along well during the Norton Professorship in 1936, or perhaps because the break from Amherst had soured him on all college employment, Frost procrastinated for more than six weeks before sending his formal acceptance to Conant.[19] In a letter to Louis Untermeyer from South Shaftsbury on June 26, he seemed to imply that the Harvard offer was little more than a distraction from more urgent problems in his private life:

"You are said on good authority to have said of me that I am dangerously apt to get anything I want. Don't worry about me then, but accept the risk that what I want may prove too much for your sense of propriety. There is an old proverb that goes Half a cake, especially if it be the upper half frosted, is better than no bread. But assuming for the sake of argument that for the moment I am at a loss to know what I want, what as a friend do you want for me? What or whom would you prescribe for my unhappiness. For I confess I am not as pleased with myself as I might be. Would you suggest either of the Worlds Fairs or Soviet Russia or farming with a farmer and his wife to take care of me. This new Harvard entanglement is no help. None at all. I am going to say in my letter of acceptance that I wonder at myself for still hanging round education after all these years; but I suppose what keeps me is the reasonable doubt that the college belongs entirely to the scholars. . . ."[20]

When he finally did get around to drafting a letter to Conant, he did not try to conceal his misgivings about the appointment he was accepting:

"I should have written you weeks ago how proud I am to be made Ralph Waldo Emerson fellow in poetry at Harvard University. Such great names as Harvard and Emerson are not just nominal. But in letting myself in for the office, I can hardly help wondering if I am fitted for the duties of a fellow. David McCord could tell you my story. My teaching in the last twenty-five years has been no more than a sequence of philosophical positions taken and rather skilfully acted out for the symbol. I havent enough going on for three classes a week forty weeks in the year or half that. I am a peculiarly advanced case of what I am, good or bad. Much of education in school I have never believed in. At the first serious suggestion of my pretending to Latinity or any other kind of scholarship I am struck as school-shy as in the nineties when I fled uneducated to the Philistines. What has brought me back in and partly disarmed me is the kindness the colleges have shown my poetry. I find myself even anxious to be useful to them in requital. I may be expected to stay round them I suppose as long as there is a reasonable doubt that they belong entirely to the sound scholars and the graduates going out into the world to earn our living. Only compromise must be made with my [cunctations?]. Nothing I am likely to do will lend itself to cataloguing; or so I fear. I wish I could throw myself on your authority to leave me at large for visiting a class, Morrisons in Eng. A for instance, giving a public lecture or sitting it out and talking it out in young society at Adams House with the

Littles when I am prompted with anything to say. In that way I could feel natural and my thinking would be more nearly at one with my teaching. Could I talk it over with you some Sunday afternoon?"[21]

While Frost was worrying over the details of his new job, he was also taking steps to find a happier place to spend his summers than South Shaftsbury, Vermont. The Morrisons, as they had informed Frost in the fall of 1938, had arranged to rent a farm situated just halfway between Bread Loaf and the nearby town of Ripton. The Homer Noble farm, as it was known locally, was owned by the widowed Mrs. Noble, and she also had for rent a small white cottage across the road from where she now lived in Ripton village, with her sister, Miss Agnes Billings. It was an easy walk from the cottage to the Homer Noble farm, almost as easy a walk to the Bread Loaf campus, and Mrs. Noble and her sister provided dinner for the summer guests they took in at the house they shared. After some consideration, Frost decided to rent the cottage, and he made arrangements with Mrs. Noble to be included at her table when she served dinner.

On many occasions, however, he dined with the Morrisons at the farm, and the more he saw of it, the more he liked what he saw. Always on the lookout for an interesting piece of property, he was impressed by the gently rolling land that had once grazed sheep on its meadows, but in recent years had been used only for occasional picnics or hayrides by summer visitors from the Bread Loaf School of English and Writers' Conference. Situated in the upper pasture, a hundred yards or more above the main farmhouse, was an attractive little guest cabin that had been built in 1928 by Mrs. Noble's adopted son, Harold Whittemore, as a "cash crop" to be used by hunters in the autumn, by fishermen in the spring, and by members of the Bread Loaf School of English during the summer. The entire farm was something more than 150 acres, and it was surrounded on three sides by government land that was part of the vast Green Mountain National Forest. Frost had reason to believe Mrs. Noble was willing to sell her farm, and he decided early that if she were, he might well be willing to buy.

In Frost's plans for the Homer Noble farm the Morrisons, of course, were central. They had refused his offer, a year ago, of a house next to his in Concord Corners, but their refusal, unlike DeVoto's, had been based on other reasons than a reluctance to be too close to him. He knew they were as fond of the Homer Noble farm as he was, and he doubted that either Kay or Ted would object to living in a farmhouse of which he was landlord. For compensation, he would ask only the same rent the Morrisons were paying Mrs. Noble, and to be fed and looked after, mostly by Kay, while he made his own home in the three-room cabin above the house. To confirm his high opinion of the farm, he set out early one morning to walk completely around the property, and when he returned late in the day, he was sure he wanted to be the owner of the Homer Noble farm. With considerable misgiving, but sensible of the advantages in terms of simplifying their own summer housing problem, the Morrisons agreed to join him, beginning next summer, in the arrangement he had in mind. When he later spoke to Mrs. Noble about selling the place, he found she was willing to accept the figure he proposed.[22]

The 1939 session of the Bread Loaf Writers' Conference began on August 15, and Frost carried out his plan of the previous November by "teaming up" with Louis Untermeyer in classes on poetry criticism, four or five a week, for the two weeks of the Conference. Despite his unusually extensive participation in the teaching activities at Bread Loaf, Frost continued to doubt that the Writers' Conference did much to improve the productions of Bread Loaf's would-be artists. He expressed his ambivalent views on the value of Bread Loaf in a preface he had reluctantly agreed to write for the forthcoming *Bread Loaf Anthology*, a collection of previously unpublished pieces of poetry and prose submitted at the Writers' Conference:

"You who are as much concerned as I for the future of Bread Loaf," it began, "will agree with me that once in so often it should be redefined if it is to be kept from degenerating into a mere summer resort for routine education in English, or worse still for the encouragement of vain ambition in literature. We go there not for correction or improvement. No writer has ever been corrected into importance. Nor do we go to find a publisher or get help in finding a publisher. Bringing manuscript to Bread Loaf is in itself publication. . . ."

Continuing the piece, which was largely a restatement of the ideas he had expressed in his National Institute speech and at Colorado Springs, he offered his wry assessment of what went on at the Writers' Conference:

"Bread Loaf is to be regarded then as a place in Vermont where a writer can try his effect on readers. There, as out in the world, he must brave the rigors of specific criticism. He will get enough and perhaps more than enough of good set praise and blame. He will help wear out the words 'like' and 'dislike.' He will hear too many things compared to the disadvantage of all of them. A handkerchief is worse than a knife because it can be cut by a knife; a knife is worse than a stone because it can be blunted by a stone; a stone is worse than a handkerchief because it can be covered by a handkerchief; and we have been round the silly circle. All this is as it has to be where the end is a referee's decision. There is nothing so satisfactory in literature as the knock-out in prize fighting. . . ."[23]

At the end of the Conference, Frost returned to Boston, rested for one month, and then set out on a whirlwind lecture tour in which, by his own count, he "did fourteen lectures and travelled two thousand miles in fifteen days."[24] When he returned he was exhausted, but he at once began preparing for his debut as Harvard's Emerson Fellow. His plans for his course in "Poetry" were revealed in an interview he gave before the first class meeting in mid-November:

". . . Mr. Frost has not thrown in the sponge on his ideas that education should be a take-it-or-leave-it business instead of a day-after-day quizzing of boys with questions to which he already knew the answers. His belief is in an 'education by presence'—the stimulation of students to enterprise by the mere presence in their midst of men who have done things and have wide intellectual horizons. He will give marks of a sort, but they will be secondary. Mr. Frost will do most of the talking, but if mere talking will not stir up some enterprise among his hearers, he will 'just keep silent, or even lie down on the desk until it is realized that what I want is self-starters, not followers of a set routine. . . .'" Further developing the automotive metaphor, he said his objective was to help colleges become "factories for turning out human self-starters."

The Associated Press interview, which appeared in the New York *Times*, included Frost's thoughts on a variety of subjects, among them the world political situation in the wake of the recent German invasion of Poland:

"'The world is swaying to the left and to the right. It is a drunken world, going home we know not where, but the important thing to realize is that it is not swaying too far to the left or too far to the right. . . . My life has been all holidays, whether it has been work or play. The secret? I say it is this: Never allow yourself to become a "case" if you can help it; and never froth at the mouth about things. That's the trouble with too many people. They froth at the mouth because they're reading the same newspaper too much. They get all scared about what they think Germany's going to do. They get all worried about "reds" in the country. They get frothed up about what's going to become of democracy. And all the time they forget that there are limitations to all things; that there always is a balance to everything. . . .' "

Frost's notion that there was "a balance to everything" was strongly reminiscent of the Emersonian doctrine of compensation, and he may well have been re-reading Emerson's essay on the subject while thinking about his new job.[25] The interview concluded, however, with ideas that were pure Frost:

"Although the catalogue lists his course as poetry, he remarked: 'I can talk politics under that heading. I'll tell the boys the world speaks to them and they have to answer back. I'll tell them always to have something to say or they will be on their way to become "cases." Say something to Hitler, to Chamberlain or to the drama, but say something—something with a kick in it.'

"He suggested that the things most like the arts in a college were the college sports. 'It's live or die in a football game,' he said, 'and that's the way it should be with writing. One should not write just for the practice of writing, as is done in classroom routine. One should write only when he has something to say, and then it should be live or die, as in the football game.' "[26]

The "Poetry" seminar, consisting of forty undergraduate and graduate students, met Thursday nights in the Upper Common Room of Adams House, whose Master, David H. Little, had been one of the "Friends of Robert Frost." Putting his educational theories into practice, Frost began the course by asking his students to put down "boastfully," on the three-by-five cards he distributed, something of their own which they had said—a phrase, a sentence, an epithet. For several moments, the boys sat staring nervously at their blank cards, not knowing what to do. Finally, Little spoke up and suggested that perhaps Mr. Frost was asking too much of them. No, he didn't think so. He could try the same test on himself. In fact, he would give them two lines that he had made up over fifty years ago, and had never since used in a poem or even written down. Gathering himself up, he quoted the lines:

> *Save of trees chafing, interlocking,*
> *And a woodpecker knocking*

"Is that something?" asked Master Little.

"Yes," said Frost, "that's something."[27]

Late in the semester, Frost told his class that he would not be able to meet them the following week, but would return to continue the course two weeks hence. He then issued a directive that confused a few of them as much as they had been on the first day of class: "Now the modern psychiatrist would try to do something for you by saying, 'Don't worry; work.' But I'm going to treat you like normal healthy Harvard boys. I'm going to leave you with the motto: 'Don't work; worry.'" After the class had broken up, Frost was walking along the street toward the subway when one of the boys overtook him. "Mr. Frost," he said, with a troubled look, "I don't quite understand the assignment." "About worry?" "Yes, what should I worry about? You see, I'm a senior and I need to get a B in this course if I'm to graduate so—"

"All right," said Frost. "Worry about that."[28]

FRIENDS AND NEIGHBORS

Well it seems well settled that we are to be settled down near each other for some months a year for the duration. As you are a cross between a Maryland farmer and a Florida farmer, I am now a cross between a Vermont farmer and a Florida farmer. Some figures ought to [be] derivable of value to future agronomy.[1]

HIS HARVARD STUDENTS were probably not aware of it, but as Robert Frost taught the closing weeks of his course in "Poetry," he was suffering from an increasingly painful and debilitating illness. The trouble had started in October, after his return from his fall round of readings. At first, he had dismissed it as a minor kidney infection, not serious enough to warrant medical attention. Left untreated, however, it had continued to worsen, and by early December the pain was so intense that Frost did see a doctor, before taking to bed. From the Morrison home on Walker Street, Cambridge, where Kay had put him up and engaged two nurses to help her give him full-time care, he dictated on December 13 an account of his condition to Louis Untermeyer:

"I have been too sick to write you the letter I owed and I am too sick to write it myself now. I assume responsibility in it for nothing but the sentiments. When I say that K. has been my nurse and saviour—the English spelling is hers! My disease I guess is accidia (Fr. acedie) contracted I fear from having tried to get too much meaning out of the word in a lecture . . . at the Grolier Club recently. It is closely related to acidosis, for which I am being treated by a doctor. He has a right to complain that I have held something back from him and not laid all my cards on the table. But accidia it really is and as you will fully understand not a disease I could bring myself to be confidential about with any but those who love me. Don't think of me any oftener than usual on this account. . . ."[2]

Frost assumed Untermeyer would know what he meant by "accidia," or would take the trouble to find out. Acedia, as it was properly spelled, was a disease not of the body but of the spirit, the symptoms of which, as first diagnosed in students, monks, and other medieval contemplatives, were "a loss of faith, undue retreat into one's self, a sense of futility, and a paralyzing estrangement from God and man."[3] In his Grolier Club talk on November 16, Frost had discussed "accidia" in a more secular sense, as the affliction he and other artists suffered in periods of "sullen lethargy" between spells of creative effort. Addressing a select audience of 400 book-collectors, at the invitation of his young bibliophile-friend, Frederick B. Adams, Jr., he had begun by announcing as his subject "the flight from vanity or the pursuit of humility," and had gone on to speak of the "vanity" implicit in an artist's decision to loaf and invite his soul. "Loafing has a good deal to do with being an artist," he asserted. "No good writing can be done in a continuous stream. All writers who have struggled with ideas have suffered from these terrible lulls. It is called temperament."[4]

The cure for acedia, traditionally, was "hard and unremitting prayer." For Frost it was "honest work." With his own "accidia" complicated by acidosis, however, he was already beginning to worry about what would happen in the event that his illness continued to worsen, and kept him away from the numerous income-producing lectures he had planned for the months ahead. Though the purchase of the Homer Noble farm was well within his means, it did represent an expense. His intention to buy property in Florida, when he went down in January, would involve further outlays. Considering also his financial commitments to Carol, Irma, and the rest of his family, he began to realize that if he did not recover quickly, his funds would soon be dangerously low.

In the context of these worries over money and illness, the recent proposition of a man named Earle J. Bernheimer had begun to seem more attractive than it had at first. An avid collector of the first editions and first appearances of Robert Frost, Bernheimer had been sending Frost items from his collection, to be signed and returned, since 1936.[5] Impressed by his obvious dedication, and amused perhaps by his self-consciously formal letters of thanks, Frost had always signed or inscribed whatever items Bernheimer sent for improvement. When the collector visited him at Bread Loaf in August 1939, however, their association had taken a new direction. Carrying with him a suitcase full of more items he wished to have signed, Bernheimer was eager to discuss an item that he did not possess, but which he coveted as an item he knew would be the crowning jewel of his, or any, Frost collection. It was the slender little volume called *Twilight*, which Frost had had privately printed in 1894 in an edition of two copies, only one of which survived. Was there any possibility, Bernheimer had inquired during his visit, that Frost might be willing to part with the precious volume? Frost had said no, he could not, the book had been a gift to Elinor before they were married, and in a way it still belonged to her. If he parted with it at all, it must be to some college or university library where it would be safely and permanently preserved. With that, the conversation had turned to other subjects.

A few days after Bernheimer's departure from Bread Loaf, Frost had received an interesting letter from the collector. "Driving my car the long road home," Bernheimer wrote, "I thought many times of your conversation—especially of the volume of your poems titled 'Twilight.' I planned plans and thought of many things so that I might eventually own it. I hope you will not be perturbed when I bring up the subject again. I had one thought that might appeal to you. Would you let me 'rent' that book from you during my lifetime? By written agreement, consent to will it to any library or institution you name, in your honor? That way, I would have the pleasure of owning 'Twilight' so long as I lived. You would have whatever convenience the 'rent' would get and also know, definitely, the volume would finally find a permanent place of your choosing. Please, Mr. Frost, consider this and then kindly let me know."[6]

Away from the pressures and frictions of the Writers' Conference, Frost had found himself giving Bernheimer's offer more thought than he had first intended. Whatever the book had meant to Elinor, whatever it now meant to collectors like Bernheimer, *Twilight*, for him, had always been surrounded by intensely unpleasant associations. He still remembered vividly that day in the fall of 1894 when he had thrust it into the hands of Elinor White, the girl who had promised to become his wife. She had refused to let him into her house at college in Canton, New York, despite his protests that what he had to say was of great importance to them both. She had taken his gift, indifferently it seemed to him, and watched him run away to destroy his own copy and seek to destroy himself in Virginia's Dismal Swamp.[7] It was all of a piece, he now thought, with the way Elinor had used silence as a weapon to punish him during their marriage, and to punish him again most awfully at the time of her death. Why not then sell the book, he asked himself, what did it mean to him? Surely he had good use for the money.

Thus, on November 18, 1939, Robert Frost answered Bernheimer's letter with a short one of his own: "I might not be able to refuse serious money for the unique *Twilight*, but it would have to be really serious money that would mean something to my family. You say what you think could be done. There may be merit in your suggestion that you could buy or lease the book with an agreement to leave it in the end to some person or institution by me designated."[8]

Bernheimer arrived in Boston on January 6, 1940, and went directly to 88 Mt. Vernon Street. There he found Frost, still ill with acidosis, but well enough to hold his own in the business arrangement he had come to close. At first Frost talked only about the history of the volume, informing Bernheimer of all it had come to mean in the forty-five years since its creation. Finally, Bernheimer suggested they discuss figures. Frost thought a moment, knitted his brow, and said he had four families to take care of, Marjorie's, Irma's, Carol's, and Lesley's. What would Bernheimer say to a thousand for each of them? Having come prepared to spend a good deal more for the volume—as Frost was prepared to take considerably less—the collector immediately agreed to the figure. He telephoned his business partner in Kansas City, and instructed him to send Frost at once a check for $4,000. Then, receiving Frost's assurance that the volume, suitably inscribed, would soon be mailed to him in Kansas City, Bernheimer happily departed.

If Frost had any sense of triumph for having sold *Twilight* for the figure he asked, he did not have long to enjoy it. The next night, while alone in his apartment, he suffered a violent gastroenteritic attack and delirium, with pain so intense that, to relieve it, he began smashing chairs over one another until he had broken several to bits. Had he been left alone for long in this condition, the consequences might well have been grave. But by a fortunate coincidence, his friend and physician, the poet-psychiatrist Merrill Moore, happened to call, and Frost's voice on the telephone was so strange that Moore rushed over at once. He found Frost almost unconscious, and immediately ordered an ambulance, which took him to the emergency room of Phillips House, Massachusetts General Hospital.

By morning Frost had recovered considerably, and several tentative diagnoses had been made. The attack may have been brought on by intestinal flu, by food poisoning, or, most likely, as a reaction to sulfa drugs that had been prescribed for his cystitis. Whatever the cause, what was certain was that the attack had aggravated an already present hemorrhoid condition, and that surgery would likely have to be performed. After another day at Phillips House for observation, and one day more at the Morrisons' home, Frost reentered Massachusetts General, and underwent a hemorrhoidectomy.

The operation was successful, and within a few days Frost was well enough to begin joking about his condition and treatment. On January 12, he supplemented the terse hospital reports on his condition with a "bulletin" of his own, passed to the press by his private nurse and referring to the doctor who had performed the surgery. "Mr. Frost," it went, "is resting on his laurels after a legal operation for asteroids at the hands of Dr. Henry Faxon."[9]

He recuperated in Phillips House for some three weeks, slowly regaining his strength after the "minor" but painful operation. Finally, on February 1, after being pronounced well enough to travel, he left Boston with Mrs. Morrison and her son Bobby to complete his recuperation in Key West, Florida. Kay was able to remain with him, at the Casa Marina Hotel, for only the first two weeks of his stay. She had arranged, however, to have Frost looked after for another month by his newly appointed "official biographer," Lawrance Thompson, who met him in Coconut Grove the day after Kay's departure from Miami.[10] On the morning of February 17, Frost rode back with Thompson in a hired limousine for another few weeks in Key West.

The 178-mile drive to the southernmost of the Florida Keys took all day, and they arrived at the Casa Marina after dark. Going straight to the hotel dining room, they enjoyed a leisurely dinner. Then Thompson left to unpack, and Frost went to sit by the hotel's open fireplace. After a few minutes, a young man in his early twenties who had quietly watched them from his seat in the dining room came up and stood by the fire. "You're Robert Frost, aren't you?" he shyly inquired. "Yes," Frost smiled, happy to be recognized in such an out-of-the-way place. "Who are you?" The young man said his name was Hyde Cox, and added that he had attended Frost's Norton lectures at Harvard in 1936. Prompted by Frost's questions, he then explained what had brought him to Key West.

He had, he said, inherited from his grandfather enough money to make him financially independent. But after graduating from Harvard, he had decided to travel around the country, living on what he could earn by hawking newspapers on street corners and by other menial jobs. He craved this kind of experience as an antidote to his sheltered and bookish childhood, a need that Frost understood perfectly. Cox had been on the road now for several months, and planned to visit all forty-eight states before going home to New England. He was staying at the Casa Marina, he told Frost, while recuperating from influenza. As soon as he was well, he planned to resume his travels and his adventures as before.

Frost listened, fascinated, as Hyde Cox described the unusual path he had chosen to follow after completing his formal education. Curious to know more about this young man and wishing to help him in any way he could by sharing his own experiences, he took him for a long walk around the island and invited him for breakfast the next morning. As they talked that night and on several days and nights following, Frost took pleasure in discovering all that he could about his new friend. He found that Hyde Cox shared his love for poetry, that their family backgrounds were in some ways similar, and that Cox, like him, was experiencing difficulties in adjusting to the circumstances of his life. Before Cox left Key West, Frost made him promise to call on him in Boston. Thus Frost began a friendship with a man forty years younger than himself which was to grow for more than twenty-three years and endure to the end of his life.[11]

In addition to developing his new friendships with Hyde Cox and Thompson, Frost had an opportunity while in Key West to renew an acquaintance that had begun at the same Casa Marina Hotel five years before. Soon after his arrival, he learned that Wallace Stevens was again staying at the Casa Marina, with the same Judge Powell who had been his companion when Frost first met him in 1935. A dinner meeting was arranged, and at it Frost and Stevens traded literary gossip before resuming the playful teasing of each other they had started in 1935.

"The trouble with you, Robert, is that you're too academic," said Stevens.

"The trouble with you, Wallace, is that you're too executive," retorted Frost.

"The trouble with you, Robert, is that you write about—subjects."

"The trouble with you, Wallace, is that you write about—bric-a-brac."[12]

Frost knew from his last meeting with Stevens and Powell that a highlight of any evening they spent together would be the riotously funny off-color anecdotes which were Judge Powell's particular specialty. By the end of his first week in Key West since Kay's departure, however, Frost was more interested in another kind of "humor," the practical joke, which numbered among its uses the punishment of secretaries who failed to write letters to their employers. On February 22, Frost decided that he had waited for Kay's first letter long enough, and that retaliatory action was in order. He knew Kay had given Thompson instructions not to permit him to buy property while he was in Key West. He also knew, or at least suspected, that she had told Thompson to telegram her at once should Frost suffer a physical relapse or a serious emotional depression while he was in Thompson's charge. Summoning Thompson, then, Frost instructed him to send Kay at once a telegram message of only two words, "GETTING SERIOUS," which she could take as referring to an impending purchase of real estate, or in any other way she liked.

Thompson did as he was told, and Frost awaited the results. If his intention was to cause Kay agonies of worry over what had happened to him, he could not have been disappointed. Not knowing if the apparent crisis in Florida was mental or physical, she telephoned doctors of the mind and body in Boston and Miami, seeking advice and making contingency arrangements for treatment. She telegraphed Hervey Allen to say the situation in Key West was out of hand, and telegraphed Thompson for further information. Finally, after a day of uncertainty, she received a telegram of explanation. Nothing was wrong with Frost. It had all been an unfortunate misunderstanding.

On February 24, the day the flurry subsided, Hervey Allen appeared unexpectedly at the Casa Marina with his friend Henry Seidel Canby. Happy to see Allen again for the first time since his visit to the Glades a year before, Frost was equally happy when Allen invited him back to the Glades for another visit. On the twenty-sixth, Frost, Thompson, Canby, and Allen checked out of the Casa Marina, and drove together in Allen's car back to the Florida mainland.

His telegram notwithstanding, Frost had failed to find a house to his liking on Key West, and he soon began scouting the neighborhood around Hervey Allen's estate for a piece of property he could develop himself. One lot he and Allen examined, belonging to a man named Paige, adjoined Allen's, but Paige was asking a steeper price than Frost was willing to pay. He continued his search elsewhere, without immediate success. Finally, in mid-March, he announced it was time for him to go. Mrs. Morrison, he said, had made arrangements for him to lecture his way up the Atlantic Coast, and he was expected to speak shortly at a women's club in Palm Beach.

To satisfy herself that there was nothing wrong with Frost, Kay had also arranged for him to see a Palm Beach doctor named Waterman before he subjected himself to the rigors of another series of lectures. Frost knew that Kay's fears were groundless, and he was too eager to return to his home and secretary to permit good health to delay him. After his return to Boston, he described to Louis Untermeyer the result of his examination:

"In all that concerns me," he began, "trust your poetic imagination more than anything you hear from my over-anxious friends. I was willing the doctors down in Florida (Dr Waterman to be precise) and the doctors up here (Dr Moore to be precise) should have me as sick as they pleased if it would get the prescription out of them that I wanted, namely, that I should 'go back north where I was born bred look to die.' I told Dr Watermans wife in his presence and hearing that he had better look out for me: I wasnt above using him merely to get out of work or get round a woman. She answered I would have to be a pretty smart man to get anything out of her husband that he didnt see me getting and intend me to get. I ventured to say I was a pretty smart man when I had been up awhile and was well awake. Well the result of our fencing was that my aches and pains were authenticated and I got my order to go North for my health instead of further South. Looking each other wickedly in the eyes we both laughed. No money passed between us. In exchange for his treating me I treated him for not knowing infallibly enough how to tell a good quatrain from a bad quatrain; a discrimination I demonstrated that lies at the very root of all poetry appreciation. A bad quatrain consists of an epigram of about the extent of two lines which the poet thinks of first but saves for the last two lines preliminary labored into some semblance of validity or at least plausibility to round out the form. A good quatrain keeps you from knowing which member of the rhyme-twins the poet thought of first. I had the doctor's acknowledgement of value received."[13]

He wrote at the same time to Hervey Allen, beginning with a less incriminating account of his visit to Dr. Waterman, and continuing with remarks relating to his real-estate plans in Coconut Grove. As his letter implied, he had already intimated to Allen his reasons for wanting a vacation retreat in southern Florida:

"I'd be a bad man as well as a bad author if I couldn't squeeze a report for you out of my pen on how I came out after I left you. Dr. Waterman at Palm Beach thought he didn't think me too bad yet didn't think me quite good enough to face the lectures in North Carolina and Virginia. So I made a long hop for here and the source of the letters I was always waiting for at The Glades. Soothing converse and time have brought me along till I begin to believe I may yet live to resemble my old self. But never mind if I dont. You and I won't care will we, please? All I need is a very few friends to set their hearts right on me just as I am without one plea. I refuse to be taken as promising. I have been all through that and I have had enough of it. It makes me sick in the nerves to be counted on for anything. Cheers for my moral improvement would start me down hill on the road to ruin. This time with you I began to be sure you understood. And I was encouraged to advance a step toward buying the Page acres. I dont see how we could hurt each other by being conterminous. Your neighborhood would give me pleasure. My devoted secretary to whom my problems are an open book likes the things I have told her you say to me. They abet me and I might have acted on the realization last year. If I hesitated to buy land near you it was from fear that you would take me as a serious responsibility. I was foolish. You are not the kind to take me and I am not the kind to be taken too seriously. Pleasure decides for us which being the case I don't see why I should be squeamish about asking you to press the business a little further with Page. I'd probably listen to an offer of five acres for twenty five hundred, five hundred to be refunded me when I built a house. Would it be too much trouble for you to get the other man's terms across the road from you for comparison? A graceful way to get out of all this lies open to you if I seem unwise. All you have to do is ignore my inquiry and broach a new subject next time you write, or let the matter rest till the child forgets his whim."[14]

A few weeks later, when he returned from a two-week lecture tour in the Midwest made possible by his complete recovery from surgery, he found among his mail Allen's answer:

"Thank you for your fine, frank letter. It is a great relief to know that you are feeling better. I am glad the Doctor at Palm Beach advised you not to take those lectures in on the way north. I was really anxious about that because, while it seemed to me that you were coming along while you were with us, frankly I was ascared that you would overdo it on the way North and undo your time in Florida.

"I don't feel we really have to do much explaining of ourselves to each other. I have no moral program for other people and I really don't go through life giving folks good and bad marks for the emotional events which overtake them. To do so would imply two things, either that I was possessed of some peculiarly superior type of holiness, or that I regarded myself as the recipient of some authority or wisdom that conferred upon me the capacity to arrange my friends and acquaintances in a moral hierarchy. Well, I just don't. The truth is, I feel, that what we all need is a hell of a lot of loving kindness both in deed and attitude—a constant attitude of warm sympathy. I do not mean something soft and glowing, but a sympathy that is hard and durable. It is only fatigue that occasionally makes me shy off, or break out in irritation, both in the family and to my friends. On certain days I like to complain. In the final analysis it is the quality of being of a person that I care or do not care about, and, to a great extent, I feel that is entirely above, or rather beyond any code of action or manners. . . ."

The letter continued with more mundane matters:

"Now as to the land down here. Having you as a neighbor would be delightfully full of that pleasure which, as you say, is the only thing upon which people can get along. I will therefore see Paige again and try to persuade him on the basis of your suggestion. . . ."[15]

The deal with Paige did not materialize, but in late April, with the help of a local real-estate agent, Allen found a five-acre tract of undeveloped pineland on Davis Road in South Miami, within a mile of his estate in Coconut Grove. It was available for purchase at $400 an acre, and Allen recommended it to Frost as the property he should buy. A month later, having rejected several other possibilities that arose, Frost informed Allen of his decision to buy, sight unseen, the property on Davis Road.

"Well," he wrote, "it seems well settled that we are to be settled down near each other for some months a year for the duration. As you are a cross between a Maryland farmer and a Florida farmer, I am now a cross between a Vermont farmer and a Florida farmer. Some figures ought to [be] derivable of value to future agronomy. I mean we ought to be able to find out what sets a poet back most: farming in Maryland, Vermont or Florida. My check for the binder is enclosed. This is just a word of thanks to you and Ann [Mrs. Allen] for choosing the plot. . . ."[16]

By the end of May, Frost and the Morrisons were installed at the Homer Noble farm in Ripton, Vermont, Ted and Kay and their children for the second year in a row, Frost for the first time. The cabin he had chosen to make his home, while the Morrisons lived in the farmhouse below, was as snug and comfortable as he could wish. It was a rustic-looking log structure, lined inside with brown Beaverboard. Also inside, a stone fireplace warmed the main living room, off of which were a small bedroom, a central kitchen area with a small stove and hot-water heater, a small room suitable for bookshelves or storage, and a bathroom. In front, facing the pasture, was a large, screened-in porch.

Down the hill, the farmhouse was home for two people besides the Morrison family. As she had in previous summers in

West Dover, and last year in Ripton, Kay employed the Sages' daughter, Bunty, to look after her children and to care for the pony the Morrisons planned to rent. Also employed as housekeeper-cook was Mrs. Mary Jenkins, who had served the Sage family in a similar capacity until they gave up West Dover for another summer place. Known familiarly and affectionately by all as "Ma Jenks," the portly, warm-hearted widow was a Canadian by birth and loyalty, and on many evenings, often far into the morning hours, Frost could see her light from his cabin as she listened to her radio for some comforting and favorable news of the Canadian troops fighting in Europe.

Within a short time, a pattern of living had been established at the farm. Frost slept late, and rising, fixed himself a breakfast of raw egg, orange juice, and coffee or milk. He then worked for a few hours on a new poem or his next lecture, awaiting the arrival up the hill of Mrs. Morrison carrying a basket lunch. They talked or conducted whatever business needed to be done, and in midafternoon she returned to the farmhouse, leaving Frost to amuse himself with his garden, with a walk, with his chickens, or with training his new and remarkably intelligent companion, a young black-and-white Border collie he had given the name Gillie. Descending in late afternoon for dinner with the Morrison family, Frost then returned to his cabin with any guest who might be visiting, talking and walking until well past midnight.

Before the end of the summer, Frost increased his property holdings in Ripton by purchasing the thirty-seven-acre Euber farm, a mile through government land from his own, which commanded from its farmhouse a fine view of the Adirondack Mountains to the west. The farmhouse was badly in need of repair, and Frost arranged for extensive renovations to be made so that the "U-Bar" could be used next summer by one of his friends. He was equally concerned with his Florida property, on which he hoped to have erected some kind of living quarters by the time he went South for his winter vacation. There was only one obvious obstacle to his plans: he did not yet own the land he hoped to build on.

"I want to tell you something," he wrote to Hervey Allen on September 6. "There remains a slight flaw in the title to the five acre farm I am buying by you in Florida. I judge from the Judge's letter enclosed that it is only a slight flaw. I am not afraid of it, and unless I hear reason from you or the judge to dissuade me I shall go ahead with the business right away so we can get started with some sort of shelter down there for the winter. Suppose the Judge tells me the only waiver we lack is that of the only living nephew of say ten living aunts and uncles who have signed off and he is with the French foreign legion still a young man and they are all over seventy. I can see the possibility of their all dying inside of seven years and his turning up the sole heir and claiming the whole property. I might hesitate in such a situation. I must ask the Judge if the legionnaire would be heir to any buildings and improvements. I wouldn't like to lie awake even with a fence around me thinking of his return at the eleventh hour of the last day of the seven years. But there are such terrible possibilities in every prospect nowadays that I find it hard to take any small risk of my own very seriously. . . ."[17]

Three weeks later, the matter of the title had been resolved, and Frost, now back in Boston, was able to write enthusiastically to Allen:

"The deed is done—at least the money is passed for it. The small risk is cheerfully taken. What's a small personal risk in these times? We mean to do a whole lot of the building ourselves—at least Carol does with his own hands. What I need to ask you now is information about lumber and other building supplies. . . . I think I shall follow your example and use a small Hodgson unit for a start. If the whole region becomes an airport, I suppose we can hope to sell out at a profit short of profiteering. We ought to have a pull with A. MacLeish who I noticed spent the week-end with the President both or all at sea."[18]

Saying Archibald MacLeish and President Roosevelt were both "at sea" was the kind of joking in which Frost routinely engaged when poets or politicians chanced to expose themselves to his barbed wit. The phrase would have taken on a much less humorous connotation, however, had Frost applied it to his own son Carol, who was now very much "at sea" with a recurrence of one of his oldest mental irregularities. It soon became clear to Frost that Carol was in no position to do anything "with his own hands"—anything, that is, but an act his father and family had been dreading for years.

THE DEATH OF THE DARK CHILD

I took the wrong way with him. I tried many ways and every single one of them was wrong. Some thing in me is still asking for the chance to try one more. There's where the greatest pain is located. I am cut off too abruptly in my plans and efforts for his peace of mind.[1]

TO SOME EXTENT, at least, Robert Frost's son Carol had been "at sea" for all the thirty-eight years of his life. From childhood on, he had been plagued by persistent fears and anxieties which his parents, and later his wife, eventually came to recognize with painful clarity as symptoms of mental illness. His paranoia led him to suspect potential friends of seeking to take advantage of him, and he suspected strangers of plotting to spy on him or worse. He refused to believe, at times, that even the closest members of his family loved him, and he found little to love in himself. Craving perfection from his youth, much as his father had done, he found that his achievements always fell far short of his expectations. When they did, he was frequently plunged into deep depression. What was most disturbing of all to his parents and wife, he would frequently speak of taking his own life, not just to escape from the demons that tormented him, but whenever he felt that his life had attained "fulfillment."

Much in his son's troubled mind seemed to have no specific origin, but Frost believed he could trace the origin of Carol's obsession with suicide to a particular event in his life. In June of 1911, the Frost family was living in Derry Village, New Hampshire, in a house owned and occupied by an affable young lawyer named Lester Russell. One day, Russell was arrested for misusing funds which had been entrusted to him, and before he was taken to jail, he drank enough arsenic to cause his death next day. Frost tried to comfort and reassure his children by telling them that Russell's life had been a happy one, that it had reached a kind of fulfillment, and that God had called him home to heaven. But the children, in their play with neighborhood friends, soon heard the word "suicide," and gradually they picked up the details of how Lester Russell had killed himself. For nine-year-old Carol, there seemed to be a curious problem in trying to correlate his father's word "fulfillment" and the other word, "suicide." Thereafter, at various turning points and crises in his life, he often spoke of committing suicide when it seemed to him that he, too, had reached "fulfillment."[2]

The most recent episode of such talk, prior to 1940, had followed the death of Carol's mother in 1938. Preoccupied as she was by the sufferings of those around her, Elinor had taken a special interest in Carol's difficulties, and had tried to help and protect him whenever she could. Where, for example, Frost had persisted in frowning on the artistic ventures of his children, saying that "one artist in the family is enough," Elinor had encouraged them to try their hands at various art forms of their own choosing. Carol had turned to poetry, and while Frost could see that his son's poems showed not the least talent, Elinor always gave them lavish praise. As a result of this and other factors, Frost and his son had never developed any sustained affection in their relationship, but Carol and his mother became exceptionally close. When Elinor died, Carol's grief was so intense that he began to speak vehemently of suicide, until his wife Lillian feared that the son would not long survive the mother.

The two and a half years that had passed since Elinor's death had not been happy ones for Carol. He had tried to succeed at various business ventures, all centered on the farm in South Shaftsbury, but at none of them had he even reached the break-even point. Sinking deeper than ever into his delusions of persecution and into financial dependence on his father, he became increasingly morose and withdrawn as he despaired of ever achieving the success he coveted for the sake of his wife and son. Frost had already begun to wonder if Carol would not eventually be better off, and safer, in a mental institution, when a new crisis occurred. In the summer of 1940, Lillian Frost developed a condition that made a complete hysterectomy advisable in the near future. In view of his wife's history of heart trouble and tuberculosis, Carol's apprehensions for her safety were entirely reasonable. But as he continued to brood over the approaching operation, Carol became more and more obsessed by its obvious corollary: Lillian would never again be able to bear a child. Once again, he began to speak of suicide.

Carol's talk so frightened Lillian that a few days before she entered the House of Mercy Hospital in Pittsfield, Massachusetts, on the first of October 1940, she wrote to her father-in-law asking for help. Could Frost, she inquired, possibly spend a few days with Carol and Prescott when she underwent surgery on the second or third of October? She explained that Carol was "pretty nervous about it," and assured him that fifteen-year-old Prescott was "a pretty good cook." No further explanation was required. Frost immediately telephoned Carol in South Shaftsbury, and made arrangements to join his son and grandson as soon as he could leave Boston.[3]

When he reached South Shaftsbury around the third of October, he was shocked by how completely Carol had slipped into the depths of a suicidal depression. For the next two or three days, he listened to a litany of failures, fears, and frustrations. He reasoned, cajoled, and argued with his son, trying to make him give up the idea that he was a hopeless failure, that his life had reached "fulfillment" now that Lillian would never again have a child, that everyone would benefit if he were no longer alive. Carol's reasoning was so mired in confusion, however, that Frost could not be sure his son even understood what he was saying and hearing. Finally, when he had exhausted all the arguments he could think of, Frost persuaded Carol to repeat to him the promise he had made to Lillian just a few days before: that under no circumstances, whatever he might wish to do, would he ever do more than talk about taking his own life.

Having visited Lillian with Carol on several successive days following her operation, and having spent an entire Saturday night in close conversation with his son, Frost was convinced that the worst of their two very different crises had passed, and that it was safe for him to leave. Carol's last sullen remark, "You always win an argument, don't you?" was disquieting but seemed, at least, to indicate his grudging willingness to go on with life. Two days later, however, Carol appeared in an agitated state in Lillian's hospital room, and stayed just long enough to blurt out a few ill-connected remarks. One of them was that he was going to break two promises he had made.

Carol returned that night to his home and son in South Shaftsbury, and in the upstairs bedroom that they shared in Lillian's absence, he began to talk to Prescott about suicide. Hours passed, and more hours, until finally, when it was almost dawn, Prescott could stay awake no longer. As the boy slept, Carol burned all his old letters and his poems, went downstairs, and loaded the deer-hunting rifle he had given Lillian as a wedding present seventeen years before. Some time later, Prescott was startled from sleep by the sound of a shot. He ran downstairs to find his father lying dead on the kitchen floor, the rifle by his side.

"I'm cursed. God, if I don't believe I'm cursed." So the bereaved father had complained in Frost's early poem, "Home Burial."[4] When Prescott telephoned his grandfather on the morning of October 9 with the news of Carol's death, Frost had reason enough to say the words anew. He had lost his favorite daughter, Marjorie, in 1934, his wife in 1938, and now his last surviving son. But too many people were depending on him, and too many plans needed to be made, for Frost to permit himself as yet the luxury of mourning in bitter solitude. By early afternoon of the same day, he was in South Shaftsbury making arrangements for a funeral and cremation, comforting Prescott, and planning the best way to break the tragic news to Lillian.[5]

As for Prescott, Frost was pleased to learn that throughout his ordeal, he had conducted himself with remarkable character for one so young. After his all-night vigil with his father, and his discovery of the suicide, he had immediately telephoned the police, then his grandfather, then the family doctor, and then waited at home until the police came. By the time Frost arrived in South Shaftsbury, Prescott had even called a friend of the family, Floyd Holliday, and made tentative arrangements to live with the Holliday family until his mother was out of the hospital. A few days later, after his return to Boston following the funeral, Frost wrote a letter to his grandson praising him for having shown so much of the quality Frost had always valued most in life:

"Disaster brought out the heroic in you. You now know you have the courage and nerve for anything you may want or need to be, engineer, inventor or soldier. You would have had plenty of excuse if you had gone to pieces and run out of that house crying for help. From what Lesley reported to me of her talk with Lillian in Pittsfield Friday I judge you were in actual danger there alone with your unhappy father—unhappy to the point of madness. You kept your head and worked your faculties as cooly as a clock on a shelf. You've been tried more than most people are in a whole lifetime. Having said so much, I shan't bring up the subject again (for a long time anyway) either of your bravery or the terrible occasion for it. Let's think forward—I don't mean in big terms all at once, but just taking the days as they come along with a more natural and comfortable interest than I fear you have been permitted for some years past. You are fortunate in the friendship of such splendid people as the Hollidays. I took a great liking to them. They are a new beginning for you. The spell you and Lillian have been under is broken. You and she can think with some sanity now. So can I with you.

"Lillian says Carol thought nobody loved him. Pitiful! His mind was one cloud of suspiciousness. And we cared so much for him that his cloud was our cloud. We tried to enter into his affairs and sympathise with him. We spent hours, you and Lillian of course more hours than I. We could do him no good. Well he has taken his cloud away with him. His difficulty was too hard for us to understand. We never gave it up. He ended it for us. We shall have difficulties of our own ahead, but they will be simple and straightforward I believe. You and I and your mother have the healthy clearness of ordinary plain people. Lesley is that way too. So also is the Kathleen who has set me on my way onward again. We are the tough kind. . . ."[6]

At the same time Frost wrote a letter to Lillian, which began with an assurance that she and her son could continue to count on him for support now that Carol was dead:

"You're going to make it easy for me from now on by telling me always right straight out what you think best for yourself and Prescott and then if it is within my means and ability I will do it. I shan't have to guess so miserably any more. That is the great gain for me from our tragedy. I'll make suggestions if you want me to and I won't if you don't want me to. I suspect you will be making plans as you lie there in bed. But don't think you have to hurry. The immediate future is taken care of. You are to stay where you are till you are strong and then you are to live with Prescott at the Hollidays for awhile. . . ."

Carol had never, at any time in his life, threatened to harm anyone but himself, but when Lesley had visited her sister-in-law to tell her the news of Carol's death, Lillian's immediate reaction had been to fear that Prescott, too, was dead. That reaction, reported by Lesley to her father, partially accounted for Frost's erroneous belief that Carol had threatened the lives of his wife and son, as well as his own. He had expressed this view in his letter to Prescott, and he repeated it in the continuation of his letter to Lillian:

"I mustnt blame you for not making me realize the actual danger you and Prescott have been living in. You couldn't tell me. You didn't know yourself any too clearly. You were of course kept in confusion of mind by Carol's confused suffering. We forgive the poor boy. I'm sure he was fond of both of you. His desperation was due to his not being able to accomplish anything for you. He couldnt be sensible about his ambition for you. He overworked and he thought too terribly hard. I see now that his overstrained reasoning tended toward his destroying you all together as included in his failure. Still he said things to me when I was up there a week ago that indicated a wish (I see now) to save you and Prescott from his own doom. You know better than I what he thought about. None of us will ever understand him entirely. There is no use in going over and over it. Two things are sure: he was driven distracted by life and he was perfectly brave. I wish he could have been a soldier and died fighting Germany. . . ."[7]

Perhaps there was "no use in going over and over" the circumstances surrounding Carol's death, but as Frost brooded alone in his Boston apartment, searching for the reasons why his son had been driven to unreason, he found it impossible to avoid doing just that. Within a few weeks of his first letter to Lillian, he wrote and sent another, in which he recounted, perhaps more for himself than for Carol's widow, the last months and days of his son's life:

". . . You will realize more and more that Carol's misunderstandings of life had been growing rapidly worse in the last year. I spent most of Saturday night when I was up there trying to clear his conscience of guilt and his mind of worry. I thought I had done him some good. We had a pleasant ride down to see you and we had a natural good dinner together at the Hotel. But he spoiled my confidence in the end by saying that I had got the better of him in argument. He wasnt satisfied. It had got so nothing satisfied him. What showed he wasnt right in the mind was his returning again and again to your not being able to have any more children. I tried to make him laugh at his own foolishness there. That wasnt all. He said many things that I didnt know what to make of. He had many fine qualities. He was devoted to work, he was fond of little children and animals he was idealistic truthful and brave. And he thought everything of you and his mother. But his mind had in it a strange twist from childhood that no wrench we could give it could seem to straighten out. You helped him of course more than any of us. I failed with him. Do my best with money or advice it was always the wrong thing. I dont mean I think he resented my kindness. I wanted more than anything to soothe his anxiety, and he wouldnt be persuaded. Apparently he talked all his last night with Prescott the same way he talked all his last night with me. Prescott will probably tell you about it. But probably you know what it was already. A mixture of unreasonable guilt and anxiety. He couldnt seem to hold in mind anything comforting said to him. I tried to make him look forward to Florida. Florida was all right but he said he didnt see where the money was coming from to get back from there. I was in a terrible state of wondering if it wasnt my duty to have him examined by a mental doctor. But where might that have landed him? Better this way than a life in an institution. I am not going to keep on with this kind of talk. . . ."[8]

Before he finally did manage to put an end to "this kind of talk," Frost wrote also to Louis Untermeyer, expressing more openly than he could to a member of his own family his conscience-stricken sense of failure as a father for having failed to prevent Carol's death:

"I took the wrong way with him. I tried many ways and every single one of them was wrong. Some thing in me is still asking for the chance to try one more. There's where the greatest pain is located. I am cut off too abruptly in my plans and efforts for his peace of mind. You'll say it ought not to have come about that I should have to think for him. He really did most of his thinking for himself. He thought too much. I doubt if he rested from thinking day or night in the last few years. Mine was just an added touch to his mind to see if I couldn't make him ease up on himself and take life and farming off-hand. I got humbled. Three weeks ago I was down at Merrills telling Lee [Simonson] how to live. Two weeks ago I was up at South Shaftsbury telling Carol how to live. Yesterday I was telling seven hundred Harvard freshmen how to live with books in college. Apparently nothing can stop us once we get going. I talk less and less however as if I knew what I was talking about. My manner will be intended to indicate henceforth that I acknowledge myself disqualified from giving counsel. Kay says I am not to give myself up. Well then I'll be brave about this failure as I have meant to be about my other failures before. But you'll know and Kay will know in what sense I say things now. . . .

"I failed to trick Carol or argue him into believing he was the least successful. Thats what it came down to. He failed in farming and he failed in poetry (you may not have known). He was splendid with animals and little children. If only the emphasis could have been put on those. He should have lived with horses."[9]

Heartbroken as he was, Frost was determined not to let Carol's death disrupt, as had the death of his wife, his normal activities. Only a week after the tragedy in South Shaftsbury he informed his publisher, William Sloane, that he would have two books to offer him for publication in the coming year: one, a volume of prose that would be a selection of his previously published prefaces, talks, and essays; and the other, a new volume of poetry whose appearance would coincide with and help celebrate the seventy-fifth anniversary of the founding of Henry Holt and Company.[10] Frost worked so hard at putting together the new verse volume after Carol's death that by the time he was ready to leave for a visit to the University of Iowa in late October, he was able to tell Mrs. Morrison just where in his study she would find the completed manuscript should anything happen to prevent his return.

He came back refreshed and ready to take up his duties at Harvard for the second and last year of his Emerson Fellowship. By Christmas 1940, he had gone so far toward regaining his equilibrium that he was able to send out to his friends and associates a Christmas poem which asserted that, taken all in all, the forces of light still held a slight edge over the forces of darkness in the world. Against the dark backdrop of the Nazi advance across Europe, the title, "Our Hold on the Planet," had many levels of possible meaning:

We asked for rain. It didn't flash and roar.
It didn't lose its temper at our demand
And blow a gale. It didn't misunderstand

And give us more than our spokesman bargained for;
And just because we owned to a wish for rain,
Send us a flood and bid us be damned and drown.
It gently threw us a glittering shower down.
And when we had taken that into the roots of grain,
It threw us another and then another still,
Till the spongy soil again was natal wet.
We may doubt the just proportion of good to ill.
There is much in nature against us. But we forget:
Take nature altogether since time began,
Including human nature, in peace and war,
And it must be a little more in favor of man,
Say a fraction of one percent at the very least,
Or our number living wouldn't be steadily more,
Our hold on the planet wouldn't have so increased.[11]

On the fifteenth of January 1941, after dismissing his Harvard students at the end of his second course in "Poetry," Frost headed for Florida to direct the building of the two prefabricated houses he had ordered from a firm in New England some months before. When he arrived at Hervey Allen's estate, however, he discovered that the houses had not yet been delivered, having been delayed in transit for reasons related to the heavy flow of war materials up and down the coast. He had thus to content himself with clearing unwanted palmettos from his property and planting the first young orange trees in what he hoped would someday be a grove. His next-door neighbor, a retired professor at the University of Miami named Elmer Hjort, provided helpful information concerning the secrets of gardening in the thin soil of lime-based South Miami: how, for example, one had to prod the ground with a stick until one found a pocket of dirt deep enough for a young tree to send forth roots. So, between gardening, relaxing, and visiting with Hervey Allen, just a short walk away, Frost spent his winter vacation at the Florida "farm" he had already decided to call "Pencil Pines."

The delay in the erection of his prefabricated houses might have been more disappointing had Frost not decided, even before leaving for the South, to look for a new home in the North. The lease on his Mt. Vernon Street apartment was just about up when he concluded that, instead of renewing it, he would ask Mrs. Morrison to find him a house with more room for his books, his guests, his dog Gillie, and himself, and with stairs front and back on which he could exercise by climbing and descending. By the time he came back to Boston, Kay had succeeded in finding him a place that perfectly suited his needs. It was an old Victorian-style double house, of three stories, in a quiet, residential neighborhood of Cambridge known locally as Brewster Village. After a two-week lecture trip to Texas early in March, Frost locked the door of his first city apartment and moved to his new residence at 35 Brewster Street.[12]

On the twenty-sixth of March, the day he celebrated his "sixty-seventh" birthday, Frost went to Washington, D.C., to visit with his daughter Lesley, to inspect an exhibition of his works that she had helped prepare in the Library of Congress, and to give a talk the following day in the Coolidge Auditorium of the Library of Congress. Eugene Meyer, the publisher of the Washington *Post*, had had the idea some time before of sponsoring a series of personal appearances by major American poets at the Library, and Frost had been invited to appear in the second program of the series. The title he gave his talk was "The Role of a Poet in a Democracy."[13]

His position, he began, was analogous to what "a good churchman" had once said regarding Jesus Christ:

> *Thou art the Way.*
> *Hadst Thou been nothing but the goal*
> *I cannot say*
> *If Thou hadst ever met my soul.*[14]

Democracy as a way, he said, had always interested him more than democracy as an end in itself. He was not one to say, as some parents did of their children, that the more he loved it, the more he saw its faults. "Hell! You know, it's a lie to begin with; it's an affectation. The more I love my country the less I've seen its faults and I'm not ashamed to say it. It is the way; had it been nothing but the goal, democracy and I would probably never have met. I'm not far-seeing enough for goals."

The focus of his remarks was the truncated pyramid with an eye at the apex, which appears on the Great Seal of the United States. It was a figure, he said, and "all figures, all figurative things in verse or in prose, may be taken more than one way." But the way he preferred to take it was as meaning that "democracy would always mean refraining from power beyond a certain point; that we would never in this country have anybody at the apex but God." That was why he so much admired George Washington, because he had had the chance to seize power, but had refused to go beyond a certain point. As a humorous illustration of "the kind of nationalist" he was, Frost read his poem called "Triple Plate," which was reminiscent in many ways of "A Drumlin Woodchuck," though it was far more obviously political:

The Infinite's being so wide
Is the reason the Powers provide
For inner defense my hide.
For next defense outside

I make myself this time
Of wood or granite or lime
A wall too hard for crime
Either to breach or climb.

Then a number of us agree
On a national boundary
And that defense makes three
Between too much and me.[15]

The Library of Congress talk did much to bring Frost into public notice as a commentator on the American political scene, a role to which he had increasingly aspired in recent years. He received further help and encouragement in that direction a few months later when President Conant invited him to stay on at Harvard for an extra year as a "Fellow in American Civilization," or as Frost described it, a "roving consultant in History and Literature." The annual stipend of $3,000 was half again as much as he had received in his Emerson Fellowship, and the duties were no more rigorous: all he would have to do would be to make himself more or less regularly available for "group discussions on American Civilization in the larger sense of the word" in each of Harvard's seven houses, rather than merely the one house, Adams, where his Emerson classes had been held. Frost cheerfully accepted Conant's invitation.[16]

His first opportunity to speak on American civilization came little more than a month later. On the twentieth of June, he delivered to the Phi Beta Kappa Society at Harvard a new poem on which he had been working, irregularly, since 1935. It was called "The Lesson for Today," and in it Frost took a stand, in his half-joking, half-serious way, against those poets and prophets of doom who were suggesting that in 1941 the world was beyond question passing through the darkest age in human history. Such people, Frost said, were off the mark in several respects. First, it was impossible for them to judge how bad the times really were without the perspective of hundreds of years of ensuing history. Second, in their condemnation of human suffering and adversity, they failed to realize that "the groundwork of all faith is human woe."

> *Earth's a hard place in which to save the soul,*
> *And could it be brought under state control,*
> *So automatically we all were saved,*
> *Its separateness from Heaven could be waived;*
> *It might as well at once be kingdom-come.*[17]

Until that day arrived, Frost was inclined to scoff at those who shed "literary tears" over the fact that they, the nation, the human race, even the earth itself, were "doomed to broken-off careers":

> *I may have wept that any should have died*
> *Or missed their chance, or not have been their best,*
> *Or been their riches, fame, or love denied;*
> *On me as much as any is the jest.*
> *I take my incompleteness with the rest.*
> *God bless himself can no one else be blessed.*

But the epitaph that Frost would choose to be remembered by would be no more bitter than the single line: "I had a lover's quarrel with the world."[18]

After his Harvard appearance Frost returned to Ripton, where Lillian and Prescott were spending part of the summer, Prescott haying with a friend during the day and staying with his mother in rented rooms in town. With Frost's assistance and encouragement, both Lillian and her son had emerged as successfully from the dark period of Carol's death as Frost himself had done. But there was still one more sad duty to be performed before they could feel that the whole sad business was behind them. Carol's ashes as well as Elinor's were still in the hands of the Bennington undertaker where they had both been since Carol's cremation. The interment had yet to take place.

Some months before, with Lillian's permission, Frost had purchased a large plot in the cemetery of Old Bennington's First Congregational Church, for use as the Frost burial ground. He had also arranged for several stones to be made that would bear the names of all the Frosts, including those already buried elsewhere, and his own.

In September, he learned that the stones had been delivered to the cemetery, and that two recesses had been prepared to receive the urns of Carol and his mother. He completed arrangements with the minister of the church and set a time for the interment. As they entered the churchyard at the appointed hour, they caught a glimpse of the minister talking to a parishioner. They walked on to the gravesite to await his arrival. Ten minutes passed, then twenty, then thirty. Thinking the minister was for some reason deliberately ignoring them, Frost became increasingly furious, until at last he decided they had waited long enough. "We don't need any help to do what we came here for," he said to Lillian and Prescott. He instructed his grandson to place Carol's urn in the space that had been prepared for it, then he did the same with the long-unburied urn of his wife. As they watched, two workmen who were standing by came forward and set the stones in place. Then the three Frosts turned and walked away.[19]

A WITNESS TREE

Thus truth's established and borne out,
Though circumstanced with dark and doubt—
Though by a world of doubt surrounded.[1]

THE EUROPEAN WAR that had begun in the fall of 1939 was two years old when Robert Frost began his third consecutive year at Harvard as its new "Fellow in American Civilization." Since the collapse of Poland before the German advance, Belgium, France, and the Netherlands had also fallen, and England itself had only narrowly escaped catastrophe by the RAF's stunning performance in the Battle of Britain. Thus far the United States had managed to stay out of the fighting, and many at home were content that America should continue to isolate itself from the conflagration abroad, whatever the consequences. Frost was not one of these, for he was willing to see his country go to war against Hitler's Germany. He needed, however, a better reason for doing so than merely the salvation of Great Britain.

"Our seaboard sentimentalists think of nothing but saving England," he wrote to his son-in-law, Willard Fraser, in November 1941. "Some of them would go so far as to sacrifice America to save England. They are the Anglophiles with an English accent. One of the seven colleges of Harvard is presided over by such a patriot. Only one. But there are more who act and talk from a fear that to save America we must save England. I brush all this aside. We are able to fight and we are not afraid to fight. My only doubt is whether we need to join in England's fight. I should like it better if we had it all to ourselves and if we won we would get the loot the glory and the self-realization.[2] That last is the great thing. I don't want to see a lot of bloody trouble unless we are going to bring America out a nation more distinct from all other nations than she is already. But as I am in the hands of my government in business so am I in war. I rather hope from certain signs he has given that the President would let the British merge us in their empire. I mean he will take care to get something out of this war for us. He made a good beginning in the swap of destroyers for island bases. You see I am not much worked up over politics. There are some people round I can't bear to listen to—that's all that ails me. I heard two commencement addresses the argument of which was that this was a war to make the world safe for Shakespeare. The Athenians might have made the rhetorical claim that the object of their war with Sparta was to make the world safe for Thucidides and Sophocles. They lost to Sparta, but the great dramatists were still the great dramatists over and above the conflicts of politics and nations. There's where the only peaceful brotherhood of man will ever be, above opinion and parliaments in the realm of music poetry science and philosophy. Religion ought to be included in my list and might be if it would only behave religiously and cease to try to pray God on one side or the other. Men should be able to kill each other in settling differences of opinion, but at the same time recite and sing to each other the same poems and songs of international greatness."

Lest his son-in-law conclude from his remarks that he was hoping for the defeat of England, Frost added a postscript to help clarify his position:

"I don't know whether I made it clear in all the foregoing that my international politics were in no way hostile to England. I admire England beyond any great power since Rome. Benny DeVoto goes round saying he wishes the war was over so we could go back to hating England. He means twisting the Lion's tail. I have never been a Lion's-tail-twister. I am for the moment impatient with the mighty nation that it should be crying baby to us to come and save it again. I wish it would try to keep my admiration by winning its own war: or else get clear off the field and out of our way so we could win the war not for England but for ourselves."[3]

Frost had a fire-fight of his own a few weeks later when he and Kay Morrison went up to Ripton to open the Homer Noble farmhouse for the Thanksgiving holiday. Soon after their arrival, Frost discovered in a wastepaper basket some old lesson books Mrs. Morrison's son, Bobby, had used and discarded.

When he opened one, Frost found it contained such multiple choice questions as, "A cow gives: a) ink b) water c) milk. Check right answer." Disgusted by what seemed to him thoroughly inane questions, he took the basket outside to the incinerator behind the garage and set fire to its contents. There was a considerable blaze but it soon died down, and Frost thought no more about it. Later that afternoon, however, as he and Mrs. Morrison were starting toward the Euber place to inspect it before leaving for lunch in the village, they got half-way across the field when Frost looked back and saw a great cloud of smoke coming from the tall dry grass beside the garage. They ran back and tried to beat the fire out, but it spread into the field and, with the help of a stiff breeze, began to roar up the slope toward the cabin and the woods. They ran back to the house and telephoned for help. The flames were burning rapidly up the field toward Frost's cabin. They tried to outrace the advance. Sighting some men who had been chopping wood nearby, Frost started toward them shouting, "Help, fire! Help, fire!" before continuing on his way. When the men arrived, the fire had reached the cabin and had ignited the steps. They helped to pull the steps down, and the cabin was saved. The flames now struck off into the government property above the cabin. A considerable crowd had now assembled, both curious onlookers and forest rangers of the government park service. The fire burned all that afternoon and into the night, and continued to smolder underground for three days. Later, Frost received a bill from the Forest Service for some $200, and a letter apologizing for the necessity of charging him with the costs of his "trespass" into government land. "Mr. Frost is decidedly an asset to Vermont," the Forest Supervisor wrote, "and, in a larger sense, he has contributed much to human happiness. For this reason I can say with the utmost sincerity that everyone associated with this matter is truly sorry that it occurred." As for Frost, sorry as he was, he was glad when pneumonia did not result from all the smoke he had taken into his lungs. His exertions were followed by nothing worse than a hearty Thanksgiving dinner with the Morrison family.[4]

On December 5, 1941, Frost went to Williamsburg, Virginia, to serve as the Phi Beta Kappa poet at the annual meeting of the society's mother chapter at William and Mary College. He chose to read for the occasion three short poems he had written over a period of many years. The earliest, "To a Moth Seen in Winter," dated from the turn of the century, and the latest, "Time Out," had been written within the past three or four years.[5] The third poem he read was the second oldest, having been written around 1935, and like the other two it had never before been given to the public. Unlike the others, however, its theme was clearly historical, in a way which no poem of his had been since his first poetic composition, "La Noche Triste," back in 1890. He called it "The Gift Outright," and in it he celebrated the process by which America had ceased to be merely a group of English colonies, and had begun to take shape as a nation in its own right:

The land was ours before we were the land's.
She was our land more than a hundred years
Before we were her people. She was ours
In Massachusetts, in Virginia,
But we were England's, still colonials,
Possessing what we still were unpossessed by,
Possessed by what we now no more possessed.
Something we were withholding made us weak
Until we found out that it was ourselves
We were withholding from our land of living,
And forthwith found salvation in surrender.
Such as we were we gave ourselves outright
(The deed of gift was many deeds of war)
To the land vaguely realizing westward,
But still unstoried, artless, unenhanced,
Such as she was, such as she would become.[6]

Two days after Frost's Williamsburg visit, the Japanese attacked Pearl Harbor and thrust the United States overnight into active participation in the Second World War. When news of the war broke, Frost lectured his secretary for nearly an hour on the need for courage in the face of the present crisis. He was, however, far more upset by the turn of events than he wanted to admit. The outbreak of war, as he well knew, was likely to result in the serious curtailment of his extensive lecture schedule, upon which he greatly depended to help provide an income for his financial outlays to his family and for his farm. In his excited reaction to the declaration of war on Japan, and subsequently on its European allies, Frost bitterly blamed President Roosevelt for getting the United States into a fight for which the country was not adequately prepared. Even more bitterly, he accused England of starting something she could not finish, and then appealing to America for help. He despised the way in which Prime Minister Churchill had come to America to tell how it could be of help, and he saw the whole thing as connected with America's insistence on commercial expansion into parts of the Pacific where it did not belong. But whatever or whoever the cause or culprit, Frost felt sure that the advent of war would mean a drastic reduction in his income for the duration of the hostilities.[7]

Fortunately, relief was available in the form of an unusual arrangement he had recently entered into with Earle J. Bernheimer, the collector who had purchased the unique copy of *Twilight* just a year ago. Back in June, Frost had sent Bernheimer a proposal he hoped would find acceptance:

"I am rather in need of about two thousand dollars right now and would like to sell you two of my most valuable manuscripts at one thousand dollars apiece. One would be the original manuscript of my only full length play to date ['The Guardeen'] with all its emendations crude upon it. The other would be the Robinson preface [to *King Jasper*]. I thought perhaps your interest in collecting me would go to this length. You already have so much more than anyone else except perhaps the Jones Library at Amherst. I dont want to make you feel bothered. I value your friendship too much and appreciate what you are doing for my perpetuation."[8]

There was little that Bernheimer would not have done to please Frost or to improve his own collection, but $2,000 for those particular items seemed a steep price even to him. He had, moreover, become enmeshed in a legal quarrel that for the moment made such an outlay next to impossible. He replied, therefore, by offering Frost a loan of one thousand dollars, to be cancelled in the near future by the "purchase" of literary manuscripts such as those Frost had already offered.[9]

The poet's silence was so loud that Bernheimer asked their mutual friend, the rare-books dealer Louis Henry Cohn, if Frost had been offended by his refusal to accept the original proposition. Cohn's answer reflected the amusement he felt at Frost's propensity for horse trading:

"I cannot see how you could possibly have offended Frost by offering to advance him a thousand dollars. He may be slightly annoyed that you did not fall for his little game of getting two thousand out of you for a couple of manuscripts not worth half the sum. He may have thought that you were more naive than you are. Obviously he did not need the money as much as he pretended as he would have jumped at the chance of getting the thousand or would have suggested that you stretch it a bit as he really needed the larger sum. . . ."[10]

Thus encouraged, Bernheimer had requested a personal interview with Frost. They met in Ripton on July 28. Frost's manner was now so cordial that Bernheimer made bold to suggest an arrangement with the poet that would be mutually profitable. Bernheimer would take the two manuscripts and would give Frost the thousand dollars of his original counter-offer. But he was willing to go much further. In return for whatever literary documents, original drafts, galley proofs, or anything else Frost felt he could spare, with whatever personal signature or inscription he might choose to add, Bernheimer would quietly and regularly send him a monthly check for $150, until such time as one or the other of them saw fit to terminate the arrangement. Frost had scarcely believed that the collector would be willing to relieve him so handsomely of materials he would otherwise have merely stored or destroyed. He had accepted Bernheimer's proposal and sent him off to await the first bundle of desiderata.

One significant new contribution to Bernheimer's collection was offered in December 1941 shortly after the Pearl Harbor disaster:

"We have now two versions of the play ['The Guardeen'] ready for you in two volumes," Frost wrote. "The second is better because more compact. There may yet be a third. If so, you shall have it. From your point of view I know the more versions the merrier. I never have versions of a poem or hardly ever; so I will try to have as many versions of this play as I possibly can. We would like to get the two we have off our hands and into your safekeeping where the Japanese bombs are falling and the earthquake shaking your house down but we hesitate to consign them to the Railway Express when clogged with Christmas presents. But if you say the word by return air mail they will come along."[11]

Much as Bernheimer's checks were a comfort to Frost, they did not remove his deep fear that, because of the war, his old age would be marked by the same kind of want he had known earlier in his life. The new book he was working on, he believed, contained some of his best poetry, but what would that matter from the standpoint of financial worries if the war made money even tighter than it already was? Frost's fears continued to build until Kay Morrison decided to reveal them to William Sloane, his editor at Holt, in the hope that he might be able to reassure the poet. Sloane responded early in January 1942:

". . . Kay tells me," he wrote, "that you are worried about the situation as regards the way it might affect the reception of this book. I want to give you an optimistic prognosis about that with the understanding that if I am wrong you won't hold it against me. I believe that the next months are going to see an intensification of the better kind of patriotism in this country, a renewal of the average American's love for the things which are distinctly his own. Your poetry is one of those things, and I do not believe that in the case of this book of all others the situation is going to prove unfavorable. Of course heavier taxes will mean less luxury money, and books are to a certain extent luxuries; but I think this will be more than offset by the other tendency which I have mentioned. We are planning our sales campaign so as to secure an advance sale of 7500 copies of *Witness Tree* if we can, and I can see no reason why we cannot."[12]

Under the circumstances, Frost could hardly have wished for a stronger vote of confidence from his publisher. The size of the anticipated advance sale was scarcely smaller than it would have been if there had been no war at all. But whether such confidence was justified remained to be seen.

Unhappily, the fact that his public career had survived Pearl Harbor did not mean that the problems of Frost's private life were at an end. In the early weeks of America's involvement in the war, a personal crisis of unclear nature but apparently major seriousness threw him into a depression deep enough for him to toy—though surely no more than toy—with the idea of committing suicide. The mood soon passed, and in a few days he returned to business as usual—at least outwardly. Inwardly, it would seem, he was not without self-pity. He soon sent Louis Untermeyer a new version of a poem he had sent also on two previous occasions to mark his passage through some crisis in his spiritual or emotional life:

To prayer I think I go,
I go to prayer—
Along a darkened corridor of woe
And down a stair
In every step of which I am abased.
I wear a halter-rope about the waist.
I bear a candle end put out with haste.
For such as I there is reserved a crypt
That from its stony arches having dripped
Has stony pavement in a slime of mould.
There I will throw me down an unconsoled
And utter loss,
And spread out in the figure of a cross.
Oh, if religion's not to be my fate
I must be spoken to and told
Before too late!

He added a message that hinted at the nature of the crisis just past: "You had the first of this from me long ago and I recently had a copy of it back from you. You never saw the end of it. You never saw how it came out. There was no end to it till now that I could write that I *had* been spoken to and told—you know by whom. This is merely the letter I always owe you and it's all my news for the moment—if it can be called news. It's not such as to get me into the newspapers. I believe I am safely secular till the last go down—that's all. I decided to keep the matter private and out of my new book. It could easily be made too much of. I can't myself say how serious the crisis was and how near I came to giving in. It [death] would have been good advertising."[13]

Having decided to let William Sloane find less dramatic ways of selling the new book, Frost went about his normal activities as if nothing dire had occurred. After attending a P.E.N. banquet in his honor on the night of January 20, he headed for Florida to inspect his newly erected prefabricated houses and to await the arrival of Mrs. Morrison. Frost living in a small rented cottage on Ohio Street in Coconut Grove, and Kay in a boarding house nearby, the poet and his secretary were presently hard at work furnishing, planting trees around, and otherwise improving his future winter headquarters.

"We've brought the two small houses on a little way further," he reported to Lesley sometime in February. "We've had three and five weeks in them and now leave them to our neighborly neighbors the Hjorts to keep an eye on till we come back next year. . . . The three-room house is already almost too pretty to abandon. The two room house exactly twenty five feet across a grassy and flowery court from it is comfortable and convenient. The three-room is to have an open fireplace soon. The two room has a small woodstove against the blue norther. . . ."[14]

Mrs. Morrison left Florida for Cambridge on the twenty-fifth of February, and Frost remained behind to fulfill a few lecture commitments in the South. A summer cold, however, soon forced him to return to South Miami for a few days before starting North once again. Relaxing at Pencil Pines, he decided to pass the time by answering some of the letters he owed. One of these was a reply to a recent letter of Lesley's, in which she harshly criticized the British for their willingness to trade increased political freedom for India in return for active support of the Allied war effort. Lesley liked neither the British handling of the Indian situation nor the way in which England seemed to be fawning on the United States. To her verbal attack Frost added a few observations of his own.

"You mustnt be too hard on the British in their day of adversity. I hate to hear them starting to free India under fire. If one were fanciful he might venture the figure that it sounds like the Empires death bed repentance. Neither do I like their fawning on us at such a time. Still it ill becomes a Frost not to sympathise with a nation that has done so much for our family. Possibly you calculate it has not been all good—good only for me and not for the rest of the family. I have no answer for that. Anyway I am on their side. But what would Rudyard Kipling say—Had he lived to see this day—of having his poems edited by worlds-end-whimper T. S. Elliot—to rouse the spirit of the British to the Natzi level to meet the Natzi-greatness?

"There are sarcastic things I could say to our own campaign. For instance: the New Deal has won one more victory than was to be expected of them in the field of internal politics over real men. Churchill won't last much longer unless his affairs take a turn for the better: and if he goes it will be too bad for the Groton boys who love the mother country like a mother."[15]

Frost's sarcasm was by no means confined to political subjects. Shortly after he came home to 35 Brewster Street, Mrs. Morrison showed him an article by Carl Sandburg in the March 1942 issue of the *Atlantic Monthly*. The aging poet whom Frost had long since decided was one of his major rivals had taken issue with his recently quoted statement that he would as soon write free verse as play tennis with the net down. Without mentioning Frost by name, Sandburg had written what amounted to a self-defense as well as a defense of free verse against its detractors:

"That a large body of English teachers in high schools, colleges, and universities have been kindly and favorable to my work in the field of free verse, more than occasionally one of them maintaining this or that student's saying, 'Until we got into Sandburg, I was never interested in poetry'—this I do not forget. That some of the professional reviewers and critics have been both kindly and eloquent toward my work as a verse writer—this too I do not forget.

"Recently a poet was quoted as saying he would as soon play tennis without a net as to write free verse. This is almost as though a zebra should say to a leopard, 'I would rather have stripes than spots,' or as though a leopard should inform a zebra, 'I prefer spots to stripes.'

"The poet without imagination or folly enough to play tennis by serving and returning the ball over an invisible net may see himself as highly disciplined. There have been poets who could and did play more than one game of tennis with unseen rackets, volleying airy and fantastic balls over an insubstantial net, on a frail moon lit fabric of a court.

"The arguments against free verse are old. They are not, however, as old as free verse itself. When primitive and prehistoric man first spoke with cadence or color, making either musical meaning or melodic nonsense worth keeping and repeating for its definite and intrinsic values, then free verse was born, ages before the sonnet, the ballad, the verse forms wherein the writer or singer must be acutely conscious, even exquisitely aware, of how many syllables are to be arithmetically numbered per line.

"The matter should not be argued. Those who make poems and hope their poems are not bad may find readers or listeners —and again they may not. The affair should rest there. Nothing can be proved except that some poets have one kind of readers or listeners—and other poets have other kinds. . . ."[16]

Frost's reaction to Sandburg's defense of his craft was as full of sarcasm as the remark that had prompted it. In a letter to Lawrance Thompson he wrote:

". . . Kathleen says I am challenged to single combat by Carl Sandburg in an article in the *Atlantic* for March. His works prove you can play tennis more imaginatively with the net down, or so he maintains. He suspects me of having meant him in my witticism: and merely incidentally to his patriotic campaign to help Archie [MacLeish] save the country he rushes to the defense of himself as an American poet. Sauve qui peut (sp.) It is something if he saves one poet in the general wreck. Kathleen says he says many a teacher says her average pupil often says he never liked poetry till Sandburg came and his own failed to receive him not. (sic-k). Did I never tell you how his daughter once caught a magnate reading my NoB [*North of Boston*] early one morning before he thought anyone was up. Why father she stinted, I thought you never read poetry. This isn't poetry he said crossly throwing it in the open fire. The great object of great art is to fool the average man in his first or second childhood into thinking it *isnt* art. . . ."[17]

Though Frost always found some excuse to mock poets who, like Sandburg, presented what seemed to him a genuine threat to his own literary reputation, he was often willing to do what he could to help a young and promising writer find his way to publication, or otherwise advance in his career. One such was an Iowan named James Hearst, who was the subject of a letter Frost sent to William Sloane on the occasion of his own so-called sixty-eighth birthday on March 26:

"I'm sending you separately some poems I have had on my mind on my conscience and on the shelf for too long a time. I didn't write them. But I like them rather well though not nearly as well as I like the fellow who did write them. He is the interesting Iowa farmer I may have spoken to you about. Many of us are his admiring friends including the Iowan Vice president of the United States [Henry Wallace]. His name is James Hearst and it is already known for one volume of verse (Prairie Press publishers) that went through an edition. The story that goes with him helps sell the verse. He is partly paralyzed from a diving accident and only holds up his end with his brother farming a big Iowa farm by virtue of what he can do with the big machinery once he is lifted into his seat by someone else. His brother has devoted himself to giving him a share in the farm life and has stayed unmarried, I suspect at a sacrifice. They are a noted pair. Their farm is one of the best in Iowa. I tell you all this for obvious reasons. And I might add that I have wondered if Henry Wallace mightnt be induced to go on the jacket of his book with the idea of bringing Hearst out of his regional existence into a national. Now you've got all the elements, you can be left to judge for yourself. Only please deliver judgment quickly—Hearst mustnt be kept waiting cruelly long. Mind you I am not pressing. Some of the poems I like very well. May be the book would gain by the elimination of the poems that echo Spoon River."[18]

Within a month, Frost's interest in the careers of young poets was pushed into the background by the appearance of his own book, *A Witness Tree*, his first collection of new verse since *A Further Range* in 1936. Dedicated "To K. M. for her part in it," *A Witness Tree* contained forty-two poems grouped in five sections, with two introductory poems that gave readers to understand just what Frost meant to imply by the book's title. The first introductory poem, called "Beech," Frost fancifully attributed to "The Moodie Forester"—Moodie having been his mother's maiden name—and in it he provided essential clues for understanding the symbolic levels of the "witness tree" metaphor that governed the organization of the entire book:

> *Where my imaginary line*
> *Bends square in woods, an iron spine*
> *And pile of real rocks have been founded.*
> *And off this corner in the wild,*
> *Where these are driven in and piled,*
> *One tree, by being deeply wounded,*
> *Has been impressed as Witness Tree*
> *And made commit to memory*
> *My proof of being not unbounded.*
> *Thus truth's established and borne out,*
> *Though circumstanced with dark and doubt—*
> *Though by a world of doubt surrounded.*[19]

Having thus evoked the simplest secular dimension of the "witness tree" as the scarred-trunk-and-iron-stake marker identifying the corner of a piece of country property—in this case the Homer Noble farm—and the symbolic dimension of the tree as marker between the poet's finite, troubled inner world and the only less-chaotic world around him, Frost added a second "tree" poem he borrowed from *The New England*

Primer, to which he added his own title, "Sycamore." Here, the "witness tree" became not a marker but a vantage point, from which to see beyond the finite world to the infinite, God:

> *Zaccheus he*
> *Did climb the tree*
> *Our Lord to see.*[20]

With these two poems, Frost established for his readers the notion that the others which followed were themselves, taken separately and as a whole, a kind of witness tree, demarcating the secular and spiritual boundaries of the poet's life and times. It was an ambitious design, yet he felt that it was fully justified by the poems he had chosen to include.

The first of the book's five sections, after the two introductory poems, was called "One or Two," and it included fourteen poems, beginning with "The Silken Tent," each of which contributed a different perspective to the question implied by the section's title. The second grouping, "Two or More," began with "The Gift Outright," and contained five poems including "Triple Bronze," "Our Hold on the Planet," and "The Lesson for Today." Next was "Time Out," with eight poems including "To a Moth Seen in Winter," "A Considerable Speck," "November," and "It Is Almost the Year Two Thousand." In the last of these, Frost seemed to anticipate scientific developments that were still three years away from fiery fulfillment over Hiroshima and Nagasaki:

> *To start the world of old*
> *We had one age of gold*
> *Not labored out of mines,*
> *And some say there are signs*
> *The second such has come,*
> *The true Millennium,*
> *The final golden glow*
> *To end it. And if so*
> *(And science ought to know)*
> *We well may raise our heads*
> *From weeding garden beds*
> *And annotating books*
> *To watch this end deluxe.*[21]

In "Quantula," the next section, Frost grouped nine short poems, ranging from the gnomic couplet, "The Secret Sits,"

We dance round in a ring and suppose,
But the Secret sits in the middle and knows.[22]

to the two eight-line ventures into political commentary, "An Equalizer" and "A Semi-Revolution." In the latter Frost pretended, with characteristic wit, to be one of those political thinkers who prided themselves on having all the answers to the social and political ills of the age:

I advocate a semi-revolution.
The trouble with a total revolution
(Ask any reputable Rosicrucian)
Is that it brings the same class up on top.
Executives of skillful execution
Will therefore plan to go halfway and stop.
Yes, revolutions are the only salves,
But they're one thing that should be done by halves.[23]

As much as any poem in the collection, "A Semi-Revolution" was linked thematically to the second of the introductory poems, "Sycamore." Throughout his life, Frost consistently scoffed at the notions of social planners who believed imperfection could be legislated out of existence. For him, there was only one "salve," and it was the same "Secret" who sat in the middle and knew: God. But only one who, like Frost, had climbed the tree our Lord to see would know that. All others must endlessly "dance round in a ring and suppose," spinning out one theory after another to repair what it was God's pleasure to set asunder.

The last section, entitled "Over Back," began with a poem linked even more closely to "Beech" than "A Semi-Revolution" was linked to "Sycamore." Entitled "Trespass," it concerned one who had chosen to ignore the message of the speaker's witness tree:

No, I had set no prohibiting sign,
And yes, my land was hardly fenced.
Nevertheless the land was mine:
I was being trespassed on and against.

Whoever the surly freedom took
Of such an unaccountable stay
Busying by my woods and brook
Gave me a strangely restless day.

He might be opening leaves of stone,
The picture book of the trilobite,
For which the region round was known,
And in which there was little property right.

'Twas not the value I stood to lose
In specimen crab in specimen rock,
But his ignoring what was whose
That made me look again at the clock.

Then came his little acknowledgment:
He asked for a drink at the kitchen door,
An errand he may have had to invent,
But it made my property mine once more.[24]

Five poems more and the book was complete. Published on the twenty-third of April 1942, it did so well commercially that by mid-June Holt sales stood at 10,000 copies. Informing Frost of the great success of *A Witness Tree*, William Sloane added that he had decided to let Louis Untermeyer go ahead with a project he had proposed some time ago, his own selection of Frost's poems especially designed for young and new readers[25]; this in addition to Untermeyer's huge new Simon and Schuster anthology, which itself contained a generous selection of Frost's verse. At Holt, Sloane's plans included the soon-to-be-published *Fire and Ice: The Art and Thought of Robert Frost*, written by Lawrance Thompson, the first full-length study devoted not to Frost the man but to his poetry. So much excitement gave Frost a feeling of elation as great as the misgivings he had once felt for the success of *A Witness Tree*. He did not conceal his enthusiasm when he wrote to Sloane on the sixteenth of June:

"Really ten thousand in less than two months beats everything. Larry's book ahead, and then these books of Louis', and then my prose book, and then a volume of plays, and then another volume of poetry, and then somewhere in the middle of all this the definitive augmented 'North of Boston,' should assure us of sustaining this excitement for a while yet. You were right about publishing this Spring and we are glad you stuck to it—war or no war."[26]

8

ON THE HOME FRONT

I can talk about the war upon occasion, but what unfits me for most platforms is that most people believe in this war whereas I believe in any and all wars. I mean I sympathize with all the brave people who go out to die for causes.[1]

THE SUCCESS of *A Witness Tree* freed Robert Frost from enough of his anxiety over how the war would affect his career to permit him to regard the Allied war effort with far less cynicism than before. By the late summer of 1942, he was willing to admit to Lawrance Thompson, who had recently been commissioned an officer in the United States Navy, that the British were "all right as allies," though he could not resist qualifying that statement with the wry observation, "You have to take comfort from any animal heat you can snuggle up to in a cold storm." He was even willing to express limited praise for the third major partner in the anti-Axis alliance, the Russians, who had suffered and inflicted enormous losses in their effort to stop the Nazi drive toward the oil fields of the Caucasus. Having just read the news that the Germans, after an apparent retreat, were again launching a major attack near Stalingrad, Frost wrote: "The Russians I admire for having stuck at nothing to accomplish nothing. It is a privilege to have been let look on at their spectacle of ruthlessness for its own sake (as it turns out). I accept but dont rejoice in them as allies. . . ."

He was also willing to admit, now, that his response to the war in the first months after Pearl Harbor had been deficient compared to the sense of involvement he now felt:

"But until I had you in the fight," he told Thompson, "I seemed to suffer from the sinfulness of the accidia I once lectured on at the Grolier Club. I didnt seem to stir up. I went back to old wars for my fabulae. The professional emotionalists filled me with Cordelian shame that I could not rise to the occasion. I judge from what you had to say for me on the jacket [of *Fire and Ice*] that you may have been worried just a tiny little bit about how I might look to Carl [Sandburg] and Archie [MacLeish]. Dorothy Thompson has just summoned me to sing out for her Land Army. If I remember rightly it was Mrs Roosevelt herself that asked me a month ago to set something about the future to rhyme and meter. I dont want to write poetry. I want to lick somebody. And since I can't do it myself, I want you to do it for me. My satisfaction depends entirely on you."[2]

Earlier in the letter, Frost had called Thompson "my one soldier at the front in this war, and my clearest reason for wanting to win."[3] Flattering though the statement was, it would have been more accurately applied to Frost's son-in-law, Willard Fraser, who was currently serving as a private with the American infantry in Europe. Among the letters the late Marjorie's father and her husband exchanged on the subject of the war was the one Frost wrote in September at the Homer Noble farm, a few days before he left it for the year:

"I've heard from you directly several times as well as indirectly through your sister and sisters-in-law. So it's about time you heard from me in reply to any question you may have asked. One question was: How is our war going in upstate Vermont? We think we are beginning to win it. At any rate I think we are as of September 26 1942 and may as well put it in writing. The only time I have said as much before was last year when the Russians made me think they were breaking the Germans winter line and were coming right through to the English Channel, bringing their typhus with them. I wish I knew better how the Vermonters were taking the war. Our few young men of Ripton are dutifully but very quietly winding up their affairs and disappearing for the camps. They say little. They have none of the encouraging bravado you can get any hour of the day or night over the radio—I mean the gay songs and big talk about our celebrating Christmas in Berlin and next Fourth of July in Tokio or vice versa. I should probably feel more excitement if I were in the city. I am told that in New York and Washington you are no longer free not to proclaim this a Holy War. I am told that real mobs gather there to demand an immediate second front for the relief of the Russians. The tendency of people in crowds is to hold each other up to their ideals. One suspects another of not pressing his tin cans [for scrap metal drives] and asking a third if he ought not to be reported. We live so scattered that we have to get along without the help of crowd psychology. Not that we make no effort to understand the war. Mrs. Homer Noble the older lady than I am who sold me this farm recently read me out of a local paper that our able Governor had been saying it was a Christian war we and the Russians were waging. He made out a perfect case to her mind.[4] I had to confess that if it was a Holy War what made it so for me was what seemed to make it so for Henry Wallace, namely, its promise for the common man all over the world including India, Egypt, Mexico, Abyssinia, Jave, Korea, the Phillipines, Ashantes, Liberia, the Gold Coast, Porto Rico, Devil's Island, Tristan da Cuna and the Andamans. Don't doubt I am aware of the sentimentality this verges on. It is nearer Carl Sandburg than me in philosophy. To get right down to my way of thinking the most I count on from the war is an improvement of our National position with friend and foe. We are a great democracy now. I trust the President's leadership to make us a greater. I should regard it as too bad if we hoped the war would leave us without a foe in the world. Everything has its opposite to furnish it with opposition. There are those in favor of democracy like you and me and there must always be the contrary minded. With us the emphasis is on the answerability of the ruler to those he rules; with our opponents the emphasis is on the answerability of the ruler to the highest in himself and to God. The conflict is a matter of emphasis. Each side has something of both principles in it. It flatters my patriotism to believe our system has both in the happiest proportion. But no victory however complete must make us forget that enmity to our faith is deeply grounded in human nature and will always be there ready to take arms against us. . . ."[5]

Many of Frost's fellow artists, Louis Untermeyer, Archibald MacLeish, and Carl Sandburg among them, had decided to turn their own views on the war to useful purpose by joining in the propaganda efforts of the Office of War Information. Untermeyer, in particular, wanted, and even expected, Frost to do likewise. But Frost was aware, more acutely than Untermeyer was now in a position to be, of what an artist lost by yoking himself to any official line of reasoning, and he flatly rejected all invitations to hurl his words and thoughts as weapons against Japan or Nazi Germany. So foreign to Frost was the idea of an artist churning out government propaganda that, in a letter he wrote to Lesley a few days before Christmas 1942, he even speculated Untermeyer himself had selfish reasons for going to work in the New York City–based OWI:

"Once you start reasoning you never know where you will end up," he began. "That's why I refrain from reasoning too much about the Germans. Louis is down living alone in the Webster Hotel on the regular government job that Archie and Carl and Elmer Davis are on. I couldn't bring myself to it if I tried. Louis is writing a primer of Americanism to be translated into all the languages of Europe and distributed to the peoples of Europe. How can he?—unless as an excuse to flee the failing farm and rest from his wife. He says [his wife] Esther blames him for a deserter. Deserter is a bad word in war time. But as long as he isnt a deserter of his country and his country's cause or causes.

"Becauses!" he continued. "Why are we at war? The best construction I can put on it is that we and the British have a property and a position the Germans would give anything to get away from us: and that we arent fools enough to let them. The position and the airs of easy assurance that go with it are even more enviable than the property. They would fain try how it feels to sit on top of the world—recline on top of the world. It gives beautiful the manners of the non-upstart and non-climber. Well if I dont look out I'll be writing a primer myself. Whence the Natziism? That grows naturally and swiftly out of the desperation of what the poor fools are attempting against a world roused from peace and comfort to meet them in arms. Louis now speaks with the official We. He says We expect the war to last about another year. I am only too willing to have them proved right. I wonder how much of a soldier Prescott will have been made into by then. I'm glad he got in in time to choose his service."[6]

That service, in which Prescott Frost, just turned eighteen, had chosen to enlist on 7 December 1942, was the Army Signal Corps. Back in September, Frost had expressed to Lillian the belated desire that the boy might have finished his secondary schooling at a military academy, perhaps even going on from there to a college program at the Army's service academy. "I could wish Prescott could have got an appointment to West

Point," Frost had written to Lillian. "But it is not for me to wish my own out of heroic danger. You know best how his spirit is tuning up."[7] Lillian did indeed know, and she soon explained that, when the time came for her son to enter military service, Prescott would be unlikely to choose a course leading to his use of firearms against other men. "I have a long letter from her," Frost wrote of Lillian a short time later, "in answer to my question whether she and Prescott had any notion of preparing him for the thought of war by sending him to a military school. She says Jack Holliday finds his a strict dull place he may not stay in and then again he may. She says Prescott will have had so many hours of shop work in the B. H. S. [Bennington High School] that he can count on getting into some such service as ground work on the airplanes. Not that he would avoid duty at the front. Only of course he would want to be where his abilities and training would help most. He had been out hunting and had killed a grey squirrel. I shall say nothing more on the subject. Not everybody can be expected to like war. . . ."[8]

If Frost felt any disappointment that his grandson did not, apparently, "like war," he soon received word of a far more disturbing nature. In mid-January 1943, just a few weeks after arriving in Colorado for his basic training, Prescott was overtaken by a serious illness, the details of which arrived in Cambridge only after the worst of the crisis had passed. Unable to go to Colorado himself, Prescott's worried grandfather asked for the help of his Boulder friend, John Bartlett, who he knew would help the boy for his sake in any way he could:

"This is just to tell you and Margaret there's another Frost in trouble in your region. I hope the trouble isnt going to prove very serious. Prescott, just past eighteen, enlisted a month or so ago in the Signal Corps and was sent to Camp Carson for his basic training. All well and good so far. But now comes word that he has gone down with pneumonia and partly recovered—all in one message. Probably he has been given some of the new medicine I won't attempt to spell. There is nothing you can do. But I thought if he was invalided out temporarily and not sent clear home he might find time on his hands and you might help him spend it by asking him for a night's visit at Boulder. I reminded him in my only letter so far that he had you or the thought of you for moral support not too far off. I don't know what such a sickness means to the army doctors and how it will affect Prescott's career as a soldier. I wait for further news with some anxiety."

He resumed: "The further news has just this minute come in through the slot in the front door. The pneumonia was the bad kind and he was probably only saved by the drug I can't spell the name of. That changes nothing I have said above. Prescott may write to you some time along. He may sign his name Prescott as of old, but it is to be noticed that the army has decided to know him as Private William P. Frost. His great grandfather, my father, was always called William Frost though he had the same Prescott for a middle name.

"I wish I could see you," Frost added to Bartlett. "There is some chance of my going by and dropping in on my way to engagements in California next fall if the war doesnt cancel them. I thought I would be out entirely but I am still hired now and then by people who can bear to hear something talked about besides the war. I can talk about the war upon occasion, but what unfits me for most platforms is that most people believe in this war only whereas I believe in any and all wars. I mean I sympathize with all the brave people who go out to die for causes. They are the great boys, beside whom I am nothing."[9]

By late January, Frost had heard enough of Prescott's improving health from Lillian, from Lesley, and from Prescott himself to be fully satisfied that his grandson, though still weak from the effects of his illness, was out of all danger. He saw no reason, therefore, to delay further his departure for Florida, where he planned to spend the month of February gardening, relaxing, and writing at his five-acre "farm" in South Miami. He was soon busy tending tropical fruit trees at Pencil Pines with the same loving attention he gave to his annual garden of peas, beans, and potatoes in Ripton, Vermont. A few days after his arrival, he interrupted his activities long enough to write one of his first letters to the grandson with whom he had communicated mainly through Lillian since the boy left home for basic training:

"(Private William)," he began, after the more accustomed greeting, "Dear Prescott," "I shall have to get used to these formidable army addresses before I venture to write to you directly. But you might write me directly some time when you are in the mood. You can help me get into closer communication with you by printing very plainly all I must put on an envelope for you. I haven't heard from your mother for a week or so. When I do I hope it will be with good news about your health. The last was that you were up around and all right. I suppose the sulphur medicine may take longer to recover from than the pneumonia.

"I am down here again for the old climate. My exact address is Route 2 Coconut Grove Florida. I shall stay for about four weeks and Kathleen will keep me company most of the time. I have three or four oranges, two or three grapefruit, one mangoe, two loquat two calomondon and one banana to water. I may not be able to keep them alive if the govt decides to stop all fertilizers for citrus fruit. That will mean cutting off the orange juice and starving everybody of their vitimines A B C D E F G H I J K L M N O P Q R S T U V W X Y Z. The V for Victory vitimine is the one we shall miss most. The sun is warm here this year. I am getting more summer heat this winter in Florida than I got all summer in Vermont.

"Speaking of Vermont, I wonder if you have noticed the Govt report that Texas and Vermont lead all the states of the Union in percentage of enlistments. Your state is a proud little state to belong to. I wonder if the explanation isnt that Texas and Vermont were once nations by themselves, won their own independence, and had each a flag of its own—a national flag not just a state flag. A history like that is bound to linger in the minds of its people and show itself in their character. That winter we all lived in Texas I heard plenty of proud talk about the state. When I told a Texan I thought Vermonters hated the idea of Govt relief, he said Texans were the same. Absolutely no one at first would volunteer to go on relief and a posse had to be organized to run someone down to be the first victim of Govt paternalism. Massachusetts is pretty well up on the roster and so is my birth state California. It surprises me to see states like Virginia and South Carolina once so warlike (in '61) now away down. New Hampshire was next below Vermont.

"The sky overhead is almost never free from the noise of planes. They are of all kinds, from the big South America passenger planes we used to see off from the Coconut Grove airport to all sorts I dont know the name of. They say the boys who flew over Tokio trained here; also many of the British now flying in Europe and Africa. . . ."[10]

Prescott presently answered his grandfather's letter by announcing that he was about to begin a furlough which would permit him just enough time to make his way home to South Shaftsbury before returning to camp for further training. He hoped he would somehow be able to see his grandfather when he was home. He realized, however, as did Frost himself, that that would be next to impossible. Prescott would be arriving in Vermont in just a few days, and would be leaving again before the end of February. Previous commitments would necessitate Frost's remaining in the South until after his grandson was gone. Disappointed, Frost confirmed the bad news in a letter addressed jointly to Lillian and her son:

"I am sorry sorry the furlough comes so soon and lasts such a short time. I wanted to see the soldier in uniform, the first in our family for a hundred years. I mean in the direct Frost line.[11] But I have a lecture to give at the University of North Carolina (Chapel Hill) on March 1st which determines the date of my journey north. I am lucky to be getting lectures still at here and there a college and feel I mustn't pass any of them up. I shall miss the chance to hear about soldiering at first hand. You must write to me Prescott. My chief interest in the war comes from your being in it. I don't listen to the radio commentators and I hardly look at the papers. The headlines seem to be written by people who don't know anything about war. I hope you get information in camp that means something. I think of you every day."[12]

Among the other things Frost thought about every day was whether and how he could find some kind of long-term teaching appointment to replace the now-defunct Emerson Fellowship at Harvard. The Fellowship in American Civilization that had succeeded it at the same college was now entirely honorary, and it was limited to only a few lectures during the academic year. So great was Frost's fear of running out of money for his extensive outlays for his family and his farms, so fresh was the memory of his early years of want in San Francisco and Lawrence, that he was prepared to do much, even to swallow his considerable pride, to secure a job that would meet his requirements. His letter of October 9, 1942, to his still-close Amherst College friend, Professor George Roy Elliott, seemed to imply that if Amherst, through its President, Stanley King, approached him concerning a resumption of his teaching career at the college of his longest employment, he was ready to forgive King, and to forget his repeated assertion that King had plotted to get rid of him as being "more trouble than he was worth":

"I have decided to break the ice by setting foot in Amherst before all hearts are completely frozen over against me," Frost informed Elliott. "I may be making a mistake. But no matter: it wouldn't be the first time. Don't let me sound as if it had been a hard decision to make. It comes about as the naturalest thing in a careless life. Harriet Whicher asks me to lecture at Mt. Holyoke and then spend the night with them at Amherst. Rand asks me to read at Massachusetts State and spend the night with him. This Thursday and Friday the fifteenth and sixteenth are accounted for. And I am wondering if you mightn't be induced to seize the occasion to have me Saturday night. You could get Otto over to your house alone perhaps and obtain merit in the next world after the world war by presiding over our reconciliation.[13] I am somewhat alarmed at myself for the ease with which I relinquish my Christian disapprovals. It must mean my native fibre is weakening. After all these years of estrangement, I made up with Alec Meiklejohn at St. Johns under the auspices of your St. Thomas Aquinas and the presidence of Scot Buchanan last spring.[14] It ought not to make me feel better, but it does. I may as well go ahead and forgive everybody while the enthusiasm for peace is on me. Everybody, mind you. Of course I shall want to see the Bairds, the McKeons, the Browers and the Craigs too. Not that I love my friends less but enemies more. You know how mixed up it is possible to get with mercy and justice. If you don't know it is because you are inexperienced in abstract thinking and need to read my play on the Forty-third Chapter of Job.[15] If my application for an invitation in these terms appeals to you please let me know by telegram in care of Bill Snow at Wesleyan where I shall be reading Tuesday. . . . Believe me none of this is said lightly with the easy assurance you will like it and fall in with it."[16]

Elliott did indeed like it, but he was unable at the moment to fall in with it. Away in Maine on personal business, he was forced, upon receipt of the forwarded letter, to wire Frost and tell him that he could not get home in time for Frost's long-hoped-for Amherst visit. The disappointment Frost felt at the failure of his Amherst overture was somehow conveyed to Elliott: commenting on Frost's response to the telegram he had lately sent, Elliott said, echoing the language of Frost's message, "He did not like it."[17]

Several months went by during which it seemed to Frost that only an end to the war would bring about his return to college teaching on a regular basis. He had all but given up hope for an early appointment when, in March 1943, he had a visit at 35 Brewster Street from Ray Nash, a member of the faculty at Dartmouth College, whom he had befriended when Nash was teaching his graphics course at the New School in New York: "In Cambridge the other night," Nash afterward wrote to Dartmouth president Ernest Martin Hopkins, "I had a long visit with Robert Frost. It transpired that he is finishing up his work there as Ralph Waldo Emerson Fellow in Poetry [*sic*]. I said I wished Harvard's loss might be Dartmouth's gain. Then he surprised me by saying thoughtfully that it would be kind of nice to end up where he started out fifty years ago."

Nash left no room for doubt in President Hopkins's mind as to the import of Frost's "thoughtful" comment. His own expressed wish, Nash assured Hopkins, was "purely personal." But he could not conceive of "a more significant step in the direction of fitting Dartmouth for the coming fight" for postwar academic superiority than to bring Frost into the Dartmouth fold. Frost's appointment might also be useful in the attempt, already under way, to enrich student use of Baker Library. "To a large number of students and many of the faculty," Nash concluded, "the presence of Frost would be certain proof that Dartmouth holds the fort for liberal education."[18]

Hopkins readily agreed to take the matter up at the next meeting of the Board of Trustees. The exigencies of the war had obliged them to impose a freeze on new faculty appointments except where "excessive demand" could be proved. But, according to Hopkins, the idea of appointing Frost to some position on the Dartmouth faculty was not a new one: it had been discussed in administrative circles on the several occasions when word of Frost's possible availability had reached them. Nor did it seem to Hopkins that he would meet with serious opposition from the Board if, as Nash assured him, "Frost wouldn't be expensive."[19]

Frost's appointment to a position at Dartmouth was still under discussion when, in late March, he left New England for a three-week session as writer-in-residence at the Bloomington campus of the University of Indiana. If he did not know it before his arrival, he learned soon afterward that another visitor to the campus was Bernard DeVoto, the end of whose month-long series of Patten Lectures coincided with the beginning of Frost's Bloomington stay. Having never acknowledged the estrangement that DeVoto so acutely felt, Frost was in a better position than his once-devoted friend to take the initiative during the three days in which they shared the Bloomington campus. Seeking DeVoto out, Frost unburdened himself on three successive nights of talk so highly personal that DeVoto could not help wondering if he were being encouraged to undertake a biography. The attention, however, was far from flattering. DeVoto, according to Wallace Stegner, felt as if Frost were trying to "ingest" him, and he could not wait to make his escape from Bloomington.[20] Soon after he returned to Cambridge, DeVoto received news from Bloomington that was even more upsetting: Frost, after saying good-bye to him, had entertained a dinner party with talk of their relationship, in a way so marked that some of those present felt obliged to write to DeVoto, informing him of what Frost was saying behind his back. DeVoto minced no words in the letter he shortly directed to Frost:

"Various remarks you made about me in Bloomington have been faithfully reported to me. I find myself not liking one of them, one of which you have been making for a number of years in various parts of the country. It is reported to me from Bloomington by one of the eight faculty men at the dinner where you made it in words which he says are exactly or substantially yours, as follows:

" 'DeVoto, you know, has been under the care of a psychiatrist, who has told him that I am not good for him, that if he is ever to succeed, he must not cultivate my company: I am too strong for him and have a bad effect on him. . . .'

"Another guest at that dinner separately reports you in almost exactly the same words. Over a period of some years various friends and acquaintances of mine have reported your saying the same thing, or variants of it, in a good many places.

"The statement is altogether false. No part of it is true. I think you know that. What satisfaction you get from circulating a false and damaging statement about me I don't know or care, but I have made no earlier protest out of respect to years of friendship with you. I have decided, however, that I no longer care to submit to it. I do not want to hear of your making that statement again in public or in private. Please see to it that I do not have to act any further in the matter than thus calling it to your attention."[21]

With this letter threatening, in effect, legal action for slander, DeVoto clearly intended to leave no doubt in Frost's mind that he now considered their friendship finally and irreconcilably at an end. Frost, however, saw nothing in DeVoto's remarks that he could not defuse by providing his own version of the Bloomington evening in question. With the same mixture of surface humor and subsurface malice that had characterized his offending remark, Frost drafted a letter which, as Stegner says, was "as ambiguous and confusing as the motivation of his original jibe":

"Benny Benny!" it began. "The first thing Kay did when she got here was to give me what you in your unconventional Western way would call Hell for talking about you too much in company. (She did not say in public.) And now comes your letter to give me more Hell for the same thing. I feel injured and misunderstood. You bring up an evening at Bloomington when the conversation not unnaturally got round more than once to your lectures there and to your latest book. In any 'faithful' report of that evening I should have ranked as second to none in praise of the lectures and of the book. When never mind who said the book might be something better than history but it wasn't history I asked if he meant in the sense that Herodotus Plutarch and Tacitus weren't history or had he in mind the sense in which Frude [James Anthony Froude] didn't seem history to the partizans of [Edward Augustus] Freeman. When somebody else said he had stayed away from your lectures because you hadnt found anything nice to say about life on the Mississippi I answered neither had Mark Twain himself. I said I had to laugh at your being shunned as a disparager of anything American: my admiration for you had begun in an article you wrote in admiration of life on submarginal Vermont farms where the cash income was something like three hundred dollars a year. What was more your lectures had been one hammering denunciation of disparagers in general. I never speak of you but to praise. I have been mentioning you for membership in the Academy. I have predicted that you would have to be called back to Harvard. But I am nobody's propagandist. You know my danger. I am prone to think more things are funny than you would. I suppose it may have been in self defence, but the disappointed novelist pent up in me started to play with the idea the minute I heard that your doctor had advised you not to associate with me. You say the story isn't true and I take your word for it but I had it on the best authority and your attitude toward me for the last two years has tended to make it seem plausible. I don't see why you want to spoil it. By changing your name to John August you can write a twenty thousand dollar novel for Colliers any time you please. An Italian Catholic English Mormon blend in birth you are neither a Catholic nor a Mormon in religion but a Freudian in philosophy. I don't think these facts take away from your greatness as a writer. They do add to your interest as a character. Just so with the story you so much object to. I wouldnt have thought it hurt either of us and it makes us both more amusing. Get it straight from me though. For you I played up the absurdity of your letting any extraneous doctors come between us to tell you I was too strong for you—a gentle versifier like me too strong for a powerful prose man like you. Rats. But true or not I wouldnt for the world go on repeating the story if it bothers you or anybody else. You want to be friends I can tell by your manner in Bloomington. I want to be friends as you can tell by my manner in this letter. Now lets forget differences and get to writing again."[22]

Despite Frost's letter, DeVoto was for the present no more willing to "forget differences" than he was to allow himself to be further humiliated by his once-dear friend Robert Frost. It seemed likely to Frost, when DeVoto failed to respond to his letter, that their relationship had suffered a blow from which it was unlikely, even with further conciliatory gestures by him, to recover.

In early May, two weeks following Frost's return to Cambridge from his three weeks in Bloomington, came the culmination of efforts by another friend who, more than DeVoto, was willing by nature to forgive and forget differences. Louis Untermeyer, in 1943, besides serving in the OWI Frost had refused to join, was also on the Advisory Committee of Columbia University responsible for recommending to the Board of Trustees a winner of the Pulitzer Prize in poetry. As perturbed as he was by Frost's refusal—"I am nobody's propagandist"—to take any active part in the war effort, Untermeyer could not, and did not, deny that Frost's *A Witness Tree* deserved the coveted award more than any other poetry book published in 1942. His fellow committee members, Bliss Perry and Wilbur L. Cross, agreed with him that *A Witness Tree* was the best volume under consideration. They believed, however, that the three Pulitzer Prizes Frost had won already were all that any artist should receive in a lifetime—be his subsequent work ever so good. They voted, therefore, to recommend for the 1943 prize the volume that all three men agreed was the second best under consideration: *Have Come, Am Here*, by the young poet José Garcia Villa.

In his minority report, Untermeyer explained the predicament of his colleagues, and urged the trustees not to deny Frost his fourth Pulitzer Prize simply because he had won three before. Convinced by Untermeyer's argument, the Board decided to take a step that was also unprecedented. It overrode the majority vote of the advisory committee and awarded *A Witness Tree* the Pulitzer Prize as the best volume of poetry published in 1942.[23] The news reached Frost on the third of May, soon after he had spoken with Untermeyer about his prospects for winning despite the contrary vote of the committee. He soon sent off a letter to the friend responsible for his latest triumph:

"The prize came as a genuine surprise," he told Untermeyer, "after what you said about the committee's having decided I couldn't have it though I deserved it. You had prepared me to be satisfied with the golden opinion of the committee. Kay woke me with the news. It struck her breathless and me rather pleasantly thoughtful. Bliss Perry has just been in to explain his vote for *Have Come Am Here*—his and Cross's. I eased him of his embarrassment. He didn't know how much I knew and I didn't tell him. His conscience wanted him to confess that the authorities at Columbia whoever they are were the ones I had to thank for the award. They had gone over the heads of the committee and it was for the first time. I could see that he had been as surprised as I was. But really it is you I have to thank for this as for so many other things. Your accompanying letter to the authorities whoever they are and your coming out so honestly in *The Yale Review* no doubt brought the result. My only objection to it is that my fourth time estops me from saying much if Roosevelt tries for a fourth term. What I like best about it is that it defends my old age from the undertakers. I don't have to tell *you* who renewed my youth."[24]

In a letter to Professor George F. Whicher of Amherst College more than a week later, he was still exuberant about his

Pulitzer victory, and portraying it as a kind of heroic triumph against insuperable odds:

"Yes I seem to be one up even on the President of the United States. After this I can't say much if he tries for a fourth term to tie me. I have just had the story of how it happened from Bliss Perry of the committee of award. He says the recommendation of the committee to the Pulitzer authorities at Columbia whoever they are, was to encourage the young by giving the prize to *Have Come Am Here*, though mine might be the better book. The authorities whoever they are doubtless wondered what kind of a decision that was and went over the committee's not unwilling heads by giving the prize to mine. I value it chiefly as a vindication of three score and ten. You are a witness to how far down I had to come up from to win it. And you know but for whom I wouldnt have come up to write any more poems at all. . . ."

His remarks in the continuation of the letter suggest he had forgotten, conveniently, his repeated utterance in Colorado Springs and elsewhere that there was nothing in poetry so satisfying as the prize ring of boxing:

"Prizes are a strange thing for me to have come by, who have hated competition and never wanted to be anybody's rival. I could never have written a single poem if I had had to have even in a remote corner of my mind the least thought that it might beat another poem. Poetry is 'too high for rivalry.' It is supposed to differ in kind rather than degree. Still I can accept the fate of prize winners with fortitude and if my victory pleases my friends, not care too much if I annoy my enemies. . . ."[25]

By the end of the month Frost had another, though less dramatic, victory to celebrate: the culmination of his efforts to secure permanent employment in a college setting despite the economic strictures imposed by the war. For some time President Hopkins of Dartmouth had been perfecting his plans for Frost's appointment in conversations with Ray Nash, George C. Wood, Francis L. Childs, and other members of the Dartmouth faculty, as well as with Frost himself. The last remaining obstacle was the position of Harvard University, conveyed through one of its Fellows, Grenville Clark, that that institution still had claims on Frost's services, and that it would not relinquish them unless Dartmouth permitted Frost to deliver several lectures at Harvard during the coming academic year.

The matter was finally resolved when, on a Sunday morning, Hopkins telephoned Clark, his good friend, and teasingly assured him that Dartmouth would be glad to do anything it could at any time "for the cultural uplift of Harvard."[26]

The letter Ray Nash sent to Hopkins on June 24 stipulated what were to be the eventual terms of Frost's appointment. His duties would be "entirely extra-curriculum. Regular hours to meet students in his study three days each week (Friday, Saturday and Sunday) during autumn and early winter (October, November, December, January—until his usual trip South); again, in the spring, several visits for work with students or perhaps a public appearance; attendance at important gatherings like commencement. His responsibilities to Dartmouth would not interfere with occasional lectures elsewhere." The salary was to be $2,500 per annum, with an expense allowance of $500—an amount which Hopkins considered nominal, and which would come out of a special fund not part of the college's regular budget. The term of the appointment would be one year, with the understanding that it would be renewable from year to year for an indefinite period.[27] Finally—and this detail was not in Nash's letter—the title of the appointment would be one personally chosen by Hopkins: Ticknor Fellow in the Humanities, after George Ticknor, an early Dartmouth graduate who was "the foremost exponent of the humanities in the college world of his time."[28] At their June meeting, the executive committee of the Dartmouth trustees voted to approve Frost's appointment, and except for the public announcement, Frost was officially a member of the Dartmouth family. In his letter of July 9 to President Hopkins—who had presented him with an honorary Litt.D. from Dartmouth ten years before—Frost expressed his pleasure at, and his hopes for, his latest role at Dartmouth, which he had attended as a freshman for less than one semester in the fall of 1892:

"From the first I have thought I could see where the specialities I have developed in my college wanderings might be made to count a little in your new plan at Dartmouth. I like the title you would give me and I like everything you and Ray Nash tell me about the plan from its connection with the Library to its possible connection with a second-hand book store. But I wasn't as free from Harvard to take up with it as I had assumed, and as I can now say I am after my talk with Grenville Clark. I am accepting your call back to Dartmouth with pride and satisfaction. Let's make it mean all we can. Call back, I call it. I once went to school at Dartmouth. As you know I am one of your alumni, though without benefit of graduation. I had my degree at your hands. I have been at Hanover to read many times in the last twenty five years and the boys have given me some of my best occasions.

"The idea is that, in addition to what I do at Dartmouth for Dartmouth, I shall belong to Dartmouth in what I do for my publishers and my public. The bulk of my college time is to be spent at Dartmouth. Grenville Clark has your consent for me to give a few, say half a dozen, talks to the student soldiers at Harvard as a sort of honorary leave-taking there. I shall look forward to my beginning with you in October."[29]

9

DABBLING IN DRAMA

> *Last night I finished writing the* Forty-third Chapter of Job, A Masque of Reason. *You may have to listen to it sometime when I have done its companion piece* The Whole Bible, A Masque of Mercy. *Neither may ever see the light. I* will *dabble in drama.*[1]

ROBERT FROST'S incumbency as Dartmouth's George Ticknor Fellow in the Humanities began on the first of October 1943, and was marked that Friday evening by a reception open to members of the Humanities Division in the Tower Room of Baker Library. President Hopkins's plan to deliver some remarks during the evening welcoming Frost back to Dartmouth collapsed at the last minute when an important emergency meeting called him out of town. So many of Frost's Dartmouth friends and acquaintances came up to offer their own enthusiastic words of welcome, however, that the gap created by Hopkins's absence was more than adequately filled. By the time the party broke up, well past midnight, Frost had been told many times that Hopkins was not alone in regarding his appointment to the first Ticknor Fellowship as heralding a new period of importance for the humanities at Dartmouth, and for Dartmouth among the liberal arts colleges.

Frost's primary association was to be with Baker Library, and Study Room 215, specially furnished with money from the Ticknor Fund, had been set up there for his use as a private office and place for meeting, Saturdays and Sundays, with those individual students who wished to see him. Seminar Room 216, next door, had been designated his classroom, and there he was to lecture Friday nights, during the fall semester, to those undergraduates and Naval trainees in the Dartmouth V-12 program lucky enough to gain admission to his course. According to the design of the Ticknor Fellowship and following Frost's own academic preferences, it was to be a nondepartmental course, with a leaning only to the humanities in the broadest sense. How nondepartmental it proved found reflection in an account of the first regular meeting written by Charles G. Bolté, a young Dartmouth alumnus who had obtained permission to attend:

"His conversation, the best I've ever heard, carries the wisdom of a thousand and the vitality of 25. He looks about 68, when he thinks you're not looking. His face then is pure New England, a sort of massive granite front with shaggy brows and brooding eyes, a strong chin, and the farmer's weather-beaten look. Then he thinks of another approach to whatever he's been talking about, and turns to you with Puck's gleam in his eyes and a sly, humorous, winking expression of delight. That night his conversation ranged over war, politics, farming, poetry, education, social change, personalities, biography, autobiography, industrial developments in Vermont, the possibility of selling unsprayed apples, the advantages of living on a non-farming farm, the definition of democracy as the best form of government because power was divided against itself and no one could gather too much of it, the riddle of Jeffersonian policy, and the proper way to build a log fire. It went on for nine hours, goaded occasionally by his listeners, but mainly unwinding effortlessly and without the use of stimulants. . . ."

Bolté continued by summarizing what were probably Frost's opening remarks at the first meeting of his Ticknor seminar:

"Mr. Frost is interested in clear thinking, and thinks that one way to get it is to learn politeness—the kind of politeness which lets another man have his say without an angry rebuttal in the middle. He also wants his pupils to know when they're talking in quotation marks and when they're thinking for themselves—freshness again. They can write for him, but that's not the only thing; good conversation will be accepted, and good reading. Probably even good listening. The substance of his informal assignment is that he will be on hand in Hanover, to talk to anybody who cares to come in, alumni and faculty as well as undergraduates and trainees. . . .[2]

"I know," Bolté added, "of at least two instructors who plan to keep on going to school to him; and I can think of at least one alumnus. . . ." One of the two instructors was undoubtedly the professor of English whose friendship with Frost went back at least ten years further than did that of any other member of the Dartmouth faculty. Sidney Cox had first met Frost in 1911, in Plymouth, New Hampshire, when Frost was teaching at the New Hampshire State Normal School and Cox at Plymouth High. At first Cox, then twenty-two, had found the thirty-seven-year-old poet-instructor "uncouth," and had even wondered if alcohol might account for his having made so little progress in life. But soon, as they continued to meet for games of tennis, long walks, and long evenings of conversation, a deep friendship developed that was to last as long as Cox lived. By the time of Frost's arrival in Hanover for the Ticknor assignment, Cox was already recognized there as the poet's devoted disciple, as well as his intimate friend.[3]

Other friends in the Dartmouth English Department included Stearns Morse, David Lambuth, George Wood, Francis Childs, and Hewette Joyce, and any one of them might have been the second instructor to whom Bolté referred.[4] More likely, however, it was a member of the Art Department, Ray Nash, who, from his first talk with Frost concerning his possible return to Dartmouth, had continued to be of great service both to Frost and President Hopkins by acting as liaison between the two, and by seeing to it that Frost's needs—for transportation, for food, for shelter, for companionship—were looked after from his Friday afternoon arrival at the White River Junction station until his departure for Cambridge Sunday night.[5]

Among Nash's many acts of devotion, none did more to win him a place in Frost's affection than the Baker Library exhibition he assembled, in collaboration with Dartmouth librarian Harold Goddard Rugg, entitled "Fifty Years of Robert Frost."[6] Commemorating the half-century association of poet and college, the exhibition opened fifty-one years after Frost first came to Dartmouth as a freshman in 1892. It included the most extensive collection of his books and manuscripts ever gathered together up to that time. Many items, including the unique *Twilight*, were supplied on loan at Frost's personal request by Earle J. Bernheimer, the excellence of whose private collection made him almost indispensable to the assembling of a major Frost exhibition.[7] One item that Bernheimer did not own, however, commanded the particular interest of Nash, who wished to display it prominently as a work representing the fiftieth year of Frost's artistic career. A play in blank verse of one act and of some 400 lines, it was one of a pair Frost planned to write on the linked subjects of justice and mercy, and the reason men applied toward the understanding of both. "Last night I finished writing the *Forty-third Chapter of Job, A Masque of Reason*," Frost had told a friend in April of 1943, in announcing completion of the first of the two plays. "You may have to listen to it sometime when I have done its companion piece *The Whole Bible, A Masque of Mercy.* Neither may ever see the light. I *will* dabble in drama."[8]

From April to October, Frost had continued to tinker with the first "masque," had made some progress on the second, and in the interest of succinctness, had shortened the title of each. His attitude toward the eventual publication of *A Masque of Reason* and *A Masque of Mercy*, meanwhile, underwent considerable change from the position that "neither may ever see the light." In October, he impulsively went with Kay Morrison to speak to a leading director about a future Broadway production of the two masques. It was only after he returned that he realized how far ahead of his plays his ambitions for them had progressed. "Don't I beseech you," he implored Louis Untermeyer after confiding in him, "say a word to anybody about my juvenile dream of Broadway. And dont let Esther. Be sure. Kay and I may repent and want it forgotten. Im scared already. There are plenty of reasons why we shouldn't tempt fate with another ambition. I want to stay totally uncommitted till I can think what I am doing. Paul (Osborn) asked if he might drop a hint in the right quarter. But I positively forbade it. I must at least wait till I am entirely extricated from the second piece, the *Masque of Mercy.* It was unlike me to run down there with half a scheme in my pocket. I never seem to complete anything that gets talked about and demanded before it is done. So protect me. It may well be we shall decide in the end to content ourselves with the pair of masques as poems and merely publish them as such."[9]

The pair of masques, which had originally been conceived as poems in dramatic form, were nonetheless like no such poems Frost had written or read before. He called them "masques," but they bore little resemblance to the opulent court spectacles of sixteenth and seventeenth-century England. Though nominally belonging to the same genre as Milton's *Comus*, they were closer in underlying purpose to *Paradise Lost*: if not quite to "justify the ways of God to man," at least, by retelling and extending familiar biblical stories in an engagingly witty fashion, to show men how to take the mysterious ways of God.[10]

A Masque of Reason grew out of Frost's lifelong fascination with the Book of Job, whose basic narrative line, that of a man forced to suffer a prolonged period of undeserved adversity, carried for Frost great emotional appeal. Having suffered half a lifetime of frustration and neglect before achieving recognition as a poet, having lost his first child, Elliott, to *cholera infantum*, and later a daughter, wife, and son within a space of six years, Frost had little difficulty in identifying elements of his own experience with those of the archetypal sufferer of the Old Testament. Job's ultimate restoration to health and wealth also strongly appealed to his imagination and invited analogies with his own life. It was because of the opportunity it presented to explore the "reason" behind human suffering, however, that Frost had chosen, audaciously, to fashion a "forty-third chapter of Job."[11]

Four characters, Job, his Wife, God, and the Devil, constitute the dramatis personae of the play, which is set in "a fair oasis in the purest desert"[12] a thousand years after the end of Job's earthly torments. The first extended speech is God's and in it Frost presented a deity whose essential nature, divine but less than omnipotent, Frost may have derived from his early reading of William James. "I've had you on my mind a thousand years," God says addressing Job,

To thank you someday for the way you helped me
Establish once for all the principle
There's no connection man can reason out
Between his just deserts and what he gets.
Virtue may fail and wickedness succeed.
'Twas a great demonstration we put on.
I should have spoken sooner had I found
The word I wanted. You would have supposed
One who in the beginning was *the Word*
Would be in a position to command it.
I have to wait for words like anyone.
Too long I've owed you this apology
For the apparently unmeaning sorrow
You were afflicted with in those old days.
But it was of the essence of the trial

You shouldn't understand it at the time.
It had to seem unmeaning to have meaning.
And it came out all right. I have no doubt
You realize by now the part you played
To stultify the Deuteronomist
And change the tenor of religious thought.
My thanks are to you for releasing me
From moral bondage to the human race.
The only free will there at first was man's,
Who could do good or evil as he chose.
I had no choice but I must follow him
With forfeits and rewards he understood—
Unless I liked to suffer loss of worship.
I had to prosper good and punish evil.
You changed all that. You set me free to reign.
You are the Emancipator of your God,
And as such I promote you to a saint.[13]

For dramatic as well as thematic reasons, Frost did not permit God's expression of gratitude to terminate Job's search for the "reason" behind his "apparently unmeaning sorrow." Rather, Job and his waspish wife, Thyatira, proceed to engage in a witty conversation with God by means of which Frost, like the author of the Book of Job, was able to explore the complex of issues all conjoined under the heading "The Problem of Evil." At times, as when he says "God needs time just as much as you or I/ To get things done," Job's position and God's are one. Generally, however, Frost represented Job as God's persistent questioner, continuing to search out the "reason" for his suffering much as his biblical original did before finally repenting "in sackcloth and ashes."

At one point, Frost's Job utters a very biblical–Job-like complaint:

We don't know where we are, or who we are.
We don't know one another; don't know You;
Don't know what time it is. We don't know, don't we?
Who says we don't? Who got up these misgivings?
Oh, we know well enough to go ahead with.
I mean we seem to know enough to act on.
It comes down to a doubt about the wisdom
Of having children—after having had them,

So there is nothing we can do about it
But warn the children they perhaps should have none.
You could end this by simply coming out
And saying plainly and unequivocally
Whether there's any part of man immortal.
Yet You don't speak. Let fools bemuse themselves
By being baffled for the sake of being.
I'm sick of the whole artificial puzzle.

The cynical comment of Job's wife is, "You won't get any answers out of God." Almost at once, however, answers to the mystery of Job's undeserved suffering do begin to appear, the first such offered by Thyatira herself. Quoting her husband Job, and nearly quoting an open letter Frost sent in 1935 to the Amherst *Student*, she tells God:

Job says there's no such thing as Earth's becoming
An easier place for man to save his soul in.
Except as a hard place to save his soul in,
A trial ground where he can try himself
And find out whether he is any good,
It would be meaningless. It might as well
Be Heaven at once and have it over with.[14]

God follows with an explanation of his own, which at first glance seems to fall far short of the explanation Job has just provided. God says:

I was just showing off to the Devil, Job,
As is set forth in Chapters One and Two.

Frost meant God's remark, however, to be taken as much more than a wisecrack. By it, and by the symbolic grouping of God, Job, and the Devil onstage at the end of the play, he was suggesting what he felt to be a profound truth concerning the nature of evil: God requires the Devil—or evil—to be present in the world, and for the same reason he needs man: both help him realize his goals. Human reason, as Frost saw it, could not grasp what those goals were, but man must accept evil and suffering as an integral part of God's plan that no amount of "progress" would ever eradicate. It was a repudiation of the New Deal and the liberal reformers who were expecting science and government to invent and institute Utopia. Nowhere but in heaven, for Frost, and no way but by the grace of God, could one hope to realize the peace and contentment everywhere denied to men on earth.[15]

In mid-December 1943, a month after he began another phase of the Ticknor Fellowship by delivering a lecture in Hanover open to the general public, Frost came down with an illness which, had he been so inclined, he might have interpreted as yet another in the Job-like series of torments that had marked his life. Indeed, when he contracted a case of pneumonia in Hanover serious enough to require a month-long confinement in Dick Hall's House, the Dartmouth College Infirmary, he could not help wondering during the worst of it if God had misunderstood his devout intentions in *A Masque of Reason,* and decided to punish him for sacrilege he had never intended. After the fever passed, he convinced himself that God had indeed understood, and so had spared his life.[16] But he decided, then, that when he resumed work on the second play, *A Masque of Mercy,* he would leave no room for doubt in the mind of man or God that he continued to be what he had always been: a man who, though he had no use for calcified church ritual or narrowly pious orthodoxy, would not object to being regarded as one of the most profoundly religious men of his age.[17]

By the end of January 1944, he had recovered sufficiently to go to Florida and to begin only somewhat later than usual his annual winter vacation at Pencil Pines. Lillian Frost and her son, who had been living in the two small bungalows since Prescott's medical discharge from the Army in July, moved into a cottage on the property of Frost's neighbor, Professor Hjort. From there they paid daily visits to Pencil Pines to see how Frost's recuperation was progressing, and to help him with gardening chores around his modest orchard. Kay helped too, and worked with him on the manuscripts and letters he had carried with him to South Miami. Because of family responsibilities in Cambridge, and her promise to visit Lesley on her way home, she left without him after three weeks, and left a gap behind that Lillian and Prescott could not completely fill.

"My chronic deserter has just deserted me in Florida again," Frost wrote to his sometime companion Lawrance Thompson after her departure, "and there seems nothing I can ask you to do about it this time since you wont cant and shouldnt desert the Navy. She went north on a passenger train as long as a freight and rudely crowded full of Hialeah race track sports who as it comes out in today's Sunday paper have been paying a hundred dollars apiece extra for their berths. The F.B.I. has arrested thirty railroad ticket office employees and hotel clerks for having taken the money. I don't hope my deserter had a rough ride and in fact I have already heard with a pleasure unaccountable in a person of my temperament that Henry Wallace's common people treated her very well and she got to Lesley in Washington without indignity. It's as yet uncertain how I am going to find a berth to follow her. I am threatening from the public platform next Monday night that I will hitchhike and see if I can't make Henry Wallace's common people ashamed of themselves for not taking care of such an old man of twenty (honorary) degrees above zero. My best bet is the respect I am still held in in certain quarters in spite of everything. Someone on some high place who has read my book may save me.[18] The General Passenger Agent of the Pennsylvania for instance (he is in New York) has interceded with the Atlantic Coast Line for me. My engagements to read to the boys of the Army and Navy at Dartmouth and Harvard can be pled as quasiwareffort deserving priority—or quasi priority. My ostensible however is not my real reason for wanting to get north. Lets be honest. . . ."[19]

A few days later, when he wrote a long-owed letter to Earle Bernheimer, he could report no progress in finding a train that would take him North to his lecture engagements and to Mrs. Morrison: "Florida has been a terribly hard place to get into and out of, this year. I am not safely out of it yet. I should get away on March 14th but here it is the 7th and no reservation on the trains has been found for me. I lecture at the University of Miami on the night of the 13th on some such subject as Where is the Place of Ideals and Who is Their Keeper. If I don't use it then I will a month later either at Chicago University, Rockford College, Miami University (at Oxford Ohio), University of Cincinnati, Kenyon College, Dartmouth, or Harvard. There you have my schedule for the spring subject to correction by my secretary if she were here.

"She deserted me about a week ago," he continued, "after three weeks of the most perfect—well weather. The weather (if that were all) is still perfect. There is no use in trying to deny it, my native state can't compare with Florida at this season. To keep from letting my impatience to follow north get the best of me I water our citrus trees and plant new ones. I haven't written much. I seem pretty well. The pneumonia didnt hurt my wind that I can see. I felled a pine tree today and swung the big pick ax half an hour enlarging pot holes. You never saw such land as this for farming. It is all coral rock under or partly under thin sand and but for the said pot holes would be hopeless. These are scattered irregularly four or five or six feet apart (you have to feel them out), are as large as large flower pots (but deeper) and can be widened by chopping or blasting. It amuses me because it is so different from any farming I ever did before. . . ."

Continuing the letter, he expressed disappointment that he had been unable to visit with Bernheimer and his wife when they, like him, came to Florida for their winter vacation. He gave Bernheimer reason to hope that, could train reservations be made, he might indeed travel to California in June to receive "the big degree" he had been offered by the University of California. Then, as the object of the letter was partly to breathe new life into a friendship which in recent months had suffered an apparent decline, he favored the collector with his latest thinking on the war, carefully counting Bernheimer among those who, like himself, had rejected the liberal sentimentality that anticipated universal peace and brotherhood as one result of the approaching Allied victory:

"The war moves slow if it moves at all. I keep changing my expectations about it. At first I thought it would be long; then I thought it would be short, now it begins to look long again. Im not worried about it. Neither am I troubled about the future in general. Things are coming out our way. I feel more and more sure. Our kind of people are beginning to speak up for our kind of world. Take Louis Bromfield for instance. And more particularly because more philosophically the John Chamberlain who regularly reviews books for *Harpers Magazine*. I'm glad there is such a fellow as that writing. I've just begun to watch him there and in the N. Y. *Times*. I was coming to think there was no use in my contending in my unaggressive way against the Predominant Nonsense: I was so much alone in my instinctive prejudices. I was resolved not to lose my temper and get going. But I decided to give the immediate future up as lost to the bad thinkers crusted from the Social Settlements and leap forward to set my heart on vindication from the more distant future when I shant be here to triumph. I sold out too easily. There's more of us than just me and you. . . ."[20]

If his relationship with Bernheimer had indeed deteriorated of late, Frost knew he had no one but himself to blame. For the past several months, he had continued to accept without compunction Bernheimer's monthly checks for $150. By mid-1943, however, he had begun to take those "gifts" for granted, and had come to concern himself less and less with the quality of those few "items" he sent in return. Mrs. Morrison, more often than not, was the one who acknowledged receipt of Bernheimer's checks, and Frost's personal letters to Bernheimer, collector's items of a sort themselves, became increasingly rare. Frost began one letter after a silence of some six months, "It's a long time since you had any news from me direct. There should be a lot to tell if I can assemble it."[21]

In that letter, written in July 1943, Frost had informed Bernheimer, with studied casualness, of the existence of his first masque. "I have published nothing since *Come In*, either in a book or in a magazine. I have written little but a masque of four hundred lines. I may send you a copy by and by. I call it *A Masque of Reason*." The Masque came up again two months later, when Bernheimer asked if he might use a facsimile reproduction of Frost's unpublished prose play, "The Guardeen," as a Christmas remembrance for his friends. "How would it be to use a leaf out of the *Masque of Reason* manuscript (which as you know is yours) instead of 'The Guardeen'?" Frost replied. "The Masque has the advantage of being more concise and in verse." He continued: "I assume you will be willing the Masque should stay here for the exhibition at Dartmouth beginning October first. They are making big plans up there but won't really succeed without your help. (You have me so nearly cornered, Kathleen says). . . ."[22]

Such flattery, gratifying as it was to Bernheimer, could not entirely make up for the decline in the quality or quantity of Frost's contributions to Bernheimer's collection. It could not relieve Frost of the feeling that, for some time, he had not been earning the money Bernheimer had been sending. When, in early March, Frost tried to deposit Bernheimer's check for the previous month, only to learn from his bank that payment had been stopped and the check cancelled, he could only draw one conclusion: Bernheimer was punishing him for failing to hold up his end of their collectibles-for-cash association.

Suddenly faced with the prospect of losing what, in the course of a year, amounted to a substantial sum of money, Frost tried to put himself in the collector's place, and to imagine which of his own actions might have caused the greatest offense. Was it that he had so far failed to deliver, as long ago promised, the manuscript of *A Masque of Reason*? Was it that his "gifts" had, in general, fallen behind? Or had he, perhaps, angered Bernheimer by supplying a rival collector in California—Louis Mertins by name—with items Bernheimer felt should have gone to him? Bernheimer soon wrote to Frost explaining the stopped check in terms only of a crisis within his own house that had necessitated the closing of his bank account. Before the explanation reached him, however, Frost sent a letter to Bernheimer the contents of which, though it apparently does not survive, can be deduced from the collector's reply:

"I just received your letter this morning, and I can not begin to tell you how low it made me feel. But all I can say is—I hope I have explained away the reason. Were there any other, I would not hesitate to tell you. I hardly see how you could believe there was! If there is some slight doubt in your mind about a retaliation for something you have done please dismiss it. Naturally, I would like every mail to bring me something from your pen but I understand how many different things occupy your time and mind. I feel quite satisfied with your attentions to me. . . ."[23]

As soon as Frost received Bernheimer's first letter of explanation, he sent off a conciliatory telegram:

HAD BEGUN TO THINK SOMETHING LIKE THAT SO DON'T WORRY. GOOD JOKE BETWEEN FRIENDS.[24]

He added, after the arrival of the second, "Don't imagine for a moment the accident can make any difference in our friendship. You have the chief collection of me and I mean to keep it the chief. Ray Nash is slow with his catalogue but you shall have your *Masque of Reason* pretty soon. . . ."[25] It took several more months for Frost to deliver the *Masque of Reason* manuscript, but for a time he was careful to be more sensitive of Bernheimer's feelings. "I'm not keeping the Masque back to tease your interest," he closed one letter in June. "It is yours and so marked. I simply want it for some possible alteration I may make in it in the next week or two. I'll let you know when I consign it to the mail or express. . . ."[26]

In August 1944, at the Bread Loaf Writers' Conference, Frost found another and more important of his friendships in trouble, and requiring extraordinary measures to preserve. For some time, he had been aware of Louis Untermeyer's displeasure at his refusal to join him in the Office of War Information, or to take any formal role in the efforts to defeat Nazi Germany. At their infrequent meetings during the first years of the war, Frost had tried to explain to Untermeyer that he was no less loyal in his sympathies, no less opposed to Hitler, no less sympathetic to the lot of the Jews of Europe, for all his determination to remain "above the battle." Perhaps he reminded Untermeyer at some point that his own ideal was accurately represented in one of his favorite poems, Ralph Waldo Emerson's "Saadi," which read in part:

Gentle Saadi, mind thy rhyme;
Heed not what the brawlers say,
Heed thou only Saadi's lay.[27]

Faced with the enormity of the Nazi crimes against his fellow Jews, however, Untermeyer was outraged by what he could not help interpreting as Frost's indifference to the lot of his people. His hostility the one weekend he spent at Bread Loaf was so glaring that, in an effort to save their friendship, Frost wrote him a letter which, for added impact, he chose to write as an epistle in blank verse. In it, he set down more completely than he had done anywhere else just what his feelings were concerning the Second World War, and just what obligation he was under to participate somehow therein. He began by addressing himself to what was, for Untermeyer, the heart of the issue:

I'd rather there had been no war at all
Than have you cross with me because of it.
I know whats wrong: the war is more or less
About the Jews and as such you believe
I ought to want to take some part in it.
You ought to know—I shouldn't have to tell you—
The army wouldn't have me at the front.
And hero at the rear I will not be—
I mean by going berserker at home
Like a post warden bashing in a door
To put a light out some fool family

Has treasonably left burning in a blackout
To go off on a round of night-club parties.
I couldn't bring myself Tyrtaeus like
To sing and cheer the young men into dangers
I can't get hurt in. I am too untried
A soldier to preach soldiering to others.
And then please recollect I'm not a writer.
I'm good at most things as I ever was
I can't deny (you may deny it for me).
But I was never any good at routine writing.
I always hate in filling out a form
To call myself a writer. It would sound
Pretentious now to call myself a farmer,
But when it was a modest claim to make
I liked to make it. I'm a lecturer
And teacher now on income tax returns,
Though lecturer's another parlous word.
I could no more have taken pen to Hitler
Than taken gun (but for a different reason).
There may have been subconscious guile at work
To save my soul from the embarrassment
Of a position where with praise of us (US)
I had to mingle propaganda praise
Of a grotesque assortment of allies.
False friendships I accept for what they're worth
And for what I may get out of them in peace and war,
But always with a minimum of talk
And not for long. I'm bad at politics.
I was born blind to faults in those I love,
But I refuse to blind myself on purpose
To the faults of my mere confederates. . . .

Frost continued by deflating the paternalistic pretensions of the United States, England, and Russia, thereby implicitly demonstrating how unsuited he was to be a writer of wartime propaganda. He spoke of how he "took sides" with all peoples—including the Jewish—who wanted "a platform country" to "speak their language from." He spoke of "us (US) the mighty upstart, full of upstart people Or Shoe-string Starters as I like to call them," and of "the democracy in me" which demanded only that "I get surprised at where men come from." Then, as he brought his discursive epistle to a close, he appealed to Untermeyer not to give up, for mere political differences, the friendship they had shared unbroken since 1915:

Aw come on off your cosmic politics.
Not having heard from you for very long
Sets us to going over what a friend
How many kinds of friend I've had in you—
She who should be the great authority
Says no one else I know knows who I am
As well as you. That in itself would put
My debt to you so far beyond my power
To pay I can but turn up now and then
And by acknowledging the debt renew it.
I trust the explanations given you here
You only—no one else—will satisfy you
I am entitled to a day of grace.
I'll pay a first instalment pretty soon
I promise you. Hold on! Here's one right now,
An idea for one more anthology.
You say no more anthology, you're wrong.
I know the very name to call your next.
I'll tell you more about it when I see you
I'd take a hand in it if you would let me.[28]

Untermeyer could not help being moved by Frost's poetic peace offering. When he returned to New York after the Conference, and gave Frost's letter-poem the careful reading it demanded, he soon found himself writing to Frost that he was not only delighted with it, but amazed. "Once more," he said, "you accomplish that miraculous thing of saying profound things as though you were not saying anything at all, as though you were musing for the sake of musing—and being amusing. I don't know when you have packed so much thinking in so lightly running a speech."[29]

The praise was appreciated, the friendship at least provisionally restored. Untermeyer's words reminded Frost, however, that he had miles to go on another undertaking which, he hoped, would draw a response not unlike Untermeyer's to his letter-poem. He was thinking not only of the *Masque of Reason,* whose publication had by now been set to take place on the date of his "seventh" birthday, but of the *Masque of Mercy,* which he had yet to complete.

ONE STEP BACKWARD TAKEN

But with one step backward taken
I saved myself from going.
A world torn loose went by me.
Then the rain stopped and the blowing,
And the sun came out to dry me.[1]

THE ROUND of parties and social calls occasioned by his "seventieth" birthday left Frost so exhausted that he came down with a cold and spent much of the next few weeks in bed, but by the twelfth of April 1945 he had recovered sufficiently to fulfill an engagement his friends in Amherst would have hated to see him miss: his first visit to, and first reading at, Amherst College since his resignation from that college in the summer of 1938.[2] Roy Elliott, George Whicher, Reuben Brower, and others who had a hand in the invitation went out of their way to guarantee the success of Frost's first official visit to the campus in seven years. Knowing that the biggest risk they ran was a meeting between Frost and the man he blamed for his departure—President Stanley King—they declined, through English Department Chairman Brower, King's offer to return from an out-of-town trip to be on hand for Frost's visit. They chose not to cancel the evening lecture when, hours before it was scheduled to begin, word came of the death of President Franklin Roosevelt that afternoon. They decided as well to keep from Frost news of the death, apparently assuming it could do nothing to improve his nerves or the quality of his public performance. One result was that Frost's audience, while enjoying immensely his poems and most of his typically witty remarks, wondered why he did not have kinder things to say about the President who had led them through the Great Depression and most of the Second World War, and whose death they, if not he, had already begun to mourn.

Leaving Amherst after the brief but successful visit, Frost spent three weeks in Hanover to conclude his second year as George Ticknor Fellow in the Humanities, then retired to the Homer Noble farm for a summer of work on his unfinished *Masque of Mercy*. By August 8, he could report to Earle Bernheimer that he had "at last had the idea I needed for the final touch" to the play, which he promised to add to Bernheimer's collection after reading it at the impending session of the Bread Loaf Writers' Conference.[3] He did read it at the Conference, but he soon decided that the "final touch" was not so final as he had thought, and that something more—he did not know what exactly—was lacking in the second masque to bring it to a close on just the note he wanted. Except for a speech or two, in any case, the play was done.

Like the earlier masque, *A Masque of Mercy* was loosely based on an Old Testament story, this time the Book of Jonah. The action was set in a small bookstore in Frost's modern equivalent of Nineveh, New York City, where, just at closing time, a conversation between the store's owner, his wife, and a lingering customer is interrupted by the frenzied entrance of a fugitive who announces fearfully, "God's after me!"[4] He shortly introduces himself as the archetypal fugitive of the Bible, "Jonas Dove."

The other characters quickly learn his motivation for flight, which, says Jonah, is that

> *I've lost my faith in God to carry out*
> *The threats He makes against the city evil.*
> *I can't trust God to be unmerciful.*[5]

The "Keeper" of the bookstore—his full name is "My Brother's Keeper"—can scarcely understand the nature of Jonah's Old Testament indignation. Keeper's wife, Jesse Bel by name, is a neurotic "solitary social drinker"[6] who generally stays out of the discussion. Paul, however—"the fellow who theologized / Christ almost out of Christianity"[7]—has much to say about Jonah's demand—not fundamentally unlike Job's—for divine justice. Speaking to Jonah early in the play, he overtly establishes the central theme of the masque:

> *You are the universal fugitive—*
> *Escapist, as we say—though you are not*
> *Running away from Him you think you are,*

But from His mercy-justice contradiction.
Mercy and justice are a contradiction.
But here's where your evasion has an end.
I have to tell you something that will spoil
Indulgence in your form of melancholy
Once and for all. I'm going to make you see
How relatively little justice matters.[8]

With his puritanical sympathy for the "jealous God" of the Old Testament, Frost could and did join Jonah in questioning

This modern tendency I find in Him
To take the punishment out of all failure
To be strong, careful, thrifty, diligent,
Anything we once thought we had to be.[9]

When Paul picks up Jonah's complaint that he cannot "trust God to be unmerciful," by asking him "What would you have God if not merciful?" Jonah's response is clear: "Just, I would have Him just before all else. . . ."[10] But Paul, in a speech reminiscent of God's remarks to Job early in *A Masque of Reason*, shows the prophet that he has not properly understood the import of his role in religious history:

You should be an authority on Mercy.
That book of yours in the Old Testament
Is the first place in literature, I think,
Where Mercy is explicitly the subject.
I say you should be proud of having beaten
The Gospels to it. After doing Justice justice
Milton's pentameters go on to say,
But Mercy first and last shall brightest shine—
Not only last, but first, you will observe. . . .[11]

If at any earlier time in his life Frost might have rested in Jonah's notion of the primacy of justice, now, at seventy, his sympathies leaned rather toward the position advanced by (Saint) Paul. By the end of the masque, Frost permitted Paul to convince Jonah that the Sermon on the Mount was

. . . just a frame-up to insure the failure
Of all of us, so all of us will be
Thrown prostrate at the Mercy Seat for Mercy. . . .[12]

Says Paul: "Mercy is only to the undeserving. / But such we all are made in the sight of God."[13] Then, in a climactic moment of the play, Jonah is led to admit "I think I may have got God wrong entirely. . . . Mercy on me for having thought I knew."[14] As his Old Testament "sense of justice" begins to fade and die, so does he, with a plea for "mercy" on his lips.[15]

Although the masque was all but finished by the end of the summer of 1945, the something Frost felt to be lacking in the final scene, in which Paul and Keeper, standing over the fallen Jonah, discuss the need for courage in carrying out human responsibilities, kept him from sending the masque away to Holt or to Bernheimer. He was still working on the scene when, in early August, a pair of events halfway around the globe gave him new food for thought on the paired subjects of justice and mercy. On August 6, an American airplane dropped an atomic bomb on the city of Hiroshima, Japan. Three days later a similar weapon was turned against the city of Nagasaki. Both cities were destroyed, and the atomic age had begun.

While Frost, like many of his countrymen, had mixed feelings about the use of such awful weapons of destruction against civilian populations, he rejoiced, as did they, at the peace that soon followed, and at the first opportunity in four years to engage in business-as-usual. In mid-October, he visited in Hanover with the retiring President Hopkins and his newly named successor, John Sloan Dickey, discussing what form his third Ticknor year was going to take. He then hastened to Ohio for an honorary degree at Kenyon College.[16] Upon his return to Cambridge, he set down, at Hopkins's request, his recollection of their recent meeting:

"The possibilities came up in pairs—Should I come for week-ends part of the year or make a solid thing of it for a few weeks twice a year? We decided for the latter. Should we open the class to a large number or restrict it to a few? We decided for the latter. Should I mark like teachers of regular courses or should I merely tell the boys what I thought of them as in a progressive school. We decided for the latter. And then I'm to think of myself as belonging to the Library."[17]

A few days later, he interrupted his activities in Cambridge long enough to write a letter to Lesley. He had not, it was clear, been neglecting his own education on the subject of atomic power:

"With things like the atomic bomb I pride myself on putting

them in their relative place a priori without ever having been in a physics laboratory. I said right off uranium was only a new kind of fuel. Wood will rot down to ashes in a few years. It can be touched off and reduced to ashes in a few minutes. It can be touched off and let down with a bump—exploded. Uranium will rot down to radium in a few million years if left to itself, and from radium to lead in a few thousand more. Lead is the ashes, the dead end. It can no more be touched off than the ashes of wood. Most of the matter we live with on and among has long since spent its radioactiveness. We don't have to be afraid of anybody's setting it going: any radiomaniac. Uranium is a strange rare survival from a world once generally active with alpha beta gamma delta and other rays. We live comfortably with practically nothing but the end products. Now Einstein speaks up and tells the hysterical: no new principle is involved. It is just a bigger explosive we have got. We have found a way to let uranium down all those million years with a bang. Of course very magnificent on the part of man. The mind keeps penetrating deeper into matter. I knew at once that the important question was how much uranium there was left in the world, and how many elements there were still left that hadn't levelled off. Einstein says not many. Maybe two or three of those in very small quantities like uranium. So the imagination can rest from getting up doomsdays. The new explosive can be bad for us. But it can't get rid of the human race for there would always be left, after the bomb, the people who fired it—enough for seed and probably with the same old incentive to sow it. There's a lot of fun in such considerations."[18]

There was a lot of fun, as well, in trying to express in poetry his belief that the world was making far too much of a fuss over this new weapon that let uranium down millions of years with a bang. By Christmas time 1945, Frost had written and sent to his friends a poem "On Making Certain Anything Has Happened," in which he advised them, as he elsewhere put it, to "make sure they have something to get hysterical about before they do it":[19]

I could be worse employed
Than as a watcher of the void,
Whose part should be to tell
What star if any fell.

Suppose some seed-pearl sun
Should be the only one;
Yet still I must report
Some cluster one star short.

I should justly hesitate
To frighten church or state
By announcing a star down
From, say, the Cross or Crown.

To make sure what star I missed
I should have to check on my list
Every star in sight.
It might take me all night.[20]

If in this poem Frost adopted a posture of effortless equanimity, other poems he was writing at about the same time suggested that the slightly bemused detachment he now felt had been achieved only after some not insignificant difficulty. "One Step Backward Taken," published early in 1946, presented the powerful, nightmarish vision of a world being swept off its foundations, and of a destruction only survived by a last-minute strategic retreat:

Not only sands and gravels
Were once more on their travels,
But gulping muddy gallons
Great boulders off their balance
Bumped heads together dully
And started down the gully.
Whole capes caked off in slices.
I felt my standpoint shaken
In the universal crisis.
But with one step backward taken
I saved myself from going.
A world torn loose went by me.
Then the rain stopped and the blowing,
And the sun came out to dry me.[21]

A related poem of the same period, whose genesis can be traced to the same sense of terrifying dislocation, was "Directive."[22] Where the speaker in "One Step Backward Taken" had saved himself *from* going by spatial retreat, salvation here is to be achieved *by* going—on a ritualized journey whose direction is backward in time, but also inward to levels of perception unaffected by external circumstances. The opening passage of "Directive," with its hypnotic succession of monosyllables followed by a succession of apparent contradictions, quickly established the poem's peculiarly dream-like mood:

> *Back out of all this now too much for us,*
> *Back in a time made simple by the loss*
> *Of detail, burned, dissolved, and broken off*
> *Like graveyard marble sculpture in the weather,*
> *There is a house that is no more a house*
> *Upon a farm that is no more a farm*
> *And in a town that is no more a town.*

What followed was a kind of preview of a journey to that town, farm, and house, presented by a guide who will "direct you" but "Who only has at heart your getting lost." If he has followed the directions of this ambiguous guide, the prospective journeyer will reach a "height of country" which is "the height of the adventure."

> *And if you're lost enough to find yourself*[23]
> *By now, pull in your ladder road behind you*
> *And put a sign up* CLOSED *to all but me.*
> *Then make yourself at home. . . .*

The journeyer, alone now on a site where once "two village cultures faded / Into one another" and are now themselves "lost," will next encounter a "children's house of make-believe" and then the "house that is no more a house." Proceeding past these, he will reach the goal of his quest:

> *Your destination and your destiny's*
> *A brook that was the water of the house,*
> *Cold as a spring as yet so near its source,*
> *Too lofty and original to rage.*[24]

The guide concludes his preview of the journey with a final directive:

I have kept hidden in the instep arch
Of an old cedar at the waterside
A broken drinking goblet like the Grail
Under a spell so the wrong ones can't find it,
So can't get saved, as Saint Mark says they mustn't.[25]
(I stole the goblet from the children's playhouse.)
Here are your waters and your watering place.
Drink and be whole again beyond confusion.[26]

What was this brook whose waters, attainable only by a chosen number and then only after a proper initiation, contained such power to restore to wholeness? What was "the source"? A Christian reader, noticing that the poem contained echoes of more than one passage in the New Testament and that it alluded to the legend of the Holy Grail, might be led to assume that Frost had God in mind as the "source," and a stream endowed with the power to provide a specifically Christian salvation. The first of these two conclusions, more than the second, probably has some validity. But in a conversation with Hyde Cox some time after the appearance of "Directive" in the winter of 1946, Frost responded to the comment that "some people interpreted the poem as more Christian than most of his work" by suggesting a multiplicity of possible meanings: "The poet is not offering any general salvation—nor Christian salvation in particular," Cox later paraphrased Frost as saying. "In the midst of this now too much for us he tells everyone to go back . . . to whatever source they have. The source might even be a conventional religion . . . but religion is most of all valuable when something original has been contributed to it. . . . It would be the poet's directive that one must go back to what he believes to be the source; and to the extent that he had saved something aside, removed from worldly experience—unpolluted, he would be able to contribute something himself."[27] Frost needed only to add to this comment (and he did in various ways throughout his life) that his own "contribution" to the "source / Too lofty and original to rage" was the poetry which issued from the wellsprings of his own imagination.

Even as he was articulating ways of coping with the confusion and hysteria of the "universal crisis," Frost found himself faced once again with a family crisis that demanded a practical rather than a poetic solution. In the fall of 1944, Irma and John Cone, having passed through a series of marital crises since their marriage in 1926, separated, Irma remaining with her two children at their home in Hanover, New Hampshire, and Cone moving to New York City. After nearly two years of estrangement, Cone, in May 1946, wrote to his father-in-law explaining the reasons he felt compelled to seek a divorce. Frost had seen enough of his daughter in Hanover to sympathize with Cone, and he promptly informed his son-in-law that he would do nothing to impede a divorce action.[28] When Irma learned of her husband's plans, however, she insisted on leaving Hanover and coming to Ripton, where her father could look after her and her younger son, five-year-old Harold. Though he did not relish the prospect of "protecting" Irma from the phantoms that beset her, Frost stoically agreed to her coming, and even went up with Kay to Hanover to bring her and Harold down.

Irma's tendency to hysterical displays of temper, and other unmistakable signs of her worsening mental condition, made Frost sure he did not want his daughter living under the same roof with him. He did agree to put her up in Mrs. Homer Noble's boarding house for the summer, while he considered how he should take care of her thereafter. But even this temporary arrangement did not succeed. Suffering increasingly from paranoid delusions and expressing her fears and obsessions in a number of unpleasant ways, Irma became more and more difficult for Mrs. Noble to manage. Out of loyalty to Frost, she put up with Irma as long as she could. Finally, however, she had to ask Frost to find Irma some other place to live.

Over the next several months, Irma was a constant source of anxiety to her father. With Mrs. Morrison's help, he found one place for her to stay after another, always with like results. Irma would find her present situation unbearable, or the proprietors of her current home would find her so. Frost finally decided he would have to find Irma a home she could not be asked to leave: he would have to buy her a house of her own. By October, when he had to leave New England for a series of engagements in the Midwest, his search had narrowed down to a few towns in the vicinity of Boston. A satisfactory house, however, had not as yet been found.[29]

The major stop in Frost's midwestern trip was Gambier, Ohio, where his friend Gordon Chalmers, President of Kenyon College, had arranged a week-long conference on "The Heritage of the English-Speaking Peoples and Their Responsibilities," and invited him to attend. Frost had chosen to ignore the first invitation Chalmers had proffered in May, partly out of reluctance to participate in any forum, one of whose basic assumptions was that the English-speaking peoples had any "responsibility" to the rest of the world. Another cause for reluctance was the number of speakers Chalmers had invited: twelve in all. Frost's unofficial motto had always been, "I only go when I'm the show," and nothing in Chalmers's invitation had suggested that he would be given a starring role. When Chalmers, however, renewed his invitation in July, adding that he would be "much put out" if Frost were unable to come, Frost decided that he would have to make an appearance at the conference with the unappealing title.[30]

Arriving in Gambier on October 7, he soon wished he had maintained his initial silence and stayed away. Harold J. Laski, the British Socialist, was, he learned, to be the speaker he would follow to the rostrum next day. A former chairman of the British Labour Party, Laski had lately been expressing publicly his conviction that Russian foreign policy was primarily motivated by a desire not for global hegemony but for national security, a conviction for which Frost had but little sympathy. Matters were further complicated when a young man he knew from Dartmouth came up to him saying Laski was not, in fact, pro-Russian as Frost imagined. Sure that Laski had sent the young man to smooth his obviously ruffled feathers, Frost was all the more ready to drop out of the Conference before his turn came to speak.[31]

A last-minute change in the order of speakers, enabling Frost to follow not Laski but Senator Robert A. Taft, saved the day. His topic was one he had spoken on often in recent months, in lectures entitled, as this one was, "The Separateness of the Parts." Running directly counter to the views expressed by most of the Conference participants, Frost began by delineating what he considered a fundamental human dichotomy. On one side, there was "the Western idea that we must master nature, and get such a grip on it that we can make ourselves all happy and make the universe a brotherhood of unconflicting love." In opposition to this, he said, was the Eastern belief that "nature is too much for us, and that we may as well throw ourselves on God and Christ or some savior." His own inclination, he freely admitted, was "toward Asia."

Continuing his talk, he explained what he meant by "the separateness of the parts" and its opposite, another way of discussing his basic dichotomy. "I won't go any further than to say that the separateness of the parts is as important as the connection of the parts. That is my gospel. There are those who were called to take care of the connection of the parts and there are those who were called to take care of the separateness of the parts, and I don't believe I am called upon to do either. I was just watching those things with a little anxiety for the separateness because everybody is talking unity so hard—just a little anxiety, that's all, and a little bit of fear of mob thinking." Despite his disclaimer, few participants in the Conference doubted that Frost leaned markedly toward "the separateness of the parts," and that he looked not to the infant United Nations Organization or other political inventions, but heavenward, for solutions to the political and economic disunity of so much concern to the liberal members of the Conference.[32]

After his one day in Gambier, Frost went on to Cincinnati, where his plans included a visit with one of his Ripton neighbors and friends, Rabbi Victor E. Reichert. During their summers together in Vermont, Frost and Reichert, leader of Cincinnati's Rockdale Avenue Temple, had passed many evenings discussing the relative merits of the Old and New Testaments and other theological matters of interest to them both. In inviting Frost to spend an evening with him and his wife at his home, Reichert knew they would be likely to engage in yet another lively discussion on some problem of biblical interpretation or comparative religion. Fond of teasing Frost that he was really "an Old Testament Christian," if not a Jew at heart, Reichert also knew that Frost's interest in the Jewish religion went further than that of most other Christian believers. After several hours of talk, Reichert announced that he must retire to prepare for a sermon he was giving next day on the eve of Succoth, the Feast of Tabernacles. With studied casualness, Frost announced in turn that he himself had once preached for a friend at a Congregational church back home.

"You never preached for me," the Rabbi ventured.

"You never asked me," answered Frost.

"I'm asking you now."[33]

Next morning there were two sermons delivered at the Rockdale Avenue Temple, one by Robert Frost. Scarcely more sermon-like than many of the talks he had given in recent months, Frost's remarks were mechanically recorded without his knowledge at the instance of Reichert, who later had them privately printed to commemorate the unusual event.[34]

Frost began by saying he sometimes found himself thinking courage was the greatest of all virtues. But he had read an ancient Roman poet, Ennius, who said that it was only the second greatest of virtues. Many bad men, Frost quoted Ennius, have been brave. Wisdom is better than bravery.

"Now religion," Frost continued, "always seems to me to come round to something beyond wisdom. It's a straining forward to a wisdom beyond wisdom. Many men have the kind of wisdom that will do well enough in the day's work, you know, living along, fighting battles, going to wars, beating each other, striving with each other, in war or in peace—sufficient wisdom. They take their own side, naturally, and do well enough. But if they have religious natures . . . they constantly tremble a little with the fear of God. And the fear of God always has meant the fear that one's wisdom . . . one's own human wisdom is not quite acceptable in His sight. Always I hear that word 'acceptable'—'acceptable' about offerings like *that* [indicating the fruit-filled cornucopia gracing the pulpit for the holiday], like offerings like mine. Always the fear that it may not be quite acceptable. That I take it, is the fear of God, and is with every religious nature, always. . . ."

Frost had, perhaps, "always" heard the word "acceptable," but he had heard it used in a specifically religious context only minutes before, during the reading by Rabbi Reichert and his congregation of a passage from the *Union Prayer Book*, and ultimately from Psalm 19:14: "Look with favor, O Lord, upon us, and may our service ever be acceptable unto Thee. Praised be Thou, O God, whom alone we serve in reverence." When Frost heard this, he knew he had a focus for his talk to those who were gathered there that morning. Only later did he realize that he also had more: a way of bringing his *Masque of Mercy* to just the kind of conclusion he wanted, but which he had heretofore been unable to find. Soon after he returned to Cambridge, he drafted speeches for his characters Paul and Keeper that were a kind of benediction to his ventures into religious drama. The first of these, Paul's, most clearly grew out of his visit to Cincinnati:

We have to stay afraid deep in our souls
Our sacrifice—the best we have to offer,
And not our worst nor second best, our best,
Our very best, our lives laid down like Jonah's,
Our lives laid down in war and peace—may not
Be found acceptable in Heaven's sight.
And that they may be is the only prayer
Worth praying. May my sacrifice
Be found acceptable in Heaven's sight.[35]

Keeper picks up the same idea, in the speech which ends the play:

Let the lost millions pray it in the dark!
My failure is no different from Jonah's.
We both have lacked the courage in the heart
To overcome the fear within the soul
And go ahead to any accomplishment.
Courage is what it takes and takes the more of
Because the deeper fear is so eternal.
And if I say we lift him from the floor
And lay him where you ordered him to lie
Before the cross, it is from fellow-feeling,
As if I asked for one more chance myself
To learn to say (He moves to Jonah's feet.)
Nothing can make injustice just but mercy.[36]

A Masque of Mercy now was finished. Within a month, Frost had not only sent it to Holt for publication in a separate volume early in the new year; he had also gathered together many of his wartime lyrics and decided to bring out a new collection of these as well. Two books in one year: not bad for a poet just turned seventy. He could only hope that his offerings would be found acceptable to the critics, to the reading public, and not least of all, in the sight of heaven.

MY FAMILY LUCK

Cast your eye back over my family luck and you will wonder if I haven't had pretty near enough. That is for the angels to say. The valkyries and the eumenides.[1]

WELL IN ADVANCE of the last day of 1946, Kay Morrison let Frost know that she and her husband planned to spend New Year's Eve with some Cambridge friends whom Frost did not know well. Though she invited the poet to join them, she was not surprised when he declined to do so. A few years before, when he had gone with them to a similar gathering, he had been too ill at ease to enjoy himself, so much so, in fact, that Kay had afterward suggested to Frost that henceforth he get up his own New Year's celebration, inviting friends of his own choosing.

Arriving for work at 35 Brewster Street on the afternoon of New Year's Day, 1947, it appeared to Kay that this year Frost had followed her advice. The shades were still drawn. The house was suffused with the stale reek of cigar smoke. The chairs in the living room were out of their usual position and the table in the dining room was wet with spilt whiskey. There was broken glass on the carpet and a plate held the crumbled remains of crackers and cheese.

She found Frost upstairs in his study. He greeted her cheerfully.

"I see you had a party," she said.

"Yup."

"Who was here?"

"People from Chicago," Frost said. "A couple of old friends who happened to be in town. I had them over."

"Your friends smoked a lot of cigars."

"Yup."

"And cigarettes."

Frost nodded.

"And spilled so much liquor on the table that it's spoiled the finish."

"Guess we got a little careless," Frost said.

Kay searched his eyes, and shook her head. "Robert," she said at last. "You know perfectly well there was no one here last night but you. You made all this mess just so I wouldn't know you spent New Year's Eve alone."

Frost chuckled and, after some hesitation, admitted the party had indeed been a hoax. He told how he had stood over the gas stove holding cigars and cigarettes in pincers until they were reduced to ashes, how he had filled the ashtrays, broken the glass on the floor, and poured whiskey onto the table top. He thought it was all a great joke, and invited Kay to tell him if she really had been fooled. Yes, she said, thinking what a hopeless child her employer could be at times, she really had. Then, with his help, she proceeded to clean up the debris of his New Year's Eve "party."[2]

Apart from his domestic depredations, Frost had really spent the last hours of the old year, and the first of the new, composing a long letter to his old friend Untermeyer. Had he permitted Kay to read it before he posted it a week later, she might have suspected that he had not poured all the whiskey on the living-room table. Beneath the printed letterhead of "The George Ticknor Fellowship in the Humanities" Frost had penned, "—and in opposition to the Sciences by contract. I am not supposed to use electric light to read or write by. I use Roman candles in preference to tallow candles." Then:

"Dear Louis Untermeyer: As I sit here alone watching the old year out with nobody to get ahead of me in exclaiming Happy New Year on the last stroke of twelve (or should it be on the first? Has any custom been established?), but after all come to consider me by and large, none so forlorn in my emotional life (there would be no mockery in my being wished a Happy New Year or at any rate a Happy-go-lucky New Year—nor in your being, either, I take it)—let's see where was I?—as I sit here on this anniversary of nothing but one of Time's new beginnings it comes over me with a young freshness to write one more letter to the friend I have written more letters to than any one else. (Kay and I promised permission to look those letters over for anything they ought not to contain. Dull with propriety and discretion as I am in public on the platform, my breaks in private are as the waves on the shore. I get going wild, more stimulated than hindered by any guardian of my accuracy present who tries to laugh me down. I havent meant harm in such a character as I may have given Amy Lowell for instance and if she had been half a man she would have liked it for its strength of chiaroscuro. This is too parenthetical.) . . ."[3]

For several pages running, he rambled on with a succession of jokes and witticisms as if determined to provide Untermeyer with enough material for a new edition of his recent *Treasury of Laughter*. When fatigue began to overtake him, however, he remembered that he had not yet said a word about the "family troubles" this letter, and the "party" hoax, had helped him temporarily to forget. They concerned Irma, who, divorced now from John Cone, showed every sign of heading for a complete mental breakdown:

"My daughter has lived in ten houses in the last six months from sheer unhappiness," Frost told Untermeyer. "Kay and I have found most of them for her. We are buying her a small one right now in Acton Mass where her ancestors on the other side landed from the Mayflower. The wear and tear on Kay and me has been considerable. Merrill is for having Irma brought to rest in an institution or at least under a guardian. I find it hard to end anyone's freedom to range to waste and to ruin. Take that away from anyone and what is there left? Let them run I say till they run afoul. . . ."[4]

The specter of Carol's final insanity and death, as Frost had hunted with Kay in recent weeks for a house they had at last found and made arrangements to buy, had continued to haunt him through the holiday season. So had memories of Frost's sister Jeanie, whose own illness, so much like Irma's in its obsession with sexual violation, had resulted in her commitment to a mental institution where she had spent the rest of her short life.[5] What could he do, Frost had asked himself repeatedly, beyond buying Irma a house where she could care for her younger son Harold with a minimum of disturbance from the outside world? Merrill Moore, the poet who was also a practicing psychiatrist, had told him the prognosis for Irma was not good, that she would probably slip further and further into her paranoid delusions until there was no other recourse than committing her, probably for the rest of her life. What should he do, when Moore also told him that others who suffered from a malady like Irma's often ended up doing harm to themselves, or to those with whom they had the strongest emotional bonds? Was six-year-old Harold, whom Irma fussed over endlessly day and night, in danger? Was Frost himself? Was he, as he had often wondered before Carol's death, somehow to blame? He had no answers. He had only a sense of dread of what was to come, and of frustration that nothing he could do would alter for the better his younger daughter's fate.

Having gotten Irma settled in the two-story frame house he had found for her in Acton—a town just near and far enough to and from Cambridge—Frost prepared to leave for a much-needed month-long vacation at his winter retreat in South Miami, Florida. In gathering together the correspondence he wanted to take with him, much of which concerned the trip to California he was to make in March around the time of his so-called seventy-second birthday, he remembered that he had not yet thanked Earle Bernheimer, whom he would be seeing in San Francisco, for the Christmas present he had recently sent: a check, his first to Frost since the monthly "gifts" stopped coming in mid-1945, for $250. "That was a startlingly pleasant remembrance," Frost wrote the collector on January 14. "It seems like old times again. I'm headed your way and shall be seeing you in your home pretty soon now. I can tell you more exactly when after I see my arrangements a little more clearly in mind. I've been kept off the subject by distresses in the family I wont go into except to say they had to do with the divorce of my daughter and getting her settled in a house of her own where she can rest from her unhappy wanderings of the last six months. . . .

"I shall be having a good look at the streets I ran as a youngster: Le[a]venworth, Washington, Broadway, Polk, Larkin, Clay, California, Van Ness, Steiner, Sutter, Bush, Farrell, Kearney, Valejo, DuPont—but I of course had nothing to do with DuPont except to cross it at right angles in fear and wonder. I wish they hadnt put Alcatraz to such terrible use. I shant want to look in that direction. Why couldnt they have hid their Devils Island somewhere out of sight?—instead [of] spoiling the best bay in the world with it?"[6]

Touring streets he had walked in as a child was but the least of the activities that were planned for him during his visit to the San Francisco area. The major event, his main reason for going to California in the first place, was a Charter Day ceremony on March 22 at the Berkeley campus of the University of California, in which he would accept an honorary LL.D. from the University's outgoing President Robert G. Sproul. Then, as his California trip would coincide with his birthday on March 26—it would be his first in his native San Francisco in sixty-two years—a celebration had been planned by President Sproul and others, including Bernheimer's principal Frost-collecting adversary, Louis Mertins, to take place at the Bohemian Club just before he left San Francisco a few days before the 26th. Informed by Mertins in mid-January of the proposed prebirthday party, Frost realized that Bernheimer would have to be included in the planning stages to avoid potentially awkward jealousies. He immediately wrote to both collectors:

"This celebrating my birthday in San Francisco sort of discombobulates my schedule," he told Mertins. "I want to leave San Francisco on the twenty fifth at least. Could we anticipate by a few days and have the big blow-up the evening of the twenty fourth? Now I want the thing done so there are no hurt feelings and I won't suffer from the rivalries between my friends. You thought of it first but I want you to go ahead tactfully and make Earle your co-manager of whatever it is to be. Please speak to him at once and ask for his backing and his name on the program if there is to be a program. . . ."[7]

To Bernheimer he wrote: "There seems to be a movement on foot to celebrate my birthday in the city of my birth. I don't make out too clearly who is behind this, but it is partly Mr. Sproul's representative at the University and somewhat our friend, Mr. Mertins, of Redlands. Now, I won't be satisfied, in fact I'll be very dissatisfied, if you are not one of the sponsors of the affair too. I want you there in name and in person as my friend and chief collector on earth. Please make it pleasant for me by getting into communication with Mertins about particulars. . . ."[8]

Well into his Florida vacation he was still working out the details of the trip. "Apparently the date for the party at the Bohemian Club has been changed to Sunday March 23," he informed Bernheimer on February 20. "Mertins will confirm this to you. I should think it a good idea for me to leave for your place some time on March 24. How would a night train do

—starting late and not getting there too early in the morning? You know my habits but travelers must not be too particular. I am prepared to rough it a little. I am afraid I have got myself into a tighter place than I had intended. I never allow myself enough time or enough money for an expedition. We thus provide for my lecturing once on the twenty fifth or twenty sixth at one of the universities you mention. You'll have to choose the one. I don't think I ought to use myself up with too many lectures. My usual fee is three hundred and fifty but I want to make it the same as I am getting from Mertins at Redlands which is two hundred and fifty, I think. I am lecturing for Mertins on the twenty eighth and leaving those parts on a train due in Denver at 7:45 A.M.—an unholy hour. The ticket from there is being got for me by my agent in Boston. I have no ticket from San Francisco to Los Angeles. Good of you to think of my accommodations in San Francisco but I suppose the University will be taking care of me. . . ."[9]

At last, when each of his ten days in California had been accounted for, the Charter Day events in Berkeley, the tour of old haunts in San Francisco, the birthday celebration, the visit with Bernheimer in Beverly Hills, with Mertins in Redlands, the lectures, the trains back and forth, Frost could announce to President Sproul, "As far as I can think things out beforehand, my visit to California seems all provided for."[10] Leaving Florida at the end of February, he returned for two weeks to his home on Brewster Street, and on March 16 left by train for the West Coast.

Despite some last-minute editing of his schedule by Mrs. Morrison, Frost soon wished, after his arrival in San Francisco on March 19, that he had been less ambitious in making plans for his triumphal return to the state of his birth.[11] The public phase of his visit, after two days of rest at the home of Willard Durham, Chairman of Berkeley's English Department, began with an afternoon press meeting on the Berkeley campus at which he fielded predictable questions on his poetry, his geographic loyalties, and his literary preferences. Which of his own poems, he was asked, did he consider his favorite? "I couldn't tell you if I would," he said, "and I wouldn't if I could. I'm parental in that. If I liked one of my poems better than another I'd never admit it any more than a parent would about his child." Which state did he consider his home? "I vote in Vermont, but I've never been received there yet. It's a slow state.

People who know of my various places ask, 'Where do you stay?' Well, I don't much stay." What one book would you take with you to a desert island? "Well, once I came out to Monrovia, California, and I brought along a single book you could never guess. It was a book of Lucretius' poems in Latin. I wanted to see what I could dig out without a dictionary from a language in which I was once proficient. When you've only one thing that way you have to depend on memory. Good experience. This question of which books are the world's best irritates me. I get mad thinking about the one hundred best books of St. John's College. I couldn't name a hundred best ones. While I'm waiting for the fall of the British Empire, I read Gibbon's *Fall of the Roman Empire*. It took four hundred years for it to fall, really fall. So, you can see how long we've got to wait on the British. Humpty Dumpty takes his time." So it went.[12]

Later that day, he visited the University library, where he chatted with students whose immediate recognition pleased him immensely, and saw the huge new cyclotron complex, guided by its Nobel-Prize-winning designer, Ernest Lawrence. Next morning, he attended the Charter Day ceremonies at Berkeley's open-air Greek Theatre, listened with interest to an address by Douglas Southall Freeman, the biographer of his namesake, Robert E. Lee, and received from President Sproul an honorary degree, his seventeenth, along with Freeman and the Columbia economist, Frederick C. Mills. At noon, he attended a luncheon at the home of President Sproul, and afterward, accompanied by three of Sproul's aides, he had his first look in sixty-odd years at those few landmarks that were still recognizable in the San Francisco whose proud symbol was now the new bridge spanning the once ferry-crossed Golden Gate. He visited Blanche Rankin Eastman, his mother's closest friend, whose telephone call the night before was the first amazing hint in fifty years that, at nearly 100, she was still alive. He listened as the ancient lady reminded him, matter-of-factly, of her gift of second sight, and as she asked him, as a favor, to tell Governor Warren her vision of "what was going to happen" with the atomic bomb. Her recollections of his father and mother, and of himself as a child, were, he found to his pleasure and fascination, as sharp as his own.[13] Finally, in the evening, tired as he was, he attended as guest of honor the annual California Alumni Banquet at the Palace Hotel.

The gala prebirthday party was celebrated on the following

evening in the Golden Room—a name that brought back memories of Wilfrid Gibson's cottage in Gloucestershire, England—of the Hotel Mark Hopkins in San Francisco. Robinson Jeffers and Gertrude Atherton were among the sponsors, along with Sproul, Mertins, and Bernheimer, and the guest list of 100, to which Frost had contributed several suggestions, included Wallace Stegner, George Stewart, Edith Mirrielees (all at various times of Bread Loaf), Alfred Harcourt, Frost's first Holt editor, and even Earl Warren, the present governor of the state. Sproul, Jeffers, and Dorothy Canfield Fisher were unable to attend, but they, and many others not invited, sent best wishes. The huge birthday cake, embellished with a representation in frosting of "Stopping by Woods on a Snowy Evening," was a great success, and Frost felt Mertins did a creditable job as toastmaster of the evening's festivities, which ended, inevitably, with Frost "saying" several of his poems.[14]

The balance of Frost's time in California was spent, in roughly equal parts, with Mertins and with Bernheimer. Going by train next day to visit the Redlands poet-teacher-collector whose ranch home overlooked the San Bernardino Valley, Frost had his first look at the orange grove whose boxed products Mertins had frequently offered as payments in advance for Frost's signature on countless oddments of gathered "Frostana." On the morning of his birthday, Mertins drove him down to Beverly Hills, where Earle Bernheimer lived in a home that reflected his considerable wealth. There, that night, Bernheimer gave him a second birthday party of almost embarrassing opulence, to which he had invited an assortment of minor literary figures, businessmen, editors, and actors, few of whom Frost personally knew. The food was excellent and abundant, and enough champagne flowed to bring at least one heated discussion to the verge of violence. When it was over, Frost watched with a mixture of amusement and chagrin as the two collectors argued over who would enjoy the privilege of putting him up for the night.

Bernheimer won, and a disconsolate Mertins drove back to Redlands alone. Two days later he returned, to bring Frost back for a final lecture at the University of Redlands he had—as he now regretted—agreed to deliver. Fatigue, boredom, and homesickness had long since got the better of him, and he wanted nothing more than to be back under the protection of his secretary in Cambridge. Still, as he stopped at Ann Arbor for an overnight stay during the long ride from the West to the East Coast, he managed to put the hectic California visit in the best possible light. "I have just been out in California," he said in his April 1 talk-and-reading in Rackham Building of the University of Michigan, "the 'state where I was born in, early on one frosty morning,' as the song goes. They were very nice to me out there—so nice they only embarrassed me once. The Governor of the state asked me why I had left. I said I was very young—and I was carried out screaming."[15]

After a week of rest at his home in Cambridge Frost went traveling again, first to Hanover for the first spring session of his popular Ticknor seminar, then to Amherst for what was only his second visit to the College since his resignation from the faculty in 1938. Stanley King, whom Frost had never forgiven for the way he had—as Frost saw it—plotted to get him off the faculty, was now gone himself, having resigned and been replaced by one of Frost's former—and favorite—Amherst students, Charles Woolsey Cole.[16] The new president, a member of the class of 1927, had invited his former English professor to spend the four days of his visit living in his home, an offer Frost was only too happy to accept. His single regret was that he would be unable to accept a similar invitation from his best friend in Amherst, George Roy Elliott.

"Now Look, Roy," he wrote to Elliott shortly before his arrival, "Your dream of getting me where you want me long enough to do me any good is not destined to be fulfilled yet a while. My motto for today is Keep Moving. I am a nomad in my own house. I have slept in every one of its rooms but the kitchen.[17] My motto for yesterday was Dont let being mixed make you feel confused. It makes [Arthur] Koestler feel confused because he is blended of flesh and spirit, comfort and peace, like Mocha and Java. Keep moving. Keep changing your motto. I'm touching in Amherst only for four nights this time—I have decreed it and it cannot be otherwise. I can remember the time when I would have made the cowardly excuse that someone else wouldnt let me stay longer. Two world wars and a few private catastrophes have made a man of me who doesnt mind blame. Neither for my sins of omission nor commission am I afraid of being punished. All that is past like a vision of Dante or Gustave Doré. My fear of God has settled down into a deep inward fear that my best offering may not prove acceptable in his sight. I'll tell you most about it in another world. My approach to the New Testament is rather through Jerewsalem than through Rome and Canterbury. Old friend forgive me. I want to see a lot of you and Alma. But it had best be in excursion from the Presidents house. This time. I want to scatter myself somewhat. There is Otto to see. I'm not quite up to living in his house yet. Old pains come back to my mind. . . ."[18]

The visit began with a Friday-night appearance before an overflow audience in Johnson Chapel, where he had spoken many times before during his twenty-odd years of teaching at Amherst. "I do not know whether I deserve this as a reward or a punishment," he began after a cordial introduction by President Cole, "but I am back here. All of you seem to be here too." He went on to remind his audience that he was not coming before them as a complete stranger: "It is true that I think I have belonged to Amherst longer than I have to anything else. I've been here a good many times on this platform or pulpit—whatever it is. Well, I'm going to read you some new poetry, some old poetry and talk a little bit. People ask why I bother to talk. It is to show my courage. When I first read poetry here, I knew that if I just read poetry somebody might get too rapturous, so after I got through reading poetry, I talked a little on a technical level. You know how it is. It was easy enough for me to lean on a book and talk. And now here I am. So I am going to say a little to you."

Dartmouth's Ticknor Fellow in the Humanities, or "fellow humanitarian" as he jokingly called himself, then described for his Amherst listeners "the way to approach a scientist"—one of his favorite subjects in recent months of lecturing around the country: "You say to him, science is domestic science and that is all it is. It all comes down to keeping house, cooking, eating, keeping warm and, of course, domesticating ourselves on the planet, so to speak. You can always get a rise by saying that. They tell you, don't you know, science is a good deal pure science and of no earthly use."

Frost did not have to be told by a scientist, he continued, that pure science, or "curiosity," had resulted in the penetration of space and the splitting of the atom. But he was afraid that, with all the modern talk about "pure" and "applied" science, the notion of "pure" and "applied" would be carried too far, until there would be distinctions made between "pure" and "applied" religion, "pure" and "applied" athletics, "pure" and "applied" motherhood, or even "pure" and "applied" poetry: "Some people have talked about reducing poetry to more immediate use. Maybe it is not useful if it is only in a book." Of his own poems, he said, "Mending Wall" had been spoiled by being "applied," and a committee had once been sent to him to find out "what those promises were" in "Stopping by Woods on a Snowy Evening."[19]

The Johnson Chapel lecture was a great success, and so was his talk on Sunday afternoon at the Phi Psi fraternity. There, according to a report in the Amherst *Journal*, he spoke on subjects ranging from "witch tales and 'wild women' to minstrel shows," to the utter delight of his undergraduate auditors. "Mr. Frost laid stress on the need for 'a dash of chaos' in the midst of order," the account continued, "poetry having that quality. American democracy, he said, is an example of a blend of chaos, 'call it freedom if you will,' and discipline. Mr. Frost said he admired men who enjoyed working in a medium of tumult and who could still retain their composure, men such as Henry Wallace and the late President Roosevelt. Everything in life, Mr. Frost went on, contains a varying blend of order and riot, from the individual to nations. But 'to admit confusion is to admit being licked.' "[20]

The Amherst visit ended as pleasantly as it began, and Frost left for Cambridge wondering if Cole would, sooner or later, think of approaching him about coming back to the college he had left under such unpleasant circumstances nine years before. When he had taken the job at Dartmouth, in 1943, he had let it be known that he planned to remain there for the rest of his teaching career. Certainly Dartmouth had given him not the slightest hint of displeasure with the way he had performed his duties as Ticknor Fellow in the Humanities. Still, if President Cole asked him to "come home" to Amherst as he had "come home" to Dartmouth, could he say no? In the back of his mind, the idea of proving by his return how wrong Stanley King had been to let him go was attractive, almost irresistible. Well, he would have to see. If Cole wanted him back, he would, Frost supposed, say so soon enough.

In early May, less than a week after his return to Brewster Street, Frost answered a knock at his door and opened it to find, to his amazement, T. S. Eliot standing before him. "I was in town," Eliot explained simply, "and I couldn't leave without coming to pay my respects." Frost showed him in, and the visitor soon explained further how he happened to be in the country and the neighborhood. He had come from England, he said, to visit his ailing brother, and he had decided to make his passage-money by giving a few lectures and readings. One of these was in Cambridge, at Harvard's Sanders Theatre, just a few days past. Frost had been away at the time, but Eliot had stayed on with relatives. On hearing that Frost was back, he had decided to call.

They had first met in London, in 1928, at a dinner given by their mutual acquaintance, Harold Munro. Frost had not liked Eliot, then, thinking him too enamored of poetic obscurity for his own good and too "British" for one who had been born in St. Louis, Missouri. When they next met in 1932, at a banquet in Eliot's honor at Boston's St. Botolph Club, Frost's opinion of his Anglo-American rival underwent no improvement. Once again he was annoyed by Eliot's British-inflected pontifications, and now in addition by the way the guests—members of the Harvard English Department—seemed to hang on Eliot's every word. With the inevitable jealousy and tension the evening produced in Frost, it was easy for him to interpret the guests' polite attentiveness as mere slavish adulation, and to resent them almost as much as he did Eliot.

Now, however, sitting at his ease in the living room at 35 Brewster Street, Eliot seemed quite modest and natural. He said he was still working for Faber & Faber as a "publisher's assistant"—he was in fact one of the directors—to make his living. Although he was not writing anything now, he was going to take two or three weeks off after his return to England to "find a subject and write something before my vitality fails." They chatted about the old days in London before the Great War and about their most recent poetic efforts. After an hour or so Eliot said he must go, adding that he had greatly enjoyed the visit. Flattered by Eliot's interest in seeing him, and by the esteem Eliot accorded his verse, Frost had to admit, to his visitor and to himself, that he had enjoyed the unexpected visit too.[21]

Far less pleasant was another surprise visit Frost made himself a few days later, to his daughter Irma's new home in Acton. It was, more accurately, a near-visit. Having learned from Irma that she had recently asked for—and been denied—

police protection to keep people away from her house, and that she had later asked Dr. Moore to furnish her with a pistol for self-defense—a request also denied—Frost decided reluctantly that he would have to pay his daughter at least a brief visit before he left the area to spend the summer in Vermont. As he walked up from the depot and reached her street, however, his courage failed him and he stopped. What good would it do to upset his daughter with a visit, he wondered, not to mention the effect their meeting would have on himself. He and Irma never saw each other without a heated argument ensuing—she always seemed so resentful of everything he said and did for her—why not just leave bad enough alone? Instead of walking up to the house, then, he merely looked at it from down the street, hoping to catch a glimpse of his daughter working in her flower garden or tending the lawn. He saw nothing of Irma, but did notice that an upstairs window fronting the street was wide open. Coming as close as he dared, he saw in it a deliberately arranged exhibition of her grotesquely ugly sculptured heads, exposed to the view of passers-by. When he had seen enough, he turned around and walked slowly back to the depot.[22]

Another source of anxiety for Frost, that spring and on into the summer, was associated with the publication on May 28 of *Steeple Bush*, his first collection of new lyrics since *A Witness Tree* in 1942. Good as he felt the forty-three poems in the new book to be, he knew that the critics, and readers in general, would be on the lookout for signs that he was now past his poetic prime, too old, as he edged closer to his seventy-fifth year, to turn out verse that invited comparison with his best work.

Certainly he had tried, in *Steeple Bush*, to branch out in new directions, taking more direct cognizance than in previous collections of the issues affecting the contemporary world. The final grouping of six poems, for example, was called "Editorials," and contained several poems which referred in some way to that new subject for treatment in poetry, the atomic bomb. One was called "U.S. 1946 King's X":

> *Having invented a new Holocaust,*
> *And been the first with it to win a war,*
> *How they make haste to cry with fingers crossed,*
> *King's X—no fairs to use it anymore!*[23]

Another in the grouping, entitled "Why Wait for Science," seemed to have equally little to do with the themes he had been treating in poetry for fifty years:

Sarcastic Science, she would like to know,
In her complacent ministry of fear,
How we propose to get away from here
When she has made things so we have to go
Or be wiped out. Will she be asked to show
Us how by rocket we may hope to steer
To some star off there, say, a half light-year
Through temperature of absolute zeró?
Why wait for Science to supply the how
When any amateur can tell it now?
The way to go away should be the same
As fifty million years ago we came—
If anyone remembers how that was.
I have a theory, but it hardly does.[24]

When read sequentially, however, the poems of *Steeple Bush* contributed to a thematic whole dominated not by secular but by spiritual concerns. In the opening section of the book, immediately preceding "One Step Backward Taken" and "Directive," Frost placed a poem entitled "Something for Hope" in which he asserted that, contrary to the views of social reformers, men can accomplish some desirable things just by patience and hope:

At the present rate it must come to pass,
And that right soon, that the meadowsweet
And steeple bush, not good to eat,
Will have crowded out the edible grass.

Then all there is to do is wait
For maple, birch, and spruce to push
Through meadowsweet and steeple bush
And crowd them out at a similar rate.

No plow among these rocks would pay.
So busy yourself with other things
While the trees put on their wooden rings
And with long-sleeved branches hold their sway.

Then cut down the trees when lumber grown,
And there's your pristine earth all freed
From lovely blooming but wasteful weed
And ready again for the grass to own.

A cycle we'll say of a hundred years.
Thus foresight does it and laissez-faire,
A virtue in which we all may share
Unless a government interferes.

Patience and looking away ahead,
And leaving some things to take their course.
Hope may not nourish a cow or horse,
But spes alit agricolam *'tis said.*[25]

Following a second grouping of "Five Nocturnes" was a third called "A Spire and Belfry," among whose several poems was one entitled "The Fear of God":

If you should rise from Nowhere up to Somewhere,
From being No one up to being Someone,
Be sure to keep repeating to yourself
You owe it to an arbitrary god
Whose mercy to you rather than to others
Won't bear too critical examination.
Stay unassuming. If for lack of license
To wear the uniform of who you are,
You should be tempted to make up for it
In a subordinating look or tone,
Beware of coming too much to the surface
And using for apparel what was meant
To be the curtain of the inmost soul.[26]

Complementing "The Fear of God" was another fear-poem, "The Fear of Man," which—like "The Night Light" earlier in the volume[27]—skillfully presented an objective image corresponding to the poet's own inner state:

As a girl no one gallantly attends
Sets forth for home at midnight from a friend's—
She tries to make it in one catch of breath,
And this is not because she thinks of death.

The city seems in-toppling from a height,
But she can trust it not to fall tonight.
(It will be taken down before it falls.)
There scarcely is a light in all its walls,
Except beside a safe inside a bank
(For which assurance Mammon is to thank).
But there are little streetlights she should trust,
So jewel-steady in the wind and dust.
Her fear is being spoken by the rude
And having her exposure misconstrued.
May I in my brief bolt across the scene
Not be misunderstood in what I mean.[28]

Retiring to his cabin at the Homer Noble farm to await the returns, both critical and financial, on the new book, Frost's anxieties continued to mount until, by mid-June, he was nearly sick with worry. For many years, he had professed to have little or no interest in how the critics received his works. In fact, he could not rest until he had learned, usually by indirect means, what every important reviewer had to say. Knowing how Frost went into a tailspin at the least hint of an unfavorable notice, Kay protected him by screening the reviews in advance, reading to him the best ones, and reporting, sometimes with selective discrimination, on most of the rest. One review Frost was particularly anxious to know about was Randall Jarrell's, in the New York *Times Book Review*. It read, in part, ". . . most of the poems merely remind you, by their persistence in the mannerisms of what was genius, that they are the productions of somebody who once, and somewhere else, was a great poet. . . ."[29] Having to say something, Kay told Frost Jarrell's review was "all right," and hoped he would not ask to see it. Luckily, he did not. Another notice, Leonard Bacon's in the *Saturday Review*, was better. "There is no falling off. There has been no resting on oars or laurels. . . ."[30] Of this Frost was provided a full report.

Inevitably, there were times when even Kay's best efforts were insufficient to protect her employer from emotional knocks at the hands of reviewers. In Hanover on June 13 for the Dartmouth Commencement he was obliged as Ticknor Fellow to attend, Frost went with her afterward to the home of Ray Nash, where he had agreed to spend a few days. Soon after their arrival, Nash took Kay aside and warned her that the review of *Steeple Bush* in the current issue of *Time* magazine, just out, was not kind. Examining it herself in the Nash living room, Kay decided that it would surely not do to let him see it. It was, she told Frost, a typical "smart-alecky" *Time* review. He had best leave it alone. He agreed. Later that afternoon, however, when Kay announced that it was time she returned to Ripton, Frost asked her to drop him off at the grocery store, as he wanted to buy a few things for his stay at the Nashes. As soon as her car was out of sight, he went to the nearest newsstand and bought a copy of *Time*.

"Robert Lee Frost," he read, "is the dean of living U.S. poets by virtue of both age and achievement. At 72, the four-time Pulitzer Prizewinner has lost little of his craftsmanship and none of his crackling vigor. But what was once only granitic Yankee individualism in his work has hardened into bitter and often uninspired Tory social commentary. The 43 poems of *Steeple Bush* do nothing to enlarge his greatness and no one of them could begin to displace the best of his *Collected Poems. . . .*"[31]

That night Frost telephoned Kay in Ripton and, in a dark, almost growling voice, asked her if his Cambridge neighbor, friend, and lawyer, Erastus Hewitt, still had the key to 35 Brewster Street. Yes, she answered, he did. "That's all I wanted to know," said Frost. "I'm going down." But why, Kay asked. "I've got to be alone a few days. I've seen the *Time* review." Kay said he could not do that, the house had been promised to Lillian for a month of complete rest after some recent heart trouble. Well then, he said, would it be better if he came up and locked himself in his cabin instead? No. "Then you leave me no choice." But why not stay in Hanover, Kay asked. "That's all," said Frost. "Good-bye."[32]

He did remain in Hanover as planned, but when he returned to Ripton a few days later, he soon began to complain of pains in his wrists and chest. One afternoon, Mrs. Morrison came up to his cabin and found him on the floor in front of the fireplace. His head was resting on his arms, and these were draped across the seat of his Morris chair. When she went over to speak to him, he winced, and said, "Don't touch me." Where does it hurt? she demanded. "In my heart."

Familiar enough with Frost's psychosomatic ailments not to be unduly alarmed, Kay suggested he remain in bed the rest of the day, and see how he felt tomorrow. Next day he was still complaining of pains in his chest and arms, and the day after that, when Kay went to the cabin as usual around noon, she found him still in bed, not feeling well. Although he agreed to get dressed, he soon returned to his bedroom to lie down. He had been trying, he told her, to write a letter to Irma's older son Jacky, recently discharged from the Army, telling him about his mother's condition. He was feeling bitter and blue. He tried to dictate the rest of the letter to Kay, but was unable to finish it. Instead, he dictated a letter to a recent visitor to the farm, a sister of Willard Fraser, in which he said he did not care if he ever saw any of his children again as they had never been anything but a curse to him.

Mrs. Morrison wisely refused to let him send the letter. In the ensuing argument, Frost soon became so angry he fell back on the bed, coughing and choking. Kay fetched him a glass of water and he began to feel better. She wanted him, she said at last, to see a doctor as soon as possible. No, he said, he would not live on pills; it would be the end of his writing. If he was going to die, he was going to die.

Dr. William Branch Porter, a frequenter of the Bread Loaf Writers' Conference and a medical specialist, arrived next day. He found no evidence of a heart attack, but told Kay that Frost was suffering from what was commonly known as "soldier's heart": a problem more of mental and emotional strain than of physical malady. Returning for another visit a few days later, he invited Frost to tell him something of his recent physical and emotional history. After listening for some three hours, he offered an opinion.

He could, he told Frost, give a medical explanation for the pains he had been suffering, for this "soldier's heart." But before he went into that, he wanted to say something else. While he knew little of the arts, he said, he gathered from everyone, everywhere he went, that Frost was considered the poet laureate of the United States. As such he was in a position earned by his accomplishments, and it gave him certain rights he should accept. But one right, which he should accept, he did not accept, and this refusal amounted to a basic flaw in his character: he had never developed his ego to the extent that he could be free from concern for what other people thought of him.

Having been told by Mrs. Morrison, and by Frost himself, of his reaction to the *Time* review, Porter continued: Who was the author of this dread review? A nobody. Yet Frost, the poet laureate of the United States, had permitted himself to be upset by him. What Frost needed, said Porter, was more of the "old mule philosophy." Did Frost know that story? No, he did not. Well, said Porter, I'll tell you. There was an old black man who tried to sell his friend an old mule that was obviously blind, a fact the would-be seller simply denied. That old mule, he said, could see as well as any other mule, and he was willing to prove it. Giving the mule a whack across the withers he let it run down through the orchard, then watched as it ran past a few trees before colliding with one and falling over on the ground. "See," said the prospective purchaser, "I told you he's blind." "Nope," said the seller, "he ain't blind. He just don't give a damn." After assuring Frost that his physical condition was excellent for a man of his age, that he was physiologically younger than Porter himself, the doctor took his leave. Frost was soon out of bed, feeling much better in body and in mind.

A few days later, having just learned that Jacky Cone had recently spent two days with his mother in Acton, Frost wrote his grandson the letter he had previously been unable to complete:

"Perhaps you would like to tell me in a letter just how you think it is with Irma now. Our anxiety is of course chiefly for Harold. The doubt is whether in the long run it will prove good for him to have been brought up in all those fears that possess Irma. But to be frank with each other, isn't it a little worse than that? I never listen to the mad extravagance of her praise of his beauty and innocence without some fears of my own. A number of experiences have combined to put it into my head that her kind of disorder (whatever it is) is often dangerous to those it loves most. There is no use in making too much of all this. I'll take any risk that you will in consultation with John. I'll leave the whole problem to you and to him if you say so. I just want you to know that I stand ready to help in any way you'll let me. You understand my reason for keeping away from Acton. My visits seemed only to disturb her and make her worse. Here's one little piece of warning you may not need. We must take care not to alarm her about separating her from Harold. He must be sure to be off on vacation with some of his relatives when we get round (if we get round) to the proposal that she should accept mental examination or treatment. It would have to be very delicately handled. The timing is so hard to decide on. I think I ought to see you for a talk some time late in August or early in September—well before you go to Cornell. I wonder what John is advising you. He has shown such good sense in what he has said to me. This is a sorrowful business all around and I hate it that anyone of your age should have to bear so heavy a part in it. I have admired your dignity and assurance."[33]

Replying almost at once, Jacky Cone assured his grandfather that their views were the same. The main issue to be resolved was that of Irma's legal residence, for she could not receive treatment in a state hospital unless she were a resident of that state. It was agreed that the Concord State Hospital, in Concord, New Hampshire, was the best place for her to be committed, should commitment become necessary. But Irma had not lived in New Hampshire since her divorce ten months before, and it was not at all clear which state was currently her legal residence.

The matter rested until the thirtieth of July, when Mrs. Morrison received a call from Jacky Cone, saying his mother was worse and that she had asked him to come up from New Jersey, where he was staying with his father, to take her away from the Acton house. Young Harold, she had explained, was about to go and visit some of his father's relatives, and she was afraid to stay alone in the house because there were plots afoot to kidnap her. Only a few days before, Frost had asked Kay to take especially good care of him for the next two weeks, for if she did not, *he* would go crazy. On the strength of this request, Kay decided not to tell him about her conversation with Jacky Cone. Her protective efforts, however, soon proved to be in vain. The day after Jacky's call, Irma was found wandering on Brattle Street looking for the house of her cousins, Vera and Hilda Harvey, on Foster Street nearby. When she arrived at her destination, the Harvey sisters telephoned 35 Brewster Street, where Lillian, the only present occupant, had Irma taken by taxi. Lillian quickly realized that Irma's condition was much worse and, almost fearful of violence ensuing, she called Frost's lawyer-neighbor, Erastus Hewitt, who in turn called Frost.

On August 3, Frost sent a wire to Irma's ex-husband, John Cone:

AFRAID IT WON'T DO TO LEAVE IRMA ALONE IN ACTON OR ANYWHERE ELSE. . . . THIS IS VERY SERIOUS. JACK DOES VERY WELL, BUT WITH BOTH BOYS' FUTURE AT STAKE FEEL YOU SHOULD TAKE PART WITH ME IN DECIDING WHAT COMES NEXT. WHEN HAROLD IS AWAY WON'T JACK HAVE TO LEAVE WORK AND STAY WITH HER. THE OTHER ALTERNATIVE IS MEDICAL CARE. AM NOT SATISFIED WITH TELEPHONING AND TELEGRAPHING. LILLIAN WILL KEEP HER TONIGHT AT 35 BREWSTER STREET BUT LILLIAN HAS A NEW HEART CONDITION AND SHOULDN'T BE BURDENED. ANYHOW SHE IS NO MORE GOOD FOR IRMA THAN I AM. CAN I ASK YOU TO COME RIGHT UP TO SEE ME TOMORROW. SITUATION IN CAMBRIDGE REALLY BAD. PLEASE WIRE TRAIN. R. F.[34]

The bad situation soon became even worse. Instead of coming to Cambridge as Frost requested, Cone wrote back to say he was not willing to take a role in Irma's commitment, and was withdrawing from the entire matter. He added only that, under the circumstances, he did not intend to permit Harold to return to Irma's care. A few days later, Mrs. Morrison asked Erastus Hewitt to collaborate with Merrill Moore in having Irma committed to the State Hospital in Concord. This they declined to do, insisting instead that Frost return to Cambridge at once.

On August 6, Frost and Kay took a train down from Vermont and, after a ride through teeming rain and thick fog, were met at Porter Square by Hewitt. They went directly to Hewitt's home, where they were soon joined, at his request, by Merrill Moore. In the discussion that followed, Moore said he had considered the various alternatives and concluded that a suggestion previously offered by Frost was impracticable: to have someone hired to take care of Irma would be exorbitantly expensive, way beyond the poet's means. The only viable option was to take Irma to the State Hospital in Concord, where he had already made the preliminary arrangements for her admission. Now, said Moore, they must all go to Frost's house and take Irma up to Concord.

While Frost waited outside in Moore's car with Kay, Moore's wife, and Hewitt, Moore went up to the house and knocked on the door. Lillian Frost let him in, and told him that Irma was upstairs, in bed. Please tell her to get up, he said. Going upstairs, Lillian awakened Irma and told her Dr. Moore was in the living room, that he wanted to see her. "Something has happened to pa-pa!" Irma cried. But Lillian said no, nothing had happened to him. "Then why," asked Irma, "is the doctor here? Tell him to come back in the morning." Lillian said no, she would just worry about it all night, so she had best come down. A few minutes later, Irma appeared in the living room, a wrapper over her night clothes. She listened as Moore explained why he had come. He had decided, he said, that she needed the protection and rest a good hospital would afford, and he had come with her father to take her to one. Irma refused to go, but he insisted. If she did not dress, he told her gently but firmly, he would carry her upstairs and dress her himself. Two hours later, having dressed and packed her bag, Irma emerged from the house.

Frost was still waiting in the car, alone with Mrs. Moore. Presently Hewitt came up, followed moments later by Kay. They worked out the seating, putting Irma in front between Moore and his wife, and in back Kay, Frost, and Hewitt. Then they set off on the two-hour drive to Concord. Moore and the others occasionally tried to make conversation with Irma, but her answers suggested that she knew exactly what was being done to her. As they drove on through the fog and cold, she rocked forward and back in the front seat, sighing to herself as if trying to figure out a means of escape from her captors. Apart from that, she behaved well. When at last they arrived at the hospital, shortly before dawn, Moore said he hoped she had managed to get some sleep along the way. "How *very* kind of you," said Irma, bitterly.

Frost, Kay, and Hewitt waited outside the handsome hospital building as Moore and his wife took Irma inside. After some time, a doctor came out to speak to Frost. He said Irma claimed that she was a legal resident of Acton, Massachusetts. Was it indeed Hanover, New Hampshire, as Dr. Moore had said? Frost said yes. Fine, said the doctor, then he would be happy to admit her. Frost asked if he might speak to his daughter before he left. Of course, said the doctor. Going inside for the first time, Frost thought to explain to his daughter the necessity of bringing her to Concord. Only this way, he wanted to say, could she ever hope to regain her health, rid herself of all the fears she was plagued by. Only this way could she hope to get her son Harold back. When he tried to talk to her, however, she would have nothing to do with him. After listening intransigently to his pleas for understanding, all she would say was "Get out of here."

The weary travelers took rooms in a Concord hotel, and early in the morning Moore and Hewitt drove home through the continuing rain and fog to meet their morning engagements. After a miserably uncomfortable night Kay took Frost for a diner breakfast and then to the hospital to sign the formal commitment papers. Then, following a dreary wait relieved only by a hamburger in the Concord station, they took the train to Boston.[35]

"Cast your eye back over my family luck," Frost wrote to Louis Untermeyer a few days later, "and you will wonder if I haven't had pretty near enough. That is for the angels to say. The valkyries and the eumenides."[36]

12

SPEAKING OF LOYALTY

There is loyalty to chemistry, loyalty to physics, loyalty to geography, loyalty to history, and just incidentally, there might be loyalty to Amherst College and, more incidentally still, loyalty to the United States of America.[1]

AFTER ALL Frost had been through in the troubles over Irma's commitment to the Concord State Hospital, neither Kay nor Ted Morrison had the heart—or courage—to tell him that another potential source of upset awaited him at the August 1947 session of the Bread Loaf Writers' Conference. Frost had already learned from Merrill Moore that Louis Untermeyer would not be participating in the Conference, an acute disappointment in light of Untermeyer's time-tested gift for turning tears to laughter with his irrepressible sense of humor. Prior to his arrival at Bread Loaf, however, Frost had had no reason to suppose that Untermeyer's absence would coincide with the presence of Benny DeVoto, who had not participated in the Writers' Conference for the past five years. For what purpose had DeVoto come back to join the Bread Loaf staff, Frost wondered when he learned elsewhere what the Morrisons had failed to tell him. Did he want a repetition of the scene they had played out in Bloomington in 1943, when Benny had accused him of driving a wedge between himself and Kay, between Kay and Ted? Were there to be more threats for his having spoken what, after all, had been the truth about DeVoto's psychological difficulties? Entering the Little Theater on the evening of August 13 to deliver his first public lecture, Frost's questions were soon answered. He had just reached the front of the hall when DeVoto fairly jumped out of his seat and rushed toward him. "Robert," he said in a stage whisper over the din of applause at Frost's entrance, "you've been a damn fool and I've been a damn fool. Let's forget it and be friends." Permitting DeVoto to lead him to the seat he had saved beside his own, Frost turned to see where Kay was seated and said, in another stage whisper, "Now, wasn't that nice of him."[2] From there the evening, and the week that followed, proceeded as free of unusual stress and difficulty as Frost could have wished. Though the friendship was by no means fully restored, the Frost-DeVoto feud, at least, was over.

Less happy were his relations that fall with Earle Bernheimer. For the past few years, Frost knew, Bernheimer had been embroiled in a divorce and child-custody suit as costly as it was complicated. Only while visiting the collector in California in March, however, had he learned just how costly Bernheimer's legal difficulties might prove to be. There, even as he had entertained the poet with a birthday party that did not spare any expense, Bernheimer had hinted that he had begun considering the liquidation of his assets including, to Frost's dismay, his extensive literary collection. It was bad enough to hear Bernheimer speculating that *Twilight*, for which he had paid Frost $4,000 in 1940, might now fetch more than twice that amount by virtue of Frost's increased fame. What was worse, by far, was hearing him say that, were he unable to sell the collection as a whole to, say, the college library at Dartmouth, Harvard, or Amherst, the auction block might be the destiny of the collection Frost had spent a decade helping him build.

In October, responding to Bernheimer's promise of a lavish Christmas present, Frost wrote to the collector:

"I want to tell you something I have never said to anybody before and throw myself on your generosity and understanding. Don't think I haven't appreciated your generosity from the very first display of it in connection with the smallest book. At the time I was in the mood to take that as a rich man's joke between us. You were willing to be a little absurd for a poor poet's benefit. Now I hear you set a value of ten thousand dollars on the smallest book. Another pleasantry for the encouragement of the arts. Till you came along I had no notion my by-products were worth considering. And I hope you will give me credit for having tried to requite your favors. I take some satisfaction in believing that when I send you the original of the *Masque of Mercy* and another of my copybooks, I shall have put your collection beyond rivalry. You speak of a present for this Christmas that Santa Claus can't get down the chimney. That's like you in form and content. But don't send the present please. I want a chance to catch up with you. We've played an amusing game. I'm no collector and I can't say I have taken collecting too seriously. But I've attained to an experience of it that begins to tell on my nerves. There is a strain of responsibility for my waste paper and my disowned poems in print that I shall have to have a rest from. . . ."

After a digression on family problems the letter ended: "I confess to long having entertained the hope that you would deposit your collection some day where it would link our names in public for the years to come. What you said when I was out there rather was calculated to kill that hope—wasn't it? It's your collection to do what you like with. I have no more to say. I've had a lot of fun helping you to build it."[3]

Unable to exercise control over literary artifacts he now felt he had sold for far too little, Frost was thankful that he could, at least, prevent letters he had written to friends from going into print and thereby exposing to public view the often wretched details of his private and family life. One request for permission to print just such letters had come in March from Margaret, the recent widow of John Bartlett, Frost's old friend from the days at Pinkerton Academy. They had last met in Boulder, Colorado, on Frost's return trip from California, and she had then asked his help with a book her husband had intended, but not lived, to write. Now Mrs. Bartlett wrote to say that she would like to use his letters in a book on the Frost-Bartlett friendship.

"You would have several advantages over anyone else that might attempt my biography," answered Frost the day after Christmas. "I mean anyone else outside my own family. Only Lesley's memories would go back further and go in deeper than yours. That ought to make me afraid of you. But its not from fear that I must ask you to spare me another ordeal of the kind in my lifetime. It is from something I find it hard to explain or even talk about. I am sick at heart from having had my picture taken and my portrait painted. Having my life written up is as bad. I am having it right now by one and threatened by several others. Much more and I will stop being an active man and sit back in a pose merely self-conscious. Let me tell you what I wish you would do: write anything you please about me, but put off publishing it till I am dead and gone. You ought to be able to outlive me. If you find you aren't, you can pass the documents you create on to your most trustworthy heir. Then for both of us the glory will be posthumous. This is permission for you to tell anything you please on me, but to posterity. Now let's pretend you haven't spoken to me in the matter and I will try not to think about what you may be busy with. Do I seem to make too much of myself in all this talk of avoiding self-consciousness? I know it is not important whether my life is written up or not. All the same if you want to please me you will take it off my mind that I may have to face another version of my fortunes and misfortunes. The latter pile up as the years run. You may not have heard the sad ending to Irma's story. She is at once too insane to be out of an institution and too sane to be in one. So she suffers the sense of imprisonment where she is, in one. But I didn't start this letter to let you further into my dismalities. I have things to be thankful for. I have friends for instance. I have had you and John."[4]

Frost was still in Florida on his winter vacation when, in early February 1948, a letter reached him that represented the best news he had had from any quarter in several months. Signed, simply, "Charlie," it was nonetheless an official letter from the president of Amherst College, Charles Woolsey Cole:

"It is a profound satisfaction to me to advise you that the Trustees of Amherst College at their meeting on January 24 voted to confer upon you the degree of Doctor of Letters, *honoris causa*, at our next commencement, on Sunday, June 20, 1948. You know how happy this action of the Trustees will make all your Amherst friends and what a great satisfaction it will be to me to confer the degree upon you. I hope your plans will permit you to be with us at the commencement. . . ."[5]

What plans could Frost have had to render impossible his going to Amherst under such circumstances? If his April visit to the college had proved he still had many friends there, this invitation from President Cole seemed almost to prove that, given time and the right kind of hinting on his part, his return to the Amherst family, his final victory over Stanley King, might soon be made complete. He could not have been more sure of the message implicit in Cole's letter than if the President had added, ". . . and we hope your plans will permit also a resumption of your Amherst teaching career. This, after all, is where you belong." Cole's letter, of course, had said no such thing. But if his own words and actions had any power to influence King's successor and the Board of Trustees, Frost decided it would not be long before he was once again on the payroll of the college he had served longer than any other in his long college-teaching career.

In June, having fulfilled his Ticknor obligations at Dartmouth for the fifth consecutive year, and fresh from an honorary degree ceremony at Duke University, Frost journeyed to Amherst and called on President Cole. As the commencement ceremony was still a few days off, they began their visit by going with Professor George Whicher to another kind of ceremony in Marlboro, Vermont, at the fledgling college recently founded there by Frost's one-time Amherst student and sometime friend, Walter Hendricks.[6] The central event of the Marlboro ceremony, Hendricks's installation as first president of Marlboro College, provided the basis for Frost's (as usual) extemporaneous talk, after his return to Amherst, on a subject currently very much on his mind. Later reprinted in the Amherst *Graduates' Quarterly* as "Speaking of Loyalty,"[7] his Alumni Luncheon remarks may well have been calculated to plant ideas in the minds of Cole, the Trustees, and their fellow Amherst graduates:

"Charlie Cole and I, and George Whicher," Frost began, "are just back from having inaugurated the first president of a brand new college. The extenuating circumstance is that it is a seedling from Amherst College. The chief event of the occasion for me was the history of the founding of Amherst College as told by Charlie Cole, and the analogy he drew between the shoe-string start of this new college on a mountain in Vermont and the shoe-string start of Amherst College a hundred and so many years ago. My ear is always cocked for anything democratic these days, and the most democratic thing I know about America is shoe-string starts. . . .

"I'm here in a sort of grand bath of loyalties. And I'd like to say a little bit in connection with this—the founding of this new college. There someone is starting a new thing to be loyal to. And the one starting it, the president we inaugurated, was of the class, I think, of 1917, Walter Hendricks. He was a Bond Prize winner. I sat on the platform here in 1917 when his oration won the Bond Prize, an oration on 'Adventures in Education,' and right there he set out to establish something new to be loyal to.

"You often wonder about that. There are talkers abroad who confuse the word loyalty, make confusion with the word loyalty. They use Emerson and they use Josiah Royce to prove that you can be as loyal as Benedict Arnold or Aaron Burr, we'll say, and still be a loyal person. Loyal to something else, that's all they mean. The leading article in the *Harper's Magazine* a month or two ago was written to prove that.[8] I heard a speech like that here many years ago confusing the loyalties. There is loyalty to chemistry, loyalty to physics, loyalty to geography, loyalty to history, and just incidentally, there might be loyalty to Amherst College and, more incidentally still, loyalty to the United States of America. The only hitch is that the United States is in a stronger position than chemistry, physics, or history to compel loyalty. . . ."

After a long digression Frost fixed his piercing blue eyes on a Dartmouth colleague who had come down to see him, and, putting as much meaning as he could into every word, he continued:

". . . [R]ight here and now I am looking at somebody who is watching me too. He's from Dartmouth. And he's wondering how I straighten all this out with Dartmouth when I get back there. I remember once, one of the faculty members, my fellows-to-be, said to me, 'From Dartmouth!' he said. 'I never saw a Dartmouth man yet who didn't deserve to be shot.' We began like that. I was in a transition stage—it's one of the problems of life—that transition between an attraction and an attachment.

"The loyalty I'm speaking of—I don't know whether I'm permitted here to deal with it in written words of my own—I've written a great deal about it; once away back when I was very young in a stanza I'll venture to say to you.

Ah, when to the heart of man
Was it ever less than a treason
To go with the drift of things,
To yield with a grace to reason,
To bow and accept the end
Of a love or a season?[9]

"Even a season—that pain of the end of summer—is in it for me, the person, the place, friendship, parting is such sweet sorrow, and so on. One of the poems I'll say has to do with the breaking off, with the cost of breaking off with one attachment to form another. And then I'll say a couple of short ones just to wind up and say goodbye. . . ."

Reciting "The Gift Outright," he used its theme of changing national loyalty to head his talk toward its conclusion:

"And that, I take it, is the whole thing. Lately I've been thinking more and more about it. All there is is belonging and belongings; belonging and having belongings. You belong and I belong. The sincerity of their belongings is all I have to measure those people by. I hate to take great names in vain, but I am tempted to call some men quislings that perhaps some of you would not like to hear me call quislings. Men in great places. I can't quite take them. My namesake anyway, Robert Lee, never came up to Washington to curry favor with those that had licked him. He sawed wood. That was the only thing for him to do when beaten.

"You have to ask yourself in the end, how far will you go when it comes to changing your allegiance. . . ."[10]

Despite the extensive hints he dropped in his Alumni Luncheon talk, the point of which only the most obtuse listeners could have missed, Frost waited in vain for a hint from Cole—or anyone else—that his reappointment to the faculty at Amherst was under active consideration. As week after week went by with no word out of Amherst, Frost began to think that one of two alternatives must be the case. Either he had been, incredibly, too subtle in speaking of changing allegiances and attachments in his Amherst talk, or Cole had, indeed, understood what he was trying to say, and had chosen to ignore the message. In either case, it would hardly do for him to say anything more to Cole or someone else about his willingness—his desire—to return to Amherst. If Cole didn't want him, he certainly didn't want to come. It was a matter of pride, a pride intensified by his humiliation in 1938. In any case, he was sure, the next move was not his to make.

Finally, in mid-September, came a break in the silence. It was a letter to Kay Morrison, who had done her part on Frost's behalf by dropping some hints of her own into the receptive ears of George Whicher:

"Though I have nothing definite to report," Whicher told Kay, "I am willing to say that I have not forgotten the intimations you gave me last summer. I conferred with Charlie Cole as soon as he returned from his vacation and he has asked me to send him a written memorandum to be presented to the Trustees at their next meeting, late in October.

"Possibly we may get action soon after the Trustees meet, or there may seem to be reason for further deliberation. A president in Cole's position must feel his way very carefully. He cannot command the dispatch that Mr. Olds, for example, could and did exercise.

"I have made some discreet soundings and as far as I can discover there is a unanimous and excited hope that a way may be found to attach Robert again to Amherst. But securing authorization, working out financial adjustments, and the like take more time than anyone would suppose.

"You may, of course, use your judgment about communicating any part of this to Robert. He should not feel that our deliberation is an index of our desires. . . ."[11]

In early November, some weeks after Frost began his sixth consecutive year at Dartmouth with a Ticknor seminar entitled "The Theory and Practice of Historical Parallels," President Cole wrote to inform him that the Trustees of Amherst had, at last, made the decision for which he had been waiting. "As you know," said Cole, "I have been hoping that we could work out some arrangement that would bring you to Amherst for much longer periods than an annual lecture. To my mind it would be a great thing for the faculty and the students if you could be persuaded to come back home to Amherst for at least some weeks every year. . . ." He outlined a proposal that the trustees had unanimously approved: Frost would come to Amherst and stay in residence there for at least one month each semester; his title would be Simpson Lecturer in Literature; his annual stipend would be $3,000 a year, and his obligations minimal: no faculty duties requiring attendance at meetings, service on committees, or the like; at least one lecture and reading in Johnson Chapel to the entire college each year; other duties consisting of visiting classes and seminars as a guest teacher, informal conferences with faculty and students, and "such other engagements as might seem desirable to the faculty and students and acceptable to you. They might include, for example, evenings with the boys at fraternity houses." Finally, "It would be our intention to continue this arrangement as long as you were willing and able to maintain it but the appointment might as well be on an annual basis."[12]

Good as the proposal was, there were some drawbacks. The

salary was roughly the same as that of the Ticknor Fellowship at Dartmouth, and no mention was made of an annual pension, payable upon his retirement. But when Frost and Mrs. Morrison paid a personal call at the president's office, they were happy to learn that Mr. Cole was willing to be "flexible" on these two points. He soon wrote back to propose a straight five-year contract at $3,500 per annum, renewable annually thereafter. He also said that "if after July 1, 1954, it should be decided that you should not continue your duties on a year-to-year basis. . . the college would thereafter pay you an annual retirement allowance of $2,500 a year. I am very hopeful," Cole wrote in conclusion, "that you will find this offer as attractive as I think it is."[13]

Frost quickly decided to accept, but postponed notifying President Cole until he had told President Dickey that he would be resigning the Ticknor Fellowship. His letter to Dickey skirted the fact that it was he himself as much as anyone who had instigated the change of loyalties:

"Dear Mr Dickey: You have some thing to listen to that I hope will give you a little pain if only because it gives me a good deal of pain. I am being asked back to the college of my first and longest employment and on terms so extravagantly generous that I couldn't expect anyone else to match them. My recent five years back at the college of my first attendance has meant much to me under both you and Mr. Hopkins and my admiration for you both in your different ways will always come out in my talk wherever I go. I particularly admire the political stir you have given Dartmouth with the new course. I shall be proud if you will let me see you once in a while as a friend to learn of anything new—like that—you may be projecting. But I must beg you to let me leave you now with your blessing. Please understand that what takes me away is not just more money, though that has to be considered even by the most improvident. It is largely the appeal of being provided for at one stroke for the rest of my time in and out of education. The men I owe this promise of ease (haecotia) to were some of them boys I preached my heresies to from twenty to thirty years ago at Amherst. For it is Amherst calling and with a warmth I don't think you would think should be denied. There is sentiment to the situation and even something of rapprochement. I was nineteen years connected with Amherst and nineteen more should see me a nonegenarian. I will tell you the rest when we meet in April. I speak now merely to prepare you to receive me with forgiveness."[14]

A week later, and while still in South Miami on his annual vacation, Frost was presented with an opportunity to dispense forgiveness himself. Ezra Pound had once been useful to Frost when, in London in 1912, he had written a complimentary review of the newly published *A Boy's Will for* Harriet Monroe's *Poetry* magazine. Helpful as it was in introducing him to American readers, the review had seriously embarrassed Frost not only by its verbal indelicacy but also by portraying him (as he had portrayed himself, thoughtlessly, to Pound) as the victim of American editors typically oblivious to native-born talent. Before he left England in February 1915, Frost wrote to his major champion in the United States, Sidney Cox, explaining the awkwardness of his relationship with Pound:

"I fear I am going to suffer a good deal at home by the support of Pound. This is a generous person who is doing his best to put me in the wrong light by his reviews of me: You will see the blow he has dealt me in Poetry (Chicago) for December, and yet it is with such good intention I suppose I shall have to thank him for it. I don't know about that—I may when I get round to it. The harm he does lies in this: he made up his mind in the short time I was friends with him (we quarreled in six weeks) to add me to his party of American literary refugees in London. Nothing could be more unfair, nothing better calculated to make me an exile for life. Another such review as the one in Poetry and I shan't be admitted at Ellis Island. This is no joke. Since the article was published I have been insulted and snubbed by two American editors I counted on as good friends. I dont repine and I am willing to wait for justice. But I do want someone to know that I am not a refugee and I am not in any way disloyal. . . ."[15]

Thirty years later it was Pound not Frost who stood accused of disloyalty, and in a far more serious way. Having begun broadcasting his peculiar brand of political-economic propaganda over Rome Radio early in 1941, Pound in 1943 was indicted for treason *in absentia* by a District of Columbia grand jury and, two years later, imprisoned by the invading army of the country he had never, in his own mind at least, abandoned. After an eight-month incarceration in a wire cage near Pisa, Italy, Pound was returned to the United States where, still under indictment for a crime that carried a maximum penalty of death, he was remanded to St. Elizabeths Hospital, and confined to a ward for the criminally insane. In 1949 he was still under indictment for treason, and still an inmate at St. Elizabeths.

Pound the spouter of anti-Semitic, pro-Nazi utterances had few friends or none by the late 1940s, but Pound the poet still had many. Some of these friends of his verse were on the jury of Fellows in American Literature of the Library of Congress which, on February 19, voted to award his *Pisan Cantos*, written during his Italian imprisonment, the first annual Bollingen Prize, for the best poetry written in 1948.

The news, which set off a heated controversy across the country, reached Frost in Florida soon after the announcement was made. Having published nothing in 1948, he could not have been embittered that the prize had not gone to him. Still, to give it to the likes of Pound was an unendurable outrage, one compounded, in Frost's view, by the statement that had accompanied the announcement of the prize: "The Fellows are aware," it read, "that objections may be made to awarding a prize to a man situated as is Mr. Pound. In their view, however, the possibility of such objection did not alter the responsibility assumed by the jury of selection. This was to make a choice for the award among the eligible books, provided any one merited such recognition, according to the stated terms of the Bollingen Prize. To permit other considerations than that of poetic achievement to sway the decision would destroy the significance of the award and would in principle deny the validity of that objective perception of value on which any civilized society must rest."[16]

In a private memorandum to Kay Morrison, Frost unburdened himself:

"I was playing in luck yesterday. Just after stumbling on to my name mentioned in a pleasant way publically as third only to ONeil and Lewis in a poll recently taken[17] (you will say I ought to be first, thank you) it happened to me that I was out far away from here when an Associated Press man called with Hervey to get something from me about the way Auden Allan Tate Willard Thorpe Louise Bogan Whats-her-name Chapin Leonie Adams T. S. Elliot Robert Lowell Carl Shapiro Paul Green and the Ghost of Ted Spencer had just voted Ezra Pound though possibly crazy but more likely criminal a prize for the book of poetry lately.[18] With this they had thrown in extra a lecture to the United States of America on how to be civilized. My second piece of good luck was in not being caught where I had even to refuse a statement. Hervey made the mistake of trying to draw me into the mess.

"I might have been betrayed by my 'emotions' into saying that in the list of names I saw at once the Chapin lady at the heart of the list as Mrs. Francis Biddell the wife of the former Attorney General and the explanation of why Ezra had been protected by the New Deal from being tried for treason like poor friendless Axis Sally. . . .[19]

"I may still be betrayed into saying to someone somewhere:

"The white corpusticles all rush together at a point of infection and such a meeting is not properly called a meeting but a gathering. It may be healing, but another name for it is puss. In this case it may do the state good by bringing Ezra out into the open to stand trial like an honest traitor. I suppose Louise Bogan wrote the manifesto of the wild party. Well if her logic carries through it will say as we should admire Ezra for being a great poet inspite of his being a great traitor, so we must condemn him for a great traitor inspite of his being a great poet. That works both ways for anybody with a brain."[20]

While Frost spent much of the next week stewing over the Bollingen award, he also devoted considerable thought to a re-examination of his own loyalties in a sphere more mundane than that of national allegiance. For some four years now, his publishers, Henry Holt and Company, had been in a period of upheaval begun, in 1946, by the wholesale resignation of the trade department to follow to his own firm its departing manager, William Sloane. It had not been easy for Frost to decline his friend's invitation to cast his lot, as a number of Holt authors had done, with the new organization called William Sloane Associates. To be sure, his decision to remain with Holt, the only American publisher he had ever had for thirty-six years, was partly out of loyalty. Even more, however, it was a matter of prudence. Suppose the new firm should fail, even under Sloane's expert management? What would that do to the modest prosperity he had spent so many years trying to build? And what problems might there be if, at any time in the future, he decided to bring out a collected edition of poems published by two competing firms? So, in 1946, Frost had wished Bill Sloane the best of luck with his new venture, but had told him that he must stay where he was.

In his decision to continue with Holt, Frost was aided by an officer of the firm who had, like him, declined an invitation to shift his allegiance to Sloane's firm. Alfred C. Edwards had come to Holt, from a successful career in banking, in 1945, seeing in the publishing industry great possibilities for growth as soldiers returned from the war to take up books and studies once again. As treasurer of the firm, and subsequently as executive vice president and president, Edwards on numerous occasions showed the good sense and business acumen Frost wanted to see in those responsible for the production and marketing of his literary enterprises. More than that, Edwards showed qualities and had a background that soon resulted in his becoming not only Frost's business associate, but his friend. Like Edward Thomas, the most cherished friend of Frost's life, Edward's father was a Welshman; his wife, like Kay, was of Scottish ancestry, and her name, Eleanor, in no way diminished Frost's affection for her as well as her husband. Edwards's interest in sports, an interest born of firsthand experience as a college athlete and one-time professional lacrosse player, also gave him something in common with Frost. Above all, Edwards was a doer: he knew how to get things done, and done right. Although he was not a particularly bookish man, he could command the respect of men who were, and he had always had a great admiration, even as a banker, for the poetry of Robert Frost.

Despite his developing friendship with Al Edwards, Frost was less than totally pleased with Sloane's successors in the Holt trade department, beginning with his immediate successor Denver Lindley. A minor poet in his own right, Lindley was a genteel, literate man of the old school who, unfortunately, lacked not only Sloane's sensitivity to Frost's need for encouragement and praise, but also the hard-driving spirit needed to achieve commercial success in the highly competitive world of New York book publishing. After his removal in 1948, Lindley's place was taken by Glenn Gosling who, as acting-editor, was somewhat more adept in managing the trade department and Frost, its principal literary property. The new publishing contract Frost, Edwards, and Gosling worked out shortly after Gosling's accession was by and large a good one, from Frost's point of view. It took away from him, however, the voice he had always exercised in deciding when, and which, books of his should be brought out by the company, and this loss Frost was reluctant to accept. In February 1949, while the subject of loyalty was, thanks to the Bollingen judges, fresh in his mind, he decided to write to Gosling suggesting some ways he, and through him Holt, could prove as loyal to him as he had always been to the firm.

"What has slowed me down," he wrote on the 26th, "is wondering what I have a right to ask you to do next with me—you and Mr. Edwards. The next step is going to be all but all important in my career. You should be flattered by my taking my publishers so seriously. Not all authors are as just. In reading the enclosed contract I come on the passage that gives you total discretion as to how my books shall be brought out. You both make me feel however that you will want to please me all you can in the matter. Our recent talks raised my hopes that you might find it in your budget to make the Collected an entirely new book with new plates, charge fifteen dollars for the special edition to pay for the new plates and then market the trade edition at the popular price of say five dollars. You would be striking a fateful blow for me by so doing. I mean my reputation would be furthered, I'm sure, by such a mark of your belief in me. I have some repute I suspect. I'm in no position to tell how much. Large crowds come to see and hear me east and west. I avoid reviews. I never read about myself except inadvertently. But I did come across a poll last week in News Week[21] that placed my verse as third only to Lewis and ONeil's prose. Many may be against me for good or bad reasons, often party-political. But there's evidence some are for me. Of these latter it would encourage me to have my publishers show themselves the foremost. Am I asking too much? Has the indulgence of the firm little by little been spoiling me, as for instance by the expensive Christmas cards it has made of my lyrics, best of all perhaps this year. Nobody else has been treated as well in the form of his books by any other publisher.

"And to continue in the same vein if it is not too presuming. Kay tells me you might consider the possibility of having a new and more inclusive *North of Boston* with a few pictures not to[o] illustrative some holiday. That's long been a dream of mine. I tried to make Linscott do it in the Modern Library. But he was bent on more. It would bring in 'The Witch of Coos,' 'Paul's Wife,' 'Two Look at Two,' 'West-running Brook,' 'An Old Man's Winter Night,' 'Snow,' 'The Grindstone' to spread into variety, have the same little old frontis poem and for a new end piece symbolically Closed for Good. I could roll up my sleeves and write a small preface to go desperately to posterity with. That I have been stunned by the late upheaval I won't deny. But I'm all right. I begin to regain confidence. I could do with a little sense of stability somewhere of course. Why dont you folks make Edwards president and get down to business? But stability isn't everything. A fresh adventure in the big way of publishing would be more inspiring than stability—I hardly need say. I speak chiefly to show you I am still full of publishing ambition. Kay isnt here to write this for me or it would be more readably and better put. . . ."[22]

Gosling answered that Holt had decided, more out of necessity than choice, to come out with a *Collected Poems* completely redesigned and reset. "It turned out," he wrote on March 11, "that the old Collected Poems had been set in a type which Joe Blumenthal had long since disposed of, and therefore it was impossible to make even the slightest correction, to say nothing about replacing type that had become battered." As to a new *North of Boston*, expanded from the original book Holt had brought out in 1915: "I have indeed thought a good bit about another volume to be called *North of Boston*, which would possibly have illustrations of a decorative sort. I think that a very handsome and worthwhile volume of this kind could be put together. Whether it is the project upon which we will embark next, I am not certain, because I am very much intrigued too with carrying through the project of a collection of your poems for children."[23]

Happy that Gosling was, at least, giving him the all-new *Collected* he wanted, if for all the wrong reasons, Frost turned his attention away from publishing matters and toward an area where his successes tended, generally, to be of the unqualified sort. Early in April, having fulfilled a number of lecture obligations elsewhere, Frost went to Hanover to deliver, for the last time as Ticknor Fellow in the Humanities, a lecture in the Dartmouth "Great Issues" course President Dickey had established in 1947 as a requirement for graduating seniors. The political orientation of the course was well-suited to his present interests, which, more often than not, were outside the immediate domain of poetry.

"The first thing to say," he began in his lecture entitled "Some Obstinacy," to which he had brought a newspaper as an appropriate "passport for admission," "is that you've got to start getting up things to say to yourself if you want to hold your own. And the pre-first thing to say is that you've got to have an own to hold. You can have that any way you please. You can call it preconception, prejudice, but it's something that you'd rather have so than not, either about God or man or education or science or *something* you'd rather have so than not. If it's no matter to you it'd be hard for me to talk to you. There'd be nothing for me to talk up against."

Explaining the importance of having and holding ideas, "some obstinacy" he called it, Frost said that what one had to do was "get up a rigamarole," a defense against those ideas which were hostile to one's own. "Don't be afraid of the word," he said. "Get up a rigamarole. And I'm going to get up and show you some rigamaroles I got up for my own defense, you know, for the defense of my position in the course of the years, the defense of my friends' positions sometimes." The first "rigamarole" he offered was one he had "got up" many years before to protect one of his mother's cherished religious beliefs. "She encountered the idea that we were descended from monkeys," Frost explained. "This was back in the '70s and '80s—'80s, way back then. I remember the first time I heard of the missing link I saw it in the newspaper in San Francisco and had to have it explained to me. But I remember saying to her shortly after that—I've forgotten how old I was, high-school age—that I didn't see that it made much difference whether God made man out of mud as it says in the Bible or out of prepared mud as Darwin said. Just worked up a little."

He offered another "rigamarole" he had worked up to embellish a scientific fact: "I heard that the virus that we talk about so much, you know, when we don't know any better, the virus is very close to crystal form. It was shown this way. Mustn't linger over this too long, must I? . . . The disease called mosaic on potatoes, when boiled down and then dried out to crystalize and then boiled again and crystalized, would still give the mosaic to potatoes, and it made my biological friends suspicious that there must be some very close connection between the beginning of life in virus and crystals. So maybe God made us out of crystals, you see, a little rigamarole."

Continuing his talk, in which he touched upon subjects as diverse as space exploration and treason, Frost said that Shakespeare had divided the world in two with four lines from his Sonnet 116. He quoted them from memory:

O, no! it is an ever fixèd mark,
That looks on tempests and is never shaken;
It is the star to every wand'ring bark,
Whose worth's unknown, although his height be taken.

Half the world, said Frost, was given to science, the scientific spirit, which could take the height of that star but which was incapable of measuring its worth. The other half was given to "the spiritual," or "the spirit of man," in which Frost included religion, poetry, and the arts. That side, he said, was concerned with qualitative, not quantitative, measuring. Even the side he gave to science, however, was subdivided. As he had said before in many lectures touching upon the subject of science, the upper half of that aspect of human endeavor was "pure curiosity," and in its way as spiritual as religion or poetry. "All I've left for gadgeteers and engineers," Frost said at the end of his talk, "is the lower right-hand corner."[24]

Next day he concluded his participation in the Great Issues course by attending a question-and-answer session and expanding upon his remarks of the night before. On the following evening, April 13, he was in Amherst, where, after his talk-and-reading before an overflow audience in Johnson Chapel, President Cole announced that Frost would rejoin the Amherst College faculty in the fall. "Mr. Frost has long been a favorite in this vicinity," wrote an anonymous reporter in the next issue of the Amherst *Journal*, "a fact verified by the tremendous applause which greeted President Cole's announcement. . . ."[25]

At Holt, meanwhile, Frost's new collected edition had gone through the necessary steps of production and was ready for the announcement of publication, as scheduled, on May 30. The first word of the title Holt had chosen for the book, *Complete Poems of Robert Frost 1949*, was not, to be sure, the one Frost would have chosen himself. But handsomely designed, set, and bound as it was, Frost could find no other fault with the job Gosling and Edwards had done. Like the 1939 collected edition, this one began with "The Figure a Poem Makes," then followed, in chronological order, with the texts of each of the eight volumes of verse Frost had published from *A Boy's Will* in 1913 to *Steeple Bush* in 1947. Preceding the Masques of Reason and Mercy with which the volume, by Frost's choice, ended, was a section called "An Afterword" containing three poems, each of recent origin and each having appeared in some fashion prior to 1949. The first, "Take Something Like a Star," had, for example, been incorporated, under a slightly altered title, in Louis Untermeyer's 1943 compilation of Frost's verse, *Come In and Other Poems*:

> *O Star (the fairest one in sight),*
> *We grant your loftiness the right*
> *To some obscurity of cloud—*
> *It will not do to say of night,*
> *Since dark is what brings out your light.*
> *Some mystery becomes the proud.*
> *But to be wholly taciturn*
> *In your reserve is not allowed.*
> *Say something to us we can learn*
> *By heart and when alone repeat.*
> *Say something! And it says, "I burn."*
> *But say with what degree of heat.*
> *Talk Fahrenheit, talk Centigrade.*
> *Use language we can comprehend.*
> *Tell us what elements you blend.*
> *It gives us strangely little aid,*
> *But does tell something in the end.*
> *And steadfast as Keats' Eremite,*
> *Not even stooping from its sphere,*
> *It asks a little of us here.*
> *It asks of us a certain height,*
> *So when at times the mob is swayed*
> *To carry praise or blame too far,*
> *We may take something like a star*
> *To stay our minds on and be staid.*[26]

If this first poem had the quality of a benediction, the second, "Closed for Good," was closer to a valediction:

> *Much as I own I owe*
> *The passers of the past*
> *Because their to and fro*
> *Has cut this road to last,*
> *I owe them more today*
> *Because they've gone away*

And come not back with steed
And chariot to chide
My slowness with their speed
And scare me to one side.
They have found other scenes
For haste and other means.

They leave the road to me
To walk in saying naught
Perhaps but to a tree
Inaudibly in thought,
"From you the road receives
A priming coat of leaves.

"And soon for lack of sun,
The prospects are in white
It will be further done,
But with a coat so light
The shape of leaves will show
Beneath the brush of snow."

And so on into winter
Till even I have ceased
To come as a foot printer,
And only some slight beast
So mousy or so foxy
Shall print there as my proxy.[27]

The book was well reviewed, and advance sales soon indicated *Complete Poems* was going to be a best seller. In early June, with the press party Alfred Edwards had arranged on the day of publication still fresh in his mind, Frost wrote an exultant letter to the man he credited with having helped him progress from a town-and-gown poet to the national bard:

"It was great having that long pre-publication ride with you toward our better and better acquaintance. I was afraid we should have had some of that twenty-dollar shark-skin soup on the bill-of-fare at the Chinese restaurant to build up our strength for what we had to face. Just reading about it seems to have been enough. Look at the power we are showing. Dont think I would claim more than my share of the credit for it either. Friends are bobbing up in every mail and calling me up from hundreds of miles off on the telephone to compliment me on the sendoff I have had from my publishers. Nothing will satisfy the demands of friendship, I fear, but quite a number of autographed, nay inscribed copies of the important book in question. Perhaps I had better ask you right now if you will set aside for me some of both the ordinary and the special edition. I have seen neither as yet, but I have had nothing but praise for the form of both and the reviews we are getting. Kay is as happy as I am about it all."[28]

Of all the words of praise he received for *Complete Poems*, perhaps those most satisfying came from Louis Untermeyer, who, in a notice in the *Yale Review* two years earlier, had characterized *Steeple Bush* as "neither Frost's most commanding nor his most co-ordinated volume."[29] "As my chief upholder through two world wars and one and one fifth peaces," Frost wrote after a family visit in early July, "you would have reason to be proud if I ever came to anything. It is a great satisfaction to have lived to hear you say you *are* proud. Some times I've been afraid the difference between your form of patriotism and mine was bothering you when you had me to defend at some kinds of cocktail parties. But the easy talk we four had together all afternoon there at Lesley's was all the proof needed of how far we hadnt drifted apart. Your touch on my poetry has always been right on the right spot. You 'flattered to tears this aged man and poor' by asking (in good faith I took it) if my latest poem, 'Closed for Good,' was not really a product of my earlier lyric years. I've told Time (the personification) not to fail to put that into his list of cates. . . ."[30]

Untermeyer made further repentance for his critical candor in the *Yale Review* by sending Frost, later that summer, a letter again praising the new volume. Its contents can be deduced by the report Frost made of it in a subsequent letter to Lesley:

"I have had very uneven luck in my friendships," he wrote in the fall of 1949. "I have reached a poise, however, of taking them as they turn out. Louis for instance wrote me the warmest kind of an old time letter in recognition of my having brought round so many of the doubters and held my own with so many of the faithful. It is noticeable that he is saying nothing in print. I suppose he cant say much after what he did to me in the Yale Review. . . . 'Oh well,' as Justice Stone sighed over the Supreme Court and as I sighed in answer. At least

I have a vague sense of having had this year the height of my success. It is entirely beyond anything I ever dreamed of or set my heart on. Its our elders that despise our unpromising youth. So they get dead and safely out of the way before they are proved wrong in their misjudgement of us. There are a few people I regret not triumphing over. But it is with a mild regret that seldom comes over me in its unworthiness. Now would be the time for them to have to reappear and face my facts. Any earlier it wouldnt have been so hard on them. Any later we dont know what the situation might have become. 'For we are poised on a huge wave of fate. And whether it will roll us out to sea' etc. etc. as it is written in Sorab and Rustum if I remember rightly. I haven't my Arnold here to verify it. . . ."[31]

The lines of Arnold he quoted imperfectly from memory were just right for the mood he was in, feeling as he did that he was at an important turning point in his life and his career:

> *For we are all, like swimmers in the sea,*
> *Poised on the top of a huge wave of fate,*
> *Which hangs uncertain to which side to fall,*
> *And whether it will heave us up to land,*
> *Or whether it will roll us out to sea,*
> *Back out to sea, to the deep waves of death,*
> *We know not . . .*[32]

As he overtook the midcentury mark and approached his "seventy-fifth" birthday, Frost had a gathering body of evidence that the huge wave of fate would not roll him out to sea, but would deposit him, triumphantly, on dry land. In November, at a Waldorf-Astoria luncheon attended by some 300 poets, critics, publishers, and friends, the Limited Editions Club awarded him its coveted Gold Medal for *Complete Poems*, the book which, published within the past five years, was judged "most likely to attain the stature of a classic." Early in 1950, he was informed that a committee of the American Academy of Arts and Letters had nominated him as a candidate for that year's Nobel Prize for literature. Awaiting the Swedish Academy's decision, Frost tried to prepare himself for an unfavorable outcome by writing to Louis Untermeyer: ". . . you and Al Edwards have got my expectations perhaps higher than they should be. Disregard them. If nothing comes, why nothing comes. Really now, it's absurd for me to be even interested. I've come a long way on a little, a long way on plenty, and I've had this year of superabundance."[33]

When the Nobel Prizes were announced, Frost's name was not among the winners. On March 26, however, two days before his birthday, the United States Senate bestowed an honor upon him that was a satisfactory alternative to the Swedish award: a resolution which it passed by unanimous consent:

"Whereas Robert Frost in his books of poetry has given the American people a long series of stories and lyrics which are enjoyed, repeated, and thought about by people of all ages and callings; and

"Whereas these poems have helped to guide American thought with humor and wisdom, setting forth to our minds a reliable representation of ourselves and of all men; and

"Whereas his work throughout the past half century has enhanced for many their understanding of the United States and their love of country; and

"Whereas Robert Frost has been accorded a secure place in the history of American letters; and

"Whereas on March 26 he will celebrate his seventy-fifth birthday: Therefore be it

"*Resolved*, That the Senate of the United States extend him felicitations of the Nation which he has served so well."[34]

"Dear Senator Taft," Frost wrote to the resolution's principal sponsor early in April. "There is nothing I had rather be called than an American and a poet. It is my reward, I suppose, for not having presumed to give myself either title that I now receive both at once officially from the Senate of the United States. My laureation and patriation at your hands and in your warm words will go down in Frost family history as the greatest public event of my life. . . ."[35]

FRIENDS LOST AND FOUND

". . . How would it be for you to take your father
To the slave auction in some marketplace
And sell him into slavery? My price
Should be enough to set you up in business—
Or making verse if that is what you're bent on.
Don't let your father tell you what to be."[1]

THE YEAR culminating so magnificently for Frost in the birthday resolution of the United States Senate also brought to a bittersweet resolution the long legal battles of his principal collector, Earle J. Bernheimer. Having taken his complicated lawsuit all the way to the Supreme Court of Missouri, he had there won a verdict which, while denying him custody of his son, Jerry, at least guaranteed that the boy would eventually inherit his grandmother's contested estate. For Bernheimer it was, at best, a Pyrrhic victory. Two of his marriages having ended in divorce, he had spent thousands of dollars in alimony payments and thousands more on legal fees over a period of several years. By 1950, while he was by no means reduced to poverty, his assets had greatly diminished, and he was forced to a series of painful decisions.

As he told Frost in a letter in March of that year, one of these was that he was giving up his expensive home in Beverly Hills, the home where he had so lavishly entertained the poet during his birthday visit in 1947. Another, which touched Frost more directly, was that he was disposing of the art and literary collections with which the house had been filled, foremost among these his collection of the books and manuscripts of Robert Frost. Unable now to give his assemblage to an academic library, as he had always hoped and intended, he would sell it, if he could, to any library willing to pay his price of $18,000.

Could Frost help him find a buyer, Bernheimer wrote, he would be entitled and welcome to a commission for his trouble. Could he not, the collection would very likely have to be sold, piecemeal, at public auction.[2]

Frost was sympathetic to Bernheimer's complaint that material possessions, including his various collections of paintings and literary artifacts, imposed a burden of responsibility from which he was determined, henceforth, to be free. He could not help thinking, however, that Bernheimer's decision to sell his Frost collection, in which he had always professed to take the most pride and pleasure, was motivated by more than the considerations he stated. Thinking back over the course of their ten-year relationship, Frost knew how his own conduct must have irked the collector in ways he had never presumed to express. During the period in which he was accepting, month after month, Bernheimer's "gifts" of $150, he had often failed to provide items which, in quality or quantity, justified such payments. He had often kept the collector waiting a year or more for those items which were of unquestioned value. He had often left it to Kay to acknowledge receipt of the monthly checks, or failed to acknowledge receipt at all. He had sent items to Louis Mertins, Bernheimer's California rival, which Bernheimer's "gifts" had given him a right to expect. Taking all his sins of omission and commission into account, Frost concluded that Bernheimer's decision to sell his Frost collection amounted to a punishment for the many ways and times he had failed to fulfill his part in their apparently defunct relationship.

If Bernheimer sold his collection at auction—a likely prospect in view of Frost's reluctance to act as his "agent" in its sale—it would be a punishment, indeed. In inscribing so many items for Bernheimer over the years, Frost had always operated on the assumption that, someday, the entire block of inscribed books, poems, and manuscripts would be given—donated—to an academic library of his own choosing. The Bernheimer-Frost collection, then, would stand as a monument to Bernheimer's generosity and to his own poetic achievement. Should it be sold at auction, however, it would likely be dispersed in a score of public and private collections around the country, never to be reassembled. What was worse, perhaps, an auction sale might force one or the other of them to reveal the outlines of an arrangement which, by book-collectors' standards, was most irregular: the preparation of inscribed "association items," typically the outright gifts of an author or poet to his friends, in return for a collector's payments—on a more or less regular basis—of cash.

Hoping it was not too late to dissuade Bernheimer from the "absolute decision" he had made, perhaps even to rekindle the dying embers of their friendship, Frost wrote and sent, on March 19, an importunate letter to "My dear Earle":

"Please please! I had begun to infer from your silence that something must be going wrong. You make it sound like some bad domestic dinner you took satisfaction in making a scene of by suddenly avalanching all the dishes off the table with one sweep of one arm or one strong pull of the table cloth and then bursting out of the dining room (wildly) to go hunting wild game in Africa. I have felt that way myself.[3] I can see how something tragic might make you want to clear your life of everything in it. You cant be too sweeping of property for my understanding and you cant be expected to stay dispassionate all the time. Throw collecting out of your life if you must and throw away your collections. But hold on a minute. You've been my friend and I've been yours. We've exchanged favors in the largest way. How many friends have you ever had who could speak to you as I am speaking now? I make no secret of it that I have had a romantic pleasure in your being my one and only Maecenas. If anybody else had bestowed on me with your generosity I might now be rich enough to take up with your offer of your Frost collection for sale. Surely our friendship has gone too far for you to want to chuck it all along with the collection. Dont treat me like the women who have bedevilled you. Let's keep our kindness to each other in mind as the central fact in all this. You can see how you would hurt my sensibilities a little in seeming to assume that I would be willing to act for profit as a middleman between you and any purchaser of the books I have inscribed for you. You are in a petulant mood and not saying what you really mean. Of course I'll try to find you a purchaser in a creditable quarter if that is your insistance. But what I would very much rather do is what I have wanted to do all along—persuade you to end as you began ma[g]nificently by sending me that tailor made coat to replace the old one I used to stuff your bag with in returning you your books signed.[4] How do I mean magnificently? I mean becoming a man of your means and intelligence. I mean by giving the whole big rubbish heap to some one library to be preserved in your name and mine as the Bernheimer Frost Collection. Our names are inextricably woven together in it. It will never explain itself except with your name made prominent on its treasure chest, showcase or room. Come, some sentiment in the grand manner for my birthday. Why not take a plane east on the momentous errand of arranging with me which will be the institution we bless with our riches. You could afford to let me share in the gift—take part of the credit. It would lift you out of yourself and out of all those miseries of litigation and resentment. I shall be delivering a lecture at the American Academy on May 26. Come there and be my guest with Kay and my daughter Lesley. And lets snatch a little fun ourselves. Lets go to a theatre. And then maybe we could go to Amherst together with the Jones Library in mind or to Middlebury College with the Abernethy Library in mind or to Dartmouth with the Dartmouth Library in mind. I must [not] leave out the Amherst College Library. I'm inclined to think Dartmouth would give us a room all to ourselves—the room I used to teach in while there. (I belong to Amherst now.) Anyway there are four places likely to give us the prominence required. The Library [of Congress] is another possibility. The Librarian Evans is a friend and would welcome us to Washington. Only there I should be afraid of being lost in the throng. It would be novel and exciting business. We have much to talk over. Once the collection was placed you could forget or not as you pleased. I would continue to add to it in your name as I went on making. I[n]deed I would add a few items to it right now. . . ."[5]

Bernheimer's reply was friendly enough, but by no means was it the kind of turnabout for which Frost had hoped.

". . . At the outset I want to assure you that the idea of delivering the Frost collection to a reputable and deserving institution was uppermost in my mind all along. But financial conditions and other important reasons have precluded the possibility of my doing this. The money that my books will bring is of great importance to me now. I must get all that I can, in every way I can. True, the Frost volumes have been inscribed for and to me—but so have all my Tarkington volumes and Steve Benet's. I must be coldly indifferent to these memories of great friendships, it seems. I cannot deposit these collections in Libraries that might treasure them. Believe me, such was, as you know because we talked of it, my treasured idea. It has to be abandoned in favor of a way that will benefit me most considerably. I thought a long time about it before I decided to write you about selling the assemblage I took greatest pride in—my Robert Frost's. I also thought about the reaction you would have. I want you to believe anything but that I want to 'chuck' the collection and forget all about it. The associations with you will be, like the Birthday you celebrated yesterday, a diamond Jubilee in my wealth of memories of the past years.

"I am not depressed by something that another might call tragic. I never was happier nor more content, ever. My son not being under my roof is the only thing I miss at all. That does not affect my wanting to dispose of my home and library and most of the furnishings. There were many times in my life, when I felt this same way. Felt that valuable possessions were confining—too much so. A tramp, I sometimes believe, is to be envied. He carries his holdings on the end of a stick wherever he goes.

"I must emulate the tramp, slightly. Anyhow, I must shape a pattern to fit my piece of cloth. Meaning by that that I must live in a much less pretentious manner. What the general alleged friends think makes little difference to me. What a man like you thinks of me makes all the difference. I surely don't want to offend you. But I must sell ALL the things that demand so much as an extensive library. Other things, too, that will allow me to maintain a small apartment or very small house. Financial outlays must be curtailed and I can't help who knows it. I have no reason now and want to assume no false stratum of living, in future—ever again.

"So, as I wrote you without very much explanation, it is necessary that I forgo what was a cherished dream of giving several of my collections to institutions. In fact, I seem to think that it was I who mentioned to you, years ago, that such a gesture was uppermost in my mind. Certainly, I never intended to make you feel a middle man peddling something for a small profit. I really felt that such considerations as you have shown me deserved more tangible evidence of thanks than I have been able to bestow upon you. Long ago, and but now I admit it, I quit sending you monthly evidence of my gratefulness and genuine affection.[6] I believe that you are entitled to make something for efforts you can make in placing my

Frost collection. Your weighty word, in the right place, would benefit me greatly, indeed, and you should be compensated.

"Very confidentially, I am negotiating with a New York auction gallery to dispose of my collections—other than the Frost assemblage and a couple of others. I would much rather have them kept intact and carefully preserved for posterity. More than any others, your volumes deserve preservation as a whole. It is a true regret that I am at a loss as to how this should be done. You are so able to assist me, I know. It is either as a whole or by piecemeal auction, unfortunately.

"In the Fall, they say, will be as soon as a sale [can be arranged.] In the near future they want me to send my library East so the cataloguing may be done over the Summer.

"Will you let me know, without too much delay, what you are able to advise or to accomplish? . . ."[7]

Sure that he could accomplish nothing, Frost, in his final letter to Earle Bernheimer, tried one last time to advise him against selling his collection.

"All I can do then is spread the word among the benefactors of my colleges and see if I can find you a purchaser. I can tell by their looks that $18,000 is a lot of money for them to spend on collecting me. I am afraid the auction room is what it will come to. And probably you will feel better satisfied to have had the trial by market that I had told you in verse everything must come to.

"There should be nothing more to say. Nevertheless I am going to indulge in one last word of protest. I still think it would be a real triumph of sentiment if you make yourself the final benefactor by conferring the collection in your name on one of the colleges I spoke of. That would be fine for both of us. I wish I could get at you personally for a good old persuasive talk. Please go slow in taking your decision. Mind you, the sale of the collection will give me no offence. I merely speak to save you from what you might come yourself to look on as a mistake. Of course you'll tell me if there's any chance of your being East. . . ."[8]

Quite possibly, Frost initially intended to behave in a manner consistent with his statement that "the sale of the collection will give me no offence." Once the auction became a certainty, however, and word began to circulate that Bernheimer possessed an inordinate number of Frost books and manuscripts all inscribed to him, Frost's self-defensive instincts outweighed his more generous impulses. In conversations with friends and book-collecting acquaintances during the months preceding the December auction, he repeatedly hinted that Earle Bernheimer's decision to auction his collection constituted the most inexplicable kind of betrayal. He hinted, or said flatly, that much of what Bernheimer had to sell had been gifts from him, including the unique book *Twilight.* He professed to have no idea why Bernheimer should abruptly decide to dispose of what he had accumulated. He did not take issue with his friends' speculations that Bernheimer had cynically contrived to acquire his Frost treasures for the express purpose of realizing such profits as the forthcoming auction was likely to bring in.

Frost's apparent victimization by Bernheimer so outraged one of his sympathetic friends that he wrote an irate—and anonymous—letter to a well-known trade magazine, the *Antiquarian Bookman.* It read:

"In the records of 'Association Copies' the name of Bernheimer seems likely to take on special meaning. 'His remarkable collection of the writings of Robert Frost,' 230 items in all, goes on sale December 11 and 12, each item bearing the name of Earle Bernheimer—thus attesting that the Beverly Hills collector acquired and then solicited inscriptions to himself of all the important items connected with a bibliography of the outstanding literary figure in America in our century. Having achieved this notable collection, he takes the occasion, when the public and academic world are echoing with their acclaim of the poet, to place the whole 230 items on the auction market. The name Bernheimer is even written in ink on the single existing (truly unique) copy of Frost's first poems to see print (1894). Such an incident must inevitably lessen the respect in which book collecting, especially first edition collecting, is held by the public."[9]

Though aware of the attack, and of how ill-founded it was, Frost made no effort, either publicly or privately, to correct it. The public auction of Bernheimer's "remarkable" collection, at the Parke Bernet Galleries in New York, brought a total of $14,695, in a market made bearish by the widespread belief that Bernheimer was selling for profit the gifts of a victimized poet. As a final irony, the unique *Twilight,* for which Bernheimer had paid Frost's price of $4,000 in 1940, was purchased for $3,500, a figure which, according to a brief account in the New York *Times Book Review,* was "reportedly the highest price ever paid for a single work by a contemporary American author."[10]

In the months between his birthday in March and the auction in December, Frost had, of course, spent relatively little time in matters relating directly to Bernheimer and his collection. But in the only major poem he wrote during that period, "How Hard It Is to Keep from Being King When Its in You and in the Situation," the verse tale hinges on a son's sale of his father into slavery—in a public auction.[11]

First read on May 25 as the Blashfield Address of the American Academy of Arts and Letters, the poem was a humorous parable concerning a king and prince, father and son, who decide that they have had enough of royal life and flee their palace "in the guise of men." Realizing belatedly that they will need money in order to live, the ex-king offers a suggestion to the ex-prince:

> "*. . . How would it be for you to take your father*
> *To the slave auction in some marketplace*
> *And sell him into slavery? My price*
> *Should be enough to set you up in business—*
> *Or making verse if that is what you're bent on.*
> *Don't let your father tell you what to be.*"

The plan is adopted, the ex-king permits himself to be sold as a slave, and he is put to work as a cook in the kitchen of another king. Before too long, however, opportunities arise that enable him to prove the validity of his initial assertion:

> " *. . . I needn't think I have escaped my duty,*
> *For hard it is to keep from being King*
> *When it's in you and in the situation. . . .*
> *My crown shall overtake me, you will see;*
> *It will come rolling after us like a hoop.*"

His uncommon wisdom so impresses his employer, Darius, that the ex-king is permitted to lecture him on the art of government. Speaking now as an obvious mouthpiece for Frost's own political views, he contradicts Darius's shallow notion that a ruler's duty consists merely in feeding his people. Rather, he says, "A King must give his people character":

"Make them as happy as is good for them.
But that's a hard one, for I have to add:
Not without consultation with their wishes;
Which is the crevice that lets Progress in.
If we could only stop the Progress somewhere,
At a good point for pliant permanence,
Where Madison attempted to arrest it.
But no, a woman has to be her age,
A nation has to take its natural course
Of Progress round and round in circles
From King to Mob to King to Mob to King
Until the eddy of it eddies out."

Finally, the ex-king's son decides to reveal their true pedigree, in a speech Frost aimed in part at those who erroneously labeled him a writer of "free verse":

"Don't let him fool you: he's a King already.
But though almost all-wise, he makes mistakes.
I'm not a free-verse singer. He was wrong there.
I claim to be no better than I am.
I write real verse in numbers, as they say.
I'm talking not free verse but blank verse now.
Regular verse springs from the strain of rhythm
Upon a meter, strict or loose iambic.
From that strain comes the expression strains of music.
The tune is not that meter, not that rhythm,
But a resultant that arises from them.
Tell them Iamb, Jehovah said, and meant it.
Free verse leaves out the meter and makes up
For the deficiency by church intoning.
Free verse, so called, is really cherished prose,
Prose made of, given an air by church intoning.
It has its beauty, only I don't write it.
And possibly my not writing it should stop me
From holding forth on Freedom like a Whitman—
A Sandburg. . . ."

The poem concludes with the removal of Darius, who is really no king at all but a cook's son, and his replacement by the "slave" whose wisdom was his undoing. "But don't tell me it wasn't his display / Of more than royal attributes that did it," says the prince of his father in a final speech. "It's hard for kings to keep from being kings / And that is half the trouble with the world. . . ."

Two weeks before reading "How Hard It Is . . ." to the American Academy, Frost had broken the ice in a new communications medium by appearing, briefly, on John Cameron Swayze's popular television program, "Watch the World." The Blashfield Address was to have been the matter of his second television appearance later in the month. But after putting up with spotlights so blinding they almost prevented him from reading his poem, he was informed that, through a technical malfunction, the part of his reading that was to have been broadcast had been lost. Frost was so annoyed that he confined his activities for the next two years to more familiar avenues of public expression.

Thus, for the balance of 1950 and most of 1951, he did little that added more than footnotes to an already impressive academic career. In the June following his American Academy appearance, he accepted honorary degrees from Colgate and Marlboro colleges, and in August he participated as usual in the Bread Loaf School of English and Writers' Conference. In October he attended another conference in Gambier, Ohio, arranged in his honor by the president of Kenyon College, his friend Gordon Chalmers,[12] after which he returned to New England to spend a month in residence at Amherst in fulfillment of his duties as Simpson Lecturer in Literature. In the first months of 1951, he could be found, as usual, at his winter retreat in South Miami, Florida, and in the spring the pattern of readings from Florida to New Hampshire began once again.

This regular cycle of activities was temporarily interrupted by an illness that, untreated, might well have posed a serious problem. In the summer of 1951, a wen Frost had long had on the right side of his face, near his right eye, began to grow in size and ulcerate. A local doctor he went to for advice suspected an allergic reaction to some food he had taken, and told Frost to think no more about it. A week later, however, during the closing exercises of the Bread Loaf School of English, Frost was introduced to a well-known Boston doctor named Ragle whose son was a member of the graduating class. After an exchange of pleasantries Dr. Ragle took Kay Morrison aside to say the lesion on Frost's face was cancer and must have immediate attention. A few days later Frost entered the Mary Hitchcock Memorial Hospital in Hanover, New Hampshire—where he had been treated for pneumonia in 1943—and underwent facial surgery.

The operation was successful, and Frost remained in the hospital several days to give his wound a chance to mend. During his confinement, he wrote of his illness and the thoughts to which it gave rise to Earle J. Bernheimer's successor as his principal collector, the New York book-dealer Louis Henry Cohn:

"This purports to be the spurious collector's item I promised you over the telephone," he wrote while recuperating in Ripton on September 12. "The only thing to authenticate it will be the signature at the end which is a new one I have just adopted in acknowledgement of what the sculptors did to me at the Hanover Hospital. General Ridgeway in Asia would call it Operation Save Face, and that's all right with me, if it turns out that my face is saved—more or less. Anyway that is a great hospital over there as I can testify from its having saved me not only my face but now for the second time my life.

"We ought not put on humanistic airs to make fun of science because though it can postpone death, it can't do away with death. I for one, I am willing to be under obligation to it for postponing death. I count every year beyond the time I had pneumonia in 1906 as velvet. I had hardly accomplished a thing then that I had in my heart if not in my mind to do.

"No we mustnt forget to give science its due. It is much though not everything that it prolongs my individual life and yours. It is much though far from everything that it maintains the human race on the planet beyond all expectation. And now you may have noticed its mouthpiece Prexy Conant has undertaken for it to make the planet less uncomfortably crowded with a new kind of manna (manna from Hell not Heaven, a religious friend Al Edwards calls it), a contraceptive to be taken at the mouth so we can stop breeding without having to stop futution. I made a five line poem on the event entitled Pares Continuas Fututiones (Catullus XXXII). You may object to the word 'futution' as pedantic and rare even in classic Latin. But remember I have never been either a soldier or sailor like you and you must allow for the limitations of my vocabulary. I know what you are thinking. You wish I would shut up and deliver the goods. Well then—if you want the poem, here it is

Pares Continuas Fututiones

Says our Harvard Neo Malthushian
'We cant keep the poor from fututìon;
But by up to date feeding
We can keep them from breeding.'
Which seems a licentious conclusion![13]

"There I guess that's the way I want that to stand.

"I begin to wonder if I am furnishing you with any internal evidence that I am the author of this letter. Let's see what more I can say to convince you that it is I that speaketh. My predicament is like the ghost's on the Ouiga Board. I wish I could mention something nobody but you and I could possibly know the answer to: such as for instance that leaning old silo in the Elysian Fields we used to suck fermentation out of with a straw in the interval between our last two existences but one. Some philosophy warned us against it as habit forming. It proved to be worse than that. It killed us—killed us out of heaven back into life. Remember? . . ."[14]

He signed the letter "Scarface," and scarred though he was by this most recent life-threatening disease, his general health was unusually good for a man approaching eighty. True, his gait had slowed a bit, by imperceptible degrees, in the course of the past ten years. His hearing and eyesight had begun to fail him,[15] and he did not have the excess of physical energy he had once had to spend, for example, on vigorous games of softball or tennis at the Bread Loaf Writers' Conference. But his mind remained undimmed, and his gift for monologue and memorization more than adequately made up for what he had lost in his ability to hear a low-toned conversation or read unfamiliar verse on the public platform. Rarely, now, did he "read" poems to an audience. Rather, he "said" them, and did so with equal facility—though occasionally with some initial fumbling—whether they were his own or those of Shakespeare or Milton, Emerson or Longfellow.

Survivor that he was, it was inevitable that he should outlive some of his closest friends. John Bartlett had died in 1947, followed by his wife Margaret. Hervey Allen had died in 1949; early in 1952, Sidney Cox. Equally inevitably, a new generation of friends rose up, composed of young men and women who had come to know Frost as a teacher at Amherst, Dartmouth, Harvard, or any one of the score of other campuses at which he spent some time each year. His students revered him, cherished his friendship and advice, and looked upon him as a benign, loving grandfather, full of wisdom and wit. It was an image that Frost found particularly congenial.

One of his "boys" at Dartmouth was a member of the class of 1951 named Edward Connery Lathem. Undoubtedly, among the things that first caused Frost to fix his attention on this particular undergraduate was the fact that he came from Bethlehem, New Hampshire, the White Mountains community to which Frost himself had gone during the hay-fever season for several summers prior to his departure for England in 1912—and the place to which he and his family went for refuge during the late winter of 1915, immediately following their return to America. Frost also became keenly aware of Lathem's special interests outside the classroom, interests that included a concern for fine printing and a passion for digging into the historical manuscripts preserved in the college's archives. Frost's concern for Lathem and the deepening of their friendship are marked by a letter of generous encouragement, written in the autumn of 1950, as the latter was beginning his senior year:

"Research-boy, chronicler, historian all are worth being in an ascending scale. You are certainly off to a good start for the first and even second—yes and even third. It seems to me for you to decide how far you want to go. I sometimes wish there were more strict chroniclers for me to read. Though historians are my favorites they can disturb me with a tendency to be novelists. They can overindulge the dramatic and narrative faculties till I lose my confidence that there is any such thing as a fact. Maybe there isnt any such thing. For every fact of history I have had faith in a low-down has turned up to the effect that it's a lie. But examine a first class history like Bury's Greece[16] for the irreducible reality and theres really a considerable share of it to rest on. Where there are dubieties they are frankly marked. For instance we might like to think but do not know that Asia was beaten by Europe at Himera in Sicily and away off beyond communication at Salamis on the same day exactly. It shapes up fine that way. But is that enough to let it go at that? I am not satisfied to call it history when it leaves me as insecure as that. Fiction has one kind of thing it has to be true to and history another. I like the two kinds kept as separate as possible. I have been told they inevitably mingle. I may as well give in and enjoy them both for being true to ideas or to human nature or something else they may aim at. (No, I disagree. I wont give in.) . . ."[17]

Lathem's quiet integrity, in addition to his north country New Hampshire background and the nature of his intellectual enthusiasms, won for him not only Frost's regard but his affection as well. After a year away from Hanover, during which he undertook professional library training at Columbia University, Lathem was brought back to Hanover by the college to join the Dartmouth library staff, providing ample opportunity for the bonds between the two men, over half a century apart in age, to grow stronger and stronger. The poet even took an active part in encouraging his young friend's romantic interests in a physician on the staff of the Mary Hitchcock Hospital, Dr. Betty French; and when the two were married, in November of 1957, Robert Frost was there to serve as best man.

Another young man fortunate enough to have gained Frost's respect and affection was Hyde Cox, the wandering Harvard graduate Frost had first met and befriended in Key West, Florida, early in 1940. Having kept in mind the poet's invitation to visit him at the conclusion of his travels, Cox had called on him in Boston in October of that year, only a short time, as it happened, after the tragedy of Carol Frost's death. The emotional and intellectual bonds they had formed in Florida were readily renewed. Cox felt that it was the first time that anyone so much older and more important than himself had treated him as an equal intellectually and emotionally—confiding in him thoughts and doubts, and asking his advice as if they were contemporaries. In many subsequent visits by Cox to Ripton or Cambridge, and by Frost to Crow Island, Cox's home on the coast in Manchester, Massachusetts, each provided the other with a kind of companionship neither could derive in quite the same way from anyone else.

Often during his lifetime, and increasingly in his later years, Frost went out of his way to help someone whose difficulties, psychological or otherwise, were akin to problems he had confronted in his own experience. With Hyde Cox, as with many other friends over the years, Frost wanted to discover as much as he could about every aspect of his friend's existence, and to provide help and encouragement in any way he could.

Cox's family background, as he revealed it to Frost's persistent questioning in Key West and thereafter, was in some ways notably similar to Frost's own. Hyde's mother had died when Hyde was five years old. His father, like Frost's, had played a relatively small and equally unsatisfactory part in his life. Hyde was brought up by his mother's parents, and to his grandmother he was as intensely devoted as Belle Moodie Frost's son had ever been to her. Hyde's grandfather, like Frost's, seemed to his grandson rather austere, but to him, like Frost to his own grandfather, Hyde found himself owing a considerable debt of gratitude.

In personality, Hyde probably reminded Frost of no one so much as his most cherished friend, Edward Thomas. Like Thomas who, at Frost's instance, had turned to writing poetry before his death in the First World War, Hyde was extremely sensitive, easily depressed, and sometimes at a loss as to what direction his life should take. Intellectually gifted, he was obviously capable of doing almost anything he chose. The problem was, simply, just what choice to make. In the early forties, he worked in New York as an associate editor in the publishing firm of Duell, Sloan and Pearce, until he was overwhelmed by urban life. When the war came, he taught English with great success at the Phillips Exeter Academy for several years. Later, he tried his hand as a lobster fisherman in Gloucester, Massachusetts, a city with which he had had close associations from his earliest childhood. Finally, in what for him was an important decision, he involved himself actively and effectively in the cultural life of Gloucester. In the summer of 1953—at Hyde's request, and sponsored by the mayor—Frost spoke in Gloucester, and his appearance attracted one of the biggest crowds in the city's history. In 1956 Cox was elected president of the Cape Ann Historical Association, which in the years since he has guided into becoming a distinguished museum and a showplace of the city's cultural heritage.

Frost followed with interest his friend's circuitous route toward personal fulfillment, seeing in Hyde's developing career something of his own protracted struggle for self-realization. Often, when Hyde's spirits were low, Frost would manage to come forth with just the right word to set things right. For example, although Cox's appointment as a teacher at Exeter was understood to be a temporary wartime job, he did so well and found himself liking the work so much that he began to wonder if he should commit himself to teaching permanently.

Frost felt strongly that Cox was such an outstanding teacher that Exeter should make special arrangements to keep him there. In an effort to influence events, he said that if the Academy should let Cox go, he himself would never appear there again. Cox persuaded him not to be so partisan for his sake, and in the end he resigned to return to his home and to work in Gloucester.

Partisan as he was in matters touching his personal friendship, Frost often took a real or imagined slight to someone else as a personal affront to himself. In 1952, when he brought Hyde along as a companion on a visit to Bowdoin College in Maine, both he and Hyde were invited to stay with Bowdoin's retiring president Kenneth M. Sills. When next he visited that college, a year later, Frost again invited Cox to join him, and so informed the new president. This time, however, when they arrived at the president's house, they found that arrangements had been made for Cox to stay in a local—and perfectly adequate—hotel. Frost was shown to his room, by a maid—the president was out at the time—and Cox went to his hotel room in town. A short time later, while unpacking, Cox heard a knock on his door. He opened it and there was Frost.

"What are you doing here?" asked the younger man in amazement.

"I've taken a room," Frost answered. "I don't stay in houses where they don't want my friends." Cox insisted that he return to the house, and Frost did.

With such unselfish gestures in mind, Cox was particularly happy when, in late 1949, another of his friends, the noted sculptor Walker Hancock, expressed an interest in doing a head of the poet as he approached his seventy-fifth birthday. Cox soon conspired with Hancock to bring Frost to Gloucester, Massachusetts, where the artist had his studio. The head was sculpted in March 1950, and the experience was as rewarding for Frost as it was for Cox and Hancock. During the long hours of sitting in Gloucester, Frost watched Hancock demonstrate his prowess with clay as the head took shape in his hands. The poet talked all through the sittings, and there were further rich hours of conversation with Hancock at Crow Island. Frost, meanwhile, displayed prowess of his own by composing, aloud, lines for the poem he would read, in May, to the American Academy, "How Hard It Is to Keep from Being King. . . ." When the head was at last completed, Frost agreed that his likeness had never been more successfully captured in any artistic medium.

Another friendship for which Frost had Cox to thank was the one he formed with his favorite American painter, Andrew Wyeth. In May 1953, when Frost was anticipating a new, expanded edition of *North of Boston* to appear about the time of his eightieth birthday, he discussed with Hyde Cox the possibility of having some of Wyeth's paintings reproduced as illustrations in the proposed book. Cox in turn discussed the matter with Wyeth, who was greatly interested by the prospect of having his work appear in company with the poems of his favorite American poet.[18]

"Our mutual friend Hyde Cox," Wyeth wrote to Frost in May 1953, "has, I know, mentioned to you my great interest in having some of my paintings of New England reproduced in your forthcoming book *North of Boston.* I want you to know that I would certainly be greatly honored if this could come about. I realize that your work does not need illustrating to the actual poem as that would be anti-climax. My idea is that perhaps we could use several of my already completed paintings which portray the people and country you love. . . ."[19]

Frost wrote back to Wyeth in early July: "Nothing I could think of would please me more. Hyde and I have been talking about it and I have put in a word with my publishers to break the idea. Of course costs will be a consideration with them. This comes at a time when I have been thinking of a fresh edition of *North of Boston* slightly expanded by a few pieces in the same kind I have scattered through my books of later years. You wouldn't be illustrating it but gracing it with something in a spirit I can't help thinking kindred to mine. You and I have something in common that might almost make one wonder if we hadn't influenced each other, been brought up in the same family, or been descended from the same original settlers."[20]

The idea for an expanded, illustrated *North of Boston* was talked about for several more months before it was finally dropped by Holt in favor of other, less ambitious projects. Frost's disappointment was great, as was Wyeth's. But out of the talk had come, at least, a heightened sense of kinship between two artists who, though they were to meet only once in person (introduced by Hyde Cox at the American Academy in 1950, after Frost delivered his Blashfield Address), felt bound together by their common devotion to the country north of Boston.

One reason why Frost's plans for a new book fell through was that, since the publication of *Steeple Bush* in 1947, he had written too few poems to make any new volume significantly different from those that had already appeared. Besides the poem he had read to the American Academy in 1950, his productions in the years immediately following *Complete Poems 1949* rarely came to more than one a year, that one being the poem he sent forth in booklet form to his friends at Christmastime. In 1950 it was "Our Doom to Bloom," whose title referred to the inevitable proliferation of the welfare state; in 1951 it was "A Cabin in the Clearing," a dialogue between "Smoke" and "Mist" concerning the "inner haze" of a country cabin's occupants; in 1952, "Does No One But Me at All Ever Feel This Way in the Least," a complaint to the sea on its failure to isolate the New World from the Old; in 1953, "One More Brevity," concerning a dog very much like Gillie, whose death in 1949 had robbed Frost of his most constant companion since 1940. Besides "How Hard It Is to Keep from Being King . . ." the only poem he published between 1950 and 1953 that was not a Christmas offering was "For Columbus Day," first read at Amherst in December 1950, which reflected his impressive knowledge of events in pre-colonial American history.[21]

Frost wrote another poem in the early fifties, probably in 1953, but this, like others he had written in a ribald vein, was not destined for publication. Among the friends and acquaintances he saw each year during his month-long stay in Amherst as Simpson lecturer, there was a reclusive poet named Robert Francis. Something of a local celebrity, Francis lived on next to nothing in a secluded house that he called "Fort Juniper," on Market Hill Road, in town. When not writing, he spent much of his time cultivating his garden and amusing himself with a collection of praying mantises that flourished around his house. As taken by Francis's unconventional life-style as by some of his verse, Frost sometimes invited him for a visit at his room in the Lord Jeffery Inn, at other times going to Fort Juniper himself. Then, Frost would read whatever Francis had written in the past year, offering comments that were usually more flattering than those of other critics or editors.

One day, however, Frost came across a poem of Francis's called "Apple Peeler," which for a time made him sorry he had ever been kind to the hermit of Fort Juniper. It read:

Why the unbroken spiral, Virtuoso,
Like a trick sonnet in one long, versatile sentence?

Is it a pastime merely, this perfection,
For an old man, sharp knife, long night, long winter?

Or do your careful fingers move at the stir
Of unadmitted immemorial magic?

Solitaire. The ticking clock. The apple
Turning, turning as the round earth turns.[22]

To Frost, the "trick sonnet" written in an "unbroken spiral" could only be one poem, and the "old man," the "virtuoso," only one poet. After reading "Apple Peeler" over a few times, he was sure that Francis, who always praised both him and his verse whenever they met, was a hypocrite and a jealous disparager of a superior poet. There was no doubt in his mind: the poem to which Francis referred in so derogatory a manner was his own one-sentence sonnet, "The Silken Tent"; the "old man" was himself.

Frost considered various ways of punishing Francis for having written "Apple Peeler," and soon decided that the area in which Francis was most vulnerable to attack was his preference for homosexual relationships. He then recalled what Francis had told him, during a visit to Fort Juniper in October 1952, about the odd sexual habits of the praying mantis, the insect in which he took such a great interest: how the female mantis often devoured her mate alive when hunger outweighed her sexual appetite. Before long, Frost had achieved his revenge, by writing a cruelly satiric poem about Francis's "Apple Peeler," and the cannibalistic praying mantis. He called it "On the Question of an Old Man's Feeling," and in it he struck out at the unwitting offender with a bitterness and cruelty Francis would probably not have imagined possible in his beloved and revered friend. In three of the poem's least virulent lines, Frost named Francis's crime:

He found fault with an aging friend for reeling
A sonnet off with skill for lack of feeling
In one unbroken length like apple peeling.

He then attacked Francis by describing the mating habits of the praying mantis as an example of what Francis "thought of matrimony":

In his herb garden he would cultivate
The Praying Mantis for the way they mate.
After the female drains her mate by force
She eats the male up for a second course.
But whether this may be from love or hate
Or both of them combined at any rate
There must be something it's a symbol of;
Let's say the combination hate and love
Asserts Catullus whose address was Rome
If I may quote a poet in a pome. . . .[23]

Having written it, Frost was satisfied that Francis had been sufficiently punished by the mere existence of "On the Question of an Old Man's Feeling." The poem, in any case, was much too harsh to show the offending author of "Apple Peeler," even if he deserved to see it. In subsequent visits to Amherst, Frost entertained or was entertained by Francis exactly as before. Only three years later, in 1956, did Frost give Francis an indication that he even knew "Apple Peeler" existed. Then, while complaining that it was aimed at "The Silken Tent" and its creator, Frost gave Francis only the slightest hint of the hurt and resentment that had caused him to write his retaliatory poem.[24]

Despite the minor upset caused by Francis's poem, the disappointment of Frost's plans to bring out a new *North of Boston* illustrated by Wyeth, and a recurrence of face cancer which necessitated a second operation in late December, the year 1953 was by and large a good one for Robert Frost. In March, he was awarded the annual Fellowship of the Academy of American Poets, which carried a stipend of $5,000. In June, he accepted an honorary degree from the University of North Carolina, his twenty-fifth from an American college since he accepted his first such honor from Amherst, in 1918. In December, a week before the cancer surgery, he concluded an active year of lecturing by returning to California, where an audience of 2,500 at the University of California at Berkeley gave him an enthusiastic reception.

It was 1954, however, that was truly a milestone year. Only months before he reached what would have been celebrated as his "seventy-ninth" birthday, on March 26, 1954, the researches of his biographer revealed that Frost would, in fact, be eighty years old on that day.[25] While Frost recuperated from his recent operation at his South Miami retreat, plans were quickly formulated by his friends in Washington, in Amherst, in New York, and elsewhere to mark the suddenly extra-significant date with appropriate kinds of public and private celebration.

The events connected with Frost's birthday began on March 12 in Washington, D.C., where he had been invited to a White House reception by President Dwight Eisenhower's Assistant, Sherman Adams. Frost had first met Adams a year or two earlier, when the diminutive but powerful ex-marine was near the end of his term as governor of New Hampshire. On a visit to Boston, Adams had been taken to the St. Botolph Club to hear Frost give a reading of his poems, and at the end of the evening he had been called on for remarks. Much to the poet's surprise, the governor had quoted from memory several appropriate lines of Frost's poem "New Hampshire," and their friendship had thus begun. Adams's invitation to Frost to come to the White House implied that the President would be there to welcome him; such proved not to be the case. But Frost's afternoon at 1600 Pennsylvania Avenue, where he read his poems to, and was toasted on his upcoming birthday by, the assembled Presidential staff, was an exciting experience that did much to further the friendship of the politics-loving Vermont poet and the poetry-loving ex-governor of New Hampshire.[26]

In New York, on March 25, Frost's day began with a nine-o'clock press conference at his suite in the Waldorf-Astoria Hotel, where, for nearly three hours, he answered questions in a room crowded with television cameras, glaring lights, and some two dozen reporters. That evening, he attended a Holt-sponsored dinner in his honor at the Waldorf, to which had been invited some eighty select guests including poets, publishers, senators, and jurists. Each of the guests was given an autographed copy of *Aforesaid* which, published that day, was Holt's own birthday gift to Frost: a new selection of his verse, in a limited edition of 650 copies, handsomely bound as a memento of his poetic achievement as Holt's foremost author.[27]

On the big day itself, Friday, March 26, Frost went to Amherst, Massachusetts, where a second major birthday party was held that night in the dining room of the Lord Jeffery Inn. There was a touch of sadness in the gathering, for one of those who was to have spoken, George Whicher, had died of a heart attack three weeks before. (His remarks in praise of Frost, the last thing he did before his death, were read at the dinner by an Amherst colleague.) But sadness was not the reigning emotion of the party, whose guest list of eighty included more of those Frost considered his close friends than had the Holt affair the night before. One by one, the after-dinner speakers rose at the behest of toastmaster Archibald MacLeish, and offered reminiscences and praise of the poet they had come to honor. While Frost, exhausted and ill from the day before, sat pale and impassive behind a bouquet of eighty red roses, President Cole spoke of how Frost had spent twenty-three of his last thirty-eight years at Amherst, first as poet-in-residence in 1916, and most recently as Simpson Lecturer in Literature. After Cole it was Louis Untermeyer's turn to speak: he recalled how he had been one of the first in America to review the poetry of Robert Frost, whose work, in 1914, had just appeared in a British magazine. "I was amazed," said Untermeyer, "that any Englishman could write with so pronounced a New England accent." An encomium by Mark Van Doren followed, read in his absence by MacLeish. Then it was Thornton Wilder's turn, then MacLeish's, then Whicher's stand-in, Curtis Canfield. When Canfield had finished, Hyde Cox presented to the poet his birthday gift of an Andrew Wyeth watercolor, "Winter Sunlight." An account of Hyde's remarks by Robert Francis, a guest at the dinner, deserves quoting:

"Only with Edward Hyde Cox's speech of presentation . . . did Mr. Frost come to life. . . . Facing Frost and speaking very simply and with a delicate earnestness, [Cox] told how at a birthday party there should be a present, and how his grandmother had taught him years ago to pick a present that the giver himself would fall in love with, and how the opportunity to have a part in such a gift had overcome his shyness in speaking on such an occasion, and how he hoped—his pleasure being so great, so much greater than his shyness—that he could go on giving Robert Frost birthday gifts for many years to come. A most artfully artless little speech, and beautifully given. Cox had the luck to be and the wit to recognize that he was the perfect foil to the old wizard beside him. The other speakers had been under the disadvantage of trying to say wise things about a wise man. Cox did not try to be wise; he was content to be young and simple and affectionate. The visible effect on Frost was moving. The gray mask perceptibly mellowed. The great head moved as by a kind of tropism till its gaze met the speaker, and the ghost of a smile, the gentlest imaginable smile, came over the face."[28]

After Cox, Raymond Holden rose to say a few words, and to read a letter from the governor of New Hampshire. Finally, it was time for Frost himself to speak. Walking slowly to the podium, he adjusted the microphone, cleared his throat, and began by commenting on the manifold tribute he had just been accorded. "I don't read about myself very much," he said, "but I hear about it, people tell me, word comes to me: then I spend all night wondering if it's true. I've heard a lot tonight to think over, and it makes me look back, think about my poems, and think about why I wrote them."

To the frequent comment that "poets die young" he answered that poets die in many ways; not just into the grave, but into businessmen, into critics, or into philosophers—"one of the noblest ways to die." This reminded him, he said, that "what begins more ethereal than substantial often tends to end more substantial than ethereal. . . . You might say that that's the curve from the lyric to the epic. . . . But when I think of myself (I'm made self-conscious about it all) I wonder if the curve hasn't been a little different from that: it's always been very substantial, I think, from the very earliest. . . . Ethereal growing more substantial till I may be too much of a thinker. I hear the praise of my wisdom—and I once threatened to think about that a little: what begins in delight ends in wisdom. . . ."

After talking about his late interest in "collecting absolutes" —universal truths just surprising enough to give delight as well as inspire wisdom—he told of his press conference the day before, then of an encounter he had had with a local grocer, and then, to conclude, of what it was like to be called "great" so many times in one evening. "You know," he observed, "people say you're this and you're that and you wonder if you're anything—and words are strange, aren't they? Hard to get out. Perfection is a great thing. All I've wanted is to write a few little poems it'd be hard to get rid of. That's all I ask. I heard somebody say, you know, that if you don't know you're great you can't be great. This word 'great' grates on my nerves!"[29]

THE DEMAND FOR ME

It will also sort of round off my rather great academic career in general. I have had about everything I can have in my own country. Now for the mother country.[1]

LESLEY FROST was a regular summer caller at the Homer Noble farm, but when she came to Ripton in July 1954 she had a special purpose in mind. As a former employee of the U.S.I.A. in Spain, and a frequent lecturer in South America, she had been asked by her friends in the Department of State to seek her father's participation in a forthcoming good-will mission. In August, an international writers' congress was to be held in São Paulo, Brazil, as one of the principal events in the city's quadricentennial celebration. The United States was among those nations that had been invited to send a poet and a prose writer to the congress, and the State Department's choice in the former category was Robert Frost. If he agreed to go, said Lesley, his travel expenses would be paid by the State Department, all other costs by the Brazilian government. And, as an added inducement, she continued, the Department was prepared to pay her own way to South America, so that she might serve him there as his companion and interpreter.

Frost was at first reluctant to go, not only because it would require him to fly for the first time since 1939, but also because it would require a violation of one of his oldest maxims, "I only go—when I'm the show." Further conversations with two State Department officials, Muna Lee and Harold Howland, convinced him, however, that this was no ordinary good-will mission. In recent months, he was told, anti-Americanism had been on the rise in Brazil as a result of the lack of American interest shown in other quadricentennial activities. The temporary denial on political grounds of a U.S. visa to Brazilian writer José Lins do Rêgo had exacerbated an already precarious situation. By agreeing to attend the São Paulo writers' congress, Frost was assured, he would be doing much to improve the image of his country throughout South America. For this, everyone from the American Embassy in São Paulo to the White House itself would be greatly in his debt.[2]

To the government's appeal to his patriotism was added Lesley's appeal to his fatherly instincts. Since completing her tenure in the U.S.I.A. Library in Madrid, Lesley had traveled extensively in South America under State Department auspices to lecture on American literature. But she had never had occasion to visit Brazil, and the proposed trip was clearly to her liking. Having so often been reminded by Lesley of his shortcomings as a father, Frost was naturally eager to show his daughter what a good father he could be. After some consideration, therefore, he decided to please both Lesley and the State Department by going to South America.

In the midst of hectic preparations for the trip now just two weeks off, Lesley wrote excitedly to her father on July 20: "If you are in a state of turmoil over what we're planning to do, don't think I'm *not*! I guess I never thought for a minute you'd say yes, hence the excitement, pleasure, plus worry. . . . I think it's going to be simply wonderful if we can keep it under control. The State Department, the Brazilian Embassy, and the White House (Sherman) are united in thinking you are doing a good deed for your country and striking the best blow yet struck for 'inter-cultural relations.' Which is true. . . ." William Faulkner, Frost's fellow American delegate to the congress, had, she added, told Muna Lee to tell him that 'he is delighted you are going. You are his great admiration.' "[3]

The two Frosts left from New York's Idlewild Airport on August 4, and landed in São Paulo some twenty-four hours later. Then began ten days of poetry-reading, sightseeing, parties, and press conferences, through all of which Frost moved with the easy assurance of a seasoned man of the world. In both São Paulo and Rio, his lecture performances were received with unbounded enthusiasm, an adulation usually reserved for the most popular native poets. The simplicity of his poetic idiom, so much a liability in the early years of his public career, served him well in a country whose native language was Portuguese. Even those listeners whose command of English was, at best, halting, could make out, at least, the "sound of sense" in "Birches" or "Stopping by Woods on a Snowy Evening."

His talk about poetry often wandered, as it did at home, into political subjects. At a Rio press conference on August 10, he offered his wry views on a favorite topic of his fellow congress-goers, the desirability of a "one-world" approach to solving political differences. "Decency, honor, and not too much deceit," he said, "are about the best one can aspire to in international relations. Nationalism and internationalism are the same as personalism and interpersonalism. There cannot be anything interesting between persons unless they are persons. There cannot be anything interesting between nations unless they are both distinctly nations."[4]

At the congress itself, he came down hard on the frequently heard complaint that the United States dominated South America with its overwhelming economic power. "They spent most of their time worrying about us (the United States)—" he later reported, "not hating us so much as worrying. They worry about our materialism, think we lead them astray with our movies, automobiles, our chewing gum and Coca-Cola. I reassured them. If they don't trust us, they shouldn't buy our things. They shouldn't be so willing to be seduced."[5]

Having completed his Brazilian itinerary—and having succeeded in avoiding his fellow delegate William Faulkner, whose drinking habits he found as repugnant as his 1950 Nobel Prize acceptance speech[6]—Frost agreed to Lesley's request to return to North America by way of Lima, Peru. After a few days there as guest of the American Ambassador, Harold Tittmann, he was happy, however, to return to his farm and friends in Vermont. He delayed his homecoming only long enough to stop and confer in Washington with Secretary of State John Foster Dulles, to whom he offered suggestions for the improved management of "inter-cultural affairs."[7]

With scarcely a pause to catch his breath, Frost was soon back at work talking and reading on native and familiar ground. Much of the "work" consisted as well of accepting honors and awards, of which there were many in this, his eightieth year. In October he received the Distinguished Service Award of the New Hampshire Education Association, and a similar honor from the Theodore Roosevelt Association. In November he was made Honorary Associate of Harvard's Adams House, and given an honorary LL.D. by the University of Cincinnati. The new year, 1955, began with an honor that was particularly gratifying. John Dickey, the president of Dartmouth and his good friend, wrote to say that the trustees of Dartmouth, in a move unprecedented in the history of the college, had voted to grant him a second honorary doctorate at the next commencement. To the Doctorate of Letters President Hopkins had given him in 1933 would now be added a Doctor of Laws.[8]

Frost's pleasure at this latest Dartmouth honor was reflected in his playful letter of thanks to Dickey: "Nothing but great friendship would have put that into your head. We won't talk about my deserts. I am getting toward an end of advocating myself. Time I rested my case in the arts. But the law is another matter. I shall feel almost as if I had been admitted to the bar or to practice before the Supreme Court. I can't deny it gives me a surprising pleasure to get official qualification so late in life for the somewhat legalistic opinions I am so given to handing down. Even members of the Supreme Court may listen now when I flatter them for having been converted by their robes from ex parte lawyers into men of justice. I'll be with you. It will be a happy occasion for me. . . ."[9]

So great had been the number of these happy occasions in the past that, by 1955, Frost faced a unique problem. With each new honorary degree had come an academic hood, and he had put them away, one by one, in a closet at 35 Brewster Street. By the present year there were, in all, some twenty-six hoods, and the closet could hold no more.

One day the problem of the hoods came up in a conversation Frost had with his friend Howard G. Schmitt, a prosperous wholesale-grocer, Frost-collector, and fellow sports enthusiast from Hamburg, New York. In the course of the conversation the poet had a novel idea. Why not cut the hoods up and make them into one or two patchwork quilts? They would certainly make an attractive memento, and would be so much easier to store than in a closet where moths did corrupt. Schmitt thought Frost's idea splendid, and he knew just who could execute the task. Three of his own German-born aunts, he told Frost, were excellent needleworkers and would be delighted, he was sure, to do what he wanted done.

Frost had no idea where the quilting stood until the day of the Dartmouth Commencement, June 12. Then, after returning from the ceremony[10] for a reception at President Dickey's house, Schmitt reappeared in triumph, carrying a stunningly brilliant patchwork quilt.[11]

"You were a good boy," Frost wrote "Schmitty" a few days later, "you turned up at President Dickey's just at one of the highest moments of my academic career to blanket it with such a distinguished work of quilting as never was before on land or sea. Somehow it had occurred to me that somewhere in your background might lurk just the right artist to synthesize the hoods I had been getting by degrees, but I confess to my surprise to learn you had three such artists as your aunts right in your family. Your gift was a many-colored surprise to all of us, I, me and the assembled commencement company at the President's house. You capped the climax of a great day. And we mustnt forget such things have their importance though of course they are only incidental to what my life is all about."[12]

His disclaimer notwithstanding, honors and awards, the gathering of what he himself called "glory," were very much what Robert Frost's late years were "all about." Having been deprived almost totally of any kind of recognition for the first forty years of his life, he carried with him into old age a need for approbation that was almost insatiable. Each new honor did more than gratify; it was a vindication, a proof of his personal and poetic worth. The doubters now were all believers, but the old inner doubts remained. Only the steady influx of objectified praise could quiet the fear he had that everything he had achieved would somehow slip away.[13]

Frost's hunger for "glory" and his willingness to pursue it were nowhere better illustrated than in a series of events that from their simple beginning in April 1956 culminated in one of the more glorious episodes of his life. His eighty-second birthday was some two weeks behind him when a letter arrived from President Eisenhower's Assistant, Sherman Adams. "Dear Mr. Frost:" it read, "There is a matter in which the President is personally interested and about which we would like very much to talk with you in the near future. Mr. Conger Reynolds, of the U.S. Information Agency, will try to reach you for an appointment and will be available to come to Cambridge. . . . I hope it will be possible for you to see him. . . ."[14]

Having no idea what the "matter" was, but assuming it was related to his recent trip to South America, Frost answered Adams's note with more than usual dispatch: "You know how I would feel," he wrote on April 11, "about a request that comes from so close in to the center of everything going on in the world. I am yours to consult here or anywhere I happen to be on any subject you may have in mind. I can only guess it may be our cultural relations with other countries. In my report to Mr. Dulles when I came back from Brazil the one thing I was at all urgent about was the possibility of strengthening the position of our cultural attaches. From my point of view if given diplomatic status and kept as purely cultural—that is to say non-political, non-sociological as they are of course, non-religious, they could do more for international comfort than any emissaries we send abroad. But whatever the matter of state is, I shall be proud in having the first chance I ever had to more than vote in one. You tell the President with my loyal regard."[15]

In his meeting with Frost at the Homer Noble farm, Conger Reynolds had little to say about any matter in which President Eisenhower was, except in the broadest sense, "personally interested." Instead, he described various areas around the world where American prestige was threatened, and various ways in which his own agency, the U.S.I.A., was working to defend the nation's image abroad. Among the more effective ways of doing so, Reynolds explained, was to have well-known and respected public figures write essays about American life for international distribution. Perhaps, he added, Frost might wish to undertake such an essay himself.

It was the second request in as many weeks that Frost felt bound to decline. In early June, Sherman Adams had written him to invite his membership in a group called CASE, a committee of artists and scientists favoring President Eisenhower's reelection.[16] Perhaps, Frost reasoned after Reynolds's departure, the two requests were not unrelated. Was Adams trying to lure him into the Eisenhower campaign with the attentions of Reynolds and the U.S.I.A. as bait? How little, then, did Adams understand him! He was nobody's propagandist—but his own.

"Great to be named after a general so great," Frost teased in his first letter to "Sherman" following Reynolds's visit. "He and Grant were a pair. Such are the things I could wish you leisure to talk with me about sometime. Meanwhile we *should* meet if only for a hasty moment to talk over whatever it is you mean you have so close at heart for me to do. I could hardly more than guess what it is from the pleasant man that came up to see me from the State Department. I should like to think I was willing to be serviceable but I shrink from being official and using my pen on purpose to popularize my country.[17] Your messenger told me we were loved by nobody in the world. If in their small way the poems I write don't make us friends (in their small way) they at least represent the best I can think of writing. Surely I am better at verse than at prose. May I suggest that possibly the best thing *you* could do for the cause would be to keep on magnifying me the way you have been ever since you descended in state on us that night at the St. Botolph Club: for which I shall be Always gratefully yours Robert."[18]

With that audacious suggestion, Frost seemed to have brought the matter to its end. In December, however, a month after Eisenhower had managed, without Frost's help, to win reelection, a letter arrived from the man who had been instrumental in his 1954 mission to South America, Harold Howland. "Our Embassy at London has informed us," he wrote, "that it is planning an exhibition concerning your life and work some time this winter or the spring of 1957. The Embassy has further stated that a personal visit by you would enhance immeasurably the effect of this exhibit on the English public. The Department of State, recalling your splendid cooperation in visiting Latin America . . . wholeheartedly endorses the Embassy's suggestion. . . ." The letter concluded with an invitation to visit Great Britain, at government expense, sometime between February and June of the coming year.[19]

Howland's letter came as a complete surprise. Conger Reynolds, in his June visit to Ripton, had given not the slightest indication that anything like this trip to England was being contemplated by the State Department. Nor had Sherman Adams. Was this invitation unrelated, then, to the events and conversations of recent months? Frost could only guess.

What he did know was that he was interested in the proposed trip, and wanted to hear more about it. "You realize," he told Howland, "going to England on a mission so to speak would be a considerable undertaking at my age. To be sure I am kicked around at home a good deal, but that is among the home folks. . . ." What was it, then, they wanted him to do? How much did the English want him to come, and the State Department want him to go? "For confidence I must be made sure of the demand for me," he concluded. "And I must see things planned pretty well ahead."[20]

He did not sit back and wait for Howland's next letter. Instead, he wrote to the Amherst Trustee, Eustace Seligman—New York law partner of Secretary of State Dulles—and began on his own to elicit the "demand" which was his prerequisite for making the English trip: "You may remember the boy you gave the gold cuff links to on his eightieth birthday and had the almost public altercation with before the Amherst Trustees on the value of permanent peace.[21] Well, he's in trouble now you may gather from the enclosed letters we have copied out for you. I might want to go to England on the errand they are talking about if the terms were right and the behest were on a high enough level. I thought it would be a good chance for you to make it up between us by interceding in my favor a little as you and I know you could away up where it would do some real good. You can tell by the tone of voice that I do and I don't care for the prospect. I surely don't want to bestir myself for anything but big stakes for anybody less than yourself, your partner Mr. Dulles, Mr. Whitney,[22] and Sherm Adams, not to mention the President. You know all about me. What with my barding around the colleges and the poems I publish in print and by word of mouth and the build-up I get nowadays on television my ambition is pretty well sated. Still if there is any further step upward in this you think I ought to take and can take, please tell me. . . ."[23]

The letters to Howland and Seligman were written on the first and second of January 1957. On the fourth, Frost wrote to Sherman Adams: "In return for my failure to do what you wanted me to do for you"—that is, to join the Eisenhower campaign organization—"I am going to tell you what I want you to do for me. It no doubt occurred to you when you thought it over that my silence might be interpreted as an embarrassed reluctance to be drawn out into the open as a political campaigner. I might be ever so much more anti–New Deal than you and yours ever thought of being, but you must agree that as a poet so-called I should be left to vote the right way privately and even secretly if I have to invoke the Fifth Amendment. Now for what if so minded you might do for me in reprisal: without making too much fuss about it you might look into this request I have from the State Department to visit England for myself and for my country this spring. What I need to know is how much I am wanted and at what level. It would be no small undertaking for me to go abroad. I should want to be sure it would be worth the trouble all around. I suppose advice is what I am after. . . ."[24]

As a result of Frost's prodding of Seligman and Adams, Secretary Dulles wrote him on February 12, urging that he "accept this new call upon your services as a distinguished representative of the American cultural scene." The Department of State and the American Embassy in London, Dulles added, "will wish to render all possible assistance in the event that you undertake this mission."[25]

But Frost was not yet satisfied. What he still wanted—and probably had wanted from the very first mention of this English trip—was something only the English themselves could provide. To round out the public career that had begun in England before the First World War, he wanted, from the most honorable of British universities, Oxford and Cambridge, honorary degrees.

To achieve this end, Frost now turned his attention from the State Department to England itself. Acting under his instructions, Kay Morrison spoke with Jack Sweeney, Curator of the Amy Lowell Poetry Collection of the Harvard University Library, and suggested that he write to *his* friends in England and Ireland to inform them Frost might be coming in the spring. This he did and, as Frost had hoped, word soon began filtering back that both Oxford and Cambridge universities, as well as the National University of Ireland, were considering giving him honorary degrees.

The time was now right to answer Dulles's letter: "Dear Mr. Dulles," Frost wrote on February 26, "Your letter helps me to a decision. I feel better with your assurance that the State Department and our Embassy will take care of me to see that I am kept reasonably busy. I wouldn't want to be shot off as an unguided missile. I have personal friends in England and Scotland, though not so many as once upon a time when I lived with them a while before the great wars. My books are over there with Jonathan Cape and I must have some readers. But I wouldn't want it to look as if I had just come over to laze around amiably on vacation. I wish you could tell Mr. Howland that it is not overwork that I fear. I want my time planned for. . . ." He concluded: "Some day I may be thanking you for this opportunity if it works out."[26]

It did work out, precisely as Frost had hoped—and planned. On March 9, Sir Douglas Veale, Registrar of Oxford University, wrote to inform him that "the Hebdomadal Council" had "resolved to propose to the Convocation of the University that the Degree of Doctor of Letters, honoris causa, be conferred upon you." Two days later, Sir Brian Downs, Vice-Chancellor of Cambridge University, sent a similar message.[27] Only two Americans before Frost had been accorded this rare double honor: Henry Wadsworth Longfellow in 1868, and James Russell Lowell in 1873. The good-will mission would now be, as well, a major personal triumph.

"Few things could give me the pleasure of such an honor from the country ('half my own') that published my very first book," Frost wrote to Sir Douglas on the day of his eighty-third birthday. "That was nearly fifty years ago when I was living and writing not fifty miles down the line from you in Beaconsfield. I shall look at it as a rounding out that we seldom get except in story books and none too often there. Third acts and last chapters are notoriously hard to write. So much for the degree; then there is the matter of the invitation from your Assistant to read and talk to your faculty; which I shall leave to my friend, Mrs. Morrison, to tend to when she has deciphered the signature. I very much like the idea of meeting the Faculty of the University as a troubador that way. It's as a sort of troubador I've been to so many of our American colleges. She'll be writing tomorrow. I am in a very happy frame of mind over this trip to England."[28]

A few weeks later, Frost shared his good news with Lawrance Thompson, whom he would shortly invite to serve as his companion on the English trip: "I wasnt going to come clear out into open company with it like something important enough to be made much of, but I did want to tell you the other night the pleasant news of what I am really sailing (by plane) for to England on May 19. I am after degrees at both Cambridge and Oxford. The one at Cambridge they have already publicly announced in The *Times* (London) so we are free to talk about that if we like. We shall be free to mention the other after April 25. I shall probably be taking a third at Dublin too if a date can be arranged. (I shall be sorry if I cant: you know how I have always felt about Ireland.)

"Al [Edwards] and Kay know all about it all. I know you will be one of the chiefest concerned. You will start thinking with me from scratch about its meaning in the story. It will sort of round off things I initiated with Mrs David Nutt in a small office in Bloomsbury among total strangers forty five years ago already almost too old to bet on.[29] There is that in it anyway. It will also sort of round off my rather great academic career in general. I have had about everything I can have in my own country. Now for the mother country. We are not talking of deserts. No triumphs for me. But satisfactions I dont see why I shouldnt be permitted. . . ."[30]

AN ENGLISH DIARY

While serving as Frost's traveling companion on his good-will mission to Great Britain, Lawrance Thompson kept a daily record of Frost's activities and conversations. This chapter is adapted from that record, and supplemented by material from other sources indicated in the Notes.

May 18–21: THE PLANS, as worked out, called for Frost to leave for England on Sunday, May 19, and for Thompson to follow next day, meeting him in London at his hotel—the elegant Connaught, just off Grosvenor Square.[1] All worked out as arranged. Frost came to New York on Saturday, May 18, and his publisher Alfred Edwards took him to his home in Connecticut for dinner and the night. Frost's granddaughter Elinor, Lesley's elder child, came over with her husband to see him. Next day they drove into New York City, had cocktails in the home of C. Waller Barrett—a steamship executive and major Frost-collector—and went to the Metropolitan restaurant for a farewell luncheon—Frederick B. Adams, Jr. (of the Morgan Library) being the only guest not attached to Holt. Edwards then drove Frost to Idlewild Airport, where he boarded a B.O.A.C. plane which left at 5 P.M.

Twelve hours later Frost landed in London, where he was met at Heathrow Airport by Dr. Carl Bode—newly appointed head of the U.S.I.S. program in London—and by newspaper reporters and cameramen. He was rushed to a room at the airport terminal for a short television interview which was shown that night on the BBC news. Then he was taken to the Connaught Hotel.

Monday night Thompson took a Pan American flight out of Idlewild, arriving Tuesday around noon, London time. He went directly to the U.S.I.S. Library in Grosvenor Square and there met the official in charge of Frost's English itinerary, Margaret Haferd. Having just spent three hours with Frost, she told Thompson where the poet could be found. Walking to the Connaught, Thompson saw Frost alone at a table in the hotel dining room, just raising knife and fork to a hearty steak. Slipping over to where Frost was seated, he sat down opposite him before Frost looked up. Laughing, Frost said, "It doesn't seem possible, does it?"

Frost's first public appearance, a reading at the Senate House of the University of London, was scheduled for 5:30 that afternoon. A half-hour before the performance, he was given a small reception at the Senate House attended, among others, by T. S. Eliot. "It would be a great disappointment if my more or less official return to England didn't mean furthering our acquaintance," Frost had written his one-time "enemy" on May 2, "and I should be less a respector of persons than I am if I didn't hope to give you before I get through with this here world the highest sign of my regard. You and I shot off at different tangents from almost the same pin wheel. We had America in common and we had Ezra in common though you had much more of him than I. If I was ever cross with you it was for leaving America behind too far and Ezra not far enough. But such things look less and less important as we age on. . . ."[2] At the reception, Frost asked Eliot if the letter had given him any offense. Said Eliot: "I didn't mind the scolding."

The reading, attended by an overflow crowd of some 700 people, began with a graceful introduction by Professor Jack Isaacs. "This is an important day in the history of the University of London," he said. "The uncrowned laureate of the American people has consented to address us. . . . In a sense, he is coming home."

At Isaacs's invitation Frost rose to speak, and was warmly applauded. He began by recalling the Poetry Bookshop of Harold Munro, and mentioned F. S. Flint—who, like Eliot, was present in the audience—as the first person in literary circles whom he had met during his visit to England in the period 1912–1915. Flint, he said, had introduced him to Ezra Pound, who had later sent him a calling card with the unusual invitation, "At home—sometimes." There was, said Frost, a "selfish generosity" in the way Pound had helped younger poets —including himself. His reminiscences continued with an account of the publication of his first book by the London publisher David Nutt, in 1913; his reasons for coming to England the year before; the poems and friendships he had written and formed during his four-year stay.[3]

T. S. Eliot, sitting in the third-row-center beside his wife and Frank Flint, was the object of Frost's gaze and the butt of some of his more pointed remarks. "I can understand," said Frost, "how someone of another nationality might wish to become an American. But I could never see how an American chose to become, for instance—a Canadian." It was the sort of wit the British seemed particularly to appreciate, on this and subsequent occasions. Eliot, of course, had given up his American citizenship to become a British subject. Once again, he seemed not to mind the "scolding."

Frost's Senate House performance concluded with a reading of several poems, including "The Witch of Coös." He delighted in demonstrating through his poems and otherwise various "voice ways" of American speech, so different from the British in inflection. After the world had been destroyed by atomic holocaust, he said (as he often did at home), there would be an interesting "tone of voice" in the survivor's remark, "*Was*n't that *some*pin!"[4]

He was in fine form, and the audience loved him. As he finished, the applause was sustained, and many came up to ask for autographs. His first performance was an auspicious beginning for the many more to come.

Wednesday, May 22: The day began at 10:15 when Thompson met Frost at the Connaught and took him to the American Embassy for a visit with Ambassador John Hay Whitney. Their meeting, from Frost's point of view, was a failure. The ambassador seemed uninterested in initiating conversation, so Frost spent most of their visit educating him about his namesake, John Hay, the author of *Pike County Ballads*. It was apparent to Frost that the ambassador did not care much for poetry—or for him.

The rest of the day was busy—too busy. After the meeting with Whitney, Frost met and addressed the American staff of the U.S.I.S. Library, then consulted with Carl Bode about his schedule. He was taken to lunch by the head of *Time-Life*, who wanted to arrange a trip to Gloucestershire for a feature story in *Life* magazine.[5] A *Life* photographer took Frost back to the Connaught, but instead of leaving he then stayed all afternoon. With no time to rest, Frost sent word that he would be unable to attend an evening reception for Bode at the U.S.I.S. Library. He later decided to go, but by the end of the day he was exhausted. Back at the hotel, he complained to Thompson of chest pains—and said he might have to give up the whole trip.

Thursday, May 23: The schedule for this day was built around Frost's talk and reading in the Senate House at Cambridge University. When Thompson arrived at noon at Frost's room, he found him fully recovered, packed and ready to go. They went downstairs for lunch in the hotel dining room, and Frost ordered something on the menu in French because the waiter had recommended it as a "very English dish." When it was put before him, it required only one look and one taste before Frost said, "This is nothing more than a boiled dinner with corned beef and cabbage. Waiter! I can't eat this. I'll pay for it, but bring me a steak."

By two o'clock they were off for Cambridge, in an Embassy car driven by a uniformed chauffeur. Dr. Bode accompanied them, but neither he nor his companions knew at which of the University's Colleges their host, Sir Basil Willey, might be found. Fortunately, the first person on campus they asked for directions was Mrs. Willey, who rode off on her bicycle to get her husband. He soon arrived on his bicycle and led them to Pembroke College.

Frost addressed an audience of some 400 students and others at 5:30 that afternoon. He had planned to begin his talk with some remarks on Puritanism, since, as he said, so many American Puritans had been educated at Cambridge. At Thompson's suggestion, however, he spoke on "the sound of sense," using as his first example "The Gift Outright." Expanding the remarks he had made at London University, he said that a dead language was one in which perhaps everything survived except the sound of sense—the tone of voice, or speech-way, of that language. Translation failed, he said, because speech-ways could not be translated.[6]

After the talk, Frost and his companions were taken back to Pembroke College for a sherry party and dinner—tenderloin steak and burgundy—with the faculty at the high table. They then adjourned for port, apples, nuts and cigars, to the faculty room, directly under the dormitory room in which Thomas Gray had lived as a Cambridge Fellow. At nine they were taken to the University Arms Hotel, where they spent the night.

Friday, May 24: This was a day of travel, from Cambridge to Durham for a weekend visit. Rising at 7:30, Frost and Thompson were driven to Peterborough, where they were to catch the Durham train. As they had some time to spare, they stopped in Peterborough at its well-known cathedral and decided to go inside. A service was in progress at the far end of the narrow nave; a full choir was performing. Frost listened to the music for a few moments, then turned to go out. As they entered the narthex Frost turned to Thompson and said, "I hope God hears 'em. They seem to be wailing, 'Have mercy on my soul.' Silly." (He had forgotten, perhaps, that he had expressed similar sentiments in his own *Masque of Mercy*.)

In Durham, Frost's lodging was "the bishop's room" in the Castle of University College. After resting there a few hours in the afternoon, he addressed a capacity audience at Appleby Lecture Theatre. Frost had complained that it would bother him if Thompson attended all his talks and readings, so Thompson stayed away. He later learned, however, that Frost's subject had been "the venture of the spirit into the material," the theme of many of his American lectures in the past year, and of his major poem of the same period, "Kitty Hawk."

To Frost, as Thompson knew, the story of Western civilization—specifically, American—was better than the story of Oriental civilization, which he saw as based on passivity, a retreat into pure spirituality. The Western approach, Frost held, had been an attempt to blend materialism with spirituality to the greatest possible extent. The "run" of civilization, for Frost, had been west-northwest, from the Tigris and Euphrates valleys, from Israel and Asia Minor, up and across the corner of the Mediterranean to Greece and Rome, up across Europe and England to the United States: west-northwest all the time. He saw America as the high point of civilization, and the flight of the Wright brothers from Kitty Hawk as the final leap, from the ground up into space.

Frost was still working on his poem, "Kitty Hawk," but he

had already published one version of it as his Christmas poem for 1956. A key passage in the 1956—and the final—version read:

Pulpiteers will censure
Our instinctive venture
Into what they call
The material
When we took that fall
From the apple tree.
But God's own descent
Into flesh was meant
As a demonstration
That the supreme merit
Lay in risking spirit
In substantiation.
Westerners inherit
A design for living
Deeper into matter—
Not without due patter
Of a great misgiving.
All the science zest
To materialize
By on-penetration
Into earth and skies
(Don't forget the latter
Is but further matter)
Has been West-Northwest.
If it was not wise,
Tell me why the East
Seemingly has ceased
From its long stagnation
In mere meditation.
What is all this fuss
To catch up with us?
Can it be to flatter
Us with emulation?[7]

After Frost's afternoon lecture, he attended a sherry party in the Senior Common Room of the St. Cuthbert Society, then a dinner in his honor at the high table of the Castle. He later returned to the Senior Common Room, where, as decanters of port, Madeira, and claret were passed around, he entertained his hosts for some two hours with a typical witty monologue.

Saturday, May 25: The plan for the weekend was for Frost to do little but rest, in preparation for the activities of the days ahead. On Saturday morning he toured Durham with Thompson and Colleer Abbott, a retired professor. They began, at Abbott's instance, with Durham Cathedral, then drove down to the Prebends Bridge, where Thompson took photographs. One of these Frost himself asked Thompson to take. It was a picture of Frost reading an inscription on the bridge, a passage from Scott describing the group of medieval buildings on the bluff across the river: "Half church of God / Half castle 'gainst the Scot."

Abbott was not a complete stranger to Frost. When the University of Durham awarded Frost an honorary Litt.D. *in absentia* in 1952, it was Abbott who had proposed him for the degree.[8]

After lunch at high table in the Great Hall of Durham Castle, Frost adjourned to the Senior Common Room and talked there, briefly, with students and members of the faculty. Then Abbott and Thompson took Frost to his room, where they left him for an afternoon nap. By accident, Thompson picked up Frost's topcoat instead of his own, and he was down in the Great Hall before he realized his mistake. Returning to Frost's room, he exchanged Frost's coat for his and prepared to leave a second time. But Frost stopped him. "Siddown," he said. They then shared two hours of good talk.

At five o'clock that afternoon Frost and Thompson went out for a walk, so that Frost could mail some letters. On the way back from the post office he bought a box of chocolates and four bottles of Schweppes ginger beer. Back at the Castle Thompson left him to prepare for a university dinner, to which Thompson himself had not been invited.

Sunday, May 26: After spending most of the day sightseeing with Abbott in the countryside around Durham, Frost attended a garden party that had been arranged for him by the St. Cuthbert Society, late in the afternoon. Preferring a change of pattern, he declined to take dinner at high table and dined instead with Thompson at the Three Tuns Hotel. They went afterward to the home of Professor Abbott, who offered Frost Jamaica rum. To Thompson's surprise Frost accepted, saying he would like that if he could fix it himself. He took a full jigger of rum in an old-fashioned glass, added some Rose lime juice, two spoonfuls of sugar, ice, and water. This was, for Frost, a rather powerful drink. Abbott politely offered him another, and Frost accepted. By the time he had finished the second drink, he was visibly "under the influence."

At 10:30 Abbott drove Frost and Thompson back to the Castle. Thompson was prepared to carry Frost up to his room on his back, if necessary, but Frost was so embarrassed by his condition that he sent his companion home. Thompson, knowing how liquor had upset Frost's system in the past, wondered how he would be tomorrow when they returned, in the morning, to London.

Monday, May 27: Frost seemed to suffer no ill effects from his drinking the night before, and he was packed and ready to go when Thompson and Abbott picked him up at nine. He had autographed a copy of the Penguin edition of his poems as a gift to Mrs. Shaw, keeper of the Castle. By mistake, however, as he came downstairs, he gave the book to the wrong woman, one who stood on duty as guide to conduct sightseers through the Castle. Thompson saw no point in telling Frost afterward of his error.

In London by four that afternoon, Frost complained that his stomach was upset (a result, in all likelihood, of his drinking the night before), and announced that he would be unable to attend the tea to be given for him by Mrs. Whitney, wife of the ambassador. He was well enough later, however, to attend a dinner in his honor at the Athenaeum Club, given by John Lehmann and others on the staff of *London Magazine*. The guests included C. Day Lewis, who had edited the Penguin edition of Frost's poems.[9]

Tuesday, May 28: In the morning Frost met with Margaret Haferd, and interrupted a review of his schedule to educate her on his religious belief. "I tell them," Frost said, "that in matters of religion I'm like one of these new cars. I look like a convertible, but I'm actually a hard-top. I don't convert." Thompson remembered having heard Frost say that first during a ride from Ripton to Middlebury with Herbert Kenny of the Boston *Globe*. Hyde Cox had been the driver, and the car in which they were riding had matched Frost's description of himself.

After dining at the Garrick Club with Rupert Hart-Davis, Frost returned to the Connaught and happened to see Adlai Stevenson, the unsuccessful presidential candidate in the last election, crossing the lobby. Stevenson had just come from Cambridge, where he had received an honorary degree, and Frost chatted with him about why they were in England. "What did you tell them?" Frost asked, of the Cambridge ceremony. "Did you say anything about Dulles?" "Oh," said Stevenson, "I mentioned no names."

Frost had planned to open the annual meeting of the National Book League that afternoon, but he withdrew from the arrangement. Still bothered by his indisposition, he attended a dinner at London University, and went to bed early.

Wednesday, May 29: An expedition to some London bookshops was the order of the morning. The first stop was at J. & E. Bumpus, Ltd., Booksellers to Her Majesty the Queen, in Oxford Street, where the proprietor, Mr. John G. Wilson, was waiting for Frost in his office. Thompson later learned that Frost had recognized Wilson: he had called on the bookseller with Edward Thomas, in 1914, when Wilson had a small bookshop in Queens. Before leaving for another bookshop, Hatchard's, near Piccadilly, Frost bought books of poetry by Thomas Blackburn, Kathleen Raine, Stephen Spender, Edwin Muir, W. H. Auden, C. Day Lewis, and Louis MacNeice.

The next item of business was a luncheon with William Henry Beveridge, architect of the British "welfare state," at the House of Lords. Frost and Thompson were met at the Connaught by an American Embassy chauffeur, who escorted them out to the curb and into a Humber Pullman limousine bearing a sticker indicating, incidentally to its present assignment, its right to enter the grounds of the "Stassen Disarmament Conference." At the House of Lords, a red-uniformed attendant opened the car door with great elegance, and a doorman at the receiving room informed Frost, "Lord Beveridge is waiting for you." Presently the seventy-eight-year-old Beveridge came forward, thin, white-haired, limping, with a reddish complexion and smiling broadly. Thompson was not included

The poet at Bread Loaf, August 1938
(Photograph by Bernard DeVoto)

The Bread Loaf Writers' Conference staff, 1939. *Top row, left to right*: Fletcher Pratt, Gorham Munson, Herbert Agar, Richard L. Brown, Bernard DeVoto, Robeson Bailey, Herschel Brickell. *Middle row*: John Gassner, Louis Untermeyer, Frost, Edith Mirrielees, Theodore Morrison. *Foreground*: Mrs. Gassner, Mrs. Pratt, Kathleen Morrison, Mrs. Agar, Mrs. Bailey (Courtesy of Middlebury College News Bureau)

Frost's cabin at the Homer Noble farm, Ripton, Vermont (Photograph by Bernard M. Cannon)

Dartmouth's George Ticknor Fellow in Literature, with Gillie, 1944
(Courtesy of Dartmouth College Library)

Sitting for Walker Hancock, 1950
(Photograph by Hyde Cox)

A birthday gathering at Crow Island, March 1950. *Left to right*: Robert Morrison, Alfred C. Edwards, Frost, Mrs. Walker Hancock, Anne Morrison, Mrs. Erastus Hewitt, Mr. Hewitt, Kathleen Morrison, Peter Hewitt, Theodore Morrison, Mrs. Edwards, Mr. Hancock
(Photograph by Hyde Cox)

The eightieth birthday dinner, Amherst, Massachusetts, March 1954.
Left to right: President Charles Cole, Thornton Wilder, Frost, Archibald MacLeish, Louis Untermeyer, Hyde Cox, Curtis Canfield
(Courtesy Amherst College News Service)

On the way to accept an honorary degree from Cambridge University, June 1957
(Photograph by Howard Sochurek, Time-Life Picture Agency, © Time Inc.)

At the inauguration of President John F. Kennedy, January 1961
(Photograph by George Silk, Time-Life Picture Agency, © Time Inc.)

With Soviet Premier Nikita Khrushchev, Gagra, 1962
(Courtesy of Stewart Udall)

A stop on "the last go-round," November 1962
(Photograph by Joe Clark)

Frost's last Thanksgiving at the Homer Noble farm, 1962
(Photograph by Anne Morrison Smyth)

in the luncheon, but later, while Frost stepped into the gallery to listen briefly to the House debate, Beveridge approached him to say they had had a lovely time. "I never suspected," said Beveridge, "he would be so witty."

At half past five Frost and Thompson were taken to a fine old eighteenth-century house in Bedford Square for a champagne party arranged in Frost's honor by his English publisher, Jonathan Cape. Among those present were Irving Kristol, co-editor with Stephen Spender of *Encounter* magazine, and C. Day Lewis. While Lewis and Thompson chatted, in walked T. S. Eliot and his wife, in full evening dress. They were, it seems, going on after this to some other occasion, and had asked if they might be permitted to look in on their way. Eliot was wearing his Order of Merit, which hung from a ribbon around his neck. Lewis took one look before saying, to Thompson, "Why didn't somebody say to wear medals? I would have worn mine."

After the champagne party Frost went on to a dinner party, given in his honor by Miss Eunice Frost of Penguin Books. Here the guests included Mr. and Mrs. Howard of Jonathan Cape, Mr. and Mrs. Knittel (Mrs. Knittel being the celebrated German actress Luise Rainer), and the poet-critic G. S. Fraser. Thompson got on so well with Miss Frost that, when they sat down to dinner at Brusa's, she seated him on one side of her, and Frost on the other. After one pleasant exchange with Thompson, she turned to see if all was going well with Frost. He was not talking to anyone, so she tried to include Frost in the conversation by asking him to tell her more about his traveling companion. Frost answered curtly, in a sullen voice, "He's a charming man, but charm is not enough. Is it?" Later, Thompson came upon Frost in the cloak room, reciting, to a tearfully enraptured (and not quite sober) listener, his poem "Come In."

Thursday, May 30: On this day Frost made his second excursion from London, for a two-day visit to the great manufacturing center in Lancashire, the fourth largest city in England, Manchester. The trip began from Euston Station, where, on Thursday morning, Frost and Thompson boarded The Comet, the London-to-Manchester train. Shown by a porter to their reserved seats in a six-passenger, first-class compartment, Frost said, at once, "I don't want to sit here with these people.

Let's see if we can find another, empty." The porter took them up to the next car, and found another compartment without reservation tags or occupants.

When Thompson returned from buying Frost newspapers on the station platform, he found that two passengers had taken seats in their cabin. One, a short, red-faced man, was talking to Frost about his experiences as an Army doctor in India and at the Anzio beachhead. The other, with whom Frost also conversed, was a tall, dark-haired, attractive lady who was busily engaged in writing something in a notebook. When the train got under way, the doctor rose and departed, and Frost turned his attention to the woman. "Do you think," he asked Thompson, "she's writing something for the Manchester *Guardian*?" Thompson had no idea, so Frost directed the question to her: "Are you a reporter for the Manchester *Guardian*?" She looked up, and they began talking. No, she said, she was not a reporter. She was the wife of Mr. Bromley-Davenport, a Tory Member of Parliament, was an American by birth, and had been educated at Bryn Mawr. She had a son attending college in New York.

This gave Frost an opportunity to tell her about himself. He told her he was in England to pick up several honorary degrees, that he had had lunch with Lord Beveridge in the House of Lords a few days ago, that he had told Secretary Dulles thus and so, and when he got to Ireland he was going to stay with Ambassador Taft. His apparent strategy was to supply her with enough information so that she would finally say, "Oh, you must be Robert Frost," but she never did.

During the same train ride, Thompson found and showed to Frost an article in the *Spectator* by Richard Rovere, whose subject was a recent "anthology" in *Good Housekeeping* magazine.[10] The anthology was entitled "Dwight D. Eisenhower's Favorite Poetry, Prose and Prayers," and Frost thought Rovere's cruelly satiric piece on the President's intellectual tastes highly amusing. Among Eisenhower's personal favorites, Rovere reported, was an aphorism by "a former Democratic Congressman": "Democracy is a method of getting ahead without leaving any of us behind." In his Manchester talk, without referring to the Rovere piece or to President Eisenhower, Frost said our lives were lived in terms of contradictions, and we could choose between these two: "Every man for himself, and the devil take the hindmost," or, "Every man for everyone else, that there may be no hindmost."

Frost's afternoon lecture, which began at 5:30, was held in the largest available auditorium of Manchester University, the 500-seat Chemistry Theatre. Even here, the house was filled with people sitting in the aisles and standing in the rear. In another lecture hall nearby, an overflow audience of 300 more listened to Frost's talk over a public-address system.

One of the subjects he touched on in his talk was his friendship with the Welsh poet Edward Thomas, who had died at Vimy Ridge in 1914: "Edward Thomas was one of the greatest friends of my life and I am always hoping to hear that more people know about him. That is one of the wishes you have for a poet, a gentle poet, that he may be thought of." He added that he was going to collaborate with Thomas's friend, Eleanor Farjeon—whom he had met in London and would meet again later—on another edition of Thomas's poetry, "to see if we can give it another little shove." He had, he said, persuaded Thomas to turn from prose to poetry. "That was the only time I ever influenced anybody. I taught school but I have never succeeded in teaching anybody to be a poet."[11]

Friday, May 31: After a morning of letter-writing, Frost attended a luncheon in his honor at the Manchester Luncheon Club, whose members comprised a "Who's Who" of the Manchester area. Among the guests was the Lord Bishop of Manchester, with whom Frost conversed more than with anyone else. The Bishop began by congratulating him on all the honors that were lately coming his way. "Yes," said Frost, "to have so many come so fast seems almost providential." "I notice the 'almost,' " observed the bishop. "Yes," Frost repeated, "almost."

Their talk continued on religious matters, and Frost made it clear to the bishop that he had no use for all the pomp and ritual of church ceremonies. Toward the end of their conversation, the bishop said, "I believe someday you will see the light." "Oh I see the light now," Frost replied, "but I just don't pay as much attention to it as you do."

Following the small luncheon about 200 Club members assembled in the Lesser Free Trade Hall, where Frost spoke once again on "the venture into materiality." When he emerged, to wait for his host to come around with his car, a rather gushy and sentimental woman came walking around the corner with her daughter in tow. "Oh there he is," she said excitedly. "Is this the poet? Oh I do so want to *look* at the poet. Come here, dear, and look. Shake hands. Oh thank you." And away they went.

Saturday, June 1: Frost's plans for this day originally called for no more than his return, with Thompson, to London, but soon after their arrival in Manchester Frost had arranged to add a visit to one of his first English champions, Sir John Squire, once editor of the famous literary magazine *London Mercury*. Back in London by midafternoon, they returned to the Connaught, and there were joined by Frost's granddaughter, Lesley Lee Francis, who had come from Spain to spend a few days with her grandfather. After a short rest, they all set out in a chauffeured Embassy car for Diamond Cottage, Jack Squire's home in Rushlake Green, Sussex.

The cottage, on the upper side of the "green," was an ancient structure with thin red tiles for roof and sidings, and diamond-shaped windows of leaded glass. As they approached it, they saw that the door was open. Frost knocked and Sir John shouted, from a room to the left of the door, "Come in, Robert." He had seen them coming.

Sir John was seated at a table, a book in hand, with a great pile of unopened mail spread out before him. He was a sight. His Whitmanesque bald head gave way to a yellow-white flowing beard. Behind his tortoise-shell glasses his eyes appeared rheumy. He wore a baggy, loose-knit sweater, over a dirty white shirt that was open at the throat. He sat in a pair of worn and dirty gray corduroy trousers, with low sneakers on his sockless feet. What was worse, when he began to speak, his slurred voice suggested heavy drinking.

When they had all shaken hands, Squire bellowed, "Martha, bring another chair." Back came a brusque answer from the kitchen, "Go in the other room. More chairs in there." With difficulty, Squire rose from his chair and followed the visitors into a room with a fireplace, a bed on the opposite wall, a large stuffed chair and one with a straight back. Sir John shuffled to the bed, and collapsed in a sitting position on one side of it. Frost sat on the stuffed chair beside him. Presently Martha appeared, with a beer keg for Thompson to sit on. Introduced by Sir John as his "secretary," she served drinks. Then, as Frost sat close to his friend, the two old men began to reminisce.

Squire could remember, he said, that they had first met at one of T. E. Hulme's soirées, back around 1913 or 1914. Then, in the next few years, he remembered printing several of Frost's poems in the *Mercury.* Frost recalled that when Squire had just been graduated from Cambridge, he had used as a pseudonym the name "Solomon Eagle," in signing poems and reviews and brilliant parodies that he published in the *New Statesman.*

Before they had talked long—with Thompson and Lee Francis occasionally repeating for Frost Squire's heavily English-accented remarks—both men were groping sadly for a common ground for conversation. With too much laughter they remembered an occasion in Ann Arbor, Michigan, when Lesley, during a 1921 visit by Squire and a friend named Herbert to the States, had accidentally served them wine that turned out to be vinegar.[12]

When the hour of their visit was over, Frost and his companions took their leave of the pathetic old man. Squire had tried his best to put up a brave front, but he knew that it was transparent. As the party drove back to London Frost was subdued and saddened. His once-brilliant and dynamic friend had fallen on hard times. Ten years younger than Frost, Squire was now the mere shadow of what he had once been.

Sunday, June 2: In the morning, Frost was to go with Eleanor Farjeon, once a close friend of Edward Thomas, on a visit to the late poet's widow, Helen. When Thompson went up to tell Frost that Miss Farjeon was waiting with the Embassy car, Frost hoarsely announced, however, that he had caught a sore throat yesterday on the way back from Sussex, and thus could not go. Nevertheless, he dressed hurriedly and went downstairs, to greet Miss Farjeon and make his apologies. After her departure, Frost's symptoms improved so markedly that Thompson's suspicions were aroused. He knew Frost had dreaded to see Helen Thomas, having never quite forgiven her for saying too much in her autobiography about her sexual conduct with her husband before and after their marriage.

Frost remained in his room at the Connaught for the rest of the day, nursing his sore throat.[13]

Monday, June 3: When Thompson called on Frost at eleven A.M., he found the poet still in his nightgown, complaining that he was sick. His face was so pale, his words so slurred and unconnected, that Thompson suggested a doctor be called in. No, said Frost, doctors were no good. What could they do for a sore throat?

He allowed Thompson to take his pulse, which was so weak that a doctor's visit seemed, to Thompson, imperative. Before calling the Embassy, he asked Frost if he had taken any medicine for his throat. Frost said yes, he had taken some last night around one or two o'clock. What, then, had he taken? Oh, said Frost, quite a lot of morphine pills, all day, and then when he couldn't sleep two sleeping pills during the night.

The doctor, an American from Montana, confirmed what Thompson feared. The effect of the morphine and sleeping pills was synergetic—each reinforcing the strength of the other. Pneumonia, under such circumstances, was a real danger, for the slowing of the respiratory rate permitted fluids to accumulate in the lungs.

Finding no evidence of respiratory congestion, the doctor suggested that Frost simply spend the next twenty-four hours in bed. "Fine," said Frost, "I knew there was nothing you could do for me."

But the situation was not that simple. This was the day he was supposed to go to Oxford. In less than twenty-four hours, he was to be accepting his first honorary degree.

It was decided that, if he slept in the car all the way, he could probably make it to Oxford later in the day. Another consideration now was what to do about his luncheon appointment with Mrs. Michael Roberts, literary editor of the *New Statesman*, and the poet Thomas Blackburn. Frost had the answer. He would sleep for half an hour, then see them briefly in his anteroom. Thompson would wake him up.

When Thompson returned, Frost was already getting dressed. As he did so, he explained to Thompson that Einstein was all wrong; anyone with a brain could see that. The whole question of whether the universe was spending to nothing or whether new energy was coming in was just a matter of belief. Frost believed (he continued) new energy was indeed coming in. If we could only find the place where it was doing so, we would really be in business.

As he listened, Thompson wondered where Frost's new energy was coming in. That miracle seemed to be taking place before his eyes.

As predicted, Frost slept all the way to Oxford. They drove directly to the Warden's Lodge of Wadham College, where Sir Maurice Bowra awaited them. Sleeping some two more hours after his arrival, Frost was well enough recovered by evening to take dinner with Sir Maurice at the high table and to attend a reception in his honor later that evening.

Tuesday, June 4: The guests at the Monday night reception were mainly British (including W. H. Auden, since 1956 Professor of Poetry at Oxford), but among the Americans was Frost's young friend from Dartmouth College, Edward Lathem, now at Oxford for a year of post-graduate study. On Tuesday morning Lathem took Frost on a stroll around the city and its ancient buildings.

One of their first stops was Bodleian Library, where Lathem showed Frost a newspaper article from July 1869 containing an account of the Oxford Convocation for Longfellow. "They say the only thing he beats me at," Frost observed, "is being buried in Poet's Corner. So if somebody will knock me over the head while I'm in England I may come even with him."

Later, they paused beneath the windows of the room Shelley had occupied as a student at University College. Lathem recounted the old story of how Shelley wrote an atheistic article for which he was expelled from Oxford despite his vigorous denials of authorship. "Darn liar," Frost snorted. "He's like our Communists. Don't have the spunk to stand up like men and say what they are. They don't have to say they're Communists. They can say they're Marxists."

At the beautiful gardens of St. John's College (of which Lathem was a member) Frost stopped to admire and identify the many varieties of flowers and trees. "Gee, it's wonderful. Hmmph. Great. It must have cost them a lot. That looks like a beech—weeping beech, I guess it is. Beech. . . . That's laburnum, that yellow one. We don't have that in Vermont." In one particularly inviting shady recess he asked Lathem, "Are you allowed to make love here?" Lathem replied that all depended on how far you went. "It's LTD," Frost chuckled, "Love limited."

After an hour Frost declared the walk at an end. "Let's not go too far," he said. "We might get educated."[14]

At two, the Oxford Convocation ceremony began. Preceded by macebearers and escorted by Sir Maurice Bowra and the

Acting Public Orator and Principal of Jesus College, J. T. Christie, Frost walked in his red and gray academic robe to the Divinity School, where a small crowd was waiting. The citation was read by Christie, in Latin, and Frost seemed to be following it. He perked up when the statement occurred that "he would rather make a claim on our regard simply as a farmer and as a poet." The citation continued, "In truth he has for so long now devoted himself to the arts of the poet and the husbandman that his work has passed into his character, nay, into his features which reflect the genius of a poet, the sturdiness of the farmer, and the peace of old age." When that part of the ritual was over, Frost was permitted to walk forward, alone, to be greeted by the chancellor. As the ceremony ended, the small procession filed out, followed by the small crowd. Several people came up to congratulate him. Then he went back with Sir Maurice to the Warden's lodgings, to take a nap.

That afternoon, at five, Frost was ushered into a large hall called the Taylorian (or Taylor Institute) for what would be one of his best talks of the English trip. Most Oxonians had forgone the Convocation ceremony, but they attended this phase of the Oxford visit in full force. After long and enthusiastic applause when he entered the Taylorian, he began, smiling, "That's what they call British coldness."

He continued: "Little did I think when I was making a little book or two in Ledbury almost fifty years ago that I would be returning one day to all these honors. And I didn't write the poetry to get here either. . . . I'm not here to make exorbitant claims for poetry, lest they seem personal, but one thing must be said about poetry—it's the ultimate. The nearest thing to it is penultimate, even religion. Poetry is the thoughts of the heart. I'm sure that's what Catullus meant by *mens animi*. Poetry is hyphenated, like so many British names. It's a thought-felt thing. Poetry is the thing that laughs and cries about everything as it's going on—and makes you take it. A momentary stay against confusion. . . ."

After his preliminary remarks, he turned to saying his poems: first "It Is Almost the Year Two Thousand," then "Stopping by Woods on a Snowy Evening," "Tree at My Window," "The Road Not Taken," "Mending Wall," "Never Again Would Birds' Song Be the Same," "Provide, Provide," "The Star-Splitter," "Choose Something Like a Star," "One More Brevity," "Happiness Makes Up in Height for What It Lacks in Length,"

"Birches," "The Gift Outright," "Departmental," and finally, "A Considerable Speck."

As he finished after an hour and a half, Nevil Coghill of Merton College thanked him from the floor, saying it had been a very memorable, amusing, and very moving experience. To sustained applause, Frost then was escorted up the central aisle by Sir Maurice Bowra. Later that evening, he was guest of honor of the English faculty for cocktails and dinner at Exeter College.

Wednesday, June 5: The schedule for the day was relatively light. At noon, Frost addressed the American Association (of Rhodes Scholars), with W. H. Auden relaying questions from the floor. Later he dined with Lord and Lady Beveridge and their invited guests. Finally he drove (with Thompson, Lee Francis, and a reporter and photographer from *Time-Life*) to Cheltenham where, after a visit with his old friend Jack Haines, he retired to prepare for next day's tour of "old haunts" in the Dymock region of Gloucestershire.[15]

Thursday, June 6: Frost's visit to the Dymock region, where his family had lived for nine months before their return to America in 1915, began at Wilfrid Gibson's one-time home, the Old Nailshop, known to its present occupants as Wayside. The little thatch-roofed cottage had scarcely changed since the days when Gibson had entertained the Frosts, the Edward Thomases, Rupert Brooke, the Lascelles Abercrombies, and John Drinkwater in the sitting room Gibson had commemorated in his poem, "The Golden Room":

Do you remember that still summer evening
When, in the cosy cream washed living room
Of the Old Nailshop, we all talked and laughed—
Our neighbors from The Gallows, Catherine
And Lascelles Abercrombie; Rupert Brooke;
Eleanor and Robert Frost, living awhile
At Little Iddens, who'd brought over with them
Helen and Edward Thomas? In the lamplight
We talked and laughed; but, for the most part, listened
While Robert Frost kept on and on and on,
In his slow New England fashion, for our delight,
Holding us with shrewd turns and racy quips,
And the rare twinkle of his grave blue eyes.

We sat there in the lamplight, while the day
Died from the rose-latticed casements, and the plovers
Called over the low meadows, till the owls
Answered them from the elms, we sat and talked—

Now, a quick flash from Abercrombie, now,
A murmured dry half-heard aside from Thomas;
Now, a clear laughing word from Brooke; and then
Again Frost's rich and ripe philosophy,
That had the body and twang of good draught cider
And poured as clear a stream. . . .[16]

Could Frost answer in the affirmative the question posed in Gibson's first line? "You wouldn't think all those great people could fit in here," he said as he looked around, "but we had a cosy time."

After he had explored upstairs and down, Frost walked around the house to look at the field behind it. "I can remember in those fields back there," he said, "I used to entertain them all by throwing spears. I guess I've thrown stones in more rivers and oceans than any man, and I still cut spears when I see a straight one. They always thought I learned that from the Indians. How hard it is to understand people. They thought we lived close to the Indians—had them in our backyard. They used to think I was a real wild man from the West. . . . It's somethin' to see, isn't it—again. Just think, it's—we were here in 1914—that's pretty near fifty years, isn't it. Half a century."

From the Old Nailshop Frost and his companions drove the two miles up the road to Little Iddens, the house the Frost family had occupied in Gloucestershire. "Gee," Frost said as they approached, "it's further than I remember. We used to walk any distance, go out together, the six of us. It seemed such a short distance then." He stopped and tried the old pump by the back corner of the house, and said it must be the same one he had used in 1914. The kitchen stove interested him even more: "I used to get down on my knees to that stove—prayed to it. Not easy to get things going in it. Awful hard to get hot. But we had a nice time here."

Frost's next stop was at Oldfields, the house where Edward Thomas and his family had lived on the eve of the First World War. Frost got out of the car and began to approach the house, but he quickly stopped and turned back. There was no need, he said, to go in. Instead, he surveyed a nearby orchard, and told how he and Thomas heard of the outbreak of the war in which Thomas would soon perish. "Edward and I were sitting on a stile right near here on a starlit night," he said, "the night word came that the firing had started. It was August 4, 1914 . . . and we had word and were talking about it, and wondering if you could hear the guns on the continent from here. . . . That started it and it hasn't finished yet. I said before I went home, 'This will be a fifty-years' war,'—and it will." As the party left Oldfields, Frost regained the composure he had temporarily lost. "All is well, all is well," he repeated. "It's a pretty country, nice people."[17]

After a cursory glance at The Gallows, former home of the Lascelles Abercrombies, Frost dropped off his local guide, visited again briefly with Sir John Squire in Cheltenham, lunched at the Greenway Hotel, and returned by car to London. Forty-five minutes after his arrival, he was on his way with Thompson to a dinner at the Savile Club, arranged in his honor by Spender and Kristol of *Encounter* magazine. Besides Spender, Kristol, Thompson, and Frost, the guests included C. Day Lewis, Dwight MacDonald, Graham Greene, Isaiah Berlin, Arthur Waley, and Laurie Lee. There was one other guest as well, but as introductions were made Frost missed his name.

After dinner, while coffee and brandy were being served, Spender made a short speech of welcome, and invited Frost to tell the group something of his first visit to England, back in the period 1912–1915. Frost was glad to oblige. As he began to speak, however, the man whose name he had not caught began to show his amusement first by quietly smiling, then by chuckles, finally by loud and apparently deprecatory laughter. Frost ignored the stranger as long as he could, but his annoyance at last got the better of him. "What are you giggling at?" he scolded. The unknown man—who had meant no harm but was merely amused at Frost's autobiographical narrative—made no answer. It was plain that he was deeply embarrassed.

When the party broke up, the as-yet-nameless man was first to leave. As he bade goodnight to the guest of honor, Frost said, "I didn't get your name." "Forster," the man replied. "E. M. Forster." "Oh, hell," said Frost, now in his own agony of embarrassment. He went on to say that he knew Forster's work well, and had just been reading his latest book, *Marianne Thornton: A Domestic Biography.* Forster listened, and left.

Thompson noticed Forster talking darkly with Spender just after he parted from Frost. He was not surprised when Spender approached him a few moments later to make a request of him. Forster's feelings had been hurt, Spender explained, by what had occurred at the dinner. Could Thompson arrange to have Frost send Forster a note of apology? Thompson said he would try, and Frost told him later that he would be happy to write the note Spender had suggested. He really *was* sorry for the misunderstanding.

Friday, June 7: Frost spent the morning working on his note of apology to Forster. He canceled his only important engagement of the day, a sitting for the sculptor Jacob Epstein, explaining that he did not feel well.

Saturday, June 8: A day of rest for Frost, his only activity being a dinner at the home of Mr. and Mrs. C. Day Lewis.

Sunday, June 9: Another day of rest, Frost's only activities being a luncheon at the home of Mr. and Mrs. T. S. Eliot—Rosamund Lehmann also present—and a visit to his rooms by Mrs. Lascelles Abercrombie, for tea.

Monday, June 10: On this day, the English holiday Whitmonday, Frost went with C. Day Lewis, Lee Francis, and Thompson to Hyde Park, where they joined hundreds of Londoners in watching the famous Sheepdog Trials. His only other activity was an afternoon visit with Eleanor Farjeon at her London apartment.

Tuesday, June 11: Frost had become increasingly restive during the past few days, apparently feeling that he was not being paid sufficient attention by his British hosts. On this day the lull ended, with three activities including one of the most satisfying of the entire trip.

At noon he went to the huge B.B.C. office building, and recorded a half-hour question-and-answer session with C. Day Lewis as interviewer.

At five he gave a reading to the Poetry Society, attended by an overflow audience.

At 7:30 he left for the major event of the day, a formal dinner in his honor at the English Speaking Union of the Commonwealth.

This last was sponsored by Books Across the Sea, a committee within the English Speaking Union, and hostess Beatrice Warde, Chairperson of the BAS Committee, had invited some twenty guests mostly from the ranks of the Union. T. S. Eliot had agreed to serve as toastmaster, and the few Americans present included Frost's Dartmouth friend, Edward Lathem.

The after-dinner toasts began in the traditional English way. Eliot rose to his feet, raised his glass, and prepared to salute "The Queen." But Frost, sitting beside Mrs. Eliot at the opposite end of the long table, could not, because of his deafness, quite make out what Eliot was saying. When the guests rose, glass in hand, he quickly glanced down the table at Lathem, pointed to himself, and asked by a quizzical look whether it was he who at this point was being drunk to. Lathem shook his head No, and made a little motion toward his head, indicating the shape of a crown. Frost immediately understood and quickly got up, too, to join in the toast to Her Majesty.

Eliot took in this pantomime exchange, and realized that Frost, seated at such a distance, would not hear what was to be uttered thereafter. Accordingly, with great thoughtfulness, he announced that he was now going to say just a few things about the guest of honor, and invited Frost to sit by his side while he did so. After the change of seating was accomplished, Eliot began to speak:

"Mr. Frost," he said, "you have already heard a great number of speeches in your honor in the last few weeks, both in English and in Latin. I wish that I *could* make a speech in your honor in Latin, because it would, perhaps, cover up other imperfections, if my Latin was good enough. But I want to spare you that. I am merely here to propose your health, in my capacity as having been a Past-President, during the war, of Books Across the Sea. And it is, I think, appropriate that the first dinner party, I think it is, to be held in this Page Library should be a dinner given by Books Across the Sea to Robert Frost, for Robert Frost's books are very much across the sea, in both directions.

"I would like before proposing a toast merely to drop one or two grains of incense before you.

"Mr. Frost, I never heard your name until I came to this country. I heard it first from Ezra Pound of all people. He told me about you with great enthusiasm. I gathered that you were a protégé of his of whom he expected a good deal. At the same time, I gathered that your work, or what had appeared at that time, was not in Ezra Pound's opinion required reading for *me*. He may have been right, at that time, because I was still in a formative period, and goodness knows what would have happened if you had influenced me at that stage. But, you know, as one gets older, one cares less about movements and tendencies and groups. We all have our own idiom and metric and subject matter, but I have long come to feel that there are only two kinds of poetry—good and bad. And the bad poetry can be very much of one's own type, and the good poetry can be of a very different type.

"Mr. Frost is one of the good poets, and I might say, perhaps, *the* most eminent, the most distinguished, I must call it, Anglo-American poet now living. I have a special weakness, perhaps—no I shouldn't call it a weakness—I have a special understanding of a great deal of his work. Of course, I also have the New England background. But I think that there are two kinds of local feeling in poetry. There is one kind which makes that poetry only accessible to people who had the same background, to whom it means a great deal. And there is another kind which can go with universality: the relation of Dante to Florence, of Shakespeare to Warwickshire, of Goethe to the Rhineland, the relation of Robert Frost to New England. He has that universality. And I think that the beginning of his career, and the fact that his first publication and reputation was made in this country, and that he is now hailed in this country universally as the most distinguished American poet, points to that fact.

"Ladies and gentlemen, I give you Robert Frost."

Frost was moved by Eliot's remarks almost to tears. When he rose to acknowledge the tribute, the first thing he said was, "There's nobody living in either country that I'd rather hear that from."[18]

Wednesday, June 12: With Lee Francis, Edward Lathem, and Thompson, Frost left London and went to Cambridge University. He dined there with Sir Brian W. Downs, Vice-Chancellor of Cambridge University.

Thursday, June 13: After a morning stroll with Edward Lathem through the gardens of Immanuel College, Frost was escorted by Sir Basil Willey to the Senate House of King's College. There, after donning his red Cambridge gown, he was one of eight men granted Cambridge honorary degrees. The ceremonies were followed by a procession from King's to Christ's College, where a special luncheon was served.

In the afternoon, Frost returned to his room at the Garden House Hotel, and was visited there briefly by Mr. and Mrs. I. A. Richards. He later paid a visit himself to E. M. Forster who, having received his note of apology for their recent altercation, was happy to welcome him to his rooms at King's College. "If I like people," Frost explained as they greeted one another, "I like to see where they are."

They began almost at once to debate the relative merits of poetry and prose. "I only read the poetry, not the prose," Frost said, "[of] people like Emerson and Hardy. But you still like Keats's prose better than his poetry? His five odes are beautiful. I say his book of 1825 is the finest book of the century." Forster refused to change his opinion, but he was pleased to see and talk to Frost.[19]

Late in the day Frost and his party left Cambridge and returned to London. They stopped on the way in Beaconsfield to examine "The Bungalow," the house the Frost family had occupied in the period 1912–1914.

Friday, June 14: Farewells were the main business of this, Frost's last full day in England. At 12:30, a bon voyage luncheon party was given him by Sir Allen Lane of Penguin Books, at a French restaurant in Piccadilly. Next Frost attended a tea at the U.S.I.S., given by Carl Bode and attended as well by the staff of the American Embassy, their wives and their children. The day ended with a short "farewell" interview for B.B.C. television.

Saturday, June 15: After bidding farewell to Carl Bode, Margaret Haferd, and Lee Francis, Frost and Thompson boarded a green plane of the Irish line, Aer Lingus, and flew to Dublin. They were met there by Michael Tierney, President of the University College, Dublin, and by C. P. Curran, with whom Frost had stayed during his visit to Ireland in 1928. Frost later dined with his host in Dublin, the American Ambassador to Ireland, William H. Taft III—whose father had once been Frost's preferred choice for President of the United States.[20]

Sunday-Tuesday, June 16–18: Three days of relaxing and sightseeing in and around Dublin. On Tuesday evening, Frost gave a talk and reading at University College, Dublin, under the auspices of the Irish P.E.N. Club. His subject: the venture of the spirit into matter.

Wednesday, June 19: Today, after a ceremonial luncheon attended by members of the English Department, Frost was awarded his third honorary degree of the trip by the National University of Ireland. Presiding over the ceremony was the aged and renowned Prime Minister of Ireland, Eamon de Valera.

Thursday, June 20: At two in the afteroon, after a morning of sightseeing on the way to Shannon Airport, Frost and Thompson left Ireland and returned to the United States. Three degrees and many memories richer, Robert Frost, at eighty-three, had successfully completed his good-will mission to Great Britain.

WASHINGTON: THE POUND AFFAIR

None of us can bear the disgrace of letting Ezra Pound come to his end where he is. It would leave too woeful a story in American literature.[1]

IN THE FIRST public appearance of his English trip, his afternoon talk at the University of London, Robert Frost had spoken of the "selfish generosity" shown him by Ezra Pound when they first met in England in 1912. Then, Pound had taken it upon himself to "boom" Frost in the United States, by submitting reviews of his first book, *A Boy's Will*, to Harriet Monroe's *Poetry* magazine. If Frost had thereby incurred a debt to the erratically brilliant red-haired poet, it was one he eventually chose to forget. Pound's high-handed manner in London, his penchant for verbal indelicacy, and particularly his activities in the Second World War, killed whatever sense of obligation Frost may at first have felt. In the early 1950s, Frost was as satisfied as he had been in 1948 that Pound was not only mad but a traitor, deserving at the very least his punishment of indefinite confinement in the government mental institution, St. Elizabeths Hospital in Washington, where he had been placed in 1946.

Not until 1954 did Frost's attitude toward Pound begin to soften. It was in that year that there appeared in the New York *Times Book Review*,[2] on Independence Day, a review by Horace Gregory of *The Literary Essays of Ezra Pound*, edited by T. S. Eliot. In it, Gregory praised Eliot for reintroducing to the reading public "Pound the man of letters, who in 1913 and 1914 praised an unknown poet, Robert Frost, and another unknown writer, D. H. Lawrence. . . ." Gregory then quoted, in his "Treasure Chest" column, from a 1914 review by Pound of *North of Boston* which Frost had not seen before:

"Mr. Frost," Pound had written, "is an honest writer, writing from himself, from his own knowledge and emotion; not simply picking up the manner which magazines are accepting at the moment, and applying it to topics in vogue. He is quite consciously and definitely putting New England rural life into verse. He is not using themes that anybody could have cribbed out of Ovid. There are only two passions in art; there are only love and hate—with endless modifications. Frost has been honestly fond of the New England people, I dare say with spells of irritation. He has given their life honestly and seriously. He has never turned aside to make fun of it. He has taken their tragedy as tragedy, their stubbornness as stubbornness. I know more of farm life than I did before I had read his poems. That means I know more of life."[3]

The effect on Frost of the passage quoted by Gregory was most remarkable. For the first time in many years, he was forced to admit that Pound had not only been one of his earliest critics, but one of his best. How well had Pound understood what he had been "up against" at the start of his public career, the universal implications of his simple and local New England scenes! That there were "only two passions in art . . . only love and hate—with endless modifications" was precisely the way Frost himself felt about poetry, and here was Ezra Pound saying it for him. While the essay fragment scarcely left Frost with a feeling of love for Pound, it did make him feel something other than hatred. Perhaps, Frost admitted for the first time since the war, Pound deserved a fate somewhat less extreme than to languish forever in St. Elizabeths Hospital, facing indictment—if he "recovered"—for the crime of treason.[4]

Despite his new attitude, Frost did nothing to help his one-time champion for nearly three years. Then, early in 1957, he was asked by Archibald MacLeish, one of the many writers who had long been campaigning for Pound's release, to join that effort in an important way. MacLeish had written a letter to Attorney General Brownell, which T. S. Eliot and Ernest Hemingway had agreed to sign. MacLeish did not intend, he explained, to sign it himself, for he was known in Republican Washington as a staunch New Deal Democrat. That, said MacLeish, was where Frost came in. He was on good terms with Sherman Adams and others within the Eisenhower Administration. His views, if not explicitly Republican, certainly leaned toward that party's conservatism. He was, most important, the best-loved poet in the United States. His signature on the letter to Brownell, therefore, would very possibly prove decisive in winning Ezra Pound's release.

From the rising storm of opposition to Pound's continued confinement, Frost guessed it would not be long before Pound won his freedom, with or without his help. He saw no reason, then, why it should not be he who was remembered as having been instrumental in winning it for him. Thus demonstrating once again his own kind of "selfish generosity," Frost agreed to sign the letter MacLeish had drafted, and to have his name appear first of the three, as MacLeish suggested, ahead of Eliot and Hemingway. The letter, dated January 14, 1957, was soon on the Attorney General's desk.

"We are writing to you about Ezra Pound," it read, "who has been confined in St. Elizabeths Hospital in Washington for eleven years under indictment for treason.

"Our interest in this matter is founded in part on our concern for Mr. Pound who is one of the most distinguished American writers of his generation, and in part on our concern for the country of our birth. As writers ourselves we cannot but be aware of the effect on writers and lovers of literature throughout the world of Pound's continued incarceration at a time when certain Nazis tried and convicted of the most heinous crimes, have been released and in many cases rehabilitated.

"It is our understanding, based on inquiries directed to the medical personnel at St. Elizabeths Hospital, that Pound is now unfit for trial and, in the opinion of the doctors treating him, will continue to be unfit for trial. This opinion, we believe, has already been communicated to the Department of Justice. Under these circumstances the perpetuation of the charges against him seems to us unfortunate and, indeed, indefensible. It provides occasion for criticism of American justice not only at home but abroad and it seems to us, in and of itself, unworthy of the traditions of the Republic. Concerned, as we must be, with the judgments of posterity on this unhappy affair, we cannot but regret the failure of the Department thus far to take steps to nol pros the indictment and remit the case to the medical authorities for disposition on medical grounds. . . ."[5]

The triply signed letter had just the effect MacLeish hoped it would. In late February, Brownell wrote to Frost that he had "asked that a review of the matter be made. . . ." He would communicate further with him when it had been completed.[6]

The promised response came on April 11. In a letter from acting Deputy Attorney General William P. Rogers, soon to replace Brownell as Attorney General, Frost was invited to come to Washington, at his convenience and with his co-signers Eliot and Hemingway, to discuss Pound's case.[7] Preoccupied by the English good-will trip that was now just a month off, Frost made no immediate reply. On his first day in London, however, he was called on at the Connaught Hotel by MacLeish, who was staying there on his way back from visiting Pound's friends and relatives in Europe. Before MacLeish left England, he elicited a promise from Frost to visit Rogers in Washington as soon as possible after his return to the States.

Afraid, perhaps, that Frost would have second thoughts or permit himself to be sidetracked by other concerns, MacLeish next wrote, on June 17, to Kay Morrison:

"I am writing you," he explained, "because I don't know how to reach Robert who must, I suppose, be back by now. Please forgive the trouble.

"Robert told me in London he would be willing to talk to the Assistant Attorney General who wrote him about the Pound case. I said I would go down with him if he went. It's a lot to ask of him in the heat of the summer. However, if we let this chance go by it may go by for good.

"I should like to suggest two things:

"First, that Robert should reply to the Assistant Attorney General . . . Rogers—if he has not already done so. In his letter of April 10 Mr. Rogers said the Attorney General would like to meet with Frost, Eliot and Hemingway and that he, Rogers, would be writing again soon to arrange a conference. Probably Robert has already replied but if he hasn't it might be helpful to write now suggesting a time when Robert could come. Hemingway MIGHT be willing to come up too. I've written him. Eliot is, of course, in England.

"Second, I'd be grateful if you or Robert would let me know whether he feels he can go and if so when so that I can make my plans. . . ."[8]

Frost must have sensed MacLeish's anxiety, for on June 24, having obviously read the letter to Kay, he wrote "Archie": "My purpose holds to help you get Ezra loose though I won't say my misgivings in the whole matter haven't been increased by my talks with Eliot lately, who knows more about Ezra than anybody else and what we can hope to do for his salvation. I should hate to see Ezra die ignominiously in that wretched place where he is for a crime which if proven couldn't have kept him all these years in prison. So you go ahead and make an appointment with the Department of Justice. I suppose we might be prepared to answer for Ezra's relative sanity and ability to get himself taken care of out in the world. Neither you nor I would want to take him into our family or even into our neighborhood. I shall be acting largely on your judgment. I can't bear that anyone's fate should hang too much on mine.

"I am tied up here for the moment. I could be in Washington for any time on Wednesday July 17 or Friday the 19th after three o'clock or Saturday. But I should have thought that this time of year wouldn't find people in Washington and the affair might better wait until the Fall.

"So much for business—bad business. We mustn't forget the good relations we have promised to have with each other this summer."[9]

Sure now of Frost's support despite his understandable reservations, MacLeish replied at once with plans for a trip to Washington. From Uphill Farm, his home in Conway, Massachusetts, he wrote on June 28:

"Bless you. I won't forget the promise and I know you won't. I don't suppose we could tease you down here? Would you come if I drove up and got you?

"About Ezra—I agree. And I don't feel too sure of my judgment but I can't bear to have him rot. That's about all I am wholly sure of.

"I have asked Miss Geffen at the [American] Academy to write the Deputy Attorney General asking whether July 19 (late in the PM) or the 20th would do. Of course I would go along if you want me. I have also written Ernest asking him to send you a full statement of his views and I shall ask Tom to do the same so that you will go fully armed. Maybe it would be easier if their letters came to me so that I could turn the whole file over to you.

"More when I know more. It was GOOD to see you in London."[10]

On July 19, Frost and MacLeish met with Rogers at the Department of Justice in Washington, and discussed the case of Ezra Pound. MacLeish soon reported to Pound that the main obstacle to his early release seemed to be his association with a segregationist poet named John Kasper, who had recently made headlines by helping to provoke a race riot in Clinton, Tennessee:

"What the conversation boiled down to was about what we expected: though maybe a little more hopeful than we feared.

"For the immediate future and so long as the Kasper mess is boiling and stewing the Department will not move. I have never understood—and neither, incidentally, has your daughter Mary—how you got mixed up with that character.

"Beyond that though there are no commitments, the Department does not close the door provided somebody can come forward with a sensible plan for your future. The impression we got was that that future would have to be in the United States.

"Robert has some ideas about a sensible plan which he would be glad to explore if you approve and which seem promising to me: a sound professional arrangement with your publishers which might work for you as it has for him over many years.

"All this, you understand, is hypothetical as Hell. No commitments or near commitments were made. But the door wasn't closed and we were left with the impression that once the Kasper stink has blown over they would be willing to consider proposals. . . ."[11]

The "sensible plan" Frost had in mind was one based on the arrangement he had long had with Holt: a monthly amount paid by the firm as an advance against his anticipated royalties. Pound's own publisher, James Laughlin of New Directions, confirmed in September that Pound's income from royalties and permissions would permit a monthly payment to him of $300. In writing this to Frost, Laughlin added the interesting news that Frank Lloyd Wright was "very much concerned" with the outcome of Pound's case, and was even willing to have Pound come and live with him at Taliesin West, the home he had designed and built near Phoenix, Arizona.[12]

"Your magnanimous letter," Frost told Laughlin on October 8, "settles one of the three big things in the case. There is still Rogers and Overholser. I think we can count on Rogers. If I have any anxiety left it is about meeting Overholser in the right way. . . ." Dr. Winfred Overholser's cooperation was, indeed, essential. As head of St. Elizabeths Hospital, he would be required to testify as to whether Pound would ever be fit to stand trial. Only with his negative answer, and his expert opinion that Pound would pose no danger to himself or others if set free, did the campaign on Pound's behalf have any chance of success. As to the eighty-eight-year-old Wright's offer of hospitality, Frost wrote: "I can hardly resist the temptation of putting Ezra and Frank Lloyd Wright in the same gun turret but we must be serious where so much is at stake for poor Ezra. I should think we might accept a house from the great architect for the great poet at a safe distance. It is the hour of magnanimity all around. I shall be very happy if it all comes out right. . . ."[13]

Frost made his second assault on Washington, this time without MacLeish, in the third week of October. Overholser was out of town now on vacation, so no progress could be made on that important front. Rogers, however, while remaining annoyingly non-committal, seemed willing to consider Frost's suggestion that, if Pound could not be released outright because of the "Kasper mess," he could at least be transferred to a private institution until the Civil Rights crisis had quieted down. A month after his talk with Rogers, and having heard nothing from him in the interim, Frost renewed his efforts by sending now–Attorney General Rogers a note blending his most charming manner with the latest developments in the case:

"Please tell your daughter," he wrote on November 19, "how proud I am to have had my small plea listened to by the Attorney General about-to-be. Won't you ask her if she doesn't think it would be nice for us to go from this start and do a little more if only socially to satisfy your curiosity about how it goes with poets in a great nation like ours.

"I assume people are less busy the higher up they get and the bigger the questions get or I would apologize for taking your time for the rest of this Pound business. The money seems assured for the private institution and Archie MacLeish tells me this morning that he has Dr. Overholser's consent for Pound's transfer the minute he himself is released from holding Pound as a prisoner. I may have to call you on the telephone next. I grow impatient. The amnesty would be a good Christmas present."[14]

Christmas, however, brought no change in the status of Pound's case, and Frost was forced to conclude that his efforts at the Justice Department had reached an impasse. Then, on January 16, 1958, a development unrelated to Pound suggested to Frost a new way of attacking the problem. At a dinner in his honor at the New York headquarters of the Poetry Society of America, at which he was awarded the Society's Gold Medal for Distinguished Service, Frost was the subject of a telegram of greeting signed by President Eisenhower himself. It read in part:

> THE SENSITIVE AND IMAGINATIVE WORDS OF THE POET CONTRIBUTE MUCH TO THE SPIRIT OF A PEOPLE. IT IS FORTUNATE THAT OUR NATION IS BLESSED WITH CITIZENS LIKE ROBERT FROST WHO CAN EXPRESS OUR INNERMOST FEELINGS AND SPEAK SO CLEARLY TO US OF OUR LAND AND LIFE.[15]

Frost was familiar enough with such laudatory messages to guess that Eisenhower was probably not its author, and very possibly was not even aware of its existence. More likely he had only Sherman Adams to thank. In writing to Adams, however, on February 12, he glossed over the issue of authorship and used the telegram as a lever to gain access to the White House, obviously as much for his own ends as for any benefit to Pound:

"That was a splendid telegram both for me and the cause I had from you and the President. Of course I saw your hand in it. You have great influence up there. Few in your position have ever thought of the arts at all. Some day it seems as if you might want to have me meet the President to thank him in person at a meal or something, so that it needn't go down in history that the great statesman and soldier never dined socially with any but big shots, and these preferably statesmen, warriors, and Holly woodsmen. I read in today's paper that you are sending Bob Hope and Bing Crosby to represent us in the arts at the World's Fair in Brussels. And when I say this half seriously it is not just for myself that I am speaking. . . ."[16]

Frost's letter brought incredibly rapid results. Four days later, he received a telegram from the President inviting him to an "informal stag dinner" and "general chat" at the White House on February 27. Arriving the same day as Eisenhower's telegram was a note from Adams. "I understand that through some circuitous means you have been invited to come and spend the evening with the President on the twenty-seventh. I hope you may be able to do so. If you find it convenient I should hope to see you at that time, although I shall probably not be going to the dinner.

"Of course, what we really need is a person who thinks about the arts. Most of us keep our minds on more mundane problems. We miss many opportunities to promote a growing appreciation of cultural activities. Perhaps we need you on the White House staff. What think you?"[17]

On February 16, Frost wired his acceptance of the President's invitation, saying he was "only too sensible of the honor."[18] His telegram of the same day to Adams suggested that, amid the flush of excitement at the prospect of meeting the President, he had not forgotten his commitment to Pound:

> BE IT UPON YOUR HEAD BUT I AM ACCEPTING THE PRESIDENT'S INVITATION BLACK TIE AND ALL. TRUST I DON'T HAVE TO PROVE MYSELF WORTHY OF THE HONOR. WHAT'S ON MY MIND WOULD BE MORE APT TO BE BROUGHT OUT IN TALKS WITH YOU SEPARATELY. SUFFICIENT UNTO THE MOMENT THE GREAT PLEASURE OF MEETING THE PRESIDENT OF MY COUNTRY. . . .[19]

Adams came through once again by inviting Frost to lunch at the White House Mess on the same day he would dine with the President. Accepting by telephone this new invitation, Frost asked Adams to invite as well the Attorney General. Clearly, the matter "more apt to be brought out . . . separately" was Ezra Pound. A word from Adams, Frost knew, and Rogers might well abandon his intransigent position.

Just as Frost had hoped, the meeting with Rogers and Adams was the beginning of the end of the Pound logjam. When the three men met over lunch in the staff dining room of the White House, Frost learned that Rogers was at last beginning to lean toward Pound's early release. Two weeks later, on March 16, the Washington *Sunday Star* announced in a page-one headline, "Liberty Being Weighed for Poet Ezra Pound." The accompanying article began:

"A decision is near on the twin questions of freeing poet Ezra Pound of treason charges and releasing him from St. Elizabeths Hospital, it was learned today. One official close to the case of the controversial poet said discussions have gone further than ever before. He said the 'whole matter is at the boiling point.'

"An apparently effective pleader for Pound's cause has been Robert Frost, America's leading poet, who recently talked with Attorney General Rogers about the case. Mr. Frost's argument:

As a matter of justice to this country and its reputation in the world, one of its leading poets should not die in a mental hospital. . . ."[20]

On April 1 came two crucial developments. The Legislative Reference Service of the Library of Congress, which had been charged by a House Resolution in August to compile a report on the Pound case, released the completed document, "The Medical, Legal, Literary and Political Status of Ezra Pound."[21] The same day, Attorney General Rogers held a press conference and sent up a trial balloon. He said Pound might escape trial and be allowed to go to Italy, adding that his fate depended upon new diagnoses by his doctors concerning his future competence to stand trial. "Is there any point in keeping him in there," Rogers asked rhetorically, "if he can never be tried?"[22]

The public responded very satisfactorily to the test, and now all that was needed was a prominent figure to cut through the red tape. On April 14, with MacLeish's prodding, Frost went again to Washington and called on the Attorney General.

"I've dropped in to see what your mood is in regard to Ezra Pound," Frost said.

"Our mood is your mood, Mr. Frost," Rogers replied.

"Well, then," said Frost, "let's get him out right away."

At Rogers's suggestion, Frost now arranged an immediate appointment with William Shafroth, the official governmental "expediter" in legal matters. Shafroth recommended Thurman Arnold as lawyer for the defense and immediately arranged an appointment. Arnold, formerly an associate justice of the U.S. Court of Appeals and now a partner in the distinguished law firm of Arnold, Fortas and Porter, agreed, after consulting with Dorothy Pound, her husband's "committee," to take the case. In his meeting with Frost, Arnold suggested that Frost write a statement that could be read in court, when the motion for dismissal of the treason indictment was heard. This Frost agreed to do. In his hotel room that night, he wrote and tore up draft after draft until finally, almost at dawn, the statement was completed. After sending it by messenger to Arnold's office, he took a train back to Cambridge.

A day or two later, Arnold telephoned Frost at his home and asked if he could be in court on Friday, the eighteenth. No, said Frost, he could not: he had a reading on the nineteenth in New York, and he did not want to do too much traveling in too short a time. Could not the hearing be held on Monday?

No, said Arnold, Friday was the day Judge Bolitha Laws was sitting in District Court, and Laws had been the presiding judge in Pound's original hearing in 1945. Well, said Frost, do I have to appear in court? Arnold said no, that he could read Frost's statement for him. That was acceptable to Frost.

Thus, on Friday, April 18, Arnold went to court to ask for the release of Pound. After the legal and medical testimony had been presented, he read into the record a "Statement by Robert Frost":

"I am here to register my admiration for a government that can rouse in conscience to a case like this. Relief seems in sight for many of us besides the Ezra Pound in question and his faithful wife. He has countless admirers the world over who will rejoice in the news that he has hopes of freedom. I append a page or so of what they have been saying lately about him and his predicament. I myself speak as much in the general interest as in his. And I feel authorized to speak very specially for my friends, Archibald MacLeish, Ernest Hemingway and T. S. Eliot. None of us can bear the disgrace of our letting Ezra Pound come to his end where he is. It would leave too woeful a story in American literature. He went very wrong-headed in his egotism, but he insists it was from patriotism—love of America. He has never admitted that he went over to the enemy any more than the writers at home who have despaired of the Republic. I hate such nonsense and can only listen to it as an evidence of mental disorder. But mental disorder is what we are considering. I rest the case on Dr. Overholser's pronouncement that Ezra Pound is not too dangerous to go free in his wife's care, and too insane ever to be tried—a very nice discrimination.

"Mr. Thurman Arnold admirably put this problem of a sick man being held too long in prison to see if he won't get well enough to be tried for a prison offense. There is probably legal precedent to help toward a solution of the problem. But I should think it would have to be reached more by magnanimity than by logic and it is chiefly on magnanimity I am counting. I can see how the Department of Justice would hesitate in the matter from fear of looking more just to a great poet than it would be to a mere nobody. The bigger the Department the longer it might have to take thinking things through."[23]

Despite the ironic thrust at the thirteen years it had taken the government to "think things through," the motion for dismissal went unopposed by the Department of Justice, and the case of *The United States of America* v. *Ezra Pound* at last was closed.

Next morning the New York *Times* carried a front-page story on the dismissal of the indictment against Pound, and it concluded: "The person most responsible for today's announcement was not in court. He is Robert Frost, the poet, who had waged a persistent public and private campaign during the last two years for Mr. Pound's release. . . ."[24] Anyone who was aware of the behind-the-scene efforts of Archibald MacLeish might well have said that it was he, and not Frost, who was "most responsible for today's announcement." When Frost spoke that evening at the Poetry Center, however, he chose to take issue with another aspect of the newspaper's report. After finishing his reading he returned to the stage, apparently for an encore. Instead, he told his audience that though the papers said it had taken him two years to win Pound's release, it had taken him, in fact, only a week. Then he waved good night and walked briskly offstage.

He had further reason to boast a few days later, when the Librarian of Congress, L. Quincy Mumford, offered him a position in the Library that would make possible his continued involvement in the political life of Washington. It was the job of Consultant in Poetry in English, currently held by Randall Jarrell, a nine-month appointment that would be available as of the fall of 1958 and which paid the incumbent handsomely in money as well as honor. Frost had been asked to keep his discussions with Mumford in confidence until the appointment was announced, but he could not resist dropping a few broad hints when he wrote to President Eisenhower late in April thanking him—belatedly—for the White House dinner of February 27.

"To be stood up for and toasted alone in such august company by the ruler of the greatest nation in the world was almost more to me than being stood up for in acclaim by whole audiences of his people and mine. At any rate it left me with less to say for myself on the thrill of the moment and was so like the outcome of a life story, it leaves me with nothing to go on with but possibly some more of the same kind of very quiet poetry that seems to have started all this unquietness. I hope you will accept a book of it from me to take to your farm some day. I am a great advocate of some library in the farm house to mix with the life of the farm. Not that I would underestimate its value in the capitol to mix with the life of the Capitol. Books and paintings and music tend to temper the harshness of politics. I shall treasure the memory of the aside you took me on to appraise the portrait of William Howard Taft by Anders Zorn. I still see the Taft and I still see your vivid portrait of the fine young All-there-and-ready-to-take-on-the-world, your grandson."[25]

A few days later, Mumford sent him a contract specifying the terms and requirements of the post, with the request that he meet the press on May 21, the day the announcement of his appointment was to be made. He was only too happy to comply. In a high-spirited monologue-*cum*-press conference that preceded a reception in his honor at the Library's Whittall Pavilion, he answered serious questions with engaging flippancy, gave hints of the kind of Consultant he planned to be, and took every opportunity he could to steer the discussion in the direction of his late triumph in the case of Ezra Pound. Would he continue Mr. Jarrell's policies next year? "I would if I knew what they were. Is he a man of policy?" What did the job consist of? "It consists of making the politicians and statesmen more aware of their responsibilities to the arts." How do you do that? "And I wouldn't have much confidence in myself that way if I hadn't been so successful in Washington lately in a law case." A few moments later: "They say I've come home to the sticks—come back to the sticks with a reputation more for politics than for poetry. If—if you could only know the . . . my wiles." Was he referring to the Pound case? "Yes . . . Yeah," he replied, laughing. ". . . All I did was the whole thing."

Later in the conference, he addressed himself to Pound's widely quoted comment after the dismissal of his indictment that, as far as Frost's interest in his case went, "He ain't been in much of a hurry." ". . . I presumed to speak for Eliot, Hemingway, Archie MacLeish, and myself. That was the names I put into the appeal—a little about it. I haven't seen Ezra Pound since 1915. I did this on general principles and out of sentiment I have for a good poet in trouble with himself, and the world, and the law, that's all. He complains that I didn't do it fast enough. He ought to have seen me that week. He doesn't know what goes on outside, but he thinks it ought, he imagines it as having been going on ever since he was shut up, but it has just been going on lately, and I never thought of myself as the one to do it. See . . . I surprised myself by getting into a position where it looked as if somebody ought to get it over with, you know. And things are done pretty scattery and everybody writin' letters to everybody else, and you can't do it that way. I wish I could—I could tell you all the great buildings I was in that afternoon. I kept thinking about my mother —my mother's son. . . ."[26]

The high mood of the press conference was followed, weeks later, by a bitter disappointment. Sherman Adams, whose suggestions to officials in the Library of Congress had brought about Frost's appointment to the consultantship, was suddenly thrown into a political tempest by allegations that he had improperly accepted gifts and favors from an old personal friend, the New England industrialist Bernard Goldfine. Frost did not, perhaps, know Adams intimately—no one really did —but he knew him well enough to be outraged by the suggestion that the former Marine, diminutive only in physical stature, could be guilty of anything more than a minor lapse of generally impeccable judgment. At the height of the controversy in late June, Frost vented his anger in a note that roundly condemned John Fox, the Boston entrepreneur who was Adams's principal accuser, and Democratic Congressman Oren Harris, before whose Committee of Investigation Fox was presenting his damning testimony.

"Some bad dreams are so absurdly bad," he told Adams, "that I can see through them for what they are without waking up. I mean I don't have to wake up for relief. That's the point the unreality reached today with the appearance of Harris's prize Munchausen on the scene. We Bostonians of the St Botolph Club consigned Fox to the Dantesque depths long ago. I should think Harris had made one fatal mistake for his party. He himself as much [as had] his case blow up in his face today like a stench bomb. You must know without my telling you how I would feel about it all. The only thing I blame you for is the ambition to lead the life of a political hero. But what can I say who have so much ambition of my own to answer for? The excuse furnished us by Milton is that it is the last infirmity of noble minds. You are in a safe place in the confidence of the President. I know you won't be stampeded by the blatherskites. . . . I shall be counting on you in there for support when I am exposing myself as a government employee in Washington next year. Meanwhile I shall be swearing under my breath at what has happened to you. I might swear aloud if I knew you well enough to be sure you didn't approve of swearing. I know you pretty well at that, don't I?"[27]

Adams held out for another three months. But finally, in late September, the announcement was made that he had resigned, so as not to jeopardize Republican chances of gaining a congressional majority in November.

"The news of your resignation," Frost wrote him early in October, "came just in time to keep me from mailing the letter I had ready to forbid your resignation. I had hoped you would stand on your integrity and stick it out. I didn't see why you should sacrifice yourself to save the Fall elections. The elections were probably lost anyway by reason of the probably general misunderstanding of Mr. Dulles' foreign policy.

"But lets talk no more of this horrid business. I shall be in Washington all next week and look forward to finding you at worst in a state of philosophy. I'm camping out in luxury and defiance of captious criticism at the Hay-Adams. Ever yours Robert."[28]

Much as Frost grieved for Adams's downfall, he could not dwell on his friend's misfortune for long. The city in which Ezra Pound had been so long an unwilling resident now beckoned him, and with visions of greater glory dancing in his mind, he prepared to go.

POETRY AND POWER

It makes the prophet in us all presage
The glory of a next Augustan age . . .
A golden age of poetry and power
Of which this noonday's the beginning hour.[1]

IN HIS FIRST WEEK in Washington as Consultant in Poetry to the Library of Congress, Robert Frost soon made it plain that he intended to make his presence felt while he held his first official government position. At a news conference on the fifteenth of October, arranged to accommodate the large number of reporters who had sought personal interviews with the fountainhead of good copy, he announced that his own title for the new job was "Poet-in-Waiting," and that he intended to furnish his Washington office with four paintings—by Homer, Eakins, Chapin and Wyeth—that were masterpieces of American art. They would, he said, help him "get out of the small potatoes class."[2]

The Consultant's duties of lecturing at the Library's Coolidge Auditorium, helping to build up the Library's poetry collection, and answering the queries of students, professors, and would-be poets, were not nearly inclusive enough for the present incumbent of the office. He had always been deeply interested in the political process, from the days in San Francisco when, as a child, he had witnessed his father's campaign for tax collector as a candidate of the Democratic party, to the later days when he and Elinor had joined in condemning Roosevelt and the New Deal, to only recently, when he had seen how an important political decision was made at firsthand, and talked confidentially with the President of the country. He wanted the consultantship to be treated as an important political office, in which his views would be listened to by the men who were running the country, and in which he could achieve significant results for his "cause": poetry, the arts, and—not inconsequentially—his own reputation.

When he returned to Washington in December for his second week of "consulting," he called another press conference and explained, "I don't want to run for office, but I want to be a politician. I knew I couldn't run for office with all these opinions. I am not a practical campaigner like this or that politician. However, I wish that some good senator would resign about six months before the end of his term and let me finish it out."

He went on to complain, almost joking but serious underneath, that the government had failed so far to employ him in a manner commensurate with his willingness to be put to use. Since assuming office, he said, he had been consulted only a handful of times: three by the White House, once by the Supreme Court, and not at all by Congress. Such neglect, he added, was not what he had anticipated in taking the job. "I wondered if I hadn't come down here on a misunderstanding. I thought I was to be poetry consultant in everything—poetry, politics, religion, science. I'll tackle anything."

According to Mary McGrory of the Washington *Evening Star*, he then offered a summary of his consultations to date: In his first call "on the White House," he related, "I said to the White House that since Mrs. Roosevelt and Walter Reuther and all my educated friends think that socialism is inevitable . . . why don't we join up and hurry it along. It won't last, and we'll get it over with." Again at the White House, he had been asked to pick the name of one poet—whom he did not specify—from a list of thirty. "I didn't know whether it was for execution—to be shot against the wall—or to be made king of the dump." In his one inquiry from the Supreme Court, he had repeated a remark he had once made to Justice Cardozo: "You have to distinguish between being a referee and a handicapper." Asked if this had to do with the integration crisis, Frost acknowledged that it did. "I think the legislative department has been delinquent," he said. "Congress ought to have tended to things that the Supreme Court was driven to in desperation. That's tellin' them isn't it?"

Were he to be asked about education, on which he regarded himself as "the greatest living expert," he had a response already in mind: "I have long thought that our high schools should be improved. Nobody should come into our high schools without examinations—not aptitude tests, but on reading, 'riting, and 'rithmetic. And that goes for black or white. . . . A lot of people are being scared by the Russian Sputnik into wanting to harden up our education or speed it up. I am interested in toning it up, at the high-school level. . . . If they want to Spartanize the country, let them. I would rather perish as Athens than prevail as Sparta. The tone is Athens. The tone is freedom to the point of destruction. Democracy means all the risks taken—conflict of opinion, conflict of personality, eccentricity. We are Athens, daring to be all sorts of people."

Toward the end of the conference, Frost was asked if, as a would-be senator, he felt the present administration was sympathetic to the arts. It was "much more so," he promptly replied, "before a recent sad event." Asked by several reporters what that was, he admitted that he referred to the departure of Sherman Adams, who "really cares about the arts."[3]

Indeed, with Adams out of power, nothing that Frost could do or say seemed to result in the kind of notice he wanted to be paid to poetry, the arts, and himself during his year in Washington. Not until March of 1959, nearly four months later, did the calendar help him achieve what his own requests for attention had not. In that month, he celebrated the eighty-fifth anniversary of his birth, and Senator Winston L. Prouty of Vermont rose on the Senate floor and proposed a birthday resolution, S. Res. 95, honoring "America's great poet-philosopher Robert Frost." The senator hardly needed to explain, in his introductory remarks, why it was appropriate for his colleagues to honor Frost with a second such resolution—the last one having marked his "seventy-fifth" birthday. But one of his reasons must have been particularly pleasing to the poet, and that was the one which began with an excerpt from a recent article by J. Donald Adams of the New York *Times*:

"[Frost is] one of the most lovable of men and, though he would be the first to disclaim the adjective, one of the most admirable in character also. . . . I can think of no better tribute to Frost on this coming birthday than for every American who admires his work to write a letter to the Nobel Prize Committee, asking why our foremost poet has not yet been recognized in Stockholm. It is a recognition long past due, and time flies on ever-swifter wings."[4]

"The awardings of the Nobel prizes," Senator Prouty continued, "are outside the prerogatives of the United States Senate, but the unanimous passage of this resolution will inform Mr. Frost and the world of the esteem in which this great American poet is held by the members of this body. . . ."

The resolution was shortly read, with ten uses of "WHEREAS" before the final "THEREFORE," and it was quickly approved with time to spare before the twenty-sixth of March.[5]

The real celebration, however, took place in New York City, where Edgar T. Rigg, President of Henry Holt & Company, had arranged to give the company's foremost property a gala formal dinner on the evening of the twenty-sixth at the Waldorf-Astoria Hotel. The day began with a press conference at the Holt offices on Madison Avenue, where the questioning turned quickly to a subject on which Frost had much to say. With the rise of science, one reporter observed, poetry seemed to be playing a lesser role. "Poetry has always played a lesser role," Frost answered. "When you're in college, half of all you read is poetry. When you're out, not so. Funny, isn't it? Out of all proportion. When I was young, my teachers used to recite, not knowing that I was going to be a poet, a little rhyme:

> *Seven cities claimed blind Homer, being dead,*
> *Through which the living Homer begged his bread.*[6]

It's only luck when a poet gets too much notice.

"I may say I've never got on by setting poetry in opposition to science or big business or academic scholarship, although some poets seem to live on that contrast. . . . Science cannot be scientific about poetry, but poetry can be poetical about science. It's bigger, more inclusive. Get that right, you know," he said, and repeated his familiar remark.

Did these large birthday celebrations bore him? "They don't bore me, but sometimes they make me feel old. The question of deserts might bother me at night. But I like to be made of, you know. I like to be made of."

Had he any wish for the world and his country that he would like to state on this eighty-fifth birthday? "For the world, no. I'm not large enough for that. For my country? My chief wish is for it to win at every turn in anything it does. A few years ago, I summoned my family and friends and swore to them that if we lost the Olympic Games at Melbourne, I'd turn Communist. We lost. My family and friends reminded me of the oath, and asked what I intended to do about it. 'Break it,' I told them. . . . People say there's always room at the top. There isn't. There's only room for one at the top of the steeple."

Could not Mr. Frost afford to say that because he was at the top, and sitting pretty? "I was down under for many, many years," he said, "with no prospect of winning." Having "won," he gave his formula for success: "Sneak up on things. And never be caught looking as if you wanted them."

Another question concerned the present state of New England: Was it in decay? "People ask me that on my travels," he replied. "Often they ask me in the South. And I ask, 'Where did you go to school?' And they say Harvard—or Yale. And then I say the successor to Mr. Dulles will be from Boston: Mr. Herter. And the next President of the United States will be from Boston. And then I ask, 'Does that sound as if New England is decaying?' " But whom did Mr. Frost mean? "Can't you figure that one out for yourself?" The newsmen could, indeed, figure it out, but they wanted to hear Frost say the name himself. With a shrug, he obliged them: "He's a Puritan named Kennedy. The only Puritans left these days are the Roman Catholics. There. I guess I wear my politics on my sleeve."[7]

The press conference was over by eleven o'clock, and Frost had the rest of the day free until the Holt dinner began with cocktails at six-thirty. The guest list included some 100 "distinguished friends and admirers from all walks of life,"[8] but the main after-dinner speaker was neither a close personal friend nor an admirer of long standing. Rather, he was the well-known critic and contributor to the *Partisan Review*, Lionel Trilling.

Trilling began by addressing the audience at large, and speaking of how future archeologists would regard Frost as something of a mythic figure, associable with Jack Frost, the vernal equinox, and the "rite" of commencement. He went on to say that any person called upon to speak at the "momentous" occasion of the poet's "Sophoclean" eighty-fifth birthday must approach the assignment with some "diffidence."

"Yet I must be more weighed down by diffidence than many others who might speak here. I must almost entertain a doubt of the appropriateness of my speaking here at all. For I cannot help knowing that the manifest America of Robert Frost's poems is not the America that has its place in my own mind. The manifest America of Mr. Frost's poems is rural, and, if I may say so, it is rural in a highly moralized way, in an aggressively moralized way. It thus represents an ideal that is common to many Americans, perhaps especially to Americans of the literary kind, who thus express their distaste for the life of the city and for all that the city implies of excessive complexity, of uncertainty, of anxiety, and of the demand that is made upon intellect to deal with whatever are the causes of complexity, uncertainty, anxiety.

"I do not share this ideal. It is true that the image of the old America has a great power over me—that old America with which the America of Mr. Frost's poems seems to be continuous. And I think I know from experience—there are few Americans who do not—how intense can be the pleasure in the hills and the snow, in the meadows and woods and swamps that make the landscape of Mr. Frost's manifest America; and know, too, how great a part this pleasure can play in a man's moral being. But these natural things that give me pleasure constitute my notion of the earthly paradise, they are not the ruling elements of my imagination of actual life. Those elements are urban—I speak here tonight incongruously as a man of the city. . . ."

Trilling described himself as a recent convert to Frost's poetry:

"It is a fact which I had best confess as simply as possible that for a long time I was alienated from Mr. Frost's great canon of work by what I saw in it, that either itself seemed to denigrate the work of the critical intellect or that gave to its admirers the ground for making the denigration. It was but recently that my resistance, at the behest of better understanding, yielded to admiration—it is probable that there is no one here tonight who has not admired Mr. Frost's poetry for a longer time than I have."

Trilling then began to speak of "my Frost," who was "anything but" a poet who "reassures us by his affirmation of old values, simplicities, pieties, and ways of feeling." Rather, Trilling asserted, he was "a terrifying poet":

"Call him, if it makes things any easier, a tragic poet, but it might be useful every now and then to come from under the shelter of that literary word. The universe that he conceives is a terrifying universe. Read the poem called 'Design' and see if you sleep the better for it. Read 'Neither Out Far nor In Deep,' which often seems to me the most perfect poem of our time, and see if you are warmed by anything in it except the energy with which emptiness is perceived. . . ."

Finally, Trilling addressed Frost directly: "I hope that you will not think it graceless of me that on your birthday I have undertaken to say that a great many of your admirers have not understood clearly what you have been doing in your life in poetry. I know that you will not say which of us is in the right of the matter. You will behave like the Secret whose conduct you have described:

> *We dance around in a ring and suppose*
> *But the Secret sits in the middle and knows.*[9]

And I hope that you will not think it graceless of me that on your birthday I have made you out to be a poet who terrifies. When I began to speak I called your birthday Sophoclean and that word has, I think, controlled everything I have said about you. Like you, Sophocles lived to a great age, writing well; and like you, Sophocles was the poet his people loved most. Surely they loved him in some part because he praised their common country. But I think that they loved him chiefly because he made plain to them the terrifying things of human life: they felt, perhaps, that only a poet who could make plain the terrible thing[s] could possibly give them comfort."[10]

When Trilling sat down, Frost rose to deliver some remarks of his own, and it soon became apparent that he was having difficulty deciding whether to be flattered or insulted by what Trilling had said. He seemed to be not a little upset: "Well, I—ah—have enjoyed being looked into more penetratingly than ever before," he said. "The other night I got mistaken for a cattleman on the train. Now there's nothing I'd like being mistaken for more—but am I terrifying? . . . I don't mind being brought out this way. While I don't read much criticism of myself, I've heard it tonight. I never thought for a minute that I was at variance with science, with big business or literary criticism. I like to think I live in the middle. . . . Everyone wonders about his own poetry. . . . I'm puzzling about myself in public. I avoid so much writing about me that it's good to hear some of it."

Soon he began to recite his poetry, but his difficulty in remembering the familiar lines may have been a reflection of discomposure over Trilling's critical pronouncements. After one false start he explained, "I'm nervous tonight, I'm very nervous." Finishing the poem he apologized, "I didn't say that very well." After another he commented, perhaps with an implied denial of Trilling's assertions, "That's part of a long poem. It goes on and has a happy ending." Toward the end of his talk, he explained, "I know these [poems] usually, but I'm a little nervous tonight. I'm still investigating myself. I'll be investigating myself for a week. . . . I haven't been given to think about myself so much in my whole life. . . ."[11]

Trilling's intention in his birthday remarks was, of course, neither to flatter nor to insult, but rather to call attention to an aspect of Frost's poetry that he felt had hitherto been overlooked. The events of the evening had, however, a strange aftermath when J. Donald Adams, one of the guests at the birthday dinner, denounced Trilling's speech in his "Speaking of Books" column in the New York *Times Book Review*[12] and denied that Frost was at all the "terrifying" poet Trilling had made him out to be. Adams advised Trilling to "come out of the Freudian wood . . . and face the facts of life." When a number of letters appeared soon after in the *Book Review*, all expressing curiously bitter support of Adams's rebuke of Trilling and all but one based not on direct acquaintance with Trilling's actual text but only on Adams's selective report, Trilling decided to have his talk printed in its entirety in the *Partisan Review* together with a statement of his views on the meaning of the "cultural episode" to which it had given rise.[13]

Having long since recovered his lost composure—he had dined cordially with Trilling the day after his birthday[14]—Frost was delighted at the attention focused upon him by the Trilling-Adams debate. When he received from Trilling an advance copy of the *Partisan Review* piece, with a note apologizing for any distress the birthday talk had caused, he replied in a letter dated June 18: "Not distressed at all. Just a little taken aback or thrown back on myself by being so closely examined so close by. It took me more than a few minutes to change from thoughts of myself to thoughts of the difficulty you had had with me. You made my birthday party a surprise party. I should like nothing better than to do a thing like that myself—to depart from the Rotarian norm in a Rotarian situation. You weren't there to sing 'Happy Birthday, dear Robert,' and I don't mind being made controversial. No sweeter music can come to my ears than the clash of arms over my dead body when I am down. . . ."[15]

The "terrifying" debate was a local storm not destined to last. Of far greater and more continuing interest to the national press, and to the general public, were Frost's birthday predictions concerning the rising glory of New England. He had been on safe ground prognosticating the succession of Christian Herter as Secretary of State, for John Foster Dulles was ill with cancer and Herter was already Acting Secretary. But the prediction that the junior senator from Massachusetts, who had not yet even formally declared his candidacy, would be the next President of the United States, was just daring enough to make newspaper headlines across the country. Senator Kennedy, pleased though he was to learn his political future, was somewhat embarrassed to see Frost's remark widely taken as if it had been an outright endorsement.

"I just want to send you a note," he wrote Frost on the eleventh of April, "to let you know how gratifying it was to be remembered by you on the occasion of your 85th birthday. I only regret that the intrusion of my name, probably in ways which you did not entirely intend, took away some of the attention from the man who really deserved it—Robert Frost. I want to send you my own very warmest greetings on [a day] which is for all of your admirers a milestone, but for you is only another day in the life of a young man.

"I do, however, share entirely your view that the New England heritage is not a fading page but that it has continuing vitality and a distinguished future. I was more impressed than ever by this during the past fall when for the first time in six years I had an opportunity to move intensively across the state from town to town and to see again first-hand the very special qualities of the New England mind and New England heritage."[16]

Impressed himself by the young senator's letter, as well as by the publicity the prediction concerning him had generated, Frost began repeating his forecast of Kennedy's election in many, if not most, of his subsequent public lectures. He knew that if the senator did go on to become President, Kennedy just might be grateful enough to offer him a job on the White House staff, perhaps by creating a tailor-made Cabinet position of the kind Sherman Adams had half-seriously mentioned before his fall from power. In any case, Kennedy was certainly a fascinating young politician, his bandwagon sure to provide as memorable a ride as the parade float on which he had perched in San Francisco during the presidential campaign of 1880. Frost decided, therefore, to ride that bandwagon for all he was worth.

In the middle of May, he returned to Washington for his fourth and last week at the Library of Congress job. Soon after he arrived, he received a telephone call from another promising young politician, Congressman Stewart L. Udall of Arizona, who said he had recently seen it reported that Frost had yet to be "consulted" by a member of Congress, and who offered his home—including dinner—for a "Congressional consultation" later that week. Frost readily accepted, and happily regaled Udall, his family, and four or five other members of Congress with three hours of observations on poetry and politics. The evening was so successful that Udall held several more such "consultations" on subsequent visits by Frost to Washington.[17]

The introduction a month later of "A Bill to Provide for a National Academy of Culture," by Senator Francis Case of South Dakota, and the need to acknowledge the Senate's birthday resolution of March 25, led Frost to offer another "consultation" of sorts to Senator Prouty in a letter dated June 18:

"The only thing that could mean more to me than recognition by the Senate would be a seat in the Senate which I may say I have given up all hope of with two such Senators from Vermont [Prouty and George D. Aiken] already in situ. But thank the Senators for this second great honor they have crowned my days with. If it is a small matter to them in the midst of their world affairs, it is a very large one to me personally and I like to think no very negligible one to the arts in general. It is thoughts and designs for the arts that have delayed me with this letter. I have been getting up the presumption to suggest seeing you some time in Washington or at home in Vermont for a talk about some more permanent connection than mine between them and the government. It would have to be some office, appointment to which would be by some higher-ups as say, a committee of the House, the Chairman of the Senate, one member of the Supreme Court (chosen by the other members), and two editors or authors called in by my first three. All this for the protection from the spoilsmen and the literary gangsters. The term of office might well be from forty on for twenty-five years. I should want the government to impress itself with what it was doing for the arts by making this a well rewarded honor. Wouldn't it be a great thing for a latter day senator from Vermont to obtain merit in history by doing the same kind of thing to bring art and state together that an earlier senator from Vermont [Justin Smith Morrill] did to bring education and state together by his Land Grant Colleges.

"Again my thanks to the Senate. The government has gone a long way towards making this my culminating year. You perhaps know the President and his White House have come into it."[18]

The proposal to Senator Prouty was not destined to materialize. What did materialize a week later was an invitation from Quincy Mumford for Frost to prolong his formal relationship with the Library of Congress by serving for three years, beginning in 1960, in a position that had been established just for him: Honorary Consultant in the Humanities. "During your term as Poetry Consultant," wrote Mumford, "you frequently expressed the idea that you welcomed consultation in the broad realm of the humanities. It is for this reason, and because we desire your continued association with the Library of Congress, that we offer the humanities to you for your honorary consultantship."[19]

Frost was only too happy to accept Mumford's offer. "Isn't it pleasant," he wrote on the tenth of July, "that we all got to be such friends at the great Library that we want to see more of each other. You may be sure I should have to see you once in a while even if you did not summon me. And I am honored by the summons of your appointing me consultant in the humanities which I more or less arbitrarily take to mean practically everything human that has been brought to book and can be treated in poetry—philosophy, politics, religion, history, and science. Everything, everything.

"This mark of friendship is more to me than an award. It sets me up mightily that my venture into the capital of my country wasn't for nothing."[20]

Frost spent the remainder of the year doing the things he had been doing for so many years—lecturing around the country, visiting friends and being visited, teaching at Amherst, vacationing in Ripton, working on his poems—all at much the same tempo now that he was in his mid eighties that he had maintained in his seventies, his sixties, and before.

When he reached eighty-six, in March 1960, he was still going strong, and seemed determined to go on so forever.

His friends were not always so lucky. In the spring of 1960, Frost learned that J. J. Lankes, the well-known illustrator whose woodcuts had enhanced several of his books and Christmas cards, was dying of cancer in a nursing home in North Carolina. As he happened to be nearby for a lecture date at Chapel Hill, he decided to look in on Lankes and provide what little comfort he could in the face of an obviously hopeless situation. A nurse went in first to Lankes's room, coming out to say that he was awake and that he wanted to see the visitor. Then Frost went in, alone. Lankes opened his eyes just long enough to smile a greeting and to say hello. Then he closed them again. Frost took his hand and held it in his own, trying to talk with the heavily sedated man. The answers to his questions came only in nods; Lankes's eyes remained shut; he did not speak. Meanwhile, there was a commotion out in the hall: someone in pain, crying, someone screaming. Suddenly, Frost was overcome with the feeling that it had been a great mistake to visit Lankes at all. He was clearly too far gone to want anybody coming to see him. Under his breath, Frost said to himself, "God damn it," and prepared to leave. But Lankes heard him, and spoke for the first time since Frost entered the room. "God damn it," he replied. They had, after all, managed to communicate sympathetically with each other. There was nothing more or better that they could say. Gently, Frost put Lankes's hand back on the coverlet, pressed the back of his hand against Lankes's hollow cheek, turned, and walked out of the room. A short time later, he learned that Lankes was dead.[21]

Early in May 1960, Frost returned to Washington for the first series of lectures in his new role of Honorary Consultant in the Humanities to the Library of Congress. The first of several official functions arranged to hail his arrival was a luncheon in the Whittall Pavilion on May second, attended by several members of the Library staff and other invited guests. One outsider who was brought in by Roy P. Basler, chief of the Library's Manuscript Division and Frost's personal link with the Library staff, was someone Frost had no great desire to see. Carl Sandburg was in town to receive the "Great Living Americans" award from the U.S. Chamber of Commerce later in the day. Basler had had some difficulty persuading Sandburg to come to the luncheon honoring Frost, but Sandburg had agreed, and now appeared at the Pavilion wearing a wool scarf about his neck and a black fedora on his head. When Basler saw him at the door, he turned to Frost and announced, "Robert, here's Carl Sandburg come to lunch." As Basler later recorded it, Frost turned, grinned without moving or offering his hand, and said, "Don't you know enough to take off your hat when you come in the house?" Sandburg gave a throaty chuckle, and removed his fedora with an exaggerated flourish. As he did so, a lock of his silvery hair fell forward and covered his eye. "Don't you ever comb your hair?" Frost baited. Sandburg chuckled again, and without saying a word, took a comb from his coat pocket, lifted the silver forelock back into place, and offered the comb to Frost. "You could use a comb yourself," he laughingly retorted. The guests who were observing the interchange laughed, as Frost took out an ancient comb of his own and ran it through his tousled white hair with little effect. Then, to more laughter, the two poetic rivals shook hands and parted to mix with the crowd, but not before Frost reminded Sandburg, "I'd as soon play tennis with the net down as write free verse." During the luncheon, Frost aimed several more barbs in the direction of Sandburg, who did not seem to take offense at any of Frost's only half-good-natured "jokes." After lunch had been cleared, Mumford rose to invite either of the two distinguished guests to speak if he desired to do so. "Let Carl pay a tribute to me," said Frost quickly. "He oughta praise me, my poetry." Sandburg declined with another throaty guffaw, and the lunch was immediately adjourned. "Was I really bad?" Frost asked Basler later, knowing perfectly well that he had been.[22]

One of the main events of the May visit was to have been a lecture on the night of the fourth in the auditorium of the Library of Congress, for members of Congress and their wives. Frost was there, and several wives showed up, but as for members of Congress, almost none appeared. Both Houses were kept overtime in debate over an important controversial bill, and few members of either house felt free to leave the floor. The lecture went on, but it was clear that Frost was disappointed by the small turnout. "I am prepared for anything in Washington," he began, "but I expected to get a chance to tell Congress what to do next. I knew they wouldn't do it, but I thought I'd talk about that, and since they are all well occupied over there, we won't try to do too much about that. I was going to talk about anxiety. Suppose I do just the same as if they were here. Some of you tell them about it. . . ."[23] He went on with the lecture, but the evening was a great disappointment to him. "I know when I've lost," he said later. "They just didn't want to hear me."[24]

He was heard next morning, when he testified before the Education Subcommittee of the Senate Committee on Labor and Public Welfare for the Case bill to establish a National Academy of Culture. He disliked the overworked word "culture" intensely, but he liked the idea of an academy to honor the arts, and was happy to be "consulted" on the matter. Senator Ralph Yarborough's introduction suggested that, even if he had missed the lecture of the night before, the ways of the poet were not unknown to him: "You may proceed in your own way," he told Frost. "No one can tell you how to proceed. Anyway, you would proceed in your own way, but we want you to know that you comply with the rules when you do proceed in your own way."

Frost then told the senators—and the largest audience that had ever attended a hearing of the Senate Education Subcommittee—what he had recently said to many others in Washington: he wanted poetry declared equal to big business, to science, to scholarship. "When I look down the list of scholarship in the university I sometimes land, in the end, looking for what's most akin to the arts. I land in the sports department. The performance—all art is performance. It is not scholarship. The scholar people have tolerated us lately, been very nice to us. They admit that there might be such a thing as a living writer. Many of them used to boast they had read nothing later than the eighteenth century. . . . And the awareness is a great thing. . . . The foundations are getting aware of us, but I want my country officially to be aware of us so that we feel our equality. I do want you to declare our equality. We will take care of the rest." At the conclusion of Frost's testimony, Senator Yarborough thanked him and wanted to come around and shake his hand, "because I feel, when I shake hands with you and with Carl Sandburg"—who had testified earlier—"I am shaking hands with immortality." Frost's reaction to the intended compliment is not of record.[25]

He received another congressional compliment in June when the Senate passed a bill that had first been introduced in late

April by Leverett Saltonstall, the senior Republican of Massachusetts, authorizing the creation and presentation to Frost of a $2,500 gold medal "in recognition of his poetry, which has enriched the culture of the United States and the philosophy of the world." The bill was then sent over to the House of Representatives where, after consideration in committee, it was passed and sent on to the White House. President Eisenhower signed the Frost Medal Bill into law on September thirteenth.[26]

A short time later Frederic Fox, one of Sherman Adams's assistants who had remained at the White House after his resignation, called the Director of the Mint and asked when he thought the Frost Medal would be ready for presentation. Not for some time, said the Director, if ever. He went on to explain that the Mint had not yet received the $2,500 to strike it. While the Congress had authorized the money, it had forgotten to appropriate it, and until someone came up with the amount, nothing could be done but to go ahead with plans for its design. Fox telephoned Mrs. Morrison in Cambridge, and explained the situation to her. She offered the suggestion that the best likeness of Frost was the Walker Hancock bust. Fox could get a photograph of it for the government artists, either from Hyde Cox, who had the original, or from Dartmouth, which had a copy. She also thought that the medal should have a patriotic theme, though "not flag-waving," since Frost was, above all, an American patriot. She recommended using the poem "The Gift Outright," and said that Frost wanted to receive the medal from President Eisenhower before he left office.[27]

While all this was going on, Frost himself was in California on a lecture tour, traveling with his friend, the poet William Meredith. He spoke on November 7 in Los Angeles, and it was there that he delivered his first public reaction to the news that John Kennedy had won the presidential election the day before. It was, said Frost, "a triumph of Protestantism—over itself."[28] He was delighted by the outcome of the election, which had been close enough for him to feel, with some justification, that his predictions of Kennedy's victory had helped shape their fulfillment. Luckily, though the victory margin was small, it was not small enough to depend upon Frost's own vote. He had neglected to arrange for an absentee ballot before leaving for the West Coast.

Frost and Meredith made several stops on the way home, including Tucson, where they attended the opening of a new poetry center at the University of Arizona. While he was there, Frost went to call on Congressman Udall, with whom he had become increasingly cordial during each of his "consulting" visits to Washington. They toured Udall's home district, visited a local Indian museum, and speculated about the kind of President Senator Kennedy, a personal friend of Udall's, would prove to be. They agreed that Kennedy, who had occasionally quoted fragments of verse by Frost and Emerson in his campaign appearances and was himself a Pulitzer prizewinning author, would very likely pay more attention to the arts, among them poetry, than any President had done in many years.

Senator Kennedy demonstrated his willingness to give heed to the arts even sooner than Frost had anticipated. On the first of December, the President-elect summoned Congressman Udall to his Georgetown home and invited him to serve in his Cabinet as Secretary of the Interior. Udall accepted at once, and they continued to talk for some time. Then, as he rose and prepared to leave, Udall offered a suggestion. "You might consider having our mutual friend Robert Frost take part in the inauguration ceremonies." Kennedy registered surprise and asked, "Doing what?" "Why, reading a poem at the beginning, or in the middle, or at the end." "Oh, no," said Kennedy. "You know that Robert Frost always steals any show he is part of. If I did that, the same thing would happen to me that happened to Lincoln at Gettysburg, with Edward Everett." That the new President might be upstaged by the old poet was only a self-deprecatory joke, and Senator Kennedy quickly followed it by saying he was interested in the idea; Udall should find out if Frost would be interested, and report back.[29]

When Udall telephoned Frost with the good news of his own appointment to the Cabinet, he informed the poet of Kennedy's interest in having him participate in the inauguration. Frost was astonished by the idea—and delighted, both by Udall's good fortune and his own. He wasted no time in sending off a telegram to the President-elect expressing his satisfaction at the choice of the Arizona Mormon for Interior Secretary:

> GREAT DAY FOR BOSTON, DEMOCRACY, THE PURITANS, AND THE IRISH. YOUR APPOINTMENT OF STEWART UDALL OF AN OLD VERMONT RELIGION RECONCILES ME ONCE AND FOR ALL TO THE PARTY I WAS BORN INTO.[30]

The telegram, of course, served a double purpose. It also let Kennedy know, indirectly, that Frost had spoken to Udall about taking part in the inauguration, and implied that he was, indeed, available.

Two days later, with Frost at her side, Mrs. Morrison telephoned Frederic Fox at the White House to say that they had talked the matter over and had decided not to put un the money themselves for striking the Frost Medal—a possibilıty that had earlier been raised—nor did they wish to ask any of their friends to do so. Then Frost got on the line and said he had decided to wait until Congress itself got around to appropriating the funds for the medal. There was no mention now, as there had been before, of the importance of having President Eisenhower present the medal himself. "Fred," said Frost, "I need all the honors I can get," but he implied that he preferred to be honored by the new President rather than the old one.[31]

Senator Kennedy's invitation to Frost to "participate in the inaugural ceremonies January twentieth" went out by wire a few days later, and Frost answered in kind the following day:

> IF YOU CAN BEAR AT YOUR AGE THE HONOR OF BEING MADE PRESIDENT OF THE UNITED STATES, I OUGHT TO BE ABLE AT MY AGE TO BEAR THE HONOR OF TAKING SOME PART IN YOUR INAUGURATION. I MAY NOT BE EQUAL TO IT BUT I CAN ACCEPT IT FOR MY CAUSE—THE ARTS, POETRY, NOW FOR THE FIRST TIME TAKEN INTO THE AFFAIRS OF STATESMEN. I AM GLAD THE INVITATION PLEASES YOUR FAMILY. IT WILL PLEASE MY FAMILY TO THE FOURTH GENERATION AND MY FAMILY OF FRIENDS AND WERE THEY LIVING IT WOULD HAVE PLEASED INORDINATELY THE KIND OF GROVER CLEVELAND DEMOCRATS I HAD FOR PARENTS.[32]

Senator Kennedy soon telephoned to discuss what Frost was going to do when he appeared on the inaugural platform a month hence. Did he care to write a new poem for the occasion? No, said Frost, he could never be counted on for something like that. Then if he desired to read a poem that was already written, would he do "The Gift Outright," and alter the last line, if only for a day, from "such as she would become," to the more positive-sounding "such as she *will* become"? Yes, said Frost, he supposed he could do that, and the matter was settled.

Frost spent the last few days before the inauguration with Hyde Cox at Crow Island, and in the course of his visit told Cox that he had refused Senator Kennedy's request that he write a poem for the ceremony. Nevertheless, as the big day drew nearer, Frost began to waver in his reluctance to celebrate the new administration with a new composition. "Well," he thought out loud to Cox's dismay, "I guess I ought to write something."

The idea was folly from the start. For years, Frost had been depending on his memory, not his eyesight, in public readings of his verse, and to attempt to read a poem out of doors on a January day at high noon was an invitation to disaster, even assuming that he could finish it in time. When he reached Washington on the eighteenth of January, he had a few dozen lines done, but it was still far from completion. By working feverishly into the first hours of the twentieth, he managed to write forty-two lines of a poem that, while not really finished, was at least presentable. When Udall picked him up at his hotel to take him to the ceremonies, he announced, "I've decided I want to say a few things bofore reading my poem. Will that be all right?" Udall, somewhat taken aback by the surprising news, asked how long it would take. Frost was not sure; he would have to time it and see. Then, as Udall stood and listened through the door of Frost's room, Frost read aloud the poem he called, simply, "Dedication":

Summoning artists to participate
In the august occasions of the state
Seems something for us all to celebrate.
This day is for my cause a day of days,
And his be poetry's old-fashioned praise
Who was the first to think of such a thing.
This tribute verse to be his own I bring
Is about the new order of the ages
That in the Latin of the founding sages
God nodded his approval of as good.
So much those sages knew and understood
(The mighty four of them were Washington
John Adams, Jefferson, and Madison)
So much they saw as consecrated seers
They must have seen how in two hundred years
They would bring down the world about our ears

By the example of our declaration.
It made the least tribe want to be a nation.
New order of the ages did they say?
The newest thing in which they led the way
Is in our very papers of the day.
Colonial had been the thing to be
As long as the great issue was to see
Which country'd be the one to dominate
By character, by tongue, and native trait
What Christopher Columbus first had found.
The French, the Spanish, and the Dutch were downed,
They all were counted out: the deeds were done:
Elizabeth the First and England won.
Of what had been for centuries the trend
This turned out the beginning of the end.
My verse purports to be the guiding chart
To the o'erturning it was ours to start
And in it have no unimportant part.
The turbulence we're in the middle of
Is something we can hardly help but love.
Some poor fool has been saying in his heart
Glory is out of date in life and art.
Our venture in revolution and outlawry
Has justified itself in freedom's story
Right down to now in glory upon glory.
I sometimes think that all we ask is Glory.[33]

Frost emerged from his room to tell Udall that he would need only so many minutes, and was told that there was therefore no problem in having him read the new poem as a preface to his saying of "The Gift Outright." But as Udall drove him through the snow-covered streets of Washington over to the Capitol, Frost admitted that one thing still worried him about the new poem. It had been typed out on one of the hotel's office typewriters the night before, and he found it a bit difficult to make out even in good light. In the bright sunlight of the outdoors ceremony, he might have considerable difficulty reading what he had written. Udall said he knew where there was a special oversized-letter typewriter of the sort President Eisenhower used for his speeches, and that he would have the poem typed out at once on the special machine.[34]

The ceremony began at ten o'clock with an invocation by

Richard Cardinal Cushing, who was interrupted briefly when some defective wiring in the lectern began to smoke and several technicians and firemen rushed in to see what was wrong. Then Miss Marian Anderson sang the National Anthem, followed by an invocation by Archbishop Iakovos, the administering of the oath of office to Vice President Lyndon B. Johnson, and a prayer by the Rev. Dr. John Barclay. Finally, it was time for what was listed in the inaugural program as "Poem by Mr. Robert Frost."

The master of ceremonies, who had introduced each of the speakers so far, stepped to the microphone and said, "Now I have the honor to present one of our most distinguished poets who will deliver an original composition: Mr. Robert Frost." Frost, who had been shivering in the back row of the platform for nearly an hour, now rose and slowly made his way toward the lectern, with several sheets of paper clutched in his hand against the stiff breeze. Taking his time, he anchored the pages with his outstretched hands, and then, in a voice that was obviously nervous, said, "First the Dedication." The sun was glaring down on him, and the reflected light from fresh-fallen snow and fresh white paint compounded the visual difficulty. These, and his unfamiliarity with the poem he was about to read, caused him to miss the first word. "Summing . . . summoning artists to participate / In the august occasions of the state / Seems something for us all to celebrate. / And . . . today . . . is for my cause a day of days. / And his be poetry's old fashioned praise / Who was the first to think of such a thing. / This tribute to be his that here I bring / Is about. . . ." At this point, after a long pause, he interrupted himself to say directly into his typescript, but plainly enough so that the microphone picked it up, "No, I'm not having a good light here at all." A few more broken phrases from the poem, and he paused again. "I can't see in the sun." Then Vice President Johnson rose from his seat to try to shield Frost's papers from the glare with his top hat, but it did not seem to help. Half grabbing the hat away, Frost said, "Here, let me help you," a remark that broke the painful silence in the audience and brought a burst of laughter and applause. Finally, he saw that there was no point in trying to read the new poem. "I'll just have to get through as I can," he said to himself, and then into the microphone, "I think I'll say this was to be a preface to the poem I can say to you without seeing it. The poem goes like this." Another burst of applause, and then, in a voice that, unlike his performance so far, was firm and unfaltering, he began to say "The Gift Outright":

The land was ours before we were the land's.
She was our land more than a hundred years
Before we were her people. She was ours
In Massachusetts, in Virginia,
But we were England's, still colonials,
Possessing what we still were unpossessed by,
Possessed by what we now no more possessed.
Something we were withholding made us weak
Until we found out that it was ourselves
We were withholding from our land of living,
And forthwith found salvation in surrender.
Such as we were we gave ourselves outright
(The deed of gift was many deeds of war)
To the land vaguely realizing westward,
But still unstoried, artless, unenhanced . . .

Here he paused, and in slow, accentuated tones, gave his altered version of the last line: "Such as she was, such as she *would* become, *has* become, and I—and for this occasion let me change that to—what she *will* become." Without pausing, he continued to speak. ". . . and this poem—what I was leading up to—was a dedication of the poem to the President-elect Mr. John Finley." Out of kindness, or perhaps because the last two words were delivered in much lower tones than what preceded, the audience hardly remarked the final error of his uneven performance at the inaugural rostrum.[35] Instead, it gave him a warm round of applause, and the ceremonies continued immediately with the administering of the oath of office to the President-elect. Frost's official part in the day's activities was over.

He remained in Washington a few more days, long enough to attend one of the inaugural balls that night, and to see an article in the Washington *Post* next morning with the headline, "Frost's Poem Wins Hearts at Inaugural." It began, "Robert Frost in his natural way stole the hearts of the Inaugural crowd yesterday with a poem he recited and another which he couldn't read because the sun's glare hid the words. . . ."[36] In a way, Senator Kennedy's joking prediction to Stewart Udall, like Frost's own, had come to pass.

Before leaving, he went with Mrs. Morrison to call on the new President and First Lady at the White House, to receive Kennedy's thanks for taking part in his installation, and to thank him for permitting him to do so. After some picture-taking in the Green Room before a portrait of John Quincy Adams, the visitors were conducted upstairs, where Mrs. Kennedy, resting from the past two days' events and not yet fully recovered from the birth of her son, John, joined her husband in greeting them. During the conversation, Frost presented the Kennedys with a manuscript copy of the "Dedication" poem, on which he had written "Amended copy. Now let us mend our ways." He also gave the young President a bit of fatherly advice: "Be more Irish than Harvard. Poetry and power is the formula for another Augustan Age. Don't be afraid of power."

President Kennedy sent him a short thank-you letter a few days later, typed and somewhat impersonal. But in signing it, he showed that he had not forgotten the word of advice Frost had offered. Turning the letter sideways, the President had written across it, diagonally, "Power All the Way."[37]

IN THE CLEARING

The beauty of my position is I'm only listened to for amusement. But seriously you have made my life a real party for the last go-down.[1]

LESS THAN two months after President Kennedy's inauguration, and only a few weeks before his own eighty-seventh birthday, Robert Frost packed his bags and prepared to embark on a trip that would carry him farther from home than he had ever been in his life: a two-week trip, under State Department auspices, to Israel, Greece, and England. Unlike his last venture across the Atlantic in 1957, there were no honorary degrees or promises of extraordinary recognition to entice him into making the taxing and, at his age, potentially dangerous journey. Indeed, he found himself wondering before his departure on March ninth whether it had been a mistake to accept the invitation of the official from Hebrew University of Jerusalem who had come to see him in Ripton in the spring of 1960, an invitation to serve as the first lecturer in a new University program on American Culture and Civilization. At first he had hoped that the trip might also be a vacation for Kay Morrison, with whom he had never traveled abroad. But when she declined to go with him he was left, as he saw it, with at least one good reason for making the trip: it was one further opportunity to add to his store, however slightly, of that intangible commodity he called "glory."

Another reason, which itself would have been insufficient to justify so ambitious an undertaking, was that it would permit him to view firsthand two cultures from which, as he had said in his poem, "Kitty Hawk," Western civilization had taken its "running start." At a farewell luncheon in New York, sponsored, as was the Israeli phase of the trip, by the American Friends of the Hebrew University, he said as much: "I am going to make a bee-line from where the human race has come for two thousand years. And it has come in many ways—

language, the alphabet from that end of the Mediterranean, the Bible, from which so much of our own literature is made. Right there, that was the beginning of it all."

At a press conference following the luncheon, Frost's remarks suggested that his own nationalism had something to do with his going as well. "I look on Israel as a sort of American colony. They all speak English there. They have so much of the American people's spirit. They have many, many things in common with us—more than anyone else."[2]

He had a few surprises in store for him when he reached the "American colony," but the surprises of the journey began much sooner than that. After the luncheon and press conference were over, Frost spent the rest of the afternoon relaxing at the Westbury Hotel, and sharing a private dinner with his daughter Lesley, Kay Morrison, Al Edwards, and his traveling companion for the trip, Lawrance Thompson. Only when Frost and Thompson boarded the El Al Israel Airlines jet that was to leave for Israel at eight-thirty that evening did they learn that their Flight 228 was the "Sheraton–Tel Aviv Special," carrying a group of reporters and executives to the opening of the first American-owned hotel in Tel Aviv. Surprised by the prospect of an impromptu press conference as he made his way across the Atlantic, Frost was equally surprised to learn, after a nerve-racking, four-hour delay in takeoff,[3] that Holt and El Al had joined in preparing a souvenir folder for the first-class passengers "Honoring the Distinguished American Poet Robert Frost." It contained the very first printing—albeit with one of the seventy-seven lines inadvertently dropped—of his expanded and now-complete "Dedication" poem for President Kennedy.

When the plane was safely airborne, the predictable occurred. By ones and twos, the reporters and executives began congregating around Frost's seat, until he was surrounded by eager eyes and ears. Surveying the cabin of the plane, Frost noticed, however, that Mrs. Inez Robb of the Scripps-Howard syndicate had remained demurely in her seat. He remembered her well: she was the one who had asked the best questions at the 1959 Seagram symposium on "The Future of Man" and who had pleased him even more by saying in print, afterward, that he had been denied the Nobel Prize for literature long enough. Certain that she had remained in her seat only out of politeness, Frost sent Thompson to her with a message. "Mr.

Frost," he said, "would consider it an honor if you would permit him to autograph your folder for you." Mrs. Robb said that nothing could please her more, and rose at once to accept the poet's favor.

One writer present who did not wait to be asked, and who even made himself something of a nuisance with his show of admiration, was Harry Golden. Frost knew that he was the author of a best-selling collection of essays called *Only In America*, but he also knew that Golden was a close friend of Carl Sandburg's and thus, as he saw it, not one to be much suffered. When Golden presented him with a paperback copy of his book, inscribed "To Robert Frost, may you live to 120, like Moses," the poet was amused enough to reply "And like Moses with all his powers unimpaired." But as Golden persisted with his talk, comparing Frost and Sandburg as artists and finally observing, as Frost awoke disheveled from a nap, that the poets had the same kind of hair, Frost's patience wore thin. "What's he always talking about Sandburg for?" he snapped, at no one in particular. "And how dare he say I have the same kind of hair as Carl? My hair's my own, and I don't copy anybody else's haircut."

Realizing suddenly the reporters were hanging on his every word, he decided to continue his verbal barrage, aiming now not at Golden but Sandburg himself: "I've been cutting my own hair now for twenty years. Haven't been to a barber since then. Got sick and tired of those fellows. I didn't mind them talking to me. I guess every barber's supposed to do that. But I did mind them always telling me my hair was falling out. So I started cutting my own hair. As you grow older, you don't care about those things. Of course, Carl's a very careful fellow. I'm sure he goes to the barber."

The attack soon turned from Sandburg's hair to his poetry. "We're entirely different in our work. He has a good heart. He says in his poetry, 'The people, yes.' I say 'The People, Yes—and No.' I'd say Sandburg has written some good Whitmanesque verse, but I don't think he knows what form is. Our great difference is our approach to poetry. I once said when he introduced me at a dinner that I'd just as soon write free verse as play tennis with the net down. But I have no quarrel with him. He's out there in Hollywood now with his name on the door writing that five-million-dollar picture about Christ, and I suppose that's all right if you want to do that sort of thing. But I don't like people telling me we have the same kind of hair."[4]

By the time the plane approached Paris for a refueling stop, the conversation had turned to politics, but even there, Sandburg was susceptible to attack. The New Deal and the Fair Deal, Frost complained, had aimed only to send all children to school, and all people over sixty-five to hospitals. "They worried only about the helpless. I'm over sixty-five, and I don't feel helpless. Damn the helpless. That's for Sandburg."[5]

The columnist Leonard Lyons, another passenger aboard the flight, was baffled as to how, in light of his obvious conservatism, Frost had found it possible to associate himself with a liberal like John F. Kennedy. "A liberal is someone who can't take his own side in an argument," Frost responded. "Liberals are agnostic, and no Catholic can be an agnostic. Atheist, sometimes. But not agnostic. I hate stalemates, and I'd rather die than cower. I want someone to cut Gordian knots." Kennedy, he said, was such a man, and that was why he liked him.[6] More to the point, perhaps, was the further comment Frost made during the stop at Orly Airport: "I'll vote for any party," he told Lyons, "that will be nice to me."[7]

Thirteen hours out of New York, the plane landed in darkness at Lod Airport, and Frost was met as promised by representatives of the American Embassy and the Hebrew University of Jerusalem. Also as promised, he and Thompson were whisked without difficulty through the immigration office, from which they went on to their rooms at the famous King David Hotel in Jerusalem, ten miles away.

Next morning, after sleeping late and trying with some difficulty to get a hot breakfast on the Jewish Sabbath, the two visitors decided to spend a part of their free time exploring the neighborhood around the hotel. King Herod's Tomb was just down around the back, and looking north across the wadi, they could see historic Mount Zion in the distance. For more recent history, they needed to look no farther than the hotel walls. They were pockmarked with bullet holes from the 1948 war in which Israel had achieved its statehood.

After lunch, they were taken on a motor tour by an American-born poet named Robert Friend, who drove them along the boundary separating the Israeli from the Jordanian sector of Jerusalem. Over the barbed wire and the cement wall dividing the city, they could see Arab children, and on the near side, some Israeli children playing a game that resembled hopscotch. Friend stopped the car, and several of the Israeli children immediately approached it. Who was the white-haired old man? they demanded in Hebrew. "He is the American Chaim Bialik," Friend replied in kind. When they realized that this old man was the American equivalent of the greatest modern Hebrew poet, the children's eyes widened. Would he write something down on a piece of paper, and sign it? one of them asked. Friend translated for Frost, and Frost said he would. He asked Thompson to choose a line from one of his poems, write it down, and give it to him to autograph. Thompson had no trouble deciding, and wrote down the first line of "Mending Wall": "Something there is that does not love a wall." He handed the paper to Frost, and it was duly inscribed. The children, delighted, retreated with their prize.

On Sunday morning, thanks to the diplomatic efforts of the American Consul in Jerusalem, Frost and his companion were accorded the rare privilege of passing through the Mandelbaum Gate and exploring the Jordanian sector of the divided city. A camera crew of the National Broadcasting Company, which had filmed some of their earlier wanderings for use on the Chet Huntley program back home, watched as they entered Jordanian territory, were met by an Arab guide, and drove off. For the next few hours, Frost and Thompson were explorers in a fabled land. Entering the Old City through the Dung Gate, they retraced the Stations of the Cross, with their genial Arab guide pointing out historic sites along the way. There on that wall was where Jesus was tempted by Satan. Here was the Petra Hotel, named, Frost recalled, after the same Petra he had written about in 1891 in an essay published in the *Lawrence High School Bulletin*.[8] There ahead was the Mount of Calvary, where a church had been built upon the reputed site of the True Cross. The guide showed them where, behind a counter in the church, the Cross was said to have stood. The hole was there to see, and Christian believers, said the Arab, thought it beneficial to reach down into it and to pray. Did Frost wish to do so? "Oh, no," said the poet, with a mixture of amusement and embarrassment. "I'm not good enough." On the way back to the Israeli sector, Frost observed to Thompson that he was perfectly willing for anyone else to believe all the "historical" accounts the guide had been providing, even if he did not believe them himself. At least, he said, they offered greater elevation and moral significance than the evolution myths created by Charles Darwin.

During the next few days, Frost participated in a number of "talking sessions" at Hebrew University. His chief appearance came on the night of March thirteenth in the University's Wise Auditorium, where he announced at the outset that he did not intend to talk *about* American civilization because, quite simply, he *was* American civilization. With that, he said some of his poems, and then offered to take questions from the audience.

An American student began by observing that he and the poet had both flunked out of the same college back home. Before the youth had time to ask his question, Frost was off and running. "Never flunked out of anything," he said, staring into the bright lights of the N.B.C. camera crew. "Want to hear me brag? I left college because I couldn't find one that was good enough." He did not like English teachers, he said, because they were "in the business of exaggerating Shakespeare," though, he added, "all of us, you know, will go down the drain. No one will stay except for Homer and Shakespeare."

Of his own poems, he said, they all began with the same thing: "An idea—now ask me what that is." Pointing to a student but without waiting for the question to be asked, he answered it by repeating one of his time-tested formulas: "An idea is a thought-felt thing." Then, perhaps forgetting how many times he had said the same thing, he added, "Never said that before."[9]

"Yesterday I met a lot of professors and we discussed education," he continued. "Education, I said to them, elevates trouble to a higher plane. I had never said that before, either. It surprised me. Maybe one day it will start a poem."[10]

His rambling comments soon brought him from education and universities generally to Harvard University in particular. "You can measure it by the number of Presidents it has reared. Two Yanks, two Dutchmen and a Mick. Might have snobbed itself out of the world. But it didn't. It's still running, you know."[11] After two hours of what was essentially a running monologue, the session ended, and the poet retired to the King David Hotel to rest before his next meeting with the English faculty later that evening.

Over the next few days, Frost left Jerusalem for a visit to Tel Aviv, a look at the new Hadassah Medical Center, and a brief, cordial visit with the President of the country, Itzhak

Ben Zvi. An all-day drive down the seacoast was planned, as were more talks and social calls. But halfway through his ten days in Israel, fatigue, intestinal illness, and—most important—homesickness, began to get the better of him.[12] Israel had proved to be far less an "American colony" than he had anticipated. It was hotter than South Miami ever got, had more rocks everywhere than Vermont had anywhere, and fewer of the natives spoke fluent English than Bostonians spoke proper Bostonian. What he wanted now was to go home at once, where the food agreed with him, where English was the native language, and where he could be looked after by his understanding Kay. He was expected to spend a few days in Athens with the American ambassador, expected to lecture there, expected to spend his eighty-seventh birthday with E. M. Forster in Cambridge a week hence. He did not want to disappoint so many of his friends and admirers. But he did not know whether he had either the strength or the desire to continue.

Accordingly, as soon as he reached Athens, Frost asked Thompson to telephone Alfred Edwards in New York, and to say that he was seriously considering an immediate return to the States for reasons of illness. He might have done just that, had not the wife of the American ambassador, Mrs. Ellis O. Briggs, solved his digestive problem with a special diet of tea and custard. So dramatic was his recovery that, within hours of his arrival in Athens, he was well enough to hold another press conference for the score of Greek newsmen who were eager to meet him, and well enough to amuse and amaze them with his comments on international politics and his command of Greek history and literature. He was also well enough to participate in a formal reception in his honor held at the ambassador's residence, though he remained seated in the library off the drawing room while Mrs. Briggs showed visitors in to him a few at a time.

On three successive days, he gave three public lectures in Athens, all of which went extremely well. At his talk on March 22 before the Greek Archaeological Society, the subject on which he chose to speak was Plato, and more particularly his own sympathy for Platonic philosophy. Plato, he said, was "of course more of a mythologist than he was a philosopher. He was a sort of link between the almost unconscious metaphors of the earlier times and the conscious philosophy of his time and ours. But he still makes myths. I like to think that I am not quite a Platonist and then all of a sudden I find myself saying something that I myself trace right back to Plato. For instance, I say 'There's more religion outside the Church than in, there's more love outside of marriage than in, there's more poetry outside of verse than in, and there's more wisdom outside of philosophy than in.'

"I'm sort of romantic," he continued, "and if I'm romantic I'm romantic from Plato. . . . All romantic comes from the three-cornered love affair, and that's Plato again. You had Mars, see, Mars, Aphrodite and Hephaestus. That's a three-cornered love affair, and that comes clear down into all the romantic times of later. Two and one. . . . I love what I have but I love better what it's a poor imitation of. See, that's romantic again. No, I guess I put that a little wrong, didn't I? You love in a way the poor imitation, and the reality married to someone else is what you really love. See, that's from—that's all there is to romance—just that three-cornered thing. . . ."[13]

Before he left Athens for London on March 24, Frost joined vacationing friends from Amherst, the G. Armour Craigs, to climb the Acropolis that meant much to him as a symbol of Athens' ancient greatness. If he had been bored and homesick at times in Israel, he could not be so in Greece. Greek history, Greek literature, meant too much to him. Coming to Athens seemed to him, he said before leaving, a kind of homecoming.

Back in England for the first time since 1957, Frost began a limited schedule of activities by attending a prebirthday party in his honor, on the afternoon of March 25, at the residence of American Ambassador David K. E. Bruce. After a short nap, he attended as well what he supposed would be another party honoring him at the home of Sir Charles Tennyson, leading member of the Society "designed," according to Frost, "for the prevention of forgetting Tennyson." When the "party" proved to be no more than an ordinary high tea, however, the homesickness that had repeatedly overtaken Frost earlier in the trip came back in full force. He quickly returned to his rooms at the Connaught Hotel, where he told Thompson to make reservations for a flight home next day. He would not, he said, be able to spend his birthday with E. M. Forster in Cambridge as he had planned. Then, tired and ill, he went to bed.

Next morning was his birthday, but when Thompson called on him for breakfast, he found Frost in no condition for any kind of celebrating. Indeed, the poet looked so unwell that Thompson suggested a doctor be called in to examine him. The doctor's diagnosis gave little comfort: "I can tighten up his bowels all right," said the Englishman to Thompson, "but it's his heart that worries me." It was slow and irregular, and the doctor advised that Frost be taken back to America at once. Thompson told the poet what the doctor had said, and was told in turn to send a telegram to Al Edwards:

> TELL KAY I AM ORDERED HOME BY EMBASSY DOCTOR. WORN OUT.

Back in Massachusetts by the end of March, Frost recovered quickly from the various ill effects of his trip, and within a few days time was well enough to look forward eagerly to an event for which, like his role in the Kennedy inauguration, he had Stewart Udall to thank. Called "An Evening with Robert Frost," it was a reception and reading in the State Department Auditorium scheduled for the first of May, and Frost knew that not only many members of the Cabinet and the Congress, but also the Kennedys themselves, were planning to attend.

His April letter of thanks to Udall, who had just published an article on Frost's role in the inauguration, was full of cordiality: "How brotherly it all seems. By the accident of our falling in friendship with you and Lee [Mrs. Udall] we have been brought out on top of a new pinnacle of view that makes me for one feel dangerously like a monarch of all fifty states I survey. . . . You know one of my missions is to get a secretary of the arts into the President's cabinet but I am as good as in there now with you to talk to. I have been reaching the President through you for some time. Somebody's been telling him our economy is manic. I'd like to tell him that a big vigorous economy like ours can't keep itself from overstocking and so having to have a clearance sale once in so often. That's the kind of figure of speech I'm good at. The beauty of my position is I'm only listened to for amusement. But seriously you have made my life a real party for the last go-down. K. and I are looking forward to the visit to Washington and what it sounds as if you had in store for us. Roy Basler from the Library has just been talking to K. about it. You know I am consultant in the humanities. By humanities I mean parks and all that. The President wants a park made of his region on the Cape. I might want a park made of our place in Vermont. Watch out! I hear all sorts of things you are writing about fish and game and such. You like to write. So do I or I wouldn't do it. People everywhere have been talking about your piece in 'The New York *Times*.'"[14]

Much to Frost's disappointment, a government crisis involving Communist military advances in Southeast Asia prevented President Kennedy and Secretary of State Rusk from attending the "Evening with Robert Frost" on the night of May first. But in spite of their absence, and in spite of the atmosphere of crisis that overhung Washington, his talk in the new State Department Auditorium was a triumphant success. The audience was made up of ambassadors to and from the United States, generals, Supreme Court justices, senators. The Secretary of the Treasury, C. Douglas Dillon, began by introducing Secretary Udall, who in turn introduced Frost. Then, for more than an hour, the audience was completely his, as he spoke first on his favorite subject of science-versus-poetry, and then read a wide selection of some of his best-known poems. He was not permitted to leave the hall until he had returned to the stage for several encores, each preceded by a standing ovation, nor until he had spent a full hour more in the lobby, accepting the personal tribute of many of the guests.

Next day, Frost had an opportunity to repay the Interior Secretary for having arranged the "Evening" in the State Department Auditorium. While most of Washington was awaiting the outcome of the Southeast Asia crisis, Udall found himself threatened by a crisis of his own when reports appeared alleging that he had requested a Washington friend, a member of the oil and gas industry, to solicit contributions from his associates to a $100-a-plate Democratic dinner. A copy of the oilman's embarrassing letter to his colleagues had no sooner been made public when Udall resolved to deny, immediately and publicly, any involvement in its production. He wanted Frost, however, to do him a small favor. Would he be willing, before they went to lunch as planned, to join him at the front of the room when his meeting with the press took place? Frost agreed to do so, and thereby to serve as a kind of character witness for the Secretary. Though he somewhat resented Udall's willingness to involve him in his difficulty, he was prepared to do that much and more to help save his friend from needlessly going the way of Sherman Adams.[15]

As usual during his twice-yearly visits to the Library, Frost remained in Washington for two weeks, delivering a free public lecture in Coolidge Auditorium, receiving visitors, attending teas and a large formal reception, and performing other duties and social obligations in his capacity as Consultant in the Humanities. But he was glad, when the time came, to return to Vermont for his summer vacation at the Homer Noble farm. Since returning from his foreign tour, he had had almost no time to rest and write. He had high hopes of finishing the collection of new poems he had been promising Holt for the past several years. The title he had talked of using as early as 1954 was "The Great Misgiving," and it had been his own misgivings about the quality of his later poems that had prevented him from going into print much sooner with a new collection. But as he had implied in his last letter to Udall, and said elsewhere, his life had reached the phase that he called "the last go-down." Any further delay in preparing the volume might result in its being published in a way he did not want: posthumously.

The importance of finishing the book before death overtook him or his powers failed him was given a special urgency in early July when he learned of the death by suicide of Ernest Hemingway. For some time afterward, he could talk and think of nothing else, and he felt sure that he knew just why Hemingway had done what he had done: he had become convinced that he had lost his ability to write. Frost would not tolerate any criticism of Hemingway's action. He insisted that he had shown great courage in killing himself when the thing he had lived for was gone, and he spoke more than once, though not for the first time, of doing the same thing himself. He was not sure his own powers were still with him. He was not sure that he should not take the course Hemingway had chosen. In his darker moods in the weeks following the suicide, he made a gesture more than once of throwing his almost-completed book of poems into the fireplace, not so much because he feared that his powers had failed him as because he dreaded seeing his poems attacked by the critics he "never read." He did not want to be told that they were not up to his best work.

In this state of mind, he was less than pleased by a letter from Louis Untermeyer. His old friend began by acknowledging that Frost had never written anything to order and never would. "But you are the greatest player with words that our century has produced," he wrote, "and it is on this basis that I hope to interest you in a project I have undertaken." The project was a series of "Beginner Books" to be published by Crowell-Collier, which were intended to be read not to, but by, children from six to eight years old. The vocabulary in the series was limited to 250 specially selected words, a copy of which Untermeyer enclosed in his letter. He wanted to know, he said, if Frost would be interested in writing one of the books, a task for which he would be paid at least $1,000, but one that he might find an amusing diversion for its own sake.[16]

Frost was in no mood to waste his time on so trivial, even if so remunerative, an enterprise. "You cruel thing," he wrote, "to order of me the kind of book you know I could never write for love or money. You [drove] me to distraction for a few minutes. You want a whole book by me for children with a vocabulary of twenty five words beginning with the nouns 'cat' and 'dog' and the verbs 'scratch' and 'bite' or 'meow' or 'bow-wow.' The form is as strict as a limerick. The sonnet is the strictest form I have behaved in, and that mainly by pretending it wasn't a sonnet. But come up and see us and I will go to work arranging the manuscript of my next book that, until I get it out, stands in the way I feel of your publishing my letters. That ought to be an inducement. You didn't see the picture of me in the hospital, did you? I told the reporters I had my ear operated on to start a new era. For want of me the world's course will not fail. I must try work to see if it does me any good. . . ."[17]

More to his liking was the recent action of the Vermont State Legislature, which in late June passed a bill designating him "Poet Laureate of Vermont." In informing him of the honor, Governor F. Ray Keyser invited him up to Stowe in the third week of July to receive a citation thanking him for his contributions to the life of his adopted State. By the time he arrived at Stowe, where the first annual Vermont Poetry Festival was in progress, Frost had written a new four-line poem to thank the State for the honor:

Breathes there a bard who isn't moved
When he finds his verse is understood
And not entirely disapproved
By his country and his neighborhood?[18]

Frost's feelings of warmth toward his fellow Vermonters were considerably cooled by a sequence of events that began in October 1961. Stewart Udall had caught the hint when Frost had written, in his April letter, that he might want a park made someday out of his "place" in Vermont. In subsequent conversations, the poet and the politician had agreed that it would be a fine idea to have a "Robert Frost Memorial Park" created in Ripton as a living monument to the State's Poet Laureate. During a three-day visit by Udall to the Homer Noble farm, they discussed the matter further, and agreed that the best plan of attack was to arrange a trade of some of the government acreage bordering the Homer Noble farm for another piece of property Frost would purchase in or near Ripton. Government property could not be bought or sold, even if the Interior Secretary was not opposed to so doing. But if the barter of a piece of land near Ripton for part of the government pine grove near Frost's cabin could be arranged, then the "Robert Frost Memorial Park" could be formed by adding the land around the cabin, and the cabin itself, to the pine grove. It seemed simple enough, and after Udall's departure, Frost did prepare to purchase some acreage north of Ripton known as "Beaver Meadow," in order to trade it for the government land in question. But when the government land was appraised in anticipation of the trade, the value assigned to it was so astronomically high that the entire scheme had to be abandoned. For Frost, who had long hoped to see a park set up that would preserve the memory of his association with Ripton and vicinity, the disappointment was acute. "This ends a chapter in my life," he told a local forestry ranger, "and a chapter in the life of the town."[19]

Another plan that did not fall through was one initiated by the citizens of Lawrence, Massachusetts. A year or two earlier, they had authorized the construction of the Robert Lee Frost Elementary School in the town where the poet had grown up after the move with his mother and sister from San Francisco. The school opened in September of 1961, but the formal dedication was delayed until early January of the new year so that Frost could attend. In the course of the afternoon, he spoke about poetry and his early experience as a student at Lawrence High School to an audience that included a Miss Ellen Hogan, who was one of the three surviving members of the Lawrence

Class of 1892. Frost told of his excitement when his history teacher, Katherine O'Keefe, had written on the blackboard a poem by Collins that began, "How sleep the brave . . ." and how he had shortly begun to write a poem himself, "La Noche Triste," about "that terrible night when Cortez was almost wiped out in Mexico City." "It's still kicking around," he observed with a smile, "and I'm still kicking around."[20]

On January eighteenth, before leaving for his winter vacation in Florida, he attended the annual Poetry Society dinner in New York, where he knew another form of homage was awaiting him in the form of a recently completed portrait bust by the lawyer-sculptor Leo Cherne. But Frost was so far from being pleased by the finished product that the affair for him was a dismal failure. Next evening he found himself at a party in his honor at the apartment of his daughter Lesley, but again he came away feeling angry and out of sorts. Lesley had told him of her decision to sell the third of Pencil Pines he had given her and her husband, Joseph Ballantine, as a wedding present in 1953. It seemed to Frost that Lesley was deliberately setting out to hurt him, and hurt, indeed, he was.

His feeling of persecution was still strong enough several days later to convince him that even his most devoted admirers were turning against him. At Agnes Scott College in Decatur, Georgia, to which he had paid almost yearly visits on his way down to or up from South Miami since 1935, he was sure that there was disrespect intended in some of the questions he was asked after he finished his talk. One local reporter asked him if he thought poetry was going out of fashion. He did not bother to hide his annoyance: "You ought to know better than to ask me a question like that," he snapped. If he was referring to his own verse, he went on angrily, he wanted to know "who has been more popular in this country than I? Or perhaps you say because mine is popular that it is not poetry. . . ."[21] His hypersensitivity was such that when he bade farewell at last to the women of this college where he had been adored and idolized for almost forty years, he vowed privately that he would never again return.

Exhaustion and sheer rage had combined to make him virtually ill even before he reached South Miami on the night of 26 January 1962. Within a few days, he had contracted a cold and sore throat, and was feeling so poorly that he telephoned

Kay Morrison in Cambridge and tried to tell her just how sick he was. But his deafness prevented him from hearing what she was saying in response, and in disgust, he cut her off by hanging up the phone. Disturbed by this unusual behavior, Mrs. Morrison immediately telephoned one of her Miami friends, Helen Muir, who lived close by, and asked her to see what the matter was. One look at the poet was enough to convince Mrs. Muir that a doctor was needed. His diagnosis was probable influenza, but he was unable to persuade Frost to enter the local hospital. In the end, the doctor prescribed appropriate medication, and arranged for a nurse to come and take care of him while he stayed in bed at Pencil Pines.

By the third of February, he was feeling much better in body, if not in spirit. When the doctor returned and found that his temperature was normal, he suggested that Frost go outside to enjoy the sunny, mild weather with a short walk. While he was dressing, however, a brief shower left the grass soaking wet. Going out anyway, he got his feet wet and returned to the house with a chill. When the doctor came back, he assured Frost that his temperature was still normal, and that he was "coming along fine." The poet did not agree, and said he felt terrible. When he got up to shave a few hours later, he began to cough violently, and saw blood in his phlegm. Without a moment's hesitation, he walked unsteadily to the telephone, dialed Mrs. Morrison once again, and growled darkly, "If you want to see me again, alive, you'd better get down here fast. And tell Al Edwards the same." He then hung up as before.

The nurse, who had overheard all this, telephoned the doctor as soon as Frost returned to his bed, and told him that her patient was behaving "like a crazy man. He's trying to kill himself." Returning at once, the doctor found that Frost's temperature was now alarmingly high, and that his lungs were filled with congestion. The new diagnosis was inescapable: pneumonia.

An ambulance was called in, and he was taken by stretcher to the new Baptist Hospital in South Miami. There being no time to await the results of hospital tests, the doctor made an educated guess that Frost's pneumonia was of the pneumococcus variety, and treated him accordingly. That the guess was correct very likely saved Frost's life. Within a few days he was well enough to joke with the doctor about the penicillin treatments without which he would surely have died. "They say pneumonia is 'the old man's friend,' " Frost observed. "I guess that makes penicillin the enemy of the old man's friend."[22]

Despite a relapse that temporarily threw his survival in doubt, Frost was sufficiently recovered, by the sixteenth of February, to leave Baptist Hospital and retire for a month of convalescence to Pencil Pines. While there, he occupied himself by going over with Kay page proofs of the long-awaited book that he had recently submitted to Holt. His South Miami farm, nestled as it was in a clearing of scrub pine, was a particularly appropriate setting for applying the finishing touches to the new volume. The title Frost had given it, after years of intending to call it "The Great Misgiving," was *In the Clearing.*

The title was apparently derived from a poem called "A Cabin in the Clearing," which came third in the volume and which was dedicated to Frost's friend and publisher, Alfred Edwards. In it, "Smoke" and "Mist," personified but disembodied spirits, discuss the occupants of a secluded cabin who, like Job in *A Masque of Reason*, don't "know where they are."[23] When "Smoke" asks "Mist," "Why don't they ask the Red Man where they are?" "Mist" replies:

> *They often do, and none the wiser for it.*
> *So do they also ask philosophers*
> *Who come to look in on them from the pulpit.*
> *They will ask anyone there is to ask—*
> *In the fond faith accumulated fact*
> *Will of itself take fire and light the world up.*
> *Learning has been a part of their religion.*[24]

Frost had nothing against "accumulated fact" as such: indeed, as more than one scientist of his acquaintance had had occasion to observe, he himself had an unusual command of the facts and principles of modern science. But as several poems in this, as in previous, volumes suggested, he had little patience for those in or out of the sciences whose "fond faith" it was that learning generally, and science in particular, could so reduce the world to quantifiable, rational data that God would be quite left out of the universal equation. That God's purposes were served even in the most apparently accidental of natural and human events was the theme of another poem in *In the Clearing* entitled "Accidentally on Purpose":

The Universe is but the Thing of things,
The things but balls all going round in rings.
Some of them mighty huge, some mighty tiny,
All of them radiant and mighty shiny.

They mean to tell us all was rolling blind
Till accidentally it hit on mind
In an albino monkey in a jungle,
And even then it had to grope and bungle,

Till Darwin came to earth upon a year
To show the evolution how to steer.
They mean to tell us, though, the Omnibus
Had no real purpose till it got to us.

Never believe it. At the very worst
It must have had the purpose from the first
To produce purpose as the fitter bred:
We were just purpose coming to a head.

Whose purpose was it? His or Hers or Its?
Let's leave that to the scientific wits.
Grant me intention, purpose, and design—
That's near enough for me to the Divine.

And yet for all this help of head and brain
How happily instinctive we remain,
Our best guide upward further to the light,
Passionate preference such as love at sight.[25]

The notion that human instinct was man's "best guide upward further to the light" was extended in the poem "Kitty Hawk," which, despite its three-beat lines sounding half like *Beowulf* in translation and half like doggerel, Frost regarded, properly, as one of his most important poems. Beginning it in 1953 after a visit with his friends the Huntington Cairnses at Kittyhawk, North Carolina, Frost reworked and expanded the poem until it had grown to almost 500 lines, and included both a partial autobiography of his early life and the philosophy of his maturity. The autobiographical aspect of "Kitty Hawk" was contained in its first section, "Portents, Presentiments, and Premonitions," in which Frost recalled, for the first time in verse, his 1894 flight to North Carolina after his apparent abandonment by his beloved, Elinor Miriam White. It began:

Kitty Hawk, O Kitty,
There was once a song,
Who knows but a great
Emblematic ditty,
I might well have sung
When I came here young
Out and down along
Past Elizabeth City
Sixty years ago.
I was, to be sure,
Out of sorts with Fate,
Wandering to and fro
In the earth alone,
You might think too poor-
Spirited to care
Who I was or where
I was being blown
Faster than my tread—
Like the crumpled, better-
Left-unwritten letter
I had read and thrown. . . .[26]

The 1894 trip to the South, so crucial in determining the course of Frost's personal life, was also, or at least had come close to being, a turning point in his development as a poet. "Kitty Hawk" continued:

Oh, but not to boast,
Ever since Nag's Head
Had my heart been great,
Not to claim elate,
With a need the gale
Filled me with to shout
Summary riposte
To the dreary wail
There's no knowing what
Love is all about.
Poets know a lot.
Never did I fail
Of an answer back

To the zodiac
When in heartless chorus
Aries and Taurus,
Gemini and Cancer
Mocked me for an answer.
It was on my tongue
To have up and sung
The initial flight
I can see now might—
Should have been—my own
Into the unknown,
Into the sublime
Off these sands of Time . . .[27]

Frost had missed his chance, in 1894, to make the "initial flight" from the sands of Kittyhawk a "flight of words,"[28] of his poetic imagination. It had been the Wright brothers who, from the same sands nine years later, had made the initial flight of their pioneering flying machine. Yet, returning to the historic spot just half a century after the Wright brothers' achievement, Frost discovered—and expressed in "Kitty Hawk" —a new way of looking at that achievement, as part of the ongoing development of Western civilization that had begun, paradoxically, with the "fall" of man:

Pulpiteers will censure
Our instinctive venture
Into what they call
The material
When we took that fall
From the apple tree.
But God's own descent
Into flesh was meant
As a demonstration
That the supreme merit
Lay in risking spirit
In substantiation.
Westerners inherit
A design for living
Deeper into matter—
Not without due patter
Of a great misgiving. . . .

Spirit enters flesh
And for all it's worth
Charges into earth
In birth after birth
Ever fresh and fresh.
We may take the view
That its derring-do
Thought of in the large
Was one mighty charge
On our human part
Of the soul's ethereal
Into the material. . . .[29]

It was clearly Frost's intention to include the discoveries of science and technological developments among the ways men had emulated God by "risking spirit in substantiation." But it is also clear that he considered poetry, and his own verse in particular, a meritorious endeavor to apply mind, or spirit, toward the deeper penetration of the universe. Much of the extended passage just quoted appeared, as a kind of motto, at the beginning of *In the Clearing*, and it can be assumed that Frost considered the poems therein examples of how he, himself, had followed God's example by risking his spirit—in verse.

Brought back to health by Mrs. Morrison and two practical nurses, Frost was well enough by the third week in March 1962 to go as planned to Washington for the celebration of his eighty-eighth birthday on March 26. His birthday activities began with a Washington press conference in which he had an opportunity to defend former President Eisenhower from Carl Sandburg's recent statement that he had not been much of a Chief Executive. "The Old General," Frost mused aloud before the actual questioning began. "He's a friend of mine, an admiration of mine, too. I've heard all sorts of cheap things about him." In the conference proper, he was asked what he thought of Soviet Premier Nikita S. Khrushchev, of whom he had been doing much thinking of late. "Oh, what a grand man he is!" he exclaimed. "What a creature! What a creature! He's my enemy. But it takes just a little magnanimity to admire him."[30]

Later, the poet called on President Kennedy to receive from him the Gold Medal that he was once to have received from President Eisenhower. In return, he gave the President the first copy of *In the Clearing*, which was to be published later that day, and which carried an affectionate inscription:

"Great circumstances have raised this book to be almost more yours, O my President, yours and your lady's than it is the lady's who made me make it. I have admired you so much I wish I were a better Democrat than I am. I come halting along from having marched in procession over the cobblestones of San Francisco in 1884 to help elect Grover Cleveland. But let me thank you with enthusiasm for the reaffirmation in your Profiles of the brave doctrine that a ruler's answerability is but secondly to his constituents; and for much else right down to now including as it were a birthday present for George Washington—your establishment of an Office of the Fine Arts right in the White House where you and your lady can keep an eye on it toward Irish-French impulsiveness. I don't want it to get too calculated. I like your first appointments over it, the social seer and the connoisseur.

"You may notice that my dedication to you of 'The Gift Outright' has been growing into a rhymed history of the United States I may some day write for you."[31]

The President also noticed, perhaps, that the book itself was dedicated thus: "Letters in prose to Louis Untermeyer, Sidney Cox, and John Bartlett for them to dispose of as they please; these to you in verse for keeps." The "you" and "the lady who made me make it" were one and the same: Kay Morrison.

That evening, after spending the afternoon resting in his hotel room, Frost went to the Pan American Union Building for his birthday dinner. Two hundred invited guests helped him celebrate in his grandest party to date, and the after-dinner speakers who rose to praise him included Chief Justice Earl Warren, Robert Penn Warren, Adlai Stevenson, Justice Felix Frankfurter, and Mark Van Doren. Stewart Udall, who with Alfred Edwards had arranged the affair, then rose to introduce the guest of honor: Robert Frost. At five past midnight it was the poet's turn to speak, and for twenty-five minutes he did just that. Over a public-address system that was beginning to fail, he recited some of the poems in his new book, interspersed his "sayings" with his accustomed comments, and closed by praising the woman who had been his "devoted secretary" for more than twenty years. After a recitation of the sonnet he had written for her, "Never Again Would Birds' Song Be the Same," he sat down and another great evening was over.

RUSSIA: A FINAL MISSION

I go as an opportunist on the loose. I'd like a chance to ask the great Kruschev to grant me one request and then ask him a hard one.[1]

IN SPITE of his cherished belief that the battlefield was one of the best places to test the relative strength of opposing ideas, Robert Frost eventually became convinced that, in a nuclear age, it made no sense for the superpowers to go to war over some transitory world trouble spot or a difference of political ideology. His rejection of atomic combat implied, however, no acceptance of the petty squabbling and "blackguarding" of the cold war. Rivalry between the great powers was, he believed, inevitable, but the best, the highest kind of rivalry was on the level of intellectual, creative and athletic competition. It had, moreover, to contain a good measure of something Frost had come to value much in recent years, something he had once invoked in speaking of his reasons for aiding Ezra Pound and more recently in speaking of Soviet Premier Nikita Khrushchev: magnanimity.

President Kennedy, Frost was sure, believed as he did in magnanimous rivalry: it was this belief, coupled with Kennedy's much-discussed regard for courage, that had led Frost to predict the onset of "a golden age of poetry and power" under Kennedy's leadership. But what of the Russian leader, Khrushchev, of whom Frost had said in March 1962 that it took "just a little magnanimity to admire him"? Frost believed that Khrushchev, too, could be persuaded to give up "blackguarding" for magnanimous rivalry if only asked to do so in the right way. And, it occurred to Frost, an autocratic ruler like the Soviet Premier could, if he chose, do more to effect change in the conduct of world politics, to end the present cold-war stalemate, and to create a climate where nuclear war did not impend, than, ironically, even the President of the United States.

In May 1962, during a two-week stint as Consultant in the Humanities at the Congressional Library, Frost was presented with an opportunity to try out his ideas concerning magnanimous rivalry on a representative of the Soviet government. Soon after his arrival in Washington, he received a call from Stewart Udall, who began by saying that he was going to Russia in the fall to inspect Soviet hydroelectric facilities with a team of American engineers. Also, Udall continued, he was shortly to entertain the new Russian ambassador, Anatoly Dobrynin, with a small party in his Georgetown home. Would Frost care to come? Yes, said Frost, he very much would.

Though Udall's party was a great success, for Frost it led to unexpected and not entirely welcome developments. After a spirited discussion between Frost and the Russian ambassador, in which Frost presented his case for "the right kind of rivalry" between the superpowers, Udall observed that it would be greatly beneficial to international understanding if Frost could share his views with the Russian people. Perhaps, he said, an exchange could be worked out in which some Russian poet might visit the United States in return for a visit by Frost to the Soviet Union. Ambassador Dobrynin said he liked the idea very much, and promised to make inquiries about the proposed trip. Half-elated and half-terrified, Frost said that before he could agree to undertake so arduous a mission, he would have to give the matter most careful thought.[2]

When he did think about it, in Washington and back in Ripton, Vermont, he eventually decided that he was willing to go to Russia if there was a chance—even a small one—that in so doing he might be presented with an opportunity to meet Khrushchev and share with him his vision for a better world. He was past being interested in visiting new lands, seeing new people, even winning new converts to his verse. But to take a part in the shaping of history, a part that might far transcend even his participation in the presidential inauguration, that, indeed, was something! That he would meet the Premier in Russia would remain, in all probability, a "long shot"—that he would have an effect on his thinking, an even longer one. But thinking back on his long life, Frost remembered that he had achieved success, great success, when he was already "almost too old to bet on." Perhaps his luck was still running strong.

Much as he welcomed the invitation that now seemed assured, Frost could not resist playing a game he had played more than once in the past. Perhaps, he told Udall, he was not up to making so strenuous a trip. Russia was a long way off, and he had not—which was true enough—been in the best of health in recent months. But he would go, he said, if the President wanted him to. In July, after the Department of State had successfully completed preliminary arrangements, President Kennedy sent Frost the word he wanted: his personal invitation, along with an expression of his high esteem, for Frost to go to Russia in August as part of a Soviet-American "cultural exchange."

Frost's letter accepting the President's invitation only hinted at his hope to see Khrushchev while in Russia. He made no secret, however, of his boyish delight at the prospect of going: "Dear Mr. President," he wrote, "How grand for you to think of me this way and how like you to take the chance of sending anyone like me over there affinitizing with the Russians. You must know a lot about me besides my rank from my poems but think how the professors interpret the poems! I like to tell the story of the mere sailor boy from upstate New York who by favor of his captain and the American consul at St. Petersburg got to see the Czar in St. Petersburg with the gift in his hand of an acorn that fell from a tree that stood by the house of George Washington. That was in the 1830s when proud young Americans were equal to anything. He said to the Czar, 'Washington was a great ruler and you're a great ruler and I thought you might like to plant the acorn with me by your palace.' And so he did. I have been having a lot of historical parallels lately: a big one between Caesar's imperial democracy that made so many millions equal under arbitrary power and the Russian democracy. Ours is a more Senatorial democracy like the Republic of Rome. I have thought I saw the Russian and the American democracies drawing together, theirs easing down from a kind of abstract severity to taking less and less care of the masses: ours creeping up to taking more and more care of the masses as they grow innumerable. I see us becoming the two great powers of the modern world in noble rivalry while a third power of United Germany, France, and Italy, the common market, looks on as an expanded polyglot Switzerland.

"I shall be reading poems chiefly, over there, but I shall be talking some where I read and you may be sure I won't be talking just literature. I'm the kind of Democrat that *will* reason. You know my admiration for your 'Profiles.' I am frightened by this big undertaking but I was more frightened at your Inauguration. I am glad Stewart will be along to take care of me. He has been a good influence in my life. And Fred Adams of the Morgan Library. I had a very good talk with Anatoly Dobrynin in Washington last May. You probably know that my Adams House at Harvard has an oil portrait of one of our boys, Jack Reed, which nobody has succeeded in making us take down.[3]

"Forgive the long letter. I don't write letters but you have stirred my imagination and I have been interested in Russia as a power ever since Rurik came to Novogorod; and these are my credentials. I could go on with them like this to make the picture complete: about the English-speaking world of England, Ireland, Canada, and Australia, New Zealand and Us versus the Russian-speaking world for the next century or so, mostly a stand-off but now and then a showdown to test our mettle. The rest of the world would be Asia and Africa, more or less negligible for the time being though it needn't be too openly declared. Much of this would be better for not being declared openly but always kept in the back of our minds in all our diplomatic and other relations. I am describing not so much what ought to be but what is and will be—reporting and prophesying. This is the way we are one world, as you put it, of independent nations interdependent—the separateness of the parts as important as the connection of the parts.

"Great times to be alive, aren't they?"[4]

As Frost indicated in his letter, the choice of a traveling companion had by now already been made. Frederick B. Adams, Jr., Director of the Morgan Library in New York City, was a friend who had grown particularly close in the past few years, most recently participating with the poet in the filming of the Ripton portion of the documentary film, *A Lover's Quarrel With the World*. But as Adams spoke no more Russian than did Frost, it had also been decided that someone else must be brought along to serve as interpreter. Frost's friend, the poet William Meredith, suggested the name of Franklin D. Reeve, a young professor of Russian literature at Wesleyan University, who had an excellent command of the Russian language. Reeve was more than willing to serve Frost as interpreter, so the entourage was complete. Frost left it to Adams and Reeve to work out an itinerary with the State Department. He himself had only one fixed goal for the Russian expedition, and that goal appeared nowhere in his itinerary: to talk to "the great man," to Khrushchev, and to present to him his vision of a "magnanimous rivalry" that might, just might, alter the course of history.

Frost's plans called for him to go down to Washington in late August to make final preparations for the trip, but three days before doing so—on the 25th—he stayed overnight at Crow Island with his friend Hyde Cox. Hyde's island—or his

. . . isle that would be an isle
But isn't because of an isthmus.

as Frost had once written in an "envoi to Hyde the castaway of Crow Island"[5]—had come to mean almost as much to Frost as any home of his own. The beauty of its location surrounded by the sea, the atmosphere of warm hospitality that Hyde always created for his friend, had made the visit Frost always made to Hyde's at Christmas time one of the most predictably pleasant of his annual peregrinations. But this year, Frost detected a sadness in Hyde's mood, caused, as he knew, by Hyde's belief that he ought not to be making the Russian trip. Nevertheless, with stoical resignation, Hyde accepted Frost's explanation that he had to go to Russia, that he had promised the President and promised himself. In the evening, Cox helped Frost prepare for the trip by playing, at his request, some Russian music: Act II of Tchaikovsky's *Eugene Onegin*, which Frost liked, and the Fifth Symphony of Shostakovitch—which he did not. After breakfast next morning he helped the poet pack his bags.

Hyde's sadness was deepened by a feeling that when Frost left Crow Island to set off on his trip to Russia he might never return. When Frost started to leave the guest room Hyde walked behind, carrying his suitcase. Before they reached the door, Frost could sense that his friend was emotionally upset. The old man stopped, set down his bag, and put his hand on Hyde's shoulder. "Oh, it's all right," he comforted. "I know how it is. You just don't want me to go out and get lost, do you?" Outside the house, Frost lingered on the steps. Then, instead of speaking to Hyde, who shared his dislike for farewells, he bent down and patted the head of Hyde's dog, Robbie, whose breed was the same as that of Frost's own beloved Border collie, the "perfect" and now long-dead Gillie. "Good-bye—the practically perfect dog," he murmured softly. Then he abruptly climbed into the waiting car and departed.[6]

In Washington, on the twenty-seventh of August, Adams and Reeve concluded their discussions with the Soviet Exchanges Staff of the State Department, and joined Frost for dinner at the home of the Udalls. The Interior Secretary spoke encouragingly to all three of what an opportunity they had to improve understanding among the American and Russian peoples. That was agreeable enough to Frost, but it was not what interested him most. He wanted to meet Khrushchev, he kept saying, to talk bluntly with him and tell him "right off, this and that." He repeated the essence of what he had said in a recent letter to Lawrance Thompson: "I go as an opportunist on the loose. I'd like a chance to ask the great Kruschev to grant me one request and then ask him a hard one."[7] But he would not confide to any of his companions what the request was to be. To reveal it prematurely would surely diminish its impact, when, or if, the time came for it to count.

Even now, Frost's nervousness was beginning to get the better of him. A call that had come from Ambassador Dobrynin earlier in the day, asking that instead of joining him for lunch at the Soviet Embassy, Frost come for an early morning talk in his office, was still bothering him. "You see," he had said to Adams in the afternoon, "the plans are already degenerating." If a simple luncheon could not be carried off, how would he ever manage to see Khrushchev? By evening, he was so upset that Udall offered to telephone the Russians to see if it were not possible for him to lunch with Frost after all. The luncheon date was restored, but Frost continued to worry himself even to the point of illness. Next morning, Adams found him in his hotel room complaining of pains in his chest, the kind of pains he often got when something or someone was causing him anxiety. But he quickly recovered from his "heart trouble," and the lunch with the Dobrynins took place without further incident. As her guests were saying good-bye, Mrs. Dobrynin wished them a safe flight to her homeland. "Thank you," said Frost with a smile. "It's going to be some adventure." Then he added, mischievously, "I guess I can't ask you to say a prayer for me, though, or wish me Godspeed, because you don't believe in God." "I wish you a safe journey from the bottom of my heart," she replied, "which is better."[8]

The flight to Russia, with Frost, Adams, and Reeve accompanied by Udall and his party of engineers, was uneventful, and late in the afternoon of Wednesday, August 29, the Americans disembarked at Sheremetyevo Airport outside Moscow. There, Frost was greeted by a pair of American diplomats attached to the Embassy in Moscow, and a delegation of five Russians representing his official "host" on the trip, the Soviet Writers Union. Aleksandr Tvardovsky was their leader: a poet, the editor of the major literary journal *Novy Mir*, and the winner of a Lenin Prize. His companions were the poet Alexei Surkov, Secretary of the Writers Union and Deputy to the Supreme Soviet, Yevgeny Yevtushenko, the "angry young man" of Russian poetry, Mikhail Zenkevich, another poet, and a professor named Ivan Kashkin who, along with Zenkevich, had translated many of Frost's poems into Russian. There were also two women from the Foreign Section of the Union, who were specialists in American literature, and who would serve Frost as guides and interpreters: they were Elena Romanova and Frida Lurye, whose constant vigilance would soon earn them the Americans' nickname "the pendragons."

Before leaving the airport for his rooms at the Hotel Sovietskaya, where visiting dignitaries were regally lodged while in Moscow, Frost chatted with the group of Russian and foreign reporters who had come to welcome his arrival. "I am here to talk with you about science, art, athletics, great music and, of course, poetry," he told the Russians. "We can talk about these things because there is no rivalry. We admire each other, don't we? Great nations admire each other and don't take pleasure in belittling each other." But, he added, "If the Russians beat my country in everything, then I will become a Russian." His writer-hosts, who had stood by watching intently while he talked, broke into nervous laughter. But they seemed not to comprehend him when he continued, "You've got to have power to protect the language, to protect the poetry in it. You've got to be strong to protect poetry. Poetry's the most national of the arts, not so much painting or music. A great nation makes great poetry, and great poetry makes a great nation. It works both ways." He told his questioners that he had, in a way, been born in Russia: "Russia used to own the West Coast of the United States, California. That's where

I was born. I was born in Russian territory. There's a hill in San Francisco called Russian Hill. I was born right near there." "Sometime I'll go a little deeper into our approach to each other," he continued. "I've got some rather bold things to say."

After the brief interview, Udall and his engineers left for the National Hotel, and "the three" were taken to the Sovietskaya, accompanied by Jack Matlock, Second Secretary of the American Embassy, and Tvardovsky, who was to be the "other half" of the Russian-American cultural exchange. Frost knew that much about the Russian, but he was unaware of just how important a man Tvardovsky was. When the Russian quipped that he was "not only a poet myself but also a strangler of young poets," Frost took it as nothing more than the witticism of an artist competing, like him, for public attention. Reeve, at least, knew that, as editor of *Novy Mir*, Tvardovsky was a powerful figure in determining which Russian artists enjoyed the approval of the Soviet government, and—more often in recent months—which did not.

Next morning, Matlock reappeared to say that the American Embassy was working to arrange an interview with the Soviet Premier, but that it was too early to tell if their efforts would be successful. Romanova and Lurye also arrived with a lengthy program of things for Frost to do and see during his ten days in Russia. It was soon shortened considerably. "There isn't much time," Reeve explained to the pendragons, "and we must arrange things so Frost sees some people and reads his poems. He doesn't like just sightseeing and staring at monuments." That, nevertheless, was what he did for much of the morning. After several interviews with Russian newspaper reporters, he was taken in a black Zim sedan provided by the Writers Union and shown around the city. Commentary was provided by the pendragons and supplemented by Reeve. Frost joined Surkov and Tvardovsky for lunch, and in the afternoon he rested in preparation for a visit, that evening, to the city apartment of the writer Paustovsky.

Next day, after more interviews with the press, the trio was driven to dinner with Kornei Chukovsky at his dacha in Peredelkino, the writers' colony outside Moscow. At eighty, Chukovsky was Frost's counterpart among Russian writers: the "grand old man," winner of a Lenin Prize, and the receipt only a few months before of an honorary degree from Oxford

University. His book of Russian folk tales, he told Frost, had sold more than 60 million copies, and he was famous not only as a literary critic but as a writer of children's verse as well. Many children were present when Frost arrived. Seated on the floor of Chukovsky's dacha, they listened intently as the old Russian, whose hair was as white as his guest's, asked them to tell their grandchildren that they had met the great American poet, Robert Frost.

Chukovsky's English was excellent, and the pendragons were hardly required as translators. But one of them was somewhat carried away in her eagerness to be of service to Frost. During dinner, apparently assuming that Frost's deafness was preventing him from hearing what Chukovsky was saying, she began to repeat his remarks louder and louder, until she suddenly jumped from her place at the table and ran around to Frost to shout directly in his ear. Frost, who had heard less and less the higher her voice rose, reared back as if under attack, and told her flatly to go away and sit down.

Back in Moscow next morning, Frost paid a visit to an "English" school where the children were exposed to a curriculum that emphasized instruction in the English language. Since this was the first day of classes in the new term, the pupils had forgotten much of what they had previously been taught. After looking in on some elementary-level classes, Frost, followed by a number of American and Russian reporters, was taken by a rigidly proper headmistress to a group of seventh-graders, who, having been forewarned, snapped to attention beside their desks when he walked in. One boy in the front row, obviously the star pupil of the class, was instructed to ask Frost a question. "What do you think of our cosmonauts' flight?" he nervously inquired. "Great," said Frost. "Don't you think so, too?" "Of course," the boy replied. Frost asked the rest of the class how many of them would like to go to the moon, and slowly, somewhat hesitantly, they all raised their hands. "You want to get away from here any way you can," he observed, adding at once, "Oh, I'm only kidding you." Then he explained the meaning of the word "kidding."

The teacher asked the star pupil to define in English a Russian verb, and when he stumbled over the answer, she raised her voice to correct him in a manner that embarrassed all the Americans present. Then Frost was asked to recite a poem. He said a few lines from "The Pasture," but the pupils were obviously lost, and the teacher's paraphrase only emphasized Frost's failure to reach them. Suddenly, Frost turned and said to Adams, "I think we'd better go. I don't feel very well." They left at once, and returned to the Sovietskaya. Frost was visibly disappointed. He had been in Russia for almost four days, and it seemed to him that he was no closer to doing what he had come for—seeing Khrushchev—than he was when he arrived.[9]

In the evening, Frost, Adams, and Reeve visited the Aelita, a "youth café," as the guests of Yevgeny Yevtushenko. In addition to several reporters, who seemed to be present wherever he went, the company included Jack Matlock from the Embassy and three leading Soviet poets. Eduard Mezhelaitis was an older Lithuanian poet residing in Moscow, who had won a Lenin Prize. His poem entitled "The Blue-eyed Cliff," which he had written after a visit with Frost in Cambridge a few months before, had appeared in *Pravda* a day or two earlier. Yevgeny Vinokurov and Andrei Voznesensky were also present, the latter widely held to be among the most gifted of younger Russian poets. But the evening was all Frost and Yevtushenko. As a trio of musicians played American jazz on the opposite side of the room, the old American and the young Russian tried bravely to communicate across a gap of sixty years of age and light years of cultural distance. Asked what sort of wine he preferred, Frost told his host that he wanted red. Yevtushenko replied, "If you ask for red wine, people might believe you have been infected by Red propaganda." Unable to separate Yevtushenko the poet from Yevtushenko the propagandist, Frost gave no answer. Later, the conversation turned to the subject of good and bad people, and Yevtushenko suggested that there were fewer of the latter, but that their excesses provoked others into doing good. "Like killing them?" Frost teased. "Is it good to kill a bad man?" This time, it was Yevtushenko's turn to remain silent.

Afterward, the party adjourned for dinner at Yevtushenko's apartment, where several other poets and friends of the Russian were waiting. Each of them, including Frost, recited a few of his poems, and the evening ended at midnight on a much more favorable note than the day had begun. Frost could not help wondering at what sacrifice Yevtushenko managed to satisfy what were, to him, the irreconcilable demands of his art and his revolutionary politics. But his more immediate concern, on this Saturday night, was whether the Soviet Sunday would be a day of rest, giving him an opportunity to gather his strength for the meeting he hoped would soon be taking place.

Sunday proved to be sufficiently restful. In the morning, Frost and Adams attended an early performance of *Swan Lake* by the Bolshoi Ballet, accompanied by a pair of Russian guide-translators. Adams, thinking that Frost might want to leave the performance early, had made provisions for their escape. But he stayed, and enjoyed it very much, explaining afterward that the best part of it was not having to listen to spoken Russian for several hours. Back at the hotel, Frost slept for the rest of the afternoon, and following dinner at the comfortable apartment of Simonov, the Americans boarded a sleeper for the next stop on their itinerary, Leningrad.

Upon arrival, Frost went directly to his hotel room where, as he had not slept at all on the train, he spent the morning resting. Then, after lunch, he and Adams went out for a look at the restored Peterhof, the majestic estate of Peter the Great. Adams soon realized that asking Frost to come had been a mistake. The old bard walked about sullenly for a while, declined to inspect nearby Mon Plaisir, and returned to the limousine that had brought them, observing with a look of obvious boredom, "I suppose it's all very grand." Adams shot a glance over to their Russian guides, fearing that they might have been offended. Instead, they were delighted by Frost's displeasure. It proved to them that he was, after all, just a simple man, a man of the people, as the Russian press had been saying all week.

In the evening, the Americans dined at the home of novelist Daniil Granin, and although several of Leningrad's leading literary figures were present, the conversation somehow never got off the ground. Realizing that Frost's spirits were rather low, Adams and Reeve reminded him that tomorrow he would meet Anna Akhmatova, Russia's leading woman poet, and give the first public poetry reading of the trip. But neither of these filled Frost with anything like eager anticipation. He knew no more of Akhmatova than he did of any of the other Russian writers that he had met, and as for the poetry reading, he saw no point in talking to an audience that did not understand what he was saying. Khrushchev was on his mind still, and if he did not see the Premier before he went home then—as he had said more than once during his first days in Russia—"What the hell am I doing here?"

Despite Frost's ennui, a friendly meeting with Akhmatova took place next day, and after secluding himself for several hours in his hotel room, as he always did before giving a lecture, he read his poems to a politely responsive audience at Leningrad's Pushkin House. The Americans returned to Moscow that night, where Frost gave another public lecture the following afternoon. Like the first, it was received politely but with restraint. The Russian audiences, to the extent that they understood what he was saying, did not seem to trust themselves to laugh at the mild witticisms he aimed toward their society and their leadership. "Leningrad is still a royal city," he said in his Moscow talk. "It has a lingering royalism." But Moscow, he added, "is a proletarian city, and if you don't like that word too well, if it is worn out with you, why then I'll say it's a people's city." A few minutes earlier, he had aimed what seemed too much like a barb at Premier Khrushchev for the audience to laugh freely: "It is the duty of great nations to compete and see who can produce the greatest rulers," he had said. "We won't call them kings any more. You can always tell a great ruler if he is a dreamer, if he has a lot of the dreamer in him—and we won't mention any names." Realizing that he had perhaps said the wrong thing, he had quickly added: "That was an extemporaneous poem—free verse." The tension broken, his listeners finally laughed aloud.

Another sensitive moment in Moscow came when he read "Mending Wall," with its opening line, "Something there is that doesn't love a wall," and its interior lines, "Before I built a wall I'd ask to know / What I was walling in or walling out, / And to whom I was likely to give offense." With the issue of Berlin still far from resolved, and with the wall the East Germans had erected in 1961 still drawing widespread criticism in the West, Frost's choice of this particular poem seemed inescapably political to many who were present. But the poet himself implicitly denied any political motive. "I've had lots of adventures with that poem," he said after reciting it. "People are frequently misunderstanding it or misinterpreting it. The secret of what it means I keep."

At the informal reception that followed the reading, a reporter who had covered it for the New York *Herald Tribune*, David Miller, came up to Adams and asked if he, Frost, or Reeve had heard from Stewart Udall. Adams said he assumed that the Interior Secretary was on his way back from his tour of Siberian hydroelectric stations. "No," Miller informed him, "he's in Moscow, and he'll be leaving by plane early tomorrow morning for Gagra to visit Premier Khrushchev." He paused, and added, apologetically, "I thought you'd like to know."

As soon as he could get Frost away from the reception, Adams returned to the hotel and told Reeve and Matlock—but not Frost—what he had learned. By now it was too late in the evening to call Udall and ask him to communicate his plans to the poet, with perhaps a promise to do what he could toward arranging a meeting between Frost and the Premier. Matlock offered to get up at dawn and try to intercept Udall at the airport before he left for the Crimean resort where Khrushchev was to see him. But by the time he got there Udall had left, and Matlock returned disconsolately to the Sovietskaya. Frost would have to be told.

Over breakfast, Adams broke the news as gently as he could. As expected, Frost saw Udall's unheralded departure for a visit with Khrushchev as a desertion, if not an outright betrayal. Knowing that Frost was to make a television appearance later that morning, Adams tried to pacify him with assurances that, even if he did not see Khrushchev, his Russian visit had been a triumph. Frost, however, would have none of it. He forbade Adams to "preach" to him, and icily refused to talk about it any further.

Too soon, Surkov, Yevtushenko and a group of Russian translators and TV technicians began arriving for the eleven o'clock program. Adams asked them to wait until just before the appointed hour, and then went in to tell Frost it was time to dress. The poet silently complied, and they went upstairs to a makeshift studio in the hotel. Adams was apprehensive about how Frost would behave in the three-way interview with Surkov and Yevtushenko. But Frost managed to rise to the occasion. "Before I say anything about poetry," he began with a slowly broadening smile as the cameras rolled, "I want to thank my Russian hosts for their friendship and the good times they've given us. . . ." The closest he came to mentioning his crushing disappointment was when he responded to a question from Yevtushenko, who asked, "Do you feel you have had good audiences here?" "Fine," Frost replied, "despite the difficulty of language. It's always good to exchange talk about poetry, with a little talk of politics too—between poets. The exchange of poets between countries is more useful than the conversation of diplomats. It brings kindred spirits together."

That afternoon, while Frost was resting alone in his room, his telephone rang repeatedly, but he chose to ignore it. Adams and Reeve returned to the hotel in the early evening and learned at the front desk that someone had been trying to reach Frost all afternoon with no success. Fearing that something had happened to him, they rushed up to his room and knocked on the door. His step inside reassured them. When he let them in, they asked if he had not heard the telephone. "Yes," he answered, "it rang quite a lot, but I didn't bother to answer it. I knew there'd just be a voice on the other end speaking Russian, and I couldn't do anything about it."

They called the American Embassy and asked if there were any messages for Frost. There were none. They called the Writers' Union, but no one was there. Somewhat baffled, they awaited the arrival of Matlock for dinner. When he appeared, however, he could provide no information about the mysterious telephone call. Finally, as they sat over cocktails in Matlock's apartment, the diplomat received a call from which he returned with a broad smile. He had just been informed, he said, that Premier Khrushchev would see Frost tomorrow in the Crimea; reservations had already been made for the poet, Surkov, a Russian interpreter, and one member of Frost's party, on a morning flight out of Moscow.

The good news came as such a shock to the old poet that soon after Adams and Reeve returned from his hotel room he became, as Adams later described it, "actively sick." His nervous illness was, indeed, so violent that it was decided to defer until morning the final decision as to whether or not he would go at all. Several hours of sleep, they hoped, would help him recover. Unfortunately, they did not. When Adams and Reeve called on him before six next morning, he told them that he had hardly slept a wink all night, and that he felt even worse than he had the night before. He knew, and his companions knew, that he was in no condition to go anywhere, let alone to a meeting with the Premier of the Soviet Union. But as Frost remarked as they debated a course of action, "It would be hard to face my friends at home if I had a chance to do what I came to do, and then didn't do it." Adams, with some hesitation, chose not to argue the other side. With little further discussion, it was decided that Frost would go to the Premier, taking with him the Russian-speaking Reeve, instead of Adams, in case there was an emergency.

By eleven o'clock, after a three-hour flight on a regularly scheduled jet filled with Russian vacationers, Frost, Reeve, Surkov, and an interpreter named Myshkov landed at the airport outside Sochi in the Crimea. Met by the same delegation of officials and engineers that had received Udall the day before, they were driven across the border into Georgia and taken to the Guest House of the Georgian SSR Ministry of Health. Premier Khrushchev's dacha, where they were to continue after a little time to eat and rest, was a twenty-minute drive away.

Frost, who had napped during much of the flight to Sochi, lay down in his room at the Ministry and told Reeve that he was feeling worse than ever. Reeve told Surkov of the situation over lunch in the dining room, and they wondered uneasily what their next move should be. Then, returning to Frost's room, Reeve asked if the poet wanted a doctor to be summoned. After some hesitation, he said yes. Twenty minutes later, a white-frocked woman appeared at the Ministry, carrying her black doctor's bag. She took Frost's temperature—it was 101.5°—listened to his chest and back, and made her diagnosis: Frost was neither very sick nor quite well. He seemed to be suffering from nervous indigestion, probably brought on by too much traveling. Still, she agreed, if his illness became any worse, he should be returned at once to Moscow. Frost, who had watched the discussion from his bed, made his own pronouncement: he could go no further.

Once again, Reeve informed Surkov of how things stood with the poet, and then returned to Frost's room. A few minutes later, Surkov appeared and said he had just spoken by telephone with Premier Khrushchev. The Premier was sending his personal physician to look at Frost, and would soon come himself. The meeting was still on.

Frost was pleased, and in a way relieved. But the imminence of his long-sought confrontation with the Russian leader made him edgier with every passing minute. Through his mind ran all the things he wanted to say, had been planning to say ever since his first discussion of the Russian trip with Udall and Dobrynin in Washington. He tried to doze, but could not. Khrushchev's doctor now arrived, confirming his colleague's diagnosis of the poet's illness. Then, after a few minutes of waiting that were as tense for Reeve as they were for Frost, the Premier himself appeared at the house. Reeve thanked him for coming, thanked him for sending his own doctor, explained Frost's illness and said how anxious the poet was to meet him. After a word with the doctor about the state of Frost's health, the Premier, accompanied by his secretary, entered the room.

Forewarned by Reeve, Frost had sat up on the edge of his bed and put on his shoes and socks. Reeve, Surkov, and Myshkov stationed themselves around the room, as did Khrushchev's secretary and the host of the guest house. After an exchange of greetings with the poet, Khrushchev sat on a chair beside Frost's bed. Then began the conversation, an account of which was later recorded and published by Reeve:

"[Khrushchev] asked about Frost's health, chided him for not taking care of himself, expressed admiration at Frost's traveling so far, said how pleased he was to see him, reminded him to be sure to follow the doctors' orders if he was going to live to be a hundred. Frost, for his part, said that he was very glad to have come, that he was very pleased by the invitation, that you could never trust doctors anyway, and that he was certainly going to live to be a hundred because in the year he would be a hundred his country would be two hundred. It was something, he said, being half as old as your country.

"Khrushchev asked him how he had found his stay in Russia, how he had been received. Frost replied that he had had a fine time, that the Premier certainly had done a lot for poetry, judging by all the poets around. They talked briefly about art and poetry and the artist's relation to his society. Frost conveyed the President's greetings to the Premier and expressed his gratitude to those who had arranged his trip.

"And with that the real conversation began. Khrushchev wondered if Frost had anything special in mind, and Frost started talking about what had long lain closest to his heart: a way for working out an East-West understanding. . . ."

He had said much of it already, in his letter to President Kennedy, at Udall's dinner party to Ambassador Dobrynin, to the Russian literary men during his week in Russia, to the press. There must be no petty squabbling in the relations between Russia and America, but rather a noble rivalry on the level of sports, science, the arts, democracy. "God wants us to contend," he told Khrushchev, and the superpowers were destined for 100 years of competition that would determine which political system, the American or the Soviet, would come out on top. The central element had to be magnanimity: neither side must seek to blackguard the other to gain political advantage. "Great nations admire each other," said Frost, "and don't take pleasure in belittling each other."

To much of this Khrushchev readily agreed, but he also seemed particularly eager to demonstrate the logic of Soviet international politics. In Reeve's words:

"Premier Khrushchev said that the fundamental conflict between the two countries was peaceful economic competition. He said that the Soviet Union and all the Warsaw Pact nations were young countries, healthy, vital, full of energy. He said that they had made extraordinary strides forward. The United States and Western Europe, he said, were thousands of years old with a defunct economic system. This reminded him, he said, of an anecdote reported in Gorky's memoirs of Tolstoy, where Tolstoy told about being too old and too weak and too infirm to do it but still having the desire. Frost chuckled and said that might be true for the two of them but that the United States was too young to worry about that yet. . . ."

Frost now came as close as he would come in the conversation to making the hard request of Khrushchev that he had been keeping a secret from even his closest friends for months. He began by saying that the Premier was a man of great power, and that he was therefore in a position to do great good toward effecting a solution to the Berlin problem that had troubled East-West relations for the past fifteen years. All Khrushchev had to do, said Frost, was to propose a kind of horse-trade with the United States, something given up somewhere in the world by the Soviet Union in return for something given up in the matter of Berlin by the United States. He was sure the United States would accept the terms of any proposal he made. Khrushchev listened to the old man's words, and replied simply, "You have the soul of a poet." Then the conversation moved on to other subjects.

The meeting lasted ninety minutes. Finally, the Premier asked if Frost were not tired, if he had not overstayed his time. Frost said he had not, and added that he was glad to have had such a frank, high-minded discussion. Khrushchev asked that Frost give his greetings to President Kennedy and the American people, and suggested also that Frost talk to Kennedy about the issues they had just raised. "It is a great pleasure to have met such a famous poet," said the Premier. After some further exchange of pleasantries and a clasping of hands, Khrushchev, followed by his secretary and doctor, withdrew from the room.

"Well, we did it, didn't we?" Frost said to Reeve as he fell back, exhausted, on the bed. "He's a great man. He knows what power is and isn't afraid to take hold of it. He's a great man, all right."[10]

When the group returned to Moscow the following morning, the poet and Reeve went at once to the Sovietskaya, where a number of reporters, foreign and domestic, were waiting for them. Apparently fully recovered from the illness that had overtaken him two days earlier, Frost declined to take the hotel elevator to his second-floor apartment, but walked upstairs, shaved, and twenty minutes later invited the correspondents into his sitting room to hear the story of his meeting with the Soviet leader. "He's our enemy, but he's a great man," said Frost of Khrushchev. "He's a ruffian. He's ready for a fight. He's not a coward. He's not afraid of us and we're not afraid of him."

A Russian reporter suggested that perhaps he meant to say the Premier was "rough," but not that he was a "ruffian." Frost apparently did not hear her, for he kept right on talking. But it was clear he used "ruffian" as a term of admiration.[11]

"I sat on the edge of the bed and we had a good talk and went at it." He said he had been disappointed only by Khrushchev's apparent unwillingness to cut the Gordian knot of world problems—particularly in the case of Berlin. "I told him he ought to be like Alexander the Great who didn't believe in fussing with Gordian knots and untying them. He believed in cutting [them]. I just hoped a man as mighty as Khrushchev might do something even if we didn't. I was like a tramp poet who visits a great monarch. 'I've got just one little request,' the tramp asks the monarch. 'Will you grant it to me before I ask it?' Well," he conceded, "I didn't get that far."

He said he had gone to Khrushchev hoping to convince him to compete with America "in strife and magnanimity," and that the Premier was amenable: "He agrees with strife and with magnanimity. He's no saphead. No liberal sapheads for me."

Did he have any message from Premier Khrushchev for President Kennedy? he was asked. "Yes," he replied, "in a way." Adams and Reeve counseled him to save his "message" for the President's ears, but he kept on. "The Premier told me to say to the President not to do this and to do that, and that he mustn't do this and must do that, quite a few things." When pressed, he assured the reporters that the conversation had not been "on a low level of politics," but "all high level." He would say no more.[12]

Later, over lunch, Adams asked Frost if he wanted to send a cable to Mrs. Morrison, informing her of his safe return from Gagra. He thought a moment, and told his friend what message to send:

BACK FROM CRIMEA, ALL CRIMES ACCOMPLISHED.

Then they left for the American Embassy, where Frost greeted the staff with another joke that was a wry commentary on his week in Russia: "Hello, all you damn Yankees," he said, and went on to talk for an hour about politics and poetry. The day ended with a farewell visit to the apartment of Tvardovsky, attended by Surkov, the pendragons, Matlock, Adams, Reeve, and several others with whom he had come into contact during his Russian visit. On Sunday, September 9, the Americans flew home.

The story should have ended there, but it did not. When the Pan American jet carrying Frost, Udall, and their companions touched down at Idlewild Airport in New York, Frost had not slept for eighteen hours and was physically and mentally exhausted. Aware of Frost's condition, Alfred Edwards, who had come to meet him, did his best to reach the plane before Frost emerged to face the waiting press. Inexplicably, Secret Service agents prevented him from approaching the plane. A few minutes later, Frost stepped out on the arm of Stewart Udall, and happily complied with the request of the reporters that he answer just a few short questions. What had he discussed with Premier Khrushchev, what had the Premier said? "Khrushchev said he feared for us modern liberals," Frost answered. "He said we were too liberal to fight. I suppose he thought we'd stand there for the next hundred years saying, 'on the one hand—but on the other hand.' " Did he have any message from Khrushchev to deliver to President Kennedy, and if so, when did he plan to deliver it? "Yes," Frost replied, "I have a message from Khrushchev for the President. I don't 'plan' to see him. I wait for the President."[13]

In the days and weeks ahead, Frost waited for his summons

to the White House, or at least a note from the President thanking him for representing his country on the cultural mission to Russia. But nothing came. Instead, Frost began to receive mail from various quarters asking if it were true, as the newspapers all reported, that Khrushchev had said the United States was "too liberal to fight." One letter came from Dr. Charles H. Lyttle, Pastor of the First Unitarian Society of Geneva, Illinois:

"Dear Mr. Frost," Lyttle wrote, "Owing to the very high regard in which you are held in our church circle, several of our members have felt a bit distressed over certain aspects of the enclosed newspaper account of a purported interview on your arrival in New York from your visit to Russia.

"Your remarks concerning your attitude toward Socialism did not puzzle or disturb us—some of us feel as you do on that subject—but your (alleged) report that 'Premier Khrushchev believes the United States will not fight to protect its rights . . . he thought that we are too liberal to fight,' is the cause of our dismay.

"For the John Birchers in our community this is most welcome grist for their mill!

"For those of us who are striving to prevent war, the report is confusing and distressing—if the press item is accurate. We would be greatly obliged if you would, with the most convenience and positive brevity, inform us of the accuracy or inaccuracy of the press notice. Some of us suspect that the press deliberately misrepresented you, on this point at least. . . ."[14]

Unwilling to admit that he might have distorted Khrushchev's words to unburden his own obsession with "liberals," Frost answered Lyttle on September 20: "The *Sun* gets me right. Surely you can have no objection to my getting Kruschev exactly right. He is power personified ruling over four hundred million people seemingly of one accord. My stay was too brief for penetrating into any dissidence, if such exists. The Russian nation expects to try us out in one way or another. The stage or arena is set (by you-know-Whom) for a rivalry between us for the next hundred years in athletics, art, science, business, and in democracy, our kind of democracy versus their kind of democracy (so to call it by courtesy). Mr. Kruschev agreed to all this magnificently. We are confronted with a Gordian knot in the problem of whether it is as important for them to achieve great things as for us to achieve them. Liberals would rather fuss with that Gordian knot than cut it. They're wasting time in an emergency. That's the way Mr. Kruschev sees it as a nationalist. He and I didn't talk about peace or love or coexistence. We talked about surpassing excellence and the survival of the fittest. His amusing and slight contempt was for people who enjoyed wanting something they haven't the force to get. . . ."[15]

Frost came close to, but fell short of, admitting that he had put the word "liberal" in Khrushchev's mouth when he answered a letter similar to Lyttle's from the former Socialist candidate for president, Norman Thomas: "Everyone wants to start joking with me about the word 'liberal' but as you say, it's no joking matter. It was almost that with Khrushchev. I shall try to tell you the affable way he used it with me in Gagra. He was just being good natured and literary when he expressed concern for American liberality. He was quoting either Gorky to Tolstoi or Tolstoi to Gorky, I forget which, when he said there was such a thing possibly as a nation's getting like the bald headed row at a leg show so it enjoyed wanting to do what it could no longer do. I was interested to find the great old power house so bookish. People have asked me if he was literary like Kennedy and you and me. I think I broke down his figure by answering we were too young a nation for that worry.

"There are all sorts of liberals and I have amused myself with defining them. Khrushchev's was a good crack. My own latest is that they are people who have had the liberal education that I fled and have come back to assert my difference with their own stronghold, the colleges. If Matthew Arnold is their gospel, I come pretty near being a liberal myself. I have teasingly described them as people who can't take their own side in a quarrel and would rather fuss with a Gordian knot than cut it and as 'Dover Beach-combers' and as Matthew Arnold's wisest 'who take dejectedly their seat upon the intellectual throne.' They are never arbitrary enough 'to bid their will avouch it' like a real leader. But all that aside after it has entertained you enough. I yield to no one in my admiration for the kind of liberal you have been, you and Henry Wallace. . . . I can't see how Khrushchev's talk got turned into what you quote, that we weren't men enough to fight. I came nearer than he to threatening: with my native geniality I assured him that we were no more afraid of him than he was of us. We seemed in perfect agreement that we shouldn't come to blows till we were sure there was a big issue remaining between us, of his kind of democracy versus our kind of democracy, approximating each other as they are, his by easing downward towards socialism from the severity of its original ideals, ours by straining upward towards socialism through various phases of welfare state-ism. I said the stage or arena is set between us for a rivalry of perhaps a hundred years. Let's hope we can take it out in sports, science, art, business, and politics before ever we have to take it out in the bloody politics of war. It was all magnanimity—Aristotle's great word. I should have expected you to approve. Liberal in a good sense of the word. Browning tells of a post office bulletin notice in Italy, 'two liberal thieves were shot.' If only a word would stay put in basic English."[16]

President Kennedy remained silent. Frost could not have known how resentful he had been when informed by Udall that the remark attributed to Khrushchev was beyond question the sentiment not of the Soviet Premier, but of Frost himself. The only word from the White House on the subject of the Russian trip came not from the President, but from August Heckscher, Special Consultant on the Arts—a position that had been created partly as a result of Frost's prodding. "I am among the millions of your countrymen," wrote Heckscher, "who have been proud and delighted by your remarks and observations on your trip to the Soviet Union. You did wonderfully. You helped set a framework for broad and magnanimous discussion. I am sure that on both sides of the Iron Curtain your visit will be long remembered."[17]

Frost hoped that Heckscher's kind words were true. But he would have preferred, and he continued to hope, that he would soon hear similar ones from President Kennedy.

DEEPER INTO LIFE

Why will the quidnuncs always be hoping for a salvation man will never have from anyone but God? I was just saying today how Christ posed Himself the whole problem and died for it. We study and study the four biographies of Him and are left still somewhat puzzled in our daily lives.[1]

ROBERT FROST had survived grave illness to make the trip to Russia and had likewise survived the trip itself, but as he entered the fall of 1962 he was an ill and tired man. Even before leaving for the Soviet Union, he had been told by Dr. Hartwell Harrison of the Peter Bent Brigham Hospital in Boston that he had a prostatic condition which was threatening sooner or later to require surgery. He hardly needed to be told that the "cystitis" from which he had been suffering intermittently for more than twenty years had also grown worse in recent months: the constant discomfort it caused him, if not exactly a harbinger of death, at least served to remind him that he had lived a very long life. He was determined, however, not to slow down, not to end his days in a comfortable retirement surrounded by the circle of his closest friends. He had expressed the ideal he conceived for himself to one of those friends as they walked one day on a secluded path near the Homer Noble farm. "I often think that the best way to die," he said to Hyde Cox, "would be to die like this someday, out on the trail." And it was, indeed, to the well-worn academic trail that Frost once more returned as he entered the seventh month of his eighty-ninth year.

Dartmouth was the first stop on his fall itinerary; his visit, true to his custom of the past several years, coincided with the beginning of classes in the new semester. A few days later he called at Amherst, where his talk before the National

Committee of the Amherst Capital Program was preceded by President Plimpton's announcement that an anonymous gift of $3.5 million would be used to construct a new edifice: the Robert Frost Library. Lectures at other colleges followed until, after another talk at Amherst on October twentieth, he headed for Washington to speak at the first National Poetry Festival on the evening of the twenty-third.

Washington was in anything but a festive mood that week. The Cuban missile crisis, suddenly and unexpectedly, had brought the country and the world to the brink of nuclear war, and only the strong and decisive action of President Kennedy, including the blockade of Russian missile-bearing ships bound for Castro's island, seemed likely to prevent the installation of ballistic missiles seconds away from the continental United States. Into the city where the key decisions were even then being made came Frost, and in his Library of Congress talk, he demonstrated a new willingness to admit that Premier Khrushchev had not, in fact, said quite what he had earlier reported.

"I've joked about liberals a great deal," said the poet midway through his remarks, "and there's been something going around. I wonder how many of you've heard it: that I was told in Russia that Americans were too liberal to fight, or something like that. Nothing like that did I hear. What I heard was, rather, a pleasantry from the greatest ruler in the world, you know, the almighty, and in his genial way he just said, 'As Tolstoi said to Gorki'—or vice versa I've forgotten which; it was a very literary conversation—'As Tolstoi said to Gorki, "There's such a thing as a nation getting so soft it couldn't—wouldn't fight." ' See, that's all. He was just saying there was such a thing, and he might be suggesting that we better look out. See, that's all, it was a pleasantry. It wasn't a defiant thing, nothing was defiant. I'd like that straightened out, whatever happens. There might be a hint of that, but that's all; spoke of its being a matter of age, too. He says people can get to an age when they have a certain pleasure in wanting to do something they can't do, lingering in a pleasure they can't have. That's what he meant by a liberal, something like that. It was very intellectual. I knew what he meant. . . ."[2]

Clearly Frost was concerned that the present crisis might somehow be taken as having arisen from his inaccurate reporting of Premier Khrushchev's remarks to him in Gagra, that

President Kennedy had taken such a strong stand against the installation of missiles in Cuba to demonstrate that the country was not, in fact, "too liberal to fight" in defense of its principles. But it did not escape Frost that Premier Khrushchev, very possibly, had deliberately misled him by agreeing to his formula of "magnanimous rivalry" free of the kind of "blackguarding" the Cuban situation seemed to represent.

"Well, there were no lies, see," the poet continued, "it's very interesting. I couldn't go to him and say I was lied to, but I could say that there was a sort of loss of faith, that we understood each other, that I was led to understand what probably I was partly mistaken about. I wasn't very deeply, just a little. I could make that charge, that 'You've broken faith with me,' a little. I'd like to say that to him, like to see him here tonight. I admire him, admire the power and all that; but I feel a little hurt in a way."

As much as he might have liked to have Premier Khrushchev in the audience that night, Frost would have liked even more to have President Kennedy before him as he admitted, at last, that Khrushchev had not said what he had attributed to him after returning from Russia. It grieved him deeply to know that he had angered the President by his remarks, and he seemed to want Kennedy to know, if only by report, that he was sorry for what he had said, and sorry for the confusion, if not the crisis, his "liberal" remark had occasioned. Before concluding his talk, he even made a point of praising Kennedy's book, *Profiles in Courage*, as if that might somehow lead its author to relent and give him the word of friendship or forgiveness that he seemed intent on withholding. But the President was not there, and the one opportunity that Frost might have had to meet and talk with him personally was lost the day after his Poetry Festival appearance. For reasons not stated, but presumably because of the missile crisis, the White House announced next morning that a planned reception for the poets attending the Festival had been cancelled.

At the end of the week, Frost left Washington for Gambier, Ohio, and the dedication of a new library named after a president with whom his friendship had never lapsed, Gordon Keith Chalmers of Kenyon College. They had known each other since the 1930s, when Chalmers was installed as Kenyon's sixteenth president, and had remained close until 1956, the year of Chalmers's sudden death. By 1962, the library named after him was completed, and his wife, Roberta Schwartz Chalmers, asked Frost to join her in honoring her husband's memory. He had readily agreed. "He went to Kenyon to found the *Kenyon Review* that John Crowe Ransom made," Frost said of Chalmers in his Washington talk. "I was in on the beginnings of these things. John Crowe Ransom is one of my great friends, and Gordon Chalmers is one of my great friends. Gordon spent his life in education entirely. He didn't pretend to write poetry. . . ." But there was a poem that always reminded Frost of his late friend, because he had read it in public for the first time at Chalmers's inauguration in 1937. It was his own "October," and when he said it again in Gambier, its gentle cadences seemed almost prayerful:

O hushed October morning mild,
Thy leaves have ripened to the fall;
Tomorrow's wind, if it be wild,
Should waste them all.
The crows above the forest call;
Tomorrow they may form and go.
O hushed October morning mild,
Begin the hours of this day slow.
Make the day seem to us less brief.
Hearts not averse to being beguiled,
Beguile us in the way you know.
Release one leaf at break of day;
At noon release another leaf;
One from our trees, one far away.
Retard the sun with gentle mist;
Enchant the land with amethyst.
Slow, slow!
For the grapes' sake, if they were all,
Whose leaves already are burnt with frost,
Whose clustered fruit must else be lost—
For the grapes' sake along the wall.[3]

November was an unusually active month even for Frost. A week after leaving Gambier, he was in New York to receive the MacDowell Colony Medal, to say his poems to the 200 invited guests, and to hear read a number of congratulatory telegrams that included one from President Kennedy, laudatory but quite impersonal:

I AM DELIGHTED TO JOIN THE PRESIDENT AND THE DIRECTORS OF THE MACDOWELL COLONY IN THE TRIBUTE WHICH THEY ARE PAYING THIS EVENING TO THE THIRD RECIPIENT OF THE MACDOWELL MEDAL, ROBERT FROST. THE LITERARY ACHIEVEMENTS OF ROBERT FROST AND HIS PERSONAL INFLUENCE ON AMERICAN LIFE REPRESENT IN FULL MEASURE THE IDEALS OF THE MACDOWELL COLONY. BY HONORING ROBERT FROST YOU ARE EXPRESSING THE GRATITUDE OF THIS NATION AND THE ENDURING RESPECT WE ALL SHARE FOR THE CREATIVE ENVIRONMENT OF THE MACDOWELL COLONY. JOHN F. KENNEDY.

Less than a week later he was in Michigan, to receive an honorary Doctor of Laws degree from the University of Detroit after reciting his poems to what was perhaps the largest audience of his life: 8,500 people. "I thank you all," he said as he left the stage to wild applause. "This is an avalanche."[4] From Detroit he went on to Chicago for the celebration of the fiftieth anniversary of the founding of *Poetry Magazine*, and again he said his poems in a talk that focused on a defense of "the great cities of the world": "I'm not a Thoreauvian; I write about the country but I like the city. I knew very well I wouldn't sell my poetry in the country!" Then back to Greenwich, Connecticut, for a lecture and a family gathering and Thanksgiving dinner at the home of Willard Fraser's sister, Jean, attended by Lesley, her two daughters, and all their husbands. Afterward, Frost went up to Hanover for another talk, on the evening of November 27, in the handsome new Hopkins Center of Dartmouth College, named after the president who, among other accomplishments, had brought Frost to Dartmouth in 1943.

"I think the first thing I ought to speak of," he began in his talk on "Extravagance,"[5] "is all this luxuriance: all in easy chairs and a beautiful hall—and nothing to do but listen to me. Pretty soft, I call it. Pretty soft.

"I was so made that I—though a Vermonter and all that—I never took any stock in the doctrine that 'a penny saved is a penny earned.' A penny saved is a *mean* thing, and a penny spent is a generous thing and a big thing—like this. (It took more than a penny to do this. There's nothing mean about it.) . . .

"And I was thinking of the extravagance of the universe.

What an *extravagant* universe it is. And the most extravagant thing in it, as far as we know, is man—the most wasteful, spending thing in it—in all this luxuriance.

"How stirring it is, the sun and everything. Take a telescope and look as far as you will. How much of a universe was wasted just to produce puny us. It's wonderful . . . fine.

"And poetry is a sort of extravagance, in many ways. It's something that people wonder about. What's the need of it? And the answer is, no need—not particularly. That is, that's the first one.

"I've always enjoyed being around colleges nominally as a professor, you know, and a puzzle to everybody as to what I was doing—whether anything or not. (You'd like to leave that to others. Never would defend myself there.) And people say to me occasionally, 'Where *does* poetry come in?' Some of you may be thinking it tonight: what's it all for? 'Does it *count*?'

"When I catch a man reading my book, red-handed, he usually looks up cheerfully and says, 'My wife is a great fan of yours.' Puts it off on the women.

"I figured that out lately: that there's an indulgence of poetry, a manly indulgence of poetry, that's a good deal like the manly indulgence of women. We say women rule the world. That's a nice way to talk. And we say that poetry rules the world.

"There's a poem that says:

We are the music-makers,
And we are the dreamers of dreams . . .
World-losers and world-forsakers,

. . . and all that. We are 'the makers' of the future. We

Built Nineveh with our sighing,
And Babel itself with our mirth;
And o'erthrew them with prophesying
To the old of the new world's worth;
For each age is a dream that is dying,
And one that is coming to birth.[6]

That's a big claim, isn't it? An exaggerated claim.

"But I look on the universe as a kind of exaggeration anyway, the whole business. That's the way you think of it: great, great,

great expense—everybody trying to make it mean something more than it is. . . ."

Toward the end of his talk, he turned to some poems of his own composition, beginning with one from his most recent volume called, simply, "Away!":

Now I out walking
The world desert,
And my shoe and my stocking
Do me no hurt.

I leave behind
Good friends in town.
Let them get well-wined
And go lie down.

Don't think I leave
For the outer dark
Like Adam and Eve
Put out of the Park.

Forget the myth.
There is no one I
Am put out with
Or put out by.

Unless I'm wrong
I but obey
The urge of a song:
"I'm—bound—away!"

And I may return
If dissatisfied
With what I learn
From having died.[7]

Nowhere else had Frost looked forward to his own death with so much seeming equanimity. And, if it were true that he had managed to overcome much of his fear of dying, he had done so partly by returning to some of the religious beliefs which he had learned in childhood from his devout mother, principally the belief that life did not end with the grave but "went on" in a life after death.[8] In former years, he was frequently inclined to protect his religious convictions with a superficial layer of skepticism and mockery that would protect his sensitive ego from the skepticism and mockery of others less religious than himself. But now, in "the last go-down," he seemed less inclined than ever before to play at being a skeptic. His Dartmouth talk, for example, contained what amounted almost to a sermon the text of which was that key passage in his poem, "Kitty Hawk":

But God's own descent
Into flesh was meant
As a demonstration
That the supreme merit
Lay in risking spirit
In substantiation.

"That's a whole of philosophy," he said. "To the very limit, you know." He then repeated a conversation he had had a few years before with his Ripton friend, Rabbi Victor Reichert, who had started it off by observing that the best passages in the New Testament were merely quotations from the Old. Frost had asked him what, if that were so, was the best statement to be found in both Testaments.

"Love your neighbor as yourself," said Reichert.

"That's not good enough," Frost countered.

"What's the matter with it?" asked the rabbi.

"And *hate* your neighbor as you hate yourself."

"Do you hate yourself?"

"I wouldn't be religious if I didn't."[9]

He extended his remark to Reichert in the gloss he provided of a biblical passage and a Matthew Arnold poem, as he continued his Dartmouth talk:

"Some people can't go with you. Let 'em drop; let 'em fall off. Let the wolves take 'em.

"In the Bible twice it says—and I quote that in a poem somewhere, I think; yes—twice it says, 'these things are said in parables . . .' —said in this way that I'm talking to you about: extravagance said in parable, '. . . so the wrong people won't understand them and so get saved.'

"It's thoroughly undemocratic, very superior—as when Matthew Arnold says, in a whole sonnet, only those who've given everything and strained every nerve 'mount, and that hardly, to eternal life.' 'Taint everybody, it's just those only—the few that have done everything, sacrificed, risked everything, 'bet their sweet life' on what they lived. (That's again. . . . What a broad one that is: 'You bet your sweet life.' That's the height of it all, in whatever you do: 'bet your sweet life.') And only those who have done that to the limit, he says, 'mount, and that hardly . . .'—they barely make it, you know—'that hardly, to eternal life.' "[10]

Frost had bet his sweet life on poetry, sometimes at considerable expense both to those around him and to himself. By the logic that shaped his Dartmouth "sermon" he could hope to "mount, and that hardly, to eternal life." But everything depended on whether God found his poems—"acceptable"—the word he had used in *A Masque of Mercy*, and only by dying could he know how God judged his work and, through it, himself. It was therefore entirely appropriate that, in closing his talk at Dartmouth, he quoted not the poem "Away!" with its seemingly easy confidence of the continuation of life after death, but the much more somber poem, "The Night Light":

She always had to burn a light
Beside her attic bed at night.
It gave bad dreams and troubled sleep,
But helped the Lord her soul to keep.
Good gloom on her was thrown away.
It is on me by night or day,
Who have, as I foresee, ahead
The darkest of it still to dread.

"Suppose I end on that dark note," he said. "Good night."[11]

Two days later, Frost went with Kay by train to New York City to participate in a closed-circuit television broadcast raising funds for the proposed National Cultural Center in Washington. As they were leaving the train, he suddenly felt faint, and very nearly collapsed. He recovered at once, and went through with his small part in the program. But Mrs. Morrison, suspecting the momentary vertigo was related to Frost's continuing cystitis problem, was glad that a month before she had made an appointment for him to see his urologist, Dr. Harrison, at the Peter Bent Brigham Hospital on Monday, December 3.

Mrs. Morrison's plans for Frost were soon complicated, however, when on the first of December Stafford Dragon, the farmer who had served long and well as Frost's general handyman at the Homer Noble farm, telephoned to say that his son, Richard, has just been killed in an automobile accident not far from Ripton. Informed that the funeral would be on December 4, Kay assured Stafford that the three members of her family, though for medical reasons not Frost, would certainly attend. When she hung up, however, she realized that if her family did go to Vermont to attend Richard Dragon's funeral, there would be no one left in Cambridge to take Frost to the hospital on December 3.

On Sunday, December 2, Frost delivered an evening lecture at Boston's Ford Hall Forum, after which he returned home to await his examination by Dr. Harrison next day. But when Kay telephoned him at half-past nine in the morning, Frost told her he felt so ill that she would have to cancel his hospital appointment. Kay telephoned the office of Frost's personal physician, Dr. Roger Hickler, to ask if he could come at once to 35 Brewster Street. As Hickler was out of town, his colleague at Peter Bent Brigham, Dr. James Jackson, arrived in his stead.

It was soon agreed, between Kay and Jackson, that the best course of action would be to have Frost admitted to the Brigham, not just for the planned examination by Dr. Harrison, but also in order that extensive tests could be made and to ensure Frost's safety while Kay was away in Vermont. When Frost was presented with the suggestion, however, he put up more of an argument than Kay had anticipated. His initial comment, after a conversation alone with Jackson, was disturbing in its finality: "If I ever go into that place, I'll never come out alive."

Mrs. Morrison and Dr. Jackson persisted in their arguments favoring hospitalization, until Frost abruptly rose from his chair, glared at his secretary, and in his darkest voice said, as he swept upstairs to his bedroom, "This is when I walk out of your lives—all of you." The doctor was astonished, and Mrs. Morrison had to explain that such displays of temper were not unfamiliar. She suggested that Jackson go upstairs to calm him down, that he could do it better just now than she could. He found Frost stretched out on his bed, immobile. After trying several times to elicit some response from the old man, the doctor came back downstairs and said,

"He won't talk to me."

"Where is he?"

"On the bed."

"Face up or face down?"

"Nose on the pillow."

"In that case," said Kay, "it will be three hours before I can get him to the hospital. I wish it had been the other way."

Dr. Jackson soon left, as did Mrs. Morrison. When she returned later, however, after an hour or two at her home, she found Frost in the kitchen, calm now, eating a late breakfast. He asked her to help him pack his bag and to drive him to the hospital so that she and her daughter could start for Vermont. As Kay left him in his hospital room at the Brigham, he turned to her and said, "I will do this on the highest plane—don't fear."

Later that day, his examination and tests began. They revealed that the prostate was not abnormally enlarged for a man of his age, but that the bladder was obviously infected. The initial diagnosis, of which Mrs. Morrison was informed when she returned to Boston on December 5, was that Frost's problem was, indeed, chronic cystitis. But the hospital telephoned again next day to say that further tests had revealed a stoppage in the bladder. Colon bacilli had collected there which, if not removed, would poison Frost's entire system. They recommended surgery to correct the problem.

Frost was told that he had a choice: either wear a catheter for the rest of his life, or permit a complete prostate operation. Having endured a catheter for the past few days, he chose the operation.

The surgical procedure took place on December 10, and it lasted much longer than the doctors had expected: the prostate proved to be cancerous, and the cancer had spread into the bladder. But the surgeon believed that all of the cancerous tissue had been removed, and Frost came through the operation without difficulty. For two weeks, as he mended, his spirits were high, he was comfortable, and the chances of a complete recovery seemed excellent. Then, on December 23, he suffered a pulmonary embolism.

He lived through it, but only barely. His heart was damaged by the attack, and he did not have to be told by his doctors that another such was likely to be fatal. On New Year's Day 1963 came another setback, but not nearly as serious as the first.

Two days later, he was well enough to issue a statement that supplemented the terse releases of the hospital describing his "serious" condition:

"With all these countless friends in the hospital and without I find myself better than a little less than bad." His wit, and his courage, had not failed him.

Two days later, he was provided with another reason for feeling "better than a little less than bad," when he learned that he had just been awarded the Bollingen Prize for poetry. Next day, another statement came forth from his hospital room:

"A sweet coincidence to have the great doctors of this great hospital—Dr. J. Hartwell Harrison, Dr. George W. Thorn, and Dr. Roger B. Hickler—hand me a virtual new lease on life; and on the same day and hour, the Bollingen Prize Committee of Yale University Library one new reason to live.

"I am in a critical position to appreciate the committee's unanimity. It is magnificent. I was not always too sure of where all of them stood and that is as it should be—John Hall Wheelock, Allen Tate, Louise Bogan, Richard Eberhart, Robert Lowell—poets one and all of the first esteem.

"And I must not forget to thank the librarian of Yale University, James T. Babb, for rounding them up. You should have seen the excitement in the hospital when his news came.

"This year, or so, has been a year for me—taken to the President's side for his inauguration, and allowed to stand around listening when Premier Khrushchev declared Russia a Western nation to be trusted as such in heroic rivalry.

"The overwhelming wave of letters and telegrams have given me assurance of the friendship I never felt before."

On the night of January seventh, Frost was stricken by another pulmonary embolism. With the help of an oxygen tent and anticoagulants, he again survived. Next day, the doctors operated to tie off the veins in his legs, in an effort to prevent further blood clots from reaching the lungs.

Mrs. Morrison and her daughter had been Frost's only visitors up to now, but after the second embolism, with its inevitable result of weakening him still further, the doctors saw no reason to deprive him of what they knew—and he sensed—were likely to be his final meetings with his friends. Each day, as his strength permitted, he would receive one or two visitors at a time as he sat up in bed or briefly in a chair next to it, telling them of his determination to recover and saying things his reticence would not have permitted him to say were he not so obviously on the verge of death. They came in a steady stream: John Dickey, Stewart Udall, Franklin Reeve, Alfred Edwards, Hyde Cox, many more. Lesley had been one of the first to see him immediately after the first embolism, and she had returned to New York a few days later when it appeared that his condition had stabilized. But in the first week of January, she sent him a note in which she said, "I think of you as Robert Coeur de Lion." Nothing else she could have said would have pleased him more. In one of the few letters he dictated from his hospital bed to Mrs. Morrison, he returned Lesley's praise with some of his own:

"You're something of a Lesley de Lion yourself," he said. "I am not hard to touch but I'd rather be taken for brave than anything else. A little hard and stern in judgment, perhaps, but always touched by the heroic. You have passed muster. So has Prescott. You have both found a way to make shift. You can't know how much I have counted on you in family matters. It is no time yet to defer a little to others in my future affairs but I have deferred not a little in my thoughts to the strength I find in you and Prescott and Lee, and very very affectionately to K. Morrison and Anne Morrison Gentry, who are with me taking this dictation in the hospital, and to Al Edwards in all his powerful friendship. I trust my word can bind you all together as long as my name as a poet lasts. I am too emotional for my state. Life has been a long trial yet I mean to see more of it. We all liked your poems. It must add to your confidence that you have found a way with the young." Mrs. Morrison sent it along, unsigned.[12]

When he was not enduring the attentions of his doctors and nurses, receiving visitors, or resting, he was busily engaged in composing a poem that was a sequel to one he had finished shortly before entering the hospital. The first one—"The Prophets Really Prophesy as Mystics The Commentators Merely by Statistics"—had been sent out as Frost's Christmas poem for 1962:

With what unbroken spirit naïve science
Keeps hurling our Promethean defiance
From this atomic ball of rotting rock
At the Divine Safe's combination lock.

In our defiance we are still defied.
But have not I, as prophet, prophesied:
Sick of our circling round and round the sun
Something about the trouble will be done.

Now that we've found the secret out of weight,
So we can cancel it however great.
Ah, what avail our lofty engineers
If we can't take the planet by the ears,

Or by the poles or simply by the scruff,
And saying simply we have had enough
Of routine and monotony on earth,
Where nothing's going on but death and birth.

And man's of such a limited longevity,
Now in the confidence of new-found levity
(Our gravity has been our major curse)
We'll cast off hawser for the universe

Taking along the whole race for a ride
(Have I not prophesied and prophesied?)
All voting viva voce *where to go,*
The noisier because they hardly know

Whether to seek a scientific sky
Or wait and go to Heaven when they die,
In other words to wager their reliance
On plain religion or religious science.

They need to crash the puzzle of their lot
As Alexander crashed the Gordian knot,
Or as we crashed the barrier of sound
To beat the very world's speed going round.

Yet what a charming earnest world it is,
So modest we can hardly hear it whizz,
Spinning as well as running on a course
It seems too bad to steer it off by force.[13]

The new poem, or as much of it as he had composed by the beginning of the third week in January, was perhaps more redundant of the Christmas poem than Frost was entirely aware. As Mrs. Morrison's daughter recorded it, during her patient attendance at the poet's bedside, it began:

The king said to his court "Summon the prophets
I had a dream last night I want them to interpret
I want them first to tell me what the dream was."
Then he said "I told you what to do."
They said "be reasonable, oh king. Give us a chance."
They said "aw come, aw come.
We don't pretend to tell the dream as well as what it means."
He said "You are no prophets for my money
You're nothing but a lot of common commentators
Who have to have the facts. You're all false mystics.
Have them executed, every one."
And there he sat alone and dreamed his dream.
And as he sat, there wandered in a wastrel
That he became aware of.
The king said "Who are you? I thought I had you all wiped out.
False prophets."
He answered "I was not a member of the guild.
They have to have statistics to depend on."
"Tell me my dream then" said the king.
"If you're a prophet not just a commentator on the news,
You dream the only dream there is to dream."[14]

But the visits of his friends left him little time or energy to carry the poem much further or to polish the draft he had begun. On January 22, Louis Untermeyer spent nearly an hour talking about the trip to Russia, politics and poetry, and the early days of their friendship when Untermeyer had been one of the first to champion his verse. They spoke of the recent evening at the National Poetry Festival when Untermeyer had introduced him, and he had begun his talk by observing that he sometimes thought he was "a figment of Louis's imagination"; of how, long ago, the editors of the *Atlantic Monthly* had returned some of his poems with the terse note, "We regret that the Atlantic has no place for your vigorous verse"; of the disappointment that, once again, someone else had won the latest Nobel Prize for literature. Frost was obviously disheartened by that development, but as Untermeyer was leaving, he managed to look forward eagerly to another honor that he had recently got wind of: "Don't tell anyone—it's supposed to be secret—but I'm getting another prize this spring. It's to be at a reception in England, and you've got to promise to go along. It will be quite a party. Don't forget—this spring."[15]

Next day, Frost was visited by three Russians who were members of a Soviet Writers Delegation under the same U.S.-U.S.S.R. cultural exchange agreement that had taken him to Russia. These were Viktor Rozov, Valentin Katayev, whom he had met in Russia, and Frida Lurye, who had been one of the "pendragons" team. With the consent of the hospital staff, they came up to Frost's room, presented him with gifts from their homeland, and toasted him with champagne. They also listened as, once again, he explained why he had gone to their country. "I went over to Russia," he was later quoted by Mme. Lurye, "to confirm an idea I had, a feeling that Russia was drifting westward. We're rivals, in the end, in everything, war and all, to the end. One of my greatest experiences was to talk to Khrushchev, to have a heart-to-heart talk with him and to see if he was the man I thought he was. I was there to get some things corrected or confirmed. I got things confirmed but not corrected." Then, with a look at the State Department interpreter who had come up with the three Russians, he added, "Don't cheat on me!"[16]

In a final speech, after the Russians had drunk to his "good health" with champagne, Katayev summed up for the delegation: "I am happy to hold the hand of a genius and a wonderful man. If all humanity had men like Frost there would be no wars. Life would be different." Frost liked that, but he could not let the statement go uncorrected: "Men are men," the Russians later quoted him as saying. "I'm not always so hopeful. War has its rules. We must not cut down the apple trees and we must not poison the wells."[17]

The visit of the Russians touched Frost deeply. It made a proper ending to one of the great adventures of his life, supplementing a cable he had received a few days before from Yevgeny Yevtushenko:

> TODAY I READ AGAIN AND AGAIN YOUR POEMS. I AM HAPPY THAT YOU LIVE ON EARTH.[18]

But after they had gone, he kept referring to the fact that among all these greetings and tributes, not one word had come to him from President Kennedy since his return from Russia, not one word since his entrance into the hospital.

On Sunday, January 27, Frost was surprised by a visit from Ezra Pound's daughter, Princess Mary de Rachewiltz. Their conversation was recorded by Anne Morrison Gentry:

"I've come to thank you," began the princess. "I thought it was high time some member of the family did."

"This is a happy occasion for me," said Frost. "You're a dear and so is Ezra. He's a wonder—all sorts of [a?] person. A great poet and a great romantic."

"He'll be glad to know you consented to see me."

"I've never got over those days we had together."

"My father didn't say much when he got out but you understood each other, I think."

"Politics make too much difference to both of us. Love is all. Romantic love—as in stories and poems. I tremble with it. I'd like to see Ezra again."

"Come to Venice. That would be a grand occasion. We followed your travels last year. When you get your strength back you must come to us."

"Perhaps I will. The Plimptons and other young friends of his on the *Paris Review* are friends of mine, too."

They both praised Archie MacLeish, and then Frost referred to the Christmas card he had received from Pound shortly after entering the hospital.

"One of the beautiful things I had from Christmas was a nice little word from him. I wish we could see more of each other."

"Father is well now and goes to concerts and so on. He'll be glad I was able to thank you."[19]

With that, apparently, the brief visit ended.

Later in the day, Frost went back to working on his new poem about the prophet and the king, but aside from laying out the direction in which he hoped to take it, he made little progress. It was then, apparently, that he dictated to Mrs. Morrison's daughter a letter to Roy and Alma Elliott, answering a recent one of Elliott's which praised his Christmas poem as "one of your very best," adding, "We are happy in your growing health."[20]

"Oh Roy and Alma," Frost said to his old and devoted Amherst friends, "How the years have come between us. You were one of the first that gave me any stature, as they call it nowadays, and remember I went to see you at Bowdoin on purpose for your kind of recognition. Things have come out fine for you. I'm sorry you don't go to Florida any more but that's a small matter. We read each other's books and we know what we're thinking about. Metaphor is it and the freshness thereof.

"I'm mighty glad you like this poem for Christmas. Why will the quidnuncs always be hoping for a salvation man will never have from anyone but God? I was just saying today how Christ posed Himself the whole problem and died for it. How can we be just in a world that needs mercy and merciful in a world that needs justice?[21] We study and study the four biographies of Him and are left still somewhat puzzled in our daily lives. Marking students in a kind of mockery and laughing it off. It seems as if I never wrote these plunges into the depths to anyone but you. I remember our first walk to Harpswell together.

"This is being dictated to Anne Morrison Gentry who writes shorthand and her mother Kathleen Morrison who devises all my future. They are helping me through these hard days in a grand and very powerful hospital. If only I get well, with their help, I'll go deeper into my life with you than I ever have before."[22]

But it was by now too late for that. About the twenty-seventh, he began to lose strength rapidly, and it became inescapably clear that there would be no recovery.

The physician-in-chief of the Peter Bent Brigham Hospital was Dr. George W. Thorn, and by the end of January he had become something of a personal friend to the ailing poet. He had been introduced to Frost some years before by their mutual friend, Hyde Cox, who wanted to be sure Frost had a doctor he could turn to in case he took sick in the Boston area. The choice of Thorn could not have been a happier one. Soon after their introduction, Frost had taken sick in Boston, and Dr. Thorn not only had made an immediate visit to 35 Brewster Street, but had insisted on staying at the house overnight. After Frost's admission to the Brigham, Dr. Thorn, knowing that Frost really trusted himself only at the Mary Hitchcock Hospital in Hanover, had come up to welcome and reassure him, and to say, "As long as you are here, Mr. Frost, you must regard Peter Bent Brigham as an annex of Mary Hitchcock." That was the kind of man Thorn was.

As the head of the teaching hospital of Harvard Medical School, it was Thorn's custom to lead his interns around to the rooms of his patients every morning as part of their medical education. Frost was no exception, and he doubtless looked forward to the brief visitation of Thorn and his young men as they looked forward to seeing him. But the morning of January 28 was to be different. About dawn, Dr. Thorn awoke at home with an ill-defined feeling that something with Frost was not right. He drove to the hospital and went directly upstairs. Frost saw him standing in the doorway of his room, hours earlier than usual, and without his usual retinue. He instantly understood what his presence signified.

"Traveling light today, aren't you?" was all Frost said.

That day, he felt no better than he had the day before. He was unable to eat and the doctors were at a loss as to what to do. About five in the afternoon, he felt somewhat better, and a brief visit was permitted with Mr. and Mrs. Jack Sweeney. But before they left Frost told them, "I feel as though I were in my last hours."

It was true. About midnight, new blood clots reached his lungs, and within a few minutes he lost consciousness. In Manchester, shortly before two, Hyde Cox awoke in his bedroom at Crow Island. He walked to the window, and looked out across the sea to where Boston glowed in the distance. Then he somehow realized that his great friend was dead. Anne Morrison Gentry's telephone call an hour later only confirmed it.

EPILOGUE

THE TRIBUTES that had long since become an established element of Frost's life came forth in a deluge of praise after his death. From Boston to San Francisco, from Middlebury to South Miami, newspapers, radios, and television sets announced in bulletins and banner headlines the death, at eighty-eight, of "America's poet laureate," the "national bard," the "best-loved poet in the United States." Not just in his own country, but around the world, the news of Robert Frost's death elicited eulogies that would doubtless have gratified their subject as well as amused him: an embarrassment of admiration and respect. This poet who though singing had remained unsung for the first forty years of his life, this Job-like man so often tested by family tragedy, by personal doubts and frustrations, had by the time of his death reached enviable heights of public esteem.

On the afternoon of January 31, two days after the poet's death, a private memorial service was held with thirty of Frost's closest friends and relatives in Appleton Chapel of Memorial Church in Harvard Yard. While knots of students and curious onlookers idled outside, Frost's longtime acquaintance, the Rev. Dr. Palfrey Perkins, minister emeritus of King's Chapel, read selections of poetry and from the Bible, and Professor G. Wallace Woodworth of the Harvard Music Department performed organ pieces well-chosen by Anne Morrison Gentry.[1]

On the afternoon of February 17, a public memorial service was held in Johnson Chapel of Amherst College, and was attended by 700 guests ranging from the Chief Justice of the United States, Earl Warren, to many of the poets and professors, the politicians and publishers, the relatives and friends, who had touched and been touched by Frost's life and art. Mark Van Doren read a selection of the poet's verse, and remarks were delivered by President Calvin Plimpton of Amherst and the Rt. Rev. Henry Wise Hobson, the Episcopal Bishop of

Southern Ohio, who spoke with an understanding born of friendship of Frost's character and the nature of his "strong and deep religious faith."[2]

Four months later, on June 16, the poet's ashes were buried in the Frost family lot of the Old Bennington Cemetery. The simple ceremony, conducted by the pastor of the First Congregational Church of Old Bennington, the Rev. Robert P. Bell, was attended only by Mrs. Lesley Frost Ballantine and a family friend, Mrs. F. M. Simmons of North Bennington.

On October 26, 1963, many of those who had been present at the Amherst memorial service returned to the town for another ceremony, the dedication of the Robert Frost Library of Amherst College. Frost would have been particularly pleased by the choice of speaker. He was the man whose friendship he had apparently lost forever after his return from the Soviet Union, the young President whose own death was now less than a month away, John F. Kennedy. After praising the contributions of Amherst College to the life of the nation, and asserting the importance of colleges generally to that life, the President spoke of Frost in words that suggested no lingering animosity, but only genuine respect and a deep sympathy for those principles by which Frost himself had lived and written.

"This day," said the President, "devoted to the memory of Robert Frost, offers an opportunity for reflection which is prized by politicians as well as by others and even by poets. For Robert Frost was one of the granite figures of our time in America. He was supremely two things—an artist and an American.

"A nation reveals itself not only by the men it produces but also by the men it honors, the men it remembers.

"In America our heroes have customarily run to men of large accomplishments. But today this college and country honor a man whose contribution was not to our size but to our spirit; not to our political beliefs but to our insight; not to our self-esteem, but to our self-comprehension.

"In honoring Robert Frost we therefore can pay honor to the deepest sources of our national strength. That strength takes many forms and the most obvious forms are not always the most significant.

"The men who create power make an indispensable contribution to the nation's greatness. But the men who question power make a contribution just as indispensable, especially when that questioning is disinterested.

"For they determine whether we use power or power uses us. Our national strength matters; but the spirit which informs and controls our strength matters just as much. This was the special significance of Robert Frost.

"He brought an unsparing instinct for reality to bear on the platitudes and pieties of society. His sense of the human tragedy fortified him against self-deception and easy consolation.

" 'I have been,' he wrote, 'one acquainted with the night.'

"And because he knew the midnight as well as the high noon, because he understood the ordeal as well as the triumph of the human spirit, he gave his age strength with which to overcome despair.

"At bottom he held a deep faith in the spirit of man. And it's hardly an accident that Robert Frost coupled poetry and power. For he saw poetry as the means of saving power from itself.

"When power leads man toward arrogance, poetry reminds him of his limitations. When power narrows the areas of man's concern, poetry reminds him of the richness and diversity of his existence. When power corrupts, poetry cleanses.

"For art establishes the basic human truths which must serve as the touchstones of our judgment. The artist, however faithful to his personal vision of reality, becomes the last champion of the individual mind and sensibility against an intrusive society and an officious state.

"The great artist is thus a solitary figure. He has, as Frost said, 'a lover's quarrel with the world.' In pursuing his perceptions of reality he must often sail against the currents of his time. This is not a popular role.

"If Robert Frost was much honored during his lifetime, it was because a good many preferred to ignore his darker truths.

"Yet in retrospect we see how the artist's fidelity has strengthened the fiber of our national life. If sometimes our great artists have been the most critical of our society it is because their sensitivity and their concern for justice, which must motivate any true artist, [make them] aware that our nation falls short of its highest potential.

"I see little of more importance to the future of our country and our civilization than full recognition of the place of the artist. If art is to nourish the roots of our culture, society must set the artist free to follow his vision wherever it takes him.

"We must never forget that art is not a form of propaganda, it is a form of truth. And as Mr. MacLeish once remarked of poets, 'There is nothing worse for our trade than to be in style.'

"In free society art is not a weapon and it does not belong to the sphere of polemics and ideology. Artists are not engineers of the soul.

"It may be different elsewhere. But democratic society—in it—the highest duty of the writer, the composer, the artist, is to remain true to himself and to let the chips fall where they may.

"In serving his vision of the truth the artist best serves his nation. And the nation which disdains the mission of art invites the fate of Robert Frost's hired man—'the fate of having nothing to look backward to with pride and nothing to look forward to with hope.'

"I look forward to a great future for America—a future in which our country will match its military strength with our moral restraint, its wealth with our wisdom, its power with our purpose.

"I look forward to an America which will not be afraid of grace and beauty, which will protect the beauty of our natural environment, which will preserve the great old American houses and squares and parks of our national past and which will build handsome and balanced cities for our future.

"I look forward to an America which will steadily raise the standards of artistic accomplishment and which will steadily enlarge cultural opportunities for all our citizens.

"And I look forward to an America which commands respect throughout the world not only for its strength but for its civilization as well.

"And I look forward to a world which will be safe not only for democracy and diversity but also for personal distinction.

"Robert Frost was often skeptical about projects for human improvement. Yet I do not think he would disdain this hope.

"As he wrote during the uncertain days of the Second [World] War:

Take human nature altogether since time began . . .
And it must be a little more in favor of man,
Say a fraction of one per cent at the very least . . .
[Or] *our hold on the planet wouldn't have so increased.*[3]

"Because of Mr. Frost's life and work, because of the life and work of this college, our hold on this planet has increased."[4]

APPENDIX

The following essay by Lawrance Thompson is an excerpt from the "Introduction" to his unpublished "'Notes from Conversations with Robert Frost." It is his account of the circumstances that led to his appointment, in 1939, as Frost's "official biographer." As the "Introduction" was a private document not intended for publication, some minor revisions and emendations seemed advisable, and have been made.

TO THE best of my memory, it all started during my sophomore year at Wesleyan University in Middletown, Connecticut, somewhere around the "winter-dance" time of January or February 1926. I am not certain whether Frost gave any reading at Wesleyan during my freshman year; I merely remember that during the winter of 1926 I invited a blind date to a Wesleyan dance, and that I was troubled to find she was going to arrive by train so late that I would miss some of Robert Frost's reading of poetry, in the Wesleyan Chapel. I have no date for that occasion. I remember that by this time I considered myself enough of an authority on Frost's poetry so that I expected I would know almost all of the poems he would read. I met the girl at the train, I told her about the Frost reading, I told her that the dance wouldn't start before ten o'clock, and that the reading would be over about nine. Would she care to go? No, she'd rather rest in her room after a long train ride. So I left her at the room I had reserved for her, in a home near the campus, and ran for the chapel. When I got there, Frost was halfway through his reading, the chapel was jammed with people, and I went up to the balcony where I found a seat, slipped off my overcoat, sat down in a hurry, and listened. I can even remember thinking, as Frost started reading, that this was a poem I had never read. The gist of it was the pleasure in arranging to see a new moon, in different settings, with fascinating results, and the second of the two stanzas hit me just right:

I put it shining anywhere I please.
By walking slowly on some evening later
I've pulled it from a crate of crooked trees,
And brought it over glossy water, greater,
And dropped it in, and seen the image wallow,
The color run, all sorts of wonder follow.

That poem appeared later as "The Freedom of the Moon" in *West-Running Brook.* It has always held a special value for me as being the first poem I ever heard Frost read. And from the moment when I heard it, I was not only a Frost admirer but also a Frost addict, without suspecting that my addiction would make all sorts of wonder follow.

Frost was at Wesleyan for protracted periods of time during my sophomore and junior years. He had been brought there primarily by Wilbert Snow, whom I had gotten to know well as one of my teachers during my freshman year. As a result, Snow gave many of us exceptional chances to hear and talk with Frost. Those of us who wrote for the undergraduate literary magazine, the *Cardinal,* were invited to Snow's home in Portland to talk with Frost about our own writing more than once. But there was no personal contact between Frost and me during that particular kind of evening.

The first personal contact must have occurred during my junior year, when Frost was again on campus. Whether or not this was the occasion when he was present for the Wesleyan Parley on Education, and gave the talk on "The Manumitted Student," I cannot be sure, though I do remember hearing him give that talk, and I even think I remember that it was given in the Psi Upsilon House. But far more important than that conference was an announcement, posted around campus and probably run in the weekly *Wesleyan Argus,* to the effect that Robert Frost would be willing to meet with any students writing verse, and that he would offer suggestions to such writers. The place would be the Alpha Delta Phi House, the time on a certain afternoon named, and the fee of admission would be one manuscript poem written or typed, but written by the holder. Only some twelve of us showed up, placed our offerings in a wicker basket on a desk in the Alpha Delt library, took our seats around the room, and waited for the show to start. When Frost came in and began, he was extremely friendly, extremely kind, extremely gentle. And all went pleasantly for all of us until he began to read two quatrains which I had written. I could quote them word for word, now, and I will, below, after I've explained that the inspiration for what was then my latest bent in verse writing was my growing awareness that when a child made an ordinary conversation, the meaning of the child's remark had two different values: one for the innocent child, and quite a different value, possibly, for the more mature adult who might be listening. So that seemed to constitute a kind of "poetry"—the surface-meaning provided by the child's own statement, and the deeper meaning that was provided to those lines by the older listener. My subject was typically sophomoric; it was disillusionment. And quite deliberately and sarcastically and ironically I chose to risk a banal experience in childhood, to represent figuratively the child's first discovery that his family had somehow misled him about the being and attributes of a superman named Santa Claus. Now the two quatrains:

DELUSION

There isn't any Santa Claus!
I'm sure he's just a fake, because
My sister Dorothy told me so:
She said that only grown-ups know.

Of course I'm glad I'm old enough
To know the truth about this stuff:
But I keep hoping, all along,
That what my sister said was wrong.

When Frost finished reading those lines, the students burst out laughing, and the laughter was a derisive rebuke to the writer. Such silly stuff for such an important occasion! I could feel myself growing red in the face even before I noticed the way Frost's eyes were scanning faces in the front row. I was in the back row and that gave me time to protect myself as best I could by trying to join in the general laughter. But it didn't work. As Frost's eyes swept the back row I felt them linger just for a fraction of a second on my anguished face, and then move on. Then he held up one hand to stop the laughter and said somewhat reproachfully that he feared his listeners had laughed too soon, before they considered "what's going on here in these lines." Then he gave an explanatory defense of projecting and dramatizing a child's viewpoint in such a way as to make it "stand for" a more mature viewpoint. He spent quite a little while developing that idea, and as he talked he kept looking at me to see if I had begun to calm down. Then he concluded his explanation by saying, "Now let me read that again, and see what you think." He read it again, and as he finished, the students had been so persuaded by his explanations that they turned to each other, nodding their heads, and saying, "Not bad, not bad."

After that session was over, the brassy ones moved in on Frost and I hung back. But after I could see that he was fully engaged in conversation, I sneaked around behind him, and reached past him to pick up my "poem" out of the wicker basket. He must have been expecting how I would try to make my retreat, for my hand had just closed on the sheet when he looked down at the hand, then up along my arm to my face, and smiled in a kindly way. I felt as though I had been caught again, and as though I had to say something. So I turned my head away from the other students and said in his ear, almost in a whisper,

"Thanks for saving my face."

"Stick around," he said.

So I did, and after all except three of us had left he announced to us that Wilbert Snow had told him (Bill was not there for the session) that Frost could bring three boys out to his home for dinner, and we three were the ones he would bring. So out we went, in someone's car, without my saying any further words to Frost, and without his saying anything to me. But after we were getting warm before the fireplace, in Bill Snow's house on the Weathersfield Road, Frost moved around briefly to talk with each of us, one at a time. When he got to me he began,

"And where's your home when you're not at Wesleyan?"

"New Hampshire."

That gave him something to take hold of, and he said with considerable feeling,

"Well, my boy! I suppose I've slept in more New Hampshire towns and villages than you could name."

That gave me courage because the son of a Methodist minister in New Hampshire usually managed to get around the state pretty well, and I myself had slept in a good many very small towns and villages there. So I said quite boldly,

"Oh I doubt that. Name me one you think I've never heard of."

"Raymond."

"Oh I've lived there," I said. "I went to first grade in the schoolhouse just across the Lamprey River and just a little ways above the livery stable."

That was the start, and the basis for rapport. When he found that I had been born in New Hampshire, and that I knew the Raymond region particularly well—and that I had been in West Epping for a summer, and knew Derry well, and had once lived in Methuen, Massachusetts, where he had once lived, we found plenty to talk about. In fact we talked too long and Bill Snow broke it up. But after a fine evening before Bill's fireplace, as we said good night, Frost asked where I called "home" at present, in New Hampshire. East Rochester. How did I go home? I bummed rides; hitchhiked. Did I go near Amherst? Sometimes. Then next time I hitchhiked home, why not go by way of Amherst, and stop in on Frost to say hello? I would, and did. But I was only one of many students who met Frost during his bardings and who were then invited to stop in and call, and who certainly did so. Our acquaintance remained merely that, and the only unusual part of it, to which he always returned, was that he had a special pleasure in talking to any native of New Hampshire.

I was graduated from Wesleyan in 1928, and I cannot remember seeing Frost again during the next few years. But during the academic year 1935–1936 I went back to Wesleyan as a "teaching fellow" (a one-year appointment). Once again I established a friendly rapport with Bill Snow, and he was the first one to tell me that Frost had been invited back to Wesleyan to give a talk or two in April of 1936. By that time, I had progressed far enough into my doctoral dissertation, and far enough into the realms of book-collecting and auction galleries, to know quite a bit about the first editions of Robert Frost. I knew that my friend H. Bacon Collamore had a big collection; I had visited Frederick B. Adams, Jr., in New York (in connection with a Robinson exhibition for which Collamore and I did a catalogue) and knew that Adams had a good Frost collection. I knew that the most knowledgeable dealer in Frost first editions was John S. Van E. Kohn of New York City. I also knew that there was no Frost bibliography then in print. So I proposed to Bill that we get up a big Frost collection, in the Olin

Library at Wesleyan, so that the opening of the exhibition would coincide with Frost's appearance there. Maybe we could even get Frost to lend us some manuscripts.

Bill Snow hung fire on that suggestion. But I went right ahead with plans as soon as I found that the librarian at Wesleyan was interested. I even became so bold as to write a letter to Frost, while I was visiting my friends the John Kouwenhovens in Yonkers during Easter vacation, telling him of my progress and probably hinting that I wished we might show some manuscripts. He answered, on his birthday, March 26, 1936, from Cambridge, Massachusetts, where he was giving the Charles Eliot Norton lectures in poetry at Harvard. This was the first letter I had ever received from him, and I doubt very much that he remembered he had ever met (or even heard of) me before:

> Dear Mr. Thompson:
>
> Can I do anything to help you? You are so very kind. I'd like to contribute the enclosed remnant of manuscript if I knew who would act as repository. Theres probably no place for such a thing at the University. Anyway you may care to exhibit it. It is a sample of what most of my note books get reduced to in the process of revision. You say you lack the first English edition of *A Boy's Will*. I wonder if Frederick Melcher of *The Publishers Weekly* wouldn't loan you his copy. Mine is not where I can get hold of it. Dont think I dont appreciate. Sincerely yours
>
> Robert Frost

With that letter came a battered notebook containing nine leaves of manuscripts: revised versions of "The Truth of It" and "Two Tramps in Mud Time" and "A Stone Missive" and "A Record Stride." That put us over the top, in our attempt to give the exhibition a certain quality of distinction. The catalogue was written by me, and was published in time for Frost's arrival at Wesleyan on April 26, for performances on April 27 and 28. When I took him around the various cases in the library, to show him the exhibition, he was obviously pleased and excited. He had never seen any such array of his works before; there had never been such an array. So when we came finally to the manuscripts he had sent me, and I called particular attention to them as I thanked him for helping us, he said with obvious hinting that he didn't know what to do with them or who would care enough about them to keep them. I said I knew someone who would like to take good care of them, and he laughed and said,

"That settles it. They're yours."

Out of that session at Wesleyan in 1936 came two later developments. Bill Snow and I were convinced that Frost's prose had an idiom all its own; that the scattered pieces he had written as prefaces or as talks should be gathered together in book form. I said I'd do the legwork, and Bill agreed to write a preface for the book. Frost gave his permission, and we were in business. But at the same time Frost asked me if I would come over to call on him in South Shaftsbury, that summer, and added that if I had any first editions I'd like to have him autograph, he'd be glad to have me bring them along. I never got there, for reasons I've forgotten. But the plans went forward on the "Selected Prose of Robert Frost,"* and I remember calling on him in Amherst in the autumn of 1936 to discuss the project in the hope that he could tell me of any items I'd overlooked. He went over the manuscript with me and told me what he did not want used. As I was leaving, he pointed to a package on his radiator, and said that I ought to take that package along. (I wish I had taken it.) It was, he said, stenographic notes of his Charles Eliot Norton lectures, and his understanding or agreement or contract with Harvard was that he would get those lectures ready for publication. But oh gee, he said, he hated to open that package, and wasn't sure he ever would. Probably he never did. After a while he began to tell Harvard (and others, including myself) that somehow that package got "lost." It has never shown up, and the Harvard University Press insists that although it made arrangements to have the stenographer make the shorthand notes and the transcript, the carbon copy also got "lost."

Sometime in the spring of 1937 I saw Frost again. I think the occasion was a talk he gave at Hartford, and I seem to remember that Frost and I both stayed at the Collamores' home that night. In the course of conversation we got to talking about my plans and I said that I didn't have a position for the coming

* Not to be confused with the collection of the same name edited by Hyde Cox and Edward Connery Lathem (New York, 1966). Thompson never published his projected "Selected Prose."—RHW

year; that if I got one I'd let him know. He said I'd get one, and I did. As soon as I had signed up with Princeton to go there as curator of rare books, I wrote to Frost saying it was ironic that I wanted to teach literature and couldn't find anyone to hire me for that; but that Princeton was going to hire me as a curator of rare books because I had written a catalogue of an exhibition of the works of Robert Frost. He answered that letter on July 14, 1937, from South Shaftsbury:

> Dear Lawrance Thompson:
>
> You be sure to come over to see us some day before the middle of August. I want to hear about your Princeton job which I hereby approve of before I know what it is. Come and have lunch with me if Elinor isn't up to your having it with us. I know a place to take you to. Ever yours
>
> Robert Frost

Elinor was up to my having lunch with them, and I went over to the Gully House late in July, spending most of the day there, and taking my books along for autographing. Frost was deeply touched to learn that I was working on a dissertation which I was going to call "Young Longfellow," and he even gave me a first edition of *North of Boston* which he inscribed "For Lawrance Thompson, if he will not be too hard on Longfellow." It was a memorable afternoon, but I made not one single note afterward. It still had not crossed my mind that I would ever write a biography of Robert Frost.

But as soon as I had gotten to Princeton I began to urge that Frost should be brought there as a speaker. I had good luck, and a date was set for late October. In the meantime I had heard from him somehow (perhaps by phone, or perhaps by telegraph) that he would be speaking at Haverford College on October 25. I offered to drive over there to get him; offered to find a place for him to stay in Princeton. No one else did so, in Princeton, so I had my own way. Mr. and Mrs. A. E. McVitty agreed (willingly) to play host for him. At Haverford he stayed with the Lesley Hotsons, and I can remember sitting in their living room talking with them and with Frost before we started driving back. On the way back, most of his talk was about Elinor, who was chronically ill, and about his sense of guilt in leaving her alone. As we drove from Haverford out around

Philadelphia, Frost saw a sign saying that Valley Forge was only so many miles distant. His exclamation of surprise made me say

"Want to go to Valley Forge?"

"No," he said, "I've been there. I was there with Washington."

I understood that well enough, and in fact the understanding between us during that drive, even during the twenty-four hours of his stay in Princeton, seemed to indicate a considerable advance in friendship. One thing which furthered that friendship even more was my telling him, after he had completed his talk, that I had been so bold as to put a stenographer in the audience at Haverford, another in the audience at Princeton; that if he wanted the transcripts torn up, he could say the word. No, he was glad I had done that. After he had gone, I had another idea: why not have those two speeches printed in the Princeton University Library periodical, *Biblia*. It would make a nice collector's item. So I wrote to him, asking if he would give his permission, and he wrote back on November 22, from Amherst: "Yes, if you will undertake to make them read like something. Cutting might help."

Well I undertook it all right. I edited them heavily, and even took the liberty of compressing sentences where he had spoken with a certain amount of clumsiness. They were published in the issue of *Biblia* for February 1938: "Poverty and Poetry" was the title of the Haverford talk, and "The Poet's Next of Kin in a College" was the title of the Princeton talk. But before those two items could get into print I heard twice from Frost. The first was a Christmas greeting: one of his Christmas booklets, including his new poem entitled "To a Young Wretch." That was sent from Gainesville, Florida, and was postmarked December 23. Then, on January 15, he wrote the following letter:

> Dear Lawrance:
>
> I'm not anxious to hear that you printed my speech on the Poets Next of Kin but I am to hear that if you printed it or tried to print it it didn't get you in trouble with the athletic authorities. I assume you got my telegram of permission. You know my feeling about these speeches. I am getting less and less reluctant to have them published. Thats because my scattered thoughts of a lifetime are beginning to group up into natural

> shapes. You can always have the forced shape the department teaches. Give me Doors for a subject and I can elaborate it by plan till it is as big as an essay without a real sentence having been written or a happy thought having been had. I was asked the other day by an otherwise good teacher if I laid out such a thing as The Death of the Hired Man. My way of writing seemed inconceivable to him. My prose if I ever produce any will have to be written like my verse.—Not very important to us, but I confess to an uneasiness as to how bad a stir my brutal heresies left behind me at Princeton. Ever yours
>
> Robert Frost

Which, being interpreted, meant that I had failed him in not writing to tell him what a tremendous success he had been at Princeton, and of how the place was continuing to rave over him even months after he had gone. But I didn't know enough about Frost at that time to understand such an interpretation. In fact, if someone had been so unkind to him then I should have called it an unfair and inaccurate estimate. I wish I knew how I answered that letter, back there in 1938.

I am certain about one letter I wrote to him soon after that. I saw in the newspapers the announcement that Elinor Frost had died in Gainesville on March 20. I waited for perhaps two weeks and then wrote a fairly conventional letter of condolence that couldn't have been more than two sentences long. It must have touched him because he addressed to me, in his own hand, one of the printed announcements reading,

> Funeral services for Elinor Frost will be held
> at Johnson Chapel, Amherst College, Amherst,
> Massachusetts, at three o'clock in the afternoon
> of Friday, April the twenty-second.

I thought I wouldn't ask for time off to attend that service. But on April 21 Frost sent me the following telegram:

> WISH YOU WOULD ACT AS HONORARY BEARER. IF SO MEET ME AT PRESIDENT KING'S OFFICE, JOHNSON CHAPEL, NOT LATER THAN 2:45. ROBERT FROST

I was completely surprised by that invitation. Of course I went, and in the crowd of that day I scarcely had a chance to say any more than a few words of greeting to Frost. He was in good spirits, putting on as good a show as he could. I was even a bit disturbed to hear him laugh heartily at the refreshment party given for him and the honorary pallbearers at Professor Manthey-Zorn's. I remember that Bernard DeVoto was there. It was quite a crowd, and I'd never been included before in such a group—and never was again, for that matter! I stayed until Frost was driven off—by Sidney Cox, I think, but I'm not sure.

That was all, for a while. I can't remember seeing Frost again during 1938. But I do remember one other detail about the funeral services for Elinor Frost. After Frost had left, I went to the Jones Library to see the Frost collection there, and just accidentally met a man with whom I had had correspondence concerning the Frost Exhibition Catalogue I had done at Wesleyan: Professor Robert S. Newdick of Ohio State University. Newdick had published several articles on Frost and was also working on a full-length biography of him.

That last fact was all right with me, for what I had in mind to do was to write a book of essays on Frost's poetry, which I had decided to call *Fire and Ice: The Art and Thought of Robert Frost.* But I thought I shouldn't undertake such a project without first asking Frost's permission. So I wrote to him from Princeton, probably around June of 1939. No answer. I went to Maine for my vacation that summer, and while I was there I received an answer that referred to the death, in July, of Professor Newdick. It began with a reference to my having received a raise in rank, from instructor to assistant professor, with part-time teaching assignments in the English Department at Princeton. The letter was dated from Ripton on July 17, 1939:

> Dear Lawrance:
>
> Up up you go as I knew you would. We have a lot to talk over. The book you now propose can give me nothing but pleasure. That's settled before we talk. But there's all the sad problem of Newdick's literary remains to consider. I need your advice. You knew him pretty well and how completely he had thrown his life into writing mine. I am told his mind ran on

me in his last delerium. What is a miserable hero to say to a worship like his? I naturally want to deal tenderly with his memory. You be thinking my predicament over and come along when you can. A week-end (Saturday and Sunday) soon would be the best time for me. My devoted secretary Mrs Kathleen Morrison suggests that you might like to wait and look in on the Bread Loaf Conference over which her husband presides. The date of that would be from about the 15th to the 30th of August. Suit yourself and you will suit me. But there is the reason for an early visit that Mrs Newdick is coming for a visit some time in the summer and I should like to have seen you when I see her. Ever yours

Robert Frost

That one really rocked me, and I might say that here for the first time I began to think about the possibility of writing something more than a book of critical essays on Frost's poetry. Somehow or other, the rough draft of my answer to that letter has survived. It was an answer sent in the form of a telegram, and it read:

> YOUR LETTER WHICH I RECEIVED LAST NIGHT AFTER FORWARDING CONTAINED FIRST AND ONLY NEWS I HAVE CONCERNING NEWDICK AND I'M STILL BEWILDERED. SHALL OF COURSE BE WILLING TO HELP ANY WAY I CAN. SHALL BE IN DORSET ON WEDNESDAY OF THIS WEEK AND SHOULD LIKE TO RUN OVER TO TALK WITH YOU SATURDAY OR SUNDAY IF CONVENIENT FOR YOU. PLEASE SEND WORD TO DORSET, CARE OF MRS. JOHN B. KOUWENHOVEN. LAWRANCE THOMPSON

The answer was a telegram which I found waiting for me in Dorset, and which was dated July 26:

> WISH YOU COULD COME SATURDAY AFTERNOON AND STAY OVER SUNDAY NIGHT. ROBERT FROST

So I arrived on Saturday afternoon, July 29, and stayed over until Monday morning, July 31. I found Frost was spending his first full summer in Ripton, and was living in a little white guest-cottage in Ripton village, just across the second cement bridge, beyond the Whittemores' greenhouse, directly across from where Mrs. Homer Noble (widowed) and her sister Miss Agnes Billings eked out a living with a few cows and a little garden and with no men in the family to help them, only hired men. I also found that Newdick had died on July 5, 1939. Frost had reserved a room for me (at his expense) in the farmhouse home of Mrs. Noble and Miss Billings; in fact, we ate supper with the elderly ladies that first evening, in their kitchen. Then we went over to his little cottage, across the road, to talk.

In retrospect, I have difficulty understanding why I did not make a detailed set of notes on that conversation that evening; the notes I made in Cambridge under the date of August 12, 1939, are so completely lacking in the dramatic quality of that evening. But the whole thing was far too vivid for me to forget, and I can make amends by giving the high points of that evening, now.

On my way over to Vermont, from Maine, I had decided exactly what I would say about what to do with Newdick's literary remains. And my decision on that matter had been strengthened by Frost's saying to me, as we settled down to talk, that he had been troubled by Newdick's approach; that Newdick was a rather shallow person who had a nose for sleuthing and for nothing else. So he wanted to make some kind of arrangement whereby he would never again be troubled by another Newdick.

I said I thought I knew how that could be done. Frost should name his official biographer now. He should select a man whom he knew well enough to trust; a man who had a considerable literary reputation on the national scene; a man who would preferably be a poet in his own right; a man whose appreciation of Frost would not be slavish. And the value of naming the official biographer now would be this: he could explain to the man named that one part of the requirement would be that Frost did not want a biography of him published during his lifetime. (Frost had named that as one of his wishes, as we talked.) Also, he could turn away any other requests for permission to make biographical studies, on the ground that Frost had already named a biographer, and so he would have to ask the present applicant to "clear" the proposed project with the named biographer.

"All right," Frost said to me. "Name him."

"I won't name any single person," I said, "but I will name three different people who fit the qualifications I have laid down. Mark Van Doren, Bernard DeVoto, and Louis Untermeyer."

"No. No. No."

And Frost, having thus ruled out each of the three possibilities I had named, started in to do something I later became used to: he gave me the history of each and every man I had named; and particularly the history of his relationships with those men.

While Frost was talking about his "No, no, no" on Van Doren, DeVoto and Untermeyer, the hours passed. He must have digressed repeatedly. But when I finally realized that the evening had gone, and that my watch said that it was well after midnight, I felt as though I had somehow been rude in staying so late. So with some embarrassment I stood up and said I hadn't realized how late it was getting.

"Sit down," he said. "You haven't answered my question."

As I sat down I said, "I answered it; I gave you three answers to it. But you didn't like my answers. And it's a question, anyway, for you to answer."

"All right," he said. "What's the matter with my naming you as the official biographer?"

I stumbled and mumbled my appreciation before I said quite firmly,

"But I don't fit any of the qualifications I laid down. I have no reputation in letters, I'm not a poet, and you haven't any evidence, yet, that my insights on you or your poetry will please you. Why don't you wait until I finish *Fire and Ice* and then decide whether I'll qualify?"

"No," he said. "It's all settled. Your Longfellow book is enough 'evidence' for me."

NOTES

TABLE OF CONTENTS FOR THE NOTES

	Introduction	367
1 ·	A Reckless and Dangerous Mood	367
2 ·	Boston: A New Life	372
3 ·	Trials of Strength and Suppleness	376
4 ·	Hanging Round Education	380
5 ·	Friends and Neighbors	385
6 ·	The Death of the Dark Child	386
7 ·	A Witness Tree	389
8 ·	On the Home Front	392
9 ·	Dabbling in Drama	395
10 ·	One Step Backward Taken	402
11 ·	My Family Luck	407
12 ·	Speaking of Loyalty	412
13 ·	Friends Lost and Found	417
14 ·	The Demand for Me	421
15 ·	An English Diary	424
16 ·	Washington: The Pound Affair	426
17 ·	Poetry and Power	428
18 ·	In the Clearing	431
19 ·	Russia: A Final Mission	435
20 ·	Deeper Into Life	437
	Epilogue	442

In the Notes, whenever a last name or a short title is given as a reference, the Index will serve as a convenient guide to the first reference and the full citation.

KEY TO ABBREVIATIONS

When the physical location of a previously unpublished letter or manuscript is cited, one of the following abbreviations may be used for the library collection:

ACL	Amherst College
DCL	Dartmouth College
PUL	Princeton University
SUL	Stanford University
TUL	University of Texas
VaUL	University of Virginia

NOTES

INTRODUCTION

1. RF to Mr. and Mrs. G. R. Elliott, 13 April 1938; *Selected Letters of Robert Frost*, edited with notes by Lawrance Thompson (New York, 1964)—hereafter cited as *Selected Letters*—pp. 471–472.

2. This sentence contains a close paraphrase of elements in an undated journal entry made by RF not long after he arrived in England. For the text and context, see Lawrance Thompson, *Robert Frost: The Early Years* (New York, 1966)—hereafter cited as *The Early Years*—p. 427.

3. Sylvester Baxter, "Talk of the Town," Boston *Herald*, 8 March 1915, p. 9.

4. RF to LT, 16 April 1957; *Selected Letters*, pp. 565–566.

5. RF to Louis Untermeyer, 9 Aug. 1947; *The Letters of Robert Frost to Louis Untermeyer* (New York, 1963)—hereafter cited as *Letters to Untermeyer*—p. 346.

6. Quoted from *A Masque of Mercy*, in *The Poetry of Robert Frost*, edited with notes by Edward Connery Lathem (New York, 1969)—hereafter cited as *The Poetry*—p. 520.

7. The immediate source of this quotation is an anonymous syndicated article, "Frost at University of Redlands," in the Asbury Park *Evening Press*, 17 May 1958, p. 15.

1. A RECKLESS AND DANGEROUS MOOD

1. RF to Robert Hillyer, 12 Aug. 1938; VaUL.

2. For details of RF's tenure at Harvard as Charles Eliot Norton Professor of Poetry, see Lawrance Thompson, *Robert Frost: The Years of Triumph* (New York, 1970)—hereafter cited as *The Years of Triumph*—pp. 444–448.

3. The memorial service was held in Johnson Chapel, Amherst College, on 22 April 1938. The honorary bearers were Fred S. Allis, Reginald Cook, Sidney Cox, Bernard DeVoto, George R. Elliott, Donald Fisher [husband of Dorothy Canfield Fisher], Dr. Nelson Haskell, Robert Hillyer, Stanley King, Otto Manthey-Zorn, David McCord, Frederic G. Melcher, Paul E. Moody, Theodore Morrison, Wilbert Snow, Lawrance Thompson, Richard Thornton, Louis Untermeyer, and George F. Whicher. For additional details, see *The Years of Triumph*, pp. 500–502.

4. See *The Years of Triumph*, pp. 154–155; 570. Also, see Kathleen Morrison, *Robert Frost: A Pictorial Chronicle* (New York, 1974), pp. 12–13. Mrs. Morrison's sensitive and well-written

portrait of RF during the years 1938–1963 is an invaluable supplement to the present volume, well worth reading by anyone interested in the life and personality of RF.

5. For details of RF's limited association with Theodore Morrison prior to 1936, see *The Years of Triumph*, pp. 402, 462, 682–686.

6. After the death of RF's daughter, Marjorie, in 1934, her husband Willard Fraser made arrangements with the Carol Frosts to have his daughter stay with them for several months each year, in order for her to grow up in a more regular family environment. Robin's last extended stay with the Carol Frosts ended in the summer of 1940, a few months before Carol's death.

7. Holmes gave an account of his stay at the Gully in "Close-up of an American Poet at 75," The New York *Times Magazine*, 26 March 1950, p. 12: "One night in 1938 [Frost] came up from his old farm in South Shaftsbury, Vt. [the Stone Cottage] to another place he owns nearby called the Gulley, where I was living for a month, and we talked away several hours. First, the talk was in the long living room, where his books lit the walls, and a fire burned, then on the open porch that in the daylight faces down the valley, and at night up at the Vermont stars. Sometimes after midnight we went outdoors, and along the farm road to a place where it ran flat for perhaps fifty yards before it dropped and turned again. It was too dark to see one another, or the trees. Frost in the right-hand track, and I in the left, we walked slowly till our feet found the diagonal hump across the road that kept it from washing down-hill, then turned. Back and forth, back and forth we walked, disembodied in the dark, and his voice came to me from the night. Sometimes at the turn I would light my pipe, and look over the match flame at that strong tanned face under the rumpled white hair, before the light went out. And he talked.

"Like many others, I have heard Robert Frost talk half a night away, in a good many different places in the last fifteen years. But I remember that one past-midnight talk for an idea he seemed to be working out with himself, and perhaps all the better because he couldn't see his listener. He said he thought the balance of life and death—the forces of positive and negative, good and evil, success and failure, whatever one calls them—are roughly fifty-five for life and forty-five for death. He said he thought God or something else, call it what you would, had given man a slight advantage, maybe only two points over fifty.

"Maybe that is where God comes in, he said, in the dark. I asked him how he figured man's advantage at fifty-five, then. Oh, he thought man by his everlasting stubborn effort had lifted it that far. That was where man comes in, and in that narrow margin, he said, we can find almost all of what its about. We have to remember always, he said, what a small hold we have, and how hard we have to work even to keep it. I asked him, somewhere toward 2:30 or 3, if he had ever said this in a poem. He said he thought not, not that he could remember. . . ."

Some two years later RF's poem, "Our Hold on the Planet," appeared in booklet form as his 1940 Christmas poem. As later revised, and published in *The Poetry*, p. 349, the poem ends:

> *We may doubt the just proportion of good to ill.*
> *There is much in nature against us. But we forget:*
> *Take nature altogether since time began,*
> *Including human nature, in peace and war,*
> *And it must be a little more in favor of man,*
> *Say a fraction of one percent at the very least,*
> *Or our number living wouldn't be steadily more,*
> *Our hold on the planet wouldn't have so increased.*

In his *Times* article, Holmes goes on to observe, correctly, that RF had revised downward man's margin of hope, between 1938 and 1940, from 10 to less than 1 percent.

8. See *The Years of Triumph*, pp. 493–496. In a letter to LT, dated 17 Sept. 1964, Mrs. Roberta S. Chalmers, wife of the late President Gordon Keith Chalmers of Kenyon College, recorded RF's emotional state in the aftermath of Elinor Frost's death: "The two Thanksgivings after Elinor died, Frost asked to come out to us, and did. The first one was terrific in between times, and Robert would tell me to drop everything, and go walking. He had to change his underwear about three times a day because of perspiration, and was the only person I ever knew—he would not like me to say this—who had the spirit and stamina to confront and conquer what could have become, and likely was, a nervous breakdown. His feet were so bad we would sit down wherever we were, once in a while, even in the middle of a field. He sometimes wept, and once wept aloud. Finally I found out that something had been told him by a member of his family—supposedly something Elinor had said—which had 'almost killed him.'" RF's remark, almost certainly, was a reference to what Lesley, not Elinor, had said.

9. RF to Robert S. Newdick, 20 July 1938; VaUL. In this letter, RF extended the mythic account of his departure from Amherst College, in a way intended to pass the blame for his resignation from himself to Amherst President Stanley King. See *The Years of Triumph*, pp. 503 ff., 700–703.

10. The Amherst *Record*, 29 June 1938, p. 1, was one of several newspapers reporting that RF "was elected for a term of six years by the largest vote given to fourteen candidates for the five positions available."

11. Lincoln MacVeagh, at one time head of the trade department of Henry Holt & Company, was serving, in 1938, as United States ambassador to Greece. For biographical background and other information on RF's relationship with MacVeagh, see *The Years of Triumph*, pp. 156–157, and other pages cited in the index of that volume. George Santayana, whose course in the history of philosophy RF took while at Harvard in 1898, had for some time prior to

1938 been living in Rome. RF's negative reaction to Santayana's Harvard course is discussed in *The Early Years*, pp. 243–246.

12. "Waddam Jones Robinson" obviously refers to three members of the Harvard faculty. The latter two are probably Howard Mumford Jones and F. N. Robinson. "Waddam" has not been identified.

13. RF to Robert Hillyer, 20 July 1938; VaUL.

14. RF to Theodore Morrison, 29 July 1938; DCL. Harry Hopkins served in a number of public-welfare agencies before heading the Works Progress Administration (W.P.A.) under his close friend, President Franklin D. Roosevelt; hence, RF's play on the words "work" and "relief."

15. RF repeatedly used the phrase "No woman can mother me with impunity" in discussing with LT this early stage of his relationship with Mrs. Morrison. By this he meant to suggest, apparently, that an element of his initial feeling for Mrs. Morrison was a desire to punish her for her excessive solicitude.

16. John Huston Finley, Jr., was a well-known classical scholar and Eliot Professor of Greek Literature at Harvard. Finley's name reappeared in the Frost story years later when, on 20 Jan. 1961, RF inadvertently substituted it for that of another Harvard man, John F. Kennedy, at the presidential inauguration in which RF participated. For the context of this error, see p. 282 of the present volume.

17. For source, see Note 1 of the present Chapter.

18. RF's important friendships with DeVoto and Untermeyer are discussed in detail in *The Years of Triumph*.

19. Shortly after the death of Elinor Frost, Theodore Morrison informed RF that, as director of the Bread Loaf Writers' Conference, he had been authorized to grant a scholarship for study at Bread Loaf in the summer of 1938, in memory of Mrs. Frost. Touched by this gesture of affection, RF responded in an undated letter written c. 15 April 1938 (DCL): "It's more than kind of you. I'm going to let you give a scholarship in her name this year and ask your permission to give one myself in her name next year. Then there will be two boys to go forward with thoughts of obligation to her. I have in mind for the benefit this year a boy whose work in verse she has long had special hopes of. In writing to see if he can accept it, please make him realize that it is as good as if he were her personal appointment. His name is Charles Foster. . . ." The Frosts had first known Foster as an undergraduate at Amherst College, where he had demonstrated substantial talent as a poet. Morrison carried out RF's request, and Foster accepted the scholarship, spending much time with RF during the Writers' Conference. Additional details of the Foster-Frost relationship may be found in Edward Connery Lathem and Lawrance Thompson, *Robert Frost: Poetry and Prose* (New York, 1972)—hereafter cited as *Poetry and Prose*—pp. 313–328.

20. From the unpublished "Journal of Charles H. Foster," entry

dated 19 Aug. 1938. In 1970, Foster generously made a copy of his "Journal" available to LT, who here expresses his gratitude for permission to quote from it.

21. Foster, "Journal," entry dated 18 Aug. 1938.

22. Wallace Stegner, *The Uneasy Chair: A Biography of Bernard DeVoto* (New York, 1974)—hereafter cited as *The Uneasy Chair*—p. 206.

23. Ibid., pp. 206–207, from which the details of this paragraph are derived. Foster, in his "Journal" entry dated "Sunday August 28," provides a slightly different perspective on the incident: ". . . Frost did not take kindly to Archie's talk, I found out, when I met him in the kitchen of Treman. He was mixing himself a drink of a tumbler full of whiskey with a piece of ice in it. Ted Morrison asked him to be good and he said he'd be all right when he put what he had in his hand where it should go. When we went into the living room everyone felt the tension and Benny DeVoto was pacing around the room like a captain on the quarterdeck. I asked him when we'd reach port and he said 'God-damn it to hell, Charlie. Robert's acting like a fool. Archie wasn't talking against him. He knows Robert is at the bottom of the new literalness.' . . ." MacLeish now read *Air Raid*, and the reading was followed by a heated discussion mainly between Morrison and DeVoto. Foster's account resumes: "The conversation shifted from this talk across the room into little eddies and I went over to see how Frost was stirring the waters. I sat next to Frost on a davenport and after a time Archie came over and sat on the arm of it. Frost had one arm around me and as more drinks were drunk and the discussion arose, Archie balanced himself with an arm around my shoulder. With Frost's arm around my back and Archie's around my neck and with both arguing and almost meeting before my nose, I felt at least physically in the center of American poetry. Frost said that it made him mad when 'a young squirt' like Spender gave what he had worked on all his life a phrase, and tried to take the credit for it. 'I'm going to England and spank Spender.' 'Jesus H. Christ, Robert,' said Archie, 'you're the one who ought to be spanked. You're the foundation and we all know it.' 'I'm an old man. I want you to say it, to say it often. I want to be flattered.' Archie said that it wasn't that he wanted flattery. It was perfectly natural to want to get recognition for what you had started. Archie then tried to make the conversation less personal and Frost said 'God-damn everything to hell so long as we're friends, Archie.' 'We are friends, Robert.' . . ."

24. Irma, like RF's sister Jeanie, long harbored an irrational fear that men were plotting to abuse her sexually. For the eventual result of Irma's peculiar anxieties, see Chapter 11 of the present volume.

25. For source of the details of the preceding three paragraphs, see Note 19 above.

26. RF and DeVoto separately gave LT identical accounts of this incident.

NOTES

2. BOSTON: A NEW LIFE

1. RF to J. J. Lankes, c. 12 Oct. 1938; TUL.

2. For additional information on the response of RF's children to Elinor Frost's death, see *The Years of Triumph*, pp. 495 ff.

3. RF's decision to move to the Boston area predated the secretarial arrangement he worked out with Mrs. Morrison. In the unpublished "Journal of Charles H. Foster," cited in Note 21 of Chapter 1, the entry dated 18 Aug. 1938 reads, in part: "Frost said he was going to move to Cambridge this fall and try to run Harvard University. . . . His chief reason for wanting to get to town was so that he could write the Harvard lectures. He couldn't write in the country; it excited him too much." RF's election, in June of 1938, to the Harvard Board of Overseers explains the reference to "running" Harvard University. He had also agreed, in becoming Norton Professor of Poetry in 1936, to prepare his lectures for publication, a task which he never got around to completing.

4. This is apparently RF's first use of a phrase that later became the final line of "The Lesson for Today," read at Harvard University before the Phi Beta Kappa Society on 20 June 1941. Appearing in *The Poetry*, pp. 350–355, the poem ends:

> *I hold your doctrine of* Memento Mori.
> *And were an epitaph to be my story*
> *I'd have a short one ready for my own.*
> *I would have written of me on my stone:*
> *I had a lover's quarrel with the world.*

5. President King, almost certainly, never charged RF with "ingratitude." The allegation that he had was part of the myth RF created to justify his resignation from Amherst College. For additional information, see *The Years of Triumph*, pp. 700–703.

6. Herschel Brickell, Robeson Bailey, Fletcher Pratt, John Gassner, and Wallace Stegner, and presumably "Strauss," were all members of the Bread Loaf staff. "Hassell and Negli," apparently, were students.

7. The proposed month-long visit with Brickell, at his home in Ridgefield, Connecticut, never took place. In early 1939, Carol did take his family to Florida, but was unsuccessful in his search for a suitable place to live. For details of RF's 1939 trip to Florida, and his purchase, one year later, of a "farm" in South Miami, see Chapters 3 and 5, respectively.

8. RF to Kathleen Morrison, c. 1 Sept. 1938; the original, property of Mrs. Kathleen Morrison, is on deposit in DCL, and is quoted here with the kind permission of Mrs. Morrison.

9. RF to John S. Van E. Kohn, c. 24 Aug. 1938; *Selected Letters*, p. 473.

10. John S. Van E. Kohn to RF, 31 Aug. 1938; the original is in the private collection of Mr. Kohn.

11. RF to John S. Van E. Kohn, 2 Sept. 1938; *Selected Letters*, p. 474.

12. RF to John S. Van E. Kohn, 10 Sept. 1938; quoted as fragment in *Selected Letters*, p. 480.

13. The story of the DeVotos' visit to Concord Corners is more fully told in Stegner, *The Uneasy Chair*, pp. 209–210.

14. RF to David McCord, c. Sept. 1938; quoted in Elizabeth Shepley Sergeant, *Robert Frost: The Trial by Existence* (New York, 1960)—hereafter cited as *The Trial by Existence*—pp. 360–361. Because this letter repeats in slightly different form ideas expressed by RF in other correspondence from the same period, the text as quoted by Miss Sergeant is here reproduced in full:

"I feel as if getting away from a pen to a pencil would enable me to write. Sometimes a change of paper helps me get going again. I wonder what that would mean to the psychoanalysts. I would await their answer with composure. The trial would be of them not me. For I know what it means. Browning shows he knows in a passage in Pippa Passes.

"You ask where I am. I am where the wind never ceases blowing. . . . That's a characteristic of our hill top: on the stillest day in the summer the air always draws knifelike across us up here. And in the fall it is almost too disturbing a foretaste of winter. No more nakedness mowing in the sun this year for me.

"You haven't heard, but the prospects are that in spite of the way you have neglected me this summer, I am coming to live near you in Boston and attend Overseers' meetings when I am not all abroad lecturing the other colleges in Cimerian darkness. I seem to have had the narrowest escape from getting into the Latin department (har.) Pease took the suggestion I made to Robert Hillyer and was all for roping me in as an eleventh hour advertisement of a falling stock. He came to Amherst about it and wrote me a long letter. . . . My vice is that I will keep retrying everybody and everything. Every little while I have another read at Queen Mab, The Revolt of Islam, Alastor, Prometheus Unbound or Epipsychidion. Personally I have never closed my mind on Franklin D. Grotonandharvard.

"I am not going to stay up here in a bath of memories very long —I am damned if I am not for any hay fever. . . .

"To show you how restless and reckless I am let me tell you what I paid for a pair of my books the other day to give to a friend to whom I owe almost my life. I thought it would be romantic to pay the market price or the latest auction price. By special favor and with some discount I am getting from a very friendly dealer a copy of the first *North of Boston* out of his bookshop for $150. and a copy of *A Boy's Will* out of his private collection for $100. I could have bought the two books together twenty-five years ago in any English Bookstore for exactly one dollar, from my publisher for half that. How many commodities have risen in value from fifty cents to two hundred and fifty dollars in that time? I think it's fun to be so commercial about poetry. Tell it in your funeral oration over me. To hell with living on a sound financial basis or with running a country on a sound financial basis. My adventures with money make it look ridiculous. . . . But don't worry about me: this gallop will level off into the same old trot in a minute.

"Glad you are having a book."

15. RF to LU, 6 Sept. 1938; *Letters to Untermeyer*, pp. 310–311.

16. RF to Carol Frost, 26 Sept. 1938; *Selected Letters*, pp. 477–478.

17. Miss Goodwillie's association with the Frost family, going back to 1915, is treated in *The Years of Triumph*, in pages cited in the Index to that volume.

18. The "third" child, without question, was Carol. As suggested elsewhere, Carol's psychological difficulties were a constant source of anxiety to his father, whose worst fears were realized when Carol committed suicide in October 1940. The story of Carol's death and its aftermath are told in Chapter 6 of the present volume.

19. For background on "Provide, Provide" as RF's response to a particular kind of sentimental humanitarianism popularized by the New Deal, see *The Years of Triumph*, pp. 437–438.

20. RF to Mary Goodwillie, 13 Oct. 1938; *Selected Letters*, pp. 479–480.

21. For purposes of comparison, see the text quoted in Note 3 of the present Chapter.

22. For source, see Note 1 of the present Chapter.

23. RF to John S. Van E. Kohn, c. 18 Oct. 1938; *Selected Letters*, p. 481.

24. The lines occur as the closing couplet of "Into My Own," the first poem in RF's first collection of verse, *A Boy's Will*. See *The Poetry*, p. 5.

25. As Stegner observes in *The Uneasy Chair*, p. 211, there is "half-hidden mockery" in RF's remark, "You as critic and psychoanalyst will know how to do that." RF was well aware that DeVoto, far from being a psychoanalyst himself, had for some time been, and was still, undergoing psychiatric treatment. RF's mockery of DeVoto's psychological difficulties, in "humorous" remarks to various of RF's and DeVoto's friends and acquaintances, continued unabated until 1943, when DeVoto virtually threatened RF with action for slander. For further information, see Chapter 8 of the present volume.

26. RF to Bernard DeVoto, c. 20 Oct. 1938; *Selected Letters*, pp. 481–482. This important letter is one of several attempts RF made, at various times in his life, to disassociate himself from Plato and Platonism. His open letter to the Amherst *Student*, for example, written in 1935 (and discussed in *The Years of Triumph*, pp. 386–388), concludes: "To me any little form I assert upon it [upon chaos] is velvet, as the saying is, and to be considered for how much more it is than nothing. If I were a Platonist I should have to consider it, I suppose, for how much less it is than everything else." Again, in a letter to R. P. T. Coffin, written in February 1938 (and discussed in *The Years of Triumph*, pp. 490–491, 697), RF states:

"Then again I am not the Platonist Robinson was. By Platonist I mean one who believes what we have here is an imperfect copy of what is in heaven. The woman you have is an imperfect copy of some woman in heaven or in someone else's bed. Many of the world's greatest—maybe all of them—have been ranged on that romantic side. I am philosophically opposed to having one Iseult for my vocation and another for my avocation; as you may have inferred from a poem called Two Tramps in Mud Time. You see where that lands me on the subject of Dante's Beatrice. Mea Culpa. Let me not sound the least bit smug. I define a difference with proper humility. A truly gallant platonist will remain a bachelor as Robinson did from unwillingness to reduce any woman to the condition of being used without being idealized. . . ."

It is certainly true that RF "began life wanting perfection and determined to have it." He liked to say that his mother taught him to be guided by the difficult exhortation: "Be ye therefore perfect, even as your Father in Heaven is perfect." But it is equally true that, as he grew older, he more easily accommodated himself to the imperfections of this world, until he could say, of perfection, "I got so I ceased to expect it and could do without it."

After his "defense" of his "native badness" in the letter to DeVoto, RF rarely felt the need to make statements like the one contained in a 1920 letter to Untermeyer: "She [Jeanie Frost] included me in the unendurably indifferent. A mistake. I belong to the unendurably bad." (*Selected Letters*, p. 247.) On the contrary, his letters after October 1938 consistently reflect a tendency to minimize the importance of his imperfections, as a sampling of extracts will demonstrate:

a) "I am really a person of good aspirations and you know I am or you wouldn't stay my indulgent friend through all my errancies the way you do." (RF to LU, 28 Nov. 1938; *Selected Letters*, p. 483.)

b) "I am more concerned to justify my prophecies than my moral principles." (RF to LU, 12 Oct. 1939; *Letters to Untermeyer*, p. 319.)

c) "Cheers for my moral improvement would start me down hill on the road to ruin." (RF to Hervey Allen, 31 March 1940; *Selected Letters*, p. 488.)

d) "This year it is the idea in the two-word phrase *felix culpa*. It could be turned against me personally and I am willing it should be: I am less and less on the defensive." (RF to LU, 11 March 1941; *Letters to Untermeyer*, p. 327.)

e) "Oh Gee isn't it fun being discreet at last after all the folly I have escaped the penalty for?" (RF to LU, 18 July 1945; *Letters to Untermeyer*, p. 340.)

f) "Two world wars and a few private catastrophes have made a man of me who doesn't mind blame. Neither for my sins of omission nor commission am I afraid of being punished." (RF to G. R. Elliott, c. 22 April 1947; *Selected Letters*, p. 525.)

g) "But I am always happier to hear that I am liked faults and all than that I am disliked." (From RF's "Introduction" to Sidney Cox, *A Swinger of Birches* [New York, 1957], p. vii.)

Perhaps the most revealing statement by RF on the subject of "badness" is contained in the letter cited in (b) above: "Part of the time I was acting on the theory that I was plain bad—yes and *talking* in public and private on that theory. But for me to be bad somebody else had to be bad too and that was unhypotheticable."

27. RF to LU, 28 Nov. 1938; *Selected Letters*, pp. 483–484.

28. "The Silken Tent" (*The Poetry*, pp. 331–332) was first published in the *Virginia Quarterly Review*, Winter, 1939. An early version, now in the University of Buffalo Library, is entitled "In Praise of Your Poise."

3. TRIALS OF STRENGTH AND SUPPLENESS

1. RF to Lesley Frost Francis, 30 Nov. 1938; *Family Letters of Robert and Elinor Frost*, edited by Arnold Grade (Albany, 1972)—hereafter cited as *Family Letters*—p. 200.

2. "The Rambler," "Robert Frost Turns Harvard into Subway Jam with Talk," Boston *Evening Transcript*, 1 Dec. 1938, pp. 1–2.

3. This reference to a social meeting of RF and the DeVotos is strong indication that, while their friendship was strained by the events of August 1938, it was not severed. There is no reason to suppose, however, that RF and DeVoto ever returned to the level of friendship they had enjoyed from 1936 to the summer of 1938.

4. For source, see Note 1 of the present Chapter.

5. RF to Lesley Frost Francis, Dec. 1938; *Family Letters*, p. 202.

6. G. R. Elliott to RF, 15 Feb. 1938; *Selected Letters*, p. 459.

7. RF to G. R. Elliott, c. 21 Feb. 1938; *Selected Letters*, p. 460.

8. RF to Richard H. Thornton, (c. 1938); quoted, without date, in Charles A. Madison, *The Owl Among Colophons* (New York, 1966), pp. 176–177.

9. RF to LU, 12 Oct. 1938; *Letters to Untermeyer*, p. 313.

10. T. H. Wilson to RF, 28 Nov. 1938; Holt Archives, PUL.

11. Herbert G. Bristol to RF, 12 Dec. 1938; Holt Archives, PUL.

12. T. J. Wilson to RF, 12 Dec. 1938; Holt Archives, PUL. This proposal was one of two contained in Wilson's letter. The other applied if RF chose to give Holt publication rights only to his future books of verse. The two proposals were essentially similar.

13. RF to Lesley Frost Francis, c. Dec. 1938; *Family Letters*, pp. 201–202. Raymond Everitt was a literary agent for, and later vice-president of, Little, Brown and Company. He and his wife, Helen, were for many years stand-in teachers on Theodore Morrison's Bread Loaf staff.

14. RF included "The Figure a Poem Makes" not only in the 1939 *Collected Poems*, but also consistently in other volumes that constituted comprehensive gatherings of his verse. It is also reprinted in *Poetry and Prose*, pp. 393–396, and in Hyde Cox and

Edward Connery Lathem, eds., *Selected Prose of Robert Frost* (New York, 1966)—hereafter cited as *Selected Prose*—pp. 17–20.

15. The theme of "wildness" is developed most explicitly in the essay's third paragraph: "Then there is this wildness whereof it is spoken. Granted again that it has an equal claim with sound to being a poem's better half. If it is a wild tune, it is a poem. Our problem then is, as modern abstractionists, to have the wildness pure; to be wild with nothing to be wild about. . . ." In a letter to Sidney Cox, dated 18 May 1939, RF associated his private "wildness" with this theme in "The Figure a Poem Makes": "But I am very wild at heart sometimes. Not at all confused. Just wild—wild. Couldnt you read it between the lines in my Preface nay and in the lines . . ." (DCL).

16. Mrs. William Vanamee to RF, 7 Jan. 1939; DCL.

17. In his introductory remarks, Dr. Damrosch said: "This is the twenty-ninth time the Institute has awarded its Gold Medal and the third time it has awarded it for Poetry. In 1911 it was awarded to James Whitcomb Riley and in 1929 to Edwin Arlington Robinson. . . . I am sure that none of us was more gratified with the result of the balloting than the two candidates who [on the voting date, December 17] ran second and third on the ballot: Mr. Stephen Vincent Benét and Miss Edna St. Vincent Millay. . . ." Quoted from *National Institute News Bulletin*, Vol. V, 1939, p. 1. The *Bulletin* also printed the text of RF's remarks in accepting the award, as RF wrote them down from memory shortly after the dinner.

18. The text of RF's talk, which has been quoted here in full, also appears as "Remarks Accepting the Gold Medal of the National Institute of Arts and Letters," in *Selected Prose*, pp. 101–102.

19. Eustace Seligman to RF, 10 Jan. 1939; DCL. Seligman's name came up in an important way in 1957 prior to RF's trip in that year to England. See p. 218 of Chapter 14 of the present volume.

20. George Daniel Olds became President of Amherst College in 1923, and persuaded RF, who had earlier served under President Alexander Meiklejohn, to rejoin the faculty in that year. In 1926, Olds visited RF in Ann Arbor and again persuaded him to return to Amherst. Dwight Morrow, the distinguished financier, was a trustee of the college.

21. The rough draft, written on the recto and verso of Seligman's letter to RF dated 16 Jan. 1939, is in DCL.

22. RF first became well-acquainted with Allen in Miami in 1936, when both were serving on the staff of the Winter Institute. In 1938, Allen was among the first to arrive in Gainesville after Mrs. Frost's death, and his condolences moved RF so much that he later wrote, "I shall never forget your coming to me with such sympathy." For additional information, see *The Years of Triumph*, pp. 436, 498–500.

23. One of the minor upsets of the Florida visit was reported by RF to Louis Untermeyer in a letter dated 17 Feb. 1939. As silently

expurgated by Untermeyer, the relevant passage (*Letters to Untermeyer*, p. 316) reads: "My chief signs of life are shown in any debate. He [my opponent] interrupted me in company the other night to ask while I was reciting Raleighs The Wood the Weed the Wag what in the world was meant by Wag. I had got to the first time it occurs in the poem: 'And they be these, the wood the weed the wag.' My answer was the poem itself would have told you if you had had the manners to wait and hear it out. It goes on to say The Wag, my pretty *knave*, betokens *thee*. I put plenty of accent on where it was needed."

According to Theodore Morrison, with whom RHW discussed the matter in Sept. 1975, such outbursts by RF—from which no friend of his, however close, was ever entirely immune—did not represent studied attempts to punish or humiliate, but rather reflected RF's tendency to hold up his own position in a discussion with the readiest means at hand. Morrison offered two similar instances from his personal experience in support of his view: On one occasion, in a group that included Morrison, RF expressed one of his pet themes: that we're all in this world to show what we're good for, and so are nations; that war is the ultimate test, and therefore war is good. Morrison was strongly opposed to this line of argument, and felt obliged to refute it. Trying to be polite as possible, he asked: "Wasn't it Ben Franklin who said there never was a good war or a bad peace?" "He was a fool, whoever said it," RF snapped. A few minutes later, however, he looked at Morrison quietly and asked with perfect cordiality, "Who was it said that?"—as if the outburst of a few minutes before had never occurred.

On another occasion, RF was informally talking at Bread Loaf—not in an evening lecture—and again riding a pet theme, that literature and writing are "play." Morrison ventured that all could agree to that up to a point, but wasn't RF pushing a sound view to an extreme? Don't we need some other word than "play," he asked, to describe our response to, say, *King Lear*? "It's a play, isn't it?" said RF instantly. Again, according to Morrison, he was not trying to humiliate or punish, but was simply defending his position with the first response that came to his mind, in this case a pun.

24. RF to Lesley Frost Francis, 3 Feb. 1939; *Family Letters*, pp. 203–204. Quotations immediately preceding are from the same letter.

25. In a letter, dated 12 Aug. 1938 (SUL), to Norman Foerster of the Iowa Department of English, RF wrote: "All those in favor of my coming to Iowa settle the question. You, Paul Engle, Wilbur Schramm, Edwin Ford Piper, Charles Foster, my long lost Helene Magaret and Grant Wood. In what University has such an array been got together on the artistic side? . . ." He concluded: "I look forward with all my heart to being with you out there. I feel more than a usual warmth of friendship for several you name. Paul Engle has become very dear to me." RF's affection for Engle was in part attributable to a flattering essay the latter had contributed to an English edition of RF's poetry: *Selected Poems*, by Robert Frost. With Introductory Essays by W. H. Auden, C. Day Lewis,

Paul Engle, and Edwin Muir (London, 1936). For information on RF's first awareness of Paul Engle, see *The Years of Triumph*, pp. 433–434.

26. RF to Robert S. Newdick, 12 Feb. 1939; VaUL. A slightly different account of the Cuban trip was contained in the letter cited in Note 31 below: "Did I tell you I went to Cuba for a week with Paul and Mary Engle. We went down to Camaguey saw several cities besides Havana and plenty of sugar cane and royal palms. The land is rich; the people are miserably poor. Everywhere beggars and beggar-vendors. We saw one great beach to beat the world and on it a car with a Vermont license which on inquiry proved to belong to friends of yours [Lesley's] the heads of the art department at Bennington College—Bee's friends—I forget their name. It was one of the only two American cars we saw outside of Havana. We had a pleasant more than pleasant meal with them by the most transparent ocean water I have ever looked into. Paul and Mary had two long swims in it. I am not much on foreign parts. I favor that beach for you to resort to someday though. To me the best of the excursion was the flight both ways in the big Pan American plane and especially the swoop and mighty splash into the bays on arrival."

27. The telegram, a copy of which was made available to LT by Hervey Allen in 1940, is dated 9 Feb. 1939. It began,

ARRIVE ON PLANE · FRIDAY NOON

28. RF to LU, 17 Feb. 1939; *Letters to Untermeyer*, pp. 314–315. The letter begins: "I seem as bad in some ways as when you saw me last. I dragged both Morrisons south with me to Key West and then here to Hervey's for a week's stay. After their desertion I was sent to Cuba for five days for obvious reasons and then for the same reasons when I got back was removed from the small house where I had lived with them to another without associations. I am not supposed to be in on the secret of what people think is the matter with me. It's pretty ill we all dissemble [See Matthew Prior, "Song"]. I go north to some more of my fate next Friday morning and should be at my office . . . with my secretary not a minute later than Monday morning February 27th. I have been talking of you with the Chapins who are living in another of Hervey's little houses. . . ." In April 1967, Henry Chapin generously supplied LT with his written recollections of RF's 1939 stay at Hervey Allen's ranch. Despite certain obvious inaccuracies, these recollections provide a valuable glimpse of RF at the Glades by one who had only limited understanding of RF's emotional condition:

"About thirty years ago Paula [Mrs. Chapin] and I were staying in a small bungalow on Hervey Allen's place in Florida, called the Glades. Why, God knows, for the Glades at that time were a happy tropical fiction in Hervey's active imagination, a few lean and hungry pines, some struggling Hibiscus etc. laid out along a tortuous drive that led to the main house. This house started as a Hodgson prefab and was overlaid with local rock and anchored with piano wire against hurricanes. The drive had been made purposely narrow to protect the children from fast driving and possible kidnappers. We lived down the drive in a dark but adequate cottage used as a guest house.

"Frost came to visit Hervey shortly after Mrs. Frost died and was deeply depressed. Hervey asked us to board him in the cottage while he looked around for a place of his own. At this time the area was strictly Florida pine backwoods just outside Coconut Grove, rather wild and inhabited by rabbits, snakes, a few wild-cats and an occasional panther, all harmless if left alone. The primitive nature of the surroundings appealed to Robert.

"He moved into our spare room and was very shy and quiet as we were strangers to him and also, as you know, he was wary of all personal contact. He started to learn the recorder and in a few days could master The Keeper of the Eddistone Light, to which he added various verses not quite fitting for his collected works. The possibilities and inabilities of mating with mermaids was hard to solve.

"Ted and Kay Morrison came through about this time from Boston and, as I recall, Kay had not at this time decided to become Robert's secretary and see him through this period when he felt a good deal at sea after his wife's death. He stayed on with us for about ten days and then, I think, Hervey arranged for him to go to Havana with Paul Engle. This trip I am told had its difficulties but what wouldn't at that particular time. . . ."

29. William M. Sloane III to RF, 16 Feb. 1939; DCL. The Latin was an adaptation of Carmen XXX Liber III of the *Odes* of Horace, with the second person singular substituted for the first.

30. RF to William M. Sloane III, 17 Feb. 1939; DCL.

31. RF to Lesley Frost Francis, 25 Feb. 1939; *Family Letters*, p. 207.

4. HANGING ROUND EDUCATION

1. RF to LU, 26 June 1939; *Letters to Untermeyer*, pp. 316–317.

2. RF to Lesley Frost Francis, 25 Feb. 1939; *Family Letters*, p. 209. The remark is contained in a postscript which RF added, as an afterthought, to an account of his Florida vacation. As it casts further light on the difficult relationship of RF and his son, the passage is quoted here in full: "I ought to add that Carol Lillian Prescott and Robin seem better than in the years when we were too much with them for our good. Carol came down perverse and surly, but he improved on being let alone. Or so I imagine. I have played cards with them six or eight nights and had a couple of long rides with them. They have been fishing on their own considerably. They are not lucky so far in life. They catch no fish. The mongrel dog has just brought forth eight more, much more, mongrel pups, for them to drown. Nobody else's experience profits them the least. I told them they couldn't take care of a bitch. I couldn't. You could see a little of them—not too much."

3. RF tried to communicate some of his complex feelings about

his marriage to Elinor in a conversation with his poet-friend, Raymond Holden. After he had listened to Holden read before the Phi Beta Kappa Society at Tufts College, on 24 May 1939, the two men drove into Boston by taxi and had dinner at the St. Botolph Club, where RF put Holden up for the night. As told by Holden in his tape-recorded "Reminiscences of Robert Frost" (DCL), the talk soon turned to personal matters: "He was in a very friendly and mellow mood, having worked out his resentment of my absence from Elinor's funeral—or else, having come to think it had no importance. He sat up in my room until after two o'clock talking about old times and, for almost the first time in my experience with Robert, discussing personal emotion as it applied to each of us. Robert questioned me. I had been twice divorced by that time, and he seemed to want to know about the compulsion behind my mistaken marriages, and talked about his own emotions quite freely. He told me in his lightest, aphoristic manner that he had had many troublesome feelings about different women, but had loved only one. I do not know why I felt that he was meaning to imply that that one was not Elinor. Perhaps I mistook his emphasis. I didn't feel like questioning him to find out what he really meant. I had always assumed that in his curious and somewhat egocentric way he was completely devoted to Elinor as she was to him. . . ."

4. RF to Lesley Frost Francis, 1 March 1939; *Family Letters*, pp. 209–211.

5. The status of the anthology, as of 16 Dec. 1938, was discussed in a letter of that date from T. J. Wilson of Holt to RF (Holt Archives, PUL): "Confirming our telephone conversation this morning, I wish to state that we fully understand your obligation to Harvard University and the Harvard University Press in the matter of the six lectures you delivered some time ago. We understand it is your plan, and theirs, that you reduce the essence of these six lectures to one fairly long essay to be published as the preface or introduction to an anthology of verse, probably to be called "The Harvard Book of Verse," or "The Harvard Anthology of Poetry," or some similar title. This is entirely satisfactory to us and will not be considered in any way a contravention of any one of our agreements." Despite the amenability of Holt and the announced intentions of RF, the task was ever completed.

6. Details of RF's first White Fund lecture are derived from an anonymous article, "Teacher Inspired Frost with Love for Poetry" in the Lawrence *Evening Tribune*, 3 March 1939, p. 6. The five lectures, delivered between 2 March and 11 May 1939, were entitled: "The Success of a Single Poem, such as Collins' 'How Sleep the Brave' "; "To Find the New in Old Poets: Emerson, Longfellow, Poe, Bryant and Sill"; "The Difficulty with Contemporary Poets arises from having known them personally"; "The Anthology as the Highest Form of Criticism; survival and revival tell the story"; and "If the Anthologist Includes His own Writing; with liberal quotations from his latest book."

7. In the letter to Norman Foerster cited in Note 25 of Chapter 3, RF agreed to visit the University of Iowa in November 1938. Three

weeks later, on 5 Sept. 1938, RF wrote back to Foerster saying he had changed his mind: "The warmth of your invitation makes me impatient to be with you out there soon. But November is my bad month to be in other people's houses where I can't govern the heating and it is the decline of the year when I am most liable to the germs in railway beds. I believe it would be better if after my Ohio lectures I came back east for a few easy things near home and had you wait for me till April. It will be spring before we elders know it. I sent enough love by Charlie Foster last week to hold you and Paul Engle in our friendship till I can get there. Dont you think I am right? Not only would I be better in the spring, but I presume Iowa would be—you want me to enjoy the country as well as its inhabitants." (SUL)

8. The details of this incident are recorded in a letter from Doris Foster (Mrs. Charles H. Foster) to her parents, written in April 1939, a copy of which was supplied to LT by Mrs. Foster.

9. "About Robert Frost," *American Prefaces*, Vol. 4, No. 7 (April 1939), p. 100.

10. Ibid., pp. 105–107.

11. The friendship of RF and Engle did not die at this time, but it suffered a blow from which it never fully recovered. Apparently aware that something had upset RF during his Iowa visit, Engle wrote to him on 23 April 1939, apologizing for everything but what had upset RF the most: "This is just to tell you that nothing has made me as sore for years as not being here for your visit. Had those lectures not been booked a year ahead, I would have crawled out of them. I'm equally sorry about some things in the American Prefaces. Although it was my original idea to dedicate the magazine to you, I had nothing to do with editing it. I don't want to evade any responsibility, but my job there is simply to turn over manuscripts to Schramm, who has the final word. . . . Further, the title of my poem to you was R. F., and not 'Homage etc.' . . . I'm sorry about the lecture being held where it was. The last thing I urged on both Schramm and Foerster was that they move it to the larger auditorium. . . . But I only hope you weren't too much worried by these things. . . ." (DCL)

RF was apparently somewhat placated, for he offered Engle and his wife the use of the Gully farm during the 1939 session of the Bread Loaf Writers' Conference. But gradually, over the next few years, the two men grew further and further apart, until virtually all personal contact ceased. In a letter dated 26 Dec. 1945 (DCL), Engle wrote: "Our sad estrangement has been a constant grief to me. I am writing this letter to say that I hope time has softened whatever outrage you felt. . . . This comes with the hope that these latter years have not been too disagreeable for you, and the firmer hope that I shall have a friendly word from you."

Engle's friendship with RF suffered another blow in the mid-1940s when RF saw another of the Iowan's poems, this one entitled "Cuban Voyage" and based on the visit the Engles made with RF to that island in 1939. Again taking exception to Engle's treatment of their conversations and shared experiences, RF once more made known to Engle his marked displeasure.

Finally, in July 1947, after being told that Engle had just written a highly complimentary review of his latest book, *Steeple Bush*, RF relented and sent Engle the following note: "I have it on the best authority that I was mistaken about the dread poem you sent me in print. K. has insisted all along that you were my friend and could not possibly mean what I took you to mean. She has what you have been saying about my new book to sustain her. The moral is don't go too far in these experiments in obfuscation. You have a way of your own in prose and verse that I believe in and should suppose you could trust your future to. Let's forget Our Cuban Journey. My best to Mary and yourself." (RF to Paul Engle, 5 July 1947; rough draft, dictated by RF to Kathleen Morrison, in DCL.)

12. Anonymous article, "Robert Frost Will Be Honored at Banquet, Talk in Auditorium," *The Branding Iron*, 13 April 1939, p. 1.

13. RF to John Bartlett, 23 April 1939; Margaret Bartlett Anderson, *Robert Frost and John Bartlett: The Record of a Friendship* (New York, 1963)—hereafter cited as *Frost and Bartlett*—p. 194.

14. Edward Davison, "'Trial By Market Best Test of Art,'" Colorado Springs *Gazette*, 29 April 1939, pp. 1, 3.

15. "Frost Regrets the Arts Lack 'Prize Ring' Fight," The New York *Times*, 30 April 1939, p. 15: "Robert Frost would like to see the superiority of artists determined in 'something like the prize ring.' At present the best test of a piece of art is the cash it brings its creator, Mr. Frost told a fine arts conference today, but for the artist, 'the inner assurance of excellence is still lacking. I wish we had something like the prize ring, where we could fight to a finish, where work went down on the mat and had its arm lifted by the judges at the end.'"

16. The New York *Times*, 1 May 1939, p. 22.

17. Anderson, *Frost and Bartlett*, p. 196. This is a variant of RF's half-playful, half-serious claim, "I only go / When I'm the show."

18. James B. Conant to RF, 4 May 1939; DCL.

19. Either because RF orally accepted the appointment prior to submitting his written acceptance, or because his acceptance was tacitly assumed, the announcement of his appointment was released as early as 11 May. As carried by the New York *Times* on that date, it read: "Establishment of a new Ralph Waldo Emerson fellowship in poetry, and the appointment of Robert Frost as first incumbent, were announced today by Harvard University. Mr. Frost will be in residence at Harvard under the fellowship for two years, beginning next September. The purpose of the fellowship is to enable distinguished poets to come to Harvard for one or two years, to meet informally with students interested in poetry, and perhaps to give formal courses. Funds for the fellowship were raised by a committee composed of Howard Mumford Jones, Professor of English; Robert S. Hillyer, Boylston Professor

of Rhetoric and Oratory; Archibald MacLeish, poet and journalist, curator of the Nieman collection of contemporary journalism; David M. Little, secretary to the University and master of Adams House; and David McCord, poet, executive secretary of the Harvard Fund Council."

20. For source, see Note 1 of the present Chapter.

21. RF to James B. Conant, n.d.; rough draft in DCL. From the letter cited in Note 20, it can be assumed that RF wrote this one around, and probably after, 26 June 1939.

22. RF paid for the farm after leaving Ripton at the end of the Writers' Conference. He soon received a letter from Mrs. Noble saying she had used the money to buy another farm, because she couldn't get along "without having something to worry about."

23. "The Doctrine of Excursions," *Bread Loaf Anthology* (Middlebury, 1939), pp. xix–xx. The Preface is reprinted in *Poetry and Prose*, pp. 397–399.

24. RF to Lesley Frost Francis, 9 Nov. 1939; *Family Letters*, p. 215.

25. "Whilst the world is thus dual, so is every one of its parts. The entire system of things gets represented in every particle. There is somewhat that resembles the ebb and flow of the sea, day and night, man and woman, in a single needle of the pine, in a kernel of corn, in each individual of every animal tribe. The reaction, so grand in the elements, is repeated within these small boundaries. For example, in the animal kingdom the physiologist has observed that no creatures are favorites, but a certain compensation balances every gift and every defect. A surplusage given to one part is paid out of a reduction from another part of the same creature. If the head and neck are enlarged, the trunk and extremities are cut short. . . . The true doctrine of omnipresence is that God reappears with all his parts in every moss and cobweb. The value of the universe contrives to throw itself into every point. If the good is there, so is the evil; if the affinity, so the repulsion; if the force, so the limitation. . . ." ("Compensation," in *Essays: First Series.*)

26. "Robert Frost Aims to 'Stir' Students," The New York *Times*, 12 Nov. 1939, p. 12. An expanded version of this interview by Frances E. Carey is reprinted in Edward Connery Lathem, ed., *Interviews with Robert Frost* (New York, 1966)—hereafter cited as *Interviews*—pp. 101–103.

27. This story was told to LT by RF in Key West, Florida, Feb. 1940. The two lines of poetry were inscribed by RF on the back flyleaf of "Twilight," his unique first "book," prior to its delivery to the San Francisco businessman-collector, Earle J. Bernheimer. (For details, see Chapter 5 of the present volume.) It was first printed in Ray Nash, ed., *Fifty Years of Robert Frost: A Catalogue of the Exhibition Held in Baker Library in the Autumn of 1943* (Hanover, 1944).

28. This story was told to LT by RF in Key West, Florida, 24 Feb. 1940, at which time RF also expressed an opinion on educational theory. The old-fashioned method of teaching, he said, was to get

a hundred boys in a room and tell them something; but the modern method was to have each boy meet with you privately, sitting down and putting his feet on your shoulders so you could give him personal attention. Wasn't it better, he asked, if you had something to say, to say it once to a hundred boys instead of wasting time saying the same thing a hundred times to each of them individually?

5. FRIENDS AND NEIGHBORS

1. RF to Hervey Allen, 23 May 1940; *Selected Letters*, pp. 489–490.

2. RF to LU, 13 Dec. 1939; the original of this letter, in Mrs. Morrison's hand and signed "Robert" by RF, is in the Louis Untermeyer Papers, Manuscript Division, Library of Congress.

3. So defined by Professor Robert A. Nisbet of the University of California at Riverside, in a review of Kenneth Keniston's *The Uncommitted: Alienated Youth in American Society*, the New York *Times Book Review*, 14 Nov. 1965, p. 1. RF's spelling is apparently phonetic; the standard form is "acedia."

4. RF's appearance at the Grolier Club coincided with a major exhibition there entitled "Four American Poets." These included, besides RF, Stephen Vincent Benét, Edna St. Vincent Millay, and Edwin Arlington Robinson. Regrettably, no stenographic or electronic recording of RF's remarks was made. The quoted passage is derived from notes made during the lecture by Mr. Harold J. Baily, Esq., who generously supplied a copy to LT.

5. The earliest known correspondence from RF to Bernheimer is a letter dated 2 March 1936, which begins: "The Gold Hesperides you have is a first. You may always send me anything you please for my autograph. . . ." This and numerous other letters from RF to Bernheimer are located in the Robert Frost Collection, Clifton Waller Barrett Library, VaUL. Letters from Bernheimer to RF are in DCL.

6. Earle J. Bernheimer to RF, 17 Oct. 1939; DCL.

7. For additional information concerning the creation of *Twilight* in 1894, and the events immediately following, see *The Early Years*, pp. 173 ff.

8. RF to Earle J. Bernheimer, 18 Nov. 1939; *Selected Letters*, pp. 486–487.

9. The "bulletin" was widely quoted, as an Associated Press release, on 13 Jan. 1940.

10. RF appointed LT as his "official biographer" in July 1939, following the death of Professor Robert S. Newdick. While not RF's authorized biographer, Newdick had for some years been working with the poet's knowledge and consent on a biography that was unfinished at the time of Newdick's death. See Appendix.

11. This and subsequent information concerning RF's friendship with Hyde Cox is based on several extended interviews granted by the latter to RHW beginning in September 1972.

12. For details of RF's first meeting with Stevens in 1935, see *The Years of Triumph*, pp. 665–666.

13. RF to LU, 31 March 1940; *Letters to Untermeyer*, pp. 321–322.

14. RF to Hervey Allen, 31 March 1940; *Selected Letters*, p. 488.

15. Hervey Allen to RF, 8 April 1940; *Selected Letters*, p. 489.

16. RF to Hervey Allen, 23 May 1940; *Selected Letters*, pp. 489–490.

17. RF to Hervey Allen, 6 Sept. 1940; University of Pittsburgh Library.

18. RF to Hervey Allen, 30 Sept. 1940; University of Pittsburgh Library.

6. THE DEATH OF THE DARK CHILD

1. RF to LU, 26 Oct. 1940; *Selected Letters*, p. 491.

2. For additional information on the death of Lester Russell and its effect on the Frost family, see *The Early Years*, pp. 365–366. Details concerning Carol Frost's suicidal obsession were told to LT by Mrs. Lillian LaBatt Frost (Mrs. Carol Frost), on 19 Feb. 1963.

3. Lillian Frost's letter to RF, dated 28 Sept. 1940, is in DCL.

4. *The Poetry*, p. 54.

5. Mrs. Morrison accompanied RF by train as far as Springfield, Massachusetts, before returning alone to Boston. On the way, they happened to meet a young poet named Daniel Smythe, whom RF had first encountered at the home of John Holmes several months before. Smythe and RF talked for some time on a variety of subjects, without any reference by RF to his son's death. The train reached Springfield and RF escorted Mrs. Morrison to the platform. Then, returning to his seat, he startled Smythe by saying "My son Carol died last night. He killed himself." A detailed account of this episode can be found in Smythe's book, *Robert Frost Speaks* (New York, 1964), pp. 59–68.

6. RF to William Prescott Frost, 12 Oct. 1940; *Family Letters*, pp. 218–219.

7. RF to Mrs. Lillian LaBatt Frost, 12 Oct. 1940; *Family Letters*, pp. 219–220. Despite Louis Untermeyer's unsubstantiated assertion, in *Letters to Untermeyer* (p. 322), that Carol "even threatened his father's life" before taking his own, there is no reason to believe that any such threat was ever made. Lillian Frost, in a letter to LT dated 3 Sept. 1963, stated unequivocally, "Carol never threatened his father's life." She continued: "Carol had talked to me many, many hours. There was never a time but what he had a great deal of love and honor for his father. He did speak of the difficulties of being the son of a great man, but the thought of killing his own father was never in his mind. While I was in the hospital and Prescott, not quite sixteen, was with him, he never spoke ill of his father, and he talked to Prescott every night the way he did with his father the night he was there, and the way he

had talked to me many nights before. Prescott never had a bit of fear of his father, he knew he was greatly loved. Can you imagine any grandfather whose life had been threatened by a son who had lost his mind going away and leaving a much loved grandson alone in the house with him? I can't."

Further proof of the fact that Prescott's life or his grandfather's had not been in any danger is provided by a letter from William Prescott Frost to Arnold Grade, dated 5 Feb. 1971. As quoted by Grade (in *Family Letters*, p. 219) it reads: "My memory is clear . . . I was nearly sixteen . . . there was never any violence or threat of physical harm to be inflicted on anyone except by my father on himself."

8. RF to Mrs. Lillian LaBatt Frost, Oct. 1940; *Family Letters*, pp. 221–222.

9. RF to LU, 26 Oct. 1940; *Selected Letters*, pp. 491–492.

10. RF's letter to Sloane, dated 17 Oct. 1940 (*Selected Letters*, pp. 490–491) is worth quoting here in full for the light it casts on RF's state of mind in the aftermath of Carol's death:

"I hereby promise in the presence of Kathleen, my secretary, that I will give you both the books you want, prose and verse, at approximately the times you name. Tell me right back in your next letter what's the latest you can wait for the prose book. I, of course, want to do all I can to celebrate your (I was going to say our) seventy fifth anniversary. You know me well enough to know that I wouldn't make these undertakings if I hadn't the books practically written already. I could hope the poetry book would get a little fatter before next June. I am sure it will if I am kept happy enough by you and my secretary and such outlying friends as Bill Snow.

"We are sending in this letter—but hold on a minute, maybe we're not sending the one I was going to name. It has just occurred to us that we might offer you something longer than usual [for the annual Christmas poem]. What should you say to a rather amusing skit in blank verse of one hundred and fifty lines. It is called THE LITERATE FARMER AND THE PLANET VENUS, A DATED POPULAR SCIENCE MEDLEY ON A MYSTERIOUS LIGHT RECENTLY OBSERVED IN THE WESTERN SKY AT EVENING (from TALKS WALKING). If length isn't fatal let us know and we'll send it down. Otherwise we'll find you the shorter one. Don't worry about not seeing them both! You will in the end. And don't worry about me too much. But thanks for caring."

The volume of prose mentioned in this letter never materialized. The volume of poetry, "Talks Walking," was retitled *A Witness Tree* before its publication in April 1942 (see next Chapter). The concluding poem in that volume is "The Literate Farmer and the Planet Venus."

11. *The Poetry*, p. 349. For the origins of this poem, see Note 7 of Chapter 1.

12. A partial transcript of a letter from RF to Mrs. Lillian Frost, dated 9 March 1941, was supplied by the latter to LT, and refers

to RF's move to 35 Brewster Street: "I get out of 88 Mt. Vernon St. toward the end of the week. I have had a good home for the likes of me at 88 Mt. Vernon. But I have grown restless again. The new place will have room for any of you when you come visiting. But Gee the number of places I have on earth."

13. The Library of Congress exhibition, which coincided with RF's talk, was composed largely of materials supplied on loan by Mrs. Lesley Frost Francis. One item on view was a first draft manuscript of a poem RF never published, and apparently never completed. Called "Tendencies Cancel," it was reproduced in the Washington *Post* on 27 March 1947, as follows:

Thats where the one comes in.
Tendencies Cancel
ever
If ~~any~~ tendential force
~~Ever~~ Ran out its logical course
The alarmist might well be
There were reason for being *scared*
But tendencies seem to be paired
And there seems to be provision
The pairs shall be in collision
And many collisions shall lace
Entangle and mass in space
To make a bristling sun.
It's then comes in the One.
Thats where the One comes in
He has let the action begin
And let a lot get done
And been at no least expense
[incomplete]

RF seems to have been trying here to explain the paired forces of nature in terms of an essential dualism ultimately under the control of the great One, God. The idea of the universe being composed of counterbalancing opposites was a favorite one of RF's. See, in this regard, Note 5 of Chapter 8 below.

14. In fact, the "churchman" was the churchwoman, Alice Meynell. The passage is the first stanza of her poem, "I Am the Way."

15. "Triple Plate," which had been RF's Christmas poem for 1939, appeared as "Triple Bronze" in *A Witness Tree* (1942). Aside from the change in title, the poems were identical. See *The Poetry*, p. 348.

16. James B. Conant to RF, 15 May 1941; DCL.

17. This passage in "The Lesson for Today", *The Poetry*, p. 353, bears striking resemblance to one in RF's "Letter to the Amherst *Student*," [c. 21 March 1935]; *Selected Letters*, p. 418: "All ages of the world are bad—a great deal worse anyway than Heaven. If they weren't the world might just as well be Heaven at once and have it over with. One can safely say after from six to thirty thousand years of experience that the evident design is a situation here in

which it will always be about equally hard to save your soul. Whatever progress may be taken to mean, it can't mean making the world any easier place in which to save your soul—or if you dislike hearing your soul mentioned in open meeting, say your decency, your integrity. . . ." The passage also anticipates a similar one in *A Masque of Reason* (1945), spoken by the character called "Job's Wife":

> *"For instance, is there such a thing as Progress?*
> *Job says there's no such thing as Earth's becoming*
> *An easier place for man to save his soul in.*
> *Except as a hard place to save his soul in,*
> *A trial ground where he can try himself*
> *And find out whether he is any good,*
> *It would be meaningless. It might as well*
> *Be Heaven at once and have it over with."*
> (*The Poetry*, p. 484, ll. 315–322)

18. "The Lesson for Today," *The Poetry*, p. 355.
19. This episode was described by Mrs. Lillian LaBatt Frost to LT, 19 Feb. 1963.

7. A WITNESS TREE

1. Quoted from "Beech," *The Poetry*, p. 331.
2. RF had said much the same thing, in virtually the same words, in a note he slipped under Untermeyer's door on the night of 22 August 1941, during the Bread Loaf Writers' Conference. Entitled "A Manifesto of Manifest Destiny," the note was characterized by the kind of half-humorous punning RF often used in his communications with Untermeyer:

"Having got up a momentum of expansion into territories occupied by none but Indians and not knowing how to curb it or where next to turn it unless into territories occupied by Greasers and Kanucks I have decided to move my Capital of the World to the Noble Homeric farm (for the night) at Ripton Vermont (rather than to Berlin Moscow London or Washington) and clarify the present world situation by offering to take over everybody's quarrel with Hitler and to fight the war out with American forces and resources alone. I can see no other way to establish our national identity and define Democracy. I would say to all my adherents and coherents, Come ye out from among the fools who would lose in the confusions of old European casuistry. Give the present war up as a hopeless mess and begin all over with a plain statement of who is opposed to whom and what to what. Then if we win ours will be the loot the glory and the self-realization. If we fail the Indians will have their chance to come back. The Fearer." (*Letters to Untermeyer*, pp. 328–329.)

3. RF to Willard E. Fraser, 2 Nov. 1941; *Selected Letters*, pp. 494–495.

4. This incident was described by Mrs. Kathleen Morrison to LT on 27 Dec. 1941.

5. "To a Moth Seen in Winter" appeared first in the *Virginia Quarterly Review*, Spring, 1942, where it was dated "Circa 1900." "Time Out" also appeared there for the first time; when RF wrote it into LT's copy of the Halcyon House edition of *Collected Poems* (1939), he gave as its title "On the Ascent," and dated it "1939."

6. *The Poetry*, p. 348. According to Charles R. Green, Librarian of the Jones Library, a fair copy of "The Gift Outright" was presented to that library in 1936. At that time, RF urged Green to use the manuscript in reproduction in the Jones Library Bibliography for that year. Green decided to reproduce instead the manuscript of "A Time to Talk," because RF had made revisions therein. As an indirect result, "The Gift Outright" was not published for another six years.

In 1936, RF also presented to LT a fair copy of the poem, in which the last line occurs as a variant of the final published form: "Such as she was, such as she might [as against "would"] become." A second variant of the final version was read at the inauguration of President John F. Kennedy on 20 January 1961, when the poem came into particular prominence. For details of this variant, see page 282 of Chapter 17.

Accompanying the three poems in the *Virginia Quarterly Review* was an introductory note provided by RF: "The Virginia Quarterly . . . is a favorite place of publication with me. You may of course put the poems in any order you please. At Williamsburg I read the one about my right to Time Out for considering; then the one about considering humanitarianism, On a Moth Seen in Winter, and the last the one about meditating my country, The Gift Outright. It may mean something to you (it does to me) that the line in The Gift Outright, 'In Massachusetts, in Virginia' was not an introduction of afterthought for the purpose of a Virginia occasion. The poem exactly as submitted to you has been in the possession of the Jones Library at Amherst for six or seven years. I take pride in having thought of a thing before I had to think of it under fire."

7. Mrs. Kathleen Morrison described RF's reaction to the events following Pearl Harbor to LT on 27 Dec. 1941.

8. RF to Earle J. Bernheimer, 1 June 1941; *Selected Letters*, p. 493.

9. This offer was made by Bernheimer in a letter to RF dated 9 June 1941; DCL.

10. Louis H. Cohn to Earle J. Bernheimer, 2 July 1941; DCL.

11. RF to Earle J. Bernheimer, 16 Dec. 1941; *Selected Letters*, pp. 495–496.

12. William M. Sloane III to RF, 6 Jan. 1942; PUL.

13. RF to LU, 15 Jan. 1942; *Selected Letters*, pp. 497–498. RF first sent a version of the poem, which he never published, to LU in a letter dated 7 July 1921 (*Selected Letters*, pp. 270–271). He sent it again in a letter dated 26 September 1921—less than three months after the first. There it appeared after this paragraph: "I'm

in earnest. Just as the only great art is inesthetic so the only morality is completely ascetic. I have been bad and a bad artist. I will retire soon to the place you wot of. Not now but soon. That is my last, my ultimate vileness, that I cannot make up my mind to go now where I must go sooner or later. I am frail."

Repeatedly, throughout his life, RF indulged in a spoiled-child attitude toward any major crisis that thwarted his own wishes; he seemed to feel, at least temporarily, that such a crisis denigrated him to a point at which he was justified in throwing his life away as "an unconsoled and utter loss." An early example of this tendency occurred in 1894, when RF, in his despondency over Elinor White's attitude toward him, attempted to throw his life away in an unconvincing fashion by making a mysterious trip to and through the Dismal Swamp in Virginia. For details, see *The Early Years*, pp. 173–189.

In the present crisis, which may somehow have involved Kathleen Morrison, RF goes so far as to permit the poem by extension to imply an analogy between his own predicament and that of one crucified. Given his apparent emotional state, the sentimental fusion of suicide and crucifixion is not a paradox. But notice the self-conscious ambivalence established by the line, "Oh, if religion's not to be my fate," and his comment in the letter, "I believe I am safely secular till the last go down." Fear of death seemed to keep RF from ever being "safely secular."

To listeners whose sympathetic insights he trusted, RF was outspoken concerning his own religious beliefs and affirmations; increasingly so, as he approached "the last go down." To others, he self-protectively masked his religious beliefs behind postures of profane and seemingly blasphemous secularity.

14. RF to Lesley Frost Francis [Feb. 1942]; *Family Letters*, pp. 229–230.

15. RF to Lesley Frost Francis, 6 March 1942; *Family Letters*, pp. 232–233.

16. Carl Sandburg, "Those Who Make Poems," the *Atlantic Monthly* (March 1942), pp. 344–346. Efforts to determine when and where RF first uttered the statement, "I would as soon play tennis without a net as write free verse," have not been successful, but after the initial occasion, RF repeated the remark in many of his public lectures until the end of his life.

17. RF to LT, c. 21 March 1942; *Selected Letters*, p. 499.

18. RF to William M. Sloane III, 26 March 1942; *Selected Letters*, pp. 499–500.

19. *The Poetry*, p. 331.

20. Ibid., In *The New England Primer*, this poem was the paradigm for the letter "Z."

21. *The Poetry*, p. 361.

22. Ibid., p. 362.

23. Ibid., p. 363. Some time after this poem appeared in *A Witness Tree*, the poet and anthologist Oscar Williams wrote a rebuttal that he called "A Total Revolution":

I advocate a total revolution.
The trouble with a semi-revolution,
It's likely to be slow as evolution.
Who wants to spend the ages in collusion
With Compromise, Complacence and Confusion?
As for the same class coming up on top,
That's where the poor should really plan to stop.
And speaking of those people called the "haves,"
Who own the whole cow and must have the calves
(And plant the wounds so they can sell the salves)
They won't be stopped by doing things by halves.
I say that for a permanent solution
There's nothing like a total revolution!
P. S. And may I add by way of a conclusion
I wouldn't dream to ask a Rosicrucian.

24. Ibid., p. 364.
25. The volume, entitled *Come In*, was published in April, 1943.
26. RF to William M. Sloane III, 16 June 1942; PUL.

8. ON THE HOME FRONT

1. RF to John T. Bartlett, 20 Jan. 1943; *Selected Letters*, p. 507.

2. RF to LT, 20 Aug. 1942; *Selected Letters*, pp. 503–504. The dust jacket for the first edition of LT's *Fire and Ice: The Art and Thought of Robert Frost* (1942) carried a "Message to the Reader from Lieutenant (j.g.) Lawrance Thompson, USNR," which read, in part, as follows: "Robert Frost is a fighter, and he knows the value of the war. A champion of individualism, he also knows the extent of the individual responsibility, in times of war. Briefly summarized, the essence of Robert Frost's ideas would have been these. Human beings give an intelligible structure to their own lives only after they learn to accept the inevitable triumphs and defeats of individual struggle. Always the struggle and the conflict of opposing forces remain essential and rewarding factors in 'the evident design' of the universe. Beyond the basic conflict, waged incessantly by any individual who seeks to express his own personality, men in every age have discovered a larger and higher conflict, waged for beliefs so important to the individual that he is willing to give his life to protect the existence of those beliefs. . . ."

3. RF had made a similar statement a few weeks before in a letter to his Dartmouth College friend, Sidney Cox. As it reflects the way in which RF shaped his attitude toward the war, the relevant passage is worthy of quotation: "He [LT] has been close to me in my latter days and come closer still in going out to be the only soldier I can call my own at the front. He is on sea duty and as I think on a merchant vessel gunning for submarines. I seem to want to win the war not for the Russians, nor yet for the British (much as I admire the Russians for sticking at nothing to accomplish nothing and much as I owe the British for my start in life) I

want to win it for the U.S.A. in general and for Larry Thompson in particular." (*Selected Letters*, p. 502.)

4. RF despised the Russians for the atheism of their Communist doctrine, and he had little sympathy for those in the United States who were willing to forget fundamental ideological differences for purposes of maintaining Allied unity. In a letter to Lesley Frost Francis, dated 8 Oct. 1942, RF again expressed his scorn toward those who were willing to forget what Russia under Stalin was really like: "I have to laugh at the ingenuities of our rulers in making it out that our differences with the Russians never existed. I cant admit the differences dont exist. But tonight I am willing to waive them. Lets call it this as a Christian War because it is so Christian an act for the Russians to be fighting it for us and lets call it a Democratic War because I cant learn that Stalin has been elected as often as Roosevelt. But whats all that compared to the friendship of people? After we have shown our intelligence by judging lets abdicate judgement and have a good time together." (*Family Letters*, p. 234.)

5. RF to Willard E. Fraser, 26 Sept. 1942; *Selected Letters*, pp. 504–505. The idea that "everything has its opposite to furnish it with opposition" was a favorite of RF's, and he expressed it repeatedly in poems, essays, letters, and public and private utterances throughout his life. In one instance, his "Introduction" to *Threescore: The Autobiography of Sarah N. Cleghorn* (New York, 1936), RF expressed his notion of opposites in a way which clearly revealed its roots in the Puritan concept that all fundamental opposites are extensions of the warfare between God and the Devil: "I don't know what makes this so nettling unless it is that it ignores so superciliously the strain we may have been under for years trying to decide between God and the Devil, between the rich and the poor (the greed of one and the greed of the other), between keeping still about our troubles and enlarging on them to the doctor and—between endless other things in pairs ordained to everlasting opposition." For further discussion of this passage, see *The Years of Triumph*, pp. 413 ff. See also Chapter 9 of the present volume, where the God-Devil opposition is examined as a major component of RF's verse play, *A Masque of Reason* (1945).

6. RF to Lesley Frost Francis, 21 Dec. 1942; *Family Letters*, pp. 237–238.

7. RF to Lillian LaBatt Frost, 22 Sept. 1942; *Family Letters*, p. 233.

8. RF to Lesley Frost Francis, 8 Oct. 1942; *Family Letters*, p. 235.

9. For source, see Note 1 of the present Chapter. RF's lifelong interest in heroes and the heroic went back to his early childhood, when his mother entertained him and his sister with stories featuring heroes of classical myth, battles and leaders of her native Scotland, and battles and leaders of the American Civil War—after one of whose heroes RF was named. To trace the early development of RF's attitude toward bravery, see pages cited under the headings "Courage and Daring" and "Heroes and Hero-Worship" in the Index

to *The Early Years*, pp. 620–622. See also the discussion of courage as it relates to RF's *A Masque of Mercy*, in Chapter 9 below.

10. RF to William Prescott Frost, 1 Feb. 1943; *Family Letters*, pp. 239–240.

11. RF is referring here to Samuel Abbott Frost (1795–1848), who served in the War of 1812. See the "Genealogy" to *Selected Letters*, p. 601.

12 RF to Lillian LaBatt Frost and William Prescott Frost, Feb. 1943; *Family Letters*, p. 241.

13. Harriet Whicher was the wife of RF's Amherst College friend, George Frisbie Whicher. Rand was Frank Prentiss Rand of the University of Massachusetts in Amherst, and Otto was Otto Manthey-Zorn, a German professor at Amherst and RF's close friend until he failed to condemn President Stanley King following RF's resignation from Amherst in 1938.

14. For details of RF's relations with President Alexander Meiklejohn of Amherst prior to Meiklejohn's dismissal in 1923, see *The Years of Triumph*, pp. 101 ff.

15. An early reference by RF to his recently completed and still unpublished play in verse, *A Masque of Reason* (1945), which is discussed at length in Chapter 9 of the present volume.

16. RF to G.R. Elliott, 9 Oct. 1942; *Selected Letters*, p. 506.

17. Elliott's comment is recorded at the end of the letter cited in Note 16. It reads, in its entirety, "Unfortunately I was in Maine and could not get home in time. I wired him. He did not like it. G.R.E." (ACL)

18. Ray Nash to Ernest M. Hopkins, 28 March 1943; DCL.

19. Ibid. That Nash approached Hopkins with RF's knowledge and consent is suggested by Nash's letter to RF dated 12 April 1943 (DCL), some two weeks after their Brewster Street meeting: "Following the good visit I had with you in Cambridge, you can be sure I lost no time in passing on to President Hopkins the suggestion that you might be willing to accept an invitation to join this College. From his response I could see that he is personally keen on the idea. He said that although the trustees have adopted a strict war-time policy of no new faculty appointments this might well be an exception they would endorse and I personally feel confident that he'll get their approval at the scheduled meeting late this month. . . ."

20. Stegner's excellent account of the Bloomington clash and its aftermath is contained in *The Uneasy Chair*, pp. 246–251.

21. Bernard DeVoto to RF, 7 June 1943; *Selected Letters*, pp. 508–509.

22. RF to Bernard DeVoto, c. 10 June 1943; *Selected Letters*, pp. 509–510.

23. Untermeyer briefly describes his participation in the events leading up to the awarding of RF's fourth Pulitzer Prize in *Letters to Untermeyer*, p. 333.

24. RF to LU, 6 May 1943; *Letters to Untermeyer*, pp. 332–333. In the "New Books in Review" section of the Winter 1943 issue of the *Yale Review*—which, incidentally, was founded by Wilbur

Cross—LU wrote, in part: "As the year [1942] draws to a close it appears that no volume of poetry surpassed, or even approached, Robert Frost's "A Witness Tree" (separately reviewed in these pages a few months ago), a book which, published in the poet's sixty-eighth year, was one of his richest collections in wit, ripest in philosophy, and youngest in spirit. . . ." LU goes on to observe that "the strangest and most vivid book by any newcomer" published in 1942 was José Garcia Villa's *Have Come, Am Here.*

25. RF to George F. Whicher, 15 May 1943; ACL.

26. Ernest M. Hopkins to George C. Wood, 26 July 1943; RF's carbon copy in DCL.

27. Ray Nash to Ernest M. Hopkins, 24 June 1943; DCL.

28. The phrase occurs in a letter from President Hopkins to RF, dated 29 June 1943, which began by informing RF of his election as Ticknor Fellow in the Humanities. (DCL)

29. RF to Ernest M. Hopkins, 9 July 1943; DCL.

9. DABBLING IN DRAMA

1. RF to George F. Whicher, c. 2 April 1943; ACL.

2. Charles G. Bolté, "Robert Frost Returns," in Dartmouth *Alumni Magazine* (November 1943), pp. 13–14.

3. For details of the early friendship of RF and Sidney Cox, see *The Early Years*, pp. 371, 375. For details of their relations in later years, see *The Years of Triumph*, pp. 321, 523, 634, 637, 699.

4. The recollections of several of RF's Dartmouth colleagues are contained in articles in the October 1966 issue of the *Southern Review*, one of which, by Hewette E. Joyce, describes a phase of RF's Ticknor activities not included in the terms of his appointment:

"When Robert Frost was Ticknor Fellow, it was the faculty's privilege to ask him, now and then, to take a class for us. I asked him one day if he would talk to my Seventeenth-Century Literature class. 'Yes,' he said. 'What are they reading?'

" 'Milton,' I replied.

" 'I'll talk about the short poems, not the long ones.'

" 'We have just come to *Lycidas*,' I said. Knowing that *Lycidas* was a favorite of his, I had planned carefully.

"That was a really memorable class hour. I had put a text, open at *Lycidas*, on the desk; but he closed it, saying, 'If you really like a poem, you remember it. You have your books. If I forget or make mistakes, you tell me.' As far as I can remember, he needed no help.

"He began reciting, stopping for comments every line or so, one poet talking about another poet's work. He had fun with 'Hence with denial vain, and coy excuse . . .' ('Don't be coy now, Muse; you can't back out of this.') I have often wished that I had a tape recording of that brilliant and fascinating hour. When the bell rang, he had 'covered' perhaps half of the poem. It was Frost as teacher, at his best." ("A Few Personal Memories of Robert Frost," in *Southern Review* [October, 1966], pp. 847–848.)

5. RF refers to his newly established routine in a letter to his South Shaftsbury neighbor, Charles Monroe, dated 9 Nov. 1943: "I am back at my original college—and first college I ever ran away from. You may have heard. But I keep my home at 35 Brewster St. in Cambridge and go up to Hanover only for the weekends. I lecture Friday evening and sit round with the boys Saturday. I seem not to be able to let the colleges alone. I seem divided pretty equally into three parts, teaching, farming and poetry. . . ." (A copy of the original, unidentified as to its source, was found by RHW in LT's letter-files. The copy was made by LT, presumably, while Mr. Monroe was living, and while he retained personal possession of the original. Its present whereabouts are unknown.)

6. A catalogue of the Dartmouth exhibition, compiled by Ray Nash, was printed in 1944 under the title, *Fifty Years of Robert Frost: A Catalogue of the Exhibition Held in Baker Library in the Autumn of 1943*, ed. Ray Nash (Hanover, N. H., 1944).

7. The existing tensions in the RF-Bernheimer relationship, which are discussed later in the present Chapter, were further exacerbated by the manner in which Bernheimer's participation in the Dartmouth exhibition was solicited. An early discussion of Bernheimer's loan to Dartmouth of parts of his wide collection, including *Twilight*, was contained in RF's letter to him of 12 Sept. 1943: "I assume you will be willing the Masque should stay here for the exhibition at Dartmouth beginning October first. They are making big plans up there but won't really succeed without your help. (You have me so nearly cornered, Kathleen says). . . ." (*Selected Letters*, p. 514.) A somewhat peeved Bernheimer answered RF by saying in part, "I have heard nothing from the College, as you may know, and do not feel like sending so valuable a collection there without some slight evidencing of desire to have it. . . . I just feel that some expression should be forthcoming from Dartmouth. When an institution such as the Library of Congress is interested so much that they write me two long pages, with only the hope that I eventually consider that repository . . ." (DCL). RF quickly sought to correct the oversight in a fence-mending letter: "The Dartmouth people are anxious enough to get your collection—never doubt that. They'll write to you the moment I let them. They'll do anything for your favor. They will be found just as appreciative of what you can bestow as the United States Government in the person of Joseph Auslander. If you want to wait till you hear from them, it will be perfectly all right. Your loan will merely be a little bit late. They can leave a place vacant for it in the cases. It will have to be a little bit late anyway now; I have been so slow in getting started. I will mark on your list the items I particularly want them to see at this time and you can send them direct by Railway Express to Mr. Ray Nash, Dartmouth College, Hanover, New Hampshire, or direct to me. You will get your acknowledgement from him all right. He is the great authority up there on all such matters and the one who had the most to do with my having been made the George Ticknor Fellow in the Humanities. I will add to the exhibit in your name the original manuscript (in my hand writing) of the new blank-verse

Mask of Reason which you haven't read yet. . . ." (RF to Earle J. Bernheimer, n.d. but c. Sept. 1943; DCL.)

8. For source, see Note 1 of the present Chapter.

9. RF to LU, 27 Oct. 1943; *Letters to Untermeyer*, pp. 333–334.

10. RF may never have said that his aim, in either or both of the masques, was "to justify the ways of God to man." He was fond of saying, however, that in *A Masque of Reason* he had taken a dramatic risk Milton had never dared take in *Paradise Lost*, by putting God the Father Himself on stage.

11. As noted, RF dropped the phrase from the title at an early stage. The finished masque, however, concludes with "Here endeth Chapter Forty-three of Job."

12. This and all subsequent quotations of *A Masque of Reason* follow the standard text in *The Poetry*, pp. 473–490.

13. RF first read the writings of William James while a student at Harvard from 1897 to 1899, some perhaps even earlier. Repeatedly, in later years, he enjoyed the paradox of saying in effect that his greatest inspiration when he was a Harvard student came from a man whose classes he never attended: William James. (See *The Early Years*, pp. 230 ff.) RF's readings in *The Principles of Psychology* (1890, 1892), in *The Will to Believe* (1897), in *The Varieties of Religious Experience* (1902), and in *Pragmatism* (1907) had a profound and lifelong impact on his art and thought, nowhere more so than in the area of religious belief. Not surprisingly, then, both *A Masque of Reason* and *A Masque of Mercy* reflect strongly the influence of James's religious views. A few passages from James's writings that may have helped shape RF's religious thinking and thereby helped shape his two masques are gathered here for comparison with various passages in RF's masques:

(a) *A Masque of Reason* (God speaking): "[I want] to thank you . . . for the way you helped me. . . ."

The Varieties of Religious Experience (Conclusion): "Who knows whether the faithfulness of individuals here below to their own poor over-beliefs may not actually help God in turn to be more effectively faithful to his own greater tasks?" (Mentor edition [1958], p. 391.)

Pragmatism (Lecture Eight: "Pragmatism and Religion"): "What now actually *are* the forces which [the pragmatist] trusts to co-operate with him, in a universe of such a type? They are at least his fellow men, in the stage of being which our actual universe has reached. But are there not superhuman forces also, such as religious men of the pluralistic type we have been considering have always believed in? Their words may have sounded monistic when they said, 'there is no God but God'; but the original polytheism of mankind has only imperfectly and vaguely sublimated itself into monotheism, and monotheism itself, so far as it was religious and not a scheme of classroom instruction for the metaphysicians, has always viewed God as but one helper, *primus inter pares*, in the midst of all the shapers of the great world's fate." (Meridian edition [1955], pp. 191–192.)

(b) *A Masque of Reason* (God speaking): "You would have supposed / One who in the beginning *was* the Word / Would be in a position to command it. / I have to wait for words like anyone."

The Varieties of Religious Experience (Postscript): "The ideal power with which we feel ourselves in connection, the 'God' of ordinary men, is, both by ordinary men and by philosophers, endowed with certain of those metaphysical attributes which in the lecture on philosophy I treated with such disrespect. He is assumed as a matter of course to be 'one and only' and to be 'infinite'; and the notion of many finite gods is one which hardly any one thinks it worth while to consider, and still less to uphold. Nevertheless, in the interests of intellectual clearness, I feel bound to say that religious experience, as we have studied it, cannot be cited as unequivocally supporting the infinitest belief. The only thing that it unequivocally testifies to is that we can experience union with *something* larger than ourselves and in that union find our greatest peace. . . . All that the facts require is that the power should be both other and larger than our conscious selves. Anything larger will do, if only it be large enough to trust for the next step. It need not be infinite, it need not be solitary. It might conceivably even be only a larger and more godlike self, of which the present self would then be but the mutilated expression . . ." (pp. 395–396).

(c) *A Masque of Reason* (Wife speaking): "It's God / I'd know Him by Blake's picture anywhere." (Same scene, God now speaking): "Oh, I remember well: you're Job, my Patient. . . ."

The Will to Believe and Other Essays in Popular Philosophy ("Reflex Action and Theism"): "Now, as regards a great many of the attributes of God, and their amounts and mutual relations, the world has been delivered over to disputes. All such may for our present purpose be considered as quite inessential. Not only such matters as his mode of revealing himself, the precise extent of his providence and power and their connection with our free-will, the proportion of his mercy to his justice, and the amount of his responsibility for evil; but also his metaphysical relation to the phenomenal world, whether causal, substantial, ideal, or what not, —are affairs of purely sectarian opinion that need not concern us at all. Whoso debates them presupposes the essential features of theism to be granted already; and it is with these essential features, the bare poles of the subject, that our business exclusively lies.

"Now, what are these essential features? First, it is essential that God be conceived as the deepest power in the universe; and, second, he must be conceived under the form of a mental personality. The personality need not be determined intrinsically any further than is involved in the holding of certain things dear, and in the recognition of our dispositions toward those things, the things themselves being all good and righteous things. But, extrinsically considered, so to speak, God's personality is to be regarded, like any other personality, as something lying outside of my own and other than me, and whose existence I simply come upon and find. A power not ourselves, then, which not only makes for righteousness, but means it, and which recognizes us,—such is the definition which I think nobody will be inclined to dispute." (Dover edition [1956], pp. 121–122.)

(d) *A Masque of Reason* (Job speaking of the Devil): "He's on that tendency that like the Gulf Stream, / Only of sand, not water, runs through here. . . ." Job's Wife continues: "Oh, yes, that tendency!—Oh, do come off it. / Don't let it carry you away. I hate / A tendency. The minute you get on one / It seems to start right off accelerating. . . ."

The Varieties of Religious Experience (Conclusion): "It is in answering these questions [concerning an objective basis for religious belief] that the various theologies perform their theoretic work, and that their divergencies most come to light. They all agree that the 'more' really exists; though some of them hold it to exist in the shape of a personal god or gods, while others are satisfied to conceive it as a stream of ideal tendency embedded in the eternal structure of the world. They all agree, moreover, that it acts as well as exists, and that something really is effected for the better when you throw your life into its hands" (p. 385).

(e) *A Masque of Mercy* (Paul speaking, in the penultimate speech of the masque):

> *We have to stay afraid deep in our souls*
> *Our sacrifice—the best we have to offer,*
> *And not our worst nor second best, our best,*
> *Our very lives laid down in peace and war—may not*
> *Be found acceptable in Heaven's sight . . .*

In the final speech, Keeper says, in part:

> *We both have lacked the courage in the heart*
> *To overcome the fear within the soul*
> *And go ahead to any accomplishment. . . .*

Pragmatism (Lecture Eight: "Pragmatism and Religion"): "What we were discussing was the idea of a world growing not integrally but piecemeal by the contributions of its several parts. Take the hypothesis seriously and as a live one. Suppose that the world's author put the case to you before the creation, saying: 'I am going to make a world not certain to be saved, a world the perfection of which shall be conditional merely, the condition being that each several agent does its own "level best." I offer you the chance of taking part in such a world. Its safety, you see, is unwarranted. It is a real adventure, with real danger, yet it may win through. It is a social scheme of co-operative work genuinely to be done. Will you join the procession? Will you trust yourself and trust the other agents enough to face the risk?' " (p. 187).

The reader may judge for himself which, if any, of the passages in James RF echoed, consciously or not, in his two masques. Even if none of the juxtaposed passages represents a James-to-Frost borrowing, however, two central facts remain: RF was deeply influenced by James's approach to God and to religion generally; and

James's "pragmatic" approach to religious belief made it much easier for RF to fashion a "home-made" religion out of elements of several different religious systems, selecting and rejecting various tenets according to his particular spiritual or psychological requirements.

14. In early 1935, the editors of the Amherst College undergraduate newspaper sent birthday greetings to RF well in advance of his so-called sixtieth birthday. His reply was printed in the Amherst *Student* for 25 March 1935, and read, in part, as follows: "But speaking of ages, you will often hear it said that the age of the world we live in is particularly bad. I am impatient of such talk. We have no way of knowing that this age is one of the worst in the world's history. Arnold claimed the honor for the age before this. Wordsworth claimed it for the last but one. And so on back through literature. I say they claimed the honor for their ages. They claimed it rather for themselves. It is immodest of a man to think of himself as going down before the worst forces ever mobilized by God.

"All ages of the world are bad—a great deal worse anyway than Heaven. If they weren't the world might just as well be Heaven at once and have it over with. One can safely say after from six to thirty thousand years of experience that the evident design is a situation here in which it will always be about equally hard to save your soul. Whatever progress may be taken to mean, it can't mean making the world any easier a place in which to save your soul—or if you dislike hearing your soul mentioned in open meeting, say your decency, your integrity. . . ." (*Selected Letters*, pp. 417–418.)

RF was so fond of the lines in question that he used them more than once in his poetry. In "The Lesson for Today," which he read before the Phi Beta Kappa Society at Harvard University on 20 June 1941, his theme parallels that of his letter to the Amherst *Student*, and lines 98 to 103 read as follows:

Earth's a hard place in which to save the soul,
And could it be brought under state control,
So automatically we all were saved,
Its separateness from Heaven could be waived;
It might as well at once be kingdom-come.
(Perhaps it will be next millennium.)
(*The Poetry*, p. 353)

15. In a late poem entitled "Quandary" (*The Poetry*, p. 467), RF considerably expanded his theme, in *A Masque of Reason*, that bad was essential to good in the divine scheme of things:

Never have I been sad or glad
That there was such a thing as bad.
There had to be, I understood,
For there to have been any good.
It was by having been contrasted
That good and bad so long had lasted.
That's why discrimination reigns.

That's why we need a lot of brains
If only to discriminate
'Twixt what to love and what to hate.
To quote the oracle of Delphi,
Love thou thy neighbor as thyself, aye,
And hate him as thyself thou hatest.
There quandary is at its greatest.
We learned from the forbidden fruit
For brains there is no substitute.
"Unless it's sweetbreads," you suggest
With innuendo I detest.
You drive me to confess in ink:
Once I was fool enough to think
That brains and sweetbreads were the same,
Till I was caught and put to shame,
First by a butcher, then a cook,
Then by a scientific book.
But 'twas by making sweetbreads do
I passed with such a high I.Q.

16. RF told LT of his fears concerning God's reaction to *A Masque of Reason* in a bedside interview in January 1944. The conversation began in an unusual but not, for RF, uncharacteristic way. Putting his thumb to his nose, and wagging his outstretched fingers heavenward, RF said, in a nasal tone, "Fooled Him that time." He had fooled God, that is, by not dying of pneumonia.

17. LT infuriated RF with a review of *A Masque of Reason* that appeared in the New York *Times Book Review* on 25 March 1945. In it, LT said in part that the masque was an "unholy" play, and that RF would inevitably "catch hell from his more orthodox admirers because he has dared to make light of sacred themes." RF soon after took LT aside to assert the piety, if not the "orthodoxy," of his play. He was careful to explain that God's "I was just showing off to the Devil, Job" meant Evil was a necessary part of the great Design, helping Good to show off better in contrast to it, and providing the raw materials out of which God might fashion Good.

18. This is an early expression of the thought implicit in Paul's final speech in *A Masque of Mercy*, the beginning of which is quoted in section (e) of Note 13 above. When RF wrote Paul's prayerful utterance, "May my sacrifice / Be found acceptable in Heaven's sight," he was thinking that his own sacrifice was "the book" of verse he had spent a lifetime writing, and that that, more than anything else he could look to, would prosper his chances for salvation. While *A Masque of Mercy* was being readied for publication, in April 1947, RF wrote to G. R. Elliott, one of his most devout friends, "Neither for my sins of omission nor commission am I afraid of being punished. All that is past like a vision of Dante or Gustave Dore. My fear of God has settled down into a deep inward fear that my best offering may not prove acceptable in his sight. I'll tell you more about it in another world. . . ."

(*Selected Letters*, p. 525.) A year later, RF specifically identified his "offering" as his poetry: "I doubt if I was ever religious in your sense of the word. I never prayed except formally and politely with the Lord's prayer in public. I used to try to get up plausible theories about prayer like Emerson. My latest is that it might be an expression of the hope I have that my offering of verse on the altar may be acceptable in His sight Whoever He is. . . ." (RF to LT, 12 June 1948; *Selected Letters*, p. 530.)

19. RF to LT, 4 March 1944; *Selected Letters*, pp. 515–516.

20. RF to Earle J. Bernheimer, 7 March 1944; *Selected Letters*, pp. 516–517.

21. RF to Earle J. Bernheimer, 15 July 1943; *Selected Letters*, p. 512.

22. RF to Earle J. Bernheimer, 12 Sept. 1943; *Selected Letters*, p. 514.

23. Earle J. Bernheimer to RF, 17 March 1944; DCL. This letter of Bernheimer's followed by four days the collector's initial explanation of the stopped check: "While I was away, I had trouble with my secretary and it was necessary that I close my bank account as well as discharge her by long distance. It is quite a story but suffice it to say that everything is tranquil now and straightened out. If you will be so kind as to present the old check for payment again—along with the enclosed one—they will both be honored. I ask that you excuse the annoyance and inconvenience I have caused you. Attribute it to no reason other than stated above. . . ." (Bernheimer to RF, 13 March 1944; DCL.) That RF, in a letter of c. 15 March, rejected Bernheimer's first explanation is indicated by the much longer explanation which opens Bernheimer's letter of 17 March.

24. RF to Earle J. Bernheimer, 21 March 1944; VaUL.

25. RF to Earle J. Bernheimer, 22 March 1944; VaUL.

26. RF to Earle J. Bernheimer, 20 July 1944; *Selected Letters*, p. 520. RF inscribed the *Masque of Reason* manuscript to Bernheimer on 26 May 1944, about which time, presumably, delivery was made. Most or all of RF's so-called "gifts" to Bernheimer are bibliographically described in the sale catalogue issued by Parke Bernet Galleries, Inc., entitled "The Earle J. Bernheimer Collection of First Editions of American Authors / Including his remarkable collection of the writings of Robert Frost" (New York, 1950). For details of the sale, see Chapter 13 of the present volume.

27. "Saadi," in *The Complete Writings of Ralph Waldo Emerson* (New York, 1929), pp. 871–873.

28. RF to LU, 12 Aug. 1944; *Letters to Untermeyer*, pp. 335-340.

29. LU to RF, 31 Aug. 1944; DCL.

10. ONE STEP BACKWARD TAKEN

1. Quoted from "One Step Backward Taken," in *The Poetry*, p. 376.

2. For details of RF's resignation from Amherst College, see *The Years of Triumph*, pp. 503 ff., 700 ff.

3. RF to Earle J. Bernheimer, 8 Aug. 1945; *Selected Letters*, pp. 520–521. In this letter, RF told Bernheimer that "you very well may have decided that you have made me presents enough." By its writing, the latter had apparently ceased to donate monthly "gifts" to RF, which gives RF's promise to send the *Masque of Mercy* manuscript particular significance.

4. *A Masque of Mercy*, in *The Poetry*, pp. 493–521. For the reader's convenience, citations from the text will include pagination and lineation, in this case, p. 493, l. 20.

5. Ibid., p. 497, ll. 114–116.

6. Ibid., p. 496, l. 86.

7. Ibid., p. 498, ll. 128–129.

8. Ibid., pp. 498–499, ll. 137–146.

9. Ibid., p. 505, ll. 312–315.

10. Ibid., p. 507, ll. 361–363.

11. Ibid., p. 508, ll. 374–382. See Note 15 below.

12. Ibid., p. 511, ll. 483–485.

13. Ibid., p. 512, ll. 500–501.

14. Ibid., p. 518, ll. 654, 660.

15. RF's letter to Wilbert Snow, written in January 1938 and appearing in Snow's article, "The Robert Frost I Knew" (The *Texas Quarterly*, Vol. XI, No. 3 [Autumn 1968], pp. 33–34; reprinted in *The Years of Triumph*, pp. 656–657), contains RF's fullest statement on justice vs. mercy outside his two masques. Because of its importance to the genesis of RF's masques, and to an understanding of the themes therein, the letter is worth quoting here. It should be noted, first, that RF and the liberal Snow had often argued over the meaning of Milton's lines, in *Paradise Lost*, ". . . in Mercy and Justice both, / Through Heav'n and Earth, so shall my glorie excel, / But Mercy first and last shall brightest shine." (Book 3, ll. 132–134):

"Bill Bill

"Use your brains a moment while we brush up on your vocabulary. You simply must not quibble in a serious matter like a win-at-any-cost public debater. Don't pretend you don't know what Milton meant when he said mercy was always first. You know your Milton and your Puritanism. He used it in the sense of first aid to what? To the deserving? No, to the totally depraved and undeserving. That's what we are and have been since the day Eve ate the rotten apple. . . . 'In Adam's fall We sinned all.' Mercy ensued. There could be nothing for us but mercy first and last and all the time from the point of the religious pessimist. . . . There is the presupposition of a whole setup of sin, failure, judgment, and condemnation. Mercy comes in rather late to prevent execution—sometimes only to delay it. It is too easy to understand Milton. He faced and liked the harshness of our trial. He was no mere New Testament saphead. (I should like to think Christ was none; but have him your own way for the time being. You'd better read up on your Deuteronomy before I see you again.) Milton loved Cromwell for his Ironsides and Michael for licking the Devil. He had a human weakness for success; he wanted the right to prevail and was fairly sure he knew what right was. With certain limits he believed in the rewards of merit. But after all was said for the best of us he was willing to admit that before God our whole enterprise from the day we put on fig leaves and went to work had been no better than pitiful.

"I'm like that with a class in school. I see the boys as comparatively good and bad but taken as a job lot in the absolute so really good for nothing that I can bring myself to mark them with nothing but mercy and I give them all A or at worst B. Your sense of justice is shocked. You can hardly credit my claim to godlike illogical kindness. . . .

"Illogical kindness—that is mercy. Only those are likely to act on it who know what it is in all its subordination. It was just and logical that a man's body should be taken in slavery when he went beyond his depth in debt. It was illogical that his creditor couldn't take him in slavery and the state should take him merely as a prisoner. It was another step in illogic when it was decided his person should never again be taken at all. Another when it was decided that he shouldn't be reduced by the sheriff below a certain amount of personal property. At every step there were warnings from the conservative that character would be demoralized by the relaxation of strict logical justice. People would go in debt on purpose it was feared to abuse the rich and thrifty. We are now in our lifetime seeing a great next step taken in this long story of debt—and it will be something if it is all that comes of your New Deal. It is going to be settled once for all that no man's folly or bad luck can ever reduce him to no income at all. A chicken is hatched with enough yolk in its guts to last it several days. Henceforth not only the rich but everybody born is to be sure of at least a few dollars a week as long as he lives. Never more quite down to the quick. That is in America—and while we can afford it. We are all going to fetch in and make that come true. But don't call that social justice. Keep your words in their places. It is illogical kindness. It is mercy. And you and the Lord have mercy on my argument.

Ever yours
R. F."

16. RF's honorary Litt.D. from Kenyon College was to have been presented on 12 May 1945, but on 11 May RF called President Gordon Chalmers and informed him that he had been sick for several days and had a fever. At that time, Chalmers told him not to run the risk of a journey to Gambier, and promised to arrange a special degree-granting ceremony. This was held on 20 Oct. 1945.

17. RF to Ernest M. Hopkins, 30 Oct. 1945; DCL.

18. RF to Lesley Frost Francis, 5 Nov. 1945; in possession of Willard E. Fraser.

19. An account of RF's talk at Agnes Scott College on 30 Jan. 1946, written by an undergraduate reporter on the staff of the

Agnes Scott *News* for 6 Feb., reads in part as follows: "'. . . I always advise my friends to be sure they have something to get hysterical about before they do it.' This idea of the poet's was the theme of one of his newest works which he read, called 'On Making Sure Something Has Happened.' "

20. *The Poetry*, pp. 383–384.

21. *The Poetry*, pp. 376–377. On 28 May 1947, the day *Steeple Bush* was published, LT talked with RF about the book and, in praising his favorites, neglected to mention "One Step Backward Taken." RF countered by saying he thought that poem was about as close-packed as anything he had ever written. From the way he talked, LT knew RF considered it one of his own favorites.

22. *The Poetry*, pp. 377–379.

23. Compare the lines, "Who only has at heart your getting lost" and "And if you're lost enough to find yourself" to the following passage from Mark 8:35: "For whosoever will save his life shall lose it; but whosoever shall lose his life for my sake and the gospel's, the same shall save it."

24. Compare the following passage from RF's earlier poem, "West-Running Brook" (*The Poetry*, pp. 257–260):

> *Our life runs down in sending up the clock.*
> *The brook runs down in sending up our life.*
> *The sun runs down in sending up the brook.*
> *And there is something sending up the sun.*
> *It is this backward motion toward the source,*
> *Against the stream, that most we see ourselves in,*
> *The tribute of the current to the source. . . .*

LT discusses this passage, and others in "West-Running Brook," in *The Years of Triumph*, pp. 299 ff., 624–626.

25. An obvious reference to Mark 4:11–12: "And he said unto them, unto you it is given to know the mystery of the kingdom of God; but unto them that are without, all these things are done in parables: That seeing they may see, and not perceive; and hearing they may hear, and not understand; lest at any time they should be converted, and their sins should be forgiven them." Theodore Morrison, in an excellent essay entitled "The Agitated Heart" (The *Atlantic Monthly*, July 1967, pp. 72–79), has recorded the conversation which familiarized RF with this passage from Mark, and which may well have been responsible for the existence of "Directive":

". . . Hyde Cox has written me that during an evening early in the forties he asked Frost whether he remembered the reply Jesus gave his disciples when they asked why he always spoke to crowds in parables. In Hyde Cox's words, 'R. F. did *not* remember. Like many other people, it was his recollection that Christ said something about parables being easier to understand. I pointed out that this was just the opposite of what Jesus had said, and I read to R. F. the 4th Chapter of the Gospel according to Saint Mark. He was delighted and said at once "Does that occur anywhere else?" I then read him the thirteenth Chapter of Matthew especially verses 11–13! The rest of the evening was spent discussing the wisdom and the hardness of this thought. R. F. pointed out that it is the same as for poetry; only those who approach it in the right way can understand it. And not everyone can understand no matter what they do because it just isn't in them. They cannot "be saved." . . . And R. F. quickly connected this quotation with the thought that unless you come to the subject of poetry "as a child" you cannot hope to enter into "the kingdom of heaven." ' "

26. Compare Revelation 7:14–17: "These are they which came out of great tribulation. . . . They shall hunger no more, neither thirst any more. . . . For the Lamb . . . shall feed them, and shall lead them unto the living fountains of waters; and God shall wipe away all tears from their eyes."

27. Morrison, "The Agitated Heart," p. 79. Morrison goes on to quote further from Hyde Cox's nearly verbatim record of RF's remarks: " 'Not everyone can get saved as Christ says in Saint Mark. He almost says, "You can't be saved unless you understand poetry—or you can't be saved unless you have some poetry in you." . . . The waters and the watering place are the source. It is there that you would have to turn in time of confusion to be made whole again: whole again as perhaps you haven't been since leaving childhood behind. Aging, you have become involved in the cobwebs and considerations of the world. . . . People miss the key to the poem: the key lines, if you want to know, are "Cold as a spring as yet so near its source, / Too lofty and original to rage." . . . But the key word in the whole poem is source—whatever source it is.' "

28. John Cone's letter to RF, and a copy of RF's reply, are to be found in DCL.

29. In a conversation with LT on 10 Jan. 1947, RF sheepishly admitted that there was one consolation in all his recent difficulties connected with finding Irma a place to live: he was thereby enabled to engage in one of his favorite pastimes, that of searching for a piece of real estate he could buy and then develop or renovate.

30. Chalmers's first letter of invitation to RF was dated 23 May 1946, the second 16 July. Both are in DCL.

31. The young Dartmouth man was Charles G. Bolté, author of the article cited in Note 2 of Chapter 9 of the present volume.

32. RF's remarks at Kenyon College, apparently recorded stenographically, were partially reported in a pamphlet entitled "The Heritage of the English-Speaking Peoples and Their Responsibility," published by Kenyon College in 1947. It summarized the highlights of the Conference.

33. The details of this exchange are recorded in an article by Rabbi Reichert in the Cincinnati *Enquirer*, 1 Nov. 1959, p. 1–J.

34. *Sermon by Robert Frost* (1947) was issued in a privately printed, limited edition, published by Spiral Press, at the instance of

Victor E. Reichert. Quotations and paraphrasing which follow are derived from that text.

35. *A Masque of Mercy*, in *The Poetry*, p. 520, ll. 717–725. Six years after the publication of the masque, in a letter dated 5 Nov. 1953 (*Selected Letters*, p. 555), RF wrote to Rabbi Reichert for guidance. He had apparently forgotten and wanted to be reminded of the precise biblical passage that had provided the inspiration (and some of the wording) for Paul's climactic speech. "Do you want to tell me," RF asked, "where in the Bible if at all the idea occurs as a prayer that our sacrifice whether of ourselves or our property may be acceptable in His sight? Have I been making this up out of nothing? You know how I am about chapter and verse—somewhat irresponsible some would say. I went wielding the phrase *culpa felix* to my own purpose for a long time before I pinned myself down to what it may originally have meant in Church history.

"Someone may be getting after me in the matter of this prayer I have gone about so cheerfully quoting as the heart and center of all religion. It is kindred in spirit to 'Nevertheless not my will but Thy will.' But that isn't enough. I feel sure it occurs more than once. . . ."

Reichert replied, ". . . you most assuredly have not been making this up out of nothing. On the morning, memorable to us of the Rockdale Avenue Temple, the First Day of the Feast of Tabernacles, Thursday, October 10, 1946, you read these words of prayer out of our Union Prayer Book:

" 'Look with favor, O Lord, upon us, and may our service ever be acceptable unto Thee. Praised be Thou, O God, whom alone we serve in reverence.'

"In our morning service for the Sabbath, there is also a prayer that begins:

" 'Our God and God of our fathers, grant that our worship on this Sabbath be acceptable to Thee.'

"Turning now to the Bible, the prize passage that completely supports your view . . . the key passage is Psalm 19, verse 14:—

" 'Let the words of my mouth, and the meditation of my heart be acceptable before Thee, O Lord, my Rock, and my Redeemer'. . . ." (*Selected Letters*, p. 556.)

36. *A Masque of Mercy*, in *The Poetry*, p. 521, ll. 726–738.

11. MY FAMILY LUCK

1. RF to LU, 9 Aug. 1947; *Letters to Untermeyer*, p. 346.

2. Kathleen Morrison told LT the details of this incident on 10 Jan. 1947.

3. RF to LU, 9 Jan. 1947; *Letters to Untermeyer*, pp. 341–342.

4. Ibid., pp. 345–346.

5. For additional information, see pages cited under "Frost, Jeanie Florence" in the Index to *The Years of Triumph*, p. 715.

6. RF to Earle J. Bernheimer, 14 Jan. 1947; *Selected Letters*, pp. 522–523.

7. RF to Louis Mertins, 20 Jan. 1947; *Robert Frost: Life and Talks-Walking* (Norman, Oklahoma, 1965), p. 256—hereafter cited as Mertins, *Life*. Mertins's efforts to bring RF to California, beginning around 1941 and continuing up to their fulfillment in 1947, formed the basis of a lengthy correspondence between Mertins and RF. Among the highlights of that correspondence (which is discussed by Mertins in *Life*, pp. 253–257) are the following letters by RF, pertaining to a proposed visit to California in 1942:

(a) "Say, before I start correlating the dates [of engagements proposed by Mertins] you must correlate them a little more yourself. You mention times as far apart as February, March and April. Of course I can't be spread out over months and you wouldn't want me to be. Please begin with the most important date and try to pack as much money in around that as possible. You don't even say when in March the founders' day at the University of California comes. One thing more, my dear friend. I must ask you not to press too hard for me in these and other matters. I should think some of them out there would be writing to me directly sooner or later if they wanted me very cordially. Please protect my feelings. I know you act only from enthusiasm for me, but don't let your enthusiasm run away with you. The world owes me nothing and my friends mustn't make me look as if I thought otherwise." (8 Oct. 1941; Mertins, *Life*, p. 254.)

(b) "Now listen. You don't want me kicking round at my age for nothing. I can't run here and there for the sake of running. There must be some return proportionate to my expenditure of strength. Seven hundred dollars won't be enough to bring me to the coast. And there must be some warmth of assurance that somebody wants me besides you and Earle Bernheimer. I haven't had one word of invitation yet from anybody but you. Unless you make things look better—more inviting—right away, I'm afraid you'll have to give me up, and make up your mind to get along with only my ghostly presence at your conference with Earle over my first editions. . . ." (n.d. [c. Jan. 1942]; Mertins, *Life*, pp. 254–255.)

(c) "I don't see how you could expect me to come out there for only two things. I am slow about poetry. I don't earn much a month from that. But it was part of the original bargain with myself that I shouldn't. Lecturing and teaching are another matter. I like them. But not so well I will do them for nothing. I look to them to yield me the considerable money I need for my family. I ought not to have to tell you I have a good deal on me. My responsibilities refuse to grow less with my advancing years. I'm not trying to scare you. Im hard to scare myself. Still I should think my friends would show concern enough for my poetry not to want me to spend time and strength away from it except for substantial pay. Let me not have to seem ridiculous. The pay I call substantial is nothing compared with what your colleges out there pay Englishmen and even other Americans who come to you through the agencies. I wont be treated shabily. I hate it that the question of money should be brought to the point of embarrassment in my literary life.

"I suppose I am not much wanted out there. And there's an end. I have never yet begged and besought to be invited where I wasnt much wanted.

"As I said in my telegram to the president of Redlands, I might have taken up some standing invitation I have to lecture in various places between here and California if I had waked up to the situation soon enough. I didn't get it through my head that your campaign for me had broken down in time to do anything to help you this year.

"I have never said a word against business. I admire businessmen and treat business with real respect. But I cant let business take me from my leisure except for money with which to buy more leisure. Dont think I am piling up an estate for my heirs. And now lets never let money be mentioned between us again. Mind you I didnt ask to come west." (27 March 1942; DCL.)

8. RF to Earle J. Bernheimer, 20 Jan. 1947; *Selected Letters*, p. 524.

9. RF to Earle J. Bernheimer, 20 Feb. 1947; *Selected Letters*, pp. 524–525.

10. RF to Robert G. Sproul, 20 Feb. 1947; Mertins, *Life*, p. 257.

11. Shortly before RF's departure for the West Coast, Mrs. Morrison wrote to Mertins and said, in part, "The program sounds pretty stiff to me:—Friday 21st—Press, cyclotron. Please *nothing* more. Dinner with President Sproul. Press *must* be short. Saturday. Ceremony. Luncheon. Visit to old haunts. Gertrude Atherton call. Dinner for Charter Day. This is too much. An impossible day. Can you cut the dinner? He says he doesn't want to die in California—bad enough to be born there. Sunday—please *nothing* but the library and the dinner and a long rest between the library and party. By this I mean alone by 4:30. This sounds pretty dictatorial but it's only haste that makes it so. Robert has had a tough winter and although he is well, he is tired. He can do only so many things a day and needs solitude to recover himself." (Reprinted without date in Mertins, *Life*, p. 258.)

12. RF's remarks are reported in Mertins, *Life*, pp. 258–260.

13. At one point in his visit, which RF described to LT on 10 June 1947, Mrs. Eastman told RF he had been such a sickly child she and his parents had feared he would not grow up. This interested RF, he told LT, because in recent years he had come to think many of his childhood illnesses were feigned. For a discussion of RF's early illnesses in relation to psychological pressures, see *The Early Years*, pp. 18–22.

14. During the party, RF learned, to his extreme consternation, that an admission charge of five dollars per plate had been levied on all those who attended, even those he had personally invited. His anger at Mertins for this and other offenses was reflected in a letter RF wrote him sometime in 1948, but never sent: "Your oranges accepted this time though I thought I told you to send no

more. We won't stand on the niceties. They are here and we will eat them to your health and ours. But they must be looked on as the last payment in advance or arrears for autographing. You speak too lightly of the penalties I have to pay for success. It is not for you to impose them whatever they may be. You wouldnt claim it was for you, would you my kind friend? I tried to make you see in my last letter that I was determined to escape from further autographing. I mean to rest from the effort of tending to the needs of collectors for ten years. You have rounded out quite a collection with my signature to it. Surely you can get along without bothering me with any addenda. You must. At least you must have been prepared for this discipline by my last letter. I was calling a halt. So stay friends if you possibly can, but resign yourself to submission. California finished me off last year. The whole expedition turned on your collection. I was slow to get it through my head. The worst blow to my self respect was when I learned that the Stuarts the Stegners and Miss Mirrelees had had to pay five dollars for the dinner I had invited them to. Goodness sakes! In all my life lecturing I have never asked a soul to come and listen to me even when there was nothing to pay at the door. I don't blame you for the humiliation. I put it all down to the rough and tumble of collecting. But tomorrow to fresh thoughts and impulses. You won't presume to try to reduce me to the stature of a collectors item. With this understanding I can remain your friend R. F." (DCL)

15. Quoted from a stenographic transcript prepared for LT by Anne B. Comstock, to whom gratitude is here expressed. The exchange to which RF refers took place at the prebirthday party in San Francisco, which Governor Warren attended and at which he spoke briefly.

16. RF told LT he remembered Cole as a bright boy at Amherst; remembered that Cole had roomed with the boy to whom Frost had given the highest mark in one of his courses, because the boy had answered his examination, "Do something which will please me," by quoting entire a Hardy poem he had recently seen printed in a current magazine.

17. There was perhaps unintentional irony in RF's remark that he had slept in every room but the kitchen. For some time his daughter Irma had been sleeping *only* in the kitchen of her Acton house, that being the only room in which she felt safe from her imaginary pursuers.

18. RF to G. R. Elliott, [c. 22 April 1947]; *Selected Letters*, pp. 525–526. Elliott, a devout Anglican, often discussed his religious beliefs with RF in letters and in conversation. RF's last letter, dictated just before his death in 1963 and intended for Elliott and his wife, Alma, included an expression of RF's own deeply felt religious convictions. See pp. 343–344 of the present volume.

In another connection, the "Otto" RF refers to is Otto Manthey-Zorn, a professor of German at Amherst, who, though long one of RF's closest Amherst friends, infuriated RF by his refusal to join him in condemning President King in 1938. Manthey-Zorn offered

RF an invitation similar to Elliott's, and on 22 April 1947, RF declined it with the following letter: "Your invitation has been waiting for my answer till I should know what sort of a visit to Amherst this was to be. The new President seems to want to make a little ceremony of it by having me in his house. That's nice of him —really nice. A good many things I have no heart for any more, but I still like marked attention that savors of affection. I must get over the strange feelings I have about Amherst. I want to see you and Ethel. Perhaps you'll have me for dinner some evening. And we can talk as of old. I've just been in San Francisco that has far older reminiscences for me than Amherst or anywhere else." (ACL)

19. RF's Johnson Chapel talk was stenographically recorded, and a copy was subsequently made available to LT.

20. "Frost Attracts Overflow Audience," in The Amherst *Journal*, 2 May 1947, p. 1. RF enjoyed playing what he called "the game of confusion," which he began by asking his opponent, "Are you confused?" More often than not, his victim would respond, "Why, yes." "I'm not," RF would gleefully counter. "I win!"

21. For details of RF's 1928 and 1932 meetings with Eliot, see *The Years of Triumph*, pp. 333, 337–338, 402–403.

22. RF supplied LT with the details of his visit to Acton in a conversation on 15 Aug. 1947.

23. *The Poetry*, p. 399.

24. Ibid., p. 395.

25. Ibid., pp. 375–376.

26. Ibid., p. 385.

27. According to Hyde Cox, the first of the Five Nocturnes, "The Night Light," was written in the following way: Cox rented the Euber house from RF several summers during the mid-forties, and while living there he was taken care of by his (and formerly his grandmother's) black cook, Mary Douglas. Mrs. Douglas had spent her childhood on a farm in Maryland, but for the rest of her life she had lived only in urban or suburban environments. Frightened by the foxes and raccoons which often approached the Euber farmhouse at night, she comforted herself during her stays there by leaving a small lamp burning all night beside her bed. RF was a frequent visitor to Hyde's and had many meals with him, often returning on foot to the Homer Noble farmhouse hours past midnight. When he did, he always noticed the light in Mary's window as he started back. RF's observation, and Hyde's explanation of Mary's light-burning habit, gave rise to a poem whose third and fourth lines echo that familiar source of nocturnal consolation, the children's poem which begins, "Now I lay me down to sleep . . .":

THE NIGHT LIGHT

She always had to burn a light
Beside her attic bed at night.
It gave bad dreams and broken sleep,
But helped the Lord her soul to keep.

Good gloom on her was thrown away.
It is on me by night or day,
Who have, as I suppose, ahead
The darkest of it still to dread.
(*The Poetry*, pp. 382–383)

28. *The Poetry*, p. 386.
29. The New York *Times Book Review*, 1 June 1947, p. 4.
30. The *Saturday Review*, 31 May 1947, p. 12.
31. *Time*, Vol. XLIX, No. 24 (16 June 1947), pp. 102, 104.
32. Kathleen Morrison described this episode to LT in June 1947.
33. RF to John Cone, Jr., 17 July 1947; DCL.
34. A draft of the wire in Mrs. Morrison's hand, but dictated, as usual, by RF, is in DCL. It is marked by Mrs. Morrison as having been sent on 3 Aug. 1947.
35. Except as otherwise stated, the details of the events leading up to, and including, Irma's commitment were variously supplied to LT by Mrs. Morrison, Hewitt, Moore, and RF himself.
36. RF to LU, 9 Aug. 1947; *Letters to Untermeyer*, p. 346. At the present time, Irma Frost Cone continues to live in a nursing home in Vermont, one chosen by Lesley after several attempts at boarding out. She has an apartment there with her own furniture, a doctor on call, nursing care, and freedom to walk in the town. Her share of income under RF's will is more than sufficient to cover her expenses.

12. SPEAKING OF LOYALTY

1. Amherst *Graduates' Quarterly*, Vol. XXXVII, No. 4 (August 1948), p. 271.
2. LT personally witnessed this incident as a member of the Little Theater audience.
3. RF to Earle J. Bernheimer, 16 Oct. 1947; *Selected Letters*, pp. 526–527. In the auction catalog cited in Note 29 of Chapter 9 of the present volume, Item 279 is "A Ms. entitled 'A Masque of Mercy.' Written in ink on 40 pp., 4to, with some writing on a few additional pages. About 6,000 words. In a copy book. In a cloth case." The bibliographical description continues: "With a few corrections. On the page preceding the beginning of the manuscript is the following presentation inscription: 'To E. B. to keep and call his. It is the original manuscript from which K[athleen] M[orrison] typed the copy for the printers. R. F. March 26, 1948. Cambridge, Mass.'" During the auction sale, on 11–12 Dec. 1950, this item fetched $450.
4. RF to Margaret Bartlett, 26 Dec. 1947; *Selected Letters*, pp. 527–528. Nearly two years later Mrs. Bartlett informed RF that she was dying of cancer but that she still had time to edit and publish RF's letters to John Bartlett, if she could have permission. RF's answer, in a letter written c. 22 Nov. 1949, reads as follows:

"All the more in an emergency like this I seem disinclined to let you make a publisher's venture of the letters I wrote you and John in the simplicity of the heart back there when none of us was anybody. I take it your main idea is to put the record of our friendship beyond danger of being lost. Let me suggest one way you could do that without sacrilege. You could deposit the letters as a lot with one of the three or four collections of me I consider most important, the Jones Library of the town of Amherst (which is A No I). The Amherst College Library (because I have spent half my time at Amherst College in the last thirty five years), the Middlebury College Library (because John went to Middlebury a little) or the Dartmouth College Library (because I went to Dartmouth a little). The Jones Library's collection is going to be the one most visited by investigators into my past if I remain at all interesting to posterity. But any one of the four libraries would be sure to treasure anything you gave it. Nor need you give complete possession of the letters. You could keep for your heirs the right to publish them in a book whenever they should get my heirs' permission. Your heirs would probably be your daughter Margaret; mine would be Kathleen Morrison and my daughter Lesley. I'm not forgetting the property value in the letters that may be greater now than it will be later. But you are not dying indigent, you are not thinking of money. You have more serious thoughts to think of than money.

"Your fortitude in the face of approaching death makes it hard not to grant you the permission you ask as a last favor. I am in deep mourning for you. But even so I remain enough myself to shrink from wearing my heart on my sleeve. I say to myself if you can be so sensible about leaving this world it cant be too cruelly much for me to ask you to be sensible about a small matter like these letters. They are even trivial at a time like this. I wonder at your coolness—like Bennen's on the avalanche in Sills fine poem. If I seem to speak with the least coolness, I have caught the tone from your courage." (*Selected Letters*, pp. 539–540.)

Mrs. Bartlett died close to the time RF's letter arrived. In 1963 her daughter, Margaret Bartlett Anderson, published *Robert Frost and John Bartlett: The Record of a Friendship*, thus fulfilling her mother's intention as RF had suggested.

5. Charles W. Cole to RF, 28 Jan. 1948; DCL.

6. Following his graduation from Amherst in 1917, Hendricks spent a summer in Franconia, New Hampshire, to pay homage, as it were, to his Amherst professor, RF. An unfortunate incident soon interrupted their budding friendship. One evening, RF and his wife went out to visit their friends the Fobeses, leaving Hendricks in charge of the four Frost children. When they returned, Irma complained to her father that Hendricks had acted in a way which RF construed as a sexual advance. With his characteristic habit of believing his children and defending them on every possible occasion (outdone in this regard only by Elinor) RF became incensed with Hendricks and carried his anger even to the point of physical action. (So, at least, he told LT.) For several years thereafter, RF completely lost touch with his former student, until one day Hendricks came up to talk to him after a poetry reading in Chicago.

RF then told Hendricks, who was teaching English at the Illinois Institute of Technology, that he regretted the incident in Franconia, that he had come to see Irma had made the whole thing up. Hendricks accepted his apology, and their friendship, at last, was restored. In a subsequent visit to Ripton, Hendricks told RF that he was planning to start a college in Vermont. "I'll be durned," RF responded. "I always wanted to, myself." Out of their conversation came RF's offer to lecture at Marlboro College, once Hendricks had brought his plans to fruition. (RF gave LT the details of his fight with Hendricks in 1948. The quotation is contained in an article on Hendricks and the founding of Marlboro College in *Time* magazine, Vol. L, No. 10 [September 8, 1947], p. 14.)

7. Amherst *Graduates' Quarterly*, Vol. XXXVII, No. 4 (August 1948), pp. 271–276.

8. In the September 1947 issue of *Harper's Magazine*, Henry Steele Commager, the distinguished historian, had published an article entitled "Who is Loyal to America?" in which he criticized the "new loyalism" and "new Americanism" that equated loyalty and conformity, "the uncritical and unquestioning acceptance of America as it is—the political institutions, the social relationships, the economic practices." Attacking as false the concept that loyalty was conformity, Commager quoted Emerson and Royce in support of his position: " 'Enlightened loyalty,' wrote Josiah Royce, who made loyalty the very core of his philosophy, 'means harm to no man's loyalty. It is at war only with disloyalty, and its warfare, unless necessity constrains, is only a spiritual warfare. It does not foster class hatreds; it knows of nothing reasonable about race prejudices; and it regards all races of men as one in their need of loyalty. It ignores mutual misunderstandings. It loves its own wherever upon earth its own, namely loyalty itself, is to be found.' " Later: "Who are those who would set the standards of loyalty? They are Rankins and Bilbos, officials of the D.A.R. and the [American] Legion and the NAM, Hearsts and McCormicks. May we not say of Rankin's harangues on loyalty what Emerson said of Webster at the time of the Seventh of March speech: 'The word honor in the mouth of Mr. Webster is like the word love in the mouth of a whore.' " For some time after reading his article, RF publicly and privately attacked Commager's position, often denouncing the man privately as a "Red."

9. From "Reluctance," in *The Poetry*, pp. 29–30.

10. Soon after RF's Alumni Luncheon talk, George Whicher sent him a transcript of his remarks and suggested that he permit their publication in the next issue of the Amherst *Graduates' Quarterly*. RF's response, undated but probably written in June 1948, reads as follows: "The temptation is to go even further than you with this and round it into a real piece. But perhaps that wouldn't be fair to those who heard it as a speech or talk. They might feel bamboozled. It hurts like everything not to bring my point out more sharply. Loyalty is simply to those you have given a right to count on you—your country family friends gang church firm or college. The difficult thing is to straighten it out with them God

and yourself when your fancy falls a turning. If it is your country in time of war or if it is your gang you are deserting you may get yourself shot. Loyalty is as simple a thing as that. It takes a lightening change artist to make it out the same thing as disloyalty. The transition from an attachment to an attraction would be the interesting thing to talk about. The break with England probably distressed every single colonial 'patriot' but Tom Paine. It proved too much for Arnold and he repented of his unfaithfulness and backed out of the rebellion. But there is a whole article in this for another day. I was threatening a dire essay on Traitors and Quislings in my travels last year. Robert Bruce was a redeemed Quisling. Then there is Smuts. When the British want to hear themselves praised they send for him. Dont you think it a little hard on my free rendering of ideas to confront it with the studied sophistries of the Commager fellow? You'll notice I stayed purposely vague about him. But I suppose I mustn't mind. You might enjoy a row between him and me if you could get us into one. I listen to the fights myself sometimes on the radio.

"I am still dazed with what happened to me in Amherst. I am in no state to have to eat my own words like this. Ever Amherst's (and yours) R. F." In the left margin of the letter RF added: "Kay thinks I must be brave and stand by my indiscretions. The only reason I go on the platform at all is to show my bravery. I must remember that. I do it to make up for never having faced bullets like the real hero. I suffer more before and after than during action."

RF's letter, and a transcript of his Alumni Luncheon talk containing revisions in his hand, are in ACL.

11. George F. Whicher to Kathleen Morrison, 12 Sept. 1948; DCL.

12. Charles W. Cole to RF, 2 Nov. 1948; DCL. The name "Simpson" for RF's lectureship was derived from the John Woodruff Simpson endowment at Amherst, income from which was to be used "to secure from time to time from . . . elsewhere scholars for the purpose of delivering lectures or courses of instruction at Amherst College." (Terms quoted in "Robert Frost to Lecture Here During Two Months Next Year," The Amherst *Student*, 18 April 1949, p. 1.)

13. Charles W. Cole to RF, 2 Feb. 1949; DCL.

14. RF to John S. Dickey, 14 Feb. 1949; *Selected Letters*, p. 534.

15. RF to Sidney Cox, 2 Jan. 1915; *Selected Letters*, pp. 147–148. For details of RF's early relationship with Pound, see *The Early Years*, pp. 405–407, 410–423, 440, and other pages indicated in the Index to that volume.

16. Quoted from "Pound Wins Prize for Poetry Written in Treason Cell," in the New York *Times*, 21 Feb. 1949, pp. 1, 14.

17. "Eugene O'Neill, who ranked No. 3 on a similar poll in 1936, edged out Sinclair Lewis (previously No. 1) as the American author most likely to achieve immortality. A poll of readers of the *New Colophon*, a book-collectors' quarterly, also listed in the order

of finish: Robert Frost (No. 5 in 1936); Ernest Hemingway (No. 13 in 1936); Carl Sandburg (No. 17 in 1936); Nobel prizewinner T. S. Eliot (No. 20 in 1936); H. L. Mencken; George Santayana; Edna St. Vincent Millay (No. 4 in 1936)." From *Time* magazine, Vol. LIII, No. 8 (Feb. 21, 1949), p. 40.

18. The 1949 Bollingen jury consisted of the following members: Conrad Aiken, W. H. Auden, Louise Bogan, Katherine Garrison Chapin, T. S. Eliot, Paul Green, Robert Lowell, Katherine Anne Porter, Karl Shapiro, Allen Tate, Willard Thorp, Robert Penn Warren, and Leonie Adams, then Consultant in Poetry at the Library of Congress. Also serving was Theodore Spencer, who died suddenly on January 18, soon after casting his vote.

19. "The Chapin lady" was, indeed, the wife of Francis Biddle, who served as Attorney General of the United States from 1941 to 1945. "Axis Sally" was the cognomen of Mildred Gillars, an American who broadcast Nazi propaganda from Berlin during the Second World War. Her trial for treason was in progress at the time RF was writing.

20. This letter, or memorandum, written c. 22 Feb. 1949, is in the private collection of Mrs. Kathleen Morrison on deposit in DCL. Quoted by permission of Mrs. Morrison, to whom gratitude is here expressed.

21. See Note 17 above. The *Newsweek* and *Time* items were essentially alike.

22. RF to Glenn Gosling, 26 Feb. 1949; Holt Archives, PUL.

23. Glenn Gosling to RF, 11 March 1949; Holt Archives, PUL.

24. Quotations from RF's "Great Issues" talk are derived from an unedited transcript of a recording of the talk prepared under the supervision of Edward Connery Lathem, Librarian of the Dartmouth College Library. Punctuation, omitted in the transcript, has been supplied by the present writers. The transcript, along with those of many other talks by RF at Dartmouth and elsewhere, is in DCL.

25. "Robert Frost Returning to Amherst as Simpson Lecturer in Literature," in Amherst *Journal*, Vol. III, No. 32 (April 15, 1949), p. 1.

26. *The Poetry*, p. 403. In *Come In and Other Poems*, the poem bore the title, "Choose Something Like a Star," and contained a corresponding variant in the penultimate line.

27. *The Poetry*, pp. 415–416, where it occupies its final position among the poems of *In the Clearing* (1962). It appeared originally in booklet form, being RF's 1948 Christmas poem.

28. RF to Alfred C. Edwards, 5 June 1949; *Selected Letters*, p. 535.

29. Louis Untermeyer, "Still Further Range," in The *Yale Review* (Autumn, 1947), pp. 138–139.

30. RF to LU, 5 July 1949; *Letters to Untermeyer*, p. 350.

31. RF to Lesley Frost Francis [Fall, 1949]; *Family Letters*, pp. 257–258.

32. Matthew Arnold, "Sohrab and Rustum," lines 390–396.
33. RF to LU, 27 Feb. 1950; *Letters to Untermeyer*, p. 361.
34. *Congressional Record*, Vol. 96, No. 6 (24 Mar. 1950), p. 4057. Also quoted in part in *Letters to Untermeyer*, pp. 361–362.
35. RF to Robert A. Taft, 10 Apr. 1950; DCL.

13. FRIENDS LOST AND FOUND

1. Quoted from "How Hard It Is to Keep from Being King When It's in You and in the Situation," *The Poetry*, p. 454, ll. 31–36.
2. Earle J. Bernheimer to RF, 3 March 1950; DCL.
3. Throughout his life, RF repeatedly threatened or pretended to run away from problems that caused him frustration or anxiety. His most decisive gesture of escape from an untenable situation was made in 1894, when he fled to Virginia's Dismal Swamp following his apparent jilting by his future wife, Elinor White. (See *The Early Years*, pp. 173 ff.)
4. Sometime in the late 1930s, RF used an old discarded topcoat belonging to his son-in-law, John Cone, to cushion a shipment of books he had autographed at Bernheimer's request. Several weeks later, he received in the mail a new coat, tailor-made, which Bernheimer had ordered thinking the old one belonged to RF himself. It did not, of course, fit the poet, but it did serve to plant the initial idea in his mind that his friendship with the collector might result in personal gain.
5. RF to Earle J. Bernheimer, 19 March 1950; *Selected Letters*, pp. 540–542.
6. Bernheimer's $150 check to RF dated 1 May 1945 was apparently the last of the collector's monthly "gifts." During a visit with Bernheimer in 1961, LT was shown twenty-six cancelled checks for the same amount, the earliest of which was dated 1 January 1943, a year after the monthly payments began. Thus, between 1942 and 1945, Bernheimer's cash outlays to RF, excluding his large payments for specific manuscripts such as that of *Twilight* and "The Guardeen," totaled at least $3,900 and almost certainly $5,700. The surviving cancelled checks are currently deposited in the Robert Frost Collection, Clifton Waller Barrett Library, VaUL.
7. Earle J. Bernheimer to RF, 27 March 1950; *Selected Letters*, pp. 542–544.
8. RF to Earle J. Bernheimer, 15 April 1950; *Selected Letters*, pp. 544–545.
9. The letter appeared in the "Mail Box" column of the *Antiquarian Bookman* for 2 Dec. 1950, p. 1424. It was followed by an editor's note stating that the letter had come signed, but with the request that the author's name be withheld.
10. Arthur Dempsey, "About Books," New York *Times Book Review*, 24 Dec. 1950, p. 12.
11. All quotations from "How Hard It Is . . ." are derived from *The Poetry*, pp. 453–462. The poem's first appearance, in *Proceed-*

ings of the American Academy of Arts and Letters and the National Institute of Arts and Letters, Second Series, Number One (1951), differed slightly from the final version.

12. The "conference in honor of Robert Frost" was entitled "The Poet and Reality," and was held at Kenyon College on October 6–8, 1950. In inviting LT to attend, President Chalmers explained: "We are inviting a small group of leaders in American life to be present, picking them from among the representatives of ideas and pursuits with which Mr. Frost had been most actively concerned: letters, publishing, politics, science, the arts, and affairs." Speakers included J. Donald Adams of the New York *Times*; Thomas Reed Powell, Professor of Law Emeritus, Harvard University; L. A. G. Strong, British novelist and poet; Kenneth B. Murdock, Professor of English Literature, Harvard University; Marston Morse, a mathematician at the Institute for Advanced Study, Princeton; and the Right Rev. Henry Wise Hobson, Bishop of Southern Ohio. Several speakers, in the course of the conference, formed warm friendships with RF. Bishop Hobson was to serve, in 1963, as RF's eulogist at the memorial service following his death.

13. President James Bryant Conant of Harvard, a distinguished scientist whose research included the area of oral contraception, was first the butt of RF's ironic teasing in 1936, when he made the mistake of defending, in the poet's presence, President Roosevelt and the New Deal. For details, see *The Years of Triumph*, p. 448.

A rough translation of the title RF gave his limerick is "Preparations Bordering on Copulation." RF's statement that "fututionʺ is a rare word even in classic Latin is supported by the *Oxford Latin Dictionary*, which lists only two uses of "fututio": in Catullus 32:8 and in Martial I, 107:6.

14. RF to Louis H. Cohn, 27 July 1951; *Selected Letters*, pp. 549–550. As proprietors of House of Books in New York, Captain Cohn and his wife, Marguerite, had sold Earle Bernheimer most of the books in his Frost collection and had arranged to have RF autograph many of them for Bernheimer. Over the years, in return for all his services to them, RF received many gifts from the Cohns, with whom he became good friends. (See RF to Louis and Marguerite Cohn, 14 Sept. 1950, *Selected Letters*, pp. 545–546.)

After the Bernheimer auction, in which the Cohns purchased several important items including *Twilight*, RF turned to them to dispose of manuscripts he would previously have offered Bernheimer. In 1951, he offered the Cohns the first-draft manuscript of his Modern Library preface, "The Constant Symbol," and a manuscript of his unpublished one-act play, "In an Art Factory," for $1,200 apiece. He may have merely been horse trading or simply underestimating Cohn's grasp of market prices. In any case, Cohn discussed these prices with the collector RF had in mind as a possible buyer, and after amicable negotiation paid $1,000 for the unpublished play and $500 for the preface. (See two letters, RF to Louis Henry Cohn, 18 and 27 July 1951, *Selected Letters*, p. 548.)

The Cohns' Christmas gift of a case of wine led RF to write them the following letter in January 1952: "Your Christmas present this time beat all that went before. It must mean religion and wine have some necessary connection. I'm no wine-bibber as you know. But I'll say this for wine: it doesn't cloy. Candy cloys, cheese cloys, fish cloys. We have tried them all and I can report on them. The worst that wine does on top of a good meal and after a good meal has almost put you to sleep is put you to sleep entirely. I should say the best it does. And that I've figured it out at last was what it was sent into the world for by way of the grape. I've been awfully slow in my realizations. It just dawned on me late in life putting away those pint sauternes one a day at noon in the best company that wine was intended to promote carelessness. I always thought I didn't care enough but after this week's experience I don't care if I don't. We have you to thank for my edification. From now on I expect to be an easier man to live with. It is out of sheer newly acquired good nature that I am sending you as a gift to treasure or sell for yourself off the counter what I take to be the first edition of a book [Edna St. Vincent Millay, *A Few Figs from Thistles*] that expresses what I take to be the gospel of carelessness. All I have left to care for in this world is a few friends. You're two of them." (*Selected Letters*, p. 550.)

One of the fanciest pieces of bibliophilic horse trading between RF and Cohn occurred in the summer of 1953. After a public reading in New York City, RF showed Cohn the copy of *Complete Poems* which the poet had used on the platform that night, a copy into which RF had written some unpublished poems. It made an interesting "association copy," and in a moment of weakness Cohn offered $500 for it. The offer was immediately accepted and the exchange was completed. Some time later, however, Cohn sent the "association copy" back to RF requesting that RF enrich it a bit more with some additional manuscripts and notes useful for future readings. RF complied, and soon wrote Cohn the following letter:

"The book you sent back for more signs and marks of usage, having now been through another campaign, looks to me in as ideal a condition for your purposes as you could expect me to make it. You dont want me to go on with it till you and I and it fall to pieces. A lot has got crowded into it on flyleaves and elsewhere because as I tell my audiences the very name of the book forbids my having any more poems outside its covers. That's a poetic fiction I play with till I can get around to having another book in the spirit of 'The Gift Outright,' 'For Columbus Day,' and 'The Cabin in the Clearing.'

"I had my conscience tweeked by a nice letter from Freddy Adams about you and some items you let him have. . . . Otherwise you might not be getting your property so suddenly. I shall mail it today." (RF to Louis H. Cohn, 4 Aug. 1953; *Selected Letters*, p. 554.)

15. Beginning in the mid-1950s, RF tried to wear a hearing aid in his left ear. Unable to get used to it, he soon gave it up.

16. In a letter to Louis H. Cohn dated 14 Sept. 1950, RF thanked Cohn for the gift of a copy of J. B. Bury's *History of Greece*. (*Selected Letters*, p. 545.) His letter to Lathem, it will be noted, was dated 15 September.

17. RF to Edward C. Lathem, 15 Sept. 1950; *Selected Letters*, p. 546.

18. As stated elsewhere, information in this chapter (and others in the present volume) concerning the RF–Hyde Cox friendship was supplied by Mr. Cox in several personal interviews with RHW beginning in 1972. Profound gratitude for Mr. Cox's generosity and patience is here expressed.

19. Andrew Wyeth to RF, 16 May 1953; DCL.

20. RF to Andrew Wyeth, 2 July 1953; the original, in the private collection of Mr. Wyeth, is quoted here by permission and with gratitude.

21. Each of these poems was subsequently published in *In the Clearing* (1962). For a discussion of "A Cabin in the Clearing," see Chapter 18 of the present volume.

22. "Apple Peeler" was first published in *New Poems by American Poets* (Ballantine Books, 1953), where RF undoubtedly saw it for the first time. It also appears, among other places, in Robert Francis, *Frost: A Time to Talk / Conversations & Indiscretions* (1972), p. 37.

23. The original rough draft of "On the Question of an Old Man's Feeling" is among the Robert Frost papers in DCL. It was copied by LT in May 1963.

24. In *Frost: A Time to Talk* (cited in Note 22 above), Francis described a meeting with RF that took place on 30 Oct. 1956: ". . . Then he turned to my poems [in the *Faber Book of Modern American Verse*]. He seemed familiar with the first two. When he came to the third, 'Apple Peeler,' something remarkable happened. I was still sitting beside him. *Oh*, he exclaimed with a mischievous smile and looking round at me as if he had caught me in the act, *this poem*. At first I hadn't the faintest idea of what he was getting at. But he kept smiling at me and making hints, and at last I caught on. He thought I was taking a dig at him in the poem, possibly that the whole poem was really about him. He supposed that his sonnet 'The Silken Tent' was the only sonnet in one sentence in the English language. He suspected, therefore, that he was the 'virtuoso' turning out 'trick' poems after his real inspiration had been exhausted. What a thought! I hardly knew what to say to disabuse him. I didn't deny that I knew about his sonnet and that it might have been in my mind when writing the poem. But I insisted that I had not been thinking of him in particular, certainly not trying to disparage him, or that I used the word 'trick' in a disparaging sense even as applied to the actual apple peeler. I could see he was not entirely convinced. *Mr. Frost*, I said, *your poem 'The Silken Tent' is as beautiful as anything you ever did, and there is no trick about it. As for sonnets in one sentence, David Morton does them all the time.*

"He does, does he? asked F. with the trace of mischief in his smile. *Then that makes it all right."* (Francis, *Frost: A Time to Talk*, pp. 37–38.)

25. In the course of biographical research in the Harvard University Library, LT discovered a letter of RF's father, William Prescott Frost, Jr., in a Harvard Class of 1872 report, which set the year of RF's birth as 1874. The poet's birth records were destroyed in the great fire in San Francisco in 1906.

26. Much as RF enjoyed the reception-and-reading Adams had arranged, he was quite annoyed by the absence of President Eisenhower. What peeved him most was that, instead of coming to see him, the President sent an autographed photograph of himself.

27. RF's Preface to *Aforesaid* was first printed as "A Poet, Too, Must Learn the Magic Way of Poetry," in the New York *Times Book Review*, 21 March 1954, p. 1. It is reprinted as "The Prerequisites" in *Selected Prose*, pp. 95–97, and in *Poetry and Prose*, pp. 416–418.

28. Francis, *Frost: A Time to Talk*, pp. 79–80.

29. Quoted from "Amherst Honors Robert Frost," in Amherst *Alumni News* (April 1954), p. 3.

14. THE DEMAND FOR ME

1. RF to LT, 16 April 1957; *Selected Letters*, p. 565.

2. Similar appeals prompted William Faulkner to attend the conference as a representative of American prose writers. See Joseph Blotner, *Faulkner: A Biography* (New York, 1974), Vol. II, p. 1503.

3. Lesley Frost Ballantine to RF [20 July 1954]; DCL.

4. Quoted in "Robert Frost, 80, Gives a Recipe for Diplomats," the New York *Times*, 10 Aug. 1954, p. 5. RF expressed a similar view of international relations when he spoke in April 1961 to a New York gathering celebrating the centennial of the great Indian poet, Rabindranath Tagore. After saying Tagore was a nationalist as well as a poet, RF continued: "I'm a terrible nationalist myself—formidable . . . and I can't see how one can be international unless there are some nations to be 'inter' with, and the clearer and distincter the better. . . ." RF's 1961 talk was printed as "Remarks on the Occasion of the Tagore Centenary," in *Poetry Magazine* (Nov. 1961), pp. 106–119, although the passage quoted here is based on a transcript of the tape recording in DCL.

5. Quoted by Markham Ball in "Robert Frost . . . Reminisces on His Life," the Amherst *Student*, 1 Nov. 1954, p. 2. See also "From Beyond the Andes" [Brazilian interview with RF] in Lathem, *Interviews*, pp. 138–141.

6. After going out of his way to avoid Faulkner during the several days they were both in São Paulo, RF was quoted as saying, after Faulkner's departure, "I looked forward so much to meeting Faulkner, and I was so disappointed because I never saw him." (Blotner, *Faulkner*, p. 1506.) According to Blotner, RF then said to

Lesley, while making a gesture of drinking, "I think he'd been doing something naughty." (Ibid.)

As for Faulkner's Nobel Prize speech, in which he had expressed the belief that mankind would not only "endure" but "prevail," RF told LT that he thought it insincere and full of cant.

7. The gist of RF's post-Brazil conversation with Dulles can be inferred from the letter cited in Note 15 below, and from a remark in RF's letter to Harold E. Howland, cited in Note 20 below: ". . . You exaggerate the importance of what I did in South America. As I told Mr. Dulles when I came back a little Spanish and Portuguese would have given me better entree down there. I was none too satisfied with my results. . . ." For additional details of RF's Brazilian trip see Kathleen Morrison, *Robert Frost: A Pictorial Chronicle* (New York, 1974), p. 79.

8. John S. Dickey to RF, 19 Jan. 1955; DCL.

9. RF to John S. Dickey, c. Feb. 1955; typed draft, unsigned, in DCL. The letter ends, "Troublous family matters have kept me from writing sooner." This, apparently, is a reference to the death of the Morrisons' son, Robert, in a road accident late in December 1954.

10. RF's commencement address was printed in the Dartmouth *Alumni Magazine* (July 1955), pp. 14–16, and excerpted in *Poetry and Prose*, pp. 419–421. RF began his address by speaking of the significance of the day's events to the graduating class and to him: "This is a rounding out for you, and a rounding out is the main part of it. You're rounding out four years. I'm rounding out something like 63, isn't it? But it is a real rounding out for me. I'm one of the original members of the Outing Club—me and Ledyard. You don't know it, and I shouldn't tell it perhaps, but I go every year, once a year, to touch Ledyard's monument down there, as the patron saint of freshmen who run away. And I ran away because I was more interested in education than anybody in the College at the time. . . ." RF's idealized explanation of his departure from Dartmouth in 1892 leaves out a number of important factors. See *The Early Years*, pp. 138–146.

11. The quilting project was carried out by Miss Ida and Miss Louise Schmitt and Mrs. Anna Schmitt Braunlich in Hamburg, New York. Two complete quilts—the larger for RF, the smaller for Schmitt—were made, as well as a small throw that Schmitt gave to Hyde Cox. Stitched into each quilt was a chronological list, printed in India ink, of the institutions represented, the degrees, and the dates awarded.

Because the quilts were presented to RF on the day when Dartmouth awarded him still another hood, RF immediately requested that Schmitt take the quilts back to his aunts to have the new hood incorporated somehow. This was done by sewing triangle-shaped patches of green on all four corners of each quilt.

12. RF to Howard G. Schmitt, 17 June 1955; *Selected Letters*, p. 558.

13. In the context of RF's craving for recognition, a remark he made to a friend in 1960 is particularly interesting. Speaking by

telephone to Frederic Fox, a clergyman working in the Eisenhower White House, he said, "Fred, I need all the honors I can get." The circumstances that occasioned the remark are discussed on p. 278 of Chapter 17.

14. Sherman Adams to RF, 5 April 1956; DCL.

15. RF to Sherman Adams, 11 April 1956; typed draft in DCL.

16. Adams wrote to solicit RF's participation in CASE on at least two occasions, first on 7 June 1956 and again on 3 July. The former letter is in DCL; the latter is quoted in *Selected Letters*, pp. 559–560.

17. RF's refusal to do what Adams and Reynolds wanted was consistent with his refusal to join the Office of War Information, as Louis Untermeyer wanted, during World War II. See pp. 128ff in Chapter 9 of the present volume.

18. RF to Sherman Adams, 21 June 1956; *Selected Letters*, p. 559.

19. Harold E. Howland to RF, 10 Dec. 1956; *Selected Letters*, p. 560.

20. RF to Harold E. Howland, 1 Jan. 1957; *Selected Letters*, pp. 560–561.

21. The nature of the "almost public altercation" to which RF refers is not known; presumably it took place when he celebrated his eightieth birthday in Amherst on 26 March 1954. It is certain, however, that in debating "the value of permanent peace," RF ridiculed the concept and argued that war would never be eliminated completely as a means of settling political differences.

Conflict—including war among nations—was, RF believed, an inherent part of nature, and he was always ready to say so. In August 1956, an official of the United Nations, Professor Ahmed S. Bokhari, visited him in Ripton and invited him to write a poem for a new Meditation Room in the UN headquarters in New York. In the room was to be placed a massive block of iron which had been given by the King of Sweden, and Bokhari explained that what was wanted was a poem which took the block as an appropriate symbol of the choice men had to make between the "swords" and "ploughshares" into which iron could be made. RF at first declined to have anything to do with the United Nations, whose ideals he thought naïve and worthy of scorn, but he liked Bokhari and soon sent him a poem called "From Iron / Tools and Weapons" (*The Poetry*, p. 468):

Nature within her inmost self divides
To trouble men with having to take sides.

RF thus meant to suggest that, just as basic iron ore could be made into tools or weapons, ploughshares or swords, matter itself was divided into two irreconcilable opposites, the positive and negative charge. The implication, that men had to take sides because it was the nature of all matter to do so, did not escape Bokhari. He rejected RF's couplet, saying, "Mr. Frost, you have written better poems."

22. John Hay Whitney, American Ambassador to England.

23. RF to Eustace Seligman, 2 Jan. 1957; *Selected Letters*, p. 561.

24. RF to Sherman Adams, 4 Jan. 1957; typed draft in DCL.

25. John Foster Dulles to RF, 12 Feb. 1957; *Selected Letters*, p. 562.

26. RF to John Foster Dulles, 26 Feb. 1957; *Selected Letters*, pp. 562–563.

27. Both letters are in *Selected Letters*, p. 562.

28. RF to Sir Douglas Veale, 26 March 1957; *Selected Letters*, pp. 564–565.

29. The woman RF calls "Mrs. David Nutt" was in fact Mrs. Alfred Nutt, widow of David Nutt's successor in the firm David Nutt and Company. It was this publishing company which brought out RF's first book, *A Boy's Will*, in 1912. See *The Early Years*, pp. 400–401.

30. RF to LT, 16 April 1957; *Selected Letters*, pp. 565–566. The last paragraphs of the letter are worth quoting:

"If I ever have the least danger of feeling successful it is from the growing evidence that America has accepted me as one of her poets. What the British are doing is in foreign recognition of this fact. Kay seems even gladder of it than I am as yet. She had both father and mother from over there. Also she was partly educated over there. I had only a mother. And I never so much as set foot in Oxford or Cambridge before.

"Many many thoughts! I wanted you to share them."

15. AN ENGLISH DIARY

1. The idea of separate departures was RF's. So many volunteers had stepped forward to serve as his traveling companion that the poet had felt forced into a slight subterfuge in making a choice. He had quietly asked LT to go with him, but had also asked that he tell no one he had been chosen, that he pretend he was going to England on business unrelated to RF, and that he leave for London a day later than himself. LT agreed to do as RF wished. The subterfuge and the backstage arrangements are hinted in RF's letter to LT dated 24 April 1957:

"It has been brought to my attention that you are to be in England when I am there this spring. What a happy coincidence! We should find all sorts of ways of getting together. For good collusion perhaps we should get together here [in Cambridge] in advance. I am disinclined to create literature by writing it all out in letters. Is there any chance you could come up to Amherst for a little talk on the quiet on Monday, May 6, Tuesday May 7, or Wednesday May 8 when I shall be there saying some goodbys? These are strenuous excitements." (*Selected Letters*, p. 566.)

2. RF to T. S. Eliot, 2 May 1957; *Selected Letters*, pp. 566–567. Eliot answered RF's letter on 7 May: "I was very happy to get your letter of May 2nd. Of course, I had already heard some time ago

from private sources that you were coming over to take a Cambridge degree, and I have since heard that you are collecting several others: my warmest congratulations, though I feel that these honors are long overdue. My wife and I have been invited to a party at Jonathan Cape's to meet you on May 29th, and we are hoping to hear you lecture at London University on May 21st, but I hope there will be more to it than that. Indeed I hope that you will have time, amongst your numerous engagements, to have a meal with my wife and myself. I shall communicate with you at the Connaught Hotel, on, or after, the 20th. . . . We are all looking forward most eagerly to greeting you." (*Selected Letters*, p. 567.)

3. For an account of the period RF described in his talk, see *The Early Years*, pp. 392 ff.

4. RF's interest in "tones of voice" was directly related to his theory, formulated early in his career, of "the sound of sense." See *The Early Years*, pp. 417–419.

5. The picture story, entitled "A Poet's Pilgrimage," appeared in *Life*, Vol. 43, No. 13 (23 Sept. 1957), pp. 109–112.

6. See Note 4 above.

7. From "Kitty Hawk," in *The Poetry*, pp. 434–435, ll. 213–245. For a discussion of "Kitty Hawk" in relation to the poems with which it appears in *In the Clearing* (1962), see Chapter 18 of the present volume.

8. Before his departure from Durham, RF participated in a simple ceremony in which he was formally awarded the degree he had been granted in 1952.

9. *Robert Frost: Selected Poems* (London, 1955).

10. Richard H. Rovere, "Another Man's Flowers," in the London *Spectator*, 24 May 1957, p. 669.

11. Quotations in this paragraph were recorded by "our own Reporter" [William Weatherby] in "Robert Frost Still 'Goes On and On for our Delight,'" in the Manchester *Guardian*, 31 May 1957, p. 16.

12. For a reference to Squire's 1921 trip to the United States, see *The Years of Triumph*, pp. 576–577.

13. The books which RF found so offensively lurid were *As It Was* (London, 1931), and its sequel *World Without End* (New York, 1931).

14. Quotations in this section were derived from notes taken by *Time-Life* correspondent Bea Dobie, who followed RF and Lathem along their tour of Oxford on assignment for *Life* magazine. Dobie graciously arranged for LT to be provided with a draft copy of her report.

15. RF first met Haines, a Gloucestershire barrister and botanist, in 1914. They renewed their acquaintance in 1928, when RF and his wife revisited Gloucestershire during a vacation trip to England. See *The Early Years*, pp. 450–451; *The Years of Triumph*, pp. 328–332.

16. W. W. Gibson, "The Golden Room," quoted from J. E. Gethyn-Jones, *Dymock Down the Ages* (Dymock, 1951), p. 140.

RF's stay in the Dymock region of Gloucestershire is described in *The Early Years*, pp. 445–468.

17. For the source of quotations in this section, see Note 14 above.

18. A transcript of Eliot's remarks was prepared by Edward C. Lathem from a tape recording made by Mrs. Warde. Lathem provided LT with the transcript, and with a description of the RF-Lathem exchange which proceeded Eliot's speech, in a letter dated 8 Sept. 1972.

19. Forster wrote to RF thanking him for his visit on 18 June 1957. The letter (in DCL) reads in part: "What a pleasure to see you in my room, and to give you a cup of tea, even though I made it rather strong. Take no notice of anything I said about Keats. I am far away on the prose side, with all the limitations, and I was thinking after you left that the only poets of this country to whom I 'turn' are Shakespeare, Wordsworth, Hardy, and Auden—if the last named may be called of this country. After asking you how you made your money (a question you most graciously answered), I had intended to tell you how I made mine, but our talk moved elsewhere. I do very briefly tell at the end of Marianne Thornton. . . ."

20. Taft had written to RF in April 1957 saying that he would be completing his tenure as ambassador in mid-June but that he hoped to remain in Dublin long enough to greet him when he arrived. A rough-draft of RF's reply, undated but probably written in April, begins as follows: "This will be [almost] like a special dispensation for me that you are staying on in Dublin. I look forward to seeing something of you in and out of company. Your father came to mean more to me personally than anybody else in our world of politics. . . ." (DCL)

16. WASHINGTON: THE POUND AFFAIR

1. From "Statement of Robert Frost," a document filed in U.S. District Court for the District of Columbia, 14 April 1958.

2. The New York *Times Book Review*, 4 July 1954, p. 2.

3. The review first appeared in *Poetry*, Vol. V (Dec. 1914), p. 3. It was reprinted in *Literary Essays of Ezra Pound* (London, 1954), p. 384.

4. RF's change of attitude was revealed in a conversation with LT on 6 July 1954.

5. Quoted from Harry M. Meacham, *The Caged Panther: Ezra Pound at St. Elizabeths* (New York, 1967), pp. 118–119. Meacham's excellent study is the most complete and accurate account to date of the circumstances leading to Pound's release from St. Elizabeths Hospital. Readers who wish a more detailed discussion than that provided in the present Chapter are advised to consult it.

6. Herbert Brownell, Jr., to RF, 28 Feb. 1957; *Selected Letters*, p. 563.

7. William P. Rogers to RF, 10 April 1957; DCL.

8. Archibald MacLeish to Kathleen Morrison, 17 June 1957; *Selected Letters*, p. 568.

9. RF to Archibald MacLeish, 24 June 1957; *Selected Letters*, p. 569.

10. Archibald MacLeish to RF, 28 June 1957; *Selected Letters*, pp. 569–570.

11. Archibald MacLeish to Ezra Pound, 22 July 1957; *Selected Letters*, p. 570.

12. James Laughlin to RF, 24 Sept. 1957; DCL.

13. RF to James Laughlin, 8 Oct. 1957; first draft in DCL.

14. RF to William P. Rogers, 19 Nov. 1957; *Selected Letters*, p. 571.

15. Quoted from *Selected Letters*, p. 571.

16. RF to Sherman Adams, 12 Feb. 1958; *Selected Letters*, pp. 571–572. RF was correct in assuming that President Eisenhower was not the author of the telegram. In fact, it was written by Frederic Fox, a clergyman then on the White House staff, whose duties included writing such perfunctory presidential messages.

17. Sherman Adams to RF, 15 Feb. 1958; *Selected Letters*, p. 572.

18. RF to Dwight D. Eisenhower [16 Feb. 1958]; *Selected Letters*, p. 574.

19. RF to Sherman Adams [16 Feb. 1958]; *Selected Letters*, p. 573.

20. Miriam Ottenberg was the author of the *Sunday Star* article.

21. On 21 August 1957 Congressman Usher L. Burdick of North Dakota had introduced House Resolution 403—which was passed—authorizing a full-scale investigation of all aspects of the Pound affair. As a first move the Legislative Reference Service of the Library of Congress was directed to compile a full report on the case. It was this report that was released on April 1.

22. "Ezra Pound May Escape Trial and Be Allowed to Go to Italy," in The New York *Times*, 2 April 1958, p. 16.

23. For source, see Note 1 of the present Chapter. To the statement were appended added comments favoring Pound's release by John Dos Passos, Van Wyck Brooks, Marianne Moore, Ernest Hemingway, Carl Sandburg, W. H. Auden, T. S. Eliot, Archibald MacLeish, Robert Fitzgerald, Allen Tate, Dag Hammarskjøld and Richard H. Rovere. These had been compiled by MacLeish from a brochure issued on Pound's seventieth birthday, and from correspondence which had appeared in *Esquire* magazine following an article therein by Rovere in September 1957.

24. Anthony Lewis, "Court Drops Charge Against Ezra Pound," in the New York *Times*, 19 April 1958, pp. 1, 23.

25. RF to Dwight D. Eisenhower, 29 April 1958; *Selected Letters*, p. 578. In a press conference on May 21 at the Library of Congress, RF's comments on his evening with the President included an account of their conversation over the Anders Zorn portrait: "You want to hear one amus——interesting thing that he said to me? He said the most beautiful portrait in the White House is by somebody named Zorn, and to show my aptness, I said 'Anders Zorn?',

see, and he said, 'yes, Anders Zorn.' I said I knew him as an etcher. He said his portrait is the best one in the White House. We went and looked at it, together, and then he said . . . 'Where does all that light come from—all that light in that portrait?' It was a picture of William Howard Taft—magnificent thing to a magnificent. Right opposite in the room was . . . Sargent's Teddy Roosevelt, and that's a fine vigorous thing, but this is of a handsomer man, of course. . . . You could see the President lingered over it." (Quoted, with minor revision, from transcript cited in Note 26.)

RF sent his letter to Eisenhower by way of Adams, for reasons he explained in a covering letter: "This is no more belated than might be expected from such a staggering experience. Since it is all your doing from the start I naturally ask you to see it through the rest of the way. My obligation is first to you and by way of you to the ruler of the greatest nation in the world. I wish you would take a look of indulgence at my words to him to make sure they will do. I shall hope to see you before long. The Pound affair came off with dignity." (*Selected Letters*, pp. 577–578.)

26. Quoted from a transcript of RF's press conference prepared by the Library of Congress staff, and made available to LT by Roy P. Basler.

27. RF to Sherman Adams, 27 June 1958; rough draft in DCL.

28. RF to Sherman Adams, 8 Oct. 1958; *Selected Letters*, p. 580. The letter RF planned to send Adams, undated and unfinished, is in DCL. It reads as follows: "Dear Sherman If you will let my regard for you speak out you wont let them scare you out of office to save their reelections this fall. Stand fast in your integrity. They have probably lost their elections anyway on the probably prevalent misunderstanding of Mr Dulles' foreign policy. The public nerves are too shaky right now for sound judgment between war and peace. It's hard to make out from day to day what would satisfy the columnists, more to Munichward or less to Munichward. As Consultant to the Library of Congress and as such a qualifying if not qualified bureaucrat myself and also as twice an emissary of good will abroad under his auspices once to England and once to Brazil and Peru I wish I could get word to Mr Dulles that I think when all is said and done he will be seen to have managed magnificently. This by way of the report he should have had twice over from me." (Here the manuscript breaks off, and at the bottom of the sheet, RF wrote, "Never sent because of the bad news.")

17. POETRY AND POWER

1. Quoted from "For John F. Kennedy His Inauguration," in *The Poetry*, p. 424, ll. 70–71, 76–77.

2. Bess Furman, "'Poet in Waiting' Bids for a Rating," in The New York *Times*, 16 Oct. 1958. Also excerpted in Lathem, *Interviews*, pp. 182–183. During the conference, RF identified the four paintings as follows: "Winslow Homer's 'Four Bells'; Andrew Wyeth's 'Sea Wind' ['Wind from the Sea']; Thomas Eakins' paint-

ing of boatmen on the Schuylkill; and James Chapin's—that Negress of his, that girl singing." (Ibid.)

3. Mary McGrory, "Poet Frost Aspires to Be a Senator So He Can Give Advice on Anything," in the Washington *Evening Star*, 10 Dec. 1958, p. 29. Also in Lathem, *Interviews*, pp. 192–194.

4. J. Donald Adams, "Speaking of Books," the New York *Times*, 22 March 1959, p. 2.

5. *Congressional Record*, Vol. 105, Pt. 4 (25 March 1959), pp. 5160–5162.

6. RF's version of the two-line poem he remembered having heard as a child combines elements of two similar poems of different authorship, the earlier of which was written by the English poet Thomas Heywood (d. 1650?):

> *Seven cities warr'd for Homer, being dead,*
> *Who, living, had no roof to shroud his head.*

The "Epilogue" to *Aesop at Tunbridge; or, a Few Selected Fables in Verse,* "By No Person of Quality" (1698), contained this poem:

> *Seven wealthy Towns contend for HOMER Dead*
> *Through which the Living HOMER begged his Bread.*

7. Quotations from article by Maurice Dolbier in the New York *Herald Tribune Book Review*, issue of 5 April 1959, excerpted in Lathem, *Interviews*, pp. 195–198. Another report of the same interview is that by Anna Peterson, "Robert Frost, on 85th Birthday, Romps Through Interview Here," in the New York *Times*, 27 March 1959, p. 21.

8. The phrase occurred in the invitations sent out by Rigg.

9. "The Secret Sits," in *The Poetry*, p. 362.

10. Lionel Trilling, "A Speech on Robert Frost: A Cultural Episode," *Partisan Review*, XXVI (Summer 1959), pp. 445–452. Reprinted in James M. Cox, ed., *Robert Frost: A Collection of Critical Essays* (Englewood Cliffs, 1962), pp. 151–158. For a similar viewpoint that predated Trilling's talk by some six years, see "The Other Frost" in Randall Jarrell, *Poetry and the Age* (New York, 1955), pp. 26–33.

11. The New York *Times Book Review*, 12 April 1959, p. 8.

12. Ibid., p. 2.

13. In his *Partisan Review* article, cited in Note 10 above, Trilling introduced the text of his birthday speech by discussing the response to Adams's column, which column, he said, "created the impression with some people that, so far from my having paid tribute to a venerable man at a celebration of his life and achievement, I had actually offered him an affront." Trilling was disturbed not only that his speech should have been so represented by Adams, but that so few of the writers who responded to Adams's column had bothered to inform themselves of the actual content of his speech.

14. In a letter to LT dated 10 Feb. 1963, Stanley Burnshaw,

a Holt Vice-President, wrote: ". . . Robert knew that I was responsible for getting Trilling to speak that night—and I spent hours with him after the dinner, talking and talking and listening. And then the next day . . . by a curious chance, we ran into Trilling again, at the Century Club at noon, and I brought the two of them together into what turned out to be an almost loving embrace."

15. RF to Lionel Trilling, 18 June 1959; *Selected Letters*, p. 583.

16. John F. Kennedy to RF, 11 April 1959; *Selected Letters*, pp. 580–581.

17. Stewart L. Udall, "Frost's 'Unique Gift Outright,'" the New York *Times Magazine*, 26 March 1961, p. 12.

18. RF to Winston L. Prouty, 18 June 1959; *Selected Letters*, p. 582.

19. L. Quincy Mumford to RF, 26 June 1959; *Selected Letters*, p. 583.

20. RF to L. Quincy Mumford, 10 July 1959; typed draft in DCL.

21. RF described this incident to LT a few days after it took place.

22. Roy P. Basler, "Yankee Vergil—Robert Frost in Washington," *Voyages*, Vol. II, No. IV (Spring, 1969), pp. 8–22.

23. Quoted from a transcript of RF's talk in DCL.

24. For source, see Note 17 above.

25. Quotations from "'I Want Poets Declared Equal to—'," the New York *Times Magazine*, 15 May 1960, pp. 23, 105–106.

26. The Frost Medal Bill, when passed, became Public Law 86–747.

27. Information in this paragraph was supplied to LT by Frederic Fox, in a memorandum dated 8 Feb. 1965.

28. Judy Seaborg, "Poetry, Philosophy Presented by Frost," the Stanford *Daily*, 10 Nov. 1960, p. 1.

29. This conversation was reported to LT by Udall in January 1961.

30. RF to John F. Kennedy [c. 1 Dec. 1960]; *Selected Letters*, p. 585.

31. This conversation was reported to RHW by Fox on 30 May 1972.

32. RF to John F. Kennedy, 14 Dec. 1960; *Selected Letters*, p. 586.

33. RF's first "completed" version of "Dedication," later revised, expanded and retitled "For John F. Kennedy His Inauguration." This early version appeared, among other newspaper appearances, in the Washington *Post*, 21 Jan. 1961, p. 8. The final version appears in *The Poetry*, pp. 422–424.

34. Details in this and preceding paragraphs are derived largely from the article cited in Note 17 above.

35. John Huston Finley, Jr., was long a professor of Classics at Harvard, but besides this Harvard connection with Kennedy there is no obvious reason why RF should have confused their names. For an early reference by RF to Finley, see the passage cited in Note 16 of Chapter 1.

36. For source, see Note 33 above.
37. RF was particularly fond of President Kennedy's remark, and told the anecdote many times in subsequent public appearances.

18. IN THE CLEARING

1. RF to Stewart L. Udall, 5 April 1961; *Selected Letters*, p. 587.
2. Quoted by Irving Spiegel, in "Frost Takes Off for Jerusalem Lecture Series," the New York *Times*, 10 March 1961. See also two other accounts of RF's departure for Israel, in Lathem, *Interviews*, pp. 255–258.
3. During the delay, RF conversed over dinner with fellow passenger Leavitt Morris, a reporter for the *Christian Science Monitor*. Morris's subsequent account is reprinted in Lathem, *Interviews*, pp. 259–264.
4. Quoted by Art Buchwald, in "Poet Gets Rather Frosty When He Is Compared to Other Poets," the Atlanta *Journal*, 20 March 1961, p. 24 (and elsewhere in Buchwald's syndicated column on March 14).
5. Quoted by Leonard Lyons, in "The Lyons Den" (syndicated column), the New York *Post*, 17 March 1961, p. 10.
6. Ibid.
7. This remark did not appear in print, but was overheard by LT as he walked behind RF and Lyons during the stop in Paris.
8. See *The Early Years*, p. 114, where "Petra and Its Surroundings" is briefly discussed.
9. One of the many times when RF used the phrase was in England, in his talk at Oxford on 4 June 1957: "Poetry is hyphenated, like so many British names. It's a thought-felt thing. . . ." See p. 238 of Chapter 15.
10. RF never started a poem with the phrase, "Education elevates trouble to a higher plane." After his return to the United States, however, he did alter the aphorism to read: "Education lifts grief to a higher plane of regard." He repeated the improved version in many of his subsequent talks.
11. RF's remarks at the Hebrew University lecture were reported by Rina Samuel in "Robert Frost in Israel," the New York *Times Book Review*, 23 April 1961, p. 42.
12. RF alluded to his occasional sourness in a note to his American-born Hebrew University host, dated 5 April 1961: "Dear David Fineman: The way you turned on me on the platform [of the University auditorium] to make your introduction personal is one of my chief memories. I got a lot more out of Israel than you might think from my ornery resistance. It was much that I saw why you were there—you and your wife. I am always more for insights than for sights. But I saw countless stones and the evidence that they had been re-used in many buildings and I heard tell that Jerusalem was a Canaanite high place before ever the Jews came to it. And the guide won my affection. You are only

more an Israelite than you are an American. I am more an American than I am an Israelite. I'm all for nationalities. Keep thinking of me as I will keep thinking of you. . . ." (VaUL)

13. The transcript of RF's talk before the Archaeological Society is in DCL.

14. RF to Stewart L. Udall, 5 April 1961; *Selected Letters*, pp. 586–587. The piece to which RF refers is "Frost's 'Unique Gift Outright,'" the New York *Times Magazine*, 26 March 1961, pp. 12–13, 98.

15. Secretary Udall's press conference, and the circumstances that led to it, were reported by David Halberstam in "Udall Accused of Seeking Party Aid From Oil Man," the New York *Times*, 2 May 1961, p. 1. A picture of Udall, with RF seated at his left, accompanied the story.

The New York *Herald Tribune*, on May 3, carried a short item with the headline "Robert Frost Supports Udall" alongside its main account of the Udall controversy. It reported that RF had been Udall's luncheon guest that afternoon, and concluded with an exchange that took place before the conference began. "I know how to handle the press," RF was quoted as saying. "Then lend me your powers," Udall replied. RF, however, remained silent throughout the conference.

16. LU to RF, 5 July 1961; DCL.

17. RF to LU, 11 July 1961; first draft, in Mrs. Morrison's hand, in DCL.

18. "On Being Chosen Poet of Vermont," *The Poetry*, p. 469.

19. RF reported his comment in a letter to Udall dated 11 July 1962 (DCL). For the light it sheds on the complications that wrecked the park project, it is worth quoting in full:

"It looks as if this might not be a go up here. Of course you are a better judge than we are,—K. and I are. This little Republican state seems to be all stirred up about declaring parks and wildernesses, the local Forestry Department particularly. The piece of land immediately adjoining me that I thought to acquire in exchange for similar wild land somewhere else adjoining them they have set an absurd value of $135 an acre (100 acres) either to flatter me or insult me or end all further talk. It couldn't be worth more than $10 or $12 an acre at most unless our presence here made it so. We find the right going price $6 or $7 an acre. Of course one would expect to pay more for the small plantation of red pine, pulp wood size, that we've been trimming for your picture. It takes the Forestry Department not to know such things but red pine is not rated very high in the pulp or lumber market. You needn't think we are all worked up by this display of whatever it is. It may be partisan Republicanism, petty localism, or departmental rivalry between the Forestry Department and the Interior though the head man at Rutland, Mr Paul Newcomb, has been very nice to us but it has its dangers. Your campaign for the wilderness has been getting a bad press in Vermont. There is real hostility that could act up if we went ahead right now by main force to carry out your generous project. Probably we need to see you to talk it all over. There is a certain insecurity when a mere match can set off as much destruction as a bomb. We're well settled in here among people friendly to us but I'm not the kind of Democrat to say 'the-people-yes' in general. Sometimes I want to tell some of them to go to Hell for me. But on the whole we laugh with relief at having our little land deal with the government ended. We know this is a very small matter in your great affairs. You can take it in your stride as we take it in our affairs philosophically. I told the local ranger here, 'This ends a chapter in my life and a chapter in the life of the town.'"

The "picture" to which RF refers was *A Lover's Quarrel with the World*, produced for television and general distribution by Edward Foote. RF had also referred to it in a letter he sent to Secretary Udall in January 1962, when the Frost Memorial Park project still seemed assured of success:

"If I am made to connect your documentary film of me with your crusade for wildernesses or virgin grass and woods as much as I long to, I must be getting the scene ready up there in Ripton to have my picture taken at work outdoors in some natural way on the land. The particular land I have designs on is just north of my cabin owned now by Uncle Sam. You told me I couldn't buy it but might obtain it from the government in exchange for land elsewhere. To show you how business-like I am, I have gone right at it and bought a hundred acres adjacent to the National Forest to offer for the piece of theirs adjacent to me. Wouldn't it be great if you could bring the exchange about right away? Then we could say so far so good and let what will follow. What do you say, great man of great affairs? Is this too small a matter for attention?

"We read about you kiting round on the great affairs. Things for both parties (Frost and Democratic) seem to be going more than pretty well. Hurrah for freer trade in being closer every day to Grover Cleveland under whom I served my novitiate. New Deal, auld Deil, ordeal—you takes your choice. Friendship and brotherhood and all. You realize how much you and this administration mean to me." (RF to Udall, 16 Jan. 1962; rough draft in DCL.) It is interesting to note that, although he came close to doing so, RF never bought the hundred acres known as "Beaver Meadow." As he often did, RF slightly rearranged facts so they might serve his best advantage.

20. Quoted in unsigned article, "Frost Thrills Audience With Poetry and Wisdom at Dedication of Elementary School in his Honor," Lawrence *Eagle-Tribune*, 8 Jan. 1962, p. 3. A transcript of RF's Lawrence talk is in DCL.

21. Quoted from the Sunday (Atlanta) *Times-Observer*, 28 Jan. 1962, p. 10.

22. Details of RF's illness were told to LT by Helen Muir in March 1962.

23. Compare "Mist's" thrice-repeated statement that "the sleepers in the house . . . don't know where they are" with the following

lines spoken by Job in *A Masque of Reason* (*The Poetry*, p. 483, ll. 285–290):

> *We don't know where we are, or who we are.*
> *We don't know one another; don't know You;*
> *Don't know what time it is. We don't know, don't we?*
> *Who says we don't? Who got up these misgivings?*
> *Oh, we know well enough to go ahead with.*
> *I mean we seem to know enough to act on. . . .*

24. *The Poetry*, p. 414.

25. "Accidentally On Purpose," *The Poetry*, p. 425. One of the first occasions when RF used the phrase "passionate preference" was in September 1959, during a symposium sponsored by Seagram Distilleries in New York on "The Future of Man." The geneticist Ashley Montague, an advocate of birth control, artificial insemination, and other eugenic techniques, was one of the participants in the symposium, and RF, in his introductory statement, was implicitly attacking Montague's position when he said: "Now science seems about to ask us what we are going to do about taking in hand our own further evolution. This is some left-over business from the great Darwinian days. Every school boy knows how amusingly short the distance was from monkeys to us. Well it ought not to be much longer from us to supermen. We have the laboratories ready and willing to tend to this. We can commission them any day to go ahead messing around with rays on genes for mutations or with sperm ovules for eugenics till they get us somewhere, make something of us for a board or foundation to approve of. But I am asked to be prophetic. As far into the future as I can see with my eyes shut people are still pairing for love and money, perhaps just superstitious enough to leave their directions to what the mystic Karl Marx called historical necessity but what I like to call passionate preference to the taste there's no disputing about. I foresee no society where artificial insemination won't be in bad taste." (Quoted from a copy of RF's opening statement lent to LT by Mrs. Morrison.)

RF expanded his comments on "passionate preference" in the interview that followed the reading of opening remarks. See "Of Passionate Preference" in Lathem, *Interviews*, pp. 207–213.

26. "Kitty Hawk," *The Poetry*, pp. 428–429, ll. 1–21. For background on the events to which RF refers in the first part of "Kitty Hawk," see *The Early Years*, pp. 173 ff. See also pp. 517–518 of that volume, where LT analyzes the opening lines of "Kitty Hawk" in terms of RF's conflicting attitudes toward Elinor White.

27. Ibid., ll. 22–47.

28. Ibid., l. 187.

29. Ibid., ll. 213–229, 246–257.

30. Quoted by Dan Gottlieb in "Poet Is Still Writing at 88," the Washington *Evening Star*, 26 Mar. 1962, p. B1.

31. Quoted from draft of RF's inscription, dictated to Mrs. Morrison and in her hand, in DCL. Mrs. Morrison noted on the draft

that RF spoiled Copy Number 1 of the special edition, which he had intended to give to the President, and gave him instead a copy of the regular edition.

19. RUSSIA: A FINAL MISSION

1. RF to LT, 15 Aug. 1962; *Selected Letters*, p. 591.

2. The RF-Udall-Dobrynin meeting is described by Udall in "Robert Frost's Last Adventure," the New York *Times Magazine*, 11 June 1972, p. 18.

3. John Reed (1887–1920) was an American journalist and poet whose book *Ten Days That Shook the World* (1919) was an eyewitness account of the Russian Revolution. After helping to found the Communist party in America he returned to Russia, where he remained until his death.

4. RF to John F. Kennedy, 24 July 1962; *Selected Letters*, pp. 589–590. RF's plans were at a somewhat more advanced stage when he wrote to his grandson, William Prescott Frost, on 17 August: ". . . I have to report for myself that I also am on the move to go places. You probably won't have heard because it is a sort of state secret not meant to get out in general that on August 28th I am off to Russia to live there ten days and then come back here not to go on anywhere else. . . . As you may guess, this is a sort of errand I am on, not a sight-seeing junket. I shall have an interpreter with me and Freddy Adams to keep me from falling out of the plane. And Stewart Udall will be on board on his way to Siberia. I shall be doing the usual thing—the preliminary talk and the reading from my book to audiences, many of whom will not understand my English. I can be a little political but I mustn't be too political. I let myself in for getting into such a big thing by accidentally getting friendly with the Russian Ambassador. Put your mind on supporting me. . . ." (*Family Letters*, pp. 269–270.)

At about the same time that he wrote to his grandson, RF sent a similar letter to LT which began with an explanation of why he had not invited his biographer on a trip as important as the approaching Russian venture. Implicit in his explanation is RF's awareness that, in failing to take LT along, he was going back on a long-standing promise to include LT in any major international trips he should happen to make:

"Who's told you that I was afraid that I had hurt you by not bringing you with me to Russia. Could it have been someone with awkward good intentions? I easily assumed that you would understand. A first thought is that I want a variety in the followers on my trail and I want some of them to be not too critically intent on who and what I am. I can take Freddy Adams to keep me from falling out of the plane. I didn't want to be made too self conscious in this momentous expedition. I got into it by the accident of an almost too genial evening with the Russian Ambassador to this country. The President and Stewart Udall are in it too and I am committed. I must lean pretty heavily on reading my poems to people who don't understand English. I am given a faint hope that I may meet and talk with some important people but to avoid disappointment I must stay in a mood to take it all off-handed. You would have seen nothing in me that you haven't seen many times before. I shall read them 'The Lost Follower.' Bill Meredith doesn't believe anyone ever gave up writing poetry for sociology to make a better world. The two I speak of [in 'The Lost Follower'], Jean Flexner and Carter Goodrich, may have been rare cases but some of the poems in the Russian anthology I have been reading seem to be saying in verse they were making the same sacrifice. My two before they gave up wrote better poems than many who kept on. I have never been without sympathy for the equalitarians who pray or act for the Kingdom of Heaven on earth. What makes the angels something special is that they have no physical wants-appetites. The issue before Russia and us is which comes nearer—their democracy or ours—placating everybody. I may tell them what the issue is but won't claim it is nothing to fight about. Let's be great about it, not petty with petty twits. We both have a mighty history. I hope we can show ourselves mighty without being ugly. I get round once in so often to the word magnanimity, don't I? I shall be prophesying not just predicting from statistics—talking of the next hundred years ahead. I may tell them theirs is an imperial democracy like Caesar's Rome, ours a senatorial democracy like the Roman republic. I have been having all sorts of ideas but as I say for dignity I shall depend on the poems few will understand. I guess you pretty well know my attitude. I shall praise them for art and science and athletics. I may speak of the severity they've been easing down from towards socialism and our liberality we've been straining up from to the same socialism. And then again I may not. I go as an opportunist on the loose. I'd like a chance to ask the great Kruschev to grant me one request and then ask him a hard one. There. K. says this letter is getting to be a book." (RF to LT, 15 Aug. 1962; *Selected Letters*, pp. 590–591.)

5. See "Some Science Fiction" in *The Poetry*, p. 466.

6. The details of RF's visit to Crow Island were supplied by Hyde Cox in an interview with RHW in March 1973.

7. For source, see Note 1 above.

8. Quoted by Frederick B. Adams, Jr., in *To Russia with Frost* (Boston, 1963), p. 11. Adams's volume, along with Franklin D. Reeve's *Robert Frost in Russia* (Boston, 1963), are the major sources of information about RF's Russian trip. Unless otherwise stated, direct quotations of RF and descriptions of his activities in Russia are derived, in the present Chapter, from one or the other of these two excellent accounts.

9. RF's visit to District Primary School 7 was reported by Seymour Topping in "Robert Frost Talks and Jokes With Moscow Pupils and Poets," the New York *Times*, 2 Sept. 1962, p. 1.

10. This account of the RF-Khrushchev meeting is in Reeve, *Robert Frost in Russia*, pp. 110–115.

11. Back in New York, RF said, at a press conference, "I should

have modified that and said 'rough and ready.' 'Ruffian' is a pretty strong word." See Lathem, *Interviews*, p. 292.

12. Quotations here are derived from various press reports that appeared after the September 8 conference. For a sampling of the press coverage of RF's Russian trip, both Russian and American, see Lathem, *Interviews*, pp. 284–292.

13. Ibid., p. 291.

14. Charles H. Lyttle to RF, 13 Sept. 1962; *Selected Letters*, pp. 592–593.

The general concern about the implications of Khrushchev's alleged remark to RF was reflected in an editorial that ran in the New York *Times* on 15 September 1962. Unlike Lyttle's letter, the *Times* editorial accepted as accurate RF's report of what Khrushchev had said:

"Nikita Khrushchev's remark to Robert Frost that the United States was 'too liberal to fight' contrasts almost ludicrously with the Soviet Union's charge that the same United States was plotting to plunge the world into nuclear war.

"While the United States and the free world may by now take Communist propaganda contradictions as a matter of course, Mr. Khrushchev's comment does conjure up uncomfortable echoes of attitudes that helped precipitate the second World War. Hitler also believed that the 'liberal' democracies wouldn't fight under any circumstances even as he accused Britain and France of aggressive designs. Mr. Khrushchev, who is, we hope, a more diligent student of history than Hitler, ought to know that it would be hazardous in the extreme to equate Western 'liberalism' with lack of determination to defend our freedom and security.

"The Soviet Premier knows very well that Americans, like sane people anywhere, prefer the competition and cooperation of peace to the potential oblivion of war. He should also recall the lesson of history that the philosophy of liberalism and the willingness to stand fast under threats of force are not mutually exclusive."

15. RF to Charles H. Lyttle, 20 Sept. 1962; *Selected Letters*, p. 593.

16. RF to Norman Thomas [c. 28 Sept. 1962]; *Selected Letters*, pp. 594–595.

17. August Heckscher to RF [c. October, 1962]; DCL.

20. DEEPER INTO LIFE

1. RF to G. R. and Alma Elliott [c. 27 Jan. 1963], *Selected Letters*, p. 596. This letter, according to Anne Morrison Gentry, is "one of the last things Mr. Frost did." It is incorrectly dated in *Selected Letters* as having been written on 12 January.

2. RF's remarks were electronically recorded and subsequently reprinted in a government publication entitled *National Poetry Festival / Held in the Library of Congress / October* 22–24, 1962 / *Proceedings* (Library of Congress, Washington, 1964), pp. 228–259.

RF was not the only one who sought, in the weeks and months after his return from Russia, to set the record straight about what had and what had not been said to him by Premier Khrushchev. In an article in the Washington *Post* of 16 December 1962, several weeks after the end of the Cuban missile crisis, Chalmers M. Roberts reported corrective statements that had recently been made both by RF's interpreter in Russia, Franklin Reeve, and by Premier Khrushchev himself: ". . . A check has now been made with the interpreter in that Frost-Khrushchev interview. [. . .] He says flatly that Khrushchev did not make the remark. It appears that Frost felt that Khrushchev felt that way—but Khrushchev didn't say it. Indeed, on Nov. 12 Khrushchev went out of his way in a farewell talk with the retiring British Ambassador, Sir Frank Roberts, to deny he had ever said the U. S. was 'too liberal to fight.' That, of course, was after he concluded that the U. S. was indeed prepared to fight. . . ." Earlier in the article, Roberts made an observation which points up the potential gravity of RF's misquotation of the Soviet leader: "Naturally enough, it [RF's account of his meeting with Khrushchev] added to the sense of resolve here in Washington when Khrushchev's missiles were discovered in Cuba five weeks later. . . ."

3. "October," in *The Poetry*, p. 27. For some additional comment by LT, see *The Early Years*, p. 570.

4. "Frost Warms 8,500," in the *Varsity News* (University of Detroit student newspaper), 16 Nov. 1962, p. 1.

5. RF's remarks, in this the last of his college lectures before his death, were electronically recorded and reprinted as "Extravagance" in the Dartmouth *Alumni Magazine*, Vol. 55, No. 6 (March, 1963), pp. 20–24.

6. RF is quoting from the opening lines of Arthur William Edgar O'Shaughnessy's "Ode," the first poem in the latter's *Music and Moonlight* (1874). The passage, correctly quoted and in its entirety, reads as follows:

We are the music-makers,
   And we are the dreamers of dreams,
Wandering by lone sea-breakers,
   And sitting by desolate streams;
World-losers and world-forsakers,
   On whom the pale moon gleams:
Yet we are the movers and shakers
   Of the world for ever, it seems.

With wonderful deathless ditties
We build up the world's great cities,
   And out of a fabulous story
   We fashion an empire's glory:
One man with a dream, at pleasure,
   Shall go forth and conquer a crown;
And three with a new song's measure
   Can trample a kingdom down.

We, in the ages lying
In the buried past of the earth,
Built Nineveh with our sighing,
And Babel itself with our mirth;
And o'erthrew them with prophesying
To the old of the new world's worth;
For each age is a dream that is dying,
Or one that is coming to birth.

7. *The Poetry*, pp. 412–413. RF probably derived the words "I'm—bound—away" from the well-known folk song "Shenandoah," one of several songs he was fond of singing aloud. The pertinent refrain in this song is "Bound away, I'm bound away, 'cross the wide Missouri."

8. RF often attempted to hide various of his religious beliefs from friends he felt to be less believing than himself, but on three occasions, he made remarks to friends who were believers which suggest he held strongly to a conviction that there was a life after death. On one of these occasions, he was driving with Rabbi Victor Reichert and Hyde Cox on a moonlit night near Ripton when, apropos of nothing that had preceded, Reichert, at the wheel, turned to RF and asked, "Robert, do you ever feel that you don't have time? I feel that there are so many things I want to do, and should do, and I never seem to have enough time for them." After a long pause, RF replied, "The surest sign of immortality I have is that I've always known somehow that I had time to burn . . . time to burn."

On another occasion, RF was visiting Hyde Cox at Crow Island and asked him, impulsively, to "play me some great music, something you think is great." Cox played, on his phonograph, part of Handel's *Messiah*. When the record ended with the aria, "I know that my redeemer liveth," RF listened intently and then asked, half-teasingly, "Hyde, do you know that your redeemer liveth?" "Sometimes I think so," he replied, "do you?" "Oh, I don't know," said RF. "But I do know there's such a thing as redemption."

Most directly bearing on RFs belief in life-after-death is an anecdote related by Rabbi Reichert in his essay, "The Faith of Robert Frost," in *Frost: Centennial Essays* (Jackson, Mississippi, 1973), p. 418: ". . . Frost had come back from Russia and there was a gathering in our Ripton home. Suddenly, out of nowhere, sitting side by side and chatting, Frost said to me, 'Victor, what do you think are the chances of life after death?' I teased Frost by reminding him that when you ask a Jew a question, you don't get an answer; just another question. In the Book of Job, God never answers Job. Instead, God belabors Job with one great question after another. So I said to Robert, 'What do you think?' Frost became deeply silent and then said to me, 'With so many ladders going up everywhere, there must be something for them to lean against.' "

9. For an earlier and probably more nearly accurate account of

this conversation, which took place in July 1960, see *The Early Years*, p. 516.

10. The poem from which RF quotes is Arnold's "Immortality," which, for the light it sheds on RF's own religious beliefs, is worth quoting in full:

> *Foil'd by our fellow-men, depress'd, outworn,*
> *We leave the brutal world to take its way,*
> *And,* Patience! in another life, *we say,*
> The world shall be thrust down, and we up-borne.
>
> *And will not, then, the immortal armies scorn*
> *The world's poor, routed leavings? or will they,*
> *Who fail'd under the heat of this life's day,*
> *Support the fervours of the heavenly morn?*
>
> *No, no! the energy of life may be*
> *Kept on after the grave, but not begun;*
> *And he who flagg'd not in the earthly strife,*
>
> *From strength to strength advancing—only he,*
> *His soul well-knit, and all his battles won,*
> *Mounts, and that hardly, to eternal life.*

Another poem which RF was fond of quoting was Richard Blackmore's "*Dominus Illuminatio Mea,*" which, like Arnold's poem, comforted him with the promise of a glorious afterlife at the end of his earthly career:

> *In the hour of death, after this life's whim,*
> *When the heart beats low, and the eyes grow dim,*
> *And pain has exhausted every limb—*
> *The lover of the Lord shall trust in Him.*
>
> *When the will has forgotten the lifelong aim,*
> *And the mind can only disgrace its fame,*
> *And a man is uncertain of his own name—*
> *The power of the Lord shall fill this frame.*
>
> *When the last sigh is heaved, and the last tear shed,*
> *And the coffin is waiting beside the bed,*
> *And the widow and child forsake the dead—*
> *The angel of the Lord shall lift this head.*
>
> *For even the purest delight may pall,*
> *And power must fail, and the pride must fall,*
> *And the love of the dearest friends grow small—*
> *But the glory of the Lord is all in all.*

11. For the origin of this poem, see Note 27 of Chapter 11 of the present volume. In an interview with Robert Peterson, given

about the same time as his Dartmouth talk but not published until December 10, RF concluded his response to a question about his good health with another "dark note": "I guess I don't take life very seriously. It's hard to get into this world and hard to get out of it. And what's in between doesn't make much sense. If that sounds pessimistic, let it stand. There's been too much vaporous optimism voiced about life and age. Maybe this will provide a little balance." (Lathem, *Interviews*, p. 295.)

Throughout his life, RF consistently refused to be caught, or to catch himself, in extreme positions concerning good and evil, optimism and pessimism, or other "things in pairs ordained." Viewing truth as a continuing dialectic of opposites, he rarely took an extreme position except, as he says here, for purposes of counterbalancing its equally extreme antithesis. Truth, for RF, was always somewhere in the middle—and he would never presume to say exactly where. See the passage cited in Note 26 of Chapter 4; also Note 25 of the same Chapter; Note 13 of Chapter 6; Note 5 of Chapter 8.

12. RF to Lesley Frost Ballantine, 12 Jan. 1963; *Selected Letters*, pp. 595–596.

13. The poem had appeared first in the fiftieth-anniversary issue of the magazine *Poetry* (October-November 1962). As RF's Christmas greeting for 1962, it was mailed out shortly after he entered the Peter Bent Brigham Hospital on 3 December. It is reprinted in *Robert Frost: Poetry and Prose*, pp. 460–461.

14. The partial text of this poem, dictated by RF and recorded by Anne Morrison Gentry, is in DCL.

15. Untermeyer's last meeting with RF is reported in greater detail in *Letters to Untermeyer*, pp. 385–387.

16. RF's remark, "Don't cheat on me," to his Russian visitors may reflect his feeling that he had been somewhat betrayed, specifically by Premier Khrushchev, in being led to believe the Russian supported "magnanimous rivalry" even as he was preparing to perpetrate the military build-up in Cuba that resulted in the missile crisis of October 1962. After the crisis was resolved late that month, with Khrushchev's apparent retreat before the American blockade of Cuba, RF drafted a letter to Khrushchev that expressed his renewed admiration of, and faith in, the Soviet leader: "You are splendid. I knew from the harmony of our talk that you wouldn't try us in our politics more than as men we could bear. No petty squabble is to divert us from the great issue of the years ahead of our democracy versus your democracy in sports, art, science, and government. I count on you to keep faith with me." The typed draft of this letter, undated and unsigned, is in DCL.

17. This meeting was reported in the Boston *Herald*, 23 Jan. 1963, p. 1.

18. Soon after the telegram's arrival, RF was visited in the hospital by his friend, the Boston news commentator Louis M. Lyons. With RF's permission, Lyons later read the text of the telegram over a Boston radio program largely devoted to RF, and in it made reference to the poet's bravery in the face of his serious illness

while quoting a poem whose theme was, again, "bravery." RF listened to the program, and on 12 January dictated a short note of thanks: "Your brave talk buoys me up. Bravery is all. How I love to hear a poem quoted to some purpose. Affectionately, R. F." (DCL)

19. Anne Morrison Gentry's longhand transcription of this conversation, apparently made while RF and Princess de Rachewiltz spoke, is in DCL.

20. G. R. Elliott to RF, 14 Jan. 1963; DCL.

21. RF's thoughts on Christ, mercy, and justice had been expressed earlier in the week to Anne Morrison Gentry in the context of the new poem RF was working on. Her rough notes, made as they spoke about the direction he wanted the poem to take, read as follows:

> *tells king 'only dream' is difficulty*
> *between mercy and discipline—like Christ*
> *who died for it.*
>
> *What a wonder you are how did you know?*
>
> *dream of everyone to be higher than*
> *judge who can be reversed by absolute*
> *monarch*
>
> *king says to prophet youre a real prophet*
> *a wonder, whats your name?*
> *he says my name is Daniel, call me Dan.*
> *I am the author of the famous letters*
> *from Dan to Beersheba*

Mrs. Gentry's notes are in DCL.

22. See Note 1 of the present Chapter.

EPILOGUE

1. Family members present at the January 31 service included: Mrs. Joseph Ballantine (Lesley Frost) and her husband and grandchildren; William Prescott Frost; Mrs. David Hudnut (Marjorie Robin Fraser) and Mr. Hudnut; Mrs. Malcolm Wilber (Elinor Frost Francis) and Mr. Wilber; Mrs. Stanislaus Zimic (Lesley Lee Francis); a cousin, Joseph Frost; a niece, Vera Harvey; and the husband of Frost's daughter Marjorie, Willard Fraser.

Those present who were not members of Frost's family included: Hyde Cox; John Sloan Dickey; Mrs. Chisholm Gentry (Anne Morrison) and Mr. Gentry; Mr. and Mrs. Erastus Hewitt; David McCord; Mr. and Mrs. Theodore Morrison; Mr. and Mrs. I. A. Richards; Lawrance Thompson; Louis Untermeyer.

2. Quoted from a transcript of Bishop Hobson's remarks in ACL. Bishop Hobson's considerable understanding of the com-

plicated subject of RF's religious belief makes his remarks at the Amherst memorial service worth quoting at greater length:

". . . That there are a good many people who think of Robert Frost as an agnostic—or as non-religious—amazes me. A man I met a few days ago said: 'I just read in the paper that you're going to be at a memorial service for Robert Frost and I wondered what you'd be doing there. I didn't think he had much of any religion.' Several others have made similar remarks. To back up what he'd said one man quoted those delightful lines:

Forgive, O Lord, my little jokes on Thee,
And I'll forgive Thy great big one on me.

"This man represents a considerable group which thinks Mr. Frost had little or no religion because they lack both his and his God's sense of humor. There's a much larger group made up of those who accuse Robert Frost of being deficient in religious faith because they confuse a valid faith and theological orthodoxy. The latter he did not have, the former he had to a greater degree than almost any man I have ever known. His chief quarrel with dogmatic and traditional orthodoxy was that it too often tells us what we should and must think and thereby deprives us of the discovery of the truths through the process of doing a lot of hard thinking for ourselves. He was against dogma and routine because he saw so many people go to sleep in it. To a friend he said: 'What an enemy of dead and stultifying tradition Jesus was, and how he constantly worked to get people to discover the truths from within. People won't do this because it takes energy and sacrifice and suffering and education of the will to set aside one's will—or bring it into line with God's will, so that His desires are our desires. After years and years of hard work and struggle we have a habit of right desire and an educated will—and then we'll not have to struggle against ourselves as much any more.' Robert Frost had the spirit of a true Protestant in that he thought all valid belief had to be suffered for and 'hard won.' . . .

"Robert Frost's search for truth was constant and unwavering. He believed that the source of all truth is God, and the passion of his life was to discover more truth. This led him not only to read the Bible but to study it constantly, to meditate upon it, to 'inwardly digest it.' He knew the Bible as few—even the professionally trained ministers—do. At home, or away, he was never without this book while he lived, and because he worked hard, and reflected deeply, reading it was for him an adventure leading to always new discovery.

"Yet he never felt it was possible to gain more than a very partial knowledge of the whole truth. 'There is such a thing,' he said, 'as not being old enough to understand.' He realized that 'My thoughts are not your thoughts.' He recognized the value of 'the mystery withheld from us.' He sought for more light but even when it seemed dim, he bravely went forward determined to [use] what light he had. He accepted having to 'see through a glass darkly.' On a visit in the President's house at Kenyon College he sat up until about two o'clock in the morning discussing religion. When he finally started to bed, he stopped half-way up the stairs, thought for a few moments, then turned to his hostess and said, 'Well, at least you [ought] to live so's if there isn't Anything, it will be an awful shame.' He knew every man could start here even though he could find no other secure foundation, and many a lost person has been thankful for this place to begin.

"It was during this same visit, I think, that Mr. Frost was walking in the night with his close friend Gordon Chalmers. He suddenly stopped, as he often did when he wanted to think hard about something which was important, and then he said to President Chalmers, 'He's up there all right.' He didn't need theological terms to express his conviction that God is. This strong conviction that God is, and that he was dependent upon God, and must be true to him, were really at the heart of Robert Frost's faith. He once said to Mrs. Chalmers: 'The only fear I have is that I won't be true, every minute.' As part of the 125th anniversary celebration at Mt. Holyoke, Mr. Frost had an evening at the college. In his address he reported what was evidently much on his mind since he said the same thing on a number of occasions and in speaking with several individuals. He gave what he called 'the greatest prayer': 'May my sacrifice be acceptable in Thy sight.' He then added: 'That's your life, your poem, your everything.' . . ."

3. President Kennedy's quotation is a condensation of the last six lines of "Our Hold on the Planet," which is quoted accurately and in its entirety in the present volume, pp. 75–76. The other poems from which the President excerpted lines in his talk were, respectively, "Acquainted with the Night," "The Lesson for Today," and "The Death of the Hired Man."

4. The text of the President's address at Amherst appeared in full in the New York *Times*, 27 October 1963, p. 87.

INDEX

NAMES, PLACES, DATES are correlated with topics, interpretations, and conclusions—all previously deployed on three separate levels: Introduction, Central Narrative, Notes. Because this Index makes available some configurations and summaries which are not explicitly given elsewhere, it provides a fourth level of ordering.

Readers are particularly invited to browse through the Robert Frost entries under the thirty-five topical subheads which help to illuminate the complicated and contradictory responses of Frost as man and as artist. To expedite reference and cross-reference, the topical subheads are grouped here with page numbers:

AMBITION 452
ANTI-PLATONIST 452
BADNESS 452
BOOKS OF POETRY 452
BRAVERY 453
COMPETITOR 453
CONFUSION 453
COWARDICE 453
DEATH 454
FEAR 454
FRIENDSHIP 454
INSANITY 454
JUSTICE VS MERCY 454
MAGNANIMITY 454
NATIONALIST 455
OPPOSITES 455
PERFECTION 455
POEMS 455
POETIC THEORIES 456
PROPHET 456
PROSE 457
RECKLESSNESS 457
RELIGIOUS BELIEF 457
RESTLESSNESS 457
ROMANTIC 457
SADNESS 458
SATISFACTIONS 458
SCIENCE 458
SPOILED CHILD 459
SUCCESS 459
SUICIDE 459
TALKS, TITLES OF 459
TEACHER 459
WAR, ATTITUDE TOWARD . . 460
WILDNESS 460

A

Abbott, Colleer, 228
Abercrombie, Lascelles, 241
Abercrombie, Mrs. Lascelles, 242
Academy of American Poets, the
RF wins Fellowship of, in 1953, 206
Adams, Frederick B., Jr.
invites RF to lecture at Grolier Club, in 1939, 56; attends farewell luncheon on the eve of RF's English trip, in 1957, 222; RF invites, to go on Russian trip, in 1962, 308; accompanies RF to Russia, in 1962, 310ff
RF mentions, in 1953 letter to Cohn, 419; RF mentions, in 1962 letter to Thompson, 435
To Russia with Frost by, cited, 436
Adams, J. Donald
attends 1950 conference at Kenyon "in honor of Robert Frost," 418; an article by, praising RF, is quoted, 264; clashes with Trilling over the latter's speech at RF's eighty-fifth birthday dinner, 269

INDEX

Adams, Leonie, 175
Adams, Sherman
(Assistant to President Eisenhower), first meeting with RF, in the early 1950s, described, 207; invites RF to the White House, in 1954, 207; asks RF to receive visitor from the State Department, in 1956, 215
RF thanks, for telegram signed by Eisenhower, in 1957, 254; meets with RF and Rogers, in 1957, 255
RF tells, in 1958: "My obligation is first to you and by way of you to the ruler of the greatest nation in the world." 428
RF, in 1958 letter he never sent, urges Adams not to resign, 428; resigns position as Assistant to Eisenhower, 260–261; RF laments resignation of, 264
Agnes Scott College
RF's regular visits to, beginning in 1935, 297
Aiken, George D., 271
Akhmatova, Anna, 315–316
Alexander the Great, 322, 340
Allen, Ann
(Mrs. Hervey Allen), 65
Allen, Hervey
background of RF's friendship with, 377; RF and the Morrisons visit the Florida home of, in 1939, 35; arranges visit by RF and the Engles to Cuba, in 1939, 37
RF expresses gratitude for the friendship of, to Untermeyer, in 1939, 38; sees RF in Key West, in 1940, 62; RF buys property near, in Florida, in 1940, 65; RF visits, in Florida, in 1941, 76
RF mentions, in connection with the 1948 controversy over Pound's Bollingen Prize, 176; death of, in 1949, 198
American Academy of Arts and Letters
RF delivers Blashfield Address of, in 1950, 194
Amherst College
RF appears at, after seven-year absence from, in 1945, 129; RF is appointed Simpson Lecturer in Literature at, in 1948, 172–173; RF celebrates his eightieth birthday at, in 1954, 208ff; plans for the Robert Frost Library at, announced, in 1962, 328; President Kennedy speaks at dedication of Frost Library at, in 1963, 347–350
Amherst College *Student*
resemblance of RF's 1935 letter to, to a speech in *A Masque of Reason*, 389; resemblance of RF's 1935 letter to, to a passage in "The Lesson for Today," 400
Anderson, Margaret Bartlett
RF mentions, in a letter to her mother, 413
Robert Frost and John Bartlett by, first cited, 383; quoted, 45, 47
Arnold, Benedict, 170, 415
Arnold, Matthew
RF quotes from "Sohrab and Rustum" by, 185; RF glosses "Immortality" by, in November 1962, 334–335; "Immortality" by, quoted, 439–440
RF mentions, in 1962 letter to Norman Thomas, 325
Arnold, Thurman, 256–257
Atherton, Gertrude, 149
Auden, W. H.
RF mentions, in letter concerning Pound's Bollingen Prize, in 1948, 175; RF visits at Oxford, in 1957, 237, 239
Auslander, Joseph, 396

B

Babb, James T., 338
Bacon, Leonard
writes favorable review of *Steeple Bush*, in 1947, 157
Bailey, Robeson, 14, 372
Baird, Theodore, 105
Ballantine, Joseph W., 297, 442
Ballantine, Lesley Frost
visits South America with RF, in 1954, 211ff; RF visits, and is upset by, in 1961, 297; visits RF during his final illness, in 1962, 339; calls RF "Robert Coeur de Lion," in Jan. 1963, 339; attends burial ceremony of her father, 347; attends memorial service for RF, in 1963, 442
Barrett, Clifton Waller
RF visits with, on eve of his 1957 English trip, 222
Bartlett, John T.
in 1939, sees RF for the first time since 1935, 45; RF writes to, concerning illness of Prescott Frost, in 1943, 101; death of, in 1947, 198
Bartlett, Margaret
(Mrs. John T. Bartlett), RF visits, in Colorado in 1939, 45; RF writes to, concerning illness of Prescott Frost, in 1943, 101
RF denies request of, to publish a memoir of RF, in 1947, 167–168; RF denies request of, to publish his

Bartlett, Margaret (*cont.*)
letters, in 1949, 412–413; death of, in 1949, 198, 413
Basler, Roy P., 273–274, 292
Bell, Robert P., 347
Benét, Stephen Vincent, 377
Ben Zvi, Itzhak
(President of Israel), RF meets, in Israel in 1961, 289–290
Bernheimer, Earle J.
RF's early acquaintance with, 56–57; RF's earliest known correspondence with, in 1936, 385; in late 1930s, orders a tailor-made coat as gift for RF, 417
RF sells the unique copy of *Twilight* to, in 1940, 57–58; RF attempts to sell two manuscripts to, in 1942, 85; RF enters into unusual business arrangement with, in 1942, 86; RF discusses the loan of *Twilight* for a 1943 Dartmouth exhibition with, 396; lends *Twilight* to Dartmouth, in 1943, 116
in 1944, explains reasons for a stopped check to RF, 402; deterioration of RF's relationship with, 124–125; RF informs of plans for his visit to California, in 1947, 145; holds birthday party for RF, in California in 1947, 149;
threatens to sell his collection, in 1947, 166; offers to sell RF his Frost collection, 187–188; Frost collection of, auctioned, in 1950, 193–194; cash outlays to RF of, estimated, 417
Berlin, Isaiah, 241
Beveridge, William Henry, Lord
RF meets, in London, in 1957, 230
Bialik, Chaim, 288
Billings, Agnes, 50
Blackburn, Thomas, 236
Blackmore, Richard
"*Dominus Illuminatio Mea*" by, quoted, 440
Blotner, Joseph
Faulkner: A Biography by, first cited, 421
Blumenthal, Joseph, 179
Bode, Carl
aids RF in England as head of U.S.I.S. Library there, in 1957, 222ff
Bogan, Louise, 175, 176, 338
Bokhari, Ahmed S.
invites RF to write poem for U.N. Meditation Room, in 1956, 423; declines to make use of RF's poem, "From Iron," in U.N. Meditation Room, 423
Bollingen Prize
Pound wins, in 1949, for *Pisan Cantos*, 175; RF wins, in 1963, for *In the Clearing*, 338
Bolté, Charles G.
Dartmouth *Alumni Magazine* article by, quoted, 115; cited, 395
encounters RF at Kenyon in 1947, 138
Boston, Massachusetts
RF's residence at 88 Mt. Vernon Street in, 17, 388
Bowra, Sir Maurice
RF visits with, at Oxford, in 1957, 237
Bread Loaf Anthology, The
RF contributes preface to, in 1939, 51
Bread Loaf Writers' Conference
RF attends, in 1938, 7ff; RF "teams up with" Untermeyer at, in 1939, 51; RF encounters DeVoto at, in 1947, 165–166
Brickell, Herschel, 9, 14, 372
Briggs, Mrs. Ellis O.
RF attends reception at Athens home of, in 1961, 290
Bristol, Edward N., 29
Bristol, Herbert G., 28, 29
Bromfield, Louis, 123
Brooks, Van Wyck, 427
Brower, Reuben, 105, 129
Brownell, Herbert G.
RF signs letter to, concerning Pound, in 1957, 248–249
Browning, Robert, 326, 373
Bruce, David K. E., 291
Bruce, Robert, 415
Bryant, William Cullen, 41
Buchanan, Scott, 105
Bunyan, John, 32
Burnshaw, Stanley
arranges to have Trilling speak at RF's eighty-fifth birthday dinner, in 1959, 429
Burr, Aaron, 170

C

Cairns, Huntington
RF's visit to, in 1953, leads to the creation of "Kitty Hawk," 350
California, University of, at Berkeley
RF receives honorary degree from, in 1947, 148; RF lectures at, in 1953, 207
Cambridge, Massachusetts
RF's residence at 35 Brewster Street in, 77; RF, in 1946, fakes New Year's Eve party at 35 Brewster Street in, 142–143

INDEX

Cambridge, University of
RF speaks at, in 1957, 225; RF receives honorary degree from, in 1957, 244–245
Canby, Henry Seidel, 62
Canfield, Curtis, 208
Cape, Jonathan, 219, 231
Cardozo, Benjamin, 263
Catullus, Gaius Valerius, 197, 206, 238
Chalmers, Gordon Keith
(President of Kenyon College), RF's 1945 visit at Kenyon with, 404; RF is invited to Gambier conference by, in 1946, 137; arranges conference in honor of RF, at Kenyon in 1950, 196; death of, in 1956, 329
RF attends dedication of library at Kenyon named after, 329–330
RF tells Chalmers, during a Gambier visit, "He (God) is up there, all right." 444
Chalmers, Roberta Teale Swartz
(Mrs. Gordon K. Chalmers), describes RF's emotional state in the period after the death of Elinor Frost, 369
invites RF to speak at dedication of Chalmers Library, in Gambier, in 1962, 330
Chamberlain, John, 123
Chamberlain, Neville, 53
Chapin, Henry
recalls encounter with RF in Florida, in 1939, 379–380
Chapin, James, 262, 428
Chapin, Katharine Garrison, 175
Cherne, Leo
RF's negative response to a portrait of himself by, in 1962, 297
Childs, Francis L., 111, 116
Christie, J. T., 238
Chukovsky, Kornei, 312–313
Churchill, Winston
RF vilifies, when war breaks out in 1941, 85; RF aims barb at, in 1942, 89
Cincinnati, University of
RF receives honorary degree from, in 1954, 214
Clark, Grenville, 111, 113
Cleghorn, Sarah N.
RF writes introduction to *Threescore* by, 393
Cleveland, Grover, 304, 432
Coghill, Nevil, 239
Cohn, Louis Henry
In 1942, writes to Bernheimer concerning RF's attitude toward sale of manuscripts, 85; RF's dealings with, after 1950 Bernheimer auction, 418–419; RF writes to, after facial surgery, in 1951, 197
Cohn, Marguerite
(Mrs. Louis H. Cohn), RF's dealings with, after 1950 Bernheimer auction, 418–419
Cole, Charles Woolsey
(President of Amherst College), RF recalls, as Amherst student, 410; invites RF to his home, in 1947, 150; informs RF of his second honorary Amherst degree, in 1948, 168; speaks at RF's eightieth birthday celebration, in 1954, 208
Colgate University
RF, in 1950, receives honorary degree from, 196
Collamore, H. Bacon, 355
Collins, William
RF lectures on, in 1939, 41; "How Sleep the Brave" by, 297
Colorado, University of
RF receives honorary degree from, in 1939, 45
Commager, Henry Steele
RF attacks, after reading an article on loyalty by, 414; "Who is Loyal to America?" by, quoted and cited, 414; RF mentions, in 1948 letter to Whicher, 415
Conant, James Bryant
(President of Harvard University), is the butt of RF's teasing, in 1936, 418; offers RF appointment as Emerson Fellow in Poetry, in 1939, 48; invites RF to become Harvard's "Fellow in American Civilization," in 1941, 78; RF mocks contraceptive research of, in 1951, 197
Cone, Harold (1940–   )
(grandson of RF), mentioned, 137, 161
Cone, Irma Frost
(Mrs. John Paine Cone), RF quarrels with Hendricks over, in 1917, 413–414; RF visits at Concord Corners, in 1938, 9; emotional and marital difficulties of, 39; undergoes surgery for removal of a tumor, in 1939, 40; separates from her husband, in 1944, 136–137
RF expresses concern over mental state of, in 1947, 144; RF goes to Acton to visit, in 1947, 153–154; is committed to the State Hospital in Concord, N. H., by RF, in 1947, 162ff; living arrangements of, since 1947, 412
Cone, "Jacky"
see Cone, John Paine, Jr.
Cone, John Paine
growing success as an architect,

Cone, John Paine (*cont.*)
39; separates from Irma, in 1944, 136–137; informs RF he intends to seek a divorce, in 1946, 137
Cone, John Paine, Jr. (1927–)
(grandson of RF), RF writes to, concerning Irma, in 1947, 160–161
Coulter, Vincil C., 44
Cox, Edward Hyde
RF meets, in Key West in 1940, 60; background sketches of, 60, 200–201; RF's developing friendship with, 200ff; accompanies RF to Bowdoin College, in 1953, 202
presents Wyeth watercolor to RF, in 1954, 208; RF visits home of, in 1961, 279; RF's last visit at Crow Island with, in 1962, 309–310; visits RF in hospital, in 1963, 339; attends memorial service for RF, in 1963, 442
RF, about 1946, discusses the meaning of "Directive" with, 136, 405–406; describes genesis of RF's "The Night Light," 411
and Lathem, eds., *Selected Prose of Robert Frost,* first cited, 376–377
Cox, Sidney
RF's early friendship with, 116; RF's 1915 letter to, concerning Pound, quoted, 174; death of, in 1952, 198
RF's introduction to *A Swinger of Birches* by, quoted, 375–376
Craig, G. Armour, 105, 291
Cross, Wilbur L.
serves on the Pulitzer Prize committee that, in 1943, is overruled in its decision not to give Prize to RF, 109ff
Curran, C. P., 245

D

Damrosch, Walter J., 31, 377
Dante, 375, 401
Dartmouth College
RF, in 1943, makes known his interest in teaching at, 106; RF is appointed Ticknor Fellow in the Humanities at, in 1943, 112; RF begins teaching at, in 1943, 114; RF delivers "Great Issues" lecture at, in 1948, 179ff
RF receives an unprecedented second honorary doctorate from, in 1955, 214; RF gives an idealized version of his 1892 departure from, in 1955, 422; RF speaks at dedication of the Hopkins Center at, in Nov. 1962, 331ff
Darwin, Charles
RF, at Dartmouth, in 1949, mentions, 180; RF, in Jerusalem, in 1961, debunks the evolutionary theories of, 288–289; RF mocks, in "Accidentally on Purpose," 300
Davis, Elmer, 100
Davison, Edward
RF sees, in Colorado, in 1939, 46
Detroit, University of
RF receives honorary degree from, in Nov. 1962, 331
de Valera, Eamon, 246
DeVoto, Avis
(Mrs. Bernard DeVoto), 21
DeVoto, Bernard
in 1938, attends Bread Loaf Writers' Conference, 7; tells RF, "You're a good poet, Robert, but a bad man," 10
RF, in 1938, fails to sell a house to, 16; RF apparently intends DeVoto to be recipient of a gift of books, in 1938, 20; RF writes letter "in defense of my native badness" to, in 1938, 21;
RF mentions anti-British sentiments of, in 1941 letter to Fraser, 82; RF encounters during visit to Bloomington, in 1943, 107; RF provokes infuriated letter from, in 1943, 107; RF in 1943 letter, attempts to pacify, 108–109; attends Bread Loaf Writers' Conference, in 1947, 165–166
is quoted in Foster's "Journal," 371
Dickey, John Sloan
(President of Dartmouth College), RF meets, in 1945, 132; RF writes letter of resignation to, in 1949, 173; visits RF in hospital, in Jan. 1963, 339; attends memorial service for RF, in 1963, 442
Dobie, Bea, 425
Dobrynin, Anatoly
(Russian Ambassador to U. S.), discusses Russian trip with RF, 306; RF lunches with, on eve of Russian trip, 310
Dobrynin, Mrs. Anatoly, 310–311
Doré, Gustave, 401
Dos Passos, John, 427
Douglas, Mary
inspires RF's poem "The Night Light," 411
Downs, Sir Brian, 220, 244
Dragon, Richard
death of, in 1962, 336
Dragon, Stafford, 336
Duke University
RF receives honorary degree from, in 1948, 169

Dulles, John Foster
RF meets with, after his South American trip, in 1954, 213, 216; urges RF to visit England as good-will ambassador, in 1957, 219; RF mentions, in 1958 letter to Adams, 428; RF predicts Herter will succeed, 266–270
Durham, University of
RF is granted honorary degree by, *in absentia*, in 1952, 228; RF speaks at, in 1957, 226
Durham, Willard, 147

E

Eakins, Thomas, 262, 428
Early Years, The, first cited, 367
Eastman, Blanche Rankin, 148, 409
Eberhart, Richard, 338
Edwards, Alfred C.
joins Henry Holt and Company, in 1945, 177; RF forms close relationship with, 177; RF mentions, in 1951 letter to Cohn, 197; RF visits, on eve of 1957 English trip, 222; RF orders Thompson to telephone, from Athens, in 1961, 290
RF dedicates "A Cabin in the Clearing" to, 299; helps arrange RF's eighty-eighth birthday party, in 1962, 304; is prevented from intercepting RF after his return from Russia, in 1962, 323; visits RF in hospital, Jan. 1963, 339
Edwards, Eleanor
(Mrs. Alfred C. Edwards), 177
Einstein, Albert, 133, 236
Eisenhower, Dwight D.
(President of the U. S.), RF is annoyed by failure of, to welcome him to the White House, in 1954, 420–421; Adams fails to enlist RF in campaign to re-elect, in 1956, 216; invites RF to the White House for a "stag dinner," in 1958, 255, 258–259; RF, in 1962, expresses admiration for, 303
Eliot, T. S.
RF, in 1942, refers to, with the derogatory epithet "worlds-end-whimper," 89; RF, in 1947, receives surprise visit from, 152–153; in 1949, serves on jury that awards Bollingen Prize to Pound, 175
congratulates RF for winning a Cambridge honorary degree, 424; meets RF in London, in 1957, 223; RF teases, in London, in 1957, 224; attends champagne party honoring RF, in 1957, 231; RF dines at home of, in 1957, 242; serves as toastmaster at dinner honoring RF, in London, in 1957, 243–244
joins RF, in 1957, in signing letter concerning release of Pound, 248
Elliott, George Roy
urges RF to leave Henry Holt and Company, in 1938, 28; RF, in 1942, writes to concerning a visit to Amherst, 105; is one of several who arrange RF's 1945 visit to Amherst, 129; RF receives invitation to visit home of, in 1947, 150
RF composes his last letter to, in Jan. 1963, 343–344; devout religious views of, 410
Emerson Fellowship in Poetry, Ralph Waldo
RF is offered appointment to, in 1939, 48; RF, after six-week delay, accepts appointment to, 49; RF, in 1940, begins second year of, 76
Emerson, Ralph Waldo
RF mentions, in 1948 talk on loyalty, 170; RF mentions, in 1957 conversation with Forster, 245; RF mentions, in 1948 letter to Thompson, 402
"Saadi" by, quoted, 126; "Compensation" by, quoted, 384
Engle, Mary
(Mrs. Paul Engle), 37
Engle, Paul
RF, in 1939, visits Cuba with, 37; RF writes of Cuban trip with, 379; "For an Apple Grower" by, upsets RF, in 1939, 42ff; continuing attempts of, to repair his friendship with RF, 382–383; RF is angered by "Our Cuban Journey" by, 383; reconciliation with RF of, in 1947, 383
Ennius, Quintus, 140
Epstein, Jacob, 242
Everett, Edward, 277
Everitt, Helen, 376
Everitt, Raymond, 30, 376

F

Family Letters, first cited, 376
Farjeon, Eleanor, 233, 235, 242
Faulkner, William
Lesley tells RF he is Faulkner's "great admiration," 212; RF succeeds in avoiding, during 1954 South American trip, 213; RF professes disappointment at his failure to meet, in 1954, 421; RF alludes to the drinking habits of, in 1954, 421

INDEX

Faxon, Dr. Henry, 59
Ferril, Thomas Hornsby
RF visits, in Colorado, in 1939, 48
Fineman, David, 431
Finley, John Huston, Jr.
Professor of Greek at Harvard, 370, 430; RF mentions, in 1938, 6; RF, at Kennedy inauguration, accidentally substitutes name of, for Kennedy's, 282
Fire and Ice, cited, 392
Fisher, Dorothy Canfield, 149
Fitzgerald, Robert, 427
Flexner, Jean, 435
Flint, F. S., 223–224
Foerster, Norman
RF is angered by, in 1939, 42; RF, in 1938, writes to, concerning his coming Iowa visit, 378; RF writes to, in 1938, to postpone his visit to Iowa, 382
Foote, Edward
A Lover's Quarrel with the World, 1962 film by, mentioned, 432–433
Forster, E. M.
RF, in 1957, inadvertently embarrasses, 241–242; RF visits rooms of, at Cambridge, in 1957, 245; writes to RF after their 1957 visit, 426; RF, in 1961, is prevented by illness from calling on, 290
Foster, Charles H.
background sketch of, 370; RF, in 1938, nominates, for the first Elinor Frost Memorial Fellowship at Bread Loaf, 370; RF mentions affectionately, in 1938 letters to Foerster, 378, 382
"Journal of Charles H. Foster" cited, 370–371; passages from quoted, 7, 8, 371, 372
Foster, Doris
(Mrs. Charles H. Foster), 382
Fox, Frederic
Assistant to Sherman Adams, mentioned, 276, 278, 422, 427
Fox, John, 260
Francis, Elinor Frost
see Wilber, Elinor
Francis, Lesley Frost
(Mrs. James Dwight Francis), biographical sketch of, 36, 39; joins RF on visit to Untermeyer home, in 1938, 17; RF, in 1938, defends Mrs. Morrison in letters to, 27; RF visits, in Washington, D.C., in 1941, 77; Mrs. Morrison visits, in Washington, in 1944, 121
see also Ballantine, Lesley Frost
Francis, Lesley Lee (1931–)
(granddaughter of RF), joins her grandfather in England, in 1957, 234
see also Zimic, Lesley Lee
Francis, Robert
background sketch of, 204; RF, in 1953, is angered by "Apple Peeler" by, 205–206; RF punishes, by writing retaliatory poem, "On the Question of an Old Man's Feeling," 205–206
Frost: A Time to Talk by, cited, 420; and quoted, 208–209, 420
"Apple Peeler" by, cited, 420; and quoted, 205
Frankfurter, Felix, 304
Fraser, G. S., 231
Fraser, Marjorie Frost (1905–1934)
(Mrs. Willard E. Fraser), death of, in 1934, mentioned, 36, 71, 368
Fraser, Marjorie Robin (1934–)
(granddaughter of RF), stays with the Carol Frosts after her mother's death, until 1940, 3, 368; RF mentions, in 1939 letter to Lesley, 380
see also Hudnut, Robin Fraser
Fraser, Robin
see Fraser, Marjorie Robin
Fraser, Willard E.
RF writes to, in 1941, concerning the war effort in Vermont, 81–82; RF again writes to, in 1942, concerning war effort, 98; attends memorial service for RF, in 1963, 442
Freeman, Douglas Southall, 148
Freeman, Edward Augustus, 108
Friend, Robert, 287–288
Frost and Bartlett, first cited, 383
Frost, Carol (1902–1940)
drives RF to Bread Loaf, in 1938, 7; offers to take RF in at the Stone Cottage, in 1938, 12; RF, in 1939, is disturbed by the erratic behavior of, during Florida visit, 35–36; plans to help RF erect a prefabricated home in South Miami, in 1940, 67
psychological difficulties of, 68ff; RF attempts to relieve suicidal depression of, in 1940, 70; suicide of, in Oct. 1940, 71, 386; RF, in 1941, buries ashes of, 80
Frost, Elinor White
(Mrs. Robert Frost), RF's emotional collapse after death of, in 1938, 1ff; RF, in 1939, writes about the influence on his verse of, 40; intense relationship of Carol Frost with, 69; RF recounts his 1894 flight from, in "Kitty Hawk," 300ff

INDEX

Frost, Elliott (1896–1900)
RF's and Elinor Frost's first child, mentioned, 118
Frost, Eunice, 231
Frost, Jeanie Florence
RF's sister; similarities of, to Irma, 144, 371
Frost, Isabelle Moodie
(Mrs. William Prescott Frost, Jr.), mother of RF; RF uses maiden name of, in "Beech," 92; mentioned, 201
Frost, Joseph, 442
Frost, Lillian LaBatt
(Mrs. Carol Frost), illness of, in 1940, 69ff; RF writes to, after Carol's death, 72–74; spends summer of 1941 at Homer Noble farm, 79; accompanies RF and Prescott to burial of her husband's ashes, in 1941, 80
denies that Carol ever threatened his father's life, or his son's, 386–387
FROST, ROBERT LEE
(26 March 1874–29 Jan. 1963)

AMBITION

"I say I have nothing left but work and ambition. But I sometimes doubt I have even those. I show no disposition to work and I have only ambition when it is summoned by an audience present to get me talking." 3
"His desperation was due to his not being able to accomplish anything for you." 72
"Don't I beseech you say a word to anybody about my juvenile dream of Broadway. . . . Kay and I may repent and want it forgotten. Im scared already. There are plenty of reasons why we shouldn't tempt fate with another ambition." 117
"What with my barding around the colleges and the poems I publish . . . and the build-up I get nowadays on television my ambition is pretty well sated. Still . . ." 218
"The only thing I blame you for is the ambition to lead the life of a political hero. But what can I say who have so much ambition of my own to answer for?" 260

ANTI-PLATONIST

"My philosophy, non-Platonic but none-the-less a tenable one, I hold more or less unbroken from youth to age." 21
"Then again I am not the Platonist Robinson was. By Platonist I mean one who believes what we have here is an imperfect copy of what is in heaven." 375
"I like to think that I am not quite a Platonist and then all of a sudden I find myself saying something that I myself trace right back to Plato." 290–291

BADNESS

RF, in conversation with Foster, calls himself "a God-damned son-of-a-bitch." 8
"Being out here with my faithful biographer inevitably puts me on the defense of my native badness." 21
"I mean I am a bad bad man . . ." 21
"There's a vigorous devil in me that raises me above or drops me below the level of pity." 23
"I am a particularly advanced case of what I am, good or bad." 49
"I'd be a bad man as well as a bad author if I couldn't squeeze a report for you out of my pen . . ." 63
RF in 1921: "I have been bad and a bad artist." 391
see also the various passages quoted in Note 26 of Chapter 2, pp. 375–376

BOOKS OF POETRY

Collected Poems (1939)
Holt permits cheap reprint edition of, 29; RF, at the request of Sloane, writes a preface for the Holt edition of, 30–31; is praised in Latin by Sloane, 38
A Witness Tree (1942)
early title of, 387; RF's fears for war-time success of, 87; RF dedicates to Kathleen Morrison, 92; is a marked success, 95–96; is awarded Pulitzer Prize, 110; is reviewed by Untermeyer in the *Yale Review*, 394–395
A Masque of Reason (1945)
RF, in 1943, announces completion of, 117; RF, in 1943, discusses possible Broadway production of, 117; discussed, 118ff; RF's devout intentions in, 120; RF, in 1943, speaks of having written, 124; RF, in 1943, promises Bernheimer he will deliver the manuscript of, 125
A Masque of Mercy (1947)
RF, in 1943, alludes to, as companion piece to *A Masque of Reason*, 117; RF, in 1945, prematurely announces the completion of, 130; discussed, 130–132, 140–141

FROST, ROBERT LEE (*cont.*)
Steeple Bush (1947)
RF's anxiety over success or failure of, in 1947, 155; themes underlying structure of, 154–157; mixed reviews of, 157; RF's reaction to reviews of, 157–160; RF learns that Engle has written complimentary review of, 383
Complete Poems 1949
is published, 181ff; impressive success of, 183; RF receives Gold Medal of the Limited Editions Club for, as the work "most likely to attain the stature of a classic," 185; RF speaks of, in letter to Edwards, 184–185
In the Clearing (1962)
reasons for long delay before the appearance of, 294; themes and poems in, discussed, 299–303; is published on RF's eighty-eighth birthday, 303–304; RF presents inscribed copy of, to President Kennedy, 303–304; RF dedicates, to Kay Morrison, 304

BRAVERY
"Disaster brought out the heroic in you. You now know you have the courage and nerve for anything you may want or need to be . . ." 71
"Two things are sure: he was driven distracted by life and he was perfectly brave. I wish he could have been a soldier and died fighting Germany." 73
"Kay says I am not to give myself up. Well then I'll be brave about this failure as I have meant to be about my other failures before." 75
"I mean I sympathize with all the brave people who go out to die for causes. They are the great boys, beside whom I am nothing." 102
"I wonder at your coolness—like Bennen's on the avalanche in Sills fine poem. If I seem to speak with the least coolness, I have caught the tone from your courage." 413
"The only reason I go on the platform at all is to show my bravery. I must remember that. I do it to make up for never having faced bullets like the real hero." 415
"I am not hard to touch but I'd rather be taken for brave than anything else." 339
"Your brave talk buoys me up. Bravery is all." 441
RF's lifelong interest in the heroic, discussed, 393
see also COWARDICE and FEAR

COMPETITOR
"You should see me in trials of strength and suppleness with men much younger. I even excel in some events." 26
"My chief signs of life are shown in any debate." 378
"I hate prize fights where the victory is dependent on the referee's decision; it seems too much like the arts." 46
"Kathleen says I am challenged to single combat by Carl Sandburg in an article in the *Atlantic Monthly* for March." 91
"Prizes are a strange thing for me to have come by, who have hated competition and never wanted to be anybody's rival." 111
"They say the only thing he beats me at is being buried in Poet's Corner. So if somebody will knock me over the head while I'm in England, I may come even with him." 237
"People say there's always room at the top. There isn't. There's only room for one at the top of the steeple." 266

CONFUSION
RF says poetry ends "in a momentary stay against confusion." 31
"But I am very wild at heart sometimes. Not at all confused. Just wild—wild." 377
"You were of course kept in confusion of mind by Carol's confused suffering." 73
"Drink and be made whole again beyond confusion." 136
"My motto for yesterday was Dont let being mixed make you feel confused." 150
". . . but to admit confusion is to admit being licked." 152
RF plays "the game of confusion." 411

COWARDICE
"I'm touching in Amherst only for four nights this time. . . . I can remember the time when I would have made the cowardly excuse that someone else wouldn't let me stay longer." 150
RF says, of Khrushchev, "He's not a coward. He is not afraid of us and we're not afraid of him." 322
see also BRAVERY and FEAR

FROST, ROBERT LEE (*cont.*)

DEATH

"Your fortitude in the face of approaching death makes it hard not to grant you the permission you ask as a last favor." 413

"I often think that the best way to die would be . . . out on the trail." 327

Death as theme of RF's poem, "Closed for Good," 182–183; as theme of "Away!" 333–334

see also SUICIDE AND FEAR

FEAR

"I shall never be the scared fool again that I used to be. Nothing can more than kill me." 26

RF, in 1941, signs his "Manifesto of Manifest Destiny" "The Fearer." 389

"And the fear of God always has meant the fear that one's wisdom . . . is not quite acceptable in His sight." 140

Fear as theme of *A Masque of Mercy*, 141; as theme of "The Fear of God," 156; as theme of "The Fear of Man," 156–157

"Neither for my sins of omission nor commission am I afraid of being punished. . . . My fear of God has settled down into a deep inward fear that my best offering may not prove acceptable in his sight." 150, 401

"Only Lesley's memories would go back further and go in deeper than yours. That ought to make me afraid of you." 167

"I am frightened by this big undertaking but I was more frightened at your Inauguration." 308

see also BRAVERY and COWARDICE

FRIENDSHIP

"It is an unusual friendship. I have come to value my poetry almost less than the friendships it has brought me. I say it who wouldn't have believed I would ever live to say it." 23

"All I need is a very few friends to set their hearts right on me just as I am without one plea." 63

"False friendships I accept for what they're worth, and for what I can get out of them." 127

"I have things to be thankful for. I have friends for instance." 168

"All I have left to care for in this world is a few friends. You're two of them." 419

"I have had very uneven luck in my friendships. I have reached a poise, however, of taking them as they turn out." 184

INSANITY

"I've been crazy for the last six months. I havent known what I was doing." 17

"I judge you were in actual danger there alone with your unhappy father —unhappy to the point of madness." 72

"I was in a terrible state of wondering if it wasnt my duty to have him examined by a mental doctor. But where might that have landed him? Better this way [i.e., death] than a life in an institution." 74

"I find it hard to end anyone's freedom to range to waste and to ruin. Take that away from anyone and what is there left? Let them run I say till they run afoul." 144

"You may not have heard the sad ending to Irma's story. She is at once too insane to be out of an institution and too sane to be in one. So she suffers the sense of imprisonment where she is, in one." 168

"I hate such nonsense and can only listen to it as an evidence of mental disorder. But mental disorder is what we are considering." 257

JUSTICE VS MERCY

"You know how mixed up it is possible to get with mercy and justice. If you don't know it is because you are inexperienced in abstract thinking and need to read my play on the Forty-third Chapter of Job." 105

"I was just saying today how Christ posed Himself the whole problem and died for it. How can we be just in a world that needs mercy and merciful in a world that needs justice?" 344

RF, in 1938 letter to Snow, explains the difference between justice and mercy, 403–404

MAGNANIMITY

"I should think we might accept a house from the great architect for the great poet at a safe distance. It is the hour of magnanimity all around." 253

"But I should think [a solution] would have to be reached more by magnanimity than by logic and it is chiefly on magnanimity I am counting." 257

RF, in March 1962, says of Khrushchev: "He's my enemy. But it takes

FROST, ROBERT LEE (*cont.*)
just a little magnanimity to admire him." 303
"It was all magnanimity—Aristotle's great word." 326
"I get round once in so often to the word magnanimity, don't I?" 436

NATIONALIST
"I should like to have it that your medal is a token of my having fitted . . . into the nature of Americans—into their affections . . ." 33
"The more I love my country the less I've seen its faults and I'm not ashamed to say it." 77
"I don't want to see a lot of bloody trouble unless we are going to bring America out a nation more distinct from all other nations than she is already." 81–82
"To get right down to my way of thinking the most I count on from the war is an improvement of our National position with friend and foe." 99
"I have decided . . . [to offer] to take over everybody's quarrel with Hitler and to fight the war out with American forces alone. I can see no other way to establish our national identity and define Democracy." 389
"There is nothing I had rather be called than an American and a poet." 186
"Nationalism and internationalism are the same as personalism and interpersonalism." 213
"For my country? My chief wish is for it to win at every turn in anything it does." 265
"I'm a terrible nationalist myself—formidable . . . and I can't see how one can be international unless there are some nations to be 'inter' with." 421
RF, in 1958, thanks Sherman Adams for giving him access to "the ruler of the greatest nation in the world." 428
see also WAR, ATTITUDE TOWARD

OPPOSITES
"It is a drunken world, going home we know not where, but the important thing to realize is that it is not swaying too far to the left or too far to the right." 52
"Everything has its opposite to furnish it with opposition." 99
". . . trying to decide between God and the Devil . . . between endless things in pairs ordained to everlasting opposition." 393
"If that sounds pessimistic, let it stand. There's been too much vaporous optimism voiced about life and age. Maybe this will provide a little balance." 440
RF writes, in "Quandary," that "It was by having been contrasted/That good and bad so long had lasted." 400
RF's belief that the universe is composed of counterbalancing opposites as theme of his unfinished poem, "Tendencies Cancel," 388

PERFECTION
RF's early attempts to live by the precept, "Be ye therefore perfect, even as your Father in Heaven is perfect." 375
"I began life wanting perfection and determined to have it. I got so I ceased to expect it and could do without it. Now I find I actually crave the flaws of human handwork. I gloat over imperfection." 21
"Perfection is a great thing." 210

POEMS
Accidentally on Purpose, 299–300
Away!, 333
Beech, 92
Cabin in the Clearing, A, 204, 299, 419
Closed for Good, 179, 182–183, 184
Come In, 231
Considerable Speck, A, 93
Death of the Hired Man, The, 360
Dedication
see For John F. Kennedy His Inauguration
Design, 267
Directive, 135ff, 405–406
Does No One at All Ever Feel This Way in the Least?, 204
Drumlin Woodchuck, A, 78
Equalizer, An, 94
Fear of God, The, 156
Fear of Man, The, 156–157
For Columbus Day, 204, 419
For John F. Kennedy His Inauguration, 279–280, 285
(Forgive, O Lord . . .), 443
Freedom of the Moon, The, 352
From Iron, 423
Gift Outright, The, 84, 93, 171, 225, 276, 278, 282, 304, 390, 419
Gold Hesperidee, The, 385
Grindstone, The, 178
Home Burial, 71
How Hard It Is to Keep from Being

FROST, ROBERT LEE (*cont.*)
King When It's in You and in the Situation, 194ff, 202
Into My Own, 21
It Is Almost the Year Two Thousand, 93
Kitty Hawk, 227, 284, 300ff, 334
La Noche Triste, 84, 297
Lesson for Today, The, 79, 93, 372, 400
Literate Farmer and the Planet Venus, The, 387
Lost Follower, The, 435
Masque of Mercy, A
see BOOKS OF POETRY
Masque of Reason, A
see BOOKS OF POETRY
Mending Wall, 152, 288, 316
Neither Out Far nor In Deep, 267
Never Again Would Birds' Song Be the Same, 304
New Hampshire, 207
Night Light, The, 335, 411
November, 93
October, 330
Old Man's Winter Night, An, 47, 178
On Being Chosen Poet of Vermont, 295
On Making Certain Anything Has Happened, 133–134, 405
On the Question of an Old Man's Feeling, 205–206
One More Brevity, 204
One Step Backward Taken, 134, 403
Our Doom to Bloom, 204
Our Hold on the Planet, 75–76, 93, 350, 369
Pasture, The, 313
Paul's Wife, 178
Prophets Really Prophesy as Mystics, The Commentators Merely by Statistics, The, 339–340
Provide, Provide, 19, 374
Quandary, 400–401
Reluctance, 170
Secret Sits, The, 94, 268
Semi-Revolution, A, 94
Silken Tent, The, 24, 93, 205, 376, 420
Snow, 178
Something for Hope, 155–156
Stopping by Woods on a Snowy Evening, 149, 152
Sycamore, 93
Take Something Like a Star, 182
Time Out, 84, 390
To a Moth Seen in Winter, 84, 93, 390
To a Young Wretch, 359
To Earthward, 21
Trespass, 94–95
Triple Bronze, 78, 93
Two Look at Two, 178
U. S. 1946 King's X, 154
West-Running Brook, 178, 405
Why Wait for Science, 154
Witch of Coös, The, 178, 224

POETIC THEORIES

RF asserts that the object in writing poetry "is to make all poems sound as different as possible from each other." 31

"It begins in delight and ends in wisdom. The figure is the same as for love. No one can really hold that the ecstasy should be static and stand still in one place. It begins in delight, it inclines to the impulse, it runs a course of lucky events, and ends in a clarification of life—not necessarily a great clarification, such as sects and cults are founded on, but in a momentary stay against confusion." 31

". . . a discrimination I demonstrated that lies at the very root of all poetry appreciation. A bad quatrain consists of an epigram of about the extent of two lines which the poet thinks of first but saves for the last two lines preliminary labored into some semblance of validity . . . to round out the form. A good quatrain keeps you from knowing which member of the rhyme-twins the poet thought of first." 63

"The great object of great art is to fool the average man . . . into thinking it *isnt* art." 91

"Poetry is the thoughts of the heart. I'm sure that's what Catullus meant by *mens animi*. Poetry . . . is a thought-felt thing." 238

PROPHET

"I have it plainly in writing that no one not even a seer can be at once an Overseer and an employee of the University." 4

"I am more concerned to justify my prophecies than my moral principles." 375

"My entanglement has had critical moments when it looked like openly declared trouble. The future of Europe is easier for me to see into than my own future." 36–37

"But I am asked to be prophetic. As far into the future as I can see . . ." 434

"I am describing not so much what ought to be but what is and will be—reporting and prophesying." 308

"God wants us to contend . . ." 320

FROST, ROBERT LEE (*cont.*)
"I shall be prophesying not just predicting from statistics—talking of the next hundred years ahead." 431
RF calls his 1962 Russian trip "a sort of errand I am on, not a sight-seeing junket." 435

PROSE
1939: "The Figure a Poem Makes," 30–31, 181
1939: "Remarks Accepting the Gold Medal of the National Institute of Arts and Letters," 32–33
1939: "The Doctrine of Excursions," 51–52
1946: "The Constant Symbol," 418

RECKLESSNESS
"I am in a reckless mood and a dangerous one left thus lying around loose in the world. Take care of me. . . ." 7
"To show you how restless and reckless I am let me tell you what I paid for a pair of books the other day to give to a friend to whom I owe almost my life." 373

RELIGIOUS BELIEF
"Religion ought to be included in my list and might be if it would only behave religiously and cease to try to pray God on one side or the other." 82
"My latest [theory about prayer] is that it might be an expression of the hope I have that my offering of verse on the altar may be acceptable in His sight Whoever He is." 402
". . . religion is most of all valuable when something original has been contributed to it." 136
"Now religion always seems to me to come round to something beyond wisdom." 140
"My approach to the New Testament is rather through Jerewsalem than through Rome and Canterbury." 151
". . . in matters of religion I'm like one of these new cars. I look like a convertible, but I'm actually a hard-top. I don't convert." 229
". . . one thing must be said about poetry—it's the ultimate. The nearest thing to it is penultimate, even religion." 238
"I doubt if I was ever religious in your sense of the word. I never prayed except formally and politely with the Lord's Prayer in public." 402
"The surest sign of immortality I have is that I've always known somehow that I had time to burn. . . ." 439
RF and Cox discuss whether the "redeemer liveth," 439
"With so many ladders going up everywhere, there must be something for them to lean against." 439
"Well, at least you [ought to] live so's if there isn't Anything, it will be an awful shame." 443
"He's up there, all right." 444
"Why will the quidnuncs always be hoping for a salvation man will never have from anyone but God?" 344

RESTLESSNESS
"I am like an ocean that in its restlessness may have brought up every imaginable shape to the surface. . . . I am still infinitely restless, but I came away from you as good as saved." 13
"I am still at a loss what harmless to do with myself." 37
"My motto for today is Keep Moving. I am a nomad in my own house. I have slept in every one of its rooms but the kitchen." 150

ROMANTIC
"Before I went thoroughly romantic about the classics I ought to go and muse part of the year in Greece . . . and a few days in Rome. . . ." 4
"And I think it would be unromantic of me not to accept ruthlessly your romantic offer. . . ." 15
"I thought it would be romantic to pay the market price or the latest auction price." 373
"Buying my own books at such an advance on the original cost was a real adventure in romantic friendship." 20
"I make no secret of it that I have had a romantic pleasure in your being my one and only Maecenas." 189
"I'm sort of romantic, and if I'm romantic I'm romantic from Plato." 291
"The woman you have is an imperfect copy of some woman in heaven or in someone else's bed. Many of the world's greatest—maybe all of them—have been ranged on that romantic side." 375
"Love is all. Romantic love—as in stories and poems. I tremble with it." 343

FROST, ROBERT LEE (*cont.*)

SADNESS

"My, my, what sorrow runs through all she wrote to you children. No wonder something of it overcasts my poetry if read aright. No matter how humorous I am I am sad. I am a jester about sorrow." 40

"I am prepared for any sadness in the structure of the universe." 41

SATISFACTIONS

"But whatever the medal may or may not symbolize, I take it as a very great honor." 33

"I got a telegram partly in Latin from the Holts yesterday saying it was their pride to let me know that my latest book was that day on the market. The Latin gave me a stir that I never expected to have again in this world from publication." 38

"The prize came as a genuine surprise after what you said about the committee's having decided I couldn't have it though I deserved it. You had prepared me to be satisfied with the golden opinion of the committee. Kay woke me with the news. It struck her breathless and me rather pleasantly thoughtful." 110

"As my chief upholder through two world wars and one and one fifth peaces, you would have reason to be proud if I ever came to anything. It is a great satisfaction to have lived to hear you say you *are* proud." 184

"There are a few people I regret not triumphing over. But it is with a mild regret that seldom comes over me in its unworthiness." 185

"A good many things I have no heart for any more, but I still like marked attention that savors of affection." 411

"My laureation and patriation at your hands and in your warm words will go down in Frost family history as the greatest public event of my life." 186

RF writes, after receiving an honorary degree in 1955, ". . . we mustnt forget such things have their importance though of course they are only incidental to what my life is all about." 215

"Few things could give me the pleasure of such an honor from the country ('half my own') that published my very first book. . . . I shall look at it as a rounding out that we seldom get except in story books and none too often there." 220

"It will also sort of round off my rather great academic career in general. I have had about everything I can have in my own country. Now for the mother country. We are not talking of deserts. No triumphs for me. But satisfactions I dont see why I shouldnt be permitted." 221

"Little did I think when I was making a little book or two in Ledbury almost fifty years ago that I would be returning one day to all these honors. And I didn't write the poetry to get here either." 238

"To be stood up for and toasted in such august company by the ruler of the greatest nation in the world was almost more to me than being stood up for in acclaim by whole audiences of his people and mine." 258

"But I like to be made of, you know. I like to be made of." 265

"The only thing that could mean more to me than recognition by the Senate would be a seat in the Senate which I may say I have given up all hope of with two such Senators from Vermont already in situ." 271

"The government has gone a long way towards making this my culminating year. You perhaps know the President and his White House have come into it." 272

RF to Kennedy: "If you can bear at your age the honor of being made President of the United States, I ought to be able at my age to bear the honor of taking some part in your inauguration. . . . It will please my family of friends and were they living it would have pleased inordinately the kind of Grover Cleveland Democrats I had for parents." 278

SCIENCE

"The only part of Genesis that has changed in three thousand years and become ridiculous is the science in it. The religion stands." 21

"The scientist seems to have the advantage of [the artist] in a court of larger appeal." 32

"With things like the atomic bomb I pride myself on putting them in their relative place a priori without ever having been in a physics laboratory." 132–133

RF speaks, in 1947, on "the way to approach a scientist," 151–152

RF offers his Dartmouth students some "rigamaroles" to embellish scientific facts, 180

FROST, ROBERT LEE (*cont.*)
"We ought not put on humanistic airs to make fun of science because though it can postpone death, it can't do away with death. I for one, am willing to be under obligation to it for postponing death." 197
"Science cannot be scientific about poetry, but poetry can be poetical about science. It's bigger, more inclusive." 265

SPOILED CHILD
"Nothing I do or say is as yet due to anything but a strong determination to have my own way." 22
"You are said on good authority to have said of me that I am dangerously apt to get anything I want. Don't worry about me then, but accept the risk that what I want may prove too much for your sense of propriety." 48
"All you have to do is ignore my inquiry and broach a new subject next time you write, or let the matter rest till the child forgets his whim." 64
"I hate so to be crossed I have come to think not being crossed is the one thing that matters in life. I can think of no blissfuller state than being treated as if I was always right." (from the letter cited in Note 3 of Chapter 11, 407)

SUCCESS
"It seems to me now that she was cumulatively laying up against me the unsuccess of the children I had given her." 40
"It cant be that what a woman lays up against a man is his success out where she can only imperfectly share it." 41
"Go out and get all your own success. But do so cooly and deliberately without importunate haste." 41
"I failed to trick Carol or argue him into believing he was the least successful. Thats what it came down to." 75
"You speak too lightly of the penalties I have to pay for success. It is not for you to impose them whatever they may be." 409–410
"If I ever have the least danger of feeling successful it is from the growing evidence that America has accepted me as one of her poets." 424
"At least I have a vague sense of having had this year the height of my success. It is entirely beyond anything I ever dreamed of or set my heart on." 185

SUICIDE
"I can't myself say how serious the crisis was and how near I came to giving in. It [death] would have been good advertising." 88
RF's habit of threatening suicide, discussed, 391
RF's response to the suicide of Hemingway, discussed, 294
see also DEATH and INSANITY

TALKS, TITLES OF
Extravagance, 331–335
Role of a Poet in a Democracy, The, 77
Separateness of the Parts, The, 138
Some Obstinacy, 179–180
Speaking of Loyalty, 169–171
Success of a Single Poem, The, 39
Trial by Market, The, 46
Where Is the Place of Ideals and Who Is Their Keeper, 122

TEACHER
"I'm like that with a class in school. I see the boys as comparatively good and bad but taken as a job lot in the absolute so really good for nothing that I can bring myself to mark them with nothing but mercy. . . ." 404
"What the hell do you think I am, a rural schoolteacher that nobody wants to hear? Last night I talked to two thousand in Philadelphia, and they turned five hundred away!" 42
"I am going to say in my letter of acceptance that I wonder at myself for still hanging round education after all these years; but I suppose what keeps me is the reasonable doubt that the college belongs entirely to the scholars." 49
"I seem not to be able to let the colleges alone. I seem divided pretty equally into three parts, teaching, farming, and poetry." 396
"Mr. Frost has not thrown in the sponge on his ideas that education should be a take-it-or-leave-it business instead of a day-after-day quizzing of boys with questions to which he already knew the answers. His belief is in an 'education by presence'—the stimulation of students to enterprise by the mere presence in their midst of men who have done things and have wide intellectual horizons." 52

FROST, ROBERT LEE (*cont.*)
"He also wants his pupils to know when they're talking in quotation marks and when they're thinking for themselves. . . . They can write for him, but that's not the only thing; good conversation will be accepted, and good reading. Probably even good listening." 115
RF says, of Edward Thomas, "That was the only time I influenced anybody. I taught school but have never succeeded in teaching anybody to be a poet." 233
"I have long thought that our high schools should be improved. Nobody should come into our high schools without examinations—not aptitude tests, but on reading, 'riting, and 'rithmetic. And that goes for black or white. . . . A lot of people are being scared by the Russian Sputnik into wanting to harden up our education or speed it up. I am interested in toning it up, at the high-school level." 263–264
"We study and study the four biographies of Him and are left still somewhat puzzled in our daily lives. Marking students in a kind of mockery and laughing it off." 344

WAR, ATTITUDE TOWARD
"We are able to fight and we are not afraid to fight. My only doubt is whether we need to join in England's fight. I should like it better if we had it all to ourselves and if we won we would get the loot the glory and the self-realization." 81
"Men should be able to kill each other in settling differences of opinion, but at the same time recite and sing to each other the same poems and songs of international greatness." 82
"Why are we at war? The best construction I can put on it is that we and the British have a property and a position the Germans would give anything to get away from us: and that we arent fools enough to let them." 100
"Not everybody can be expected to like war." 101
"I can talk about the war upon occasion, but what unfits me for most platforms is that most people believe in this war whereas I believe in any and all wars. I mean I sympathize with all the brave people who go out to die for causes." 102
see also BRAVERY and NATIONALIST

WILDNESS
"But I am very wild at heart sometimes. Not at all confused. Just wild —wild." 377
"Then there is this wildness whereof it is spoken. Granted again that it has an equal claim with sound to being a poem's better half. If it is a wild tune, it is a poem. Our problem then is, as modern abstractionists, to have the wildness pure; to be wild with nothing to be wild about." 31, 377
"To show his sympathy with me he says he hates to see one of the most powerful engines in the country wracking itself to pieces from running wild after the loss of its flywheel." 37
"Dull with propriety and discretion as I am in public on the platform, my breaks in private are as the waves on the shore. I get going wild, more stimulated than hindered by any guardian of my accuracy present who tries to laugh me down." 144
"You make it sound like some bad domestic dinner you took satisfaction in making a scene of by suddenly avalanching all the dishes off the table with one sweep of one arm or one strong pull of the table cloth and then bursting out of the dining room (wildly) to go hunting wild game in Africa. I have felt that way myself." 189

Frost, Samuel Abbott (1795–1848)
(RF's great-grandfather), mentioned, 394
Frost, William Prescott, Jr. (1850–1885)
(father of RF), mentioned, 102
Frost, William Prescott (1924–)
(grandson of RF), RF impressed by courage of, after the death of his father, 71–72; enlists in the Army Signal Corps, in 1942, 100; is discharged from the Army, 121
denies that Carol Frost ever threatened his life, 387
Froude, James Anthony, 108

G

Gassner, John, 14, 372
Gentry, Anne Morrison
(Mrs. Anne Morrison Smyth), attends RF during his final illness,

Gentry, Anne Morrison (*cont.*)
339ff; attends memorial service for RF, in 1963, 442
see Morrison, Anne
Gentry, Chisholm, 442
Gibbon, Edward
The History of the Decline and Fall of the Roman Empire by, mentioned, 148
Gibson, Wilfrid W.
"The Golden Room" by, quoted, 239–240
Gillars, Mildred
"Axis Sally," mentioned, 176, 416
Gillie
(RF's Border collie), 66, 77, 310
Golden, Harry
angers RF by comparing him to Sandburg, in 1961, 286
Goldfine, Bernard, 260
Goodrich, Carter, 435
Goodwillie, Mary
RF accepts invitation of, to lecture in Baltimore, in 1938, 19
Gorki, Maxim, 321, 325
Gosling, Glenn, 177
Grade, Arnold
ed., *Family Letters of Robert and Elinor Frost*, first cited, 376
Granin, Daniil, 315
Grant, Ulysses S., mentioned, 216
Green, Charles R., 390
Green, Paul, 14, 175
Greene, Graham, 241
Gregory, Horace
influence on RF of a review by, in 1954, 248

H

Haferd, Margaret, 223ff
Haines, John, 239, 425
Hammarskjøld, Dag, 427
Hancock, Walker
sculpts head of RF, in 1950, 202–203; Mrs. Morrison suggests use of RF likeness by, for Frost Medal, 276
Harcourt, Alfred, 149
Hardy, Thomas
RF mentions, to Forster, 245
Harris, Oren, 260
Harrison, Dr. Hartwell, 327
Hart-Davis, Rupert, 230
Harvard University
RF, in 1938, lectures to overflow audience at, 25; RF, in 1939, is appointed Emerson Fellow at, 49; RF, in 1941, is appointed "Fellow in American Civilization" at, 78; RF, in 1941, begins as "Fellow in American Civilization" at, 81; RF, in 1941, delivers Phi Beta Kappa poem at, 79
Harvey, Hilda, 161
Harvey, Vera, 161, 442
Hay, John, 224
Hearst, James
RF's efforts on behalf of, in 1942, 91
Heckscher, August, 326
Hemingway, Ernest
joins RF, in 1957, in signing letter concerning Pound, 248; RF's response to the suicide of, in 1962, 294
Hemingway, Pauline Pfeiffer
(Mrs. Ernest Hemingway), 35
Hendricks, Walter
RF's 1917 quarrel with, 413–414; RF helps install as President of Marlboro College, in 1948, 169
Herter, Christian P., 266, 270
Hewitt, Erastus
RF's Cambridge lawyer-neighbor, 158, 161, 442
Hewitt, Jane
(Mrs. Erastus Hewitt), 442
Heywood, Thomas, 429
Hickler, Dr. Roger, 336ff
Hillyer, Robert S.
title of, at Harvard, 383–384; successfully campaigns, in 1938, for RF's election to Harvard Board of Overseers, 3; RF writes to, in 1938, concerning RF's Harvard appointment, 6; RF mentions, in 1938 letter to McCord, 373; succeeds in arranging RF's Harvard appointment, in 1939, 48
Hitler, Adolf, 53, 389
Hjort, Elmer, 76, 89, 121
Hobson, Henry Wise
attends 1950 conference at Kenyon "in honor of Robert Frost," 418; speaks at RF's public memorial service, in 1963, 346, 442–443
Hogan, Miss Ellen, 296
Holden, Raymond
speaks at RF's eightieth birthday celebration, in 1954, 209
"Reminiscences of Robert Frost" by, cited and quoted, 380–381
Holliday, Floyd, 71
Holliday, Jack, 101
Holmes, John
occupies Gully farmhouse, in 1938, 3
"Close-up of an American Poet at 75" by, cited and quoted, 368

Holt, Henry, & Company
moves of, in 1938, in keep RF with the firm, 27ff; RF, in 1940, plans book to coincide with seventy-fifth anniversary of, 75; RF's near departure from, in 1946, 177ff; issues *Aforesaid* to celebrate RF's eightieth birthday, in 1954, 207; sponsors party on RF's eighty-fifth birthday, in 1959, 265
Homer, 265, 289, 429
Homer Noble farm, the
RF purchases, in 1939, 50–51; described, 65ff; RF, in 1941, accidentally starts a fire at, 82–83; RF mentions, in a note to Untermeyer, 389
Homer, Winslow, 262, 428
Hopkins, Ernest Martin
(President of Dartmouth College), is informed of RF's availability to teach at Dartmouth, in 1943, 106; Nash reports to RF on Hopkins's interest in hiring him, 394; discusses plans to hire RF with members of the Dartmouth English Department, 111; is absent from party welcoming RF to Dartmouth, in 1943, 114; retirement of, in 1945, 132
Hopkins, Harry, 5, 370
Howland, Harold, 217
Hudnut, David Beecher, 442
Hudnut, Robin Fraser
(Mrs. David Beecher Hudnut), attends memorial service for RF, in 1963, 442
see also Fraser, Marjorie Robin
Hulme, T. E., 235

I

Interviews with Robert Frost
ed., Edward Connery Lathem, first cited, 384
Iowa, University of
RF lectures to overflow audience at, in 1939, 42
Isaacs, Jack, 223

J

Jackson, Dr. James, 336–337
James, William
possible influence of, on *A Masque of Reason*, 118; influence of, on RF's religious beliefs, 397ff
Pragmatism by, quoted and cited, 397
The Varieties of Religious Experience by, quoted and cited, 397–399
The Will to Believe by, quoted and cited, 398
Jarrell, Randall
reviews *Steeple Bush*, in 1947, 157; RF succeeds, as Poetry Consultant to the Library of Congress, 258
Jeffers, Robinson, 149
Jenkins, Mrs. Mary
"Ma Jenks," 66
Johnson, Lyndon B.
at Kennedy inauguration, tries to help RF read "Dedication" poem, 281
Jones, Howard Mumford, 4, 370, 383
Joyce, Hewette E.
Professor of English at Dartmouth, 116
"A Few Personal Memories of Robert Frost" by, cited and quoted, 395

K

Kashkin, Ivan, 311
Kasper, John, 251–252
Katayev, Valentin, 342
Keats, John, 245
Kennedy, Jacqueline
(Mrs. John F. Kennedy), visits with RF and Mrs. Morrison at the White House, in 1961, 283
Kennedy, John F.
(President of the U. S.), RF predicts election of, to U.S. Presidency, in 1959, 266; thanks RF for predicting his election as President, 270; RF calls election of, in 1960, "a triumph of Protestantism—over itself," 276
agrees to RF's participation in his inauguration, 277; asks RF to recite "The Gift Outright" at his inauguration, 278; invites RF and Mrs. Morrison to the White House, in 1961, 283; RF, in 1961, expresses admiration for, 287; RF, in March 1962, receives Gold Medal from, and presents copy of *In the Clearing* to, 303–304
invites RF to visit Russia, in 1962, 307; RF, after Russian trip, says he has a message from Khrushchev for, 323; angry reaction of, to RF's report that Khrushchev said that U. S. was "too liberal to fight," 326; RF attempts to re-

Kennedy, John F. (*cont.*)
store his friendship with, in 1962, 329
sends telegram praising RF to MacDowell Colony, in 1962, 330–331; speaks at dedication of the Robert Frost Library at Amherst, in 1963, 347ff
Kenny, Herbert, 230
Kenyon College
RF receives honorary degree from, in 1945, 132; RF attends conference in his honor at, in 1950, 196, 417–418
Key West, Florida
RF visits, in 1940, 59ff
Keyser, F. Ray, 295
Khrushchev, Nikita S.
RF characterizes as his "enemy" but a "grand man," 303; RF meets in Gagra, in 1962, 320–321; RF, after Russian trip, says he has message for Kennedy from, 328; RF suggests he was deceived by, 329; reportedly denies having said that the U. S. was "too liberal to fight," 437–438; RF writes to, after Cuban missile crisis, 441
King, Stanley
President of Amherst College, mentioned, 13, 33, 34, 104, 129, 150, 394
Kipling, Rudyard, 89
Koestler, Arthur, 150
Kohn, John S. Van E.
RF orders books from, in 1938, 15; RF expresses gratitude to, in 1938, 20
Kristol, Irving, 231

L

Lambuth, David, 116
Lamont, Thomas, 34
Lane, Sir Alan, 245
Lankes, Julius John
RF's association with, 19, 20; RF pays deathbed visit to, in 1960, 273
Laski, Harold J., 138
Lathem, Edward Connery
background sketch of, 199; RF's developing friendship with, 199–200; serves as RF's guide, at Oxford in 1957, 237
ed., *The Poetry of Robert Frost,* first cited, 267
ed., *Interviews with Robert Frost,* first cited, 384
and Cox, eds., *Selected Prose of Robert Frost,* first cited, 376–377
and Thompson, eds., *Robert Frost: Poetry and Prose*, first cited, 370
Laughlin, James, 252
Lawrence, Ernest, 148
Laws, Bolitha, 257
Lee, Laurie, 241
Lee, Muna, 211, 212
Lee, Robert E., 148, 171
Lehman, John, 229
Lehman, Rosamund, 242
Lewis, C. Day
RF meets, in England in 1957, 229, 231, 242
Lindley, Denver, 177
Lins do Rêgo, José, 212
Little, David H., 50, 53, 384
London, University of
RF speaks at, in 1957, 223–224
Longfellow, Henry Wadsworth, 41, 220, 237
Lowell, James Russell, 220
Lowell, Robert, 175, 338
Lurye, Frida, 311ff, 342
Lyons, Leonard, 287
Lyons, Louis M., 441
Lyttle, Charles H., 324

M

MacDonald, Dwight, 241
MacLeish, Archibald
attends Bread Loaf Writers' Conference, in 1938, 8–9; RF mentions, in 1940 letter to Allen, 67; RF mentions, in 1942 letter to Thompson, 91, 98; serves as toastmaster at RF's eightieth birthday party, in 1954, 208; solicits RF's help in the Pound case, in 1957, 248, 250; RF praises, in Jan. 1963, 343; is quoted in Foster's "Journal," 371
MacVeagh, Lincoln, 4, 369
Madison, Charles A.
The Owl Among Colophons by, cited, 376; and quoted, 28–29
Madison, James, 195
Magaret, Helene, 378
Manchester, the Lord Bishop of, 233
Manchester, University of
RF speaks at, in 1957, 233
Manthey-Zorn, Ethel
(Mrs. Otto Manthey-Zorn), 411
Manthey-Zorn, Otto
Professor of German at Amherst, mentioned, 105, 151, 394, 410–411
Marlboro College
RF attends inauguration ceremony at, in 1948, 169; RF receives honorary degree from, in 1950, 196

Marx, Karl, 434
Masters, Edgar Lee, 92
Matlock, Jack, 311ff
McCord, David
successfully campaigns for RF's election, in 1938, to Harvard Board of Overseers, 3; RF writes to, from Concord Corners in 1938, 16; mentioned, 22, 25, 48, 49, 384, 442
McKeon, Newton, 105
Meacham, Harry M.
The Caged Panther: Ezra Pound at St. Elizabeths by, cited, 426, and quoted, 249
Meiklejohn, Alexander, 105, 394
Meredith, William, 276–277, 308, 435
Mertins, Louis
California collector, rival of Bernheimer, 125, 146, 188; RF, in 1942, discusses possible trip to California with, 407–409
Robert Frost: Life and Talks-Walking by, quoted and cited, 407–408, 409
Meyer, Eugene, 77
Meynell, Alice, 77
Mezhelaitis, Eduard, 314
Millay, Edna St. Vincent, 377, 419
Miller, David, 316–317
Mills, Frederick C., 148
Milton, John
RF's *Masques* compared to *Comus* and *Paradise Lost* by, 117–118, 397; RF quotes from *Paradise Lost* by, in *A Masque of Mercy*, 131
is subject of RF's 1938 letter to Snow, 403–404; RF, at Dartmouth, teaches a class on, 395; RF mentions, in 1958 letter to Adams, 260
Mirrielees, Edith, 149, 410
Monroe, Charles, 396
Monroe, Harriet, 174
Montague, Ashley, 434
Moore, Marianne, 427
Moore, Merrill
poet-psychiatrist, finds RF seriously ill in Boston, in 1939, 59; RF mentions, in 1939 letter to Untermeyer, 62; RF mentions, in 1940 letter to Untermeyer, 74; gives bleak prognosis for Irma, 144–145; assists RF in committing Irma to mental hospital, in 1947, 162ff
Morrill, Justin Smith, 272
Morrison, Anne, 2
see also Gentry, Anne Morrison
Morrison, "Bobby," 2
see also Morrison, Robert
Morrison, Kathleen Johnston
(Mrs. Theodore Morrison), friendship with RF before 1938, 2; visits RF in South Shaftsbury, in 1938, 1; RF, in 1938, proposes marriage to, 6; becomes secretary-manager to RF, in 1938, 12; helps RF move in at 88 Mt. Vernon Street, Boston, in 1938, 19; RF, in 1938 letter to Untermeyer, expresses gratitude for friendship of, 23; RF calls her "a friend to whom I owe almost my life," 373
with husband, agrees in 1939 to join RF at the Homer Noble farm, 50ff; RF mentions, in 1939 letter to Lesley, 27; RF mentions, in 1940 letter to Prescott, 72; reveals RF's fears concerning war to Sloane, 87; goes to New York City with RF to discuss Broadway production of *A Masque of Reason*, in 1943, 117; assists RF in finding a home for Irma, in 1946, 137
visits the Kennedys at the White House with RF, in 1961, 283; RF, ill with pneumonia, telephones, from Florida in 1962, 297–298; nurses RF back to health after pneumonia bout in 1962, 303; RF dedicates *In the Clearing* to, in 1962, 304; RF sends telegram to, from Russia, 323; attends RF during his final illness, 339ff; attends memorial service for RF, in 1963, 442
Robert Frost: A Pictorial Chronicle by, first cited, 367
Morrison, Kay
see Morrison, Kathleen Johnston
Morrison, Robert
RF mentions, in 1938 letter to Mrs. Morrison, 14; visits RF in Florida, with his mother, in 1940, 59; RF finds and burns discarded lesson books of, in 1941, 82; death of, in 1954, 422
see also Morrison, "Bobby"
Morrison, Theodore
(director of Bread Loaf Writers' Conference, Harvard professor, poet), background of RF's friendship with, 1; invites RF to participate in 1938 Writers' Conference, 2; RF mentions, in 1938 letter to Untermeyer, 22; RF mentions, in 1939 letter to Conant, 49; is mentioned in Foster's "Journal," 371
is an occasional target of RF's hostility, 378; attends RF's memorial service, in 1963, 442
"The Agitated Heart" by, quoted and cited, 405–406
Morrow, Dwight, 34, 377
Morse, Marston, 418

Morse, Stearns, 116
Morton, David, 420
Muir, Helen, 298
Mumford, L. Quincy
offers RF appointment as Consultant in Poetry at Library of Congress, in 1958, 258; appoints RF "Honorary Consultant in the Humanities," in 1959, 272
Munro, Harold, 153, 223
Murdock, Kenneth B., 418

N

Nash, Ray
RF discusses hypothetical Dartmouth appointment with, in 1943, 106; urges President Hopkins to bring RF to Dartmouth, 106; reports to RF concerning his possible hiring by Dartmouth, 394; services rendered to RF by, at Dartmouth, 116; RF visits, in Hanover, in 1947, 157–158; RF calls Nash "the one who had most to do" with his Ticknor appointment, 396
ed., *Fifty Years of Robert Frost,* cited, 384
National Institute of Arts and Letters
RF wins Gold Medal of, in 1939, 31
Newdick, Robert S.
invites RF to visit Ohio State Univ., in 1938, 3; mentioned, 20, 385
New England Primer, The, 92–93
New York *Times*, The
RF is criticized by, in 1939, for his competitive attitude toward the arts, 47; criticizes Khrushchev, in 1962, for a remark he never made, 437
Nisbet, Robert A.
definition of *acedia* of, quoted, 56
Nobel Prize for Literature
RF, in 1950, learns he has been nominated for, 185–186; RF again fails to win, in 1963, 341
Noble, Mrs. Homer, 50, 99, 137, 384
Norlin, George
RF stays at home of, during 1939 visit to Colorado, 45
North Carolina, University of
RF receives honorary degree from, in 1953, 206
North of Boston (1915)
RF's interest in a new edition of, 179; discusses a new edition of, with Wyeth, 203
Nutt, Mrs. Alfred, 220, 424
Nutt, David, 224

O

O'Keefe, Katherine, 297
Olds, George Daniel, 34, 172, 377
Osborn, Paul, 117
O'Shaughnessy, Arthur William Edgar
"Ode" by, is quoted by RF in 1962, 332, 438
Overholser, Dr. Winfred, 252–253
Oxford, University of
RF receives honorary degree from, in 1957, 237–238; RF speaks at, in 1957, 238–239

P

Paine, Tom, 415
Paustovsky, Konstanin, 312
Pease, Arthur Stanley, 4, 6, 373
Perkins, Palfrey, 346
Perry, Bliss, 110, 111
Piper, Edwin Ford, 378
Plato, 290–291
Plimpton, Calvin H.
President of Amherst College, 328, 346
Poe, Edgar Allen, 41
Poetry of Robert Frost, The
first cited, 367
Porter, Dr. William Branch, 159–160
Pound, Dorothy, 256
Pound, Ezra
RF speaks of his early relationship with, in 1957, 223; Eliot speaks of his early relationship with, in 1957, 243–244; RF is outraged by awarding of Bollingen Prize to Pound, in 1949, 174ff; RF softens his opinion of, in 1954, 247–248; RF's efforts to win the release from St. Elizabeths of, in 1957 and 1958, 248ff; RF is visited in hospital by daughter of, in Jan. 1963, 343
Powell, Thomas Reed, 418
Pratt, Fletcher, 14, 372
Prior, Matthew, 379
Prouty, Winston L.
sponsors Senate resolution honoring RF on his eighty-fifth birthday, in 1959, 264–265, 271
Pulitzer Prize
is awarded to *A Witness Tree,* 110

Q

Quisling, Vidkun, 415

INDEX

R

Rachewiltz, Princess Mary de
RF is visited in hospital by, in Jan. 1963, 343; mentioned by MacLeish, in 1957, 252
Ragle, Dr., 196
Rand, Frank Prentiss, 394
Ransom, John Crowe, 339
Reed, John, 308, 435
Reeve, Franklin D.
accompanies RF to Russia, in 1962, 310ff; travels with RF to meet Khrushchev, 318ff; visits RF in hospital, in Jan. 1963, 339
Robert Frost in Russia by, cited, 436, and quoted, 320–321
Reichert, Rabbi Victor E.
invites RF to preach sermon, in Cincinnati in 1946, 139; discusses "Golden Rule" with RF, 334; RF is reminded of a source of *A Masque of Mercy*, by, 407
Reuther, Walter, 263
Reynolds, Conger, 215–216
Richards, I. A., 245, 442
Ridgway, General Matthew, 197
Rigg, Edgar T., 265
Riley, James Whitcomb, 377
Robb, Mrs. Inez, 285–286
Roberts, Chalmers M.
reports corrective statements of Reeve and Khrushchev, after RF's 1962 Russian trip, 437–438
Roberts, Mrs. Michael, 236
Robinson, Edwin Arlington
mentioned, 85, 375, 377
Robinson, F. N., 4, 370
Rogers, William P.
invites RF to Washington to discuss Pound case, 250; RF pays second visit to, in 1957, 253; RF pays third visit to, in 1958, 255
Romanova, Elena, 311ff
Roosevelt, Eleanor, 98, 263
Roosevelt, Franklin Delano
mentioned, 67, 85, 111, 129, 152, 373
Rovere, Richard H., 232, 427
Royce Josiah, 170, 414
Rozov, Victor, 342
Rugg, Harold Goddard, 116

S

Saltonstall, Leverett
introduces Frost Medal Bill in Senate, in 1960, 276
Sandburg, Carl
in 1942, defends free verse in the *Atlantic Monthly*, 89–90; RF's response to *Atlantic Monthly* article by, 91; RF mentions, in 1942, 98, 99; RF mentions, in 1950 letter-poem to Untermeyer, 195; RF encounters, in Washington in 1960, 273–274; RF is angered when compared to, in 1961, 286–287; RF, in 1962, attacks, for his criticism of Eisenhower, 303
"Those Who Make Poems" by, cited, 391, and quoted, 89–90
Santayana, George, 4, 369–370
Schmitt, Howard G., 214–215, 422
Schramm, Wilbur, 378, 382
Selected Letters of Robert Frost
first cited, 367
Selected Prose of Robert Frost
first cited, 376–377
Seligman, Eustace
queries RF, in 1939, on his willingness to return to Amherst College employment, 33; mentioned, 218
Sergeant, Elizabeth Shepley
Robert Frost: The Trial by Existence by, first cited, 373; quoted, 373–374
Shafroth, William, 256
Shakespeare, William, 82, 180–181, 289
Shapiro, Karl, 175
Shelley, Percy Bysshe, 237, 373
Sill, Edward Rowland, 41, 413
Sills, Kenneth M., 14, 202
Simonson, Lee, 17, 74
Sloane, William M., III
successfully urges RF to write preface for *Collected Poems* (1939), 30; RF, in 1940, says he has two books ready for, 75; in 1942, assuages RF's fears for the success of *A Witness Tree*, 87; informs RF of the success of *A Witness Tree*, 95; departure from Holt of, 176
Smuts, Jan, 415
Smyth, Anne Morrison
see Morrison, Anne and Gentry, Anne Morrison
Smythe, Daniel
Robert Frost Speaks by, cited and quoted, 386
Snow, Wilbert
"The Robert Frost I Knew" by, cited and quoted, 403–404
Sophocles, 82, 268
South Miami, Florida
RF, in 1941, begins gardening at his farm in, 76; RF, in 1942, inspects his new homes in, 88
Spencer, Theodore, 175
Spender, Stephen, 231, 242, 371

Sproul, Robert Gordon, 146
Squire, Sir John, 234–235, 241
Stalin, Joseph, 393
Stegner, Wallace
mentioned, 14, 107, 108, 149, 372, 410
The Uneasy Chair: A Biography of Bernard DeVoto by, quoted, 8, 374; cited, 371
Stevens, Wallace, 60–61
Stevenson, Adlai, 230, 304
Stewart, George R., 149, 410
Strong, L. A. G., 418
Surkov, Alexei, 311ff
Swayze, John Cameron, 196
Sweeney, Jack, 219, 345
Sweeney, Mrs. Jack, 345

T

Taft, Robert A.
RF follows in program, at 1946 conference at Kenyon College, 138; RF, in 1950, thanks for sponsoring Senate birthday resolution, 186; RF praises, in letter to Taft's son, 426
Taft, William Howard, 259, 427
Taft, William Howard, III, 245
Tagore, Rabindranath, 421
Tate, Allen, 175, 338, 427
Tennyson, Alfred, Lord, 291
Tennyson, Sir Charles, 291
Thomas, Edward
mentioned, 177, 201, 230, 233; RF visits one-time home of, in England, in 1957, 240–241
Thomas, Helen
(Mrs. Edward Thomas), RF avoids meeting with, in England in 1957, 235
Thomas, Norman, 325
Thompson, Dorothy, 98
Thompson, Lawrance
"official biographer" of RF, stays with him in Florida, in 1940, 59ff; infuriates RF with review of *A Masque of Reason*, in 1945, 401; RF invites, in 1957, to go with him to England, 220; joins RF in subterfuge concerning English trip, 424; accompanies RF to Israel and Greece, in 1961, 284ff; RF, in 1962, explains why he did not invite Thompson to Russia, 435–436; attends memorial service for RF, in 1963, 442
Fire and Ice: The Art and Thought of Robert Frost by, cited, 392
Robert Frost: The Early Years, first cited, 367
Robert Frost: The Years of Triumph, first cited, 367
ed., *Selected Letters of Robert Frost*, first cited, 367
and Lathem, eds., *Robert Frost: Poetry and Prose*, first cited, 370
Thoreau, Henry David, 331
Thorn, Dr. George W., 338, 344–345
Thornton, Richard H., 28, 29
Thorp, Willard, 175
Threescore
by Sarah Cleghorn, cited, 393
Tierney, Michael, 245
Tittmann, Harold H., Jr., 213
Tolstoi, Leo, 321, 325
Trilling, Lionel
speaks at RF's eighty-fifth birthday dinner, in 1959, 266ff
"A Speech on Robert Frost: A Cultural Episode" by, cited, 429; quoted, 266–269, 429
Tvardovsky, Aleksandr, 311, 312
Twain, Mark, 108
Twilight
RF's unique first book (1894); background of, 57–58; RF agrees to sell, to Bernheimer, in 1940, 58; RF and Bernheimer discuss loan of, for 1943 Dartmouth exhibition, 116, 396; is sold at auction, in 1950, 193

U

Udall, Stewart L.
invites RF to his home for a "Congressional consultation," in 1959, 271; RF visits, in Arizona in 1960, 276–277; suggests RF's participation in Kennedy inauguration, 277; RF, in 1961, thanks Udall for having "made my life a real party for the last go-down," 292; RF, in 1961, acts as "character witness" for, 293; RF discusses idea of a Frost Park in Vermont with, in 1961–62, 296, 432; helps arrange RF's eighty-eighth birthday celebration, in 1962, 304; goes to Russia with RF, 306ff
"Robert Frost's Last Adventure" by, cited, 434
Untermeyer, Louis
attends Bread Loaf Writers' Conference, in 1938, 7ff; RF visits home of, in 1938, 17; RF, in 1942, reports his recent depression to, 87–88; is troubled by RF's refusal to join the OWI, 99–100; reviews *A Witness Tree* in the *Yale Review*, in 1942, 394–395; RF is recom-

Untermeyer, Louis (*cont.*)
mended for Pulitzer Prize by, in 1943, 109; RF, in 1944, attempts to placate, 126ff; RF, on New Year's Day, 1947, writes long letter to, 143ff; RF, in 1949, is gratified by the praise of, for *Complete Poems*, 184–185; speaks at RF's eightieth birthday celebration, in 1954, 208; in 1961, arouses RF's displeasure with invitation to write book for children, 294–295; visits RF in hospital, in Jan. 1963, 341–342
ed., *The Letters of Robert Frost to Louis Untermeyer*, first cited, 367

V

Van Doren, Mark, 208, 304, 346
Veale, Sir Douglas, 219
Villa, José Garcia
Have Come, Am Here by, 110, 111, 395
Vinokurov, Yevgeny, 314
Vosnesensky, Andrei, 314

W

Waley, Arthur, 241
Wallace, Henry
mentioned, 91, 99, 122, 152, 325
Warde, Beatrice, 243
Warren, Earl
mentioned, 148, 149, 304, 346, 410
Warren, Robert Penn, 304
Washington, George
mentioned, 78, 304, 307, 359
Waterman, Dr., 62–63
Wheelock, John Hall, 338
Whicher, George F.
RF writes to, in 1943, concerning Pulitzer Prize, 111; invites RF to Amherst, in 1945, 129; visits Marlboro College with RF, in 1948, 169; RF writes to, in 1948, concerning loyalty, 414–415; helps secure RF's reappointment to Amherst faculty, 171–172; death of, in 1954, 208
Whicher, Harriet
(Mrs. George F. Whicher), 105, 394
Whitman, Walt, 195
Whitney, John Hay, 224
Whitney, Mrs. John Hay, 229
Whittemore, Harold, 50
Wilber, Elinor (1929–)
(RF's granddaughter), RF visits with, on eve of 1957 English trip, 222; with husband Malcolm attends RF's memorial service, in 1963, 442
Wilder, Thornton
speaks at RF's eightieth birthday celebration, in 1954, 208
Willey, Sir Basil, 225, 244
William and Mary, College of
RF, in 1941, reads Phi Beta Kappa poem at, 83–84
Williams, Oscar, 391–392
Wilson, John G., 230
Wilson, T. J., 29, 381
Wood, George C., 111, 116
Wood, Grant, 378
Woodworth, G. Wallace, 346
Wright brothers
RF's comparison of his poetic flight to that of, in "Kitty Hawk," 302
Wright, Frank Lloyd, 252–253
Wyeth, Andrew
exchanges letters with RF, in 1953, 203
"Winter Sunlight" by, given as gift to RF, in 1954, 208; RF plans to provide his Washington office with a painting by, in 1958, 262
Wyoming, University of
RF helps inaugurate Frost Poetry Library at, in 1939, 44

Y

Yarborough, Ralph
RF testifies before Senate subcommittee of, in 1960, 275
Years of Triumph, The
first cited, 367
Yevtushenko, Yevgeny
RF meets in Russia, in 1962, 314, 317; RF receives telegram from, in Jan. 1963, 342

Z

Zenkevich, Mikhail, 311
Zimic, Lesley Lee Francis
(Mrs. Stanislav Zimic), attends RF's memorial service, in 1963, 442
see Francis, Lesley Lee
Zorn, Anders, 259, 427